Corel WordPerfect 7

NITA HEWITT RUTKOSKY
Pierce College at Puyallup
Puyallup, Washington

Developmental Editor	Lisa McGowan
Technical Consultant	Denise Seguin
Copy Editor	Patricia Brown
Proofreader	Susan Trzeciak Gibson
Indexer	Nancy Sauro
Art Director	Joan Silver
Cover & Text Designer	Jennifer Wreisner

Registered trademarks—Corel, WordPerfect, Grammatik, and TextArt are registered trademarks and Netscape Navigator, Presentations, and QuickCorrect are trademarks of Corel Corporation.

Permissions—Material for selected documents has been excerpted from *Telecommunications: Systems and Applications for Business* by William Mitchell, Robert Hendricks, and Leonard Sterry, published by Paradigm Publishing Inc.

Acknowledgments—The author and publisher wish to thank the following reviewers for their technical and academic assistance:

- DEBORAH C. CLEAR, Virginia Highlands Community College, Abingdon, Virginia
- DIANA R. HRYNCHUK, Northern Alberta Institute of Technology, Edmonton, Alberta
- ROSE KUCEYESKI, Owens Community College, Toledo, Ohio
- SHARON OLWIN, Consultant, Bloomington, Minnesota

Library of Congress Cataloging-in-Publication Data
    Rutkosky, Nita Hewitt.
        Corel WordPerfect 7 / Nita Hewitt Rutkosky.
           p.   cm.
        Includes index.
        ISBN 1-56118-919-7 (text alone). — ISBN 1-56118-920-0 (text with data disk)
        1. WordPerfect for Windows (Computer file). 2. Word processing.
I. Title
Z52.5.W655R865 1997   96-37497
652.5'5369—dc21   CIP

Text + 3.5" disk: ISBN 1-56118-920-0
Order number: 05276

© 1998 by Paradigm Publishing Inc.
    Published by **EMC**Paradigm
    875 Montreal Way
    St. Paul, MN 55102
    (800) 535-6865
    E-mail: publish@emcp.com

All rights reserved. Making copies of any part of this book for any purpose other than your own personal use is a violation of the United States copyright laws. No part of this book may be used or reproduced in any form or by any means, or stored in a database retrieval system, without prior written permission of Paradigm Publishing Inc.

Printed in the United States of America
10 9 8 7 6 5 4 3 2 1

CONTENTS

Preface	vii
Getting Started	ix
Identifying Computer Hardware	ix
Properly Maintaining Disks	xi
Using the Mouse	xi
Choosing Commands	xii
Choosing Commands with Shortcut Keys	xviii
Choosing Commands with Shortcut Menus	xviii
Using the WordPerfect Template	xix
Using Windows 95	xix

UNIT 1: Preparing Documents 1

Chapter 1: Creating, Saving, and Printing WordPerfect Documents 3

Creating a WordPerfect Document	3
Identifying the Parts of the Document Window	5
Completing Computer Exercises	8
Keying and Saving a WordPerfect Document	8
Closing a Document	11
Opening a Document	12
Printing a Document	13
Exiting WordPerfect and Windows 95	13
Chapter Summary	15
Check Your Understanding	17
Skill Assessments	17

Chapter 2: Editing a Document 19

Moving the Insertion Point with the Mouse	19
Moving the Insertion Point with the Keyboard	21
Moving the Insertion Point to a Specific Page	23
Inserting Text	23
Deleting Text	24
Splitting and Joining Paragraphs	24
Selecting Text	25
Using the Undo, Redo, and Undelete Options	28
Saving Documents	31
Chapter Summary	32
Commands Review	33
Check Your Understanding	35
Skill Assessments	35

Chapter 3: Formatting Characters 39

Creating Text in All Caps	39
Using the Tab Key	39
Formatting Text	39
Using Help	47
Chapter Summary	50
Commands Review	51
Check Your Understanding	51
Skill Assessments	52

Chapter 4: Formatting Lines 55

Centering Text	55
Using QuickMenus	56
Centering Text at a Specific Position	58
Changing Line Spacing	59
Changing Justification	60
Changing the Viewing Mode	66
Chapter Summary	69
Commands Review	69
Check Your Understanding	70
Skill Assessments	71

Chapter 5: Changing Margins and Indents 75

Changing Margins	75
Indenting Text	79
Creating Numbered Paragraphs	86
Creating Bulleted Paragraphs	88
Inserting Bullets and Numbers with the Bullets & Numbers Dialog Box	90
Inserting Bullets and Numbers with the Insert Bullet Button	92
Chapter Summary	93
Commands Review	94
Check Your Understanding	94
Skill Assessments	96

Unit 1: Performance Assessments 101

UNIT 2: Managing and Enhancing Documents 107

Chapter 6: Managing Documents 109

Displaying Document Information	109
Creating a Folder	110
Selecting Documents	111
Copying a Document	112
Cutting and Pasting Documents	113
Renaming Documents	114
Deleting a Document	114
Deleting to the Recycle Bin	116
Changing Properties	116
Printing a Document	117
Printing a Document List	117
Deleting a Folder and Its Contents	118
Viewing a Document	118
Changing Display Options	119
Using QuickFinder	121
Creating a Document Summary	125
Chapter Summary	127
Commands Review	127
Check Your Understanding	127
Skill Assessments	128

Chapter 7: Changing Fonts 131

Choosing a Typeface	131
Choosing a Type Size	132
Choosing a Type Style	132

Contents *iii*

Choosing a Font	133
Using the Font Dialog Box	133
Formatting with QuickFormat	146
Using the QuickFonts Button	147
Using WordPerfect Character Sets	148
Chapter Summary	150
Commands Review	151
Check Your Understanding	151
Skill Assessments	152

Chapter 8: Using Spell Checker and Thesaurus 157

Using Spell Checker	157
Spell Checking a Document	158
Editing in Spell Checker	160
Customizing Spell Check Options	161
Working with User Word Lists	163
Editing a User Word List	164
Using Thesaurus	166
Choosing Options from the Writing Tools Dialog Box with the Thesaurus Tab Selected	167
Displaying Document Information	171
Using QuickCorrect	172
Adding a Word to QuickCorrect	172
Changing QuickCorrect Options	172
Chapter Summary	175
Commands Review	175
Check Your Understanding	176
Skill Assessments	177

Chapter 9: Inserting Page Formatting 179

Changing Top and Bottom Margins	179
Keeping Text Together on a Page	181
Inserting Hard Page Breaks	183
Centering Text Vertically on the Page	184
Inserting Page Numbering	185
Chapter Summary	195
Commands Review	195
Check Your Understanding	196
Skill Assessments	196

Chapter 10: Manipulating Tabs 199

Manipulating Tabs with the Ruler Bar	199
Manipulating Tabs with the Tab Set Dialog Box	206
Visually Aligning Columns	213
Chapter Summary	216
Commands Review	217
Check Your Understanding	217
Skill Assessments	217

Unit 2: Performance Assessments 223

UNIT 3: Preparing and Enhancing Multiple-Page Documents 229

Chapter 11: Creating Headers and Footers 231

Creating Headers and Footers	231
Printing Headers or Footers	234
Creating Two Headers or Footers	236
Editing Headers or Footers	236
Formatting Headers and Footers	237
Discontinuing Headers and Footers	241
Suppressing Headers and Footers	241
Chapter Summary	242
Commands Review	243
Check Your Understanding	243
Skill Assessments	243

Chapter 12: Creating Footnotes and Endnotes 245

Creating Footnotes and Endnotes	245
Printing Footnotes and Endnotes	248
Formatting Footnotes and Endnotes	249
Editing a Footnote or Endnote	250
Deleting a Footnote or Endnote	251
Changing the Beginning Number	251
Changing Footnote or Endnote Options	252
Converting Footnotes and Endnotes	256
Chapter Summary	258
Commands Review	258
Check Your Understanding	258
Skill Assessments	259

Chapter 13: Manipulating Text within and between Documents 261

Working with Blocks of Text	261
Working with Columns of Text	265
Working with Documents	269
Working with Windows	271
Cutting and Pasting Text between Windows	277
Chapter Summary	279
Commands Review	280
Check Your Understanding	281
Skill Assessments	282

Chapter 14: Revising and Printing Documents 289

Finding and Replacing Text	289
Customizing Find and Replace	291
Using the Print Dialog Box	298
Printing Selected Text	305
Chapter Summary	306
Commands Review	307
Check Your Understanding	307
Skill Assessments	308

Chapter 15: Using Grammatik 311

Editing a Document with Grammatik	311
Analyzing Elements of the Document	320
User Word Lists	324
QuickCorrect	324
Chapter Summary	325
Commands Review	325
Check Your Understanding	325
Skill Assessments	326

Chapter 16: Merging Documents 329
Creating a Data File 329
Creating the Form File 336
Merging Files 338
Creating a Table Data File 340
Canceling a Merge 342
Formatting the Form File 342
Creating Envelopes 343
Merging at the Keyboard 344
Specifying Records for Merging 346
Chapter Summary 351
Commands Review 351
Check Your Understanding 352
Skill Assessments 353

Unit 3 Performance Assessments 357

UNIT 4: Enhancing the Visual Display of Documents 365

Chapter 17: Formatting Documents with Special Features 367
Hyphenating Words 367
Changing Line Height 373
Turning on Line Numbering 374
Using Abbreviations 376
Displaying Symbols 379
Inserting Hard Spaces 379
Inserting the Date 381
Bookmarks 383
Advancing the Insertion Point 385
Converting the Case of Letters 386
Chapter Summary 387
Commands Review 388
Check Your Understanding 388
Skill Assessments 389

Chapter 18: Formatting with Macros and Templates 391
Changing the Location of Macro Documents 391
Creating Macros 392
Using the WordPerfect Default Macros 400
Using Templates 401
Chapter Summary 406
Commands Review 406
Check Your Understanding 407
Skill Assessments 408

Chapter 19: Inserting Graphics Images 411
Inserting an Image into a Document 411
Creating a Text Box 413
Creating a Figure Box 414
Creating a Table Box 416
Creating a User Box 417
Creating a Button Box 418
Creating a Watermark 420
Editing a Box 421
Dragging a Box with the Mouse 437
Chapter Summary 439
Commands Review 440
Check Your Understanding 440
Skill Assessments 441

Chapter 20: Creating Graphic Elements 445
Creating Equations 445
Creating Inline Equations 450
Creating Borders 451
Creating Horizontal and Vertical Lines 456
Creating a Vertical Line 458
Creating Customized Lines 459
Creating Drop Caps 464
Reversed Text 468
Using Make It Fit 469
Chapter Summary 471
Commands Review 472
Check Your Understanding 472
Skill Assessments 473

Chapter 21: Using Draw and TextArt 477
Drawing Shapes 477
Drawing Freehand 483
Inserting Images 484
Creating Text in Draw 485
Editing an Object 489
Changing Attributes 498
Using TextArt 7 500
Editing a TextArt Image in the Editing Window 506
Chapter Summary 508
Commands Review 508
Check Your Understanding 509
Skill Assessments 510

Unit 4 Performance Assessments 515

UNIT 5: Enhancing the Presentation of Documents 521

Chapter 22: Changing Paper Size 523
Inserting a Paper Definition Code 523
Creating a Paper Definition 524
Editing a Paper Definition 526
Deleting a Paper Definition 527
Printing Text on Envelopes 527
Using WordPerfect's Envelope Feature 528
Creating Labels 532
Creating a Form File for Labels 535
Chapter Summary 536
Commands Review 537
Check Your Understanding 537
Skill Assessments 537

Chapter 23: Creating Newspaper and Parallel Columns 539
Creating Newspaper Columns with the Columns Dialog Box 539

Editing Text in Columns	543
Creating Parallel Columns	545
Changing Column Widths with the Ruler Bar	548
Creating Column Lines and Borders	549
Chapter Summary	554
Commands Review	554
Check Your Understanding	555
Skill Assessments	555

Chapter 24: Creating Tables — 559

Creating a Table	559
Entering Text in Cells	562
Changing the Column Width of a Table	565
Selecting Cells	570
Editing a Table	571
Deleting a Table	577
Chapter Summary	579
Commands Review	579
Check Your Understanding	580
Skill Assessments	580

Chapter 25: Formatting Tables — 587

Formatting Cells	588
Formatting Columns	592
Formatting Rows	594
Formatting a Table	597
Changing Numeric Format	599
Changing Cell Lines and Fill	602
Changing Table Border Lines and Fill	607
Inserting Formulas in a Table	609
Using the Sum Option	614
Formatting with SpeedFormat	615
Chapter Summary	616
Commands Review	617
Check Your Understanding	617
Skill Assessments	618

Chapter 26: Creating Charts — 623

Creating a Chart from Table Data	623
Creating Chart Layout and Type	631
Changing Chart Layouts	639
Chapter Summary	647
Commands Review	647
Check Your Understanding	648
Skill Assessments	648

Unit 5 Performance Assessments — 653

UNIT 6: Organizing Text in Documents — 661

Chapter 27: Outlining — 663

Creating an Outline	663
Chapter Summary	677
Commands Review	677
Check Your Understanding	678
Skill Assessments	678

Chapter 28: Sorting and Selecting — 683

Sorting	683
Sorting Considerations	692
Selecting Records	693
Chapter Summary	696
Commands Review	696
Check Your Understanding	696
Skill Assessments	697

Chapter 29: Using Styles — 699

Creating a Style	699
Applying a Style	704
Retrieving Styles	707
Editing a Style	708
Copying a Style	709
Deleting a Style	710
Chapter Summary	712
Commands Review	712
Check Your Understanding	713
Skill Assessments	713

Chapter 30: Creating Tables, Indexes, and Lists — 715

Creating a Table of Contents	715
Creating a List	720
Creating an Index	723
Regenerating a Table, List, or Index	728
Creating a Table of Authorities	728
Chapter Summary	733
Commands Review	734
Check Your Understanding	734
Skill Assessments	735

Chapter 31: Browsing the Web — 737

Understanding the Internet	737
Browsing the World Wide Web	738
Locating URLs on the Internet	738
Using Hypertext Links	741
Finding Information Using Search Engines	742
Creating a Home Page	745
Creating Hypertext Links	748
Chapter Summary	750
Commands Review	750
Check Your Understanding	750
Skill Assessments	751

Unit 6 Performance Assessments — 753

Appendix A - Proofreader's Marks	**757**
Appendix B - Formatting Business Documents	**758**
Appendix C - Graphics Images	**760**
Photo Credits	**763**
Index	**765**

PREFACE

When students prepare for a successful business career, they need to acquire the necessary skills and qualifications essential to becoming a productive member of the business community. Microcomputer systems are prevalent in most business offices, and students will encounter employment opportunities that require a working knowledge of computers and computer software. Microcomputers, with the appropriate software, are used by businesses in a variety of capacities. One of the most popular uses of a microcomputer system is word processing—the creation of documents.

Word processing certainly belongs in the business world, but it is also a popular application for home computer use. People will want to learn word processing to write personal correspondence, keep personal records, provide support for a home-based business or cottage industry, write term papers and reports, and much more.

This textbook provides students with the opportunity to learn word processing for employment purposes or home use and to utilize a microcomputer as a word processor. The Corel WordPerfect 7 program together with an IBM or IBM-compatible microcomputer system must be available for students to practice the features of the program. WordPerfect needs to be installed on a hard-drive or network system. To properly install the program, please refer to the WordPerfect documentation.

This textbook instructs students in the theories and practical applications of one of the most popular word processing programs—Corel WordPerfect 7. The text is designed to be used in beginning and advanced word processing classes and provides approximately 80 to 120 hours of instruction.

The book is divided into six units. Chapters within units each contain performance objectives, material introducing and explaining new concepts and commands, step-by-step exercises completed at the computer, a chapter summary, a knowledge self-check, and skill assessment exercises (also completed at the computer).

The step-by-step exercises integrated within the chapter provide students with the opportunity to practice using the feature(s) introduced. Skill assessments at the end of each chapter require students to complete computer exercises without step-by-step instructions. In addition, simulation exercises at the end of each unit require students to make decisions about document preparation and formatting. These practical exercises provide ample opportunity to practice new features and commands as well as previously learned material. Composing activities presented at the end of each unit provide students with the opportunity to compose and format business documents.

The textbook contains a listing of SCANS (Secretary's Commission on Achieving Necessary Skills) goals covered in each unit (see the back of the first page of each unit). The SCANS report was the result of a joint commission from the Departments of Education and Labor. The goal of the commission was to establish the interdisciplinary standards that should be required for *all* students. SCANS skills standards emphasize the integration of competencies from the areas of information, technology, basic skills, and thinking skills. The SCANS committee agreed that all curriculum can be strengthened by emphasizing classroom work that is more authentic and relevant to learners, i.e, connecting context to content. Teaching in context helps us move away from a subject-specific orientation to integrative learning that includes decision making, problem solving, and critical thinking. The concepts and applications material in each unit of this book has been designed to coordinate with and reflect this important interdisciplinary emphasis. In addition, learning assessment tools implement the SCANS standards. For example, the skill assessments at the end of each chapter reinforce acquired technical skills while providing practice in decision making and problem solving. The performance assessments at the end of each unit offer simulation exercises that require students to demonstrate their understanding of the major skills and technical features taught in the unit's chapters within the framework of critical and creative thinking. The addition of composing activities at the end of each unit makes it clear that students are not just producers, but editors and writers as well.

By the time students have completed the textbook, they have mastered most of the features and commands of Corel WordPerfect 7 and are ready to perform on the job. They will also have acquired a solid foundation in the problem-solving and communication abilities so important in the contemporary workplace.

GETTING STARTED

Identifying Computer Hardware

As you work your way through this textbook, you will learn functions and commands for WordPerfect 7. To do this, you will need an IBM PC or an IBM-compatible computer. This computer system should consist of the CPU, monitor, keyboard, disk drive, printer, and mouse. If you are not sure what equipment you will be operating, check with your instructor.

The computer system displayed in figure G.1 consists of six components. Each component is discussed separately in the material that follows.

Figure G.1

Personal Computer System

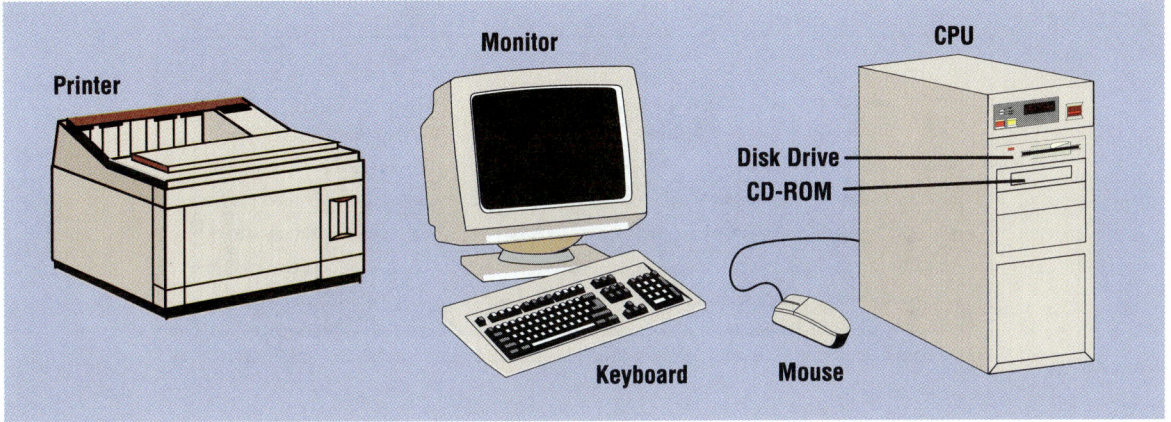

CPU

CPU stands for Central Processing Unit. The CPU is the intelligence of the computer. All the processing occurs in the CPU. Silicon chips, which contain miniaturized circuitry, are placed on boards that are plugged into slots within the CPU. Whenever an instruction is given to the computer, that instruction is electronically processed through circuitry in the CPU.

Monitor

The monitor is a piece of equipment that looks like a television screen. It displays the information of a program and what is being input at the keyboard.

The quality of display for monitors varies depending on the type of monitor and the type of resolution. Monitors can also vary in the display color. Some monitors are monochrome, displaying only one color, while other monitors display many colors. More than likely, the monitor that you are using is a color monitor.

Keyboard

The keyboard is used to input information into the computer. Keyboards for microcomputers vary in the number and location of the keys. Microcomputers have the alphabetic and numeric keys in the same location as the keys on a typewriter. The symbol keys, however, may be placed in a variety of locations, depending on the manufacturer.

In addition to letters, numbers, and symbols, most microcomputer keyboards contain function keys, arrow keys, and a numeric keypad. Figure G.2 shows an enhanced keyboard.

The 12 keys at the top of the enhanced keyboard, labeled with the letter F followed by a number, are called *function keys*. These keys can be used to perform WordPerfect functions.

To the right of the regular keys is a group of *special* or *dedicated keys*. These keys are labeled with specific functions that will be performed when you press the key. Below the special keys are arrow keys. These keys are used to move the insertion point in the editing window.

In the upper right corner of the keyboard are three mode indicator lights. When certain modes have been selected, a light appears on the keyboard. For example, if you press the Caps Lock key, which disables the lowercase alphabet, a light appears next to Caps Lock. Similarly, pressing the Num Lock key will disable the special functions only on the numeric keypad, which is located at the right side of the keyboard.

Figure G.2

Microcomputer Enhanced Keyboard

Disk Drives

Depending on the computer system you are using, the WordPerfect program is saved on a hard drive or saved as part of a network system. Whether you are using WordPerfect on a hard-drive or network system, you will need to have a disk drive available for inserting a disk, on which you will save and open documents. A disk drive spins a disk and reads information from it. Two 3.5-inch student data disks accompany this text.

The memory capacity for disks varies depending on the density of the disk. Disk memory is measured in kilobytes (thousands) and megabytes (millions). The memory capacity for a 3.5-inch double density (DD) disk is 720,000 bytes (720 kilobytes, which is written as 720Kb). The memory capacity for a 3.5-inch high density disk (HD) is 1,440,000 bytes (1.44 megabytes, which is written as 1.44Mb).

Many computers today contain a CD-ROM drive. CD-ROM stands for "Compact Disk - Read Only Memory." The Compact Disk portion refers to the disk. The Read Only Memory portion indicates that you can only "read" (receive) information from the disk and that you cannot "write" (save) information on the disk. CD-ROM disks are popular because of the large amount of information that they hold.

Printer

When you create a document at the editing window, it is considered *soft copy*. If you want a *hard copy* of a document, you need to have it printed on paper. To print documents you will need to access a printer.

Getting Started

Printing methods are either *impact* or *nonimpact*. Impact printers have a mechanism that strikes the paper to create text. Nonimpact printers use a variety of methods—heat, ink jet, laser—to print characters. These printers are much quieter and faster than impact printers; they are generally also more expensive than impact printers.

Mouse

Many functions in the WordPerfect program are designed to operate more efficiently with a *mouse*. A mouse is an input device that sits on a flat surface next to the computer. A mouse can be operated with the left or the right hand. Moving the mouse on the flat surface causes a corresponding mouse pointer to move on the screen. Figure G.1 shows an illustration of a mouse. For specific instructions on how to use a mouse, please refer to the "Using the Mouse" text later in this section.

Properly Maintaining Disks

Two 3.5-inch student data disks containing a variety of documents accompany this textbook. You will be saving on and opening documents from a student data disk. To ensure that you will be able to retrieve information from a disk, you need to follow certain rules of disk maintenance. To properly maintain a 3.5-inch disk, follow these rules:

- Do not expose the disk to extreme heat or cold.
- Keep the disk away from magnets and magnetic fields. They can erase the information saved on the disk.
- Do not wipe or clean the magnetic surface of the disk.
- Keep the disk away from food, liquids, and smoke.
- Never remove the disk from the disk drive when the drive light is on.
- Carry the disk in a plastic case to prevent damage to the metal shutter.

The disks that you will be using for saving and opening documents have been formatted and include a number of documents. If you use a blank disk with WordPerfect, that disk will probably be formatted. Formatting is a process that establishes tracks and sectors on which information is stored and prepares the disk to accept data from the disk operating system (and erases anything previously saved on the disk). If you are using a disk that is not formatted, check with your instructor on the steps needed to format. (You can also look up the steps to format in Windows 95 using the Help feature. The Windows 95 Help feature is presented later in this section.)

Using the Mouse

WordPerfect operates most efficiently with a mouse. A mouse may have two or three buttons on top, which are tapped to execute specific functions and commands. To use the mouse, rest it on a flat surface or a mouse pad. Put your hand over it with your palm resting on top of the mouse and your wrist resting on the table surface. As you move the mouse on the flat surface, a corresponding pointer moves on the screen.

When using the mouse, there are four terms you should understand: *point*, *click*, *double-click*, and *drag*. When operating the mouse, you may need to *point* to a specific command, button, or icon. Point means to position the mouse pointer on the desired item. With the mouse pointer positioned on the desired item, you may need to *click* a button on the mouse. Click means quickly tapping a button on the mouse once. To complete two steps at one time such as choosing and then executing a function, *double-click* a mouse button. Double-click means to tap the left mouse button twice in quick succession. The term *drag* means to press the left mouse button, move the mouse pointer to a specific location, then release the button.

Using the Mouse Pointer

The mouse pointer will change appearance depending on the function being performed or where the pointer is positioned. The mouse pointer may appear as one of the following images:

The mouse pointer appears as an I-beam (called the *I-beam pointer*) in the document screen and can be used to move the insertion point or select text.

The mouse pointer appears as an arrow pointing up and to the left (called the *arrow pointer*) when it is moved to the Title bar, Menu bar, or Toolbar at the top of the screen or when a dialog box is displayed. For example, to open a new document with the mouse, you would move the I-beam pointer to the File option on the Menu bar. When the I-beam pointer is moved to the Menu bar, it turns into an arrow pointer. To make a selection, position the tip of the arrow pointer on the File option, then click the left mouse button. At the drop-down menu that displays, make selections by positioning the arrow pointer on the desired option then clicking the left mouse button.

The mouse pointer becomes a double-headed arrow (either pointing left and right, pointing up and down, or pointing diagonally) when performing certain functions such as changing the size of a picture or sizing a frame.

In certain situations, such as moving a picture or frame, the mouse pointer becomes a four-headed arrow. The four-headed arrow means that you can move the object left, right, up, or down.

When a request is being processed or when a program is being loaded, the mouse pointer may appear with an hourglass beside it. The hourglass image means "please wait." When the process is completed, the hourglass image is removed.

The mouse pointer displays as a hand with a pointing index finger in certain functions such as Help and indicates that there is more information available about the item.

Choosing Commands

Several methods can be used in WordPerfect to choose commands. A command is an instruction that tells WordPerfect to do something. You can choose a command with one of the following methods:

- Click a button on a toolbar with the mouse
- Choose a command from a menu
- Use shortcut keys
- Use a shortcut menu

Choosing Commands on Toolbars

When WordPerfect is loaded, the Toolbar and the Power Bar display toward the top of the screen below the Menu bar. For example, to print the document currently displayed in the document screen, position the tip of the arrow pointer on the Print button on the Toolbar, then click the left mouse button.

Print

Choosing Commands on the Menu Bar

WordPerfect includes a Menu bar that displays below the Title bar that contains a list of options used to customize a WordPerfect document. For example, features to work with files (documents) are grouped in the File option. Either the mouse or the keyboard can be used to make choices from the Menu bar or make a choice at a dialog box.

To use the mouse to make a choice from the Menu bar, move the I-beam pointer to the Menu bar. This causes the I-beam pointer to display as an arrow pointer. Position the tip of the arrow pointer on the desired option, then click the left mouse button.

To use the keyboard, press the Alt key to make the Menu bar active. Options on the Menu bar display with an underline below one of the letters. To choose an option from the Menu bar, key the underlined letter of the desired option, or move the insertion point with the left or right arrow keys to the option desired, then press Enter. This causes a drop-down menu to display.

For example, to display the File drop-down menu shown in figure G.3 using the mouse, position the arrow pointer on File on the Menu bar, then click the left mouse button. To display the File drop-down menu with the keyboard, press the Alt key, then key the letter F for File.

Figure G.3

File Drop-Down Menu

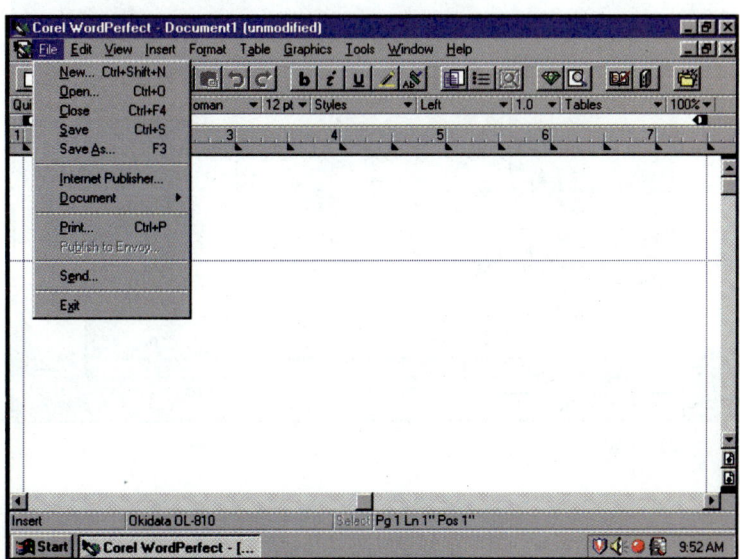

Getting Started *xiii*

Choosing Commands from Drop-Down Menus

To choose a command from a drop-down menu with the mouse, position the arrow pointer on the desired option, then click the left mouse button. You can also position the arrow pointer on the desired option on the Menu bar (such as File), hold down the left mouse button, drag the arrow pointer to the desired option, then release the mouse button. When you position the arrow pointer on an option and hold down the left mouse button, a drop-down menu appears. As you drag the arrow pointer down the menu, the various options in the menu will be selected.

To make a selection from the drop-down menu with the keyboard, key the underlined letter of the desired option. Once the drop-down menu is displayed, you do not need to hold down the Alt key with the underlined letter. If you want to close a drop-down menu without making a choice, click in the document screen outside the drop-down menu; or, press the Esc key twice.

Some menu options may be gray shaded (dimmed). When an option is dimmed, that option is currently not available. For example, if you choose the Edit option from the Menu bar, the Edit drop-down menu displays with several dimmed options, including Cut and Copy. If text is selected before the Edit drop-down menu is displayed, these options are available and display in black.

Some menu options are preceded by a check mark. The check mark indicates that the option is currently active. To make an option inactive (turn it off) using the mouse, position the arrow pointer on the option, then click the left mouse button. To make an option inactive (turn it off) with the keyboard, key the underlined letter of the option.

If an option from a drop-down menu displays followed by an ellipsis (...), a dialog box will display when that option is chosen. A dialog box provides a variety of options to let you specify how a command is to be carried out. For example, if you choose File, then Print from the Menu bar, the Print dialog box shown in figure G.4 displays (your Print dialog box may vary slightly).

Figure G.4

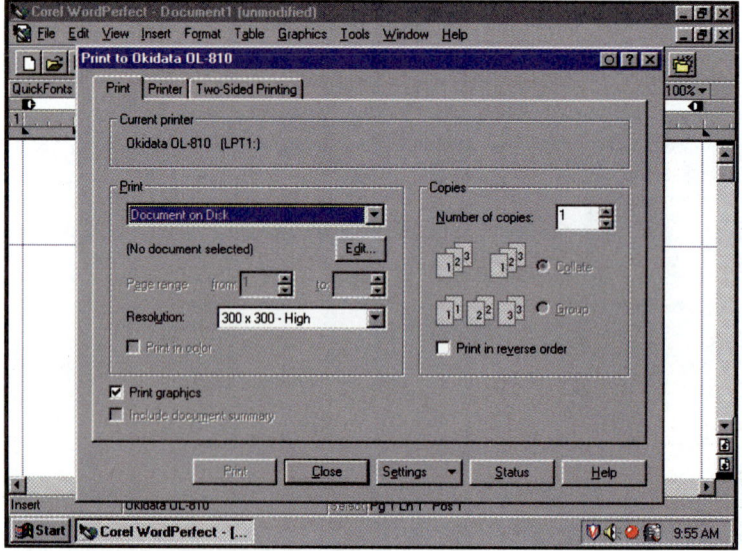

Print Dialog Box

Some dialog boxes provide a set of options. These options are contained on separate tabs. For example, the Print dialog box shown in figure G.4 contains a tab at the top of the dialog box with the word *Print* on it. To the right of that tab is another tab with the word *Printer*. A third tab displays with the words *Two-Sided Printing*. The tab that displays in the front is the active tab. To make a tab active using the mouse, position the arrow pointer on the desired tab, then click the left mouse button. If you are using the keyboard, press Ctrl + Tab.

To choose options from a dialog box with the mouse, position the arrow pointer on the desired option, then click the left mouse button. If you are using the keyboard, press the Tab key to move the insertion point forward from option to option. Press Shift + Tab to move the insertion point backward from option to option. You can also hold down the Alt key, then press the underlined letter of the desired option.

When an option is selected, it will display either in reverse video (white letters on a blue background) or surrounded by a dashed box called a *marquee*.

A dialog box contains one or more of the following elements: text boxes, list boxes, check boxes, option buttons, spin boxes, and command buttons.

Text Boxes

Some options in a dialog box require text to be entered. For example, the boxes below the F<u>i</u>nd and Replace <u>w</u>ith options at the Find and Replace Text dialog box shown in figure G.5 are text boxes. In a text box, you key text or edit existing text. Edit text in a text box in the same manner as normal text. Use the left and right arrow keys on the keyboard to move the insertion point without deleting text and use the Delete key or Backspace key to delete text.

Figure G.5

Find and Replace Text Dialog Box

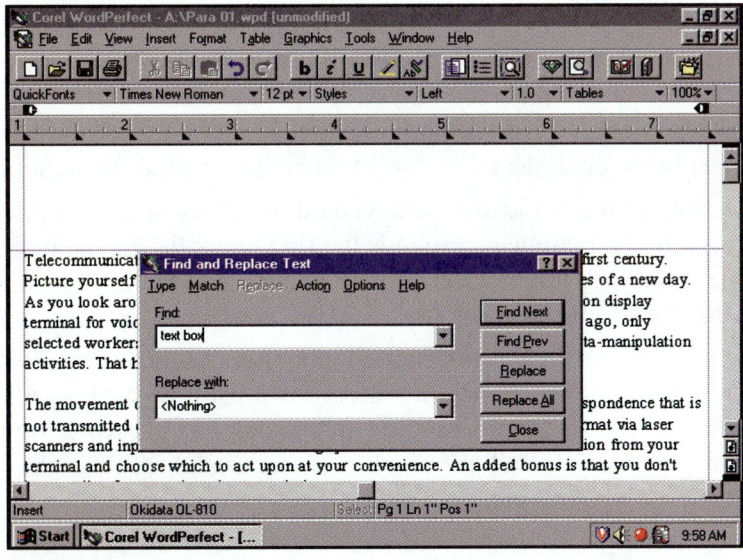

List Boxes

Some dialog boxes such as the Open dialog box shown in figure G.6 may contain a list box.

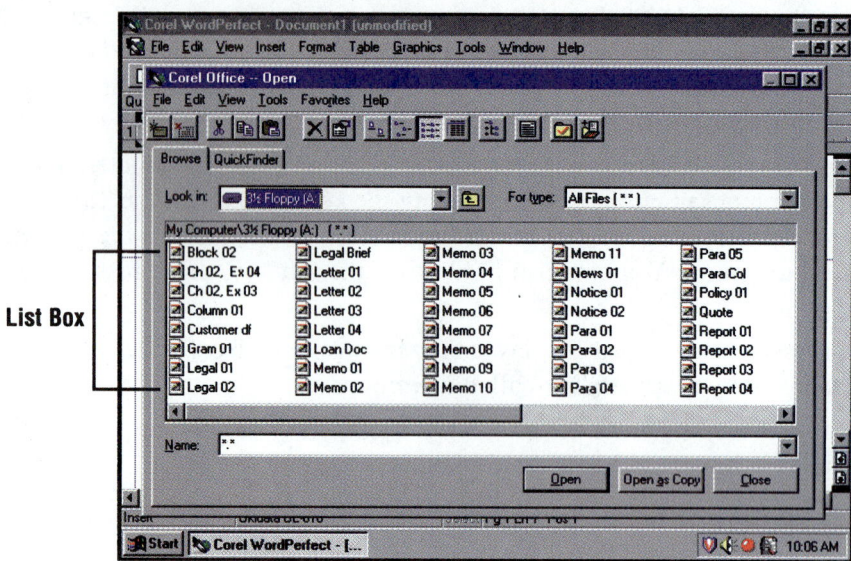

Figure G.6 — Open Dialog Box

List Box

The list of files below the Look in: option are contained in a list box. To make a selection from a list box with the mouse, move the arrow pointer to the desired option, then click the left mouse button.

Some list boxes may contain a scroll bar. This scroll bar may display at the right side of the list box (a vertical scroll bar) or at the bottom of the list box (a horizontal scroll bar). Either a vertical scroll bar or a horizontal scroll bar can be used to move through the list if the list is longer than the box. To move down through a list with a vertical scroll bar, position the arrow pointer on the down scroll triangle and hold down the left mouse button. To scroll up through the list with a vertical scroll bar, position the arrow pointer on the up scroll triangle and hold down the left mouse button. You can also move the arrow pointer above the scroll box and click the left mouse button to scroll up the list or move the arrow pointer below the scroll box and click the left mouse button to move down the list. To move through a list with a horizontal scroll bar, click the left scroll triangle to scroll to the left of the list or click the right scroll triangle to scroll to the right of the list.

To make a selection from a list using the keyboard, move the insertion point into the box by pressing the Tab key until the marquee surrounds the first option in the list box, or hold down the Alt key and press the underlined letter of the desired option. Press the up, down, left, or right arrow keys on the keyboard to move through the list.

In some dialog boxes where there is not enough room for a list box, lists of options are inserted in a drop-down list box. Options that contain a drop-down list box display with a down-pointing triangle. For example, the Look in option at the Open dialog box shown in figure G.6 contains a drop-down list. To display the list, click the down-pointing triangle to the right of the Look in text box. If you are using the keyboard, press Alt + L.

Check Boxes

Some dialog boxes contain options preceded by a box. A check mark may or may not appear in the box. The Font dialog box shown in figure G.7 displays a variety of check boxes within the Appearance section. If a check mark appears in the box, the option is active (turned on). If there is no check mark in the check box, the option is inactive (turned off). Any number of check boxes can be active. For example, in the Font dialog box, you can insert a check mark in any or all of the boxes in the Appearance section and these options will be active.

Font Dialog Box

Figure G.7

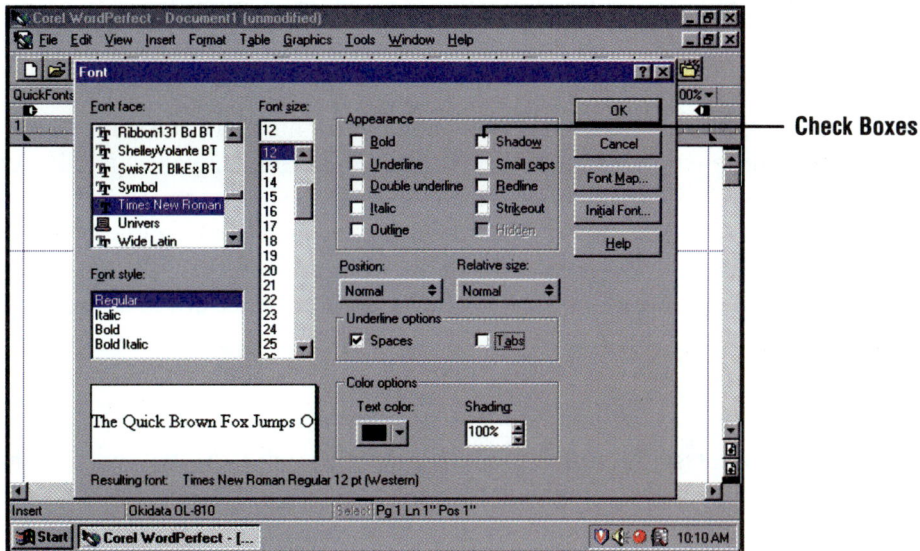

Check Boxes

To make a check box active or inactive with the mouse, position the tip of the arrow pointer in the check box, then click the left mouse button. If you are using the keyboard, press Alt + the underlined letter of the desired option.

Option Buttons

In the Center Page(s) dialog box shown in figure G.8, the options in the Center section are preceded by option buttons (also referred to as *radio buttons*). Only one option button can be selected at any time. When an option button is selected, a dark circle displays in the button.

Center Page(s) Dialog Box

Figure G.8

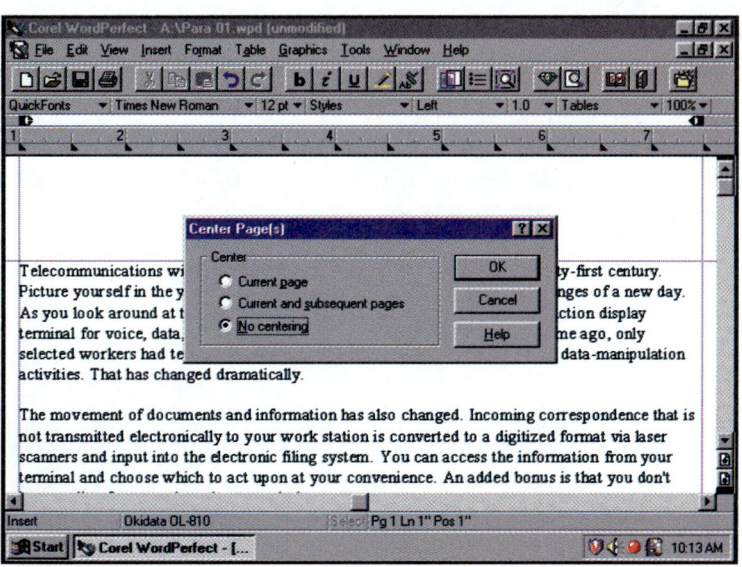

Getting Started *xvii*

To select an option button with the mouse, position the tip of the arrow pointer inside the option button, then click the left mouse button. To make a selection with the keyboard, hold down the Alt key, then press the underlined letter of the desired option.

Spin Boxes

Some options in a dialog box contain measurements or numbers that can be increased or decreased. These options are generally located in a spin box. For example, the Print dialog box shown in figure G.4 contains a spin box located after the Number of copies option. To increase a number in a spin box, position the tip of the arrow pointer on the up-pointing triangle to the right of the desired option, then click the left mouse button. To decrease the number, click the down-pointing triangle. If you are using the keyboard, press Alt + the underlined letter of the desired option, then press the up arrow key to increase the number or the down arrow key to decrease the number.

Command Buttons

In the Find and Replace Text dialog box shown in figure G.5, the boxes at the right side of the dialog box are called *command buttons*. A command button is used to execute or cancel a command. Some command buttons display with ellipses (...). A command button that displays with ellipses will open another dialog box. To choose a command button with the mouse, position the arrow pointer on the desired button, then click the left mouse button. To choose a command button with the keyboard, press the Tab key until the desired command button contains the marquee, then press the Enter key.

Choosing Commands with Shortcut Keys

At the left side of a drop-down menu is a list of options. At the right side, shortcut keys for specific options may be displayed. For example, the shortcut keys to save a document are Ctrl + S and are displayed to the right of the Save option at the File drop-down menu shown in figure G.3. To use shortcut keys to choose a command, hold down the Ctrl key, key the letter for the command, then release the Ctrl key.

Choosing Commands with Shortcut Menus

WordPerfect includes menus that contain commands related to the item with which you are working. A shortcut menu appears right where you are working in the document. To display a shortcut menu, click the *right* mouse button or press Shift + F10.

For example, if the insertion point is positioned in a paragraph of text in a WordPerfect document, clicking the *right* mouse button or pressing Shift + F10 will cause the shortcut menu shown in figure G.9 to display in the document screen.

Figure G.9

WordPerfect Shortcut Menu

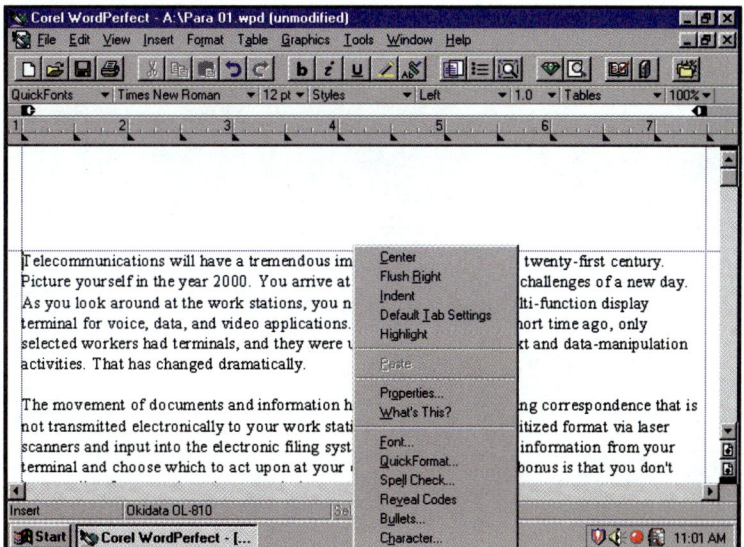

To select an option from a shortcut menu with the mouse, click the desired option. If you are using the keyboard, press the up or down arrow key until the desired option is selected, then press the Enter key. To close a shortcut menu without choosing an option, click anywhere outside the shortcut menu or press the Esc key.

Using the WordPerfect Template

Corel includes a template with the WordPerfect program that identifies the commands of the function keys. The template is placed above the function keys to provide a visual aid. A template designed by Paradigm Publishing Inc. is included with this textbook (last page in the book). You may use this template as a visual aid to WordPerfect functions.

Using Windows 95

A computer requires an operating system to provide necessary instructions on a multitude of processes, including such operations as loading programs, managing data, directing the flow of information to peripheral equipment, and displaying information. Windows 95 is an operating system that provides these types of functions (along with much more) in a graphical environment. Windows 95 is referred to as a *graphical user interface* (GUI—pronounced *gooey*) that provides a visual display of information with features such as icons (pictures) and buttons.

In this introduction, you will learn basic features of Windows 95. For a more in-depth look at Windows 95, consider reading *Microsoft Windows 95* by Edward J. Coburn published by EMC/Paradigm Publishing.

Before using WordPerfect, you will need to start the Windows 95 operating system program. To do this, turn on the computer. Depending on your computer equipment configuration, you may also need to turn on the monitor and printer. When the computer is turned on, the Windows 95 operating system is automatically started and, after a few moments, the Windows 95 desktop will display as shown in figure G.10 (your screen may vary slightly).

Getting Started

Figure G.10

Windows 95 Desktop

Start Button   Taskbar   Desktop Application Director (DAD)   Date/Time Control

The main portion of the screen that displays when Windows 95 is loaded is called the *desktop*. Think of the desktop in Windows 95 like the top of a desk in an office. A businessperson places necessary tools—such as pencils, pens, paper, files, calculator—on his or her desktop to perform functions. Like the tools that are located on a desk, the Windows 95 desktop contains tools for operating the computer. These tools are logically grouped and placed in dialog boxes or panels that can be displayed using one of the icons at the left side of the desktop. In the "Using the Control Panel" section presented after "Using Windows 95 Help," you will learn how to make changes to the screen saver by clicking the My Computer icon on the desktop.

The bar at the bottom of the desktop is called the *Taskbar*. The Taskbar will display the name of a currently open application inside a button. It also displays the current date at the right side. This is called the Date/Time Control. Position the arrow pointer on the time displayed, click the left mouse button, and the current date will display in a yellow box above the time. If you want to reset the time and or date, you would complete the following steps:

1. Position the arrow pointer on the time that displays at the right side of the Taskbar, then click the *right* mouse button (be sure to click the *right* mouse button and not the left).
2. At the pop-up menu that displays, position the arrow pointer on *Adjust Date/Time*, then click the left mouse button.
3. At the Date/Time Properties dialog box, adjust the date with options in the Date section and/or adjust the time with options in the Time section.
4. When all changes have been made, click the OK button that displays at the bottom of the dialog box.

Start

The Start button is located at the left side of the Taskbar. Use this button to start a program, use the Help feature, change settings, and open documents. To display the options available with the Start button, position the arrow pointer on the Start button, then click the left mouse button. This causes a pop-up menu to display as shown in figure G.11 (the options on your pop-up menu may vary).

xx   Getting Started

Start Pop-Up Menu

Figure G.11

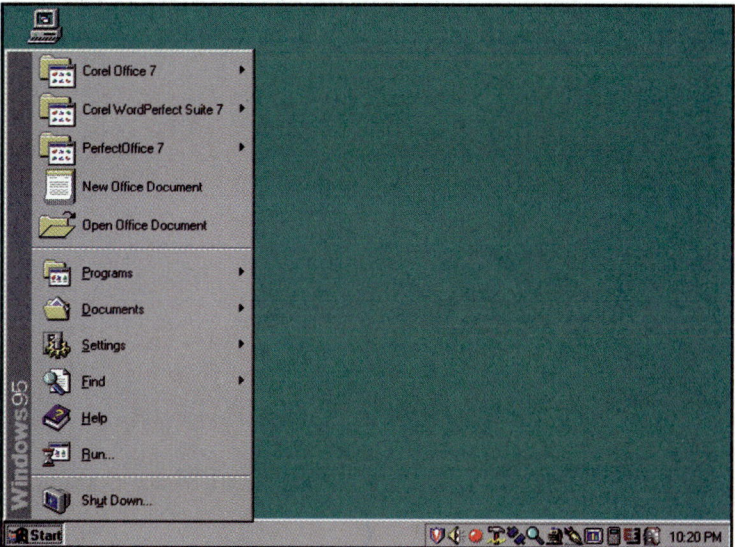

To choose an option from this pop-up menu, drag the arrow pointer to the desired option, then click the left mouse button.

Using Windows 95 Help

As you work your way through this textbook, you will be introduced to many WordPerfect features. There may be other features that you will want to research. An excellent tool for learning about a particular feature is the on-screen Help. In this introduction, you will learn about the Windows 95 Help feature. In a later chapter, you will learn how to use WordPerfect's Help feature. To begin using the Help feature, you would complete the following steps:

1. Position the tip of the arrow pointer on the Start button located at the left side of the taskbar, then click the left mouse button.
2. At the pop-up menu that displays, drag up to Help, then click the left mouse button. This causes the Help Topics dialog box with the Contents tab selected to display as shown in figure G.12.

Figure G.12 — Help Topics Dialog Box with Contents Tab Selected

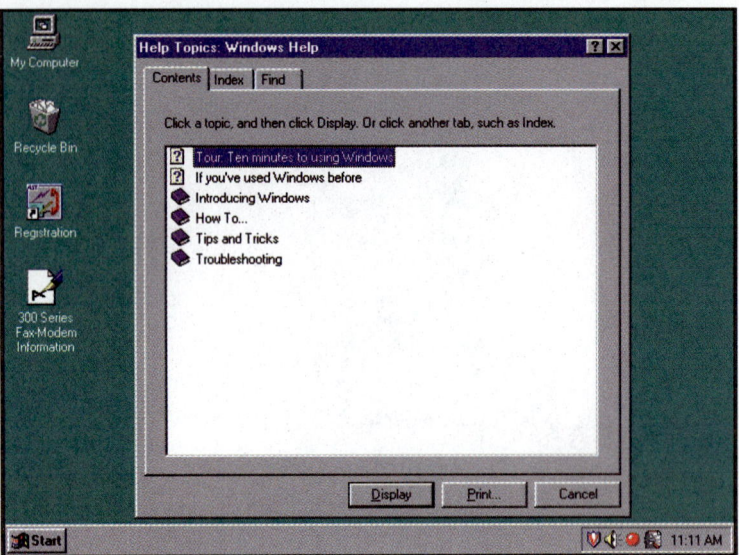

The Help Topics dialog box with the Contents tab selected displays a variety of categories, each preceded by the icon of a closed book. Most of these categories contain additional categories. To display these additional categories, double-click a category. This causes the closed book icon to change to an open book icon and the additional categories to display below the selected category. Some of these additional categories may be preceded by an icon containing a question mark.

If you choose a category preceded by a question mark, a help screen will display containing information about a topic. Some of these screens may display with text in a yellow box or icons representing features or buttons. Move the arrow pointer to one of these yellow boxes (the pointer turns into a hand), then click the left mouse button. This causes information about the topic to display on the screen. Move the arrow pointer to an icon representing a feature or button (the pointer turns into a hand), then click the left mouse button, and an explanation of the feature or a definition of the button displays on the screen.

Using the Index

Choose the Index tab at the Help Topics dialog box and a list of topics displays in alphabetical order. Key the first few letters of the topic you want to display, then double-click the desired topic. You can also click the desired topic once, then click Display at the bottom of the dialog box. When you choose a topic, another dialog box may display with a list of additional topics. Continue choosing topics until the specific information you desire is displayed.

Finding Special Words or Phrases

At the Help Topics dialog box with the Find tab selected, you can search for specific words or phrases in help topics rather than searching for information by category. The first time you use this feature, Windows must create a list containing every word from the help files. Before using this feature, please check with your instructor.

Using the Control Panel

The Windows 95 operating system contains a control panel, which you can use to view, change, and/or customize settings. To display the control panel shown in figure G.13, you would complete the following steps:

1. Position the arrow pointer on the My Computer icon that displays in the Windows 95 desktop, then double-click the left mouse button.
2. At the My Computer window that displays, position the arrow pointer on the Control Panel icon, then double-click the left mouse button.
3. At the Control Panel, double-click the icon representing the function with which you want to work.

You can also display the control panel by clicking the Start button located at the left side of the Taskbar, pointing to Settings, then clicking Control Panel.

As an example of how to use the control panel, you would complete the following steps to add a screen saver:

1. Position the arrow pointer on the My Computer icon that displays in the Windows 95 desktop, then double-click the left mouse button.
2. At the My Computer window, position the arrow pointer on the Control Panel icon, then double-click the left mouse button.
3. At the Control Panel window, double-click the Display icon.
4. At the Display Properties dialog box, position the arrow pointer on the Screen Saver tab that displays at the top of the dialog box, then click the left mouse button.
5. At the Display Properties dialog box with the Screen Saver tab selected, click the down-pointing triangle to the right of the Screen Saver text box, then click the desired screen saver that displays in the drop-down list.
6. If desired, change the number of minutes the screen must remain still before the screen saver displays. To do this, click the up- and/or down-pointing triangles that display after the Wait text box. Make any other desired changes to the dialog box.
7. Click the OK button at the bottom of the dialog box. (This closes the dialog box.)
8. At the Control Panel window shown in figure G.13, click the close button that displays in the upper right corner of the window (the button that displays with an X).
9. At the My Computer window, click the close button that displays in the upper right corner of the window (the button that displays with an X).

Figure G.13 Control Panel Window

The control panel contains many other options for viewing, changing, or customizing settings. You may want to experiment with some of the other icons that display in the Control Panel dialog box.

Unit One

Preparing Documents

In this unit, you will learn to create, edit, format, save, and print WordPerfect documents.

CREATING, SAVING, AND PRINTING WORDPERFECT DOCUMENTS

PERFORMANCE OBJECTIVE

Upon completion of chapter 1, you will be able to create, save, close, open, and print a WordPerfect document.

This textbook provides you with instructions for using a word processing program on a microcomputer system. The program you will learn to operate is the *software*. Software is the program of instructions that tells the computer what to do. The computer equipment you will use is the *hardware*.

You will be learning to operate a software program called WordPerfect for Windows, version 7, on a microcomputer system. WordPerfect 7 operates within the Windows 95 operating environment. Before continuing with this chapter, be sure to read the *Getting Started* section at the beginning of this textbook.

Creating a WordPerfect Document

Eight basic steps are completed when working with a word processing system to create a document. The steps are:

1. Load the program.
2. Key (type) the information to create the document.
3. Save the document on the disk.
4. Proofread the document, then make any necessary edits (changes).
5. Save the revised document on the disk.
6. Print a hard copy of the document.
7. Close the document.
8. Exit the program.

In this chapter, you will be provided with the information needed to complete all the steps except 4. You will complete several exercises to practice the steps.

Loading WordPerfect

The steps to load WordPerfect may vary depending on the system setup. Generally, to load WordPerfect, complete the following steps:

1. Turn on the computer. (This may include turning on the CPU, the monitor, and possibly the printer.)
2. After a few moments, the Windows 95 desktop shown in figure 1.1 displays (your screen may vary). At the Windows 95 desktop, position the arrow pointer on the Start button on the Taskbar (located at the bottom left side of the screen), then click the left mouse button. This causes the pop-up menu shown in figure 1.2 to display.
3. Position the arrow pointer on *Corel WordPerfect Suite 7* (you do not need to click the left mouse button). This should cause another menu to display to the right of the first pop-up menu.
4. Move the arrow pointer to *Corel WordPerfect 7*, then click the left mouse button.

Figure 1.1

Windows 95 Desktop

Figure 1.2

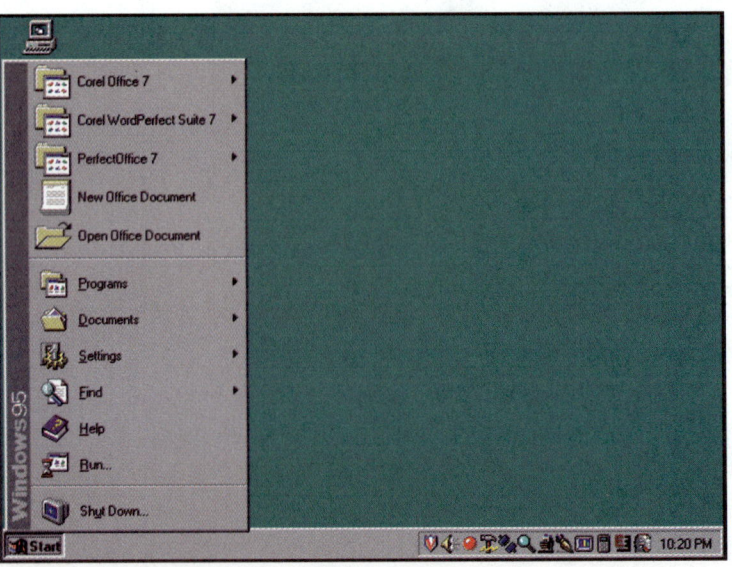

Start Pop-Up Menu

Chapter 1

If WordPerfect 7 was installed as part of the Corel WordPerfect 7 Office suite, the Desktop Application Director may have been installed also. The Desktop Application Director (called the *DAD*) displays in the lower right corner of the Windows 95 desktop (unless customized). The DAD includes icons representing different programs within the Corel WordPerfect Office suite. Another method for starting the WordPerfect 7 program is to position the tip of the arrow pointer on the Corel WordPerfect 7 icon (displays with the tip of a fountain pen), then click the left mouse button.

Corel WordPerfect

The steps for operating WordPerfect on your computer system may vary from these instructions. If necessary, ask your instructor for specific steps to load WordPerfect and write the steps here:

Identifying the Parts of the Document Window

When you load WordPerfect, you will be presented with a screen that looks similar to the one shown in figure 1.3. This screen is referred to as the *document window*.

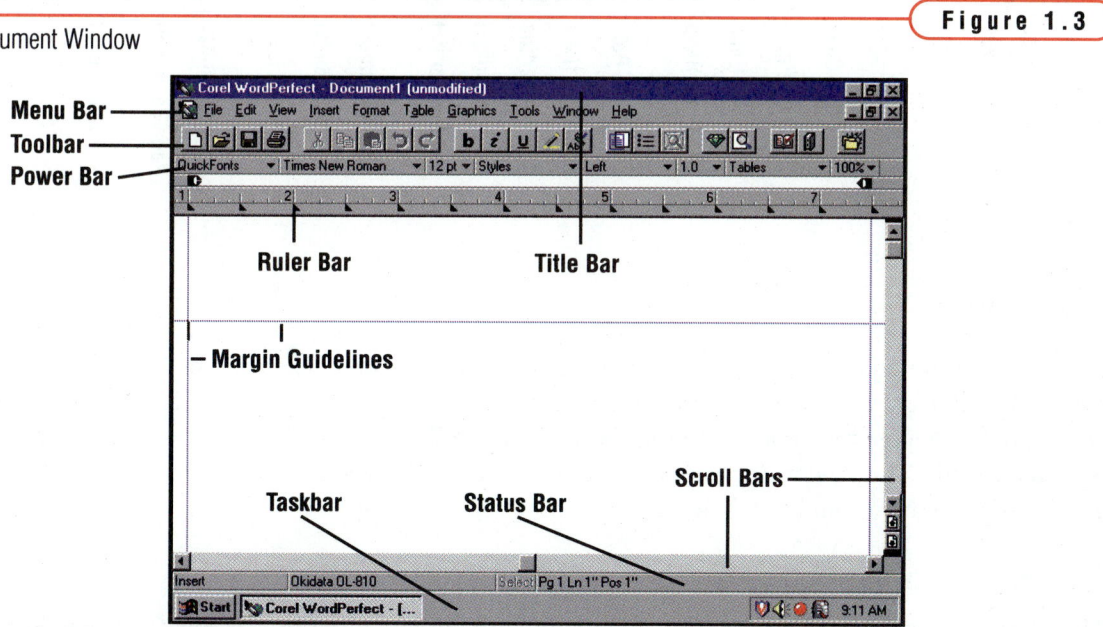

Figure 1.3

Title Bar

The top line of the document window is referred to as the *Title bar*. When you load WordPerfect, you are given a new document window with the name Document1. The word *unmodified* after the document name indicates that nothing has been entered or modified in the document. As soon as you begin keying text, the word *unmodified* is removed from the Title bar.

Creating, Saving, and Printing WordPerfect Documents

When a document is completed, it can be saved with a new name. If you open a previously saved document to the document window, the document name is displayed in the Title bar.

Menu Bar

The second line of the document window is called the *Menu bar*. The Menu bar contains a list of options that are used to customize a WordPerfect document. WordPerfect functions and features are grouped into menu options located on the Menu bar. For example, functions to save, close, or open a new document are contained in the File option from the Menu bar.

Toolbar

Bold

Italic

Print

WordPerfect includes a *Toolbar* that contains icons of common features, programs, and macros. An *icon* is a picture or image that represents a function. With this Toolbar, located below the Menu bar, you can use the mouse to execute certain commands quickly. For example, the button with the *b* bolds text, the button with the *i* italicizes text, and the button with the printer displays the Print dialog box.

WordPerfect provides a QuickTip that shows what the button on the Toolbar will perform. To view a QuickTip, position the arrow pointer on a button on the Toolbar. After approximately one second, the QuickTip displays. The QuickTip displays below the button in a yellow box. Figure 1.4 displays the names of each button on the Toolbar. The Toolbar display is on by default. You can turn off the display of the Toolbar with the Toolbar option from the View drop-down menu on the Menu bar.

Figure 1.4 — Toolbar Buttons

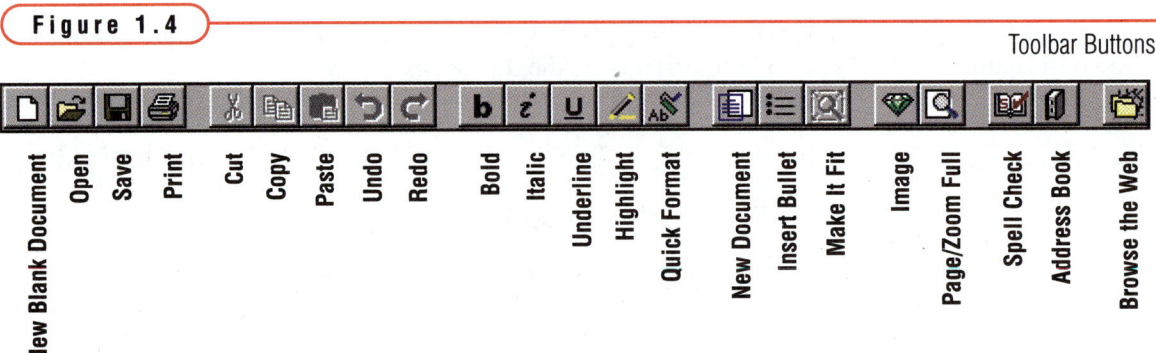

Power Bar

The series of options below the Toolbar is called the *Power Bar*. The options on the Power Bar are used to quickly access text editing and text layout features. A QuickTip will display when the arrow pointer is positioned on an option (button) on the Power Bar. The display of the Power Bar is on by default. The Power Bar can be turned off with the Power Bar option from the View drop-down menu on the Menu bar.

Insertion Point

The blinking vertical bar, located approximately an inch below the Power Bar (or Ruler Bar if it is displayed) at the left side of the document window, is called the *insertion point* (also referred to as the *cursor*). The insertion point indicates the location where the next character entered at the keyboard will appear.

The insertion point is positioned in the portion of the document window called the *editing window*. The editing window is the portion of the window where text is entered, edited, and formatted.

In addition to the blinking vertical bar, an arrow pointer will also display in the document window. When the mouse pointer is positioned in the editing window, it displays as an arrow ( ).

Shadow Pointer

As you move the arrow pointer in the document screen, a slender gray line called a *shadow pointer* will appear at the tip of the arrow. The shadow pointer shows exactly where the insertion point will be positioned when you click the left mouse button.

Scroll Bars

The gray shaded bars along the right side and bottom of the document window are called *scroll bars*. Use the scroll bars to view various sections of a document. Additional information on the scroll bars is presented in chapter 2.

Status Bar

The gray bar located immediately above the Taskbar is called the *Status bar*. The Status bar displays information about the document and the location of the insertion point.

The word *Insert* displays at the left side of the Status bar. This indicates that the Insert mode is turned on. The currently selected printer displays to the right of Insert. The word *Select* on the Status bar displays in gray. This indicates that the Select feature is off. When the Select feature is turned on, the word *Select* displays in black letters.

The information at the right side of the Status bar displays the current location of the insertion point by page number and line and position measurements.

Taskbar

The Taskbar displays at the bottom of the screen. The Start button displays at the left side of the Taskbar and the current time displays at the right side. The name of any open program displays to the right of the Start button. If more than one program is open at the same time, you can switch between open programs by clicking the program button on the Taskbar.

Word Wrap

As you key (type) text, you do not need to press the Enter key at the end of each line as you would on a typewriter. WordPerfect wraps text to the next line. A word is wrapped to the next line if it begins before the right margin and continues past the right margin. The only times you need to press Enter are to end a paragraph, create a blank line, or end a short line.

QuickCorrect

WordPerfect contains a feature called *QuickCorrect* that automatically corrects certain words as they are being keyed (typed). For example, if you key the word *adn* instead of *and*, QuickCorrect automatically corrects it when you press the space bar after the word. There are over 120 words that QuickCorrect will automatically correct.

QuickCorrect also changes formatting automatically by correcting capitalization errors (cAPS lOCK is replaced with Caps Lock), changing quotation marks (" is replaced with "), and replacing numbers with superscript ordinals (1st is replaced with 1st). Text preceded by bullets or numbers can be easily entered with QuickCorrect options. You will learn more about these options in a later chapter.

Spell-As-You-Go

A new WordPerfect 7 feature called Spell-As-You-Go automatically inserts red slashmarks below words that are not contained in the Spelling dictionary or not automatically corrected by QuickCorrect. This may include misspelled words, proper names, some terminology, and some foreign words. If you key a word not recognized by the Spelling dictionary, the red slashmarks will appear as soon as you press the space bar. If the word is correct, you can leave it as written. If, however, the word is incorrect you have two choices—you can backspace over the word using the Backspace key and then key it correctly, or you can position the arrow pointer on the word, click the *right* mouse button, then click the correct spelling in the pop-up menu.

For example, if you key the word *aplication* and then press the space bar, WordPerfect inserts red slashmarks below the word. To correct it using the mouse, position the arrow pointer on any character in the word *aplication*, click the right mouse button, then click *application* in the pop-up menu that displays. If WordPerfect inserts red slashmarks below a proper name such as *Weinburg* that is spelled correctly, you can either leave it (the red slashmarks will not print) or position the arrow pointer on any character in the name, click the right mouse button, and then click the Skip in Document option at the pop-up menu.

Spacing Punctuation

WordPefect 7 uses Times New Roman as the default typeface. Times New Roman is a proportional typeface. (You will learn more about typefaces in chapter 7.) When keying text in a proportional typeface, space once (rather than twice) after end-of-sentence punctuation such as a period, question mark, or exclamation point, and after a colon. Proportional typeface is set closer together and extra white space at the end of a sentence or after a colon is not needed.

Completing Computer Exercises

At the end of sections within chapters and at the end of chapters, you will be completing hands-on exercises at the computer. These exercises will provide you with the opportunity to practice the functions and commands presented.

Exercises in the beginning chapters present text in arranged form. Exercises in later chapters include unarranged text. This provides you with decision-making opportunities. The skill assessment exercises at the end of each chapter include general directions. If you do not remember how to perform a particular function, refer to the text in the chapter.

In the exercises in this chapter, you will be creating and saving several short documents. Press Enter only to end a paragraph or to create a blank line between paragraphs. Otherwise, let the word wrap feature wrap text to the next line within paragraphs.

The WordPerfect editing window displays between 16 and 19 lines of text at one time. When more lines are entered, the text scrolls off the top of the editing window. The text is not lost or deleted. When the document is saved, all the text is saved, not just the lines you see in the editing window.

Keying and Saving a WordPerfect Document

At the clear WordPerfect editing window, you can begin keying information to create a document. A document is any information you choose; for instance, a letter, a memo, a report, a term paper, or a table.

Saving a Document

When you have created a document, the information will need to be saved on your disk. When a document is keyed (typed) for the first time and is displayed in the editing window, it is only temporary. If you turn off the computer or if the power goes off, you will lose the information and have to rekey it. Only when you save a document on the disk (or drive) is it saved permanently. Every time you load WordPerfect, you will be able to bring a saved document back to the editing window.

A variety of methods can be used to save a document, such as the following:

- Click the Save button on the Toolbar.
- Click File, then Save.
- Press the Alt key, the letter F, then the letter S.
- Press Ctrl + S.

Save

To save a document with the Save button, you would complete the following steps:

1. Position the arrow pointer on the Save button (the third button from the left) on the Toolbar, then click the left mouse button.
2. At the Save As dialog box shown in figure 1.5, key a name for the document.
3. Click Save.

Save As Dialog Box

Figure 1.5

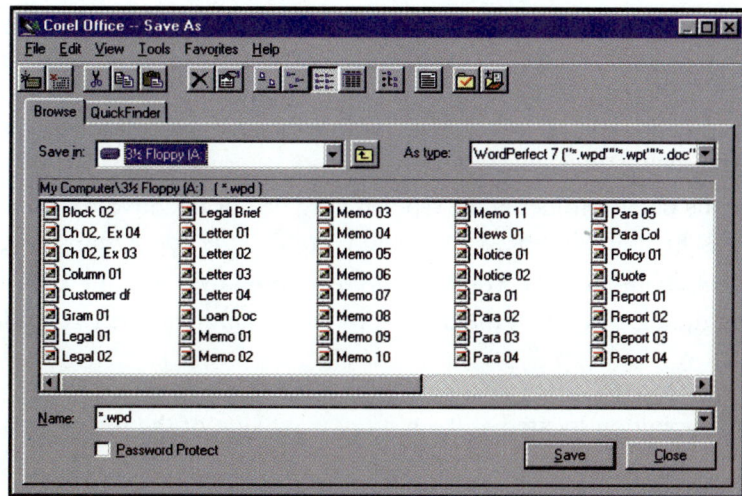

In addition to the Toolbar, a document can be saved by executing a command. There are three methods that can be used. One method uses the Menu bar with the mouse, one uses the Menu bar with the keyboard, and the other method uses function keys or shortcut keys.

The function keys can be used to execute commands. Some commands require the function key by itself, other commands require the function key together with the Alt, Shift, or Ctrl keys. In this text, commands that require two or three keys are shown with a plus sign in between. For example, the shortcut command to save a document is written as Ctrl + S. To use this shortcut command, hold down the Ctrl key, press the letter S one time, then release the Ctrl key.

To save a document using the Menu bar with the mouse, you would complete the following steps:

1. Click File, then Save.
2. At the Save As dialog box, key a name for the document.
3. Click Save.

Creating, Saving, and Printing WordPerfect Documents **9**

To save a document using the Menu bar with the keyboard, you would complete the following steps:

1. Press the Alt key, the letter F for File, then the letter S for Save.
2. At the Save As dialog box, key a name for the document.
3. Press the Enter key.

To save a document using the shortcut command, you would complete the following steps:

1. Press Ctrl + S.
2. At the Save As dialog box, key a name for the document.
3. Press the Enter key.

As you can see, there are several options for completing the same process. In this textbook, the focus will be placed on the steps that are the easiest or the fastest. For many features, instructions for using the mouse will be emphasized. You may find that you prefer other options. At times, you may want to explore the other options for completing steps or procedures not emphasized in this text.

Changing the Default Folder

In this and the remaining chapters in the textbook, you will be saving documents. More than likely, you will want to save documents onto your student data disk. Also, beginning with chapter 2, you will be opening documents that have been saved on your student data disk.

To save and open documents on your data disk, you will need to specify the drive where your disk is located as the default directory. Unless your computer system has been customized, WordPerfect defaults to the hard drive (usually c:) or the network drive. Once you specify the drive where your data disk is located, WordPerfect uses this as the default folder until you exit the WordPerfect program. The next time you load WordPerfect, you will need to specify again the drive where your data disk is located.

You can change the default folder at the Open dialog box or the Save As dialog box. To change the folder to a: at the Open dialog box, you would complete the following steps:

Open

1. Click the Open button on the Toolbar (the second button from the left).
2. At the Open dialog box, click the down-pointing triangle at the right side of the Look In text box.
3. From the drop-down list that displays, click *3½ Floppy (A:)*.
4. Click the Close button located at the bottom right side of the dialog box.

Naming a Document

A WordPerfect document name can be up to 255 characters in length including drive letter and any folder names and may include spaces. Filenames cannot include any of the following:

    forward slash (/)   question mark (?)
    backslash (\)   quotation mark (")
    greater-than sign (>) colon (:)
    less-than sign (<)   semicolon (;)
    asterisk (*)   pipe symbol (|)

Canceling a Command

If a drop-down menu is displayed in the document screen, it can be removed with the mouse or the keyboard. If you are using the mouse, position the arrow pointer in the document screen (outside the drop-down menu), then click the left mouse button. If you are using the keyboard, press the Alt key. You can also press the Esc key twice. The first time you press Esc, the drop-down menu is removed but the menu option on the Menu bar is still selected. The second time you press Esc, the Menu bar is no longer selected.

Several methods can be used to remove a dialog box from the editing window. To remove the dialog box with the mouse, position the arrow pointer on the Cancel command button, then click the left button. You can also click the button containing the "X" in the upper right corner of the dialog box (called the Close button). A dialog box can be removed from the editing window with the keyboard by pressing the Esc key. You can also remove a dialog box from the editing window with the keyboard by pressing the Tab key until the Cancel command button is selected, then pressing the Enter key.

Close

Closing a Document

When a document is saved with the Save or Save As options from the File drop-down menu, the document is saved on the disk and remains in the editing window. To remove the document from the editing window, click File, then Close; or click the Close button at the far right side of the Menu bar. (The Close button is the button containing the X. Be sure to use the Close button on the Menu bar, not the Close button on the Title bar. The Close button on the Title bar will close the WordPerfect program.) When you close a document, the document is removed and a clear editing window is displayed. At this editing window, you can open a previously saved document, create a new document, or exit the WordPerfect program.

EXERCISE 1

Creating a Document

1. Follow the instructions in this chapter to load Windows 95 and Corel WordPerfect 7.
2. At the clear editing window, change the default folder to the drive where your student data disk is located by completing the following steps. (Depending on your system configuration, this may not be necessary. Check with your instructor before changing the default folder.)
   a. Click the Open button on the Toolbar.
   b. At the Open dialog box, click the down-pointing triangle at the right side of the Look in text box.
   c. From the drop-down list that displays, click *3½ Floppy (A:)* (this may vary depending on your system).
   d. Click the Close button located in the bottom right corner of the dialog box.
3. At the clear editing window, key (type) the text in figure 1.6. Your line endings will differ from what you see in figure 1.6. If you make a mistake while keying and Spell-As-You-Go inserts red slashmarks below your text, backspace over the incorrect word using the Backspace key and then rekey the correct text. (Do not worry about doing a lot of correcting since you will learn more about editing a document in chapter 2.) Remember to space only once after end-of-sentence punctuation while keying the text.
4. When you are done keying the text, save the document and name it Ch 01, Ex 01 (for chapter 1, exercise 1) by completing the following steps:

Creating, Saving, and Printing WordPerfect Documents

a. Click the Save button on the Toolbar.
b. At the Save As dialog box, key **Ch 01, Ex 01**. (Key a zero when naming documents, not the letter o. In this textbook, the zero, 0, displays thinner and taller than the letter o.)
c. Click the Save button located in the bottom right corner of the dialog box or press Enter.
5. Close Ch 01, Ex 01 by clicking File, then Close or clicking the Close button (the button containing the "X") located at the right side of the Menu bar.

Figure 1.6

The field of telecommunications has been expanding rapidly in the past few decades. In a textbook written by William Mitchell, Robert Hendricks, and Leonard Sterry, the authors state that telecommunications systems are destined to become as common in the workplace of the nineties as typewriters were in the offices of the sixties.

The authors also state that people entering the job market now and in the future will need to understand the basics of telecommunications technology and its applications. This fundamental knowledge will prepare workers to accept and use the new products that result from each advance in technology.

Opening a Document

When a document has been saved, it can be opened at the Open dialog box. To open a previously saved document, you would complete the following steps:

1. At a clear editing window, click the Open button on the Toolbar.
2. At the Open dialog box, click once on the document name you want opened.
3. Click the Open button.

You can also open a document at the Open dialog box by double-clicking the document name. When a document is opened it is displayed in the editing window where you can make changes. Whenever changes are made to a document, save the document again to save the changes.

EXERCISE 2

Opening and Closing a Document

Open

1. At a clear editing window, open the document named Ch 01, Ex 01 by completing the following steps:
   a. Click the Open button on the Toolbar.
   b. At the Open dialog box, position the arrow pointer on *Ch 01, Ex 01*, then double-click the left mouse button.
2. Close Ch 01, Ex 01 by clicking File, then Close or clicking the Close button (the button containing the "X") located at the right side of the Menu bar.

Printing a Document

The computer exercises you will be completing require that you make a hard copy of the document. (Soft copy is a document displayed in the editing window and hard copy is a document printed on paper.) To print a document, you would complete the following steps:

1. Open the document to be printed.
2. Click the Print button on the Toolbar.
3. At the Print dialog box, click the Print button located at the bottom of the dialog box.

Print

You can also display the Print dialog box by clicking File, then Print or by pressing Ctrl + P. Before displaying the Print dialog box, check to make sure the printer is turned on.

EXERCISE 3

Printing a Document

1. At a clear editing window, open Ch 01, Ex 01.
2. Print Ch 01, Ex 01 by completing the following steps:
   a. Click the Print button on the Toolbar.
   b. At the Print dialog box, click the Print button.
3. Close Ch 01, Ex 01.

Exiting WordPerfect and Windows 95

When you are finished working with WordPerfect and have saved all necessary information, exit WordPerfect by clicking File, then Exit or clicking the Close button (contains an X) located at the right side of the Title bar. After exiting WordPerfect 7, exit Windows 95 by completing the following steps:

1. Click the Start button at the left side of the Taskbar.
2. At the pop-up menu, click Shut Down.
3. At the Shut Down Windows dialog box, make sure *Shut Down the Computer?* is selected, then click Yes.

EXERCISE 4

Creating a Document

1. At a clear editing window, key the information shown in figure 1.7. (Correct any errors highlighted by Spell-As-You-Go as they occur and remember to space once after end-of-sentence punctuation.)
2. Save the document and name it Ch 01, Ex 04 by completing the following steps:
   a. Click the Save button on the Toolbar.
   b. At the Save As dialog box, key **Ch 01, Ex 04**.
   c. Click the Save button or press Enter.
3. Print Ch 01, Ex 04.
4. Close the document by clicking File, then Close or clicking the Close button at the right side of the Menu bar.

Creating, Saving, and Printing WordPerfect Documents 13

Figure 1.7

We are living in what is called the "information age." In this age, information is regarded as a company asset or resource. The ability to access information on a timely basis is critical to an organization's ability to be competitive and to operate at a profit. Business information systems that integrate software, hardware, and internal and external communication links are continually being developed and refined.

There are many obstacles to the successful development of integrated systems. First and foremost is how to get people to change the way they communicate information. Other obstacles to improving telecommunications relate to technology.

EXERCISE 5

Opening and Closing a Document, then Exiting WordPerfect

1. At a clear editing window, open Ch 01, Ex 04 by completing the following steps:
   a. Click the Open button on the Toolbar.
   b. At the Open dialog box, position the arrow pointer on *Ch 01, Ex 04*, then double-click the left mouse button.
2. Close Ch 01, Ex 04.
3. Exit WordPerfect 7 and Windows 95 by completing the following steps:
   a. Click File, then Exit.
   b. At the Windows 95 desktop, click the Start button on the Taskbar, then click Shut Down. At the Shut Down Windows dialog box, click Yes.

CHAPTER SUMMARY

- ▼ Computer equipment is called the hardware. The program used to operate the computer is called the software.

- ▼ The Title bar displays at the top of the screen. It displays the name of the current document.

- ▼ The Menu bar is the second line on the screen. It contains a list of commands used to customize a WordPerfect document.

- ▼ The Toolbar is located below the Menu bar and displays icons of common features, programs, and macros. You can use the mouse and the Toolbar to execute these features quickly.

- ▼ The Power Bar is a series of buttons (options) below the Toolbar. These buttons are used to quickly access text editing and text layout features.

- ▼ The insertion point appears as a blinking vertical bar and indicates the position of the next character entered in the editing window.

- ▼ The mouse pointer displays as an arrow pointing up and to the left. As the arrow pointer is moved in a document screen, a slender gray line called a *shadow pointer* will appear at the tip of the arrow. The shadow pointer shows exactly where the insertion point will be positioned when you click the left mouse button.

- ▼ The scroll bars appear as gray-shaded bars along the right and toward the bottom of the document window and are used to quickly scroll through a document.

- ▼ The Status bar, positioned below the horizontal scroll bar, displays the current location of the insertion point by page number and line and position measurements. The Status bar indicates other information such as the currently selected printer and the date and time.

- ▼ WordPerfect automatically wraps text to the next line as you key information.

- ▼ WordPerfect's QuickCorrect feature will automatically correct certain errors as soon as you press the space bar. For example, if you key *adn* and then press the space bar, QuickCorrect will automatically change the word to *and*.

- ▼ The Spell-As-You-Go feature will insert red slashmarks below words that are not found in the Spelling dictionary.

- ▼ To save and open documents on your data disk, the default folder can be changed at the Open dialog box or the Save As dialog box.

- ▼ Document names can be a maximum of 255 characters in length including the drive letter and folder name. The name can contain letters, numbers, and spaces.

- ▼ Drop-down menus and dialog boxes can be removed from the editing window with the mouse or the keyboard.

- ▼ A document can be printed with the Print button on the Toolbar or the Print option from the File drop-down menu. These two methods cause the Print dialog box to display on the screen. At the Print dialog box, click the Print button.

- ▼ You should always exit WordPerfect and Windows 95 before turning off the computer.

Loading WordPerfect 7

1. Turn on the computer.
2. At the Windows 95 desktop, position the arrow pointer on the Start button on the Taskbar (located at the bottom left side of the screen), then click the left mouse button.
3. At the pop-up menu, position the arrow pointer on *Corel WordPerfect Suite 7* (you do not need to click the left mouse button). This should cause another menu to display to the right of the first pop-up menu.
4. Move the arrow pointer to *Corel WordPerfect 7*, then click the left mouse button.

Saving a Document

1. Click the Save button on the Toolbar.
2. At the Save As dialog box, key a name for the document.
3. Click the Save button.

Opening a Document

1. Click the Open button on the Toolbar.
2. At the Open dialog box, double-click the document name to be opened.

Closing a Document

1. Click File, then Close or click the Close button (contains an X) located at the right side of the Menu bar.

Printing a Document

1. Click File, then Print or click the Print button on the Toolbar.
2. At the Print dialog box, click the Print button.

Exiting WordPerfect

1. Be sure all needed documents have been saved.
2. Click File, then Exit or click the Close button located at the right side of the Title bar.

Exiting Windows 95

1. Click the Start button at the lower left side of the Taskbar.
2. At the pop-up menu, click Shut Down.
3. At the Shut Down Windows dialog box, make sure *Shut down the computer?* is selected, then click Yes.

CHECK YOUR UNDERSTANDING

Matching: In the space provided at the left, indicate the correct letter that matches each description.

- **A** Close
- **B** Cursor
- **C** Exit
- **D** FastCorrect
- **E** FastTip
- **F** Insertion point
- **G** Menu bar
- **H** Power Bar
- **I** QuickCorrect
- **J** QuickTip
- **K** Shadow pointer
- **L** Spell-As-You-Go
- **M** Status bar
- **N** Taskbar
- **O** Title bar
- **P** Toolbar

_P_ 1. This bar displays icons of common features, programs, and macros.

_G_ 2. This bar contains a list of commands used to customize a WordPerfect document.

_H_ 3. This bar contains a series of buttons (options) used to quickly access text editing and text layout features.

_J_ 4. This appears after approximately one second when the arrow pointer is positioned on a button on the Toolbar.

_O_ 5. This displays at the top of the WordPerfect screen and displays the name of the currently open document.

_L_ 6. This feature inserts red slashmarks below words not contained in the Spelling dictionary.

_F_ 7. This displays as a vertical bar and indicates the position of the next character entered in the editing window.

_M_ 8. This bar displays the current location of the insertion point by page number and line and position measurements.

_I_ 9. This WordPerfect feature automatically corrects certain words that are keyed incorrectly.

_C_ 10. One method for exiting WordPerfect is to click this button (displays with an "X"), located at the right side of the Title bar.

_K_ 11. This pointer displays as a slender gray line and shows exactly where the insertion point will be positioned when the left mouse button is clicked.

SKILL ASSESSMENTS

Assessment 1

1. Load Windows 95 and WordPerfect 7.
2. At the clear editing window, change the default folder to the drive where your student data disk is located. (Check with your instructor to determine if this step is necessary.)
3. Key the text in figure 1.8. (Correct any errors highlighted by Spell-As-You-Go as they occur and remember to space once after end-of-sentence punctuation.)

Creating, Saving, and Printing WordPerfect Documents

4. Save the document and name it Ch 01, SA 01.
5. Print Ch 01, SA 01.
6. Close Ch 01, SA 01.

Figure 1.8

For more than 100 years the U.S. public telephone system has provided the means to transmit information via voice. In the past 30 years, the public telephone system, designed for voice transmission, has also provided the means for transmitting data. Currently, 80 to 85 percent of the traffic over telephone lines is voice. Within the next few years, data traffic over the public telephone system is expected to exceed voice traffic.

Traditionally, the signals sent over the telephone system are sent as analog waves, which are fine for voice transmission. The signals for information transmitted from computers used for business applications are sent as digits that have only two values, 0 or 1.

A series of 0s and 1s are used to represent letters, numbers, sounds, values, symbols, and format codes. Since the telephone system transmits information as an analog wave, a modem (MOdulator/DEModulator) is needed to convert digits into analog waves. The modem adds to the cost of transmitting data over the public telephone system.

Assessment 2

1. At the clear editing window, change the default folder to the drive where your student data disk is located. (Check with your instructor to determine if this step is necessary.)
2. Key the text in figure 1.9. (Correct any errors highlighted by Spell-As-You-Go as they occur and remember to space once after end-of-sentence punctuation.)
3. Save the document and name it Ch 01, SA 02.
4. Print and then close Ch 01, SA 02.

Figure 1.9

Early mainframe computers consisted of a centralized system. Most computer systems resided in a separate room and were operated by a few highly trained individuals. For many companies, computers represented a large investment. The centralized organization required employees to bring individual requests to the computer room for processing.

The advent of microcomputers brought substantial computing power to the desktop. This capability was in direct contrast to the centralized mainframe computing of the past. Individual computers that operate with little or no central control are called distributed computing systems. Distributed computing allows desktop computers to perform many of the tasks formerly available only on mainframe computers.

2

EDITING A DOCUMENT

PERFORMANCE OBJECTIVE

Upon successful completion of chapter 2, you will be able to edit a WordPerfect document.

Many documents that are created need to have changes made to them. These changes may include adding text, called *inserting*, or removing text, called *deleting*. To insert or delete text, you need to be able to move the insertion point to certain locations in a document without erasing the text it passes through. For example, if you key three paragraphs and then notice an error in the first paragraph, you need to move the insertion point through lines of text to the location of the error without deleting the lines.

To move the insertion point without interfering with text, you can use the mouse, the keyboard, or the mouse combined with the keyboard.

Moving the Insertion Point with the Mouse

The mouse can be used to move the insertion point quickly to specific locations in the document. To do this, move the arrow pointer to the desired location, check to make sure the shadow pointer is in the correct location, then click the left mouse button.

Scrolling with the Mouse

In addition to moving the insertion point to a specific location, the mouse can be used to move the display of text in the editing window. This is referred to as *scrolling*. Scrolling in a document changes the text displayed but does not move the insertion point. If you want to move the insertion point to a new location in a document, scroll to the location, position the arrow pointer (and shadow pointer) in the desired location, then click the left mouse button.

You can use the mouse with the *horizontal scroll bar* and/or the *vertical scroll bar* to scroll through text in a document. The horizontal scroll bar displays toward the bottom of the document window (just above the Status bar) and the vertical scroll bar displays at the right side. Figure 2.1 displays the document window with the scroll bars and elements of the scroll bars identified.

Figure 2.1

Scroll Bars

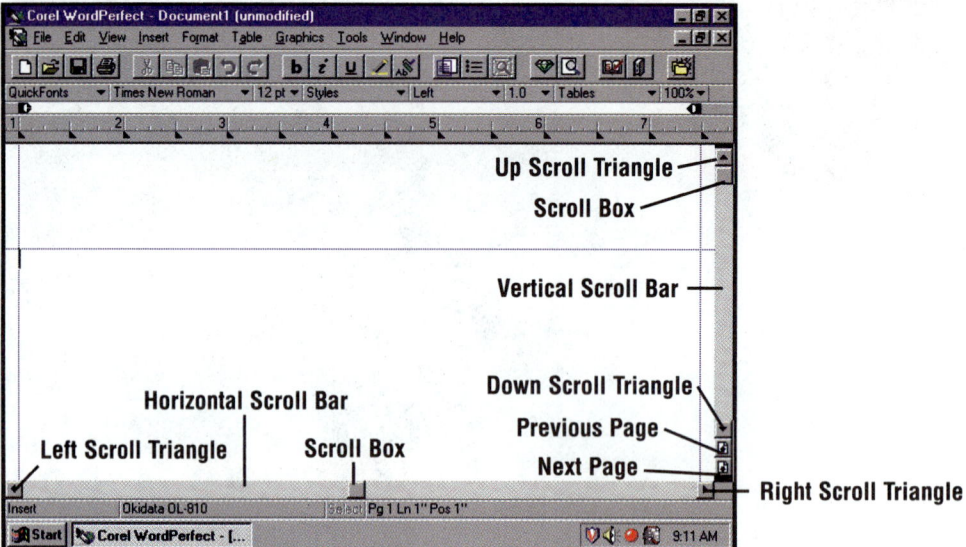

Scrolling with the Vertical Scroll Bar

An up-pointing triangle displays at the top of the vertical scroll bar. This up-pointing triangle is called the *up scroll triangle*. You can scroll up a line in the document by positioning the arrow pointer on the up scroll triangle and clicking the left button. To scroll through the document continuously, position the arrow pointer on the up scroll triangle, then hold down the left button.

The down-pointing triangle at the bottom of the vertical scroll bar is the *down scroll triangle*. Scroll down a line in the document by positioning the arrow pointer on the down scroll triangle then clicking the left button. Hold down the left button if you want continuous action.

When you begin working in longer documents, the scroll bars will be useful in scrolling to certain areas in a document. The small gray box located in the vertical scroll bar is called the *scroll box*. This scroll box indicates the location of the text in the editing window in relation to the document. The scroll box moves along the vertical scroll bar as you scroll through the document. You can scroll up or down through a document one screen at a time by using the arrow pointer on the scroll bar. To scroll up one screen, position the arrow pointer above the scroll box (but below the up scroll arrow) and click the left button. Position the arrow pointer below the scroll box and click the left button to scroll down a screen. If you hold the left button down, the action becomes continuous. You can also position the arrow pointer on the scroll box, hold down the left mouse button, then drag the scroll box along the scroll bar to reposition text in the editing window. For example, if you want to scroll to the beginning of the document, position the arrow pointer on the scroll box in the vertical scroll bar, hold down the left mouse button, drag the scroll box to the beginning of the scroll bar, then release the mouse button.

Scrolling with the Horizontal Scroll Bar

A left-pointing triangle called the *left scroll triangle* displays at the left side of the horizontal scroll bar. The *right scroll triangle* displays at the right side of the horizontal scroll bar. These scroll triangles operate in the same manner as the up and down scroll triangles on the vertical scroll bar. Click the left scroll triangle to scroll the text to the right in the editing window. Click the right scroll triangle to scroll the text to the left in the editing window. To scroll the text to the right, position the arrow pointer to the left of the horizontal scroll box (but after the left scroll triangle) and click the left mouse button. To scroll the text to the left in the editing window, position the

20 Chapter 2

arrow pointer to the right of the horizontal scroll box (but before the right scroll triangle) and click the left mouse button. You can also position the arrow pointer on the scroll box, hold down the left mouse button, then drag the scroll box along the horizontal scroll bar to reposition text in the editing window.

Scrolling with Page Icons

Previous Page

Two buttons display at the bottom of the vertical scroll bar. The button with the page and up arrow is the *Previous Page* button. The button with the page and down arrow is the *Next Page* button. Click the Previous Page button to scroll to the previous page and click the Next Page button to scroll to the next page in the document.

Next Page

EXERCISE 1

Moving the Insertion Point and Scrolling through a Document

1. Load WordPerfect 7 following the instructions in chapter 1.
2. At a clear editing window, open Report 02. This document is located on your student data disk.
3. Practice moving the insertion point and scrolling through the document using the mouse by completing the following steps:
   a. Position the arrow pointer (and shadow pointer) at the beginning of the first paragraph, then click the left button. This moves the text insertion point to the location of the shadow pointer.
   b. Position the arrow pointer on the down scroll triangle, then click the left mouse button several times. This scrolls down lines of text in the document. With the arrow pointer on the down scroll triangle, hold down the left mouse button and keep it down until the end of the document is displayed.
   c. Position the arrow pointer on the up scroll triangle and hold down the left mouse button until the beginning of the document is displayed.
4. Position the arrow pointer below the scroll box, then click the left mouse button. Continue positioning the arrow pointer below the scroll box and clicking the left mouse button until the end of the document is displayed.
5. Position the arrow pointer on the scroll box in the vertical scroll bar. Hold down the left mouse button, drag the scroll box to the top of the vertical scroll bar, then release the mouse button.
6. Close Report 02.

Moving the Insertion Point with the Keyboard

To move the insertion point with the keyboard, use the arrow keys located to the right of the regular keyboard. The illustration in figure 2.2 shows arrow keys marked with left, right, up, and down arrows.

Figure 2.2 — Insertion Point Movement Keys

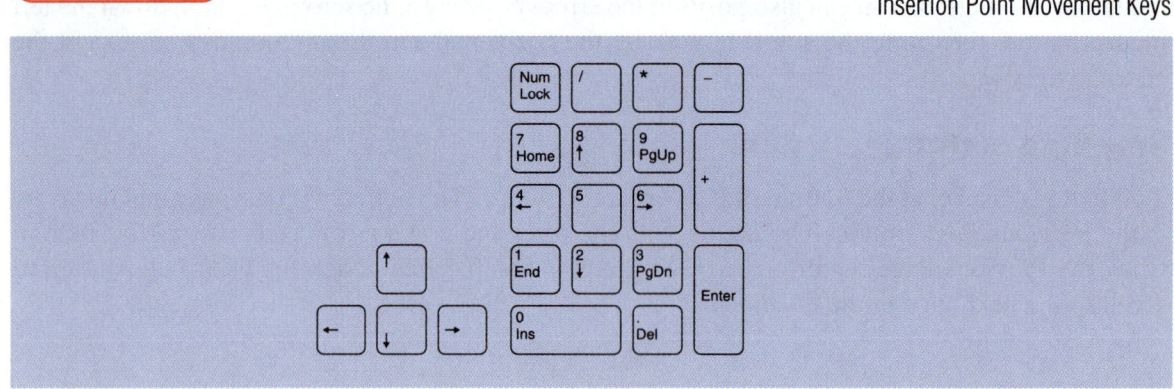

If you press the up arrow key, the insertion point moves up one line. If you press the other arrow keys, the insertion point moves in the direction indicated on the key. If you hold down an arrow key, it becomes a continuous-action key causing the insertion point to move quickly in the direction indicated. You can also move the insertion point to a specific location in a document by choosing one of the commands shown in figure 2.3.

Figure 2.3 — Insertion Point Movement Commands

To move insertion point	Press
One character left	←
One character right	→
One line up	↑
One line down	↓
One word to the left	CTRL + ←
One word to the right	CTRL + →
To end of a line	END
To beginning of a line	HOME
To beginning of current paragraph	CTRL + ↑
To beginning of next paragraph	CTRL + ↓
Up one screen	PG UP
Down one screen	PG DN
To beginning of previous page	ALT + PG UP
To beginning of next page	ALT + PG DN
To beginning of document	CTRL + HOME
To end of document	CTRL + END

Moving the Insertion Point to a Specific Page

WordPerfect includes a Go To option that you can use to move the insertion point to a specific page within a document. To move the insertion point to a specific page, click Edit, then Go To; or press Ctrl + G. At the Go To dialog box, key the page number, then press Enter.

EXERCISE

Moving the Insertion Point using Keys on the Keyboard

1. At a clear editing window, open Report 03. This document is located on your student data disk.
2. Practice moving the insertion point with the keyboard by completing the following steps:
   a. Press the right arrow key to move the insertion point to the next character to the right. Continue pressing the right arrow key until the insertion point is located at the end of the first paragraph.
   b. Press Ctrl + right arrow key to move the insertion point to the next word to the right. Continue pressing Ctrl + right arrow key until the insertion point is located on the last word of the second paragraph.
   c. Press Ctrl + left arrow key until the insertion point is positioned at the beginning of the document.
   d. Press the End key to move the insertion point to the end of the first line.
   e. Press the Home key to move the insertion point to the beginning of the first line.
   f. Press Page Down to move the insertion point to the next to last line at the bottom of the editing window.
   g. Press Page Up to move the insertion point to the top of the editing window.
   h. Press Alt + Page Down to position the insertion point at the beginning of page 2. Press Alt + Page Down again to position the insertion point at the beginning of page 3.
   i. Press Alt + Page Up to position the insertion point at the beginning of page 2.
   j. Press Alt + Page Up to position the insertion point at the beginning of page 1.
   k. Position the insertion point at the beginning of page 4 using the Go To function by completing the following steps:
      (1) Click Edit, then Go To.
      (2) At the Go To dialog box, key **4**, then press Enter.
   l. Press Ctrl + End to move the insertion point to the last character in the document.
   m. Press Ctrl + Home to move the insertion point to the first character in the document.
3. Close Report 03.

Inserting Text

Once you have created a document, you may want to insert information you forgot or have since decided to include. At the default WordPerfect editing window, the Insert mode is on. The word *Insert* is displayed toward the bottom of the document window in the Status bar. With Insert on, anything you key will be inserted in the document (rather than taking the place of existing text).

Editing a Document

If you want to insert or add something, leave Insert on. However, if you want to key over existing text, turn Insert off by pressing the Insert key. When you press the Insert key, the word *Typeover* (rather than *Insert*) displays in the Status bar. To turn Insert back on, press the Insert key again.

Deleting Text

When you edit a document, you may want to delete (remove) text. You may want to delete just one character or several lines. WordPerfect offers the deletion commands shown in figure 2.4.

Figure 2.4 — Deletion Commands

To delete	Press
Character immediately to the right of insertion point	DEL
Character immediately to the left of insertion point	BACKSPACE
Word where insertion point is positioned	CTRL + BACKSPACE
Text to the end of the line	CTRL + DEL

Splitting and Joining Paragraphs

By inserting or deleting, paragraphs of text can be split or joined. To split a large paragraph into two smaller paragraphs, position the insertion point on the first letter that will begin the new paragraph, then press the Enter key twice. The first time you press Enter, the text is moved to the next line. The second time you press Enter, a blank line is inserted between the paragraphs.

To join two paragraphs into one, you need to delete the spaces between them. To do this, position the insertion point on the first character of the second paragraph, then press the Backspace key until the paragraphs join. More than likely, you will need to then press the space bar to separate the sentences. You can also join two paragraphs together by positioning the insertion point one space past the period at the end of the first paragraph and then pressing the Delete key until the paragraphs join. When you join the two paragraphs, the new paragraph will be automatically adjusted.

EXERCISE

Editing a Document

1. At a clear editing window, open Ch 02, Ex 03. This document is located on your student data disk.
2. Make the changes indicated by the proofreaders' marks in figure 2.5. (Proofreaders' marks are listed and described in Appendix A at the end of this textbook.)
3. Save the document with the same name (Ch 02, Ex 03) by clicking the Save button on the Toolbar.
4. Print and then close Ch 02, Ex 03.

Figure 2.5

One obstacle to smooth ^telephone communications has to do with standards. ~~A procedure becomes standard through common practice.~~ A person can pick up a phone anywhere and call someone nearly anywhere in the world ~~and~~ if both people speak the same language, they can communicate.

No ¶ Conversely, not all computers made by ^various manufacturers are able to communicate with each other. ~~This is~~ because they speak different languages. Before communication can occur, special equipment is needed to "translate" the message. Solutions are being developed to correct ^and refine these and other communication obstacles. ¶ There are other operations that depend on ^an intricate system of telecommunications.

No ¶ Most major hotel chains, for example, can book reservations from any location in the United States, and increasingly from anywhere in the world. Airlines ~~also~~ use a one-location reservation service. ~~This~~ ^which gives customers the convenience of booking round-trip vacations before they ever leave home. These are just a few ways business and industry use telecommunications ^technology to gain a ~~sharp~~ competitive edge. To remain competitive, even the smallest businesses are finding themselves entering the telecommunications technology market. ~~Their aim is to increase customer satisfaction and their profit margins.~~

Selecting Text

The mouse and/or keyboard can be used to select a specific amount of text. Once selected, you can delete the text or perform other WordPerfect functions involving the selected text.

Selecting Text with the Mouse

The mouse can be used to select varying amounts of text. When text is selected it displays in reverse video in the document window as shown in figure 2.6. For example, if the document window displays with a white background and black characters, selected text will display as white characters on a black background.

Figure 2.6

Selected Text

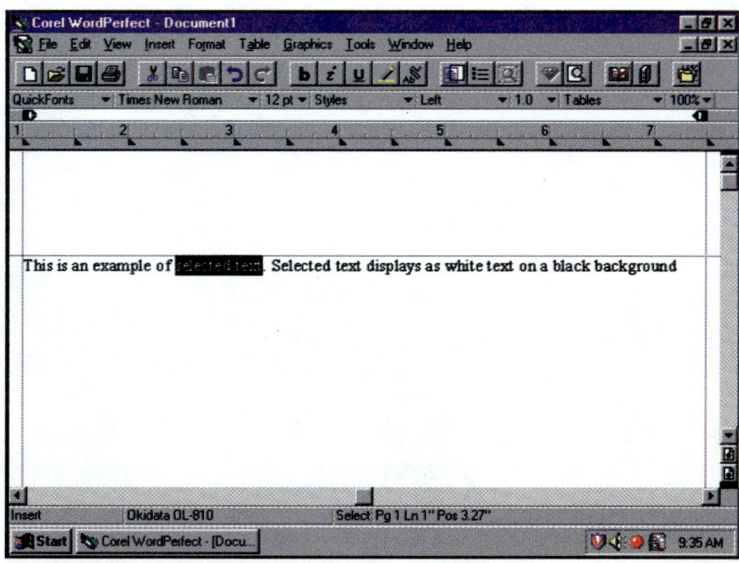

Editing a Document 25

You can use the mouse to select a word, sentence, paragraph, or an entire document. Figure 2.7 indicates the steps to follow to select various amounts of text. To select certain amounts of text such as a line, the instructions in the figure tell you to click in the selection bar. The selection bar is the space at the left side of the document window between the left edge of the screen and the vertical blue guide line. When the arrow pointer is positioned in the selection bar, the pointer turns into an arrow pointing up and to the right (instead of to the left).

Figure 2.7 — Selecting with the Mouse

To select	complete these steps using the mouse
A word	Double-click anywhere in the word.
A sentence	Triple-click anywhere in the sentence.
Multiple sentences	Click and drag in selection bar to left of the sentences.
A paragraph	Double-click in selection bar next to paragraph or quadruple-click anywhere in the paragraph.
Multiple paragraphs	Click and drag in selection bar to the left of the paragraphs.

To select an amount of text other than a word, sentence, or paragraph, position the arrow pointer on the first character of the text to be selected, hold down the left mouse button, drag the arrow pointer to the last character of the text to be selected, then release the mouse button.

When text is selected, the word *Select* displays in black in the Status bar. To delete selected text, press the Delete key. This deletes the selected text and turns off the Select mode. When the Select mode is turned off, the word *Select* displays in gray in the Status bar. To turn off the Select mode without deleting text, position the arrow pointer outside the selected text, then click the left mouse button.

Selecting Text with the Keyboard

To select a specific amount of text using the keyboard, use the Select key, F8, along with the arrow keys. If you press F8, the Select mode is turned on. With the Select mode on, press any of the arrow keys. You can also select text with the keyboard using the commands shown in figure 2.8.

Figure 2.8 — Selecting with the Keyboard

To select	Press
One character to right	SHIFT + →
One character to left	SHIFT + ←
To end of word	CTRL + SHIFT + →
To beginning of word	CTRL + SHIFT + ←
To end of line	SHIFT + END
To beginning of line	SHIFT + HOME
One line up	SHIFT + ↑
One line down	SHIFT + ↓

To beginning of paragraph	CTRL + SHIFT + ↑
To end of paragraph	CTRL + SHIFT + ↓
One screen up	SHIFT + PG UP
One screen down	SHIFT + PG DN
To beginning of document	CTRL + SHIFT + HOME
To end of document	CTRL + SHIFT + END

With the text selected, press the Delete key to remove it from the document. When selected text is deleted from the document, the text is removed and the Select mode is turned off. If Select is turned on and you decide to turn it off without deleting any text, press F8 again. This turns off Select and changes the display of Select to gray in the Status bar.

Selecting Text with the Edit Menu

The Edit drop-down menu contains an option that lets you select a sentence, paragraph, page, or the entire document. To use the Edit menu to select a sentence, position the insertion point anywhere in the sentence, then click Edit, point to Select, then click Sentence. To select a paragraph, click Edit, point to Select, then click Paragraph. To select a page, click Edit, point to Select, then click Page. To select the entire document, click Edit, point to Select, then click All.

EXERCISE 4

Selecting and Deleting Text

1. At a clear editing window, open Ch 02, Ex 04. This document is located on your student data disk.
2. Delete the name, *Mr. Gerald Koch*, and the department, *CIS Department*, using the mouse by completing the following steps:
    a. Position the arrow pointer on the *M* in *Mr.* (in the address).
    b. Hold down the left button, then drag the arrow pointer down until *Mr. Gerald Koch* and *CIS Department* are selected.
    c. Release the left mouse button.
    d. Press the Delete key.
3. With the insertion point positioned at the left margin on the line above *San Mateo Community College*, key the name, **Ms. Aleta Sauter**.
4. Delete the reference line, *Re: Telecommunications Course*, using the Select mode by completing the following steps:
    a. Position the insertion point on the *R* in *Re:*.
    b. Press F8 to turn on the Select mode.
    c. Press the down arrow key twice. (This selects the reference line and the blank line below it.)
    d. Press the Delete key.
5. Delete the first sentence in the first paragraph using the Edit menu by completing the following steps:

Editing a Document 27

> a. Position the insertion point anywhere in the sentence *The Western Computer Technology conference we attended last week was very educational for me.*
> b. Click E̲dit, point to Sel̲ect, then click S̲entence.
> c. Press the Delete key.
> 6. Delete the first sentence in the second paragraph (the sentence that reads, *The interest in the class has been phenomenal.*) using the Edit menu.
> 7. Delete the third paragraph in the letter using the Edit menu by completing the following steps:
>   a. Position the insertion point anywhere in the third paragraph (the paragraph that begins, *The instructor for the course...*).
>   b. Click E̲dit, point to Sel̲ect, then click P̲aragraph.
>   c. Press the Delete key.
> 8. Change the salutation from *Dear Mr. Koch* to *Dear Ms. Sauter*.
> 9. Save the document with the same name (Ch 02, Ex 04) by clicking the Save button on the Toolbar.
> 10. Print and then close Ch 02, Ex 04.

Using the Undo, Redo, and Undelete Options

If you make a mistake and delete text that you did not intend to delete, or if you change your mind after deleting text and want to retrieve it, you can use the Undo or Undelete options.

Undo

Redo

The Undo option will undo the last function entered at the keyboard. For example, if you just changed the left and right margins, clicking the Undo button on the Toolbar or clicking E̲dit, then U̲ndo will cause the margin codes to be removed from the document. If you just turned on bold, clicking the Undo button on the Toolbar or clicking E̲dit, then U̲ndo causes the bold codes to be removed from the document. If you just keyed text in the document, clicking the Undo button on the Toolbar or clicking E̲dit, then U̲ndo causes the text to be removed. WordPerfect removes text to the beginning of the document or up to the point where text had been deleted previously in the document. The Redo option will reverse the last Undo action. To do this, click the Redo button on the Toolbar or click E̲dit, then R̲edo.

You can use the Un̲delete option from the E̲dit menu to restore deleted text. WordPerfect retains the last three deletions made in one editing session. If you decide you want to restore text, move the insertion point to the position where you want text inserted, then click E̲dit, then Un̲delete. The Undelete dialog box shown in figure 2.9 displays in the editing window.

Undelete Dialog Box

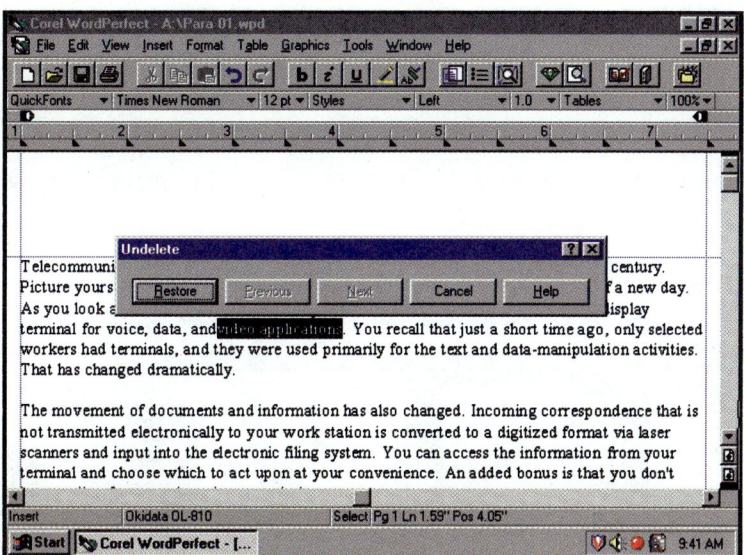

Figure 2.9

To restore the text, click Restore. If you want to see the other two deletions in memory, click Next or Previous. Clicking Next displays the next deletion in memory and clicking Previous displays the previous deletion in memory. If you want information about the Undelete feature, click Help. This displays the WordPerfect Help dialog box at the right side of the editing window. This Help screen contains information about the Undelete feature. After reading the information, remove the Help dialog box by clicking File, then Exit at the Help dialog box menu. To remove the Undelete dialog box from the editing window without undeleting any text, click Cancel. The Undelete option restores text at the insertion point while the Undo and Redo options restore information in its original location.

WordPerfect maintains actions in temporary memory. If you want to undo an action performed earlier, click the Undo/Redo History option at the Edit drop-down menu. With the Undo/Redo History option, you can reverse up to 300 actions in a document. To undo or redo a previous action, click Edit, then Undo/Redo History. This causes the Undo/Redo History dialog box to display as shown in figure 2.10. The contents of this dialog box will vary depending on what type of action has been performed in the document. Actions that have been performed in the document are displayed at the left side of the dialog box in the Undo list box. Any actions that have been redone are displayed in the Redo list box in the dialog box.

Editing a Document

Figure 2.10

Undo/Redo History Dialog Box

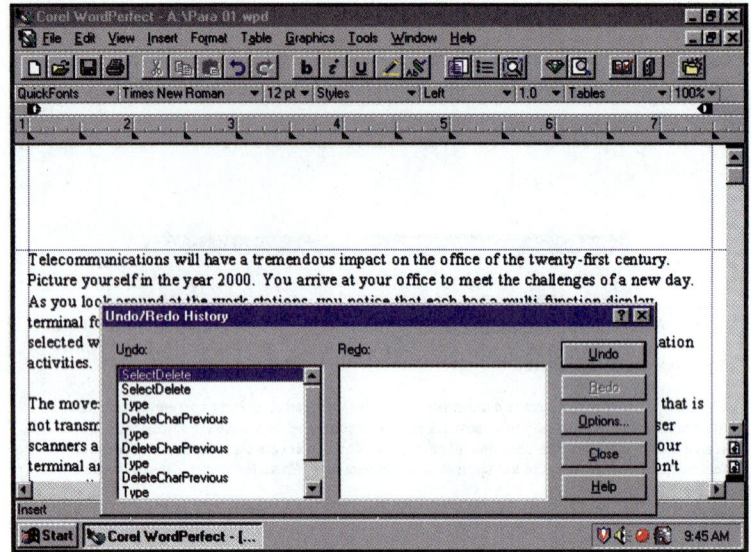

To undo or redo two or more actions, select the item to be undone or redone. This causes any actions listed above the selected item to also be selected. With the items selected, click Undo or Redo. Click Options to display the Undo/Redo Options dialog box. At this dialog box, you can specify the number of Undo or Redo items (from 0 to 300) you want to maintain. After selecting items to be undone or redone at the Undo/Redo History dialog box, click Close to return to the document.

EXERCISE 5

Deleting and Restoring Text

1. At a clear editing window, open Para 01. This document is located on your student data disk.
2. Make the following changes to the document:
   a. Move the insertion point to the end of the document. Press the Backspace key until the last three words of the document (*cluttering your desk.*) are deleted.
   b. Undo the deletion by clicking the Undo button on the Toolbar.
   c. Select the first sentence in the first paragraph, then delete it.
   d. Select the second paragraph in the document, then delete it.
   e. Position the insertion point at the beginning of the document, then insert the paragraph just deleted by completing the following steps:
      (1) Click Edit, then Undelete.
      (2) At the Undelete dialog box, click Restore.
   f. Position the insertion point at the end of the second paragraph (one space after the period), then insert the sentence previously deleted by completing the following steps:
      (1) Click Edit, then Undelete.
      (2) At the Undelete dialog box, click Previous until the sentence *Telecommunications will have a tremendous impact on the office of the twenty-first century.* is displayed in the document.

30 Chapter 2

> (3) Click <u>R</u>estore.
> 3. Save the document with the same name (Para 01) by clicking the Save button on the Toolbar.
> 4. Print and then close Para 01.

Saving Documents

In chapter 1, you learned to save a document with the Save button on the Toolbar or the Save option from the File drop-down menu. The File drop-down menu also contains a Save As option. The Save As option is used to save a previously created document with a new name.

For example, suppose you created and saved a document named *Memo*, then later open it. If you save the document again with the Save button on the Toolbar or the Save option from the File drop-down menu, WordPerfect will save the document with the same name. You will not be prompted to key a name for the document. This is because WordPerfect assumes that when you use the Save option on a previously saved document, you want to save it with the same name.

If you open the document named *Memo*, make some changes to it, then want to save it with a new name, you must use the Save As option. When you use the Save As option, WordPerfect displays the Save As dialog box where you can key a new name for the document. To save a document with Save As, click <u>F</u>ile, then Save <u>A</u>s.

In many of the computer exercises in this text, you will be asked to open a document from your student data disk, then save it with a new name. You will be instructed to use the Save As option to do this.

EXERCISE

Editing a Document

> 1. At a clear editing window, open Para 02. This document is located on your student data disk.
> 2. Save the document with the name Ch 02, Ex 06 using Save As by completing the following steps:
>   a. Click <u>F</u>ile, then Save <u>A</u>s.
>   b. At the Save As dialog box, key **Ch 02, Ex 06**.
>   c. Click <u>S</u>ave or press Enter.
> 3. Make the changes indicated by the proofreaders' marks in figure 2.11.
> 4. Save the document again with the same name (Ch 02, Ex 06). To do this, click the Save button on the Toolbar.
> 5. Print and then close Ch 02, Ex 06.

Figure 2.11

A change that is ~~occurring~~ *happening* in offices today is the ability to create documents by dictating to *a* ~~your~~ terminal through a ~~feature called~~ voice-activated display. This ~~feature~~ allows you to view dictation on your terminal for editing and revising. You also have the option of ~~dictating or~~ using your hand-manipulated input device to make corrections.

The text ~~Everything~~ you dictate is *checked by* ~~run through~~ an electronic dictionary and a grammar and syntax validator before the final draft is distributed. If you mistakenly dictate "you is" instead of "you are," the grammar and syntax validator corrects it. Once your document is complete, you control how and when it is distributed. What~~ever~~ you prepare can be sent electronically anywhere within your organization or the world at the touch of a button. ~~In addition,~~ *a* copy of what you distribute is filed automatically in *an* ~~the~~ optical disk storage system~~, making~~ *This makes* storage and retrieval compact and easy.

CHAPTER SUMMARY

▼ The insertion point can be moved throughout the document without interfering with text by using the mouse, the keyboard, or the mouse combined with the keyboard. The insertion point can be moved by character, word, screen, or page and from the first to the last character in a document.

▼ Use the horizontal/vertical scroll bars and the mouse to scroll through a document. Use the scroll box to determine insertion point location in an editing window.

▼ By default WordPerfect loads with the Insert mode on so text can easily be inserted. The Insert mode can be turned on and off with the Insert key. When Insert has been turned off, the message *Typeover* displays in the Status bar. When Insert is on, *Insert* displays in the Status bar.

▼ Text can be deleted by character, word, line, several lines, or partial page using specific keys or by selecting text using the mouse or the keyboard.

▼ To split a paragraph into two, position the insertion point on the first letter that will begin the new paragraph, then press Enter twice. To join two paragraphs into one, position the insertion point on the first character of the second paragraph, then press the Backspace key twice.

▼ A specific amount of text can be selected using the mouse or the keyboard. This text can then be deleted or manipulated in other ways using WordPerfect commands.

▼ The **U**ndo option will undo the last function entered at the keyboard or delete text that was just entered. The U**n**delete option will restore one or all of the last three deletions made in the document. WordPerfect retains the last 300 actions in temporary memory. These actions are listed in the Undo/Redo History dialog box.

▼ The Save As option is used to save a previously created document with a new name.

INSERTION POINT MOVEMENT REVIEW

Using the Mouse to Move the Insertion Point

to a specific location   Move arrow pointer to desired location, then click left button

Using the Keyboard to Move the Insertion Point

in the direction indicated	↑, ↓, ←, or →
One word right	CTRL + →
One word left	CTRL + ←
To end of line	END
To beginning of line	HOME
To beginning of current paragraph	CTRL + ↑
To previous paragraph	CTRL + ↑ ↑
To next paragraph	CTRL + ↓
Up one screen	PG UP
Down one screen	PG DN
To beginning of previous page	ALT + PG UP
To beginning of next page	ALT + PG DN
To beginning of document	CTRL + HOME
To end of document	CTRL + END

SCROLLING REVIEW

Up one line	Click the up scroll triangle on the vertical scroll bar
Up several lines	Position arrow pointer as above, then hold down left button
Down one line	Click the down scroll triangle on the vertical scroll bar
Down several lines	Position arrow pointer as above, then hold button down
Up one screen	Click with arrow pointer above scroll box on the vertical scroll bar
Up several screens	Position arrow pointer as above, then hold button down
Down one screen	Click with arrow pointer below scroll box on the vertical scroll bar
Down several screens	Position arrow pointer as above, then hold button down
To the beginning of the document	Position the arrow pointer on the vertical scroll box, hold down the left button, drag the scroll box to the beginning of the scroll bar
To the end of the document	Position the arrow pointer on the vertical scroll box, hold down the left button, drag the scroll box to the end of the scroll bar

Editing a Document

DELETION COMMANDS REVIEW

Delete character immediately to the left of insertion point	`DEL`
Delete character immediately to the right of insertion point	`BACKSPACE`
Delete word (including punctuation)	`CTRL` + `BACKSPACE`
Delete text to the end of the line	`CTRL` + `DEL`

SELECTING TEXT REVIEW

Using the Mouse

Select text	Position arrow pointer at the beginning of text to be selected, hold down left mouse button, drag the arrow pointer to end of text to be selected, then release the button
Select a word	Position arrow pointer within the word, double-click the left mouse button
Select a sentence	Position the arrow pointer within the sentence, triple-click the left mouse button
Select a paragraph	Position the arrow pointer within the paragraph, quickly click the left mouse button four times or double-click in selection bar

Using the Keyboard

Select text	Press `F8` and then use arrow keys to select text

Using the Edit Menu

Select a sentence	Position insertion point within the sentence, click Edit, Select, Sentence
Select a paragraph	Position insertion point within the paragraph, click Edit, Select, Paragraph
Select a page	Position insertion point within the page, click Edit, Select, Page
Select entire document	Click Edit, Select, All

Deleting Selected Text

Select, then permanently delete selected text		Select text, press `DEL`

OTHER COMMANDS REVIEW

Undo option	Edit, Undo
Undelete option	Edit, Undelete
Undo/Redo History dialog box	Edit, Undo/Redo History

Chapter 2

CHECK YOUR UNDERSTANDING

Matching: In the space provided at the left, indicate the correct letter that matches each description.

- **A** Backspace
- **B** Ctrl + Home
- **C** Ctrl + End
- **D** Ctrl + Delete
- **E** Delete
- **F** Insert
- **G** Redo
- **H** Save
- **I** Save As
- **J** Select
- **K** Undelete
- **L** Undo

__F__ 1. Press this key and the word *Insert* in the Status bar changes to *Typeover*.
__A__ 2. Press this key to delete text immediately to the left of the insertion point.
__K__ 3. This option from the Edit drop-down menu will display a dialog box where the last three deletions made in one editing session can be restored.
__C__ 4. Press these keys to move the insertion point to the last character in the document.
__I__ 5. Use this option from the File drop-down menu to save the currently displayed document with a different name.
__E__ 6. Press this key to delete the character immediately to the right of the insertion point.
__J__ 7. When text is selected, this word displays in black in the Status bar.
__D__ 8. Press these keys to delete text to the end of the line.
__B__ 9. Press these keys to move the insertion point to the first character in the document.
__G__ 10. Click this button on the Toolbar to reverse the last Undo.

SKILL ASSESSMENTS

Assessment 1

1. At a clear editing window, open Para 03. This document is located on your student data disk.
2. Save the document with Save As and name it Ch 02, SA 01.
3. Make the changes indicated by the proofreaders' marks in figure 2.12.
4. Save the document again with the same name (Ch 02, SA 01).
5. Print and then close Ch 02, SA 01.

Figure 2.12

In defending or prosecuting individuals, an attorney must research cases very extensively. This research is based on precedents established in cases having already been resolved before the courts. Many volumes of law books are available to search for the information needed. A number of companies have taken volumes of law manuals and recorded them electronically.

In conventional law practice, hundreds of hours are devoted to checking the indexes for the source of facts and figures and finding the pages that contain the information.

Being able to access information quickly eliminates wasted time and adds to productivity. Attorneys are now able to conduct much of their research electronically by using information databases developed for legal research. Attorneys at their law firms pay a monthly fee to access these databases, plus a per-minute charge for the electronic searches.

All the attorney needs is a computer terminal (such as a microcomputer), communication software, and a modem (a device that converts computer signals that travel over a telephone line). To use the electronically stored database of legal information, the attorney dials the telephone number of the computer that contains the database, and as soon as the connection is made, the attorney enters some key words related to the information needed.

In a matter of seconds, the computer electronically searches for the information and sends a message back to the attorney noting the information's location. The attorney can then either direct the computer to display this information on the screen or go back to the hard copy volumes of the law books to complete the research.

Assessment 2

1. At a clear editing window, open Para 04. This document is located on your student data disk.
2. Save the document with Save As and name it Ch 02, SA 02.
3. Make the changes indicated by the proofreaders' marks in figure 2.13.
4. Save the document again with the same name (Ch 02, SA 02).
5. Print and then close Ch 02, SA 02.

Figure 2.13

Imagine yourself in the year 2000. You arrive at your office to meet the challenges of a new day. As you look around at the workstations, you notice that each has a multi-function display terminal for voice, data, and video applications.

You recall that just a short time ago, only selected workers had terminals. They were used primarily for text and data manipulation functions and activities.

The movement of documents and information has also changed. Incoming correspondence that is not transmitted electronically to your workstation is converted to a digitized format via laser scanners. This is input into the electronic filing system.

You can access the information from your terminal and choose which to act upon at your convenience. An added bonus is that you don't have a pile of papers sitting around cluttering your desk. Another challenge is the ability to create documents by dictating to your terminal through a feature called voice-activated display. This feature allows you to view dictation on your terminal for editing. You also have the option of dictating or using your hand-manipulated input device to make corrections.

Everything you dictate is run through an electronic dictionary and a grammar and syntax validator before the final draft is distributed. If you mistakenly dictate "you is" instead of "you are," the grammar and syntax validator corrects it.

Assessment 3

1. At a clear editing window, compose a paragraph explaining when you would use the Save As command when saving a document and the advantages of Save As.
2. Save the document and name it Ch 02, SA 03.
3. Print and then close Ch 02, SA 03.

#) Need to complete yet. √Completed

You would use the Save As when there is a document already saved and you need to edit it and save the changes (to a new name). I like to use the Save As when ever I save a document, because it allows me to go back into that document and edit it and save it to the original "saved" name that was given, rather then using disk space, when creating new "save" names for the document and you don't need each document you edited.

3 FORMATTING CHARACTERS

PERFORMANCE OBJECTIVE

Upon successful completion of chapter 3, you will be able to enhance single-page business documents and reports with character formatting including all caps, bold, underlining, and italics. You will also learn to use WordPerfect's Help and PerfectExpert features.

As you work with WordPerfect, you will learn a number of commands and procedures that affect how the document appears when printed. The appearance of a document in the editing window and how it looks when printed is called the *format*. Formatting may include such elements as all caps, line spacing, margin settings, even or uneven margins, tabs, bolding, underlining, and much more.

Creating Text in All Caps

To key text in all uppercase letters, press the Caps Lock key. The Caps Lock key is a toggle key—press the key once to activate the Caps Lock feature, and press it again to turn it off. When Caps Lock is turned on, a green mode indicator light appears at the upper right side of the keyboard.

Using the Tab Key

The WordPerfect program contains a variety of default settings. A *default* is a preset standard or value that is established by the program. One default setting in WordPerfect is a Ruler Bar that contains tab settings every one-half inch. In a later chapter, you will learn how to change the default tab settings. For now, use the default tab settings to indent text from the left margin. To indent text, press the Tab key. The Tab key on a microcomputer keyboard is generally located above the Caps Lock key.

Formatting Text

Formatting can be applied to accentuate text, elicit a particular feeling about the text, or draw the reader's eyes to a particular word or words. There are a variety of ways that text can be

Formatting Characters   *39*

accentuated such as bolding, italicizing, and underlining. Text can be bolded, italicized, or underlined with buttons on the Toolbar, shortcut commands, or options at the Font dialog box. In this chapter, you will learn to bold, italicize, and underline with buttons on the Toolbar and shortcut commands. The Font dialog box is discussed in chapter 7.

Bolding Text

Bold

The Bold button on the Toolbar or the shortcut command, Ctrl + B, can be used to bold text. When text is bolded, it appears darker than surrounding text in the editing window and also on the printed page. Text can be bolded as it is being keyed, or existing text can be bolded. To bold text as it is being keyed, click the Bold button on the Toolbar or press Ctrl + B. Key the text to be bolded, then click the Bold button on the Toolbar again or press Ctrl + B. In addition to clicking the Bold button on the Toolbar or pressing Ctrl + B to turn off bold, you can also just press the right arrow key on the keyboard.

In exercise 1 and other exercises in this text, you will be required to create memos. Please refer to Appendix B at the end of this text for the correct placement and spacing of a traditional-style memo. Unless otherwise instructed by your teacher, use this format when creating memos. The initials of the person keying the memo usually appear at the end of the document. In this text, the initials will appear in the exercises as *xx*. Key your initials where you see the *xx*. Identifying document names in correspondences is a good idea because it lets you find and open the document quickly and easily at a future date. In this text, the document name is identified after the reference initials. Before printing any exercises, always proofread the document and correct any errors.

EXERCISE 1

Bolding Text as It Is Keyed

1. At a clear editing window, key the memo shown in figure 3.1 in the traditional-style memo format. Use Caps Lock to key the memorandum headings–*DATE*, *TO*, *FROM*, and *SUBJECT*. To align the information after *DATE:*, key **DATE:**, press Tab, then key **November 15, 1997**. (Press Tab after the other headings to align them properly. You will need to press Tab twice after *TO:*.) Bold the money amounts as shown in the memo as they are being keyed by completing the following steps:
   a. Press Ctrl + B.
   b. Key the money amount.
   c. Press Ctrl + B (or press the right arrow key).
2. Save the memo and name it Ch 03, Ex 01.
3. Print and then close Ch 03, Ex 01.

> Figure 3.1
>
> DATE: November 15, 1997
>
> TO: All School Principals
>
> FROM: Pat Windslow, Superintendent
>
> SUBJECT: BOARD OF EDUCATION MEETING
>
> Two decisions were made at the Board of Education meeting last night that I would like to bring to your attention. The board members passed a recommendation to set a Maintenance and Operations levy for February 1998. The estimated collection for 1998 is **$4,500,000** and the estimated collection for 1999 is **$4,850,000**. These estimates are based on a levy rate of **$4.20** for each **$1,000** assessed value.
>
> The Assistant Superintendent for Support Services reported that the District will save **$9,100** annually if heat pumps are installed in 23 portable buildings. The board members awarded an **$85,450** bid to Gemini Mechanics to install the pumps. You will be notified when portables at your school will be upgraded.
>
> xx:Ch 03, Ex 01

Text that has already been keyed in a document can be formatted as bold text by selecting the text first, then clicking the Bold button on the Toolbar or pressing Ctrl + B.

EXERCISE 2

Bolding Previously Keyed Text

1. At a clear editing window, open Ch 03, Ex 01.
2. Save the memo with Save As and name it Ch 03, Ex 02.
3. With Ch 03, Ex 02 displayed in the editing window, select and bold the words *Maintenance and Operations* in the first paragraph by completing the following steps:
    a. Using the mouse, position the arrow pointer on the *M* in *Maintenance,* hold down the left button, drag the arrow pointer to the end of *Operations*, then release the mouse button.
    b. With *Maintenance and Operations* selected, click the Bold button on the Toolbar.
4. Select and bold the following text in the memo:
    a. *Assistant Superintendent for Support Services* in the second paragraph.
    b. The heading *DATE:*.
    c. The heading *TO:*.
    d. The heading *FROM:*.
    e. The heading *SUBJECT:*.

Formatting Characters

5. Change the document name after your initials from Ch 03, Ex 01 to Ch 03, Ex 02.
6. Save the memo again with the same name (Ch 03, Ex 02).
7. Print and then close Ch 03, Ex 02.

Displaying the Reveal Codes Window

You can identify text that is bolded because it appears darker than surrounding text. There are special codes embedded in the text that are not visible; these codes tell WordPerfect where to start and stop bold. To display the bold codes, you must display a special window called Reveal Codes. At the Reveal Codes window, you can see the format changes that have been made to a document. To display the Reveal Codes window, click View, then Reveal Codes or press Alt + F3.

In Reveal Codes a double line is inserted toward the bottom of the screen. Above the double line the text displays normally. Below the double line, text displays with formatting codes added. Figure 3.2 shows a document with Reveal Codes displayed.

Figure 3.2

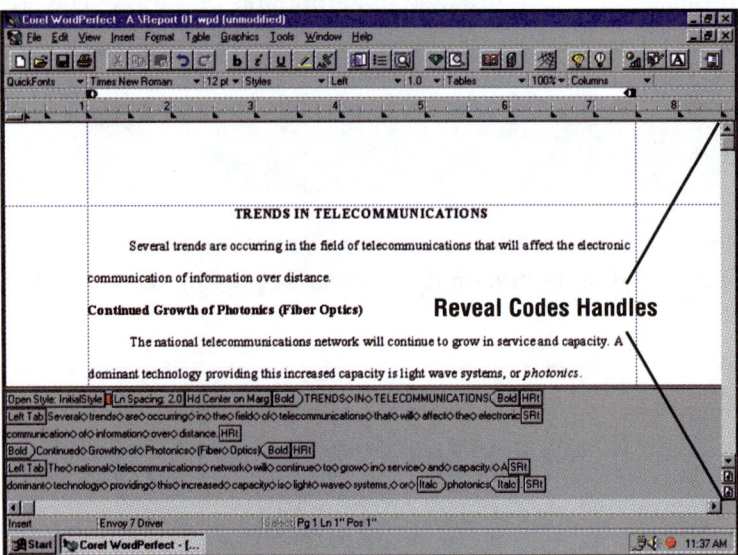

Reveal Codes

The insertion point appears above the double line as a blinking vertical bar. Below the double line, the insertion point displays as a red rectangle. The insertion point can be moved through text with the insertion point movement keys.

You can also display the Reveal Codes window using the arrow pointer on the Reveal Codes handles. The Reveal Codes handles are the small black bars at the right side of the screen immediately above the up scroll triangle and immediately below the Next Page button. (These handles are visible only at the normal editing window.) To use the mouse to display the Reveal Codes window, you would complete the following steps:

1. Position the arrow pointer on either the top Reveal Codes handle or the bottom handle until the arrow pointer turns into a double-headed arrow.
2. Hold down the left mouse button, then drag the arrow pointer up or down. (As you drag the arrow pointer, a black line appears across the screen.)

3. When the black line appears in the editing window where you want to split the display, release the mouse button.

To remove the Reveal Codes window using the mouse pointer, you would complete the following steps:

1. Position the arrow pointer on the double black line dividing the screen until the arrow pointer turns into a double-headed arrow.
2. Hold down the left mouse button, then drag the arrow pointer to the top or bottom of the screen.
3. Release the mouse button.

Codes and text can be deleted in Reveal Codes with the regular deletion commands or with the mouse. For example, the Backspace key will delete the character or code to the left of the insertion point and the Delete key will delete the character or code immediately to the right of the insertion point. You can use the mouse to "pull" codes out of Reveal Codes.

The Reveal Codes insertion point cannot be positioned on a code. Instead, the Reveal Codes insertion point moves to the left or right side of a code. To delete a code with the Backspace key, position the Reveal Codes insertion point (the red rectangle) immediately to the right of the code to be deleted, then press the Backspace key. To delete a code with the Delete key, position the Reveal Codes insertion point immediately to the left of the code to be deleted, then press the Delete key. To remove a code with the mouse, position the arrow pointer on the code to be removed. Hold down the left mouse button, drag the code into the editing window, then release the mouse button.

Special codes appear in Reveal Codes that identify functions and commands. Some of the lines of text in figure 3.2 end with the code [SRt]. This code indicates a soft return, which is an end of line created by word wrap. The [HRt] code identifies a hard return and indicates that the Enter key has been pressed. In Reveal Codes, the code [Bold] identifies the beginning and the code [Bold] identifies the end of bold text. If after bolding text you change your mind, display Reveal Codes, then delete one of the bold codes. Because bold codes are paired codes, when one code is deleted its pair is automatically deleted.

EXERCISE 3

Removing Bold Codes

1. At a clear editing window, open Ch 03, Ex 02.
2. Save the document with Save As and name it Ch 03, Ex 03.
3. Remove the bold codes from the heading *DATE:* by completing the following steps:
    a. Move the insertion point to the *D* in *DATE:*.
    b. Display the Reveal Codes window by clicking View, then Reveal Codes.
    c. Position the insertion point immediately to the right of the  code, then press the Backspace key. (This will delete the on code as well as the off code.)
4. Complete similar steps to delete the bold codes from the heading *TO:*.
5. Remove the bold codes from the heading *FROM:* by completing the following steps:
    a. Move the insertion point to the *F* in *FROM*.

      b. Display the Reveal Codes window. (Skip this step if Reveal Codes is already displayed.)
      c. Position the arrow pointer on the [Bold] code on the left side of *FROM:*.
      d. Hold down the left mouse button.
      e. Drag the arrow pointer into the editing window, then release the mouse button.
6. Complete similar steps to delete the bold codes from the heading *SUBJECT:*.
7. Change the document name after your initials from Ch 03, Ex 02 to Ch 03, Ex 03.
8. Save the document again with the same name (Ch 03, Ex 03).
9. Print and then close Ch 03, Ex 03.

Italicizing Text

Italic

WordPerfect's italics feature can be used in documents to emphasize specific text such as the names of published works. Text can be italicized using the Italic button on the Toolbar or the shortcut command, Ctrl + I. To italicize text as it is being keyed, click the Italic button on the Toolbar or press Ctrl + I. Key the text to be italicized, then click the Italic button on the Toolbar again or press Crtl + I. You can also just press the right arrow key. Text that has already been keyed in a document can be italicized by selecting the text first.

Text formatted with italics will appear in italics on the screen. In Reveal Codes, the code [Italc] identifies the beginning, and the code [Italc] identifies the end of italicized text.

EXERCISE 4

Italicizing Text as It Is Keyed

1. At a clear editing window, key the text shown in figure 3.3. Italicize the text shown as it is being keyed by completing the following steps:
    a. Press Ctrl + I.
    b. Key the text.
    c. Press Ctrl + I (or press the right arrow key).
2. Save the document and name it Ch 03, Ex 04.
3. Print and then close Ch 03, Ex 04.

Figure 3.3

Collier, Samuel G. (1991). *Educating Our Children* (pp. 56-78). Montpelier, VT: Maple Leaf Publishers.

Fjetland, Brita A. (1992). *Effective Educators* (2nd ed.). Vancouver, British Columbia, Canada: Vancouver Press.

Kitamura, Toshiki. (1990). *Managing the Classroom.* Boston, MA: Atlantic Publishing House.

Mejia, Marianna C. (1994). *Education for the Twenty-first Century.* Spokane, WA: Eastside Publishing and Printing.

EXERCISE 5

Italicizing Previously Keyed Text

1. At a clear editing window, open the document named Bibliography from your student data disk.
2. Save the document with Save As and name it Ch 03, Ex 05.
3. Select and italicize the title, *Telecommunications in Today's Businesses*, by completing the following steps:
    a. Using the mouse, position the arrow pointer on the *T* in *Telecommunications,* hold down the left button, drag the arrow pointer to the end of *Businesses*, then release the mouse button.
    b. With *Telecommunications in Today's Businesses* selected, click the Italic button on the Toolbar.
4. Select and italicize the following titles in the document:
    a. *Technological Advancements* in the second paragraph.
    b. *Computer Systems and Applications* in the third paragraph.
    c. *The Changing Business Office* in the fourth paragraph.
5. Save the document again with the same name (Ch 03, Ex 05).
6. Print and then close Ch 03, Ex 05.

Underlining Text

Text can be underlined using the Underline button on the Toolbar or the shortcut command Ctrl + U. To underline text as it is being keyed, click the Underline button on the Toolbar or press Ctrl + U. Key the text to be underlined, then click the Underline button on the Toolbar again or press Ctrl + U. You can also just press the right arrow key.

Formatting Characters

EXERCISE

Underlining Text as It Is Keyed

1. At a clear editing window, key the text shown in figure 3.4. Underline the text as shown as it is being keyed by completing the following steps:
   a. Press Ctrl + U.
   b. Key the text.
   c. Press Ctrl + U (or press the right arrow key).
2. Save the document and name it Ch 03, Ex 06.
3. Print and then close Ch 03, Ex 06.

Figure 3.4

Caprin, Heidi L. (1993). The Business Educator. Dallas, TX: Longhorn Publishing.

Landeis, Ricardo M. (1994). Total Quality Management in the Educational Environment. Columbus, OH: Midtown Press.

Verdun, Christine L. (1993). The ABCs of Integrated Learning. St. Louis, MO: Riverside Publishing.

Text that has already been keyed in a document can be underlined by selecting the text first, then clicking the Underline button on the Toolbar or pressing Ctrl + U. In Reveal Codes, the [Und] code identifies the beginning and the code [Und] identifies the end of underlined text.

EXERCISE

Underlining Previously Keyed Text

1. At a clear editing window, open Ch 03, Ex 05.
2. Save the document with Save As and name it Ch 03, Ex 07.
3. Delete all italics codes from the titles.
4. Select and underline the title *Telecommunications in Today's Businesses* by completing the following steps:
   a. Using the mouse, position the arrow pointer on the *T* in *Telecommunications,* hold down the left button, drag the arrow pointer to the end of *Businesses*, then release the mouse button.
   b. With *Telecommunications in Today's Businesses* selected, click the Underline button on the Toolbar.
5. Select and underline the title, *Technological Advancements,* in the second paragraph.
6. Select and underline the title, *Computer Systems and Applications,* in the third paragraph.

7. Select and underline the title, *The Changing Business Office*, in the fourth paragraph.
8. Save the document again with the same name (Ch 03, Ex 07).
9. Print and then close Ch 03, Ex 07.

Using Help

WordPerfect's Help feature is an on-screen reference manual containing information about all WordPerfect functions and commands. To display the Help dialog box shown in figure 3.5, click Help, then Help Topics. At the Help Topics dialog box, click the Contents tab. The options in the list box perform the action described to the right. For example, double-click *What's New or Changed* and WordPerfect will display a list of categories. Double-clicking a category will cause a further list of WordPerfect 7 enhancements to appear. Click an item in this list and then click Display and you will be presented with a summary describing how to use the new feature. Complete exercise 8 to practice using the Help feature.

Figure 3.5

Help Topics Dialog Box with Contents Tab Selected

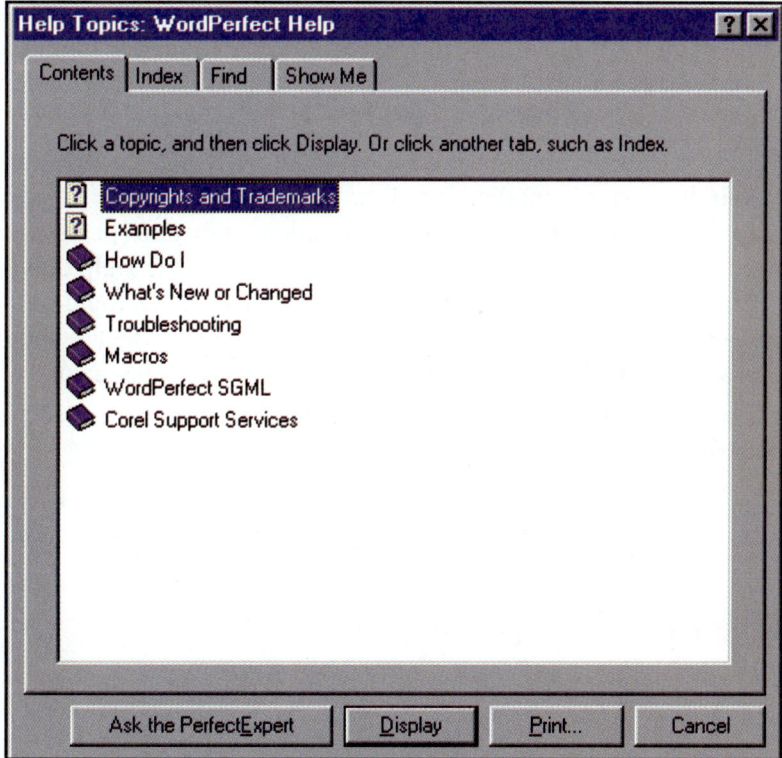

EXERCISE 8

Using the Index Feature in WordPerfect's Help

1. At a clear editing window, use WordPerfect's Help feature to read about italics by completing the following steps:
   a. Click Help, then Help Topics.
   b. At the Help Topics dialog box, click the Index tab.
   c. At the Index dialog box, key **italic**, then click Display.
   d. Read the information on the Italic feature. (Press the down arrow key or scroll with the scroll bar to view all the information.)
2. To remove the information from the screen and return the insertion point to the document, click the Close button (the button containing the X) located at the right side of the WordPerfect Help Title bar.

Using the Help Menu Options

When you click Help on the Menu bar, the drop-down menu shown in figure 3.6 displays. The first option, Help Topics, displays the Help dialog box shown in figure 3.5. The Ask the PerfectExpert option displays a dialog box that provides information on how to complete a WordPerfect function. In the next exercise, you will use the PerfectExpert. With Help Online you can go to the Documentation home page on the World Wide Web for the Corel WordPerfect Suite. The Documentation home page provides links where you can download reference manuals and technical information documents or view hints and tips on WordPerfect features.

For people who have used another word processing program or a previous version of WordPerfect, the Upgrade Help option provides information on features geared toward experienced users who just need a quick synopsis of a command. At the Upgrade Help dialog box, choose the word processing program from which you are converting, then click the topic about which you want to learn. WordPerfect will provide the equivalent feature in WordPerfect 7, mouse and keystroke summaries, and, in some cases, will provide more detail about how the feature works.

The last option, About Corel WordPerfect, displays information about the WordPerfect program, including such items as the release date and license number.

Help Drop-Down Menu

Figure 3.6

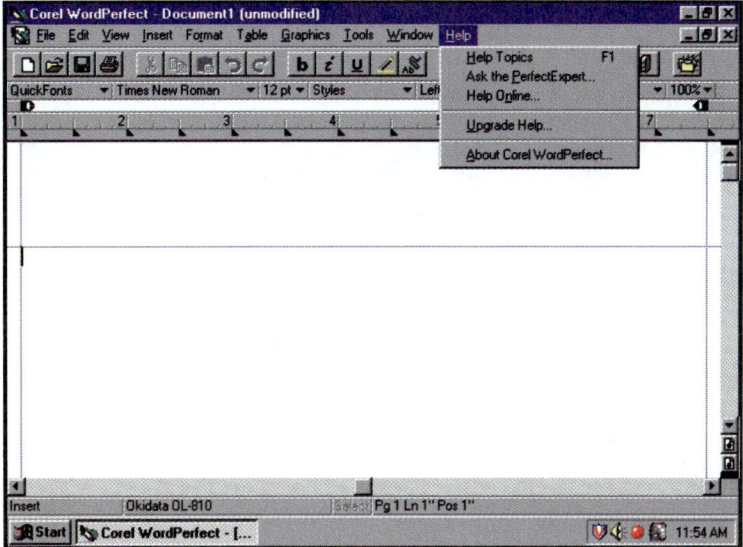

EXERCISE 9

Using the How Do I and Ask the PerfectExpert in Help

1. At a clear editing window, use the Help feature to read about how to save documents by completing the following steps:
   a. Click Help, then Help Topics.
   b. At the Help Topics dialog box, click the Contents tab. (Skip this step if the Contents tab is already selected.)
   c. Double-click the *How Do I* option in the list box.
   d. From the list of subtopics that displays, double-click *Work with Documents*.
   e. From the choices that display below Work with Documents, double-click *Save and Close Files*.
   f. Double-click *Save Files*.
   g. Read the information about saving a document that displays in the Help dialog box at the right side of the document window.
   h. After reading the information about saving documents, close the Help dialog box by clicking the Close button (button containing an X) that displays at the right side of the Help Title bar.
2. Use the Ask the PerfectExpert feature to learn about indenting text in a paragraph by completing the following steps:
   a. Click Help, then Ask the PerfectExpert.
   b. At the Ask the PerfectExpert dialog box key **Indent**, then click the Search button.
   c. At the list of related topics about indenting that displays, click "*To indent text*" and then click Display.
   d. After reading the information about indenting text, click the Show Me (light bulb) button at the top right corner of the dialog box. A pop-up box will appear with the Show Me icon.

Formatting Characters

49

e. Click the Guide Me Through It button inside the Show Me box.
   f. Read the information about the different ways of indenting text then click the "Guide me through each step of the task" button.
   g. From the next dialog box, click the button to the left of First line of a Paragraph.
   h. A help box will now appear at the bottom right corner of the screen that will provide information on each step in the task. Read the information, complete the instruction, then click the Next button to proceed to the next step. You can click the stop button at any time to exit the PerfectExpert help.
3. Close the document without saving it.

The Help feature contains a Show Me tab that will play animated demonstrations on some features if you have access to the Corel WordPerfect Suite 7 CD ROM. If the CD ROM is in the drive while you run WordPerfect, click Help, then Help Topics. At the Help Topics dialog box, click the Show Me tab. At the Help Topics dialog box with the Show Me tab selected, click the *Play a Demo* option. Select a topic that displays at the right side of the dialog box, then click the Display button. An animated demonstration of the topic will display.

If the CD ROM is not normally in the drive when you are using WordPerfect, you can insert it during a session. When the Corel Setup screen appears after you have inserted the CD ROM, click Demos, then click the topic you want to view. When you are finished, close the Setup window to return to your WordPerfect session.

CHAPTER SUMMARY

▼ To key text in all uppercase letters, press the Caps Lock key.

▼ The default or preset tab setting is one tab set every half inch. Press the Tab key to move the insertion point to the next tab to the right.

▼ Text can be bolded, italicized, or underlined with buttons on the Toolbar, shortcut commands, or options at the Font dialog box. When text has been bolded, italicized, or underlined, special codes are inserted in the document. These codes can be viewed in the Reveal Codes window.

▼ To bold, italicize, or underline existing text, select the text first, then click the necessary button on the Toolbar or press the shortcut command that will apply the desired formatting.

▼ WordPerfect's Help feature is an on-screen reference manual containing information about WordPerfect functions and commands. The Ask the PerfectExpert feature can be used to search for a topic and provide instructions on how to perform WordPerfect functions.

COMMANDS REVIEW

	Mouse (Toolbar)	Keyboard
Uppercase function		CAPS LOCK
Bold	b	CTRL + B
Italics	i	CTRL + I
Underline	u	CTRL + U
	Mouse (Menu Bar)	
Reveal Codes	View, Reveal Codes	ALT + F3
Help	Help, Help Topics	Help, Help Topics
Ask the PerfectExpert	Help, Ask the PerfectExpert	Help, Ask the PerfectExpert

Reveal Codes Symbols Review

Bolded text	Bold text Bold
Italicized text	Italc text Italc
Underlined text	Und text Und
Soft return–end of line created by word wrap	SRt
Hard return–wherever the Enter key has been pressed	HRt

CHECK YOUR UNDERSTANDING

Completion: In the space provided at the right, indicate the correct term, command, or number.

1. Press this key to indent the insertion point to the next tab to the right. _tab_

2. This code in Reveal Codes indicates the beginning of underlined text. _Und>_

3. Existing text can be italicized only if this is done first. _Select it_

4. This is the shortcut command to underline text. _U_

5. This symbol is inserted in the document each time a line of text is ended by word wrap. _SRt_

6. This is the name for the on-screen reference manual containing information about all WordPerfect functions and commands. _help_

7. This feature provides instructions on how to perform WordPerfect functions for users who have converted from another word processing package. _Upgrade help_

8. This code in Reveal Codes indicates that this key has been pressed. _Enter_

Formatting Characters 51

9. The insertion point displays as this in the Reveal Codes window.   *Red rec. bar*

10. This is the name of the small black bars that display at the right side of the screen immediately above the up scroll triangle and immediately below the Next Page button.   *Reveal codes handles*

SKILL ASSESSMENTS

Assessment 1

1. At a clear editing window, key the memo shown in figure 3.7. Bold and underline the text as shown.
2. Save the memo and name it Ch 03, SA 01.
3. Print and then close Ch 03, SA 01.

Figure 3.7

DATE: November 12, 1997

TO: Rachel Una

FROM: Chris Kuehner

SUBJECT: TELECOMMUNICATIONS

After reviewing a number of telecommunications textbooks, I have chosen <u>Telecommunications: Systems and Applications</u> for use in **CIS 120, Telecommunications**. The bookstore manager has ordered the book for next quarter.

The class was to be held in **Room 310**. Due to computer requirements, the class has been moved to **Room 428**. The classroom can accommodate 25 people. Therefore, the class enrollment has been changed from 30 to 25.

xx:Ch 03, SA 01

Assessment 2

1. At a clear editing window, open Memo 01. This document is located on your student data disk.
2. Save the document with Save As and name it Ch 03, SA 02.
3. Make the following changes to the document:
   a. Display Reveal Codes and delete the underline codes from the publication titles, *The ABCs of Integrated Learning* and *Total Quality Management in the Education Environment*.
   b. Select and italicize the publication titles *The ABCs of Integrated Learning* and *Total Quality Management in the Education Environment*.

Chapter 3

      c. Select and bold the following text:
          (1) The headings *DATE:*, *TO:*, *FROM:*, and *SUBJECT:*.
          (2) *Tuesday, November 14* in the third paragraph.
          (3) *7:00 p.m. to 8:00 p.m.* in the third paragraph.
      d. Insert your initials at the end of the document where you see the "xx." Change the document name after your initials from Memo 01 to Ch 03, SA 02.
4. Save the document again with the same name (Ch 03, SA 02).
5. Print and then close Ch 03, SA 02.

Assessment 3

1. At a clear editing window, open Ch 03, SA 01.
2. Save the memorandum with Save As and name it Ch 03, SA 03.
3. Make the following changes to the document:
      a. Turn on the display of Reveal Codes, delete all the bold and underline codes in the document, then turn off the display of Reveal Codes.
      b. Select and italicize the following text:
          (1) *Telecommunications: Systems and Applications* in the first paragraph.
          (2) *Room 310* in the second paragraph.
          (3) *Room 428* in the second paragraph.
      c. Select and bold the two occurrences of the number 25 in the second paragraph and the number 30 in the second paragraph.
      d. Change the document name after your initials from Ch 03, SA 01 to Ch 03, SA 03.
4. Save the document again with the same name (Ch 03, SA 03).
5. Print and then close Ch 03, SA 03.

Formatting Characters

4 FORMATTING LINES

PERFORMANCE OBJECTIVE

Upon successful completion of chapter 4, you will be able to enhance business memos and letters by changing the alignment of lines and paragraphs of text.

WordPerfect contains a number of features that can be used to affect the appearance or layout of a line of text. Three common line features are centering, line spacing, and justification.

Centering Text

Text can be centered between the left and right margins with the shortcut command Shift + F7 or through the Format menu. When you use the command Shift + F7 or the Format menu, the insertion point is moved to the center of the editing window. Text moves left one space for every two characters you key. If you make a mistake while keying text, backspace and rekey it. This will not interfere with the centering process.

To center text using the shortcut command, you would press Shift + F7, key the text, then press Enter. To center text with the Format menu, you would click Format, point to Line, then click Center, key the text, then press Enter. When you press Enter at the end of the text, the centering feature is deactivated. The next line you key will begin at the left margin. If you want the next line centered, press Shift + F7 again or click Format, point to Line, then click Center.

In Reveal Codes, the code [Hd Center on Marg] identifies the beginning and the code [HRt] identifies the end of centered text.

Formatting Lines 55

EXERCISE 1

Bolding and Centering Text

1. At a clear editing window, key the text shown in figure 4.1 centered and bolded by completing the following steps:
   a. Key the first line by completing the following steps:
      (1) Press Shift + F7.
      (2) Press Ctrl + B (this turns on bold).
      (3) Key **CIS 120, TELECOMMUNICATIONS**.
      (4) Press Enter twice.
   b. Key the second line by completing the following steps:
      (1) Press Shift + F7.
      (2) Key **Monday through Thursday**.
      (3) Press Enter twice.
   c. Key the remaining lines following steps similar to those in 1b(1) through 1b(3).
   d. After keying the last line, **Room 428**, press Ctrl + B to turn off bold.
2. Save the document and name it Ch 04, Ex 01.
3. Print and then close Ch 04, Ex 01.

Figure 4.1

CIS 120, TELECOMMUNICATIONS

Monday through Thursday

9:00 - 10:10 a.m.

Room 428

Using QuickMenus

WordPerfect contains a number of QuickMenus that help speed up the customizing and formatting of text. QuickMenus are pop-up menus that display when you click the right button on the mouse. The QuickMenu that displays is dependent on the position of the arrow pointer before you click the right button. A different QuickMenu will display when you position the arrow pointer at one of the following positions, then click the right mouse button:

- between the top and bottom margins and the edge of the page
- between the left and right margins and the edge of the page
- the editing window
- a table
- a graphic figure or line
- the Toolbar, Power Bar, Status bar, Ruler Bar, or scroll bars

A QuickMenu can be used to center text between the left and right margins. To use the QuickMenu, you would complete the following steps:

1. Position the arrow pointer anywhere in the editing window (except the top, bottom, left, and right margins).
2. Click the right button on the mouse.
3. At the QuickMenu shown in figure 4.2, position the arrow pointer on Center, then click the left mouse button (or press C for Center).

Figure 4.2

QuickMenu

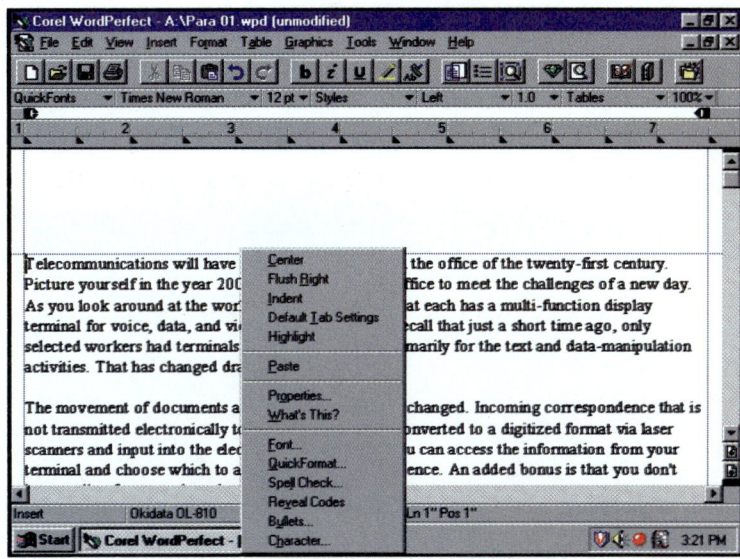

Centering Text with the QuickMenu

1. At a clear editing window, key the document shown in figure 4.3 using the QuickMenu by completing the following steps:
    a. Position the arrow pointer anywhere in the editing window (except the top, bottom, left, and right margins).
    b. Click the right button on the mouse.
    c. At the QuickMenu, position the arrow pointer on Center, then click the left button.
    d. Key **Chief Executive Officer, Chris Hedegaard**.
    e. Press Enter.
    f. Complete similar steps to center the remaining four lines.
2. After keying all lines in the document, save it and name it Ch 04, Ex 02.
3. Print and then close Ch 04, Ex 02.

Formatting Lines 57

Figure 4.3

Chief Executive Officer, Chris Hedegaard
Vice President, Robert Freitas
Vice President, Richard Dudley
Vice President, Glenna Wykoff
Vice President, Laura Culver

Centering Text at a Specific Position

The Center feature can be used to center text at a specific position on the line other than the center. To center at a specific position, you would complete the following steps:

1. Tab or space in to the position on the line where text is to be centered.
2. Click Format, point to Line, then click Center; or press Shift + F7.
3. Key the text.
4. Press Enter.

When text is centered at a specific position, the code  displays in Reveal Codes. The center on position feature can be useful for centering a heading over a column of text.

EXERCISE 3

Centering Text at a Specific Location

1. At a clear editing window, open Column 01. This document is located on your student data disk.
2. Save the document with Save As and name it Ch 04, Ex 03.
3. Bold and center the heading, *Directors,* over the text by completing the following steps:
   a. With the insertion point located on the first line in the document (this line is blank and does not contain text), press the space bar until the insertion point is located on approximately Position 2.6". (Check the Status bar; your position measurement may vary slightly.)
   b. Press Shift + F7 to access the Center command. (This does not move the insertion point. It tells WordPerfect to center text on Position 2.6.)
   c. Press Ctrl + B to turn on bold or click the Bold button on the Toolbar.
   d. Key **Directors**.
   e. Press Ctrl + B (or click the Bold button on the Toolbar) to turn off bold.
4. Save the document again with the same name (Ch 04, Ex 03).
5. Print and then close Ch 04, Ex 03.

Changing Line Spacing

By default, WordPerfect's word wrap feature single spaces text. Occasionally, you may want to change to another spacing, such as one and a half or double. Line spacing can be changed with the Format drop-down menu or the Line Spacing button on the Power Bar. To change line spacing with the Format menu, you would complete the following steps:

Line Spacing

1. Click Format, point to Line, then click Spacing.
2. At the Line Spacing dialog box shown in figure 4.4, key the number of the desired line spacing. Or you can click the up-pointing triangle to increase the number or click the down-pointing triangle to decrease the number. If you are using the keyboard, press the up or down arrow keys on the keyboard.
3. Click OK or press Enter.

Figure 4.4

Line Spacing Dialog Box

When you use the up and down triangles at the Line Spacing dialog box, line spacing is set by one-tenth line increments. You can display settings such as 0.3, 0.4, 1.2, 1.5, 2.1, 2.5, and so on; or you can key your own measurement. You can enter whole numbers or decimal numbers. You can key up to four numbers after the decimal point; however, WordPerfect will only carry the number to two decimal places.

EXERCISE 4

Changing Line Spacing at the Line Spacing Dialog Box

1. At a clear editing window, open Ch 04, Ex 02.
2. Save the document with Save As and name it Ch 04, Ex 04.
3. Change the line spacing to 2 (double) by completing the following steps:
   a. Make sure the insertion point is positioned anywhere in the first line.
   b. Click Format, point to Line, then click Spacing.
   c. At the Line Spacing dialog box, key **2**.
   d. Click OK or press Enter.
4. Save the document with the same name (Ch 04, Ex 04).
5. Print and then close Ch 04, Ex 04.

If you position the arrow pointer on the Line Spacing button on the Power Bar (sixth button from the left), then click the left mouse button, a drop-down menu displays with four options: 1.0, 1.5, 2.0, and Other. Position the arrow pointer on one of the numbers to change the line spacing,

Formatting Lines 59

then click the left mouse button. Or, if you want to change the line spacing to a number not displayed, move the arrow pointer to Other, then click the left mouse button. This causes the Line Spacing dialog box shown in figure 4.4 to display. You can also display the Line Spacing dialog box by double-clicking the Line Spacing button on the Power Bar.

When changes are made to line spacing, a code is inserted in the document that can be seen in Reveal Codes. The line spacing code is inserted at the beginning of the paragraph where the insertion point is located. Line spacing changes affect text from the location of the code to the end of the document or until another line spacing code is encountered. If a line spacing code is deleted, line spacing reverts to the default setting of single spacing or to the setting of a previously placed line spacing code. If line spacing in a document is changed to double, the code would appear in Reveal Codes as . To see the number after Ln Spacing, the insertion point must be positioned immediately left of the code, otherwise the code appears as Ln Spacing. You can also display the number in the code using the mouse. To do this, position the arrow pointer on the code, then click the left mouse button.

In chapter 3 you learned how to remove codes in Reveal Codes using the mouse. You can also use the mouse together with codes to display dialog boxes. For example, to display the Line Spacing dialog box, position the arrow pointer on a Ln Spacing code in Reveal Codes, then double-click the left mouse button. At the Line Spacing dialog box you can edit the setting as desired.

EXERCISE 5

Changing Line Spacing with the Line Spacing Button

1. At a clear editing window, open Memo 01. This document is located on your student data disk.
2. Save the document with Save As and name it Ch 04, Ex 05.
3. Change the line spacing to 1.5 for the body of the memo by completing the following steps:
   a. Position the insertion point on any character in the first paragraph of the memo.
   b. Click the Line Spacing button on the Power Bar.
   c. Move the arrow pointer to 1.5, then click the left mouse button.
4. Display Reveal Codes. Position the arrow pointer on the Ln Spacing code, then click the left mouse button. (This should expand the code to display the number 1.5.) After viewing the code, turn off the display of Reveal Codes.
5. Save the memo again with the same name (Ch 04, Ex 05).
6. Print and then close Ch 04, Ex 05.

Changing Justification

By default, WordPerfect justifies text evenly at the left margin but leaves the text near the right margin uneven. In WordPerfect it is referred to as *left justification*. Justification changes can be made in five ways: (1) shortcut commands, (2) the Justification button on the Power Bar, (3) the Format, Justification drop-down menu, (4) buttons on the Format Toolbar, or (5) the QuickSpot button.

Text in a paragraph can be justified at the left margin, between margins, at the right margin, or to the left and right margins. Figure 4.5 illustrates the different paragraph justifications.

Figure 4.5

Paragraph Justifications

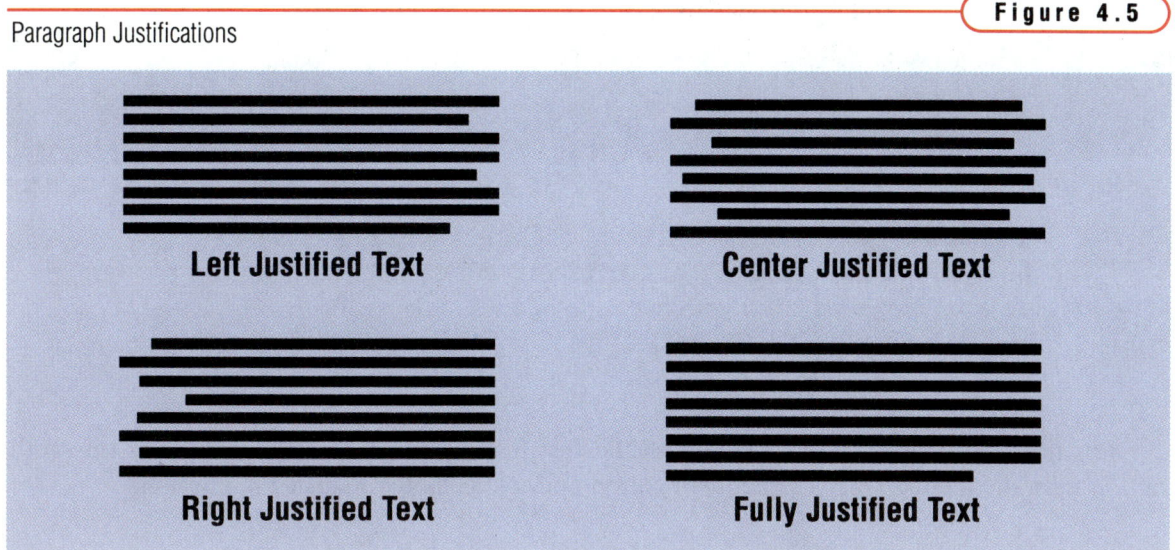

In addition to the four paragraph justifications shown in figure 4.5, you can also fully justify all lines of text in paragraphs. The difference between Full justification and All justification is that All will justify to both margins all lines of text in a paragraph, including short lines, while Full will not justify the last line of text in a paragraph to the right margin. To make changes to justification with the Format menu, click Format, then point to Justification. At the drop-down menu that displays as shown in figure 4.6, click the desired justification.

Figure 4.6

Format Justification Drop-Down Menu

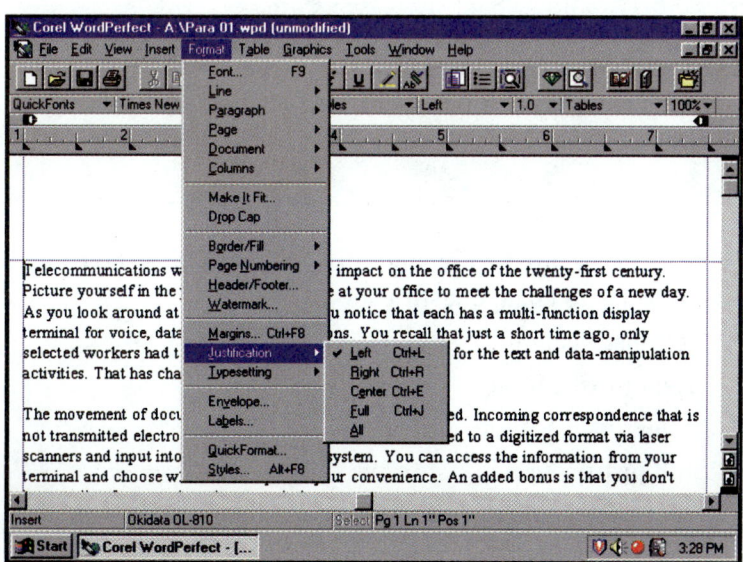

Formatting Lines

61

EXERCISE 6

Changing Justification with the Format Menu

1. At a clear editing window, open Para 03. This document is located on your student data disk.
2. Save the document with Save As and name it Ch 04, Ex 06.
3. Change to center justification using the Format, Justification drop-down menu by completing the following steps:
    a. Position the insertion point on any character in the first paragraph.
    b. Click Fo_r_mat, point to _J_ustification, then click C_e_nter.
4. Save the document again with the same name (Ch 04, Ex 06).
5. Print and then close Ch 04, Ex 06.

Justification changes can be made with the Justification button on the Power Bar (the fifth button from the left). To display the justification options, click the Justification button.

EXERCISE 7

Changing Justification with the Justification Button

1. At a clear editing window, open Para 03. This document is located on your student data disk.
2. Save the document with Save As and name it Ch 04, Ex 07.
3. With the insertion point positioned in the first paragraph, change to full justification of all lines with the Justification button on the Power Bar by completing the following steps:
    a. Click the Justification button on the Power Bar.
    b. Click All at the drop-down menu.
4. Save the document again with the same name (Ch 04, Ex 07).
5. Print and then close Ch 04, Ex 07.

Shortcut commands can be used to change the justification of text in paragraphs. Use the following shortcut commands to change justification:

Ctrl + L   =   left justification
Ctrl + R   =   right justification
Ctrl + E   =   center justification
Ctrl + J   =   full justification

There is no shortcut command to fully justify all lines of text (including short lines) in paragraphs.

EXERCISE 8

Changing Justification with a Shortcut Command

1. At a clear editing window, open Para 02. This document is located on your student data disk.
2. Save the document with Save As and name it Ch 04, Ex 08.
3. Change the paragraphs in the document to right justification using a shortcut command by completing the following steps:
   a. Position the insertion point on any character in the first paragraph.
   b. Press Ctrl + R.
4. Save the document again with the same name (Ch 04, Ex 08).
5. Print and then close Ch 04, Ex 08.

Justification changes can also be made with buttons on the Format Toolbar. By default, the WordPerfect 7 Toolbar displays below the Menu bar and above the Power Bar. WordPerfect provides a variety of other toolbars that can be used to quickly format a document. To view the names of other toolbars, position the arrow pointer on the current Toolbar, then click the *right* mouse button. This causes the drop-down menu shown in figure 4.7 to display. To display the Format Toolbar (instead of the WordPerfect 7 Toolbar), position the arrow pointer on the Format option at the drop-down menu, then click the left mouse button. This causes the Format Toolbar to display as shown in figure 4.8.

Figure 4.7

Toolbar Drop-Down Menu

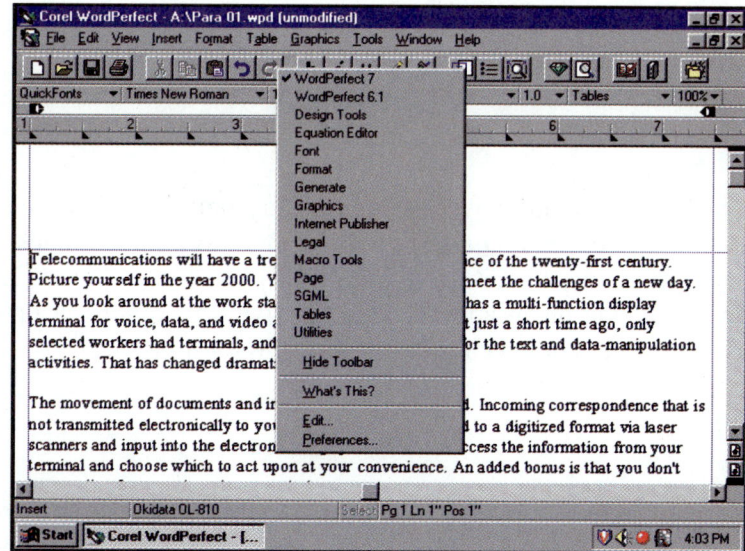

Formatting Lines **63**

Figure 4.8

Format Toolbar

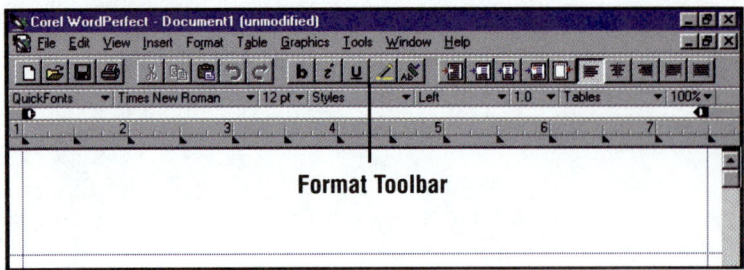

Format Toolbar

EXERCISE 9

Changing Justification with the Format Toolbar

1. At a clear editing window, open Para 04. This document is located on your student data disk.
2. Save the document with Save As and name it Ch 04, Ex 09.
3. Change to full justification using the Format Toolbar by completing the following steps:
   a. Display the Format Toolbar by positioning the arrow pointer on the current Toolbar, clicking the *right* mouse button, then clicking Format. (If the Format Toolbar is already displayed, skip this step.)
   b. Click the Justify Full button on the Format Toolbar.
4. Save the document again with the same name (Ch 04, Ex 09).
5. Print and then close Ch 04, Ex 09.
6. Change the toolbar back to the WordPerfect 7 Toolbar by positioning the arrow pointer on the Format Toolbar, clicking the *right* mouse button, then clicking WordPerfect 7.

Justify Full

When you move the arrow pointer over a paragraph, a small square appears in the left margin of the screen. This square is called a *QuickSpot*. To change justification, click the QuickSpot. A palette of frequently used options to edit paragraphs is displayed as shown in figure 4.9. Click the Justification button and a side menu appears with the five text alignment options as shown in figure 4.10. At this side menu, click the desired justification setting.

64 Chapter 4

QuickSpot Paragraph Dialog Box

Figure 4.9

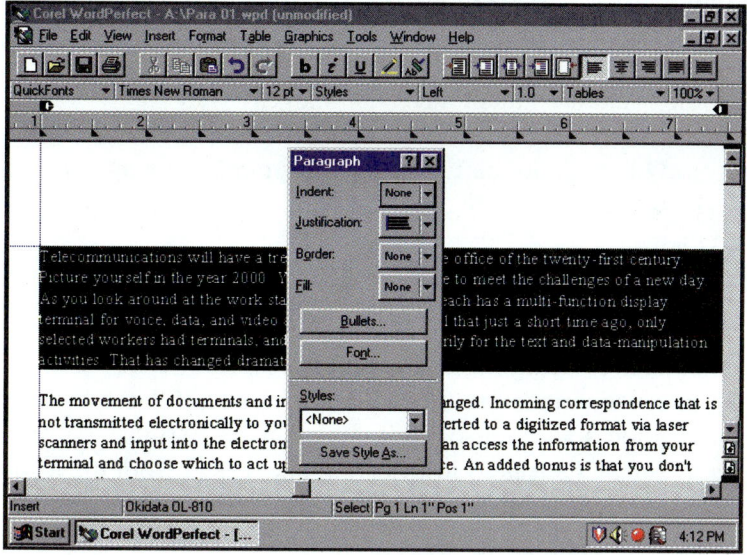

QuickSpot Paragraph Justification Side Menu

Figure 4.10

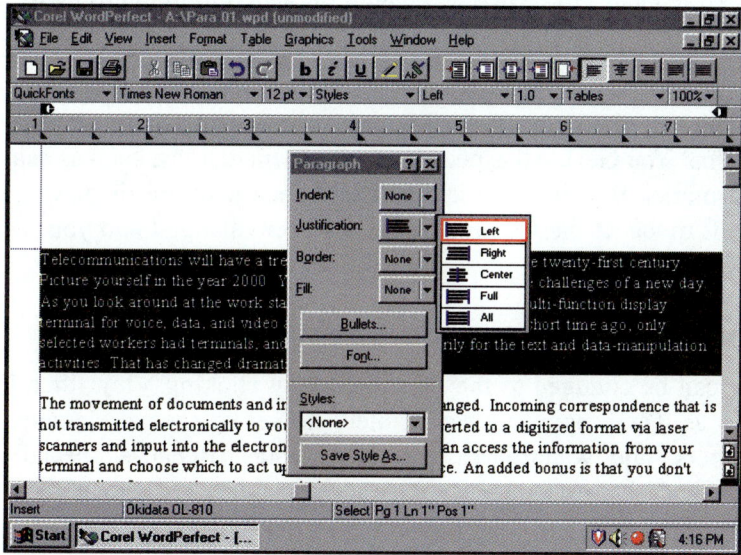

EXERCISE 10

Changing Justification with the QuickSpot Button

1. At a clear editing window, open Notice 02. This document is located on your student data disk.
2. Save the document with Save As and name it Ch 04, Ex 10.
3. Change to right justification using the QuickSpot button by completing the following steps:
    a. Move the arrow pointer to the selection bar and drag down until all five lines in the document are selected.

Formatting Lines

65

> b. Position the arrow pointer on the QuickSpot button in the left margin area and click the left mouse button.
> c. Move the arrow pointer to the down-pointing triangle next to Justification and click the left mouse button.
> d. Click the Right alignment box.
> e. Click the left mouse button anywhere in the document to close the dialog box, or click the close button in the Paragraph dialog box Title bar.
> 4. Save the document again with the same name (Ch 04, Ex 10).
> 5. Print and then close Ch 04, Ex 10.

When a change is made to justification, WordPerfect inserts the code at the beginning of the paragraph where the insertion point is positioned. For example, if the insertion point is positioned in the middle of a paragraph and the justification is changed to right, the code is inserted at the beginning of that paragraph. Changes to justification take effect from the location of the code to the end of the document or until another justification code is encountered.

Changing the Viewing Mode

The WordPerfect 7 program has more than one viewing mode. You have been using the default viewing mode, which is Page. You can also change the viewing mode to Draft or Two Page.

Viewing in the Page Mode

The Page mode, which is the default, displays a document in what is considered WYSIWYG (What You See Is What You Get). All aspects of a document display, such as headers, footers, page numbers, and watermarks. Because all elements of a document are displayed, the Page mode is slower than the Draft mode. If the viewing mode has been changed and you want to return to the Page mode, click View, then Page.

Viewing in the Draft Mode

The viewing mode can be changed to the Draft mode by clicking View, then Draft. In the Draft mode, text displays as it will appear when printed; however, special elements such as headers, footers, page numbers, and watermarks will not display. Because special elements are not displayed, the Draft mode is faster than the Page mode.

Viewing in the Two-Page Mode

In addition to the Page and Draft modes, you can change the viewing mode to Two Page. At the Two-Page viewing mode, two pages of a document are displayed side by side as shown in figure 4.11. The Two-Page mode is useful for viewing the position of elements on pages. You can edit in Two-Page mode but doing so is not practical. You may want to switch to Two-Page mode to see how elements are positioned, then switch to Draft or Page mode to make any changes.

Two-Page Viewing Mode

Figure 4.11

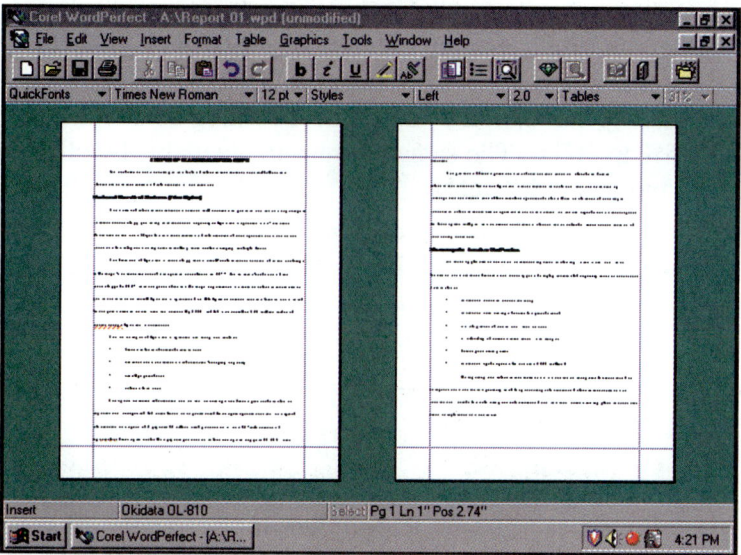

Changing the Zoom Ratio

In the Draft or Page viewing modes, you can change the size of text and document elements displayed on the screen. By default, the document is displayed at approximately 100% of the size of the document when printed. This ratio can be changed with the Zoom option from the View drop-down menu or with the Zoom button on the Power Bar. When you click View, then Zoom, the Zoom dialog box shown in figure 4.12 displays.

Zoom

Zoom Dialog Box

Figure 4.12

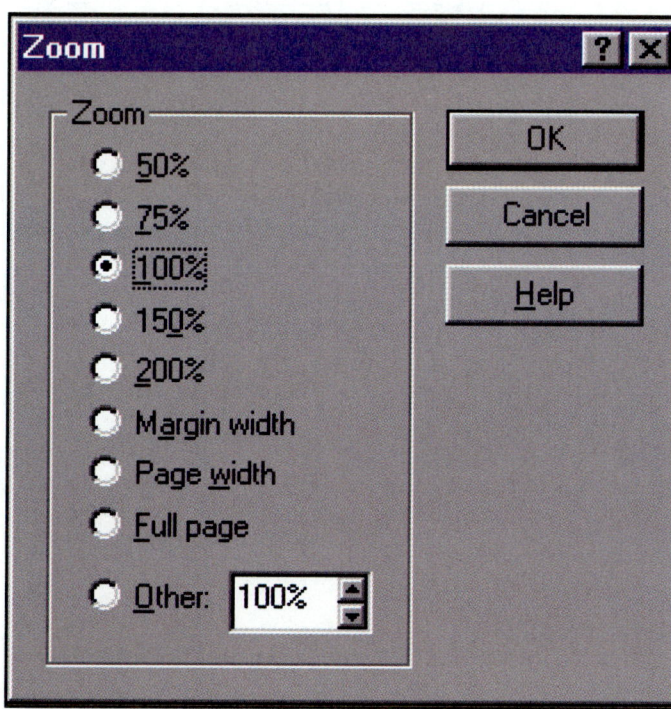

Formatting Lines

67

To decrease the display of the document, choose a percentage lower than 100% such as 50% or 75%. To increase the display, choose a percentage higher than 100% such as 150% or 200%. If you choose Margin width at the Zoom dialog box, the document displays so that all text and graphics between the left and right margins are visible. Choose Page width to display the entire document between the left and right edges of the page. If you choose Full page, the entire current page is displayed. With the Other option from the Zoom dialog box, you can decrease or increase the percentage from 25% to 400%. The same options are available by clicking the Zoom button on the Power Bar (last button on the right).

Page/Zoom Full You can also zoom to full page size by clicking the Page/Zoom Full button on the Toolbar (fourth button from right). Click Page/Zoom Full again to return to the previous viewing mode.

EXERCISE 11

Changing the Viewing Mode and the Zoom Ratio

1. At a clear editing window, open Report 02. This document is located on your student data disk.
2. Make the following view changes:
   a. Change the view to Draft by clicking View, then Draft.
   b. Move the insertion point to the end of the document page by page.
   c. Move the insertion point to the beginning of the document, then change the view to Two Page by clicking View, then Two Page.
   d. Move the insertion point to the end of the document page by page.
   e. Move the insertion point to the beginning of the document, then change the view to Draft.
   f. Change the Zoom option to 75% by completing the following steps:
      (1) Click View, then Zoom.
      (2) At the Zoom dialog box, click 75%. To do this, position the tip of the arrow pointer inside the circle before 75%, then click the left mouse button.
      (3) Click OK or press Enter.
   g. Change the Zoom option to Margin width by completing the following steps:
      (1) Click View, then Zoom.
      (2) At the Zoom dialog box, click Margin width. To do this, position the tip of the arrow pointer inside the circle before Margin width, then click the left mouse button.
      (3) Click OK or press Enter.
   h. Change the Zoom option to Full page by completing steps similar to those in 2g.
   i. Change the Zoom option back to the default of 100%.
   j. Zoom to full page size by clicking the Page/Zoom Full button on the Toolbar. Click Page/Zoom Full again to return to the previous viewing mode.
3. Close Report 02 without saving it.

CHAPTER SUMMARY

- Three common line alignment features are centering, line spacing, and justification.
- Text can be centered between the left and right margins or at a specific position.
- QuickMenus are pop-up menus that display when you click the right mouse button.
- The default line spacing, which is single, can be changed at the Line Spacing dialog box or with the Line Spacing button on the Power Bar. A line spacing code is inserted at the beginning of the paragraph where the insertion point is located.
- Justification determines how text will be aligned when it is printed. The five possible settings are left (which is the default setting); center; right; full; and full, all lines. A justification code is inserted at the beginning of the paragraph where the insertion point is located.
- QuickSpots are small squares that appear in the margin area when the arrow pointer is moved over a paragraph. Click the QuickSpot button to open a dialog box with frequently used paragraph format options.
- Three viewing modes are available with WordPerfect 7: Page (the default), Draft, and Two Page.
- By default, a document is displayed at approximately 100% of the size it will be when printed. This ratio can be increased or decreased with the Zoom option from the View drop-down menu or the Zoom button on the Power Bar.

COMMANDS REVIEW

	Mouse	**Keyboard**
Center text	Format, Line, Center	SHIFT + F7
Center with QuickMenu	Position arrow pointer within the editing window; click right mouse button, then click left mouse button on Center	
Change line spacing	Format, Line, Spacing	Format, Line, Spacing
Change line spacing at the Power Bar	Click Line Spacing button on Power Bar, click 1.0, 1.5, 2.0, or Other from drop-down menu; or double-click Line Spacing button to display Line Spacing dialog box	
Change justification	Format, Justification; or click Justification button on Power Bar; or a Justify button on the Format Toolbar	CTRL + L (Left) CTRL + R (Right) CTRL + E (Center) CTRL + J (Full)
Change Viewing Mode	View	View
Change the Zoom Ratio	View, Zoom; or click Zoom button on the Power Bar	View, Zoom

Formatting Lines

Reveal Codes Symbols Review

Beginning of centered text between margins — `Hd Center on Marg`

Beginning of centered text at a specific position — `Hd Center on Pos`

End of centered text — `HRt`

CHECK YOUR UNDERSTANDING

Completion: In the space provided at the right, indicate the correct term, command, or number.

1. This code appears in Reveal Codes before centered text. *Hd Center on*

2. At this justification setting, all lines in a paragraph, including short lines, align at the left and right margins. *Full just.*

3. To view the names of toolbars other than the WordPerfect 7 Toolbar, position the arrow pointer on the Toolbar, then click this mouse button. *Right*

4. This is the default justification type. *Left*

5. To see the number after a line spacing code in Reveal Codes, the insertion point must be positioned on this side of the code. *Left*

6. This is the shortcut command to change justification to right. *CTRL+R*

7. This is the shortcut command to change justification to center. *CTRL+E*

8. This is the name of the pop-up menu that displays when you click the right mouse button. *Quick-Menus*

9. This is the name of the small square that appears in the margin area when the arrow pointer is moved over a paragraph. *Quick-Spots*

10. Three viewing modes are available in WordPerfect: Page, Two Page, and this. *Draft*

11. Increase or decrease the size of the document display at this dialog box. *Zoom*

Chapter 4

SKILL ASSESSMENTS

Assessment 1

1. At a clear editing window, key the memo shown in figure 4.13. Bold the text as shown. Use the Center command, Shift + F7, to center the days.
2. After keying the document, move the insertion point to the beginning of the document, then change justification to full.
3. Save the memo and name it Ch 04, SA 01.
4. Print and then close Ch 04, SA 01.

Figure 4.13

DATE: January 3, 1998

TO: All College Staff

FROM: James Vaira, Training and Education

SUBJECT: WORDPERFECT CLASSES

Tampa Community College employees will have the opportunity to complete training in WordPerfect 7. This training is designed for current users of WordPerfect who want to become familiar with the changes in the new version. The WordPerfect classes will be held in Room 200 from 9:00 a.m. to 11:00 a.m. on the following days:

Monday, January 23
Wednesday, January 25
Tuesday, January 31
Thursday, February 2

Room 200 contains 15 computers, therefore, each training session is limited to 15 employees. Preregistration is required. To register, please call Training and Education at extension 6552.

xx:Ch 04, SA 01

Assessment 2

1. At a clear editing window, change the view to Draft mode.
2. Key the memo shown in figure 4.14 with the following specifications:
    a. After keying the headings, press Enter three times, then change the line spacing to 1.5.
    b. Bold and italicize text as indicated.
3. After keying the document, move the insertion point back to the beginning of the document, then change the justification to full.
4. Save the memo and name it Ch 04, SA 02.
5. Print and then close Ch 04, SA 02.

Figure 4.14

DATE: January 3, 1998

TO: Ronnie Teng

FROM: James Vaira

SUBJECT: WORDPERFECT CLASSES

A memo has been sent to all staff at Tampa Community College advertising the WordPerfect class. I am sure this memo will generate enough interest to fill the sessions. A few days before each session, I will send you a class roster. The *WordPerfect 7* program has been installed on all the computers in **Room 200**. Textbooks and disks will be available for each participant. If you need anything further, call me at extension **6552**.

xx:Ch 04, SA 02

Assessment 3

Note: In this exercise and other exercises in the text, you will be required to create business letters. Please refer to Appendix B at the end of this text for the correct placement and spacing of elements in a block-style business letter.

1. At a clear editing window, key the business letter shown in figure 4.15. Bold, center, and italicize the text as shown.
2. Save the letter and name it Ch 04, SA 03.
3. Print and then close Ch 04, SA 03.

Figure 4.15

January 11, 1998

Mr. Anthony Maloney
Tampa Community College
6100 Park Drive
Tampa, FL 33610

Dear Mr. Maloney:

The first meeting of the members of the **Outcomes Assessment Project (OAP)** was held yesterday, January 10. As you know from our conversations, the purpose of the project is to determine a process for assessing the success of graduating students as well as determining if college programs are meeting the needs of the business community. At the meeting, the members agreed that the top priority for the project is to develop a survey instrument.

With your expertise in project management, we feel you can provide us with needed information to begin the project. Our next meeting will be held at St. Petersburg College on the following day:

Wednesday, February 8, 1998
1:30 to 3:30 p.m.
Room 104

If you can attend this meeting, please call me at 555-9660, extension 1335, to determine specific topics. The input you can provide the project members will be invaluable.

Very truly yours,

Dawn Perez, Coordinator
Outcomes Assessment Project

xx:Ch 04, SA 03

Assessment 4

1. At a clear editing window, change the line spacing to double (2), then key the document in figure 4.16. Bold, center, and underline text as indicated.
2. After keying the document, move the insertion point to the beginning of the document, then change the justification to full.
3. Save the document and name it Ch 04, SA 04.
4. Print and then close Ch 04, SA 04.

Figure 4.16

DENVER MEMORIAL HOSPITAL
NURSING SERVICES
Clinical Partner

General Description

The clinical partner is a registered nurse responsible for assessing, planning, coordinating, and delegating the delivery of skilled patient care. The clinical partner is directly accountable for and responsible to the individual consumer for the quality of nursing care rendered and collaborates with team members and patients in the planning and provision of this care.

Reporting Relationship

The clinical partner reports to the clinical director or a designee determined by the clinical director.

Distinguishing Features

This position requires substantial specialized knowledge, judgment, and skill based upon the principles of biological, physiological, behavioral, and sociological sciences. The clinical partner uses critical thinking skills in making decisions regarding patient care; this critical thinking includes knowledge and integration of available standards, resources, and data. The clinical partner delegates the performance of selected nursing tasks to competent individuals in selected situations. The clinical partner delegating the task retains the responsibility and accountability for the nursing care of the patient.

Assessment 5

1. At a clear editing window, change the view to Draft mode.
2. Key the memo shown in figure 4.17 with the following specifications:
    a. After keying the headings, press Enter three times, then change the line spacing to 1.5.
    b. Center and italicize the training classes.
3. Save the memo and name it Ch 04, SA 05.
4. Print and then close Ch 04, SA 05.

Figure 4.17

DATE: January 10, 1998

TO: All College Staff

FROM: James Vaira, Training and Education

SUBJECT: TRAINING SCHEDULE

I am in the process of creating the training schedule for spring quarter. The tentative training areas include:

Effective Managing

Discipline in the Classroom

Desktop Publishing

Managing Budgets

If you have a specific training need not addressed by the above areas, please let me know. The schedule should be finalized by February 1.

xx:Ch 04, SA 05

5

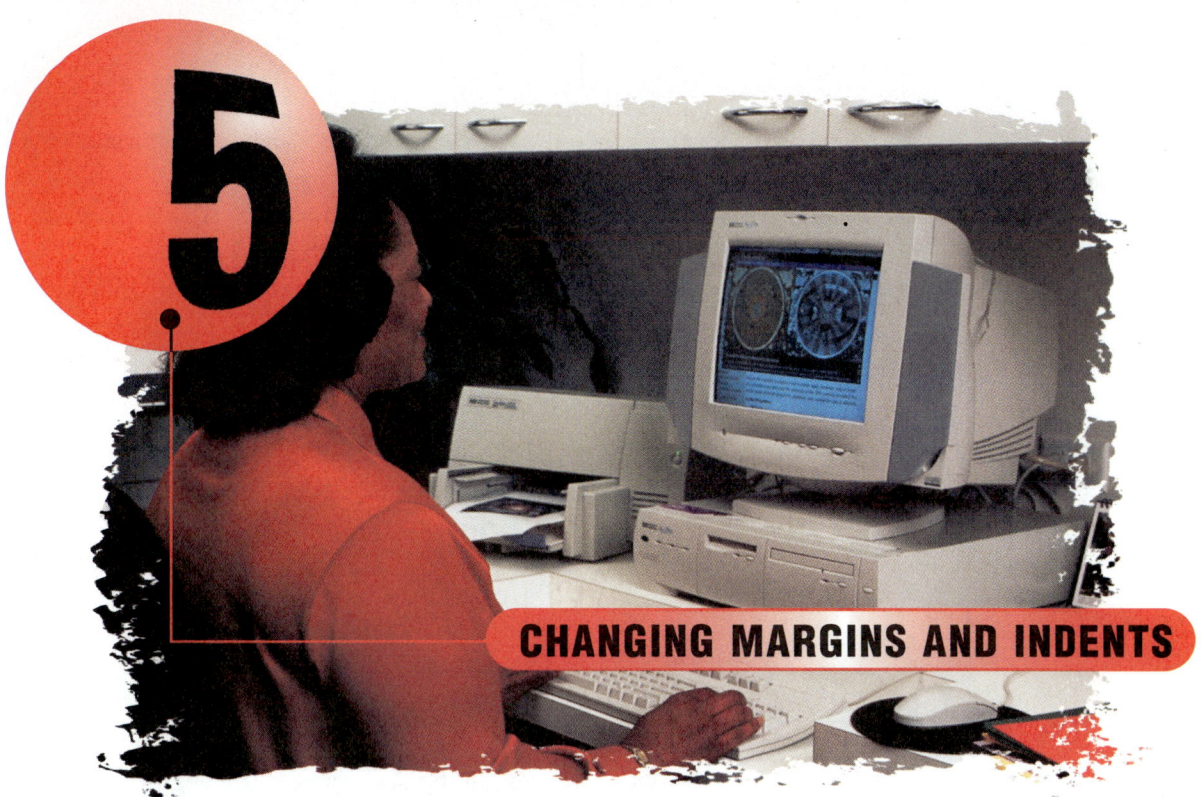

CHANGING MARGINS AND INDENTS

PERFORMANCE OBJECTIVE

Upon successful completion of chapter 5, you will be able to enhance single-page business memos and letters by changing the margins and indentations.

When you begin creating a document, WordPerfect provides default left and right margins of one inch. When text is keyed and the insertion point reaches the right margin, WordPerfect automatically wraps text down to the next line. A standard piece of paper is 8.5 inches wide. With the one-inch default left and right margins, WordPerfect begins the printed text one inch from the left edge of the paper and ends one inch from the right edge of the paper. Therefore, an actual printed text line is 6.5 inches.

Changing Margins

Even though the 6.5-inch default printed text line may be appropriate for many documents, there will be occasions when you need to shorten or lengthen margins. You can change the left and right margins using the blue margin guidelines, at the Margins dialog box, or with the Ruler Bar.

Changing Margins using the Margin Guidelines

To change the margins using the blue dotted margin guidelines, position the arrow pointer on the margin guideline you wish to adjust until the pointer changes to a left-right pointing arrow with a vertical bar between the arrows. Hold down the left mouse button, drag the guideline left or right to increase or decrease the margin, then release the mouse button. As you drag the guideline, a box will appear with the measurement of your new margin setting as shown in figure 5.1.

Figure 5.1   Margin Guideline Measurement Box

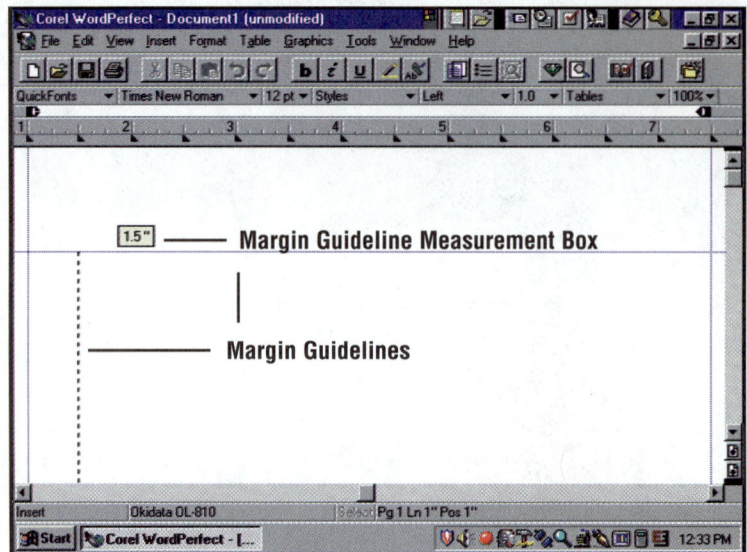

When margin settings are changed, a code is inserted in the document at the beginning of the paragraph where the insertion point is positioned. As with justification codes, margin changes take effect from the location of the code to the end of the document or until a subsequent margin code is encountered. The codes can be seen in Reveal Codes. For example, if the left and right margins are changed to 1.5 inches, the codes Lft Mar: 1.5" and Rgt Mar: 1.5" display in Reveal Codes. While in Reveal Codes, you can display the Margins dialog box by positioning the arrow pointer on the margin code and double-clicking the left mouse button.

If you want to delete a margin code, display Reveal Codes, position the insertion point immediately to the left of the margin code, then press Delete; or position the insertion point immediately to the right of the margin code, then press the Backspace key. You can also position the arrow pointer on the code, hold down the left mouse button, drag the arrow pointer into the editing window, then release the mouse button. If you delete all margin codes, the text will automatically readjust to the default settings of one inch.

EXERCISE

Changing Margins with the Margin Guidelines

1. At a clear editing window, open Para 01. This document is located on your student data disk.
2. Save the document with Save As and name it Ch 05, Ex 01.
3. Change the left and right margins to 1.25 inches using the blue margin guidelines by completing the following steps:
   a. With the insertion point positioned on any line of text in the first paragraph, position the arrow pointer on the left margin guideline until the pointer changes to a left-right pointing arrow with a vertical bar between the arrows.
   b. Hold down the left mouse button, drag the blue guideline to the right until the measurement box displays 1.25", then release the mouse button.

    c. With the insertion point positioned on any line of text in the first paragraph, position the arrow pointer on the right margin guideline until the pointer changes to a left-right pointing arrow with a vertical bar between the arrows.
    d. Hold down the left mouse button, drag the blue guideline to the left until the measurement box reads 1.25", then release the mouse button.
    e. Position the insertion point at the beginning of the document and turn on the display of Reveal Codes. Move the insertion point in the Reveal Codes window to the left of the left margin code and read the code. Move the insertion point in the Reveal Codes window to the left of the right margin code and read the code. Turn off the display of Reveal Codes.

4. Save the document again with the same name (Ch 05, Ex 01).

5. Print and then close Ch 05, Ex 01.

Changing Margins with the Margins Dialog Box

To change margins with the Margins dialog box, display the dialog box by clicking Format, then Margins. You can also display the Margins dialog box by clicking the Page Margins button on the Format Toolbar. (If the Format Toolbar is not displayed, position the arrow pointer on the current Toolbar, click the *right* button on the mouse, then click Format from the drop-down menu.)

Page Margins

The Margins dialog box contains options to change the left, right, top, and bottom margins as shown in figure 5.2. You will be working with top and bottom margins in chapter 9.

Margins Dialog Box

Figure 5.2

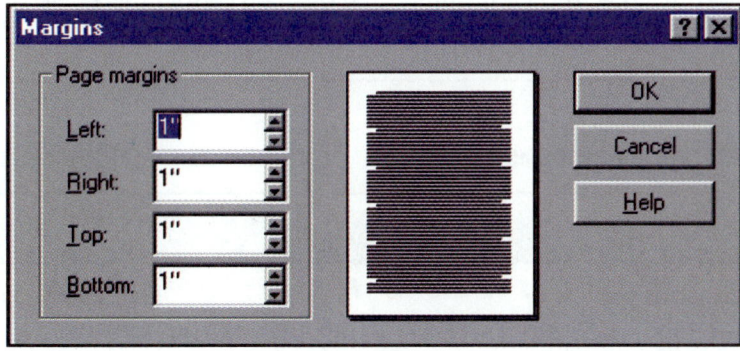

To change the left margin at the Margins dialog box, key the new left margin measurement. You can also position the arrow pointer on the up-pointing triangle beside the Left text box, then click the left mouse button to increase the number; or click the down-pointing triangle to decrease the number. Margin settings can be set by inches as well as tenths and hundredths of inches. For example, you can set a 2-inch left margin with 2; a 2½-inch margin with 2.5; and a 2 7/10-inch margin with 2.7.

To change the right margin, choose Right, then key the new right margin measurement or click the up- or down-pointing triangle.

Changing Margins and Indents   **77**

EXERCISE 2

Changing Margins at the Margins Dialog Box

1. At a clear editing window, open Para 02. This document is located on your student data disk.
2. Save the document with Save As and name it Ch 05, Ex 02.
3. Change the left and right margins to 1.5 inches by completing the following steps:
   a. With the insertion point located at the beginning of the document, click Format, then Margins.
   b. At the Margins dialog box, click the up-pointing triangle at the right side of the Left text box until *1.50"* displays.
   c. Click the up-pointing triangle at the right side of the Right text box until *1.50"* displays.
   d. Click OK or press Enter.
4. Save the document again with the same name (Ch 05, Ex 02).
5. Print and then close Ch 05, Ex 02.

Changing Margins with the Ruler Bar

WordPerfect provides a Ruler Bar that, together with the mouse, can be used to change margins and tabs. If the Ruler Bar is not displayed you can display it by clicking View, then Toolbars/Ruler. At the Toolbars dialog box that displays, click in the check box next to Ruler Bar, then click OK. The Ruler Bar, shown in figure 5.3, displays below the Power Bar.

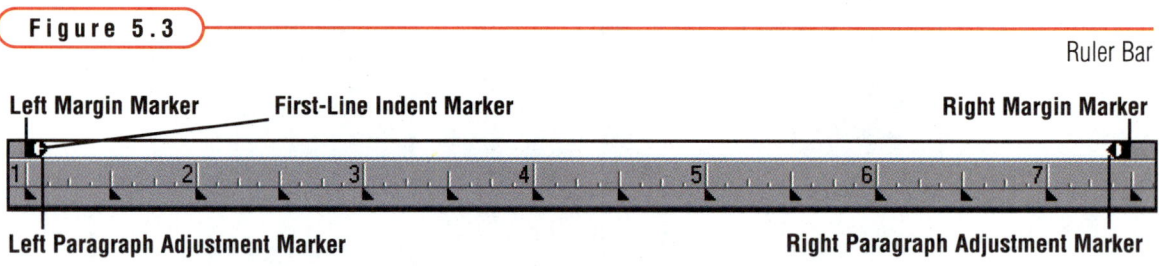

Figure 5.3

The left margin marker displays at the left side of the Ruler Bar above the one-inch mark as identified in figure 5.3. The right margin marker displays at the right side of the Ruler Bar above the 7.5-inch mark. To change the left margin in a document using the Ruler Bar, you would position the arrow pointer on the left margin marker, hold down the left mouse button, drag the arrow pointer to the desired location, then release the button. As you drag the margin marker, the margin measurement displays at the right side of the Status bar. Use this measurement to help you precisely set margins.

When you position the arrow pointer on the left margin marker, then hold down the left mouse button, the margin marker in the original position is dimmed and a vertical dashed line appears on the screen. The vertical dashed line is called the Ruler guide. Change the right margin in a document using the Ruler Bar by completing similar steps. When changes are made to the location of the left margin or right margin marker on the Ruler Bar, a margin code is inserted in the document at the beginning of the paragraph where the insertion point is positioned.

A QuickMenu can be displayed from the Ruler Bar that contains a Margins option. If you choose this option, the Margins dialog box shown in figure 5.2 displays in the editing window. To display the QuickMenu containing the Margins option, position the tip of the arrow pointer in the white area just above the Ruler, then click the right mouse button. At the QuickMenu, click Margins.

EXERCISE 3

Changing Margins with the Ruler Bar

1. At a clear editing window, open Para 03. This document is located on your student data disk.
2. Save the document with Save As and name it Ch 05, Ex 03.
3. Change the left and right margins to 1.75 inches using the Ruler Bar by completing the following steps:
   a. Click View, then Toolbars/Ruler.
   b. At the Toolbars dialog box, click in the check box next to Ruler Bar to insert a check mark.
   c. Click OK. (Skip steps 3a-3c if the Ruler Bar is already displayed.)
   d. Position the tip of the arrow pointer on the left margin marker.
   e. Hold down the left mouse button, drag the arrow pointer to the right until *Left margin: 1.75"* displays at the right side of the Status bar, then release the mouse button.
   f. Position the tip of the arrow pointer on the right margin marker.
   g. Hold down the left mouse button, drag the arrow pointer to the left until *Right margin: 6.75"* displays at the right side of the Status bar, then release the mouse button.
4. Save the document again with the same name (Ch 05, Ex 03).
5. Print and then close Ch 05, Ex 03.

Indenting Text

By now you are familiar with the word wrap feature of WordPerfect, which ends lines and wraps the insertion point to the next line. WordPerfect can force text to wrap to a tab setting instead of the left margin in three ways: (1) indenting all lines of a paragraph from the left margin, (2) indenting all lines of a paragraph on both sides (called double indenting), and (3) indenting all lines except the first line (called a hanging indent). To create these formats, use shortcut keys, the Ruler Bar, the Paragraph option from the Format drop-down menu, options from the Paragraph Format dialog box, buttons on the Format Toolbar, or a QuickSpot.

Indenting the First Line of a Paragraph

When creating certain documents, you may want to indent the first line of a paragraph to identify where a new paragraph begins. You can indent the first line of a paragraph by pressing the Tab key or with an option from the Paragraph Format dialog box.

If you use the Tab key to indent the first line of a paragraph, the insertion point is indented to the first tab setting. By default, WordPerfect contains a tab setting every 0.5 inches. Therefore, if the insertion point is positioned at the left margin and you press the Tab key, the insertion point is moved 0.5 inches from the left margin. When you press the Tab key, the code Left Tab is inserted in the document and can be seen in Reveal Codes.

Changing Margins and Indents 79

If you want to indent the first line of text to a specific measurement (other than tab settings), or you want the first line of all paragraphs indented, use the Paragraph Format dialog box shown in figure 5.4. To display this dialog box, click Format, point to Paragraph, then click Format. At the Paragraph Format dialog box, specify the first line indent measurement with the First line indent option. Changes made at the Paragraph Format dialog box affect every paragraph in the document from the location of the code to the end of the document or until another indent code is encountered.

Figure 5.4

Paragraph Format Dialog Box

EXERCISE 4

Indenting a Line to a Specific Measurement

1. At a clear editing window, open Para 04. This document is located on your student data disk.
2. Save the document with Save As and name it Ch 05, Ex 04.
3. Indent the first line of each paragraph 0.25 inches by completing the following steps:
   a. Position the insertion point at the beginning of the first paragraph.
   b. Click Format, point to Paragraph, then click Format.
   c. At the Paragraph Format dialog box, key **0.25** in the First line indent text box.
   d. Click OK or press Enter.
4. Save the document again with the same name (Ch 05, Ex 04).
5. Print and then close Ch 05, Ex 04.

The first-line indent marker on the Ruler Bar can be used to indent the first line of text in a paragraph. The first-line indent marker is identified in figure 5.3. To indent the first line of text in paragraphs using the Ruler Bar, position the tip of the arrow pointer on the first-line indent marker. Hold down the left mouse button, drag the marker to the right until the Status bar displays the desired measurement, then release the mouse button.

EXERCISE 5

Indenting Text with the Indent Marker

1. At a clear editing window, open Para 04.
2. Save the document with Save As and name it Ch 05, Ex 05.
3. Indent the first line of each paragraph 0.5 inches using the first-line indent marker on the Ruler Bar by completing the following steps:
   a. Turn on the display of the Ruler Bar. (To do this, click View, then Toolbars/Ruler. At the Toolbars dialog box, click Ruler Bar, then click OK.) (Skip this step if the Ruler Bar is already displayed.)
   b. Position the tip of the arrow pointer on the first-line indent marker on the Ruler Bar.
   c. Hold down the left mouse button, drag the first-line indent marker to the right until *First Line Indent: 1.5"* displays at the right side of the Status bar, then release the mouse button.
4. Save the document again with the same name (Ch 05, Ex 05).
5. Print and then close Ch 05, Ex 05.

Indenting Text from the Left Margin

Text in a paragraph can be indented to a tab setting or to a specific measurement from the left margin. When text is indented, all lines in the paragraph are indented to the tab or specific measurement. This is different than the Tab key, which only indents the first line of a paragraph.

Indent

To indent all text in a paragraph to a tab setting, use a shortcut command, the Indent option from a QuickMenu, the Paragraph option from the Format drop-down menu, the Indent button on the Format Toolbar, or the QuickSpot button. With any of these options, all text in a paragraph is indented to the first tab setting.

To indent text to the first tab setting from the left margin, position the insertion point at the left margin of the paragraph to be indented, then press F7 or choose Format, point to Paragraph, then click Indent.

You can also use a QuickMenu to indent text to the first tab setting from the left margin. To do this, position the insertion point at the left margin of the paragraph to be indented. Position the arrow pointer anywhere in the editing window (except the top, bottom, left, and right margins) and then click the right button on the mouse. At the QuickMenu that displays, click Indent.

The Indent button on the Format Toolbar can also be used to indent text to the first tab setting from the left margin.

The QuickSpot button in the left margin area next to a paragraph contains an indent button on the palette with various indentation options.

Each of these methods inserts a `Hd Left Ind` code in the document at the beginning of the paragraph where the insertion point is positioned. This code can be seen in Reveal Codes. The `Hd Left Ind` code only affects the paragraph where the insertion point is positioned. Text in the next paragraph will display at the left margin unless you repeat the steps for indenting.

Use the Paragraph Format dialog box shown in figure 5.4 to indent text in a paragraph and subsequent paragraphs to a specific measurement. To indent all lines of text in a paragraph and subsequent paragraphs, position the insertion point at the left margin of the first paragraph of text

Changing Margins and Indents *81*

to be indented, then click Fo**r**mat, point to **P**aragraph, then click **F**ormat. At the Paragraph Format dialog box, click the up-pointing triangle at the right side of the **L**eft margin adjustment option until the desired indent measurement displays. Click OK or press Enter to close the dialog box. You can also select the current measurement in the **L**eft margin adjustment text box and then key the desired measurement. The measurement entered at the Left margin adjustment option can be a whole number or a decimal number.

The left paragraph adjustment marker on the Ruler Bar can be used to indent all lines of text in a paragraph and subsequent paragraphs to a specific measurement. The left paragraph adjustment marker is identified in figure 5.3. To indent text using the Ruler Bar, position the tip of the arrow pointer on the left paragraph adjustment marker. Hold down the left mouse button, drag the arrow pointer to the right until the Status bar displays the desired indent measurement, then release the mouse button.

If you use the Paragraph Format dialog box or the Ruler Bar to indent text in a paragraph, each paragraph is indented from the location of the code to the end of the document or until another code is encountered.

EXERCISE

Indenting Paragraphs

1. At a clear editing window, open Memo 02. This document is located on your student data disk.
2. Save the document with Save As and name it Ch 05, Ex 06.
3. Indent the second paragraph in the document (containing the book title) to the first tab setting using the shortcut command by completing the following steps:
   a. Position the insertion point at the beginning of the second paragraph.
   b. Press F7.
4. Indent the third paragraph in the document to the first tab setting using the QuickSpot button by completing the following steps:
   a. Position the insertion point at the beginning of the third paragraph.
   b. Position the arrow pointer on the QuickSpot button in the left margin area, then click the left mouse button.
   c. At the Paragraph dialog box that displays, click the down-pointing triangle at the right side of the **I**ndent option.
   d. At the side menu that displays, click Indent.
5. Indent the fourth paragraph in the document to the first tab setting using the Fo**r**mat drop-down menu by completing the following steps:
   a. Position the insertion point at the beginning of the fourth paragraph.
   b. Click Fo**r**mat, point to **P**aragraph, then click **I**ndent.
6. Indent the fifth paragraph in the document to the first tab setting using a QuickMenu by completing the following steps:
   a. Position the insertion point at the beginning of the fifth paragraph.
   b. Position the arrow pointer anywhere in the editing window (except the top, bottom, left, and right margins) and then click the right mouse button.
   c. At the QuickMenu that displays, click **I**ndent.
7. Save the document again with the same name (Ch 05, Ex 06).
8. Print and then close Ch 05, Ex 06.

Indenting Text from the Left and Right Margins

A paragraph that you want visually set off from other text in a document or a paragraph containing a quotation can be indented from the left as well as the right margin. Indenting from the left and right margins gives a paragraph a balanced look.

Text can be indented 0.5 inches from the left and right margins in four ways: (1) the shortcut command Ctrl + Shift + F7, (2) Format, Paragraph, then Double Indent, (3) the Double Indent button on the Format Toolbar; or (4) click the QuickSpot button, click the Indent button, then click Double Indent. By repeating an indent command, text is indented 1 inch from both margins. If text is indented to the first tab setting from the left and right margins, the code  displays in Reveal Codes.

Double Indent

EXERCISE 7

Indenting Text from Both Margins

1. At a clear editing window, open Quote. This document is located on your student data disk.
2. Save the document with Save As and name it Ch 05, Ex 07.
3. Indent the second paragraph in the document to the first tab setting from the left and right margins by completing the following steps:
    a. Position the insertion point at the beginning of the second paragraph.
    b. Press Ctrl + Shift + F7.
4. Indent the fourth paragraph in the document to the first tab setting from the left and right margins by completing the following steps:
    a. Position the insertion point at the beginning of the fourth paragraph.
    b. Click Format, point to Paragraph, then click Double Indent.
5. Save the document again with the same name (Ch 05, Ex 07).
6. Print and then close Ch 05, Ex 07.

With the Left margin adjustment and Right margin adjustment options at the Paragraph Format dialog box, you can indent text a specific amount from the left and right margins. The measurement does not have to be the same for each option.

The left paragraph adjustment marker and the right paragraph adjustment marker on the Ruler Bar can be used to indent all lines of text in a paragraph and subsequent paragraphs to a specific measurement. The markers are identified in figure 5.3.

If you use the Paragraph Format dialog box or the Ruler Bar to indent text in a paragraph, each paragraph is indented from the location of the code to the end of the document or until another code is encountered.

EXERCISE 8

Indenting Paragraphs and Returning to the Default

1. At a clear editing window, open Quote.
2. Save the document with Save As and name it Ch 05, Ex 08.
3. Indent the second paragraph 0.75 inches from the left and right margins by completing the following steps:
   a. Position the insertion point at the beginning of the second paragraph.
   b. Click Format, point to Paragraph, then click Format.
   c. At the Paragraph Format dialog box, select the *0"* that displays in the Left margin adjustment text box, then key **0.75**.
   d. Select the *0"* that displays in the Right margin adjustment text box, then key **0.75**.
   e. Click OK or press Enter.
4. Return the left and right margin adjustments to 0" for the third paragraph by completing the following steps:
   a. Position the insertion point at the beginning of the third paragraph.
   b. Click Format, point to Paragraph, then click Format.
   c. At the Paragraph Format dialog box, select the *0.750"* that displays in the Left margin adjustment text box, then key **0**.
   d. Select the *0.750"* that displays in the Right margin adjustment text box, then key **0**.
   e. Click OK or press Enter.
5. Indent the fourth paragraph 0.75 inches from the left and right margins using the Ruler Bar by completing the following steps:
   a. Display the Ruler Bar. (Skip this step if the Ruler Bar is already displayed.)
   b. Position the insertion point at the beginning of the fourth paragraph.
   c. Position the tip of the arrow pointer on the left paragraph adjustment marker.
   d. Hold down the left mouse button, drag the arrow pointer to the right until *Left Margin Adjust: 1.75"* displays at the right side of the Status bar, then release the mouse button.
   e. Position the tip of the arrow pointer on the right paragraph adjustment marker.
   f. Hold down the left mouse button, drag the arrow pointer to the left until *Right Margin Adjust: 6.75"* displays at the right side of the Status bar, then release the mouse button.
6. Save the document again with the same name (Ch 05, Ex 08).
7. Print and then close Ch 05, Ex 08.

Creating Hanging Indent Paragraphs

With WordPerfect's Hanging Indent feature, you can create paragraphs such as bibliographic entries where the first line begins at the left margin, but second and subsequent lines in the paragraph are indented to the first tab setting. Figure 5.5 shows an example of a hanging indent paragraph.

Figure 5.5

Hanging Paragraph

> This is an example of a hanging indent paragraph. Create a hanging indent paragraph with the shortcut command Ctrl + F7, the Paragraph option from the Format drop-down menu, options from the Paragraph Format dialog box, or the Hanging Indent button from the QuickSpot Indent side menu.

To create a hanging indent paragraph with the shortcut command, position the insertion point at the beginning of the paragraph to be indented, then press Ctrl + F7. If you are using the Format Toolbar, position the insertion point at the beginning of the paragraph, then click the Hanging Indent button.

Hanging Indent

To create a hanging indent paragraph with the Paragraph option from the Format drop-down menu, position the insertion point at the left margin of the paragraph to be indented, click Format, point to Paragraph, then click Hanging Indent.

To use the QuickSpot button to create a hanging indent, position the insertion point at the beginning of the paragraph to be indented, click the QuickSpot button, click Indent, then click Hanging Indent.

EXERCISE 9

Creating Hanging Indents on Single Paragraphs

1. At a clear editing window, open Bibliography. This document is located on your student data disk.
2. Save the document with Save As and name it Ch 05, Ex 09.
3. Hang indent the first paragraph by completing the following steps:
   a. Position the insertion point at the beginning of the first paragraph.
   b. Press Ctrl + F7; or click the Hanging Indent button on the Format Toolbar.
4. Indent the remaining paragraphs in the document by completing steps similar to those in step 3.
5. Select and then italicize the title of the publication in each paragraph.
6. Save the document again with the same name (Ch 05, Ex 09).
7. Print and then close Ch 05, Ex 09.

When you create a hanging indent paragraph with the shortcut command, the Paragraph option from the Format drop-down menu, the Hanging Indent button on the Format Toolbar, or the QuickSpot button, the codes  and are inserted in the document at the location of the insertion point.

At the Paragraph Format dialog box, the First line indent and Left margin adjustment options can be used to create a hanging indent paragraph. To do this, position the insertion point at the beginning of the paragraph to be indented, click Format, point to Paragraph, then click Format. At the Paragraph Format dialog box, key a negative measurement in the First line indent text box. Select the current measurement in the Left margin adjustment text box, then key a positive measurement. Click OK or press Enter to close the dialog box.

Changing Margins and Indents

If you use the Paragraph Format dialog box or the Ruler Bar to indent text in a paragraph, each paragraph is indented from the location of the code to the end of the document or until another code is encountered.

EXERCISE 10

Creating a Hanging Indent for All Paragraphs

1. At a clear editing window, open Bibliography.
2. Save the document with Save As and name it Ch 05, Ex 10.
3. Hang indent all paragraphs in the document by completing the following steps:
   a. Position the insertion point at the beginning of the first paragraph.
   b. Click Format, point to Paragraph, then click Format.
   c. At the Paragraph Format dialog box, key **-0.5** in the First line indent text box.
   d. Select the current measurement in the Left margin adjustment text box, then key **0.5**.
   e. Click OK or press Enter.
4. Select and then underline the title of the publication in each paragraph.
5. Save the document again with the same name (Ch 05, Ex 10).
6. Print and then close Ch 05, Ex 10.

Creating Numbered Paragraphs

As you have learned, WordPerfect's QuickCorrect feature will automatically correct certain words that are keyed incorrectly. Additionally, the QuickCorrect feature will also automatically insert numbers in a document. If you key a number followed by a period, and then press the Tab key, the QuickCorrect feature will automatically hang indent the text (the number and period will display at the left margin while text will be indented to the first tab setting) and also insert the next number in the sequence when the Enter key is pressed. To create numbered paragraphs, you would complete the following steps:

1. Key a **1** followed by a period.
2. Press the Tab key, then key the paragraph of text. (QuickCorrect will automatically indent the text to the first tab setting.)
3. Press Enter and QuickCorrect inserts the number **2** followed by a period at the left margin and indents the insertion point to the first tab setting.
4. Continue keying paragraphs.
5. After keying the last paragraph and pressing Enter, press the Backspace key. (This deletes the automatic numbering code.)

When keying paragraphs of text, you can press Enter twice and the next number in the sequence is moved down with the insertion point. If, after entering numbered paragraphs, you want to key text that is not numbered, press the Backspace key. This deletes the automatic numbering codes inserted by QuickCorrect. These codes include a paragraph style code and another style code. Pressing the Backspace key deletes both codes.

EXERCISE 11

Creating Numbered Paragraphs

1. At a clear editing window, make the following changes:
   a. Change the left and right margins to 1.5 inches.
   b. Change the line spacing to double (2).
2. Key the document shown in figure 5.6. Center and bold the text as indicated. Create the numbered paragraphs by completing the following steps:
   a. With the insertion point positioned at the left margin of the first paragraph, key **1** followed by a period (.).
   b. Press the Tab key.
   c. Key the paragraph.
   d. Press Enter then key the text after 2.
   e. Continue in this manner until all numbered paragraphs are entered.
3. When the document is complete, save it and name it Ch 05, Ex 11.
4. Print and then close Ch 05, Ex 11.

Figure 5.6

POSITION ACCOUNTABILITIES

REGISTERED NURSE

1. Provides direct and indirect patient care using the nursing process to assess, plan, implement, and evaluate care given.

2. Analyzes the patient's condition and reports changes to the appropriate health care provider.

3. Observes patients for signs and symptoms, collects data on patients, reports and documents results.

4. Evaluates patient response to plan of care and modifies plan. Communicates modifications to other health care professionals.

5. Initiates and participates in patient care conferences.

6. Performs documentation that is timely, accurate, and complete.

7. Documents care that is reflective of patient needs, nursing action, and patient response.

Changing Margins and Indents

If you do not want the automatic numbering feature on, turn it off at the QuickCorrect Options dialog box. To turn off automatic numbering, you would complete the following steps:

1. Click Tools, then QuickCorrect.
2. At the QuickCorrect dialog box, click the Options button.
3. At the QuickCorrect Options dialog box, click the *QuickBullets* option in the Items list box.
4. Click the OK button to close the QuickCorrect Options dialog box.
5. Click the Close button to close the QuickCorrect dialog box.

Creating Bulleted Paragraphs

In addition to automatically numbering paragraphs, the QuickCorrect feature will also create bullets. QuickCorrect will automatically hang indent the text (the bullet will display at the left margin while text will be indented to the first tab setting) and also insert another bullet when the Enter key is pressed.

Different bullets can be created by keying different symbols. Figure 5.7 displays what bullet will display when a specific symbol is keyed.

Figure 5.7

QuickCorrect Bullets

Symbol	Bullet
*	•
o	•
^	◆
>	▶
+	★

To create bulleted paragraphs, you would complete the following steps:

1. Key the symbol that will insert the desired bullet.
2. Press the Tab key, then key the paragraph of text. (QuickCorrect will insert the bullet and automatically indent the text to the first tab setting.)
3. Press Enter and QuickCorrect inserts another bullet at the left margin and indents the insertion point to the first tab setting.
4. Continue keying paragraphs.
5. After keying the last paragraph and pressing Enter, press the Backspace key. (This deletes the bullet and turns off automatic bulleting.)

If, after entering bulleted paragraphs, you want to key text that is not preceded by a bullet, press the Backspace key. This deletes the automatic bulleting codes inserted by QuickCorrect. These codes include a paragraph style code and another style code. Pressing the Backspace key deletes both codes.

If you do not want the automatic bulleting feature on, turn it off at the QuickCorrect Options dialog box. To do this, you would complete the following steps:

1. Click Tools, then QuickCorrect.
2. At the QuickCorrect dialog box, click the Options button.

3. At the QuickCorrect Options dialog box, click the *QuickBullets* option in the Items list box.
4. Click the OK button to close the QuickCorrect Options dialog box.
5. Click the Close button to close the QuickCorrect dialog box.

EXERCISE 12

Creating Bulleted Paragraphs

1. At a clear editing window, change the left and right margins to 1.5 inches.
2. Key the document shown in figure 5.8. Center and bold the text as indicated. Create the bulleted paragraphs by completing the following steps:
   a. With the insertion point positioned at the left margin of the first paragraph to be preceded by a bullet, key the caret symbol (^).
   b. Press the Tab key.
   c. Key the paragraph.
   d. Press Enter twice and then key the text after the next bullet.
   e. Continue in this manner until all paragraphs preceded by a bullet are entered.
3. When the document is complete, save it and name it Ch 05, Ex 12.
4. Print and then close Ch 05, Ex 12.

Figure 5.8

ADVANTAGES OF TELECONFERENCING

There are a number of distinct advantages to using the various forms of teleconferencing. They include:

◆ Involvement in the decision-making process increases.

◆ Decisions can be made faster.

◆ Meetings are usually shorter.

◆ Interaction increases as more people are involved.

◆ Travel time and costs are eliminated.

◆ Meetings can be arranged on short notice.

◆ Project cycles shorten.

◆ Meetings can be held more frequently.

Changing Margins and Indents

Inserting Bullets and Numbers with the Bullets & Numbers Dialog Box

WordPerfect includes a variety of features for inserting numbers or bullets in a document. You have learned how to use the QuickCorrect feature to automatically number paragraphs of text in a document as well as precede paragraphs of text with bullets. In addition to the QuickCorrect feature, numbers and/or bullets can be inserted in a document with options at the Bullets & Numbers dialog box shown in figure 5.9. To display the Bullets & Numbers dialog box, click Insert, then Bullets & Numbers.

The Styles list box contains a variety of bullet and numbering options. The second through sixth options can be used to insert a bullet into a document. When a bullet is inserted with this dialog box, the bullet is inserted at the left margin and the insertion point is automatically indented to the first tab setting to the right.

Figure 5.9

Bullets & Numbers Dialog Box

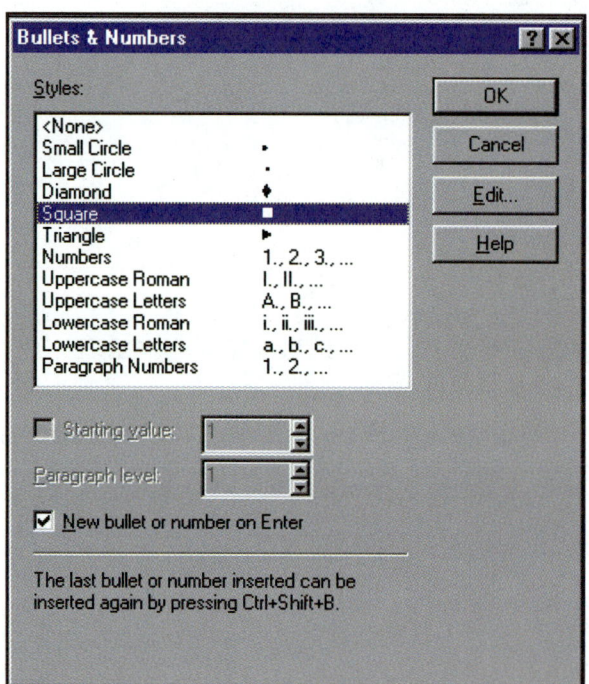

The Numbers option along with the last five options in the list box can be used to insert numbers in a document. As with bullets, WordPerfect automatically indents the insertion point to the first tab setting to the right. If you choose any of the number options, you can identify the beginning value. When a number option is selected, the Starting value option displays in black. To change the starting value with the mouse, position the arrow pointer in the check box before Starting value, click the left mouse button, then key the new starting value. If you are using the keyboard, press Alt + V, then key the new starting value.

After inserting the first bullet or number in a document, you can insert another bullet or the next number in the document with the shortcut command Ctrl + Shift + B. If you insert a check mark in the New bullet or number on Enter option, a bullet or the next number in the sequence will be inserted in the document when you press the Enter key. When you are done entering bullets or numbers in a document, display the Bullets & Numbers dialog box then remove the check mark from the New bullet or number on Enter option.

EXERCISE 13

Inserting Numbers Using the Bullets & Numbers Dialog Box

1. At a clear editing window, key the memo shown in figure 5.10 in an appropriate memo format with the following specifications:
   a. Change the left and right margins to 1.5 inches.
   b. Complete the following steps to insert the number *6.* and indent the insertion point in the first numbered paragraph below the first paragraph of the memo:
      (1) Position the insertion point at the left margin where the *6.* is to be inserted.
      (2) Click Insert, then Bullets & Numbers.
      (3) At the Bullets & Numbers dialog box, click Numbers in the Styles list box.
      (4) Change the starting value to 6. To do this, position the arrow pointer in the check box before Starting value, click the left mouse button, then key **6**.
      (5) Make sure a check mark does not appear in the New bullet or number on Enter check box. If this option is selected, remove the check mark by moving the arrow pointer to the check mark box and clicking the left mouse button.
      (6) Click OK or press Enter.
      (7) Key the text that appears after *6*.
   c. Complete the following steps to insert the remaining numbers before the numbered paragraphs:
      (1) Position the insertion point at the left margin where the next number is to be inserted.
      (2) Press Ctrl + Shift + B.
2. After keying the memo, save it and name it Ch 05, Ex 13.
3. Print and then close Ch 05, Ex 13.

Changing Margins and Indents

Figure 5.10

DATE: March 15, 1998; TO: Maggie Henedine; FROM: Katherine Brynn; SUBJECT: POSITION DESCRIPTION

At the end of last week, I sent you a position description to be included in the April newsletter. Since that time, the department manager has decided to add the following responsibilities to the list:

6. Skill in interpersonal relationships with emphasis on reaching out and being friendly

7. Ability to be sensitive and show positive regard for fellow employees, patients, and families

8. Ability to set priorities and use good judgment

9. Ability to willingly accept responsibilities

I hope these additional responsibilities can be included in the April newsletter. Please contact me to let me know if you receive this memo before the newsletter deadline.

xx:Ch 05, Ex 13

EXERCISE

Inserting Bullets Using the Bullets & Numbers Dialog Box

1. At a clear editing window, open Para 03.
2. Save the document with Save As and name it Ch 05, Ex 14.
3. Insert bullets before each of the paragraphs by completing the following steps:
    a. Press Ctrl + A to select the entire document.
    b. Display the Bullets & Numbers dialog box by clicking Insert, then Bullets & Numbers.
    c. At the Bullets & Numbers dialog box, click Square in the Styles list box.
    d. Make sure a check mark appears in the New bullet or number on Enter check box. If there is no check mark, move the arrow pointer to the check box and then click the left mouse button.
    e. Click OK or press Enter.
    f. Click outside the selected area to deselect the text.
4. Save the document again with the same name (Ch 05, Ex 14).
5. Print and then close Ch 05, Ex 14.

Inserting Bullets and Numbers with the Insert Bullet Button

Insert Bullet

In addition to the QuickCorrect feature and the Bullets & Numbers dialog box, numbers or bullets can be inserted in a document using the Insert Bullet button on the Toolbar. Click this button and a bullet or number is inserted in the document and any text keyed will be indented to the next tab to the right. What is inserted in the document is determined by what is selected in the Styles list box at the Bullets & Numbers dialog box.

92 Chapter 5

EXERCISE 15

Inserting Bullets Using the Insert Bullet Button

1. At a clear editing window, open Para 04.
2. Save the document with Save As and name it Ch 05, Ex 15.
3. Insert bullets before each of the paragraphs by completing the following steps:
   a. Press Ctrl + A to select the entire document.
   b. Click the Insert Bullet button on the Toolbar. (If the paragraphs are not preceded by a Square bullet, do the following: Click Insert, then Bullets & Numbers. At the Bullets & Numbers dialog box, click Square in the Styles list box. Click OK or press Enter.)
   c. Click outside the selected area to deselect the text.
4. Save the document again with the same name (Ch 05, Ex 15).
5. Print and then close Ch 05, Ex 15.

CHAPTER SUMMARY

▼ The one-inch default left and right margins can be changed by dragging the margin guidelines, or at the Margins dialog box. Margins can be set by inches as well as tenths and hundredths of inches.

▼ When margin settings are changed, codes such as [Lft Mar: 1.5"] and [Rgt Mar: 1.5"] display in Reveal Codes. Margin codes appear at the beginning of the paragraph in which the insertion point was located when the margins were changed.

▼ To indent the first line of a paragraph by a specific measurement (other than tab settings), use the Paragraph Format dialog box or the first-line indent marker on the Ruler Bar.

▼ The Indent feature will indent text from the left margin to the first tab setting or to a specific measurement.

▼ The Double Indent feature will indent text from both the left and right sides of the paragraph. The Double Indent code looks like this [Hd LeftRight Ind].

▼ The first line of a hanging indent paragraph begins at the left margin and the rest of the paragraph is indented. The codes [Hd Left Ind] and [Hd Back Tab] are inserted in the document at the location of the insertion point.

▼ WordPerfect's QuickCorrect feature will automatically insert numbers and bullets in a document. Any text keyed after a number or bullet will be indented.

▼ Use the Bullets & Numbers dialog box to easily insert bullets or numbers in a document.

▼ Click the Insert Bullet button on the Toolbar to insert a number or bullet in a document. What is inserted is determined by what is selected in the Styles list box at the Bullets & Numbers dialog box.

Changing Margins and Indents **93**

COMMANDS REVIEW

	Mouse	Keyboard
Change margins	Drag blue margin guidelines; Format, Margins; Page Margins button on the Format Toolbar; position tip of arrow pointer at top of the Ruler Bar, click right mouse button, then click Margins	Format, Margins
Display the Ruler Bar	View, Toolbars/Ruler, Ruler Bar	View, Toolbars/Ruler, Ruler Bar
Display Paragraph Format dialog box	Format, Paragraph, Format	Format, Paragraph, Format
Indent (tab setting)	Format, Paragraph, Indent; Indent button on the Format Toolbar; or Indent option at QuickSpot menu	F7
Indent (tab setting with the QuickMenu)	Click right mouse button, click Indent	
Double Indent (tab setting)	Format, Paragraph, Double Indent; Double Indent button on Format Toolbar; or Double Indent option from the Indent side menu at QuickSpot menu	CTRL + SHIFT + F7
Hanging Indent (tab setting)	Format, Paragraph, Hanging Indent; Hanging Indent button on Format Toolbar; or Hanging Indent button from Indent side menu at QuickSpot menu	CTRL + F7
Display Bullets & Numbers dialog box	Insert, Bullets & Numbers	Insert, Bullets & Numbers
Insert bullet or number	Insert Bullet button on Toolbar	

CHECK YOUR UNDERSTANDING

Matching: In the space provided at the left, indicate the corresponding letter of each feature described.

- A. Indenting first line of a paragraph
- B. Indenting text from left margin
- C. Indenting text from both margins
- D. Hanging indent paragraph

_____ 1. Could be used for creating a bibliography.

_____ 2. Used when inserting long quotations in a document.

_____ 3. Used when creating numbered paragraphs.

_____ 4. Used to set off one paragraph from other text in the document.

_____ 5. Can be used instead of the Tab key.

Completion: In the space provided at the right, indicate the correct term, command, or number.

1. The width in inches of a standard piece of paper.   *8.5"*

2. The default left and right margin settings.   *1"*

3. The width of the default line for text.   *6.5"*

4. The dialog box where the margins can be changed.   *Margins*

5. If, in Reveal Codes, the reveal codes insertion point was positioned immediately to the left of a 1.5" right margin code, the code would look like this.   *Rgt Mar: 1.5"*

6. The margin code would be found here in relation to a paragraph.   *Beginning*

7. This is the keyboard command to indent a paragraph from the left margin.   _____

8. This is the keyboard command to indent a paragraph from the left and right margins.   _____

9. This is the keyboard command that will create a hanging indent paragraph.   _____

10. These codes are inserted in the document when you create a hanging indent paragraph.   _____

11. Key this symbol in a document and QuickCorrect will convert it to a diamond symbol.   _____

12. Key this symbol in a document and QuickCorrect will convert it to a star symbol.   _____

Changing Margins and Indents

SKILL ASSESSMENTS

Assessment 1

1. At a clear editing window, make the following changes:
    a. Change the view to Draft mode.
    b. Change the left and right margins to 1.5 inches.
2. Key the memo shown in figure 5.11. Double indent the second paragraph.
3. Save the memo and name it Ch 05, SA 01.
4. Print and then close Ch 05, SA 01.

Figure 5.11

DATE:	December 6, 1998

TO:	Diane Tsu, Public Relations Department

FROM:	Lee Glidden, CIS Department

SUBJECT:	TELECOMMUNICATIONS COURSE

The telecommunications course, CIS 230, was a great success this quarter. The course has been added for spring quarter. Please include the following description for the course in the spring schedule:

> The fundamental ideas presented in CIS 230 will enable a student to appreciate what telecommunications is and what it encompasses; understand basic telecommunications terminology; know the business applications of telecommunications technology; understand the present status of the technology; understand events that have brought us to the present; and consider trends that will affect future telecommunications.

I would like to see the course advertised not only in the spring schedule but also through the school newspaper. Would you help me write an advertisement for the newspaper? You can contact me at extension 3320.

xx:Ch 05, SA 01

Assessment 2

1. At a clear editing window, change the left and right margins to 1.25 inches, then key the document shown in figure 5.12. Bold and center the text as indicated.
2. After keying the document, move the insertion point back to the beginning of the document, then change the justification to full.
3. Save the document and name it Ch 05, SA 02.
4. Print and then close Ch 05, SA 02.

Figure 5.12

EXPANSION AND ENHANCEMENT

OF LOCAL AND WIDE AREA NETWORKS

The foundation of the national telecommunications network is the publicly owned telephone network. This network, which was originally designed, installed, and operated by AT&T and local independent telephone companies to provide traditional voice messaging services, now offers a multitude of information services, including:

1. **Electronic Mail/Message Systems.** Individuals have an electronic mailbox in a computer that is accessed via a computer terminal such as a microcomputer.

2. **Voice Mail.** The primary difference in electronic mail/message systems and voice mail is the input/output device, which is a telephone rather than a computer.

3. **Value Added Networks.** These are special services provided by telecommunications companies in addition to transferring information, such as storing information for delivery at a later time, providing security features so that no one is able to intercept the information, and selecting alternative routes for transmitting that help reduce costs.

4. **Expanded Voice Services.** Examples include voice mail, voice responses to answer phones and direct callers to specific departments, and systems that provide callers with an electronic voice response to questions such as weather information, bank balances, and time of day.

5. **Database Services.** Examples include airline reservation systems so that individuals can reserve seats on flights.

6. **Data Networking.** This includes the connection of computers within a complex, such as a school, or connecting computers at distant sites, such as two schools located in separate areas, for the purpose of exchanging data.

Assessment 3

1. At a clear editing window, make the following changes:
   a. Change the left and right margins to 1.5 inches.
   b. Change the line spacing to double (2).
2. Key the document shown in figure 5.13. Bold, center, and italicize text as indicated. Hang indent the paragraphs as shown.
3. After keying the document, move the insertion point back to the beginning of the document, then change the justification to full.
4. Save the document and name it Ch 05, SA 03.
5. Print and then close Ch 05, SA 03.

Figure 5.13

BIBLIOGRAPHY

Brickman, Andrew C. (1992). "Networking Computers." *Power Computing,* (pp. 10-14). Omaha, NE: Myers-Townsend Publishing Company.

Daughtery, Megan A. (1994). "Managing a Local Area Network." *Computer Technologies,* (pp. 19-23). Jacksonville, FL: Macadam Publishers.

Layug, Angela M. (1992). "Wireless LANs." *Business Offices of the 90s,* (pp. 31-45). Denver, CO: Mile-High Publishing International.

Owen, Kerry H. (1995). "Interconnecting Internal LANs." *Network Management,* (pp. 22-31). Fairbanks, AK: Marsh & Monroe Press.

Assessment 4

1. At a clear editing window, key the document shown in figure 5.14.
2. After keying the document, move the insertion point to the beginning of the document, then change the justification to full.
3. Save the document and name it Ch 05, SA 04.
4. Print and then close Ch 05, SA 04.

Figure 5.14

DENVER MEMORIAL HOSPITAL

EMPLOYEE MANAGEMENT SPECIALIST

General Description

The Employee Management Specialist is responsible for coordinating employee development and training classes. This includes coordination of the Organization Management Schedule and other publications to market educational programs.

Characteristic Duties

◆ Manages employee education, development, and training classes.

◆ Develops, coordinates, and evaluates educational conferences or seminars in collaboration with departments within the Hospital using both internal and external sources.

◆ Maintains budgets for educational training for Hospital employees.

◆ Develops publications to market and promote educational trainings offered by the Organization Management Department.

◆ Facilitates training sessions in communication skills, conflict management, and assertiveness.

◆ Keeps complete training records and enters data into the system as needed.

Minimum Qualifications

◆ Knowledge of adult education theory, technique, and evaluation methodology.

◆ Skills in interpersonal communication, time management, program planning, and detail work.

◆ Ability to work efficiently under pressure, work independently, and assume initiative.

◆ Two years' experience in the design, development, and evaluation of education and training programs in the organizational setting.

◆ Four-year degree from an accredited college or university in adult education or related field.

Unit One

PERFORMANCE ASSESSMENTS

PROBLEM SOLVING AND DECISION MAKING

Assessment 1

1. At a clear editing window, key the text shown in figure U1.1 in an appropriate memo format with the following specifications:
   a. Change the view to Draft mode.
   b. Change the left and right margins to 1.5 inches.
   c. Double indent the second paragraph.
2. Save the memo and name it Unit 01, PA 01.
3. Print and then close Unit 01, PA 01.

Optional: Rewrite the memo as a letter to the district's attorney.

DATE: November 9, 1998

TO: Pat Windslow, Superintendent

FROM: Jocelyn Cook, Assistant Superintendent

SUBJECT: RESERVOIR REPAIR

As you requested, I called Jack Manuel, president of the Alderton Water Company. He explained about the problem with the spring and reservoir that serve Leland Elementary School. During our conversation, he stated:

> According to the contract between the District and Alderton Water Company, the District must pay $10,000 toward the repair of the reservoir.

I contacted the District's attorney and asked her to review the documentation referred to by Mr. Manuel. She will call me next week with her impressions.

xx:Unit 01, PA 01

Figure U1.1

Assessment 2

1. At a clear editing window, key the document shown in figure U1.2 with the following specifications:
    a. Change the view to Draft mode.
    b. Change the left and right margins to 1.25 inches.
    c. Bold and center the text as indicated.
    d. Correct spelling (proper names are spelled correctly).
2. After keying the document, change the justification to Full.
3. Save the document and name it Unit 01, PA 02.
4. Print and then close Unit 01, PA 02.

STAFF CHANGES

Update

1. **Food Service Assistants**: Two positions were added to the high scool because of Deli America's success. The assistants are **Marian Muehler** and **Nick Cittadino**.

2. **Bus Drivers:** Sevaral new bus drivers were hired, including **Jon Thach**, **Jesse Casada, Gale Rozine,** and **Douglas Mott**. All were substitute drivers.

3. **Teachers:** At Leland Elementary School, the hiring of **Regina Young** as a third grade teacher will reduce class size. Contracts for **Morrie Lamonte** and **Leslie Bryson** were converted to provisional contracts for the 1997-98 school yaer.

4. **Supplemental Contracts:** Supplimental contracts were isued to **Janine McCall**, Assistant Girl's Basketball Coach; **Ryan Kocar**, Assistant Wrestling Coach; **Daniel Teng**, Head Basketball Coach; and **Anthony Hassart**, Baseball Coach.

5. **Administrators:** Administrative contracts were issued to **Michelle Hayden**, Assistant Principal, McKnight High School; and **Nancy Cameron**, Principal, Dryer Elementary School.

Figure U1.2

Assessment 3

1. At a clear editing window, key the bibliography shown in figure U1.3 with the following specifications:
   a. Bold and center the title as shown.
   b. Italicize the text in the bibliography as shown.
   c. Hang indent the paragraphs.
   d. After keying the bibliography, move the insertion point to the beginning of the document then change the justification to Full.
2. Save the document and name it Unit 01, PA 03.
3. Print and then close Unit 01, PA 03.

BIBLIOGRAPHY

Anspaugh, Janeen A. (1997). *Communications for the New Century* (pp. 23-32). New York, NY: Liberty Press.

Davis, Jared M. (1996). *Preparing International Business Documents.* Vancouver, British Columbia, Canada: Maple Leaf Publishing.

Geiger, Ricardo J. (1997). *Communicating Internationally* (pp. 6-14). Sacramento, CA: Mainstay Publishing House.

Nakagawa, Lisa M. (1998). *Managing Conflict.* New Orleans, LA: Sutherland & Gaines Publishing.

Figure U1.3

Assessment 4

1. At a clear editing window, key the letter shown in figure U1.4 in an appropriate business letter format. Double indent the paragraphs as indicated.
2. Save the letter and name it Unit 01, PA 04.
3. Print and then close Unit 01, PA 04.

November 23, 1998

Mr. and Mrs. Paul Schadt
2311 Northeast 41st Street
St. Charles, MO 65033

Dear Mr. and Mrs. Schadt:

You are invited to participate in our mortgage life insurance plan that could leave your family a home without house payments. We recommend this program for our home loan customers because it provides important protection at an affordable price.

    While there are many types of insurance, only mortgage life insurance is designed exclusively to pay off the mortgage balance if you were to die.

Even if you already have a life insurance plan, you will want to consider mortgage life insurance as a low-cost, attractive supplement.

    Because so many households rely on two wage earners to make mortgage payments, we have selected a plan that can insure a second person at HALF-PRICE.

I think you will agree that this protection is almost a necessity, but you may be concerned about cost. We have carefully chosen a plan that can fit your budget. We are pleased to offer this important customer service and encourage you to apply today, while it is available at these attractive rates. To apply, please call 1-800-555-3255.

Sincerely,

Jonathon Baker
Insurance Products Manager

xx:Unit 01, PA 04

Figure U1.4

Assessment 5

1. At a clear editing window, key the document shown in figure U1.5.
2. Save the document and name it Unit 01, PA 05.
3. Print and then close Unit 01, PA 05.

DENVER MEMORIAL HOSPITAL

MANAGER OF EMPLOYEE TRAINING

General Description

The *Manager of Employee Training* is responsible for planning, implementing, maintaining, and evaluating employee training and education programs for Denver Memorial Hospital. The manager is also responsible for coaching and counseling individual employees.

Characteristic Duties

◆ Assists Director of the Employee Training Department in the administration, data analysis, feedback, and planned change strategies in response to results of employee relation survey.

◆ Performs in-depth analysis of education and training needs of all support and diagnostic services.

◆ Develops, implements, and evaluates educational programs and services within and across all non-nursing units in the hospital.

◆ Coordinates the design and implementation of all non-nursing education and training programs in collaboration with internal and external resources.

◆ Designs, installs, and maintains a career development program throughout the Hospital.

◆ Recognizes and participates in the organizational and departmental customer service/employee relations action plan programs.

Minimum Qualifications

◆ Master's Degree in Nursing or equivalent.

◆ Certification in area of nursing specialty and continuing education desired.

◆ Minimum three (3) years of supervision experience.

◆ Minimum two (2) years of educational experience.

Figure U1.5

WRITING

The following activities give you the opportunity to practice your writing skills along with demonstrating an understanding of some of the important WordPerfect features you have mastered in this unit. In planning the documents, remember to shape the information according to the writing purpose and the audience. Use correct grammar, appropriate word choices, and clear sentence constructions.

Activity 1

Situation: You are Jocelyn Cook, Assistant Superintendent for Omaha City School District. Compose a memo to Jennifer Stanford that includes the following information:

- Her application for a principal internship has been accepted.
- You would like to schedule an interview with her in your office on either of the following dates and times: Tuesday, May 19, 1998, at 3:00 p.m. or Wednesday, May 20, 1998, at 1:30 p.m.

Save the memorandum and name it Unit 01, Act 01. Print and then close Unit 01, Act 01.

Activity 2

Situation: You are Dione Landers of Landers & Associates. Compose a letter to Steven Ayala, director of the Training and Education Department at Denver Memorial Hospital, that includes the following information:

- Confirmation of a one-day training on telephone systems and techniques to be held on Wednesday, March 25, 1998, from 9:00 a.m. to 4:30 p.m.
- The training topics, which include:

    Handling incoming calls
    Transferring calls
    Telephone etiquette
    Articulation and pronunciation
    Handling stressful calls

Save the letter and name it Unit 01, Act 02. Print and then close Unit 01, Act 02.

RESEARCH

WordPerfect's Help feature contains an on-screen reference manual. Use the Help feature to find information on how to select text to make edits. In the space provided below, write the steps you completed to display this information.

_____

_____

_____

_____

Unit Two

Managing AND ENHANCING Documents

In this unit, you will learn to manage documents and enhance documents with customized features such as fonts, tabs, and writing tools such as spelling checker, grammar checker, and a thesaurus.

6

MANAGING DOCUMENTS

PERFORMANCE OBJECTIVE

Upon successful completion of chapter 6, you will be able to maintain documents in folders; copy, move, rename, and print documents; and create document summaries.

Almost every company that conducts business maintains a filing system. The system may consist of documents, folders, and cabinets; or it may be a computerized filing system where information is stored on tapes and disks. Whatever kind of filing system a business uses, daily maintenance of files is important to a company's operation. Maintaining files can include such activities as renaming, moving, and copying documents, creating folders, and deleting documents. These types of functions can be completed at the Open, Save As, or Insert File dialog boxes.

Displaying Document Information

The Open, Save As, and Insert File dialog boxes contain many of the same options. The Open dialog box is shown in figure 6.1. The Save As and Insert File dialog boxes are similar in appearance.

The first option, Look in, displays the current folder in the text box. Below the Look in option, the list box displays an alphabetic list of the documents in the current folder. Folder names within the current folder are listed first, then document names with numbers are alphabetized before document names with letters. For example, *Memo 01* would be listed before *Memo A*. To change to a different disk drive, click the down-pointing triangle to the right of the Look in text box and then click the desired disk drive in the drop-down list that displays.

If the disk drive displayed is the correct drive, but you need to see the folders one level above the current folder, click the Up One Level button to the right of the Look in text box. To view documents inside folders below the current folder, double-click the folder name in the list box.

Up One Level

On the last line of the Open dialog box, WordPerfect displays the total number of documents in the current folder, the total number of kilobytes (KB) used in the current folder or document, and the amount of free space left on the disk or drive you are viewing. As you select a document, or a group of documents, this line displays the total number of kilobytes occupied by the selected objects. This information is useful if you are copying a group of documents to a floppy disk—you will be able to determine if all of the documents will fit on one disk.

The For type option at the right side of the dialog box lets you choose what type of documents you want displayed in the list box. This option is available at the Open and Insert File dialog boxes but not the Save As dialog box. By default, WordPerfect will display all documents in the current folder. If you choose this option, a drop-down list displays showing a variety of document extensions. For example, if you choose *WP Documents (*.wpd)* from the drop-down menu, WordPerfect will display in the list box only those documents ending in the extension *.wpd*.

Just below the menu bar at the top of the dialog box is a toolbar used for document management operations and altering the display of the dialog box.

In chapter 1, you learned how to change the default folder with the Look in option. In this chapter you will be moving back and forth between the student data disk in drive A, and the hard drive or network drive. If necessary, your instructor will provide you with instructions on which drive and folder to select when completing some of the exercises in this chapter.

Figure 6.1

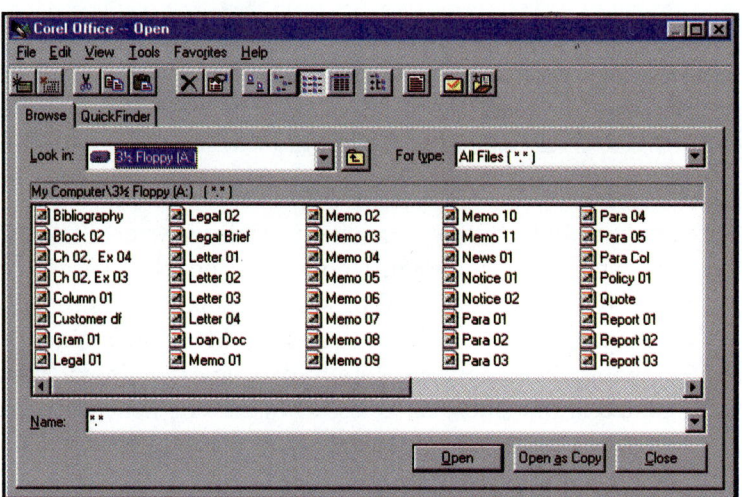

Open Dialog Box

Creating a Folder

Documents are usually filed electronically based on a cataloging system where similar types of documents are stored together. For example, all of the memos might be stored together in a folder named *Memos*. Similarly, some companies prefer to store all the documents together by department, and then further broken down by category within each department. In this case, all of the marketing department documents might be stored in a folder named *Marketing*. Within the Marketing folder there might be a folder named *Memos* to store marketing department memos, and another folder named *Reports* to store marketing department reports, and so on.

Once you start using a word processor to create a large number of files, you will want to devise your own system of storing the documents in folders that will make them easy to locate. A new folder can be created at the Open, Save As, or Insert File dialog box. To create a folder, you would complete the following steps:

1. Display the Open, Save As, or Insert File dialog box.
2. Change to the folder from which you want the new folder to branch. For example, if you want your new folder to branch from the folder *MyFiles*, make sure *MyFiles* is displayed in the Look in text box. If you want your new folder created on the floppy disk, make sure the Look in text box displays *3½ Floppy (A:)*.
3. Position the arrow pointer on a white area inside the list box and then click the *right* mouse button.
4. Point to New and then click Folder.
5. The insertion point will be positioned inside a New Folder text box. Key a name for the folder and then press Enter. A folder name can consist of 255 characters. Numbers, spaces, and some symbols can be used.

EXERCISE

Creating a Folder

1. Create two folders named *Letters* and *Memos* on your student data disk by completing the following steps:
   a. Display the Open dialog box.
   b. If necessary, change the default folder to 3½ Floppy (A:).
   c. Position the arrow pointer in a white area of the list box and then click the *right* mouse button.
   d. Point to New and then click Folder.
   e. At the New Folder text box, key **Letters** and then press Enter.
   f. Complete steps similar to those in 1c through 1e to create a second folder named **Memos**.
2. Click the Close button to close the Open dialog box.

Selecting Documents

Document management tasks can be performed on one document at a time, or you can select several documents and copy, move, delete, or print them all at once.

To select one document, position the arrow pointer on the document name in the Open, Save As, or Insert File dialog box and then click the left mouse button. To select more than one document in the Open, Save As, or Insert File dialog boxes, refer to figure 6.2.

Figure 6.2

To select documents that are...	Do this...
Adjacent to each other	Click the first document name, hold down the Shift key, then click the last document name.
Non-adjacent	Click the first document name, hold down the Ctrl key, click the second document name, click the third document name, (keeping the Ctrl key down) and so on until all the documents have been selected.

Managing Documents   *111*

Copying a Document

Copy

Paste

A Toolbar displays at the Open, Save As, and Insert File dialog boxes. This Toolbar displays toward the top of the dialog box, below the menu bar. With the Copy and Paste buttons on the Toolbar, or using the right mouse button after selecting documents, you can make an exact copy of a document and save it on the same disk, another disk, or into another folder. If you copy a document to the same folder, WordPerfect will give the duplicate copy the name *Copy of filename* where *filename* is the original document name selected to be copied. If you copy a document to another folder or drive, it can retain its original name.

To copy a document, you would complete these steps:

1. Display the Open, Save As, or Insert File dialog box.
2. Select the document(s) to be copied.
3. Click the Copy button on the dialog box Toolbar; or position the arrow pointer on the selected document, click the *right* mouse button, then click C̲opy.
4. Change to the destination folder (the folder where you want the document(s) copied to). Do this by clicking the down-pointing triangle to the right of the L̲ook in text box, then clicking the desired folder or disk name.
5. Click the Paste button on the Toolbar; or position the arrow pointer in a white portion of the list box, click the *right* mouse button, then click P̲aste.

Copying Documents to a Different Folder

1. Complete the following steps to copy the document named *Memo 01* to the *Memos* folder on your student data disk.
    a. Display the Open dialog box.
    b. If necessary, change the default folder to 3½ Floppy (A:).
    c. Click the document named *Memo 01* in the list box.
    d. Click the Copy button on the dialog box Toolbar.
    e. Change to the *Memos* folder by double-clicking the left mouse button on the folder name *Memos* in the list box.
    f. Click the Paste button on the Toolbar.
    g. Return to the previous list of documents. Do this by clicking the Up One Level button (located to the right of the L̲ook in text box).
2. Copy the remaining memo documents all at the same time to the *Memos* folder by completing the following steps:
    a. Click the document named *Memo 02*.
    b. Hold down the Shift key and then click *Memo 10*. (This will select all of the documents starting at Memo 02 and ending at Memo 10.)
    c. Move the arrow pointer inside the selected group of documents and then click the *right* mouse button.
    d. At the shortcut menu that displays, click C̲opy.
    e. Change to the *Memos* folder by double-clicking *Memos* in the list box.
    f. Position the arrow pointer in a white area of the list box and then click the *right* mouse button.
    g. At the shortcut menu that displays, click P̲aste.
    h. Click the Up One Level button (located at the right of the L̲ook in text box) to return to the previous list of documents.
3. Click the C̲lose button to close the Open dialog box.

EXERCISE 3

Copying Documents within the Same Folder

1. Copy two letters into the same folder by completing the following steps:
   a. Display the Open dialog box.
   b. If necessary, change the default folder to 3½ Floppy (A:).
   c. Select the documents *Letter 01* and *Letter 03* by completing the following steps:
      (1) Click *Letter 01*.
      (2) Hold down the Ctrl key and then click *Letter 03*.
   d. Position the arrow pointer over one of the selected documents and then click the *right* mouse button.
   e. At the shortcut menu that displays, click Copy.
   f. Deselect the document names by clicking in a white area in the list box.
   g. Click the *right* mouse button in a white area inside the list box to display the shortcut menu, then click Paste at the shortcut menu.
   h. Scroll through the list of document names to view the copied document names *Copy of Letter 01* and *Copy of Letter 03*.
2. Close the Open dialog box.

Cutting and Pasting Documents

If you decide that a document needs to be moved to a different folder or drive, select the document, and then click the Cut button on the Toolbar. Change to the folder or drive where you want to move the document and then click the Paste button on the Toolbar.

Cut

EXERCISE 4

Cutting and Pasting Documents

1. Complete the following steps to move the documents named *Copy of Letter 01* and *Copy of Letter 03* from the root folder of the 3½ Floppy (A:) to the folder named *Letters*.
   a. Display the Open dialog box.
   b. If necessary, change the default folder to 3½ Floppy (A:).
   c. Select the two documents *Copy of Letter 01* and *Copy of Letter 03*.
   d. Click the Cut button on the Toolbar.
   e. Change to the *Letters* folder by double-clicking *Letters* in the list box.
   f. Click the Paste button on the Toolbar.
   g. Click the Up One Level button to return to the previous list of document names.
2. Close the Open dialog box.

Managing Documents *113*

Renaming Documents

At the Open, Save As, or Insert File dialog boxes, you can use the Rename option from the shortcut menu to give a document a different name. The Rename option changes the name of the selected document and keeps it in the same folder.

To use the rename option, select the document, click the right mouse button, then click Rename at the shortcut menu. This positions the insertion point inside the document name text box. Key the new name for the document and then press Enter.

EXERCISE 5

Renaming a Document

1. Complete the following steps to rename the document *Copy of Letter 01* to *Denver Memorial Hospital*.
   a. Display the Open dialog box.
   b. If necessary, change the default folder to 3½ Floppy (A:).
   c. Change to the *Letters* folder by double-clicking *Letters* in the list box.
   d. Click *Copy of Letter 01*.
   e. Position the arrow pointer over the selected document and then click the *right* mouse button.
   f. At the shortcut menu that displays, click Rename.
   g. Key **Denver Memorial Hospital** and then press Enter.
2. Complete steps similar to those in steps 1d through 1f to rename the document *Copy of Letter 03* to *Facilities Dept at DMH*.
3. Click the Up One Level button to return to the previous list of document names.
4. Close the Open dialog box.

Deleting a Document

At some point, you may want to delete certain documents on your student data disk. If you work with WordPerfect on a regular basis, you should establish a system for deleting documents. The system you choose depends on the work you are doing.

Delete

To delete a document(s), display the Open, Save As, or Insert File dialog box. Select the document(s) to be deleted, then click the Delete button on the Toolbar, or click the *right* mouse button, then click Delete at the shortcut menu. At the Confirm File Delete dialog box, make sure the correct document name is displayed, and then click Yes.

114 Chapter 6

EXERCISE 6

Deleting a Document

1. Complete the following steps to delete the document named *Denver Memorial Hospital* in the *Letters* folder on the student data disk.
    a. Display the Open dialog box.
    b. If necessary, change the default folder to 3½ Floppy (A:).
    c. Change to the *Letters* folder.
    d. Click the document named *Denver Memorial Hospital*.
    e. Click the Delete button on the Toolbar.
    f. At the Confirm File Delete dialog box, make sure the correct document name is displayed, then click Yes.
2. Delete the document named *Facilities Dept at DMH* in the *Letters* folder by completing the following steps:
    a. Click the document named *Facilities Dept at DMH*.
    b. Position the arrow pointer on the selected document and then click the *right* mouse button.
    c. At the shortcut menu that displays, click Delete.
    d. At the Confirm File Delete dialog box, make sure the correct document name is displayed, then click Yes.
3. Return to the previous list of document names.
4. Close the Open dialog box.

EXERCISE 7

Deleting Selected Documents

1. Delete all documents you created that begin *Ch 01*, *Ch 02*, and *Ch 03* by completing the following steps:
    a. Display the Open dialog box.
    b. Click *Ch 01, Ex 01*. (This should be the first document in the list for chapter 1.)
    c. Hold down the Shift key and then click *Ch 03, SA 03*. (This should be the last document in the list for chapter 3. If not, click the last document name listed for chapter 3.)
    d. Click the Delete button on the dialog box Toolbar.
    e. At the question asking if you are sure you want to delete the documents, click Yes.
2. Close the Open dialog box.

Managing Documents

Deleting to the Recycle Bin

Documents deleted from the floppy disk are deleted permanently. There are some utility programs available that can recover these documents if you delete them by accident provided you do not do anything else to the disk before running the recovery program.

Documents deleted from the hard drive are sent to the Windows 95 Recycle Bin. Documents can be recovered easily from the Recycle Bin. The Recycle Bin can become full very quickly and you should empty it on a periodic basis to free up space on your hard drive. To empty the Recycle Bin, double-click the Recycle Bin icon located at the left side of the Windows 95 desktop. In the Recycle Bin window, click File, then Empty Recycle Bin.

To restore a file from the Recycle Bin, open the Recycle Bin window by double-clicking the Recycle Bin icon located at the left side of the Windows 95 desktop. Select the file(s) to be restored. Position the arrow pointer over the selected files, click the *right* mouse button, then click Restore. The file(s) will be restored to their original folder.

Changing Properties

Properties

If you click the Properties button on the Open, Save As, or Insert File dialog box Toolbar, (or click Properties at the shortcut menu) the Properties dialog box displays as shown in figure 6.3. At this dialog box, you can choose to archive or back up documents the next time you run a backup program; protect documents from being modified or deleted by clicking Read-only; hide documents in file lists; and/or identify documents as part of the computer's operating system.

Figure 6.3

Properties Dialog Box

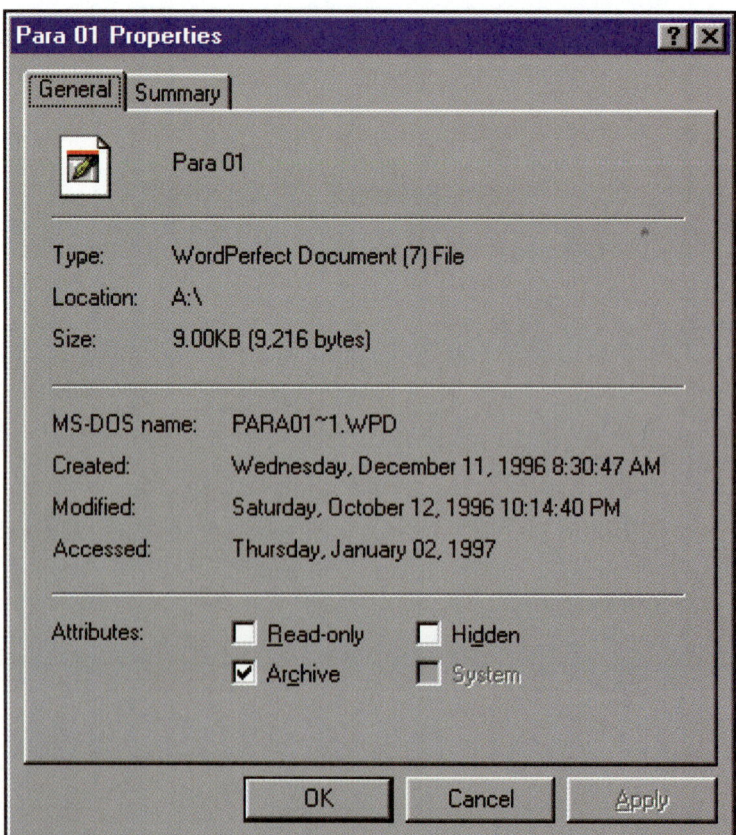

116 Chapter 6

Printing a Document

In chapter 1, you learned to print documents with the Print button on the Toolbar or at the Print dialog box. In addition to these methods, you can also print a document(s) with the Print option from the shortcut menu. To do this, click the document to be printed (or select the documents to be printed). Position the arrow pointer on the document to be printed (or one of the selected documents), click the *right* mouse button, and then click Print at the shortcut menu.

EXERCISE

Printing a Document

1. Complete the following steps to print the document named *Memo 01*:
    a. Display the Open dialog box.
    b. If necessary, change the default folder to 3½ Floppy (A:).
    c. Click the document named *Memo 01*.
    d. Position the arrow pointer on the selected document, then click the *right* mouse button.
    e. Click Print at the shortcut menu.
2. Close the Open dialog box.

Printing a Document List

At times, you may want a hard copy of folder contents as an index of the documents that are stored in the folder. To print the list of documents, display the Open, Save As, or Insert File dialog box. Position the arrow pointer in a white area of the list box and then click the right mouse button. Click Print File List at the shortcut menu. At the Print File List dialog box shown in figure 6.4, change any options as needed, then click OK.

Figure 6.4

Print File List Dialog Box

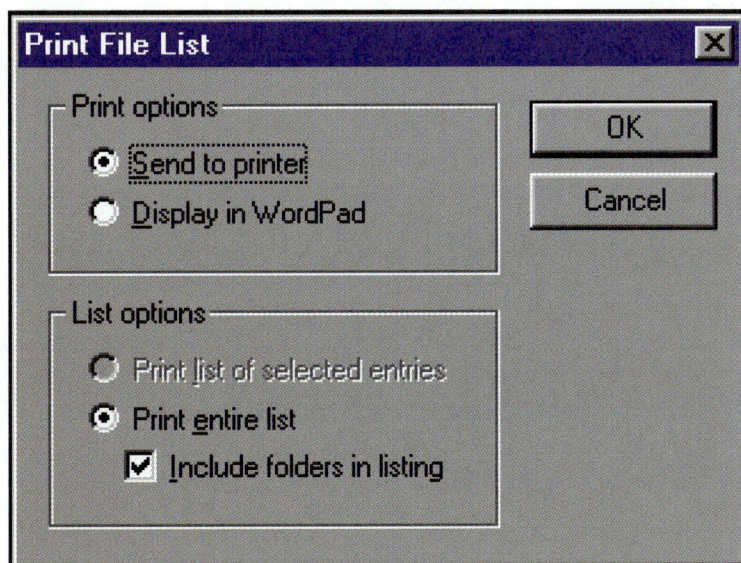

Managing Documents *117*

EXERCISE 9

Printing a List of Documents

1. Complete the following steps to print a list of the documents on the student data disk.
   a. Display the Open dialog box.
   b. If necessary, change the default folder to 3½ Floppy (A:).
   c. Move the arrow pointer to a white area inside the list box, then click the *right* mouse button.
   d. Click Print File List at the shortcut menu.
   e. At the Print File List dialog box, click OK.
2. Close the Open dialog box.

Deleting a Folder and Its Contents

A folder can be removed (deleted) from the disk or drive in the same manner that a document is deleted.

EXERCISE 10

Removing a Folder

1. Remove the *Letters* folder by completing the following steps:
   a. Display the Open dialog box.
   b. If necessary, change the default folder to the 3½ Floppy (A:).
   c. Click the *Letters* folder in the list box.
   d. Click the Delete button on the Toolbar.
   e. At the Confirm Folder Delete dialog box, make sure the *Letters* folder name is displayed, then click Yes.
2. Remove the *Memos* folder and its contents by completing steps similar to those in 1c through 1e.
3. Close the Open dialog box.

Viewing a Document

Preview

With the Preview button on the Open, Save As, or Insert File Toolbar, you can view a document without bringing it to the editing window. This feature is useful if you are looking for a particular document but cannot remember what it was named. You can check documents with the Preview option until you find the right one.

When you click the Preview button on the Toolbar, the document is inserted in a window at the right side of the dialog box as shown in figure 6.5. You can use the mouse with the up, down, left, or right scroll arrows to view different parts of the document. To magnify the text to its actual size, click the right mouse button anywhere inside the Preview window. At the shortcut menu, point to Size and then click Original Size. To remove the Preview window, click the Preview button on the Toolbar.

Preview Window

Figure 6.5

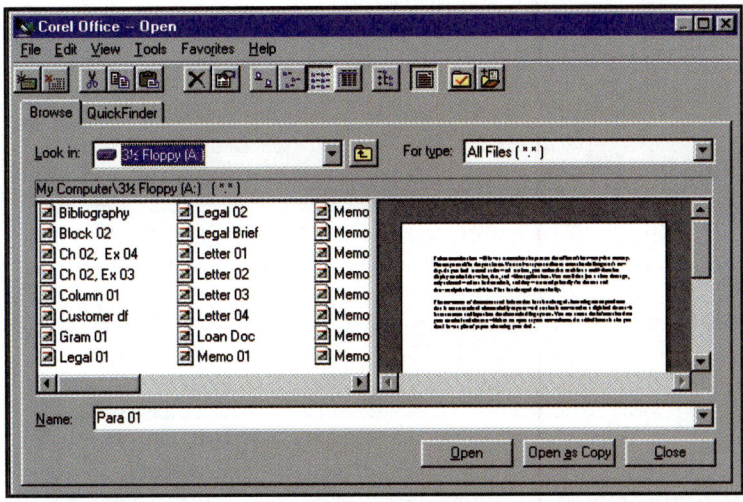

EXERCISE 11

Viewing Documents at the Open Dialog Box

1. Complete the following steps to view *Letter 01*:
   a. Display the Open dialog box.
   b. If necessary, change the default folder to 3½ Floppy (A:).
   c. Click the document *Letter 01*.
   d. Click the Preview button on the Toolbar.
   e. Change the size of the Preview text to the actual size in the letter by completing the following steps:
      (1) Move the arrow pointer inside the Preview window then click the *right* mouse button.
      (2) At the shortcut menu, point to Size, then click Original Size.
   f. Use the horizontal and vertical scroll bars to scroll through the document and view it.
2. Remove the Preview window by clicking the Preview button.
3. Close the Open dialog box.

Changing Display Options

The way document names are displayed in the Open, Save As, or Insert File dialog boxes can be altered to display large file icons, small file icons, a list of document names, or all file details. The list can be changed using buttons on the Toolbar, or with options from the View drop-down menu.

Large Icons

If you click the Large Icons button on the Toolbar, the document names are displayed as shown in figure 6.6. Small icons are similar to large icons; however, the document icons are smaller in size and more of them can fit in the window. The List button on the Toolbar allows the most document names to fit in the window as shown in figure 6.7. The Details button on the Toolbar allows you to view the document name, document size, application in which the document was generated, and the date and time the document was last modified. This display shows one document per line in the window as shown in figure 6.8.

List

Details

Managing Documents   *119*

Figure 6.6

Open Dialog Box with Large Icons Displayed

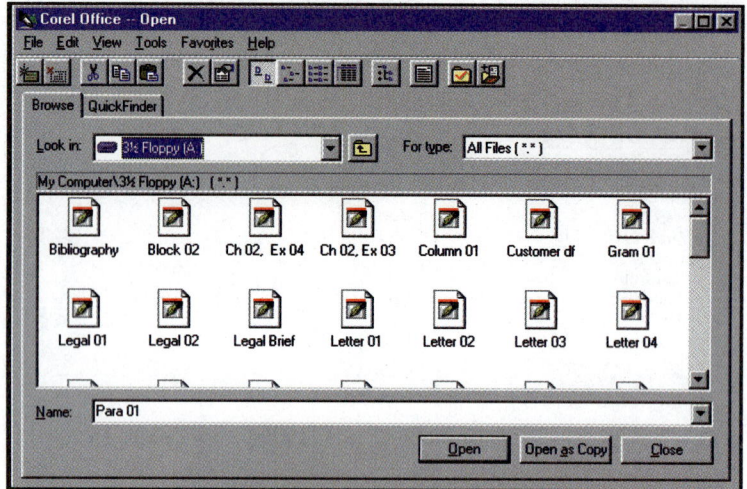

Figure 6.7

Open Dialog Box with List Displayed

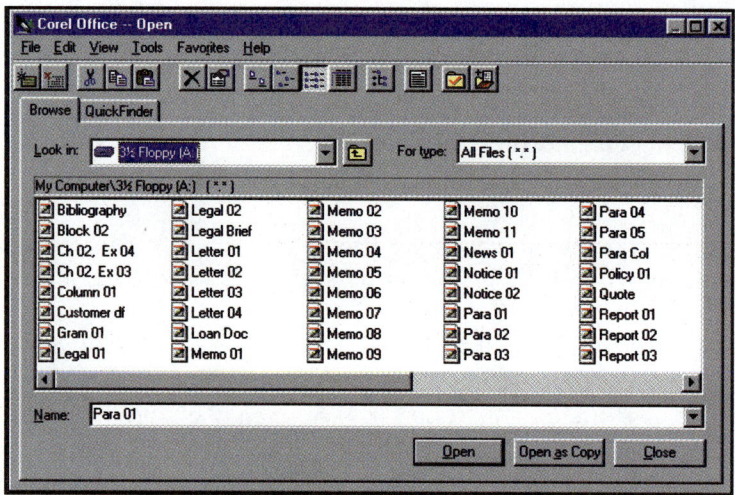

Figure 6.8

Open Dialog Box with Details Displayed

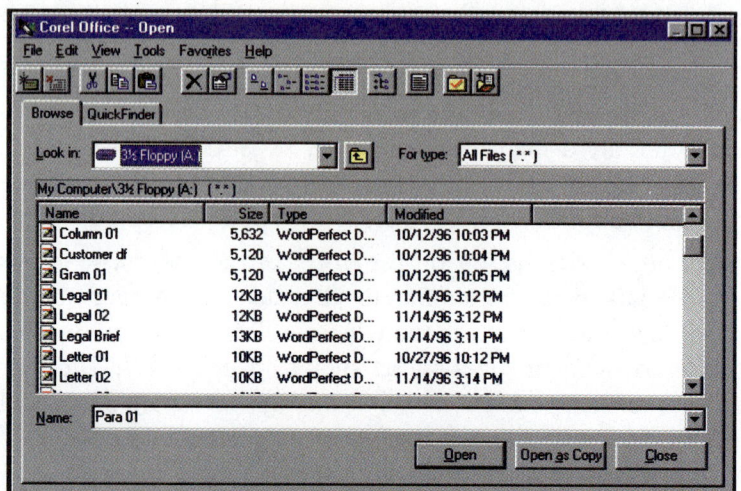

120 **Chapter 6**

The current display selection button is active (on) on the Toolbar. This setting will remain in effect until you choose an alternative display button.

Using QuickFinder

With WordPerfect's QuickFinder feature you can search a folder or specific files within a folder for a particular word pattern. This is useful in locating certain documents when you cannot remember the document name but you can remember a unique word or words contained in the document. Display the QuickFinder dialog box shown in figure 6.9 by clicking the QuickFinder tab in the Open, Save As, or Insert File dialog box.

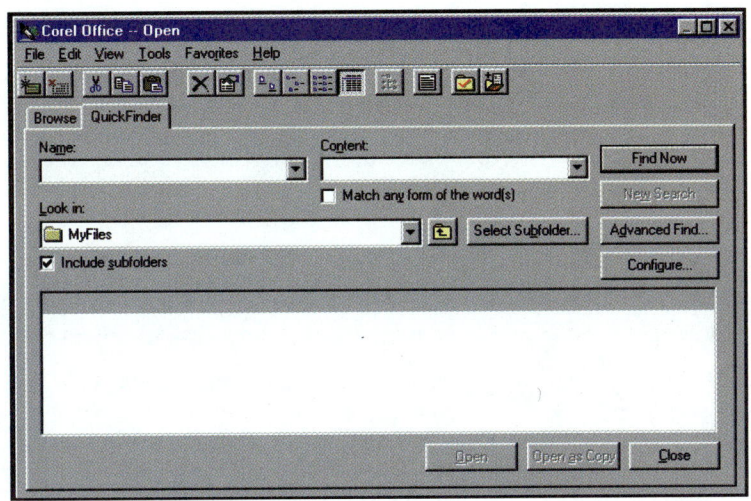

Figure 6.9

QuickFinder Dialog Box

Entering Search Text

At the QuickFinder dialog box, key the text for which you are searching in the Co*n*tent text box. For example, if you want to find all documents containing the name *Ayala*, you would key **Ayala** in the Co*n*tent text box.

You can use special operators in the A*d*vanced Find text box to locate more than one word. For example, you can search for all documents that contain the name *Ayala* and the name *Lam* by using the & operator. The list of available operators is displayed in the *O*perators list box in the Advanced Find dialog box shown in figure 6.10. Figure 6.11 shows example operators that can be inserted in the *W*ords text box of the Advanced Find dialog box, and the results the search would obtain.

Managing Documents   *121*

Figure 6.10

Advanced Find Dialog Box

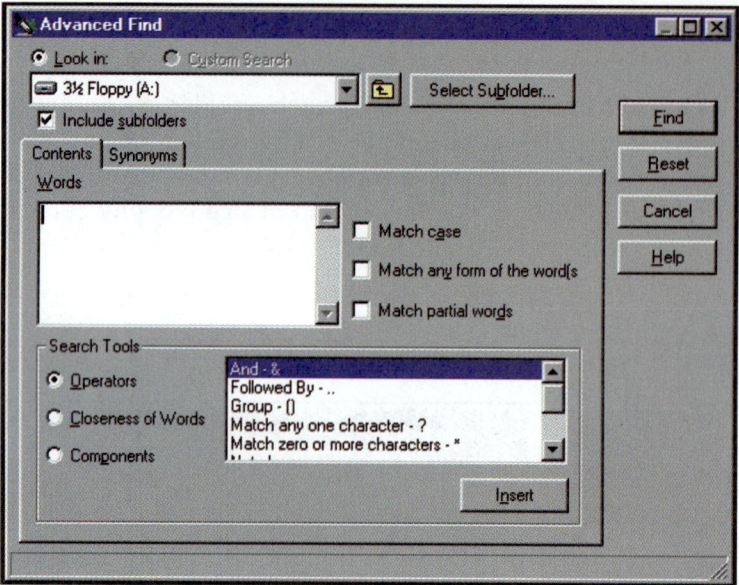

Figure 6.11

Operator Inserted	QuickFinder will find documents:
Dearing&Windslow	containing *Dearing* and *Windslow*
Dearing|Windslow	containing *Dearing* or *Windslow*
!Dearing	that do not contain *Dearing*
Dearing!Windslow	containing *Dearing* but not *Windslow*
Carey..Dearing	containing *Carey* followed by *Dearing*
(computer literacy program)	containing all three words in any order

In addition to the operators in figure 6.11, you can use the asterisk (*) symbol to indicate a combination of letters or the question mark (?) to indicate one character. For example, you can enter **educa*** in the Words text box and QuickFinder will search documents for words that begin with *educa* and end with any combination such as *education*, *educating*, and *educated*. If you enter **probabl?** in the Words text box, QuickFinder will search documents for words that begin with *probabl* and end with any one character (such as *probable* and *probably*).

Searching Specific Folder(s)

With the Look in option at the QuickFinder dialog box, you can specify the drive you want QuickFinder to search. Select a folder within the drive using the Select Subfolder button located to the right of the Look in text box. When you click Select Subfolder, a list of folders and documents on the drive or disk will display. Click the desired folder and then click the Select button at the bottom of the QuickFinder - Select Subfolder dialog box. If the Select button is not visible, drag the dialog box up or decrease its size until the button is visible.

You can also choose to search any subfolders within the selected folder with the Include subfolders check box below the Look in list box.

122 Chapter 6

Finding Documents

Once you have specified the search text in the Co<u>n</u>tent text box and the folder and/or subfolders you want searched, click F<u>i</u>nd Now at the right side of the QuickFinder dialog box. QuickFinder searches the specified folder(s) for the text and then displays documents containing the specified text in the bottom of the dialog box. Figure 6.12 shows the result of a search for documents containing the words *Denver Memorial Hospital*. The list of documents containing these words displays in a list box toward the bottom of the dialog box.

Once the search results are listed in the dialog box, you can perform on the documents any of the file management tasks learned in this chapter. You can also choose to open a document by clicking the <u>O</u>pen button at the bottom of the QuickFinder dialog box or by double-clicking the document name.

Figure 6.12

QuickFinder Search Results

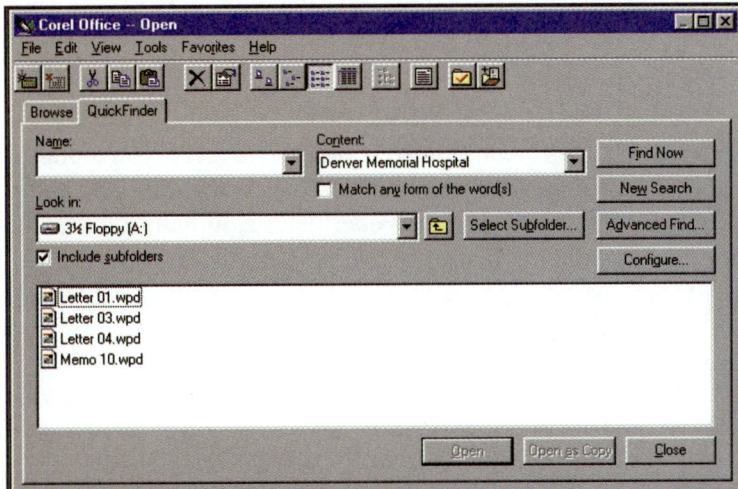

EXERCISE 12

Finding Documents Containing Specific Words

1. At a clear editing window, search for documents on your student data disk containing the words *Denver Memorial Hospital* by completing the following steps:
   a. Display the Open dialog box.
   b. If necessary, change the default folder to 3½ Floppy (A:).
   c. Click the QuickFinder tab.
   d. At the QuickFinder dialog box, press the Tab key, and then key **Denver Memorial Hospital** in the Co<u>n</u>tent text box.
   e. Make sure the <u>L</u>ook in text box displays 3½ Floppy (A:). If necessary, change the <u>L</u>ook in option to *3½ Floppy (A:)*.
   f. Click F<u>i</u>nd Now.
   g. When the search results are listed at the bottom of the QuickFinder dialog box, print a list of documents by completing the following steps:
      (1) Move the arrow pointer to a white area inside the list box.

Managing Documents   *123*

> (2) Click the *right* mouse button, then click Print File List at the shortcut menu.
> (3) At the Print File List dialog box, click OK.
> 2. Close the Open dialog box.

Entering a Path or Pattern

Use the Name option at the QuickFinder dialog box to limit the number of documents searched. For example, if you want to search only those documents with the extension *.wpd*, you would enter **.wpd* in the Name text box.

When specifying a pattern, you can use the asterisk (*) as a wildcard character. The asterisk indicates any character or any number of characters. For example, if you enter **.wpd* in the Name text box, you are telling QuickFinder to search any document with a name that begins with any number of characters but ends in the extension *.wpd*. You can also use the question mark (?) as a wildcard character. The question mark indicates a single character. For example, you can tell QuickFinder to search all document names from chapters 1 through 9 that end with *Ex 01* by entering *Ch 0?, Ex 01* in the Name text box.

You can search for documents in a specific folder by specifying a path. For example, if the disk in drive a: contains a subfolder named *Correspondence*, you could search for specific documents in the subfolder by including the path in the Name text box. Suppose you wanted to find all documents in the Correspondence subfolder that begin with *Report*. To do this, you would key **a:\Correspondence\Report*.*** in the Name text box. The first part of the text you key, *a:\Correspondence*, is the "path" or the location where you want WordPerfect to search. The rest of the text, *Report*.**, tells WordPerfect to search for document names that begin with *Report* and end in any text or extension.

EXERCISE

Specifying Documents to be Searched

1. At a clear editing window, search documents with names beginning *Ch 0* for *Leland Elementary School* by completing the following steps:
   a. Display the Open dialog box.
   b. Click the QuickFinder tab.
   c. At the QuickFinder dialog box, key **Ch 0*.*** in the Name text box.
   d. Press the Tab key and then key **Leland Elementary School** in the Content text box.
   e. Make sure *3½ Floppy (A:)* displays in the Look in text box. If necessary, change the Look in option to *3½ Floppy (A:)*.
   f. Click Find Now.
   g. When the search results are listed at the bottom of the QuickFinder dialog box, print a list of the documents.
2. Close the Open dialog box.

Creating a Document Summary

A WordPerfect feature that can help you manage your documents is the Document Summary. For each document, you can create a document summary that identifies important information such as the document's creation date and time, the author, the subject, key words, and an abstract of the document. Display the Document Summary dialog box shown in figure 6.13 by clicking File, pointing to Document, and then clicking Properties. At the Properties dialog box, click the Summary tab.

Figure 6.13

Properties Dialog Box with Summary Tab Selected

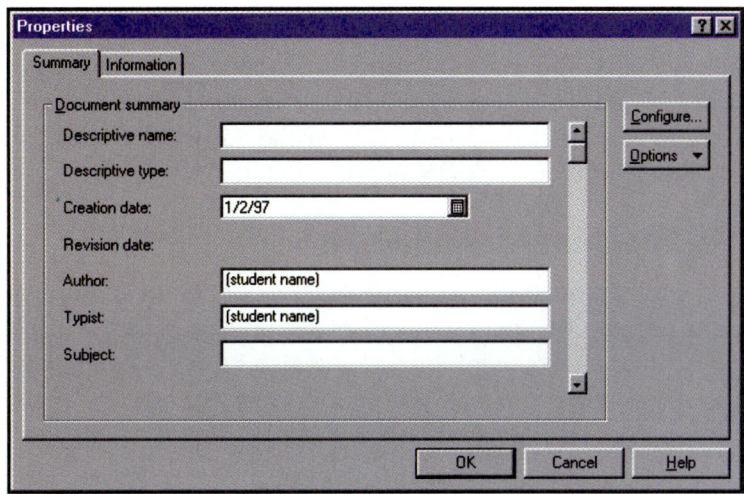

Creating the Summary

WordPerfect automatically inserts certain details about a document in the Properties dialog box with the Summary tab selected. The user adds the other information. For example, the Revision Date and/or Creation Date of the document is automatically inserted by WordPerfect. Choose the other options to insert additional information about the document. To do this, position the arrow pointer on the desired option, then click the left button.

Key a descriptive name for the document in the Descriptive name text box and key information about the type of document in the Descriptive type text box. With the Author and Typist options, identify the author of the document and the typist. Use the Subject option to identify the main point of the document. In the Account text box, key characters that might include an account name or account number. Key important words or phrases included in the document in the Keywords text box. Use the last option, Abstract, to provide a brief synopsis of the contents of the document.

The last three options, Account, Keywords, and Abstract, are not initially visible in the dialog box. To view these options, use the vertical scroll bar at the right side of the dialog box.

Using Document Summary Options

If you click the Options command button at the Properties dialog box (with the Summary tab selected), a drop-down list of options displays. With these options you can print or delete a summary, extract information from the document and insert it in the document summary, or save the document summary information as a new document.

Managing Documents

Printing a Summary: By default, a document summary does not print with the document. To print a document summary click Options, then Print Summary.

Deleting a Summary: A document summary can be deleted from a document. To do this, click Options, then Delete Summary From Document. At the *Delete Document Summary?* query box, click Yes.

Retrieving Summary Information: At the Properties dialog box, click Options, then Extract Information From Document. WordPerfect will retrieve pertinent information from the document and display it in the summary. WordPerfect searches the current document and inserts the first 400 characters of the document after the Abstract option. WordPerfect also looks for a subject in the document. WordPerfect looks for text after the letters RE:. If it does not find these letters, WordPerfect will look for the first heading in a document. This information will be inserted after the Subject option.

Saving a Summary as a Separate Document: By default, the document summary will be attached to the current document. If you want to save the summary as a separate document, click Options, then Save Summary As New Document. At the Save Document Summary dialog box, key a name for the document, then click OK or press Enter.

Customizing the Document Summary

If you click the Configure button at the Properties dialog box with the Summary tab selected, the Document Summary Configuration dialog box displays on the screen. At this dialog box, you can add or remove fields from the Document Summary dialog box. For example, you can add a field for *Client:*. Summaries for new documents will use this new setup as the default.

EXERCISE 14

Creating a Document Summary

1. At a clear editing window, open Report 01.
2. Save the report with Save As and name it Ch 06, Ex 14.
3. Create a document summary for Ch 06, Ex 14 by completing the following steps:
    a. Click File, point to Document, and then click Properties.
    b. At the Properties dialog box, click the Summary tab.
    c. Key **Trends in Telecommunications** in the Descriptive name text box.
    d. Press the Tab key. This moves the insertion point to the next field, Descriptive type.
    e. Key **Report** in the Descriptive type text box.
    f. Press the Tab key twice. This moves the insertion point to the Author field.
    g. Key your first and last name in the Author text box.
    h. Press the Tab key. This moves the insertion point to the Typist field.
    i. Key your initials in the Typist text box.
    j. Click Options, then Extract Information from Document.
    k. Click Options, then Print Summary.
    l. Click OK to close the Properties dialog box.
4. Save the document again with the same name (Ch 06, Ex 14).
5. Close Ch 06, Ex 14.

CHAPTER SUMMARY

▼ Some of the activities involved in disk and document maintenance are cutting, copying, and pasting documents, creating folders and subfolders, and deleting documents.

▼ Three dialog boxes will allow you to do all of the activities listed above. These dialog boxes are Open, Save As, and Insert File; all three contain many of the same options.

▼ Several file management choices are available at any of the three dialog boxes either through the Toolbar, or by accessing the shortcut menu with the right mouse button:

- Copy can make an exact copy of a document and save it on the same disk, another disk, or into another folder.
- Cut can place a document in another folder or drive.
- Rename allows the name of a document to be changed.
- Delete will remove unneeded documents.
- Properties allows instructions to be given regarding archiving, backing up documents, etc.
- The Print option offers an additional method for printing documents.
- Use Print File List to print a hard copy of a folder.
- Click New, then Folder to create new folders or subfolders.

▼ With the Preview option from the Open, Save As, or Insert File dialog box, you can view a document without bringing it to the editing window.

▼ WordPerfect's QuickFinder feature allows you to search a folder or specific documents for a particular word pattern.

▼ For each document, you can create a document summary that identifies important information such as the document's creation date and time, the author, the subject, key words, and an abstract of the document.

COMMANDS REVIEW

	Mouse	**Keyboard**
Open dialog box	Open button on Toolbar	File, Open
Save As dialog box	File, Save As	File, Save As
Insert File dialog box	Insert, File	Insert, File
Properties dialog box	File, Document, Properties	File, Document, Properties

CHECK YOUR UNDERSTANDING

Completion: In the space provided at the right, indicate the correct term, command, or number.

1. Most document maintenance functions can be performed at these three dialog boxes: _____

   _____

   _____

Managing Documents 127

2. If you want a hard copy of a folder, choose this from the shortcut menu. _____

3. This is a folder within a folder. _____

4. The main folder on a disk or drive is called this. _____

5. This is the button you click to move from a subfolder to the folder above it. _____

6. Click this button at the Open dialog box to view a document without bringing it to the editing window. _____

7. Click this button at the Open dialog box to display information about documents such as the size and type of document and the last date the document was modified. _____

8. With this feature you can search a folder or specific documents within a folder for a particular word pattern. _____

9. Key this in the Content text box at the QuickFinder dialog box to find documents containing the words *Workplace Literacy* or *Ayala*. _____

10. Key this in the Content text box at the QuickFinder dialog box to find documents that do not contain the words *Workplace Literacy*. _____

11. WordPerfect automatically inserts certain details about a document in this dialog box with the Summary tab selected. _____

SKILL ASSESSMENTS

Assessment 1

1. Display the Open dialog box.
2. If necessary, change the default folder to 3½ Floppy (A:).
3. Create a new folder named *Student Letters*.
4. Copy *Letter 01*, *Letter 02*, and *Letter 03* to the *Student Letters* folder.
5. With the Student Letters folder the active folder, rename the following documents:
   a. *Letter 01* to *Correspondence 01*
   b. *Letter 02* to *Correspondence 02*
   c. *Letter 03* to *Correspondence 03*
6. Print the folder file list.
7. Return to the previous list of document names.
8. Delete the *Student Letters* folder and its contents.
9. Close the Open dialog box.

Assessment 2

1. Display the Open dialog box.
2. If necessary, change the default folder to 3½ Floppy (A:).
3. Create a folder named *Reports*.
4. Select all documents beginning with *Report*, then *copy* them to the *Reports* folder.
5. With the *Reports* folder the active folder, print the file list.
6. Return to the previous list of document names.
7. Delete (remove) the *Reports* folder and its contents.
8. Close the Open dialog box.

Assessment 3

1. Display the Open dialog box and then delete all documents you created in chapter 4 that begin *Ch 04*.
2. Close the Open dialog box.

Assessment 4

1. At a clear editing window, open Report 02.
2. Save the document with Save As and name it Ch 06, SA 04.
3. Create a document summary for Ch 06, SA 04. (You determine the information for the options.)
4. Print the document summary.
5. Close Ch 06, SA 04.

Assessment 5

1. Display the Open dialog box.
2. Click the QuickFinder tab.
3. Search for all documents on the student data disk that contain the words *trends in telecommunications*.
4. Print the search results file list.
5. Close the Open dialog box.

CHANGING FONTS

PERFORMANCE OBJECTIVE

Upon successful completion of chapter 7, you will be able to adjust the style and size of type as well as the appearance of characters in standard business documents.

By default, WordPerfect uses a font that prints text with varying amounts of space. Other fonts may be available depending on the printer you are using. The number of fonts available ranges from a few to several hundred. A font consists of three parts: typeface, type size, and type style.

Choosing a Typeface

A *typeface* is a set of characters with a common design and shape. Typefaces may be decorative, blocked, or plain. Typefaces are either *monospaced* or *proportional*. WordPerfect refers to typeface as font face.

A monospaced typeface allots the same amount of horizontal space for each character. Courier is an example of a monospaced typeface. Proportional typefaces allot a varying amount of space for each character. The space allotted is based on the width of the character. For example, the lowercase *i* will take up less space than the uppercase *M*.

Proportional typefaces are divided into two main categories: *serif* and *sans serif*. A serif is a small line at the end of a character stroke. Traditionally, a serif typeface is used in documents that are text intensive (documents that are mainly text) because the serif helps move the reader's eyes across the page. Examples of serif typefaces are shown in figure 7.1.

Figure 7.1 Serif Typefaces

> Bookman Old Style
> Century Schoolbook
> Arrus BT
> Garamond
> Times New Roman

A sans serif typeface does not have serifs (*sans* is French for *without*). Sans serif typefaces are often used for headlines and advertisements that are not text intensive. Examples of sans serif typefaces are shown in figure 7.2.

Figure 7.2 Sans Serif Typefaces

> Arial
> **Swis721 BlkEx BT**
> Univers

Choosing a Type Size

Proportional typefaces can be set in different sizes. The size of proportional type is measured vertically in units called *points*. A point is approximately 1/72 of an inch. The higher the point size, the larger the characters. Examples of different point sizes in the Arial typeface are shown in figure 7.3.

Figure 7.3 Different Point Sizes in Arial

> 8-point Arial
> 12-point Arial
> 18-point Arial
> 24-point Arial

Choosing a Type Style

Within a typeface, characters may have a varying style. The standard style of the typeface is referred to as *Regular*. There are four main categories of type styles—Regular, Bold, Italic, and Bold Italic. These four main type styles are displayed in figure 7.4.

Figure 7.4

Four Main Type Styles

Arial (Regular)	Times New Roman
Arial Bold	**Times New Roman Bold**
Arial Italic	*Times New Roman Italic*
Arial Bold Italic	***Times New Roman Bold Italic***

The term *font* describes a particular typeface in a specific style and size. Some examples of fonts are *10-point Arial*, *12-point Times New Roman Bold*, *12-point Garamond Italic*, and *14-point Century Schoolbook Bold Italic*.

Choosing a Font

The printer that you are using has built-in fonts. These fonts can be supplemented with cartridges and/or soft fonts. The types of fonts you have available with your printer depend on the type of printer you are using, the amount of memory installed with the printer, and what supplemental fonts you have. A font cartridge is inserted directly into the printer and lets you add fonts. To install a font cartridge, refer to the documentation that comes with the cartridge. Soft fonts are available as software on disk. The WordPerfect 7 program comes with additional fonts that were loaded during installation.

Using the Font Dialog Box

The fonts available with your printer are displayed in the Font face list box at the Font dialog box. There are several methods you can use to display the Font dialog box shown in figure 7.5, including:

- Click Format, then Font.
- Press F9.
- Double-click the Change the font or QuickFonts button on the Power Bar.
- Display a QuickMenu, then click Font.
- Click the Font button on the Font Toolbar.
- Click the paragraph QuickSpot button, then click Font.
- Double-click a Font code in Reveal Codes.

Change the font

QuickFonts

Font

QuickSpot

The QuickFonts button is the first button at the left on the Power Bar. The Change the font button is the second button at the left on the Power Bar. To display the Font dialog box with the QuickMenu, position the arrow pointer anywhere in the editing window (except the top, bottom, left, or right margins), then click the right mouse button. At the QuickMenu that displays, click Font. To change a font for an entire paragraph, click the QuickSpot button in the left margin area next to the paragraph you want to change, then click the Font button.

You can also display the Font dialog box by clicking the Font button on the Font Toolbar. To display the Font Toolbar, position the arrow pointer on the current Toolbar, click the right mouse button, then click Font.

Figure 7.5

Font Dialog Box

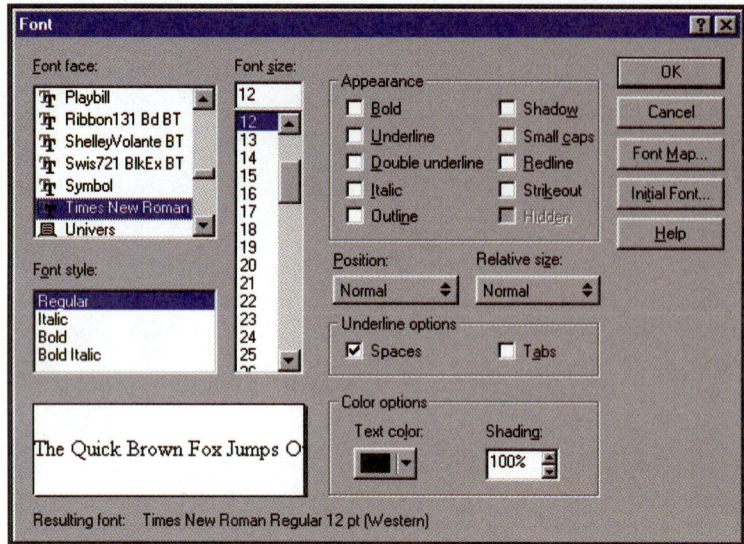

Font Face: The Font face list box at the Font dialog box displays the typefaces (font faces) available with your printer. Figure 7.5 shows the typefaces available with a popular laser printer (the fonts displayed with your printer may vary from those shown).

An icon displays before the typefaces in the Font face list box. The printer icon identifies a built-in font. These are fonts provided with your printer. The V icon and TT icon identify soft fonts. WordPerfect 7 provides a number of TrueType soft fonts that are identified with the TT icon. More than likely, these fonts were included during installation. If not, please refer to the WordPerfect documentation for directions on installing the TrueType fonts. The fonts preceded by the V indicate Vector typefaces which are generally used with a plotter (a kind of printer). The TrueType fonts are *graphically* generated while printer fonts are printer-generated. Graphically generated fonts take longer to print than printer-generated fonts.

To change to a different typeface, select the desired typeface (font face), then click OK or press Enter. When the typeface (font face) is changed, WordPerfect inserts a code in the document at the position of the insertion point. For example, the code to change the typeface to Arial would appear as Font: Arial . When different typefaces are selected, the Preview box in the lower left corner of the dialog box displays the appearance of the selected font.

EXERCISE

Changing Margins and Typeface

1. At a clear editing window, open Para 02.
2. Save the document with Save As and name it Ch 07, Ex 01.
3. With the insertion point positioned at the beginning of the document, change the left and right margins to 1.5 inches.
4. Change the typeface to GeoSlab703 Lt BT by completing the following steps:
    a. With the insertion point positioned at the beginning of the document, display the Font dialog box by clicking Format, then Font.

134   Chapter 7

b. At the Font dialog box, click the up-pointing triangle at the right side of the Font face list box until GeoSlab703 Lt BT displays, then click it. (If GeoSlab703 Lt BT is not available, choose a similar serif typeface such as Garamond.)

   c. Click OK or press Enter.
5. Save the document again with the same name (Ch 07, Ex 01).
6. Print and then close Ch 07, Ex 01.

In addition to using the Font dialog box to select a typeface, you can use the Change the font button on the Power Bar. When you click the Change the font button on the Power Bar, a drop-down menu displays as shown in figure 7.6 (your drop-down menu may vary). To select a typeface, position the arrow pointer on the desired typeface, then click the left mouse button.

Change the font Button Drop-Down Menu

Figure 7.6

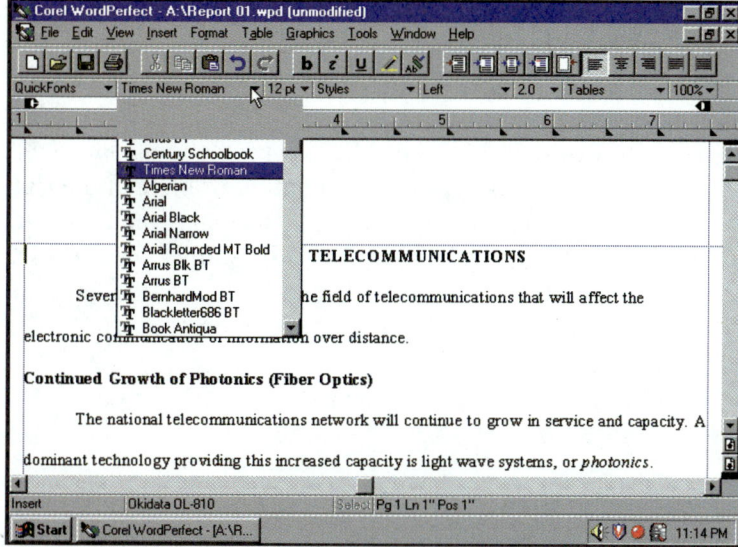

EXERCISE 2

Changing the Typeface with the Change the font Button

1. At a clear editing window, open Para 03.
2. Save the document with Save As and name it Ch 07, Ex 02.
3. With the insertion point positioned at the beginning of the document, change the typeface to Arial using the Power Bar by completing the following steps:

   a. Position the arrow pointer on the Change the font button, then click the left mouse button.

   b. At the drop-down menu that displays, position the arrow pointer on Arial, then click the left mouse button.
4. Save the document again with the same name (Ch 07, Ex 02).
5. Print and then close Ch 07, Ex 02.

Font Size: The Font size list box at the Font dialog box displays a variety of common type sizes. Decrease point size to make text smaller or increase point size to make text larger. To select a point size with the mouse, click the desired point size. If you are using the keyboard, press Alt + S, then press the up or down arrow key until the desired point size is selected.

You can also key a specific point size. To do this with the mouse, position the I-beam pointer on the number immediately below Font size, click the left button, then key the desired point size. If you are using the keyboard, press Alt + S, then key the desired point size.

EXERCISE 3

Changing the Typeface and Size

1. At a clear editing window, open Para 04.
2. Save the document with Save As and name it Ch 07, Ex 03.
3. With the insertion point positioned at the beginning of the document, change the font to 10-point BernhardMod BT using the Font dialog box by completing the following steps:
   a. With the insertion point positioned at the beginning of the document, display the Font dialog box by double-clicking the Change the font button on the Power Bar.
   b. At the Font dialog box, click the up-pointing triangle at the right side of the Font face list box until BernhardMod BT displays, then click it. (If BernhardMod BT is not available, choose a similar serif typeface.)
   c. Change the Font size option to 10. To do this, click the up-pointing triangle in the Font size list box, until *10* is visible, then click *10*.
   d. Click OK or press Enter.
4. Save the document again with the same name (Ch 07, Ex 03).
5. Print and then close Ch 07, Ex 03.

Change the font size

In addition to the Font dialog box, you can use the Change the font size button on the Power Bar to change type size. The Change the font size button is the third button from the left. To change the type size with this button, click the Change the font size button, then click the desired type size at the drop-down menu that displays.

EXERCISE 4

Changing Margins, Typeface, and Size

1. At a clear editing window, open Para 02.
2. Save the document with Save As and name it Ch 07, Ex 04.
3. Change the left and right margins to 1.25 inches.
4. With the insertion point positioned at the beginning of the document, change the font to 10-point GeoSlab703 Lt BT using the Power Bar by completing the following steps:
   a. Position the arrow pointer on the Change the font button, then click the left mouse button.

b. At the drop-down menu that displays, position the arrow pointer on GeoSlab703 Lt BT, then click the left mouse button. (If GeoSlab703 Lt BT is not available, choose a similar serif typeface.)
   c. Position the arrow pointer on the Change the font size button on the Power Bar, then click the left mouse button.
   d. Position the arrow pointer on the 10 in the drop-down menu, then click the left mouse button.
5. Save the document again with the same name (Ch 07, Ex 04).
6. Print and then close Ch 07, Ex 04.

Font Style: The Font style list box at the Font dialog box displays the styles available with the selected typeface. As you select different typefaces at the Font dialog box, the list of styles changes in the Font style list box.

EXERCISE 5

Changing the Font Style

1. At a clear editing window, open Para 03.
2. Save the document with Save As and name it Ch 07, Ex 05.
3. Change the typeface to Arrus BT and the style to Bold Italic by completing the following steps:
   a. With the insertion point positioned at the beginning of the document, display the Font dialog box.
   b. At the Font dialog box, click Arrus BT in the Font face list box. (You will need to scroll up the list to see this typeface. If Arrus BT is not available, choose a similar serif typeface.)
   c. Click *Bold Italic* in the Font style list box.
   d. Click OK or press Enter.
4. Save the document again with the same name (Ch 07, Ex 05).
5. Print and then close Ch 07, Ex 05.

Appearance: The Appearance section of the Font dialog box contains a variety of options that can be used to create different character styles. These appearances are also available on the Font Toolbar. (To display the Font Toolbar, position the arrow pointer on the current Toolbar, click the right mouse button, then click Font at the drop-down menu.)

In chapter 3, you learned to bold, underline, and italicize text with shortcut commands or buttons on the Toolbar. The shortcut commands or buttons on the Toolbar are probably the easiest to use. However, if you want to specify a variety of character styles, you can use the Font dialog box.

EXERCISE 6

Changing the Font and Character Style

1. At a clear editing window, open Report 06.
2. Save the document with Save As and name it Ch 07, Ex 06.
3. With the insertion point positioned at the beginning of the document, change the font to 12-point Century Schoolbook. (If Century Schoolbook is not available, choose a similar serif typeface.)
4. Bold and italicize the last six lines in the report by completing the following steps:
   a. Select the last six lines in the report (*increased random access memory* through *increased cycle speeds*).
   b. Display the Font dialog box.
   c. At the Font dialog box, click Bold in the Appearance section.
   d. Click Italic in the Appearance section.
   e. Click OK or press Enter.
5. Save the document again with the same name (Ch 07, Ex 06).
6. Print and then close Ch 07, Ex 06.

Double Underline

Use the Double Underline option from the Font dialog box or the Double Underline button on the Font Toolbar to insert a double underline below text. This might be useful, for example, in a balance sheet or other accounting document where you are totaling columns.

Outline

The Outline option from the Font dialog box or the Outline button on the Font Toolbar prints characters with an outline. This works if the printer you are using has an outline font. Characters that have been identified for outlining will look like this:

This is Outline text.

Shadow

The Shadow option at the Font dialog box or the Shadow button on the Font Toolbar causes characters to print with a shadow. This works for some printers, including PostScript printers. Shadow characters look like this:

This is Shadow text.

EXERCISE 7

Changing the Appearance of Text

1. At a clear editing window, open Notice 01.
2. Save the document with Save As and name it Ch 07, Ex 07.
3. With the insertion point positioned at the beginning of the document, change the font to 14-point Arial.
4. Change the appearance of the text to Shadow by completing the following steps:
   a. Select all the text in the document.
   b. Display the Font Toolbar. To do this, position the arrow pointer on the current Toolbar, click the right mouse button, then click Font at the drop-down menu. (Skip this step if the Font Toolbar is already displayed.)

      c. Click the Shadow button on the Font Toolbar.
5. Save the document again with the same name (Ch 07, Ex 07).
6. Print and then close Ch 07, Ex 07.

From the Font dialog box, the Small caps option lets you print small capital letters. You can also click the Small Caps button on the Font Toolbar. This works for some printers but not all. When text is identified for small caps, it will look like this:

THIS IS SMALL CAPS

EXERCISE 8

Using the Small Caps Option

1. At a clear editing window, open Memo 01.
2. Save the document with Save As and name it Ch 07, Ex 08.
3. With the insertion point positioned at the beginning of the document, change the font to 12-point Humanst521 Lt BT (or a similar sans serif typeface). (If necessary, properly align October 22, 1998 after DATE: by inserting a Tab.)
4. Change the appearance of all the text in the document to Small Caps by completing the following steps:
     a. Select the entire document.
     b. Click the Small Caps button on the Font Toolbar.
5. Save the document again with the same name (Ch 07, Ex 08).
6. Print and then close Ch 07, Ex 08.

The Redline option from the Font dialog box or the Redline button on the Font Toolbar lets you identify text that is added to a legal document. When text is added to a legal document, it prints with a shaded background or a vertical bar appears in the left margin. The appearance of redlined text is printer dependent—most printers will print redlined text with a shaded background. How redlined text appears when printed can be changed at the Redline dialog box shown in figure 7.7. To display the Redline dialog box, click Format, point to Document, then click Redline Method.

Redline

Figure 7.7

Redline Dialog Box

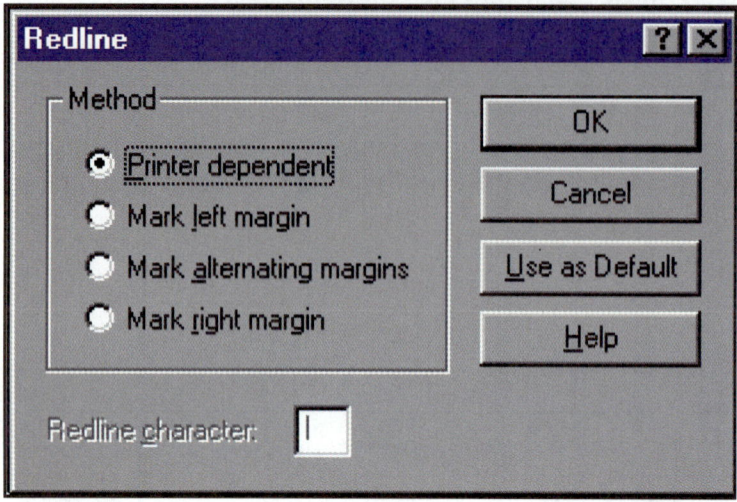

At the Redline dialog box, the default setting is Printer dependent. You can also choose to mark redlined text at the left margin of the document, alternating margins, or the right margin. If you choose Mark left margin or Mark right margin, you can change the Redline character from the default of a vertical line (|) to any other symbol with the Redline Character option at the bottom of the dialog box. WordPerfect will insert a redline mark at the left or right margin of a line where text has been added to a document. If you choose Mark alternating margins as the redlining method, WordPerfect will insert a redlining mark at the left margin for even pages and at the right margin for odd pages. If your printer supports shaded background and text is redlined in a document, it will look like this:

This is Redlined Text

Strikeout The Strikeout option from the Font dialog box or the Strikeout button on the Font Toolbar lets you show text that needs to be deleted from a document. Strikeout prints text with a line of hyphens running through it. This feature has practical application for some legal documents in which deleted text must be retained in the document. The hyphens indicate that the text has been deleted. Strikeout text looks like this:

This is Strikeout Text

EXERCISE 9

Using Strikeout and Redline

1. At a clear editing window, open Legal 01. This document is located on your student data disk.
2. Save the document with Save As and name it Ch 07, Ex 09.
3. Make the following changes to the document:
    a. With the insertion point positioned at the beginning of the document, change the font to 12-point Century Schoolbook.
    b. Select the last sentence in the second paragraph (the one that begins *A default judgment is one where the plaintiff*...), and identify it for strikeout by completing the following steps:

140 Chapter 7

> (1) Select the sentence.
> (2) Click the Strikeout button on the Font Toolbar.
> c. In the third paragraph, add the words *or a representative of the law firm* at the end of the sentence (but before the period) that reads *If you do so, the demand must be in writing and must be served upon the person signing this summons.* as redlined text by completing the following steps:
>   (1) Position the insertion point immediately to the left of the period at the end of the sentence. (This sentence is located in the third paragraph.)
>   (2) Turn on redlining by completing the following steps:
>   (a) Display the Font dialog box.
>   (b) At the Font dialog box, click Redline.
>   (c) Click OK or press Enter.
>   (3) Press the space bar, then key the words **or a representative of the law firm**.
> 4. Save the document again with the same name (Ch 07, Ex 09).
> 5. Print and then close Ch 07, Ex 09.

With the Hidden option from the Font dialog box or the Hidden Text On/Off button on the Font Toolbar, you can include such items as comments, personal messages, or questions in a document. These items can be displayed, printed, or hidden.

Hidden Text On/Off

If hidden text is displayed on the screen it is treated as regular text and it will print. To display hidden text, click View, then Hidden Text. If you do not want hidden text to print, turn off the display of hidden text by clicking View, then Hidden Text. This removes the check mark before the Hidden Text option at the View drop-down menu. To create Hidden text, you would complete the following steps:

1. Make sure there is a check mark before Hidden Text at the View drop-down menu.
2. Display the Font dialog box, then click Hidden.
3. Click OK or press Enter to close the dialog box.
4. At the editing window, key the text to be hidden.

To create hidden text with the Font Toolbar, click the Hidden Text On/Off button on the Font Toolbar. Key the text to be hidden, then click the Hidden Text On/Off button on the Font Toolbar again. To convert Hidden text to document text, delete one of the Hidden codes in Reveal Codes.

EXERCISE 10

Creating Hidden Text

> 1. At a clear editing window, open Memo 01.
> 2. Save the document with Save As and name it Ch 07, Ex 10.
> 3. Create hidden text at the end of the document by completing the following steps:
>   a. Move the insertion point to the end of the document.
>   b. Make sure there is a check mark before the Hidden Text option at the View drop-down menu. (If not, click View, then Hidden Text.)
>   c. Click the Hidden Text On/Off button on the Font Toolbar.

Changing Fonts 141

d. Key (**Check the availability of these books before sending the memo.**).
   e. Click the Hidden Text On/Off button on the Font Toolbar.
4. Save the document again with the same name (Ch 07, Ex 10).
5. Print Ch 07, Ex 10.
6. Turn off the display of hidden text by clicking <u>V</u>iew, then Hidden Te<u>x</u>t, then print the memo again.
7. Close Ch 07, Ex 10.

Position: When you click <u>P</u>osition at the Font dialog box, a drop-down menu displays with four options—Su<u>p</u>erscript, <u>N</u>ormal, Su<u>b</u>script, and Mi<u>x</u>ed.

Superscript

With the Su<u>p</u>erscript option, you can create text that is raised slightly above the line. Some mathematical expressions are written with superscript numbers. For example, the mathematical expression 4 to the second power is written as 4^2. You can create a superscript as you key text or you can superscript selected text.

Subscript

With the Su<u>b</u>script option from the Font dialog box, you can create text that is lowered slightly below the line. Some chemical formulas require the use of subscripted characters. For example, the formula for water is written as H_2O. You can create a subscripted character as you are keying text or you can subscript a selected character or characters. You can also use the Superscript and Subscript buttons on the Font Toolbar to raise or lower text in a document.

EXERCISE 11

Creating Superscript and Subscript Numbers

1. At a clear editing window, key the memo shown in figure 7.8 in an appropriate memo format with the following specifications:
   a. Change the left and right margins to 1.5 inches.
   b. Indent and italicize text as indicated. (The letters C, D, and I in the first question and the three X's in the third question are italicized.)
   c. Create the superscripted numbers in the memo by completing the following steps:
      (1) Key text to the point where superscripted text is to appear.
      (2) Display the Font dialog box.
      (3) At the Font dialog box, click <u>P</u>osition.
      (4) At the pop-up menu, click Su<u>p</u>erscript.
      (5) Click OK or press Enter.
      (6) Key the superscripted text.
      (7) Repeat steps (2) through (5) to turn off superscript.
   d. Create the subscripted numbers in the memo by completing the following steps:
      (1) Key text to the point where subscripted text is to appear.
      (2) Click the Subscript button on the Font Toolbar.
      (3) Key the subscripted text.
      (4) Click the Subscript button on the Font Toolbar.
2. Save the memo and name it Ch 07, Ex 11.
3. Print and then close Ch 07, Ex 11.

Figure 7.8

DATE: June 9, 1998; TO: Thomas Scannell; FROM: Barbara Jaech; SUBJECT: STATISTICAL ANALYSIS

The research and analysis you are conducting on medical health care is very important to the project planning. As you complete your analysis, please address the following areas:

1. What is the relationship between the indices *C*, *D*, and *I* to both r^1 and r^2?

2. What is the improvement when $r^1 = .55$ and r^2 is nearly .79?

3. What is the main effect on the scores of X_1, X_2, and X_3?

When these areas have been addressed, please give me a copy of the analysis.

xx:Ch 07, Ex 11

Relative Size: The Relative size option at the Font dialog box contains a drop-down menu with a variety of size options. The size options are used to change the size of the type based on the size of the font in the document. The selections change the size of the current font by the following percentages:

Fine = 60%

Small = 80%

Large = 120%

Very Large = 150%

Extra Large = 200%

Some printers support only a few point sizes. If your printer does not support the exact point size selected, WordPerfect tries to choose and print an approximate size.

Changing point size with a Relative size option from the Font dialog box allows changes to be made easily to text in the document. If the size of the font is changed, any type with relative size options attached is automatically updated. Also, if the typeface is changed, the size options will apply to the new typeface.

EXERCISE 12

Changing the Font and Relative Size

1. At a clear editing window, open Report 06.
2. Save the document with Save As and name it Ch 07, Ex 12.
3. Make the following changes to the document:
    a. With the insertion point positioned at the beginning of the document, change the font to 12-point Century Schoolbook.

> **b.** Change the relative size of the title, *TRENDS IN TELECOMMUNICATIONS,* to Very Large by completing the following steps:
> (1) Select the title, *TRENDS IN TELECOMMUNICATIONS.*
> (2) Display the Font dialog box.
> (3) At the Font dialog box, click Relative si_z_e.
> (4) At the pop-up menu, click _V_ery Large.
> (5) Click OK or press Enter.
> **c.** Select the heading *Continued Growth of Photonics (Fiber Optics)*, then change the relative size to Large.
> **d.** Select the heading *Microcomputer Trends in the Nineties*, then change the relative size to Large.
> 4. Save the document again with the same name (Ch 07, Ex 12).
> 5. Print and then close Ch 07, Ex 12.

Underline Options: When underlining is turned on, WordPerfect will underline spaces between words but not spaces caused by pressing the Tab key. With Underline Options from the Font dialog box, you can tell WordPerfect whether or not you want spaces between words and/or spaces created with the Tab key underlined.

Color Options: If you have a printer that can print a variety of colors, you can identify colors with the Text co_l_or button or the Define Color Printing Palette dialog box available from the Text color button.

To change the text color with the mouse, position the arrow pointer on the down-pointing triangle immediately below Text co_l_or, then click the left mouse button. If you are using the keyboard, press Alt + L, then press the space bar. At the list of color options, choose the desired color. To do this with the mouse, position the arrow pointer on the desired color option, then click the left mouse button. If you are using the keyboard, move the insertion point with the insertion point movement keys until the desired color is selected, then press Enter.

With the Shadin_g_ option at the Font dialog box, you can control the intensity of the color of text. If you use the default text color of black, the Shadin_g_ option lets you decrease the shading to create variations of gray. If you change the text color, the Shadin_g_ option can increase or decrease the intensity of the color.

If you click the Palette button at the Text co_l_or dialog box, the Define Color Palette dialog box displays. At this dialog box, you can select, create, and edit color palettes. Depending on the capabilities of your monitor and printer, you can choose from up to 16 million colors. If you are using a color printer and want to know more about color palettes, please refer to the on-line help.

EXERCISE 13

> ### Changing Margins, Font, and Color
> 1. At a clear editing window, key the memo shown in figure 7.9 in an appropriate memo format with the following specifications:
> **a.** Change the font to 12-point GeoSlab703 Lt BT (or a similar serif typeface).
> **b.** Change the left and right margins to 1.5 inches.
> **c.** Center the unit and department names as indicated.

2. After keying the document, change the color of the centered unit and department names to bright blue by completing the following steps:
   a. Select the centered unit and department names.
   b. Display the Font dialog box.
   c. At the Font dialog box, click the down-pointing triangle immediately below the Text color option.
   d. At the list of color options, click the bright blue color (the tenth option from the left in the top row).
   e. Click OK or press Enter.
3. Save the document and name it Ch 07, Ex 13.
4. Print and then close Ch 07, Ex 13.

Figure 7.9

DATE: October 12, 1998; TO: Steven Ayala; FROM: Robert Freitas; SUBJECT: CONTINUING EDUCATION CLASSES

The nursing staff in the hospital departments are required to attend continuing education classes. In the past, the classes have been scheduled by the director of each department. The Training Coordination Committee has determined that it would be more efficient to have the classes scheduled by one department. After interviewing the directors of various departments, a decision was made to have the classes scheduled by the Training and Education Department.

The following areas of the hospital require continuing education classes for nurses:

Intensive Care Unit
Labor and Delivery Unit
Coronary Care Unit
Surgical Unit
Pediatric Unit
Medical Services
Emergency Room

Please contact the director of each unit or department to determine immediate and future educational requirements. If you need additional support staff to coordinate these classes, please contact me.

xx:Ch 07, Ex 13

Formatting with QuickFormat

WordPerfect 7 contains a feature that lets you quickly copy fonts and attributes or paragraph formatting already applied to text to different locations in the document. This feature is referred to as QuickFormat.

To use QuickFormat, position the insertion point on a character containing the desired character or paragraph formatting, turn on QuickFormat, then select text to which you want the character and/or paragraph formatting applied. When you turn on QuickFormat, the arrow pointer displays with a paint roller attached.

For example, suppose you have changed the relative size of some text in a document to Extra Large and want to apply this formatting to other text in the document. To do this, you would complete the following steps:

QuickFormat

1. Position the insertion point on a character that is identified as Extra Large.
2. Click the QuickFormat button on the Toolbar.
3. At the QuickFormat dialog box shown in figure 7.10, choose to copy the Character format (font, attributes) or Headings format (paragraph format, styles, font, attributes), then click OK or press Enter.
4. Select text in the document to be changed to Extra Large.
5. Turn off QuickFormat.

Figure 7.10

QuickFormat Dialog Box

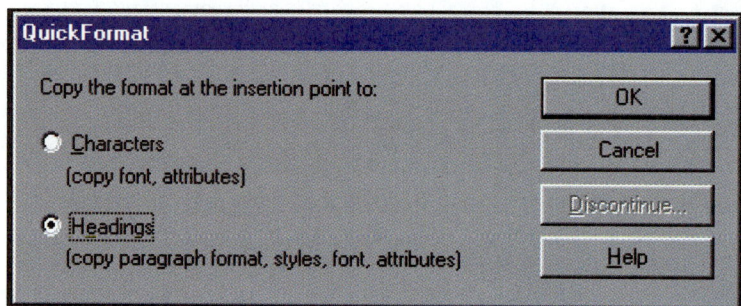

You can also display the QuickFormat dialog box with a QuickMenu. To do this, position the arrow pointer anywhere in the editing window (except the top, bottom, left, or right margins), click the *right* mouse button, then click QuickFormat at the QuickMenu. At the QuickFormat dialog box, you can identify whether you want only paragraph formatting applied, only character formatting, or both.

When you are done formatting with QuickFormat, turn it off by clicking the QuickFormat button on the Toolbar. You can also just key text to turn off the QuickFormat feature.

EXERCISE 14

Formatting Selected Parts of a Document

1. At a clear editing window, open Report 06.
2. Save the document with Save As and name it Ch 07, Ex 14.
3. Select the title, *TRENDS IN TELECOMMUNICATIONS*, then change the relative size to Large.
4. Use QuickFormat to change the two headings in the report to Large by completing the following steps:
   a. Position the insertion point on any character in the title, *TRENDS IN TELECOMMUNICATIONS*.
   b. Click the QuickFormat button on the Toolbar.
   c. At the QuickFormat dialog box, make sure Headings is selected, then click OK or press Enter.
   d. Click once on the heading *Continued Growth of Photonics (Fiber Optics)* (this will select the entire heading and apply the Large formatting).
   e. Click once on the heading *Microcomputer Trends in the Nineties*.
   f. Click the QuickFormat button on the Toolbar to turn off the QuickFormat feature.
5. Save the document again with the same name (Ch 07, Ex 14).
6. Print and then close Ch 07, Ex 14.

Using the QuickFonts Button

The QuickFonts button is the first button at the left on the Power Bar. Use QuickFonts to apply any of the fonts you have used recently to selected text. When you click the QuickFonts button on the Power Bar, as many as 20 of the last fonts you have chosen, including font style, size, and any appearance attributes are displayed in a drop-down menu as shown in figure 7.11.

Figure 7.11

QuickFonts Drop-Down Menu

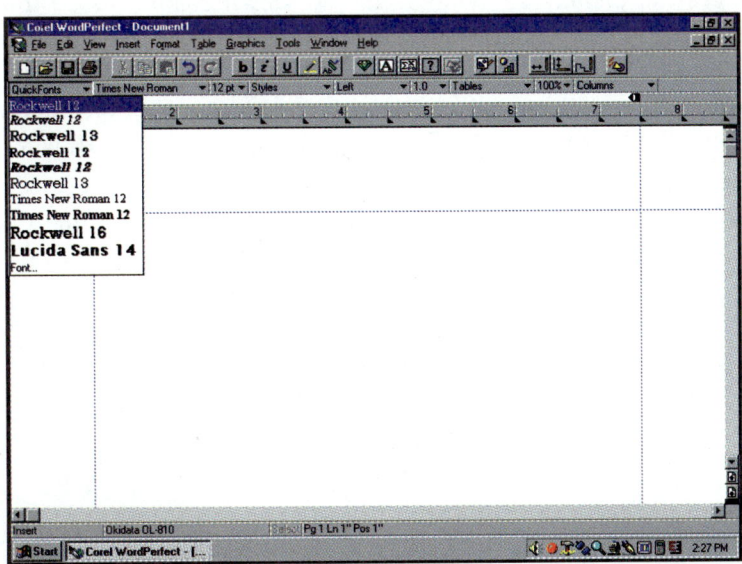

Changing Fonts 147

Using WordPerfect Character Sets

The WordPerfect program includes character sets you can use to create special letters and symbols. WordPerfect provides over 1,500 characters and symbols. Depending on the printer you are using, some or all of these symbols will be available. These symbols are grouped into 15 character sets. Each character set contains different types of symbols. For example, character set 4 contains typographic symbols and character set 6 contains mathematic and scientific symbols.

To determine the characters and character sets available, you may want to print the WordPerfect document named *charmap.wpd*. Usually this document is found in *C:\Corel\Office7\Shared\PFit7*. (This may vary depending on your system setup.) Print this document as you would any other document. When printed, the document shows the character set number, the code for the character, and the character itself in each character set.

Inserting a Symbol in a Document

You can insert a symbol in a document with the Character option from the Insert drop-down menu. You can also use the shortcut command Ctrl + W. To insert a symbol, click Insert, then Character or press Ctrl + W. At the WordPerfect Characters dialog box shown in figure 7.12, use the arrow pointer on the scroll bar to display the desired symbol, then click the symbol. This inserts a dotted box around the symbol and inserts the character set and symbol number in the Number text box. Click Insert and Close.

When you click Insert and Close, the symbol is inserted in the document and the dialog box is closed. A code can be seen in Reveal Codes. For example, if you chose the paragraph symbol ¶ (4,5) at the WordPerfect Characters dialog box, the code ¶ 4,5 displays in Reveal Codes.

At the WordPerfect Characters dialog box, you can click Insert to insert the symbol in the document and not close the dialog box. This might be useful if you are inserting more than one symbol in the document at the same time. You can also key the character set number and the symbol number in the Number text box. For example, if you want to insert a copyright symbol in the document and you know the character set number is 4 and the symbol number is 23, you would key 4,23 in the Number text box.

Changing the Character Set

At the WordPerfect Characters dialog box, you can change the character set with the Character Set option. This changes the display of symbols in the viewing box. To do this with the mouse, position the arrow pointer in the Character Set text box, hold down the left mouse button, drag the arrow pointer to the desired character set, then release the mouse button. If you are using the keyboard, press Alt + S, press the space bar once, then key the letter of the desired character set; or scroll up and down the list of character sets using the up and down arrow keys and press Enter when you have highlighted the desired character set.

After changing the character set, click a symbol, then click Insert and Close to remove the WordPerfect Characters dialog box.

Figure 7.12

WordPerfect Characters Dialog Box

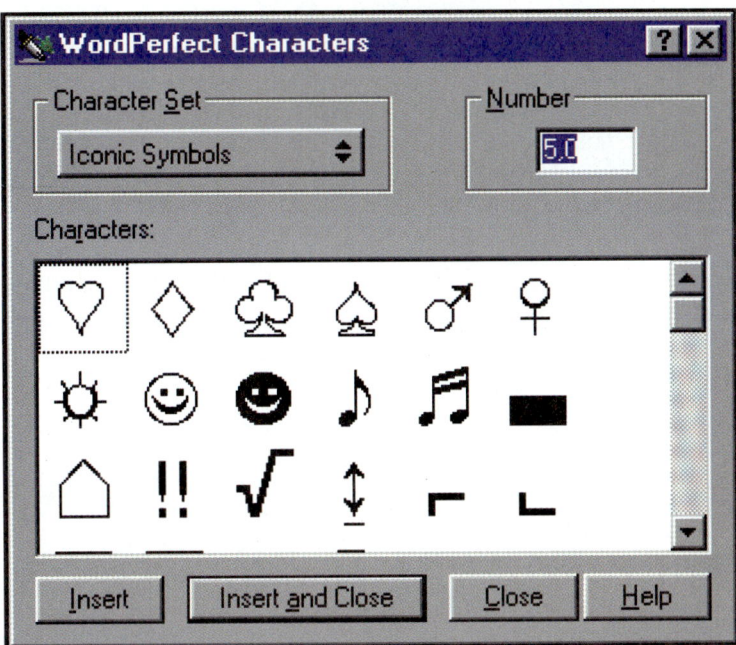

EXERCISE 15

Creating Special Symbols

1. At a clear editing window, key the memo shown in figure 7.13 in an appropriate memo format with the following specifications:
   a. Change the left and right margins to 1.5 inches.
   b. Complete the following steps to create the special symbols:
      (1) Click Insert, then Character; or press Ctrl + W.
      (2) At the WordPerfect Characters dialog box, key the character set number, a comma, the symbol number, then press Enter or click Insert and Close. Use the following numbers at the WordPerfect Characters dialog box to create the special symbol:

é	=	1,41
ñ	=	1,57
°	=	6,36
®	=	4,22

2. Save the document and name it Ch 07, Ex 15.
3. Print and then close Ch 07, Ex 15.

Changing Fonts 149

Figure 7.13

DATE: February 20, 1998; TO: Maggie Hénédine; FROM: Joni Kapshaw; SUBJECT: DISTRICT NEWSLETTER

The layout for the March newsletter looks great! I talked with Anita Nuñez about the figures. She explained how we can rotate the image inside the box by 90°, 180°, and 270°. As soon as she shows me how to do this, I will pass on the information to you.

Anita plans to offer an informal workshop on some of the graphic capabilities of WordPerfect 7 for Windows 95®. She plans to discuss customizing box borders, inserting shaded fill, rotating and scaling images, and creating drop shadow boxes. If you want her to address any other topics, please give me a call by the end of this week.

xx:Ch 07, Ex 15

CHAPTER SUMMARY

- ▼ A font consists of three parts: typeface, type style, and type size.
- ▼ A typeface is a set of characters with a common design and shape. Typefaces are either monospaced or proportional. A monospaced typeface allots the same amount of horizontal space for each character. A proportional typeface allots a varying amount of space for each character.
- ▼ The type size of proportional typefaces is a vertical measurement. The higher the point size, the larger the characters.
- ▼ A type style is a variation of style within a certain typeface. The standard style is regular. Other type styles include bold, italic, and bold and italic.
- ▼ At the Font dialog box you can change the typeface and/or the type size and see examples of the text as you make each change. You can also create different character styles such as bold, underline, double underline, and italics or a combination of these styles.
- ▼ Other options available at the Font dialog box include Outline, Shadow, Small Caps, Redline, Strikeout, Superscript, and Subscript.
- ▼ Also available at the Font dialog box are options to change the relative type size of the current font, the mode of underlining, and the color choices for color printing.
- ▼ With the Hidden option at the Font dialog box, you can include such items as comments, personal messages, or questions in a document. These items can be displayed, printed, or hidden.
- ▼ For text set in a proportional typeface, space once after end-of-sentence punctuation and after a colon.
- ▼ The QuickFormat feature lets you quickly copy fonts and attributes or paragraph formatting already applied to text.
- ▼ QuickFonts provide a list of the most recently used fonts and attributes (up to the last 20) that you can apply to selected text.
- ▼ The WordPerfect program includes character sets you can use to create special letters and symbols.

COMMANDS REVIEW

	Mouse	Keyboard
Font dialog box	Fo**r**mat, **F**ont; or double-click the Change the font button on the Power Bar	Fo**r**mat, **F**ont
QuickFormat dialog box	Fo**r**mat, **Q**uickFormat; or click the QuickFormat button	Fo**r**mat, **Q**uickFormat
Insert a symbol	Insert, **C**haracter	Ctrl + W

CHECK YOUR UNDERSTANDING

Matching: In the space provided at the left, indicate the correct letter or letters that match each description.

- **A** Arial
- **B** typeface
- **C** type style
- **D** type size
- **E** bold
- **F** proportional
- **G** serif
- **H** sans serif
- **I** italic
- **J** Garamond
- **K** font
- **L** superscript
- **M** subscript
- **N** regular
- **O** points
- **P** Times New Roman

_____ 1. Examples of different type styles.
_____ 2. A small line at the end of a character stroke.
_____ 3. A particular typeface in a specific style and size.
_____ 4. A set of characters with a common design and shape.
_____ 5. Text that is lowered slightly below the regular line of text.
_____ 6. The size of proportional type is measured vertically in units called this.
_____ 7. Examples of different typefaces.
_____ 8. Text that is raised slightly above the regular line of text.

Completion: In the space provided at the right, indicate the correct term.

1. The typefaces available with your printer are displayed in this box at the Font dialog box. _____

2. The common font sizes are displayed in this box at the Font dialog box. _____

3. A sample of text in the current font is displayed in this box at the Font dialog box. _____

4. This option lets you show which text has been deleted from a document.

5. This option lets you identify text that is added to a legal document.

6. This choice in the Relative size option box changes the size of the current font to twice its normal size.

SKILL ASSESSMENTS

Assessment 1

1. At a clear editing window, open Report 06. This document is located on your student data disk.
2. Save the document with Save As and name it Ch 07, SA 01.
3. Make the following changes to the document:
   a. Change the font for the report to 11-point Arrus BT. (If Arrus BT is not available, choose a similar serif typeface.)
   b. Change the relative size of the title to Very Large.
   c. Change the relative size of the two headings to Large.
   d. Change the font style for the last six lines of the report to italic.
   e. Insert a round hollow bullet (4,1) before each of the last six lines in the report. (Indent the bullet to the first tab setting. This will cause the lines of text to indent to the second tab setting. The bullets will be italicized.)
4. Save the document again with the same name (Ch 07, SA 01).
5. Print and then close Ch 07, SA 01.

Assessment 2

1. At a clear editing window, display the Font dialog box, then change the font to 24-point Arrus Blk BT and turn on the Shadow appearance option.
2. Key the text shown in figure 7.14 centered.
3. Save the document and name it Ch 07, SA 02.
4. Print and then close Ch 07, SA 02.

Figure 7.14

> # Intensive Care Unit
>
> # Respiratory Therapy Techniques
>
> # Tuesday, May 19, 1998
>
> # 1:00 - 3:30 p.m., Room 430

Assessment 3

1. At a clear editing window, open Legal 02.
2. Save the document with Save As and name it Ch 07, SA 03.
3. Make the following changes to the document:
   a. Change the relative size of the title, *IN DISTRICT COURT NO. 4, PIERCE COUNTY STATE OF WASHINGTON*, to Large.
   b. Following the proofreaders' marks displayed in figure 7.15, identify the text to be deleted with the Strikeout option from the Font dialog box or the Strikeout button on the Font Toolbar, then identify the text to be added with the Redline option from the Font dialog box or the Redline button on the Font Toolbar.
4. Save the document again with the same name (Ch 07, SA 03).
5. Print and then close Ch 07, SA 03.

Figure 7.15

IN DISTRICT COURT NO. 4, PIERCE COUNTY
STATE OF WASHINGTON

STATE OF WASHINGTON	)	
	)	
Plaintiff,	)	NO. NUMBER
	)	
vs.	)	**NOTICE OF APPEARANCE**
	)	**AND DEMAND FOR**
	)	**INFORMATION**
NAME1,	)	
	)	
Defendant.	)	

TO: **CLERK OF DISTRICT COURT**, AND TO THE **PROSECUTING ATTORNEY**:

   YOU AND EACH OF YOU ~~will~~ please take notice that Coburn, Raintree & Thompson hereby appear in the above entitled action on behalf of the Defendant, NAME1, *as attorneys of record*, and hereby enter a plea of **NOT GUILTY**, waive arraignment, ~~the Sixty Day Rule~~ and make the following demands:

1. That the trial of this matter be heard by jury;

2. That the undersigned *attorney* be furnished with full information concerning the ~~test or~~ tests of blood alcohol content that were submitted to by the Defendant, NAME1; ~~if any, and a copy of the alcohol influence report form~~;

3. That the undersigned *attorney* be advised as to whether or not a videotape was taken of the Defendant, NAME1;

4. That the breathalyzer operator be present at the time of trial; however, the Defendant, NAME1, may waive this request at a subsequent date ~~upon the satisfactory examination of the inspection data heretofore requested~~.

DATED this _____ day of _____, 1998.

_____
LESLIE COBURN
of Coburn, Raintree & Thompson
Attorneys for Defendant

Assessment 4

1. Create the document shown in figure 7.16 with the following specifications:
   a. Change the font to 12-point Century Schoolbook.
   b. Center and bold text as indicated.
   c. Use the greater than symbol (>) to create the first triangle bullet. QuickCorrect will insert the other triangles. (Remember, if you do not want a triangle to display at the left margin, press the Backspace key. This deletes the codes that insert the triangle.)
   d. Select the title, TECHNICAL SUPPORT PARTNER, then change the relative size to Large.
   e. Use QuickFormat to change the relative size to Large for the four paragraph headings.
2. Save the document and name it Ch 07, SA 04.
3. Print and then close Ch 07, SA 04.

Figure 7.16

TECHNICAL SUPPORT PARTNER

General Description

The Technical Support Partner is a team member working under the direction of a Registered Nurse to provide quality care that is focused on the comfort and well-being of the patient and family.

Distinguishing Features

This position requires a service-oriented individual with strong interpersonal skills for the purpose of delivering care and services to patients from diverse ethnic and social groups. Independent decision making is expected in the execution of daily routine duties. Decisions regarding patient care or services require the review and approval of the Clinical Partner.

Principal Accountabilities

▸ Performs direct patient care activities
▸ Maintains a clean and comfortable environment in assigned patient rooms
▸ Obtains blood specimens using approved procedures for venipuncture
▸ Performs simple respiratory therapy functions
▸ Assembles and disassembles specialty equipment

Minimum Qualifications

▸ High school graduate or equivalent
▸ Previous work experience in a health care environment as an Aide, Housekeeper, or Transporter preferred
▸ Previous experience in phlebotomy preferred and/or willingness to train
▸ Knowledge of communication skills with ability to listen actively
▸ Ability to work independently and take initiative

Assessment 5

1. At a clear editing window, key the memo shown in figure 7.17 with the following specifications:
   a. Change the left and right margins to 1.5 inches.
   b. Change the font to 12-point Garamond (or a similar serif typeface).
   c. Indent, italicize, superscript, and subscript text as indicated.
2. Save the memo and name it Ch 07, SA 05.
3. Print and then close Ch 07, SA 05.

Figure 7.17

DATE: June 16, 1998; TO: Barbara Jaech; FROM: Thomas Scannell; SUBJECT: STATISTICAL ANALYSIS

I have been running an analysis on the areas mentioned in your June 9 memo. Completing the computations has brought up the following questions:

1. With smaller section ratios of r^4 and r^2 (.10 to .25)[1], what will be the yield increase?

2. What is the interaction effect on the scores of X_1, X_2, and X_3?

I will try to report on the findings to these questions by the end of next week.

xx:Ch 07, SA 05

Reminder: You may want to delete outdated document files now.

USING SPELL CHECKER AND THESAURUS

PERFORMANCE OBJECTIVE

Upon successful completion of chapter 8, you will be able to proof all types of business documents with the Spell Checker and Thesaurus tools.

WordPerfect includes writing tools to help create a thoughtful and well-written document. One of these writing tools, Spell Checker, finds misspelled words and offers replacement words. It also finds duplicate words and irregular capitalizations. Another tool, Thesaurus, provides a list of synonyms and antonyms for words.

Using Spell Checker

In Chapter 1 you learned about the Spell-As-You-Go feature, which automatically inserts red slashmarks below words that are misspelled, and provides you with a menu of suggested replacements and other options if you click the right mouse button over the error. You may prefer to work with Spell-As-You-Go turned off and perform one spelling check when the document is complete. To turn off Spell-As-You-Go, click Tools, then select Spell-As-You-Go. This will remove the check mark beside the feature and any red slashmarks below words will be removed from the document screen. Spell-As-You-Go will remain turned off until you turn it on again by following the same procedure that you used to turn it off. Even if Spell-As-You-Go is turned on, you may want to complete a spell check when the document is complete to return to each word that has been marked with red slashmarks and correct any errors.

Spell Checker works mainly with two word lists—a user word list and a main word list (containing more than 100,000 words). In addition to these two word lists, a document-specific word list is automatically attached to a document where you can add words that you want Spell Checker to skip that are specific to the current document only.

When a spell check is run, Spell Checker first checks the words in the document against words in the default user word list. If a match is not found, then Spell Checker looks for the word in the main word list. Additional word lists can be purchased and used with Spell Checker for specific industries (medical, legal, scientific, etc.).

What Spell Checker Can Do

Spell Checker operates by comparing words in a document with words in the user word list and the main word list. If there is a match, Spell Checker moves on. If there is no match for the word, Spell Checker will stop and highlight a word for correction if it fits one of the following situations:

- a misspelled word if the misspelling does not match another word that exists in the word lists
- typographical errors such as transposed letters
- double word occurrences (such as *and and*)
- irregular capitalization
- some proper names
- jargon and some technical terms

Spell Checker may not stop at all proper names. For example, Spell Checker would assume the first name *Robin* is spelled correctly and pass over it because Robin would appear in the word lists as a type of bird.

What Spell Checker Cannot Do

A small number of words in the main word list are proper names. You will find that many proper names will not appear in this list. Spell Checker will not find a match for these proper names and will highlight the words for correction. Spell Checker will not identify words that are spelled correctly but used incorrectly. For example, if you want the word *from* in a document but you key it as *form*, it will be passed over because *form* appears in its word lists. Spell Checker cannot check grammar usage. For example, if the wrong verb tense is used in a document but the verb is spelled correctly, Spell Checker passes over the verb. The need for proofreading is not eliminated by Spell Checker, but it does provide assistance in editing a document.

Spell Checking a Document

Spell Check

Before operating Spell Checker, save the document currently displayed in the editing window or open a document. To begin Spell Checker click Tools, then Spell Check; or click the Spell Check button on the Toolbar. This causes the Writing Tools dialog box with the Spell Checker tab selected to display as shown in figure 8.1.

Figure 8.1 — Writing Tools Dialog Box with Spell Checker Tab Selected

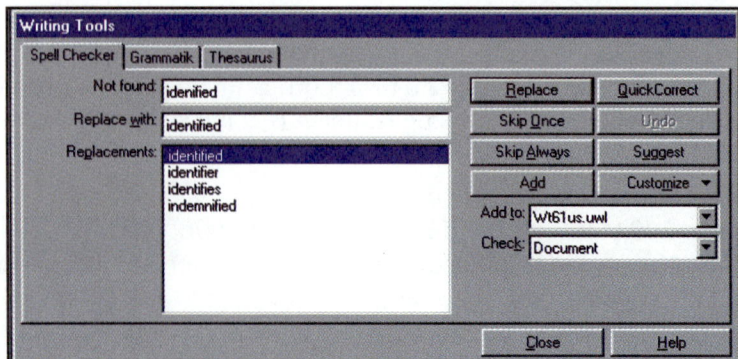

158 Chapter 8

Using Command Buttons

The Writing Tools dialog box with the Spell Checker tab selected contains several command buttons that display at the right side of the box.

Start: By default Spell Checker begins automatically. If the automatic start has been turned off, click Start to begin spell checking. If automatic start is activated, the Start button is changed to the Replace button. When Spell Checker discovers a word in the document that does not match a word in the user or main word lists, the word is selected and suggestions for spelling are inserted in the Replacements list box in the Writing Tools dialog box.

Replace: When Spell Checker encounters a word that is not in the user or main word lists, suggestions for correct spelling are inserted in the Replacements list box with the first suggestion displayed in the Replace with text box. To replace the selected word in the document with one of the suggestions, double-click the correct spelling. If you are using the keyboard, press Alt + P for Replacements, then use the arrow keys to select the correct spelling and press Enter (or Alt + R for Replace).

Skip Once and Skip Always: In some situations, Spell Checker will highlight a word for correction that you want to leave alone. This may happen with words such as proper names or abbreviations. To tell Spell Checker to leave the word alone, click the Skip Once or Skip Always command button. If you click Skip Once, Spell Checker will skip that occurrence of the word but will highlight occurrences in other locations in the document. If the word appears in other locations in the document and you want it skipped in those locations also, click Skip Always. This tells Spell Checker to skip all occurrences of that particular word.

Add: When WordPerfect is installed, a default user word list is included. If Spell Checker highlights a word for correction that will appear in many documents, such as a person's name, company name, or product, click Add. This inserts the word in the default user word list, and means the Spell Checker will not highlight it again.

QuickCorrect: In chapter 1, you learned that WordPerfect includes a QuickCorrect feature that automatically changes certain words in a document. For example, if you key *teh*, QuickCorrect changes it to *the*. You can add misspelled words with the correct spelling in QuickCorrect. To do this, make sure the proper spelling is inserted in the Replace with text box, then click QuickCorrect.

Undo: Click the Undo button to reverse the last replacement made.

Suggest: Spell Checker follows certain rules when looking for possible suggestions for correct spelling. Spell Checker will transpose the characters, make substitutions, and make additions or deletions. The possible suggestions are displayed in the Replacements list box. Click Suggest to display additional words or phrases, if there are any.

Customize: When you click Customize in the Writing Tools dialog box, the drop-down menu shown in figure 8.2 displays. The check marks in front of the options indicate that those options are active. By default, Spell Checker will check a document for words containing numbers, duplicate words, irregular capitalization, and will include phonetic suggestions in the Replacements list box. To turn off an option, click the left mouse button on the option. Customizing the spell check options will be discussed later in this chapter.

Close: Click the Close button to remove the Writing Tools dialog box from the screen.

Figure 8.2

Customize Drop-Down Menu in Writing Tools Dialog Box

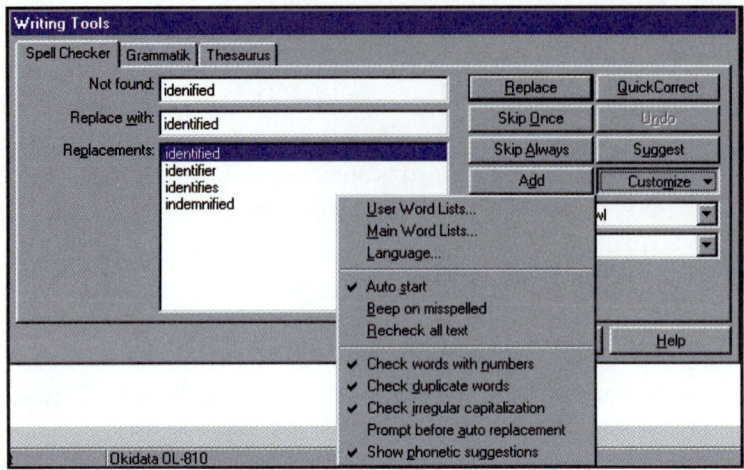

Editing in Spell Checker

When spell checking a document, you can temporarily leave the Writing Tools dialog box, make corrections in the document, then resume spell checking. For example, suppose while spell checking you notice a sentence that you want to change. To do this, move the arrow pointer to the location in the sentence where the change is to occur, then click the left mouse button. Make changes to the sentence, then click the Resume button in the Writing Tools dialog box (previously the Start button).

EXERCISE

Completing a Spelling Check

1. At a clear editing window, open Memo 03.
2. Save the memo with Save As and name it Ch 08, Ex 01.
3. Perform a spelling check by completing the following steps:
   a. Click the Spell Check button on the Toolbar.
   b. Spell Checker highlights the word *Mai*. This word is spelled properly (it is a proper name) so click the Skip Always button.
   c. Spell Checker highlights the word *Ayala*. This name is spelled properly so click Skip Always.
   d. Spell Checker highlights the word *idenified*. The proper spelling is displayed in the Replace with text box so click Replace.
   e. Spell Checker highlights the word *required*. The proper spelling is displayed in the Replacements list box. Move the arrow pointer to the correct spelling (*required*) and double-click the left mouse button.
   f. Spell Checker highlights *departmnts*. Move the arrow pointer to the correct spelling (*departments*) and double-click the left mouse button.
   g. Spell Checker highlights the word *hte*. Click the correct spelling, *the*, in the Replacements list box, then click Replace.
   h. Spell Checker highlights the word *tmies*. Click Replace.

> i. Spell Checker highlights the word *ncesary* and gives no suggestions. Correct *ncesary* in the Replace with text box by moving the insertion point and keying the letters **e** and **s** in the appropriate location in the word and then clicking Replace. (The correct spelling is *necessary*.)
> j. Spell Checker highlights *xx:Memo*. Click Skip Once.
> k. At the *Spell check completed. Close Spell Checker?* question, click Yes or press Enter.
> 4. Save the memo with the same name (Ch 08, Ex 01).
> 5. Print and then close Ch 08, Ex 01.

Customizing Spell Check Options

The Add to and Check list boxes and the Customize button allow you to change options that affect the way the Spell Checker operates.

Add to: When the Spell Checker highlights a word not found in the word list that is technical in nature, or a proper name, you can add the word to your user word list so that the Spell Checker will not stop on it again. When a spell check begins, WordPerfect first scans the user word list. If a word is not found there, the Spell Checker will search the main word list. You can activate up to ten user word lists and ten main word lists. User word lists have the file extension *.uwl*. The default user word list is *Wt61us.uwl*. The main word list that WordPerfect uses is *Wt61EN.mor*. You can create and edit your own *main word lists* using the Spell Check Utility, which is a separate program run from the Start button. Refer to the WordPerfect on-line help for more information on creating your own main word lists or converting custom lists from previous versions of WordPerfect.

Each document has its own user word list to which you can add words that pertain specifically to that document. The document word list is the first list that will be scanned if you have more than one list activated. To activate a user word list, click Customize from the Writing Tools dialog box. Click User Word Lists from the drop-down menu that appears, then click the word list you want to activate. An "x" appears in the check box next to the active word list. A check will not appear next to the name *Wt61us.uwl* or the Document word list because they are always active.

While you are conducting a spell check you can choose to add words to either the Document Word List, the *Wt61us.uwl* word list, or any other word lists that you may have activated. Change to the list to which you want the word added before you select the Add command button by selecting Add to. To do this, click the down-pointing triangle to the right of the Add to list box, which displays the default word list *Wt61us.uwl*, then click the desired word list in the drop-down list box that displays.

Check: By default, Spell Checker will check the entire document, no matter where the insertion point is positioned. If text is selected, however, the default for Spell Checker is Selected Text. How much of a document is checked can be controlled with selections from the Check option at the Writing Tools dialog box. Move the pointer to the down-pointing triangle to the right of the Check list box and press the left mouse button. A drop-down list will appear where you can select the check option you want to use.

The Number of Pages option allows you to key the number of pages to check starting from the current page. When you click the Number of Pages option, a dialog box will appear where you key the desired number of pages and then click OK or press Enter.

Check the current page where the insertion point is positioned with the Page option. The Paragraph option will check the paragraph where the insertion point is positioned. Choose Sentence to check the current sentence where the insertion point is positioned. With the To End of Document option, you can check the document from the insertion point to the end of the document. The Word option will check the word nearest to the insertion point.

Customize: As previously mentioned, a custom User Word list can be activated from the Customize button. In addition, a different Main Word list can be activated if you have created or installed additional lists. If you are working with a document that requires spell checker to check a foreign language, choose Language from the Customize button. A dialog box will appear where you can scroll through a list of foreign languages. Select the desired language and then click OK. If you want WordPerfect to check the spelling in the foreign language, additional language word lists in the foreign language selected must be installed on your system.

The Auto start option, which automatically starts spell checking, is on by default. Turn this option off if you want to control when checking begins.

The Beep on misspelled option is turned off by default. If you turn this option on, Spell Checker will beep when a word is not found in the word lists.

If you want Spell Checker to recheck new or changed text in a document, turn on the Recheck all text option.

The Check words with numbers option tells Spell Checker to stop and select any words containing letters and numbers. For example, Spell Checker will stop and highlight the function key *F3* during checking as well as a word such as *fi8nd*. If you create a document with words containing numbers such as parts numbers, Canadian postal codes, or function keys, you may want to turn off Check words with numbers. To do this, remove the check mark before the option.

The next option, Check duplicate words, tells Spell Checker to stop and highlight double words. For example, if a document contains the words *and and*, Spell Checker will stop during spell checking and ask if you want to continue (leave the double words) or delete the second occurrence.

Check irregular capitalization tells Spell Checker to highlight any words containing irregular capitalizations. Turn Check irregular capitalization off in the same manner as you would the Check words with numbers option.

If the Prompt before auto replacement option is turned on, WordPerfect will prompt you before QuickCorrect replaces words as you type them.

The Show phonetic suggestions option is on by default. With this option on, words that sound similar to the word not found are displayed in the Replacements list box. Turn this feature off if you do not want to see words that sound similar to the word not found.

EXERCISE

Changing Spell Checking Options

1. At a clear editing window, open Letter 01.
2. Save the letter with Save As and name it Ch 08, Ex 02.
3. Change spell checking options, then perform a spelling check by completing the following steps:
    a. Click the Spell Check button on the Toolbar.

      b. When Spell Checker selects *leter*, click Custo<u>m</u>ize.
      c. At the Customize drop-down menu, click Check words with <u>n</u>umbers to turn off this option.
      d. Click Custo<u>m</u>ize.
      e. At the Customize drop-down menu, click Check <u>d</u>uplicate words to turn off this option.
      f. Click Custo<u>m</u>ize.
      g. At the Customize drop-down menu, click <u>B</u>eep on misspelled to turn on this option.
      h. Click *letter* in the Re<u>p</u>lacements list box, then click <u>R</u>eplace.
      i. As Spell Checker selects other words for correction, tell Spell Checker to skip proper names. Replace misspelled words with the proper spelling and make corrections to irregular capitalizations.
      j. When the spell check is completed, click <u>Y</u>es or press Enter.
4. Proofread the letter and make corrections to mistakes not selected by Spell Checker.
5. Save the letter with the same name (Ch 08, Ex 02).
6. Print Ch 08, Ex 02.
7. Change the Spell Checker options back to the default by completing the following steps:
      a. Click the Spell Check button on the Toolbar.
      b. When asked if you want to close Spell Checker, click <u>N</u>o.
      c. At the Writing Tools dialog box with the Spell Checker tab selected, click Custo<u>m</u>ize.
      d. At the Customize drop-down menu, click Check words with <u>n</u>umbers. (This turns the feature back on.)
      e. Click Custo<u>m</u>ize.
      f. At the Customize drop-down menu, click Check <u>d</u>uplicate words. (This turns the feature back on.)
      g. Click Custo<u>m</u>ize.
      h. At the Customize drop-down menu, click <u>B</u>eep on misspelled. (This turns the feature off.)
      i. Click <u>C</u>lose.
8. Close Ch 08, Ex 02.

Working with User Word Lists

A user word list is a list of words or phrases that you want Spell Checker to skip, replace, or display alternatives for. Examples of words that you might want included in a user word list are proper names of individuals, technical jargon specific to your business, or acronyms that you use.

You can add, create, or delete user word lists, or edit words or phrases in the default user word list using the Customize button in the Writing Tools dialog box.

Adding, Creating, or Removing User Word Lists

A user word list can be added, created, or removed. To do this, click the Customize button in the Writing Tools dialog box. At the drop-down menu that displays, click <u>U</u>ser Word Lists. This causes the User Word List Editor dialog box to display as shown in figure 8.3.

Figure 8.3

User Word List Editor Dialog Box

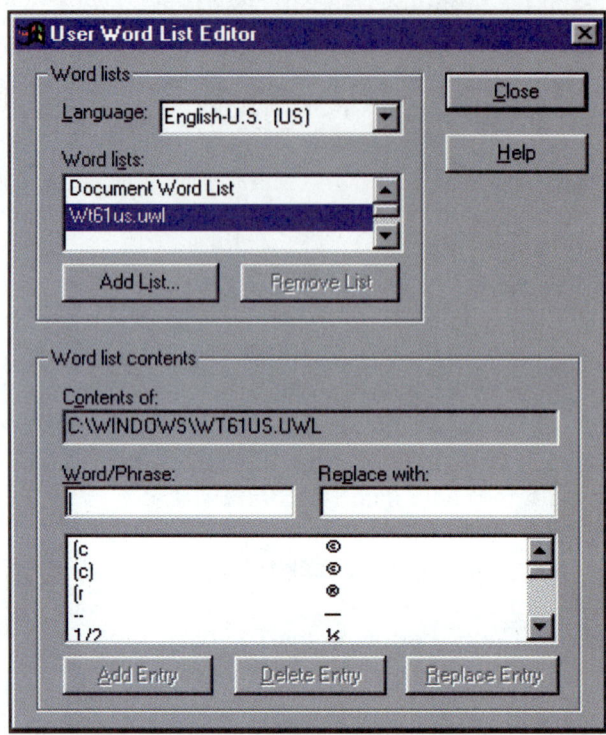

Click in the list box where you want the new user word list to be positioned. WordPerfect scans your user word lists in the order that they are presented in the dialog box during a spell check. Click Add List. Key a name for the user word list and then click Open. The new list will appear in the list box with a check mark in a box beside it. The extension *.UWL* is automatically added to the end of the document name.

Add the word or phrase you want WordPerfect to skip in the Word/Phrase text box by moving the I-beam pointer to the text box below Word/Phrase and clicking the left mouse button. Key the text and then click Add Entry. For example, suppose you want to add your last name to your user word list so the Spell Checker will not highlight it as an error. Key your last name in the Word/Phrase text box, then click Add Entry. The entry <skip> will automatically appear in the Replace with text box.

QuickCorrect replacement words are stored in the user word lists. You will work with customizing the default word list for replacement text later in this chapter.

To remove a word list, select the user word list filename in the Word lists list box and then click Remove List. Removing a user word list only removes it from the spell checking scan sequence. The file is not deleted from the hard drive.

Editing a User Word List

Words can be added, edited, or deleted from the user word lists. Access the User Word List Editor dialog box as instructed in the previous section, then select the word list you want to edit. In the Word list contents section you can scroll through a list of the words and any replacements in the selected user word list using the scroll triangles.

To change a word or phrase, select it with the mouse in the Word list contents list box. This will cause the word and any replacement text to appear in the Word/Phrase and Replace with text boxes. Move the I-beam pointer to the appropriate text box and edit the word or phrase by clicking the left mouse button in the text box, using the arrow keys, and adding or deleting characters as necessary. When you are finished, click the Replace Entry button at the bottom right of the User Word List Editor dialog box.

Add Entry will add new text entered in the Word/Phrase and Replace with text boxes to the user word list and Delete Entry will remove a selected word or phrase and its replacement text from the user word list.

EXERCISE 3

Adding Words to the User Word List

1. At a clear editing window, open Memo 04.
2. Save the memo with Save As and name it Ch 08, Ex 03.
3. Perform a spell check and add words to the *Wt61us.uwl* word list by completing the following steps:
   a. Click Tools, then Spell Check.
   b. Spell Checker selects *Hedegard.* Add this name to the user word list by clicking Add.
   c. Spell Checker selects *Lura.* Click Add to add this name to the user word list.
   d. Spell Checker selects *Bryne.* Click Add to add this name to the user word list.
   e. Spell Checker selects *xx:Memo.* Click Skip Once.
   f. At the *Spell check completed. Close Spell Checker?* question, click Yes or press Enter.
4. Save and then close Ch 08, Ex 03.

EXERCISE 4

Editing Words in the User Word List

1. At a clear editing window, open Memo 05.
2. Save the document with Save As and name it Ch 08, Ex 04.
3. Change *Bryne* in the supplementary dictionary to *Brynn* by completing the following steps:
   a. Click the Spell Check button on the Toolbar.
   b. When Spell Checker selects *Febury,* click Customize.
   c. At the Customize drop-down menu, click User Word Lists.
   d. At the User Word List Editor dialog box, make sure *Wt61us.uwl* is highlighted.
   e. In the list box that displays at the bottom of the dialog box, scroll through the list of words until *Bryne* is displayed, then click *Bryne*.
   f. Click in the Word/Phrase text box and then delete the *e* and add an *n* so the name is spelled *Brynn*.
   g. Click Add Entry.
   h. Select Bryne again and then click Delete Entry.

Using Spell Checker and Thesaurus

4. Complete steps similar to those in 3e through 3h to change the following:
   a. Change the spelling of *Hedegard* to *Hedegaard* and then delete *Hedegard*.
   b. Change the spelling of *Lura* to *Laura* and then delete *Lura*.
5. Click the Close button to close the User Word List Editor dialog box and then continue spell checking the memo. Make corrections as needed. (Proper names are spelled correctly.)
6. Save the memo with the same name (Ch 08, Ex 04).
7. Print and then close Ch 08, Ex 04.
8. At a clear editing window, delete the word *Brynn* from the *Wt61us.uwl* user word list by completing the following steps:
   a. Click the Spell Check button on the Toolbar.
   b. When asked if you want to close Spell Checker, click No.
   c. At the Writing Tools dialog box with the Spell Checker tab selected, click Customize.
   d. At the Customize drop-down menu, click User Word Lists.
   e. At the User Word List Editor dialog box, make sure *Wt61us.uwl* is highlighted.
   f. Scroll through the list box that displays toward the bottom of the dialog box, click *Brynn*, and then click Delete Entry.
   g. Complete steps similar to those in 8f to delete *Hedegaard*, and *Laura*.
   h. Click Close to close the User Word List Editor dialog box, then click Close again to close the Writing Tools dialog box.
9. Close the empty document without saving it.

Using Thesaurus

WordPerfect offers a Thesaurus program that can be used to find synonyms and antonyms for words. Synonyms are words that have the same or nearly the same meaning. Antonyms are words with opposite meanings. With Thesaurus, the clarity of business communications can be improved.

To use Thesaurus, open the document containing the word for which you want to find synonyms and/or antonyms. Position the insertion point next to any character in the word and then click Tools, then Thesaurus. This displays the Writing Tools dialog box with the Thesaurus tab selected similar to the one shown in figure 8.4. The dialog box in figure 8.4 displays synonyms and antonyms for the word *award*.

Figure 8.4

Writing Tools Dialog Box with Thesaurus Tab Selected

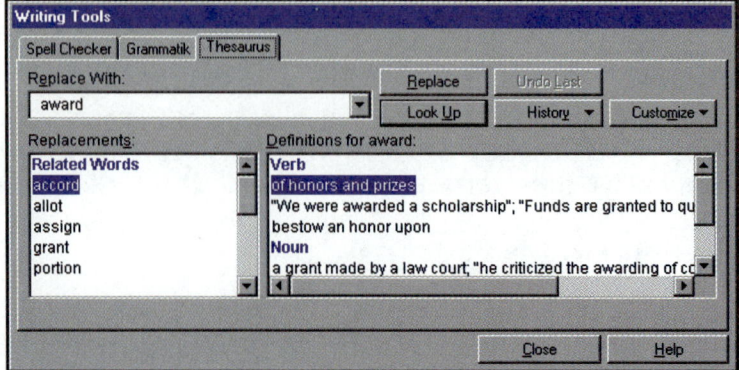

Words in the Replacements list box are arranged according to their relationship to the word looked up. Definitions and examples of selected words are displayed in the box at the right. Different definitions will display when the word selected is used as a noun, verb, adjective, etc.

EXERCISE 5

Finding Synonyms and Related Words with Thesaurus

1. At a clear editing window, look up synonyms and antonyms for the word *obsequious* by completing the following steps:
   a. Key **obsequious**.
   b. With the insertion point positioned in the word, click Tools, then Thesaurus.
   c. After viewing the synonyms and related words for *obsequious*, close the Writing Tools dialog box by clicking Close.
2. Close the document without saving it.

Choosing Options from the Writing Tools Dialog Box with the Thesaurus Tab Selected

When you click Tools, then Thesaurus, the Writing Tools dialog box with the Thesaurus tab selected displays as shown in figure 8.4. You can see only a portion of the list of words provided for the word *award*. Related words for *award* are displayed in the left section of the dialog box, called the Replacements list box.

Using List Boxes

To see the remaining list of words for *award* using the mouse, move the arrow pointer to the down scroll arrow and hold down the left button. To move back through the list, move the arrow pointer to the up scroll triangle and hold down the left button.

Using Command Buttons

The Writing Tools dialog box with the Thesaurus tab selected contains five command buttons that display at the top right side of the box.

Replace: If you find an appropriate synonym or related word for the selected text, you can replace the word in the document with the Replace command button. For example, to replace *award* with *certificate* using the mouse, click the down scroll arrow in the Replacements list box until you see the word *certificate*, click the left mouse button over the word, then click Replace.

Insert: If you open the Writing Tools dialog box with the Thesaurus tab selected when the insertion point is not positioned on or near a word, the Replace command button is changed to the Insert button. In addition, the Replace with text box is changed to the Insert text box. The insertion point will be positioned in the Insert text box. Key the word you want to look up and press Enter or click Look Up. To insert one of the suggested words in the current document, click the desired word and then select Insert.

Look Up: When Thesaurus displays synonyms and/or related words, you can continue looking further for a specific synonym for a word in the Replacements list box. For example, in the Writing Tools dialog box displayed in figure 8.4, the word *grant* appears in the Replacements list box. To look up related words for *grant*, select *grant* by clicking the left mouse button over the word and then click Look Up, or double-click *grant*. You can continue your exploration with other words by looking them up in this manner.

Undo Last: Undo Last will reverse the last word replacement or insertion. This button is only available when Auto Close is not selected. Auto Close is discussed in the Customize section later in this chapter.

History: To view a list of words you have looked up, click the History button. The drop-down list that appears will show the words you have looked up in this Thesaurus session. When you close the Writing Tools dialog box this list is removed and when you reopen the Thesaurus a new one is created.

Customize: When you click the Customize button, a drop-down menu displays as shown in figure 8.5.

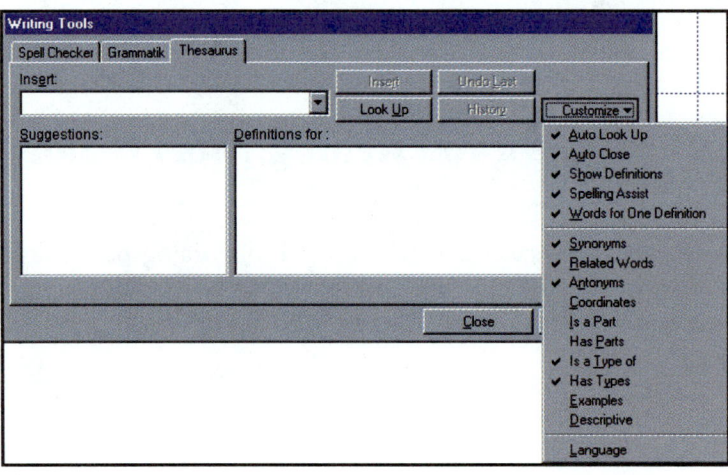

Figure 8.5
Thesaurus Customize Drop-Down Menu

Most of these options are available only if you have installed WordPerfect 7 using the Custom installation option. If you installed WordPerfect using the Typical installation, you can reinstall the program.

Figure 8.5 illustrates the default options that are active when you open the Thesaurus. An option is active if there is a check mark beside the option. To deactivate an option, position the arrow pointer over the option and click the left mouse button. This removes the check mark. To reactivate the option after it has been deactivated, follow the same procedure you used to remove the check mark.

Auto Look Up: Auto Look Up means that the Thesaurus will automatically look up the word at the insertion point when the dialog box is opened. Auto Close removes the Writing Tools dialog box automatically when you select the Replace button.

Show Definitions: With Show Definitions activated, you can click a definition in the Definitions list box and WordPerfect will automatically scroll down the Replacements list box and select the word that relates to the definition. For example, with the word *award* looked up, if you position the arrow pointer on the definition below the title "Noun" in the Definitions list box and click the left mouse button (over the text *a grant made by a law court: "he criticized the awarding of compensation"*), the word *endowment* is automatically selected in the Replacements list box.

Spelling Assist: The Spelling Assist option will display spelling suggestions when you type a word the Thesaurus does not recognize in the Replace With text box. Words for One Definition will display words for one definition at a time.

Synonyms: Synonyms are words with the same meaning. If you look up *joy,* you will see words such as *rejoice* and *triumph* listed as synonyms.

Related Words: Related words are words that have a similar meaning to the selected word. For example, if you look up *angry,* words such as *annoyed, exasperated,* and *irritated* appear as Related Words.

Antonyms: Words with opposite meaning to the selected word are displayed under the category Antonyms. If you look up *new,* some of the antonyms displayed are *creaky, decrepit, hand-me-down,* and *old.*

Coordinates: If a word is a type of another more general word, its coordinates are other words that are also types of that more general word. For example, *document* is a type of *record.* Some coordinates that display for document are *book, chronicle, file, photograph,* which are also types of records.

Is a Part: To look up what a word is a part of, select Is a Part from the Customize menu. For example, *hair* is a part of a *mammal.*

Has Parts: To look up words for specific parts that make up a whole, click Has Parts from the Customize menu. For example, if you look up the word *pie* with Has Parts selected, the Thesaurus will display the words *crumb* and *flour.*

Is a Type of: This option is on by default and will list words that are more generally related to the selected word. For example, if you look up *piano,* the Thesaurus will display *percussion instrument,* and *stringed instrument* under the heading "Is a Type of".

Has Types: Has Types is also on by default and will display more specific words related to the word selected. If *piano* is looked up, the Thesaurus displays words such as *grand, grand piano, mechanical piano, player piano,* and *upright* under the heading "Has Types".

Examples: You can view a list of specific examples of words with this option. For example if you look up *river,* the Thesaurus will list *Amazon River, Colorado River,* and *Hudson River* as just a few of the examples provided.

Descriptive: Descriptive categories for proper nouns will be displayed when this option is selected. With *Atlanta* as the selected word, the Thesaurus will display *city, metropolis, metropolitan area,* and *urban center* as the Descriptive words.

Language: If you have installed other language modules, you can direct the Thesaurus to look up words in the other language by selecting the Language module from the Customize menu. When you click Language, a dialog box will appear where you can scroll a list of foreign languages.

Close: When you replace a word, the Thesaurus is automatically closed. However, if you look up synonyms and antonyms for a word and then decide not to use any, close the Thesaurus by clicking the Close button.

Help: With the Help menu from the Thesaurus, you can access any of the Help features offered by WordPerfect 7, including specific information about Thesaurus.

EXERCISE

Using the History Option

1. At a clear editing window, complete the following steps:
   a. Key **Lugubrious**.
   b. Display the Thesaurus.
   c. After viewing the synonyms and antonym(s) for *lugubrious*, view synonyms and antonym(s) for *nascent*. To do this, click in the R<u>e</u>place With text box (this selects *Lugubrious*), key **nascent**, then click Look <u>U</u>p.
   d. After viewing the synonyms and antonym(s) for *nascent*, view synonyms and antonym(s) for *propitious*. To do this, click in the R<u>e</u>place With text box (this selects *nascent*), key **propitious**, then click Look <u>U</u>p.
   e. After viewing the synonyms and antonym(s) for *propitious*, view synonyms and antonym(s) for *imminent*. To do this, click in the R<u>e</u>place With text box (this selects *propitious*), key **imminent**, then click Look <u>U</u>p.
   f. Click H<u>i</u>story to view the sequence of words looked up. After viewing the words in the History drop-down menu, press Enter or click the arrow pointer inside the dialog box but outside the History drop-down menu.
   g. Remove the Thesaurus from the editing window by clicking <u>C</u>lose.
2. Close the document without saving it.

Replacing Words with Thesaurus

1. At a clear editing window, open Memo 02.
2. Save the memo with Save As and name it Ch 08, Ex 07.
3. Change the word *several* in the first paragraph to *numerous* using Thesaurus by completing the following steps:
   a. Position the insertion point in the word *several*.
   b. Display the Thesaurus.
   c. Scroll through the list of replacements to select *numerous*, then click <u>R</u>eplace.
4. Follow similar steps to make the following changes using Thesaurus:
   a. Change *money* in the first paragraph to *funds*. (When you replace *money* with *funds*, WordPerfect removes the *s* in *funds* and you will need to add the *s* to *fund*.)
   b. Change the first occurrence of *purchase* in the last paragraph to *buy*.
5. Save the memo with the same name (Ch 08, Ex 07).
6. Print and then close Ch 08, Ex 07.

Displaying Document Information

Information about a document such as the number of characters, words, lines, sentences, and pages can be displayed at the Properties dialog box with the Information tab selected. To display this dialog box, click File, point to Document, then click Properties. Click the Information tab and information about the document will display. Figure 8.6 displays the document information for Report 01.

Figure 8.6

Properties Dialog Box with Information Tab Selected

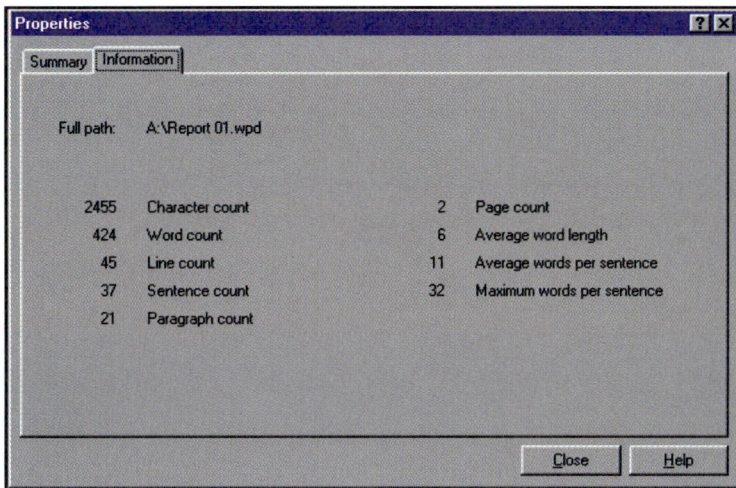

EXERCISE 8

Displaying Document Size Information

1. At a clear editing window, open Letter 01.
2. Display information about this document by completing the following steps:
   a. Click File, point to Document, then click Properties.
   b. In the Properties dialog box, click the Information tab.
   c. Read the information about Letter 01 that displays in the dialog box.
   d. After reading the information, click the Close button.
3. Close Letter 01.
4. At a clear editing window, open Report 02.
5. Display information about the report by completing steps 2a through 2d.
6. Close Report 02.

Using Spell Checker and Thesaurus

Using QuickCorrect

As mentioned in chapter 1, WordPerfect includes a feature called *QuickCorrect* that automatically corrects certain words as they are being keyed. For example, if you key the word *adn* instead of *and,* QuickCorrect automatically corrects it when you press the space bar after the word. There are numerous automatic corrections that can be seen in the QuickCorrect dialog box. To display the QuickCorrect dialog box shown in figure 8.7, click Tools, then QuickCorrect.

At the QuickCorrect dialog box, use the vertical scroll bar in the list box to view the entire list of words that WordPerfect will correct.

Figure 8.7

QuickCorrect Dialog Box

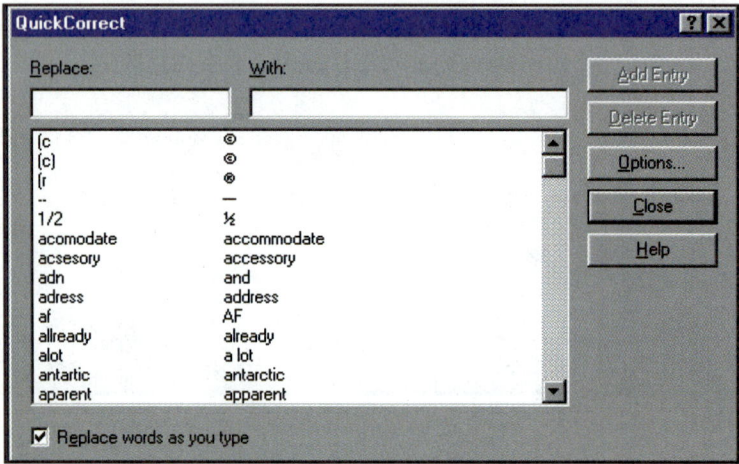

Adding a Word to QuickCorrect

Commonly misspelled words or typographical errors can be added to QuickCorrect. For example, if you consistently key *oopen* instead of *open*, you can add *oopen* to QuickCorrect and tell it to correct it as *open*. To add an entry to QuickCorrect, key the misspelling in the Replace text box, key the correct spelling in the With text box, then click Add Entry.

Entries in QuickCorrect can be deleted. To delete an entry, select the entry in the list box at the QuickCorrect dialog box, then click Delete Entry. WordPerfect will insert a dialog box asking if you want to delete the entry. At this dialog box, click Yes.

By default, QuickCorrect will automatically replace text. You can turn automatic replacement off by removing the check mark from the Replace words as you type check box that displays at the bottom of the QuickCorrect dialog box.

Changing QuickCorrect Options

The QuickCorrect feature contains a number of options that can be active or inactive. To view QuickCorrect options, click Options from the QuickCorrect dialog box. At the QuickCorrect Options dialog box shown in figure 8.8, an option is active if a check mark appears in the check box. An option is also active if a black dot appears in the radio button before it.

At the QuickCorrect Options dialog box, insert a check mark for those options you want active and remove the check mark from those options you want inactive. The End of sentence corrections box contains three choices: None, Single space to two spaces, and Two spaces to single space. The default is Nunderlined. Click one of the other options if you want QuickCorrect to correct how many spaces are inserted after punctuation at the end of a sentence.

The QuickCorrect Format-As-You-Go options allow you to alter the automatic formatting that is applied to text as you type. If you are not sure what a formatting item does, such as QuickLines, click the item. This causes a description of what the item does to display toward the bottom of the dialog box.

After making any changes to the QuickCorrect Options dialog box, click OK or press Enter. This returns you to the QuickCorrect dialog box. Click Close to close the QuickCorrect dialog box.

QuickCorrect Options Dialog Box

Figure 8.8

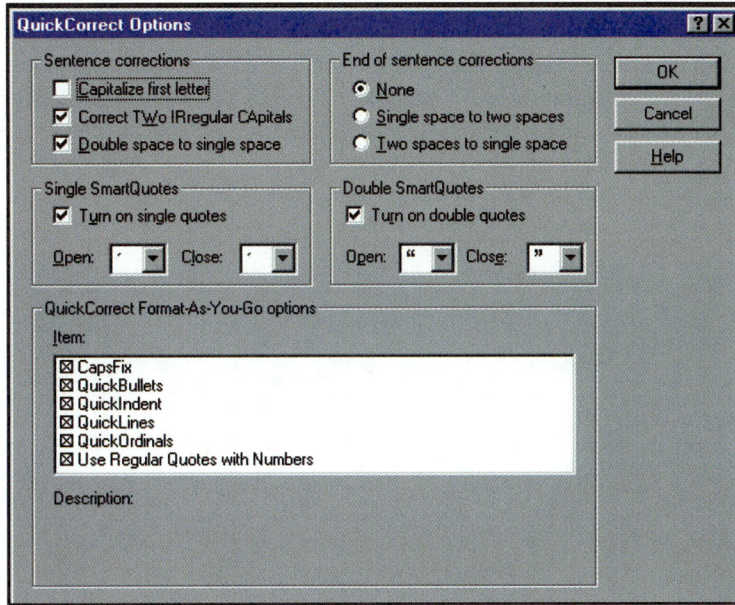

EXERCISE

Editing QuickCorrect Entries

1. At a clear editing window, add words to QuickCorrect by completing the following steps:
   a. Click Tools, then QuickCorrect.
   b. At the QuickCorrect dialog box, make sure the insertion point is positioned in the Replace text box. (If not, click Replace.)
   c. Key **efficiancy**.
   d. Press the Tab key. (This moves the insertion point to the With text box.)
   e. Key **efficiency**.
   f. Click Add Entry.
   g. With the insertion point positioned in the Replace text box, key **facters**.
   h. Press the Tab key. (This moves the insertion point to the With text box.)
   i. Key **factors**.
   j. Click Add Entry.

Using Spell Checker and Thesaurus

      k. With the insertion point positioned in the Replace text box, key **tele**.
      l. Press the Tab key. (This moves the insertion point to the With text box.)
      m. Key **telecommunications**.
      n. Click Add Entry.
      o. Click Close.
2. Key the text shown in figure 8.9. (Key the text exactly as shown. QuickCorrect will correct the words as you key.)
3. Save the document and name it Ch 08, Ex 09.
4. Print Ch 08, Ex 09.
5. Delete the words you added to QuickCorrect by completing the following steps:
      a. Click Tools, then QuickCorrect.
      b. At the QuickCorrect dialog box, click *efficiancy* in the list box. (You will need to scroll down the list box to display *efficiancy*.)
      c. Click Delete Entry.
      d. At the dialog box asking if you want to delete the entry, click Yes.
      e. Click *facters* in the list box. (You will need to scroll down the list box to display *facters*.)
      f. Click Delete Entry.
      g. Click *tele* in the list box.
      h. Click Delete Entry.
      i. Click Close.
6. Close Ch 08, Ex 09.

Figure 8.9

You consider several important facters before deciding which new tele system management you should purchase. You thoroughly study cost, efficiancy, quality, time, and ease of use. You use these facters to evaluate every tele application in terms of how well it solves a specific business problem. Later, you will be asked to rate proposed tele systems using the facters of cost, efficiancy, quality, time, and ease of use.

CHAPTER SUMMARY

- Spell Checker is a spell-checking program that consists mainly of two word lists—a main word list and a user word list. In addition, a document-specific word list is automatically attached to a document where you can add words you want the Spell Checker to skip that are specific only to that document.

- Spell Checker will not identify words that are spelled correctly but used incorrectly, nor does it identify misspellings that match other words in its word lists. Spell Checker cannot check grammar usage.

- After correcting a misspelled word, Spell Checker automatically corrects all future occurrences of that error within the document.

- Among other options in the Writing Tools dialog box with the Spell Checker tab selected, you can instruct Spell Checker to check the following: a word, a sentence, a paragraph, a page, a specific number of pages, to the end of the document from the insertion point location, or the entire document.

- Spell Checker may identify some proper names as misspelled. Frequently used proper names or other terms can be added to the user word list.

- You can add, create, or delete user word lists or edit words or phrases in the default user word list at the User Word List Editor dialog box.

- The Thesaurus can be used to find synonyms, related words, and antonyms for words in your document.

- The command buttons in the Thesaurus allow you to Replace and Look Up words, Undo Last replacement, view the History of the words looked up in the current Thesaurus session, and Customize how the Thesaurus operates and what replacement suggestions it displays.

- Use the Information tab in the Properties dialog box accessed from the Document option of the File drop-down menu to display information about your document such as the number of characters, words, lines, sentences, and pages.

- The QuickCorrect dialog box from the Tools menu can be used to add and delete words that are automatically corrected as you type. In addition, the QuickCorrect Options dialog box provides options that can be modified to change the way WordPerfect automatically formats text as you type.

COMMANDS REVIEW

	Mouse	Keyboard
Display the Spell Checker	Spell Check button on Toolbar	Tools, Spell Check
Display the Thesaurus	Tools, Thesaurus	Tools, Thesaurus
Display document information	File, Document, Properties click Information tab	File, Document, Properties choose Information tab
QuickCorrect dialog box	Tools, QuickCorrect	Tools, QuickCorrect

Using Spell Checker and Thesaurus

CHECK YOUR UNDERSTANDING

Completion: In the space provided at the right, indicate the correct term, command, or number.

1. Begin spell checking a document by clicking this button on the Standard Toolbar. _____

2. Spell Checker works mainly with two word lists—a user word list and this word list. _____

3. Click QuickCorrect from this drop-down menu to display the QuickCorrect dialog box. _____

4. If during a spelling check you temporarily leave the Spell Checker dialog box, click this button in the dialog box to continue spell checking. _____

5. These are words with opposite meanings. _____

6. These are words with similar meanings. _____

Underline the words in the paragraph below that Spell Checker *would* select for correction.

Needs assesment will be focused on determining particalar job-specific basic skills that are hindered do to lack of English skills. This will entail developement of both qualitative and quantitative instraments and methodologies. The project coordinator and instructer will analyze basic skills required inn various production area through observation of production processes and teem meetings.

Using the same paragraph above, underline twice the incorrect words that Spell Checker *would not* select.

In the space provided below, list the steps you would complete to replace the word *confident* with *assured* using the Thesaurus.

_____

_____

_____

In the space provided below, list the steps you would complete to display document information about the document named *Legal 01*.

_____

_____

_____

Chapter 8

SKILL ASSESSMENTS

Assessment 1

1. At a clear editing window, open Memo 06.
2. Save the memo with Save As and name it Ch 08, SA 01.
3. Complete a spell check on the document. You determine whether to skip words or make corrections. (Proper names are spelled correctly.)
4. After the spell check is completed, proofread the memo.
5. Save the memo with the same name (Ch 08, SA 01).
6. Print and then close Ch 08, SA 01.

Assessment 2

1. At a clear editing window, open Memo 07.
2. Save the memo with Save As and name it Ch 08, SA 02.
3. Complete a spell check on the document. You determine whether to skip words or make corrections. (Proper names are spelled correctly.)
4. After the spell check is completed, proofread the memo and make necessary changes. (There are mistakes that Spell Checker will not select.)
5. Save the memo with the same name (Ch 08, SA 02).
6. Print and then close Ch 08, SA 02.

Assessment 3

1. At a clear editing window, open Letter 02.
2. Save the letter with Save As and name it Ch 08, SA 03.
3. Change the spell check setup so that Spell Checker does not check for numbers in words or double words, then complete a spell check on the document. You determine whether to skip words or make corrections. (Proper names are spelled correctly.)
4. After the spell check is completed, proofread the letter and make necessary changes. (There are mistakes that Spell Checker will not select.)
5. Change the spell check setup so that Spell Checker does check for numbers in words and double words.
6. Save the letter again with the same name (Ch 08, SA 03).
7. Print and then close Ch 08, SA 03.

Assessment 4

1. At a clear editing window, open Para 04.
2. Save the document with Save As and name it Ch 08, SA 04.
3. Use Thesaurus to make the following changes:
    a. Change *recall* in the second paragraph to *remember*.
    b. Change *primarily* in the second paragraph to *basically*.
    c. Change *choose* in the fourth paragraph to *designate*.
    d. Change *device* in the fourth paragraph to *apparatus*.
4. Save the document again with the same name (Ch 08, SA 04).
5. Print and then close Ch 08, SA 04.

Assessment 5

1. At a clear editing window, open Letter 03.
2. Save the letter with Save As and name it Ch 08, SA 05.
3. This letter overuses the words *manage* (in various forms), *efficient* and *efficiently*. Use Thesaurus to make changes to some of the occurrences of *manage, managing,* and/or *managed* to make the letter read better. Also, use Thesaurus to make changes to one or two of the occurrences of *efficient* and/or *efficiently*.
4. Save the letter again with the same name (Ch 08, SA 05).
5. Print and then close Ch 08, SA 05.

Assessment 6

1. At a clear editing window, add the following entries to QuickCorrect:
    a. Enter *dtp* in the Replace text box and *desktop publishing* in the With text box.
    b. Enter *prouduce* in the Replace text box and *produce* in the With text box.
2. Key the text shown in figure 8.10 (Key the text exactly as shown. QuickCorrect will correct the words as you key.)
3. Save the document and name it Ch 08, SA 06.
4. Print and then close Ch 08, SA 06.
5. Delete *dtp* and *prouduce* from QuickCorrect.

Figure 8.10

In the graphic arts world, dtp is considered a prepress technology, that is, the dtp system itself is generally not used to prouduce the final multiple copies of a publication, but rather to prouduce masters for reproduction. Because it is relatively inexpensive and user-friendly, dtp has put the power of professional-quality publishing in the hands of many who are not publishing professionals. Some speak out against this trend and point to the flood of poorly designed publications produced by inexperienced publishers.

Reminder: You may want to delete outdated document files now.

INSERTING PAGE FORMATTING

PERFORMANCE OBJECTIVE

Upon successful completion of chapter 9, you will be able to adjust page breaks, turn on the Widow/Orphan feature, and number pages in a document.

WordPerfect assumes that you are using standard-sized paper, which is 8.5 inches wide and 11 inches long. By default, WordPerfect leaves a 1-inch top margin and a 1-inch bottom margin. This allows a total of 9 inches available for text to be printed on a standard page.

As you create a long document, you will notice that when the insertion point nears Line 9.83", a page break is inserted in the document. The page break is inserted at the next line (Line 10"). The line below the page break is the beginning of page 2. In the Page mode, this page break displays as a thick line that is the same color as your Windows 95 desktop color. In the Draft mode, the page break displays as a thin black line. The page break occurs at 10 inches because WordPerfect leaves the first inch of the paper blank and prints text on the next 9 inches.

While WordPerfect's default settings break each page near Line 10", there are several features that can affect the location of page breaks.

Changing Top and Bottom Margins

The top and bottom margin defaults are 1 inch. These settings are displayed at the Margins dialog box shown in figure 9.1. To display the Margins dialog box, choose one of the following methods:

- Click Format, then Margins.
- Click the Page Margins button on the Format Toolbar.
- Position the arrow pointer on the white line of the Ruler Bar, click the right mouse button, then click Margins.

Page Margins

To change the top and bottom margins, display the Margins dialog box, change to the desired measurement, then close the dialog box. When top or bottom margin settings are changed, codes are inserted in the document at the beginning of the page where the insertion point is positioned.

Inserting Page Formatting   *179*

These codes can be seen in Reveal Codes. For example, if the top and bottom margins are changed to 1.5 inches, the codes [Top Mar: 1.5"] and [Bot Mar: 1.5"] display in Reveal Codes. To see the measurement, position the insertion point immediately to the left of the code or click the code.

Figure 9.1

Margins Dialog Box

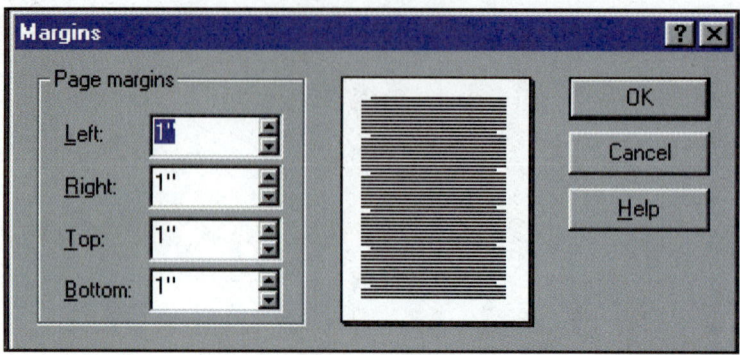

Top and bottom margin codes are inserted at the beginning of the page where the insertion point is located. For example, if the insertion point is located in the middle of page 3 when the top and bottom margins are changed, the codes are inserted at the beginning of page 3. Changes to top and bottom margins take effect from the location of the code to the end of the document or until another margin code is encountered. If you want top and bottom margins to affect the entire document, position the insertion point on page 1 before displaying the Margins dialog box.

If you change the top or bottom margins on any page except the first page, WordPerfect inserts the code at the beginning of the page where the insertion point is positioned. This code displays as a [Delay] code. Additionally, WordPerfect inserts a Delay code at the beginning of the document. For example, if you change the top and bottom margins on page 2, the code [Delay Codes: [Bot Mar][Top Mar]] displays at the beginning of page 2 and the code [Delay: 1] (this number may vary) displays at the beginning of the document. The code at the beginning of the document indicates that formatting has been added to the document that is delayed until the code is encountered. The number after Delay identifies which Delay code it relates to within the document. If you delete either of the Delay codes, the other is removed.

If you want to delete a margin code, display Reveal Codes, position the insertion point immediately to the left of the code, then press Delete. You can also drag the code out of the Reveal Codes window with the mouse. If you delete all top and bottom margin codes in a document, text will automatically readjust to the default settings of 1 inch.

EXERCISE

Changing Margins

1. At a clear editing window, open Report 01.
2. Save the report with Save As and name it Ch 09, Ex 01.
3. Make sure the insertion point is located somewhere on page 1, then change the top and bottom margins to 1.5 inches by completing the following steps:
   a. Click Format, then Margins.

> b. At the Margins dialog box, click the up-pointing triangle at the right side of the Top text box until *1.50"* displays.
> c. Click the up-pointing triangle at the right side of the Bottom text box until *1.50"* displays.
> d. Click OK or press Enter.
> 4. Save the document again with the same name (Ch 09, Ex 01).
> 5. Print and then close Ch 09, Ex 01.

Keeping Text Together on a Page

The Keep Text Together dialog box, shown in figure 9.2, contains three options you can use to keep a certain number of lines together on a page: (1) Widow/Orphan; (2) Block protect; and (3) Conditional end of page. With these features, you can control where page breaks occur in a document.

Display the Keep Text Together dialog box by clicking Format, pointing to Page, then clicking Keep Text Together. You can also display the dialog box by clicking the Keep Together button on the Page Toolbar. To display the Page Toolbar, position the arrow pointer on the current Toolbar, click the right mouse button, then click Page at the drop-down menu.

Keep Together

Turning on Widow/Orphan

In a long document, you will want to avoid creating widows or orphans. A *widow* is the last line of a paragraph that appears at the top of a page. An *orphan* is the first line of a paragraph that appears at the bottom of a page.

WordPerfect contains a feature that lets you control whether widows or orphans appear in a document. This feature, called Widow/Orphan, is off by default. At this setting, WordPerfect inserts page breaks without considering whether a widow or orphan has occurred. When working with long documents, you will usually want this feature on. WordPerfect then takes the first line of a paragraph to the next page or breaks the page a line sooner so that a minimum of two lines of a paragraph fall at the top of a page.

To turn on the Widow/Orphan feature, display the Keep Text Together dialog box, then click the check box in the Widow/Orphan section.

Figure 9.2

Keep Text Together Dialog Box

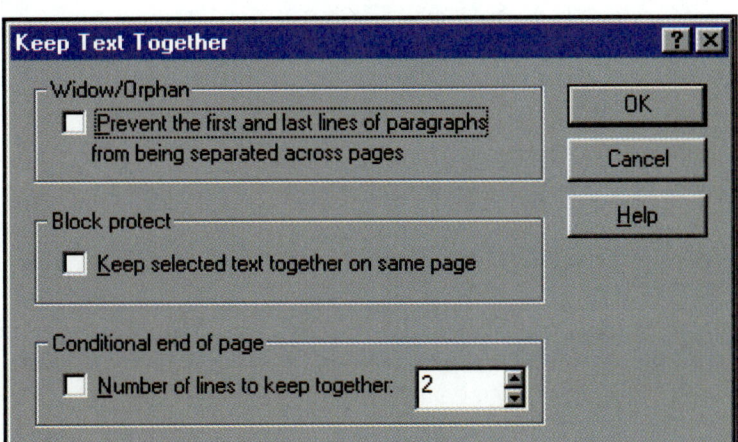

Inserting Page Formatting   **181**

When Widow/Orphan is on, WordPerfect inserts the code  at the beginning of the page where the insertion point is positioned. To turn off Widow/Orphan, complete similar steps to remove the check mark in the Widow/Orphan check box.

EXERCISE 2

Turning on the Widow/Orphan Feature

1. At a clear editing window, open Report 01.
2. Save the report with Save As and name it Ch 09, Ex 02.
3. Make sure the insertion point is located somewhere on page 1, then turn on the Widow/Orphan feature by completing the following steps:
    a. Click Format, point to Page, then click Keep Text Together (or click the Keep Together button on the Page Toolbar).
    b. At the Keep Text Together dialog box, click the check box in the Widow/Orphan section (this inserts a check mark).
    c. Click OK or press Enter.
4. Save the report again with the same name (Ch 09, Ex 02).
5. Print and then close Ch 09, Ex 02.

Protecting Selected Text

With the second option from the Keep Text Together dialog box, Block protect, you can tell WordPerfect to protect selected text from being divided by a page break. For example, you might want to keep a list of numbered items together on a page.

EXERCISE 3

Preventing Page Breaks within a Selected Block

1. At a clear editing window, open Report 01.
2. Save the report with Save As and name it Ch 09, Ex 03.
3. Make sure the insertion point is located at the beginning of the document, then change the left, right, top, and bottom margins to 1.5 inches.
4. Select the paragraph and the items preceded by bullets (•) toward the end of the first page by completing the following steps:
    a. Position the insertion point at the left margin of the line that begins *The advantages of light wave systems...*.
    b. Select the lines of text through • *relative low cost*.
    c. Click Format, point to Page, then click Keep Text Together (or click the Keep Together button on the Page Toolbar).
    d. At the Keep Text Together dialog box, click the check box in the Block protect section (this inserts a check mark).
    e. Click OK or press Enter.
    f. Turn off the select mode by pressing F8 or clicking the arrow pointer outside the selected area.
5. Save the report again with the same name (Ch 09, Ex 03).
6. Print and then close Ch 09, Ex 03.

Inserting a Conditional End of Page Code

The Conditional end of page feature is used to tell WordPerfect to keep a certain number of lines together and not to insert a page break. For example, if you create a table that is 12 lines long, you may decide that it should not be divided between two pages. To identify the table as a unit that should not be divided, you would insert a Conditional end of page code. The code is inserted in the document at the location of the insertion point. (The insertion point must be immediately to the left of the code to see the number of lines.) If a page break falls within the 12 lines, WordPerfect will break the page before the table, taking it in its entirety to the next page.

EXERCISE 4

Preventing Page Breaks within a Specific Number of Lines

1. At a clear editing window, open Report 01.
2. Save the report with Save As and name it Ch 09, Ex 04.
3. Make sure the insertion point is located at the beginning of the document, then change the left, right, top, and bottom margins to 1.5 inches.
4. Insert a Conditional end of page code for 10 lines at the beginning of the paragraph introducing the bulleted (•) items toward the end of the first page by completing the following steps:
   a. Position the insertion point at the left margin of the line that begins *The advantages of light wave systems....*
   b. Click Format, point to Page, then click Keep Text Together (or click the Keep Together button on the Page Toolbar).
   c. At the Keep Text Together dialog box, click the check box in the Conditional end of page section (this inserts a check mark and selects the number *2* in the text box).
   d. Key **10**.
   e. Click OK or press Enter.
5. Insert a Conditional end of page code for 14 lines at the left margin of the subtitle *Microcomputer Trends in the Nineties* (toward the end of the second page).
6. Save the document with the same name (Ch 09, Ex 04).
7. Print and then close Ch 09, Ex 04.

Inserting Hard Page Breaks

WordPerfect's default settings break each page after Line 9.83". If you have turned on the Widow/Orphan feature, inserted a Conditional end of page code, or changed the top or bottom margins, page breaks may vary. Even with these features, however, page breaks may occur in undesirable locations. To remedy these occurrences you can insert your own page break.

In Draft mode, the WordPerfect page break displays as a single line across the screen. The page break you insert displays as a double line across the screen. The default page break is called a *soft page break* and a page break you insert is called a *hard page break*. Soft page breaks automatically adjust if text is added to or deleted from a document. A hard page break does not adjust. If text is added to or deleted from a document with a hard page break, check the break to determine whether it is still in a desirable location.

To insert a page break, move the insertion point to the position where you want the page to break, click Insert, then Page Break; or press Ctrl + Enter. Always check page breaks in a document; some require a judgment call that only you can make.

EXERCISE 5

Inserting Page Breaks

1. At a clear editing window, open Report 01.
2. Save the report with Save As and name it Ch 09, Ex 05.
3. Insert a hard page break at the line beginning *The speed at which information...* by completing the following steps:
   a. Position the insertion point at the left margin of the line beginning *The speed at which information...* (toward the end of the first page).
   b. Click Insert, then Page Break; or press Ctrl + Enter.
4. Insert a hard page break at the left margin of the line beginning *Computing and telecommunications...* (toward the end of the second page).
5. Save the report with the same name (Ch 09, Ex 05).
6. Print and then close Ch 09, Ex 05.

Centering Text Vertically on the Page

With WordPerfect's centering pages options, you can center text vertically on the current page and/or current and subsequent pages. You may, for example, want to center vertically the title page of a report, a short letter or memo, a table, or an illustration.

With options from the Center Page(s) dialog box, shown in figure 9.3, you can center text vertically only on the page where the insertion point is positioned or center text on current and subsequent pages.

Figure 9.3

Center Page(s) Dialog Box

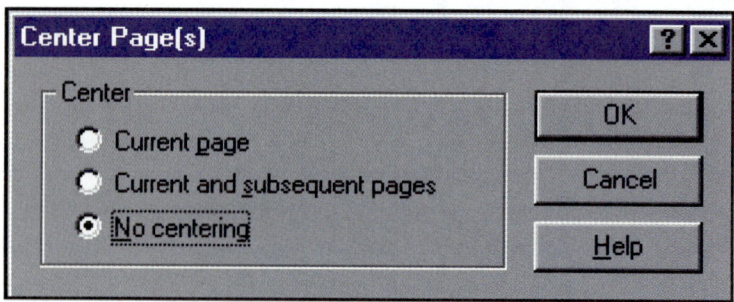

EXERCISE 6

Centering Text Vertically

1. At a clear editing window, key the text shown in figure 9.4. Center and bold the text as indicated. Press the Enter key the number of times indicated in the brackets. (Do not key the information in brackets.)
2. Center the text vertically on the page by completing the following steps:
   a. With the insertion point positioned anywhere in the page, click Format, point to Page, then click Center (or click the Center Page button on the Page Toolbar).
   b. At the Center Page(s) dialog box, click Current page.
   c. Click OK or press Enter.
3. Save the document and name it Ch 09, Ex 06.
4. Print and then close Ch 09, Ex 06.

Center Page

Figure 9.4

HISTORY OF TELECOMMUNICATIONS
[press Enter 15 times]
by Ramona Salas
[press Enter 15 times]
CIS 120
January 15, 1998

Inserting Page Numbering

WordPerfect, by default, does not print page numbers on a page. For documents such as one-page memos and letters, this is appropriate. For longer documents, however, page numbers may be needed. WordPerfect includes several options for numbering pages in documents. Page numbers can appear in a variety of locations on the page and can be turned on and off in the same document. In addition, WordPerfect includes an option that lets you force an even or odd number on a page.

Numbering Pages in a Document

When page numbering is turned on in a document, WordPerfect inserts a page numbering code at the beginning of the page where the insertion point is located. If you want page numbering to appear on all pages of the document, position the insertion point somewhere on page 1. Turn on page numbering by clicking Format, pointing to Page Numbering, then clicking Select. This displays the Select Page Numbering Format dialog box shown in figure 9.5. You can also display this dialog box by clicking the Page Numbering button on the Page Toolbar.

Page Numbering

Figure 9.5   Select Page Numbering Format Dialog Box

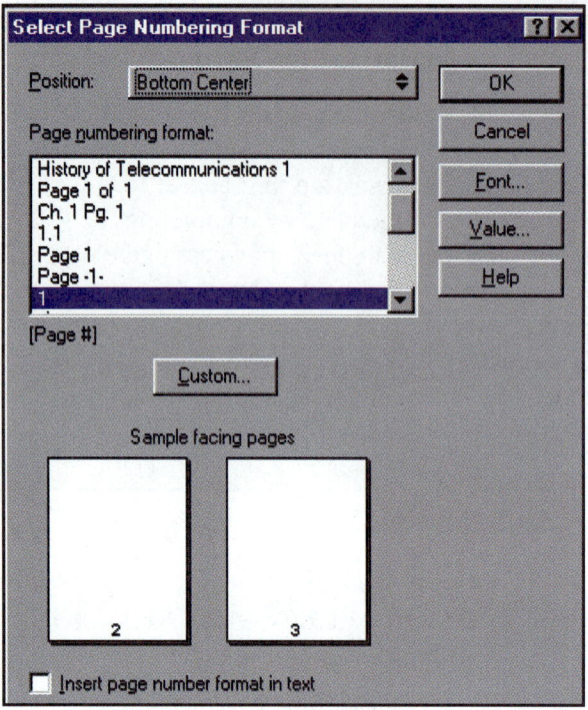

When page numbering is included in a document, a code is inserted in the document that can be seen in Reveal Codes. For example, if page numbering is turned on and numbers are to print at the bottom center of the page, the code `Pg Num Pos: Bottom Center` displays in Reveal Codes. For the page numbering position to appear, the insertion point must be positioned immediately to the left of the code.

When a document includes page numbering, WordPerfect subtracts two lines from the total number of lines printed on a page. One line is subtracted for the page number and the other to separate the page number from text. Page numbers appear on the screen in Page and Two-Page view, but not Draft view.

EXERCISE 7

Numbering Pages at the Bottom Center

1. At a clear editing window, open Report 01.
2. Save the report with Save As and name it Ch 09, Ex 07.
3. With the insertion point positioned anywhere in the first page, turn on the Widow/Orphan feature.
4. With the insertion point positioned anywhere in the first page, turn page numbering on and number pages at the bottom center of the page by completing the following steps:
   a. Click Format, point to Page Numbering, then click Select (or click the Page Numbering button on the Page Toolbar).
   b. At the Select Page Numbering Format dialog box, click OK. (The Position default is already set to Bottom Center.)
5. Save the report again with the same name (Ch 09, Ex 07).
6. Print and then close Ch 09, Ex 07.

Selective Page Numbering

Page numbering can be turned off in a document where page numbering exists. To do this, position the insertion point on the page where page numbering is to be turned off and click No Page Numbering at the Select Page Numbering Format dialog box. Page numbering will remain off from the page where the insertion point is located to the end of the document or until a page numbering code is encountered.

EXERCISE 8

Numbering Specific Pages

1. At a clear editing window, open Report 02.
2. Save the report with Save As and name it Ch 09, Ex 08.
3. With the insertion point positioned at the beginning of the document, make the following changes to the document:
   a. Change the left and right margins to 1.5 inches.
   b. Turn on the Widow/Orphan feature.
   c. Number pages at the bottom right of each page by completing the following steps:
      (1) Click Format, point to Page Numbering, then click Select (or click the Page Numbering button on the Page Toolbar).
      (2) At the Select Page Numbering Format dialog box, click the list box to the right of the Position option.
      (3) Click Bottom Right at the drop-down menu.
   d. Turn page numbering off from page 3 to the end of the document by completing the following steps:
      (1) Position the insertion point anywhere in page 3.
      (2) Click Format, point to Page Numbering, then click Select (or click the Page Numbering button on the Page Toolbar).
      (3) At the Page Numbering dialog box, click the list box to the right of the Position option.
      (4) Click No Page Numbering at the drop-down menu.
      (5) Click OK or press Enter.
4. Save the report again with the same name (Ch 09, Ex 08).
5. Print and then close Ch 09, Ex 08.

Suppressing Page Numbering

WordPerfect includes a feature that lets you suppress page numbering on specific pages. This is different from turning page numbering off. When you turn page numbering off in a document, it stays off until the document ends or until numbering is turned back on. With the Suppress dialog box, the page number is turned off for that specific page and turned back on again for the other pages. To suppress a page number on a specific page, click Format, point to Page, then click Suppress. This displays the Suppress dialog box shown in figure 9.6. You can also display the Suppress dialog box by clicking the Suppress button on the Page Toolbar. To suppress page numbering, click Page numbering at the Suppress dialog box, then click OK or press Enter.

Suppress

Inserting Page Formatting

Figure 9.6 Suppress Dialog Box

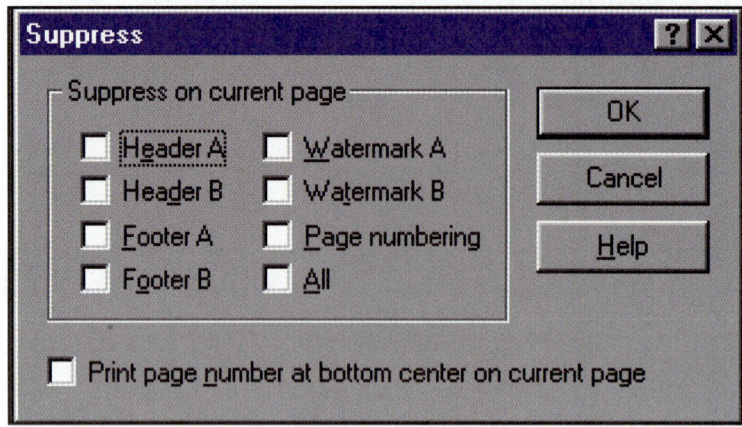

The Print page number at bottom center on current page option from the Suppress dialog box can be used to print the page number at the bottom center of the first page of a title page or report. The remaining page numbers will appear in the location identified at the Select Page Numbering Format dialog box.

EXERCISE 9

Suppressing Page Numbering

1. At a clear editing window, open Report 02.
2. Save the report with Save As and name it Ch 09, Ex 09.
3. Make the following changes to the document:
   a. Change the top margin to 1.5 inches.
   b. Turn on the Widow/Orphan feature.
   c. With the insertion point positioned somewhere on page 1, turn page numbering on and number pages in the top right corner of the page.
   d. Suppress page numbering on page 3 by completing the following steps:
      (1) Position the insertion point anywhere in page 3.
      (2) Click Format, point to Page, then click Suppress (or click the Suppress button on the Page Toolbar).
      (3) At the Suppress dialog box, click Page numbering.
      (4) Click OK or press Enter.
4. Save the report again with the same name (Ch 09, Ex 09).
5. Print and then close Ch 09, Ex 09.

Changing the Page Number

When page numbering is turned on, pages are numbered beginning with 1 and incremented. You can change the beginning page number or change the method for numbering pages by clicking the Value button at the Select Page Numbering Format dialog box. This displays the Values dialog box shown in figure 9.7. At the Values dialog box, key the new page number in the Set page number text box.

Figure 9.7

Values Dialog Box

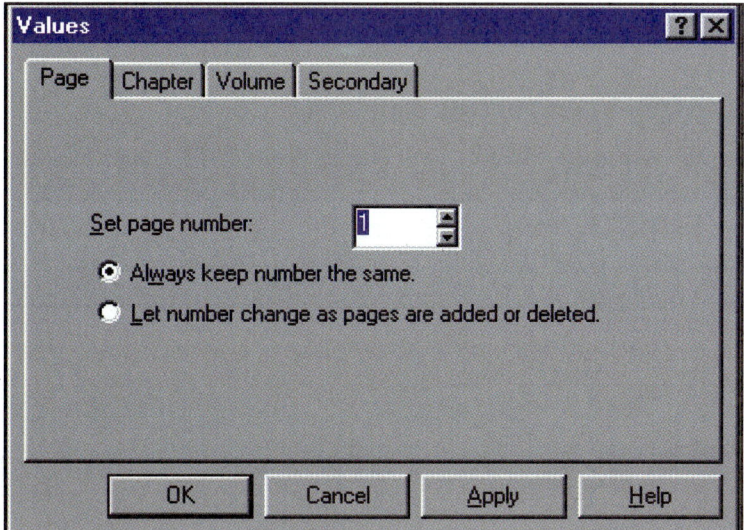

When you change the default page number, a code is inserted in the document that can be seen in Reveal Codes. For example, if you change the page number on page 5 to page 8, the code would display in Reveal Codes at the beginning of page 5 (now page 8).

EXERCISE 10

Changing the Default Page Number

1. At a clear editing window, open Report 02.
2. Save the report with Save As and name it Ch 09, Ex 10.
3. With the insertion point positioned at the beginning of the document, make the following changes to the document:
   a. Change the left and right margins to 1.5 inches.
   b. Turn on the Widow/Orphan feature.
   c. Turn on page numbering and number pages at the bottom outside of the page, alternating.
   d. Change the beginning page number to 9 by completing the following steps:
      (1) Display the Select Page Numbering Format dialog box.
      (2) At the Select Page Numbering Format dialog box, click the Value button.
      (3) At the Values dialog box key **9**. (The Set page number option is already selected.)
      (4) Click OK to close the Values dialog box.
      (5) At the Select Page Numbering Format dialog box, click OK to close the dialog box.
4. Save the report with the same name (Ch 09, Ex 10).
5. Print and then close Ch 09, Ex 10.

Inserting Page Formatting *189*

The Values dialog box can be accessed more directly by clicking Format, pointing to Page Numbering, then clicking Value/Adjust. To change the starting page number, select Set page number by clicking the up- or down-pointing triangle next to the number displayed in the text box to increase or decrease the number, then click OK.

Changing the Page Numbering Method

When page numbering is turned on in a document, WordPerfect uses Arabic numbers (1, 2, 3, etc.). With the Custom button from the Select Page Numbering Format dialog box, you can change this numbering method to lowercase letters (a, b, c, etc.), uppercase letters (A, B, C, etc.), lowercase Roman numerals (i, ii, iii, etc.), or uppercase Roman numerals (I, II, III, etc.). These choices are offered at the Custom Page Numbering dialog box shown in figure 9.8.

Figure 9.8

Custom Page Numbering Dialog Box

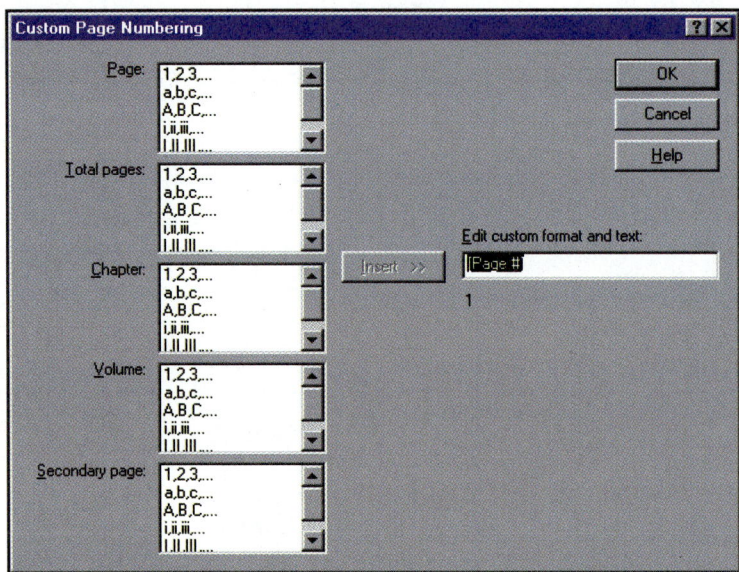

When the numbering method is changed, a code is inserted at the beginning of the page where the insertion point is located. If you changed the numbering method to lowercase Roman numerals, the code `Pg Num Meth: Lev 1;3` would display in Reveal Codes.

EXERCISE 11

Numbering Pages with Roman Numerals

1. At a clear editing window, open Report 02.
2. Save the report with Save As and name it Ch 09, Ex 11.
3. With the insertion point positioned at the beginning of the document, make the following changes to the report:
    a. Change the left and right margins to 1.5 inches.
    b. Turn on the Widow/Orphan feature.
    c. With the insertion point positioned anywhere on page 1, turn on page numbering and number pages at the bottom center.

d. Change the page numbering method to lowercase Roman numerals by completing the following steps:
      (1) Display the Select Page Numbering Format dialog box.
      (2) At the Select Page Numbering Format dialog box, click the Custom button.
      (3) At the Custom Page Numbering dialog box, click the lowercase Roman numerals option (*i,ii,iii,...*) that displays in the Page list box.
      (4) Click the Insert button.
      (5) Click OK to close the Custom Page Numbering dialog box.
      (6) At the Select Page Numbering Format dialog box, click OK.
4. Save the report with the same name (Ch 09, Ex 11).
5. Print and then close Ch 09, Ex 11.

Adding Accompanying Text

With the Custom option from the Select Page Numbering Format dialog box, text can be included with the page number. For example, the word *Page* can be included before the page number, such as *Page 3*. Or, a section heading can be included with the page number, such as *Outcomes Assessment - 5*. Just key the text you want in the Insert text box. If you want accompanying text to appear before the page number, press the left arrow key, then key the accompanying text. If you want the accompanying text to follow the page number, press the right arrow key, then key the accompanying text.

Including Text with Page Numbers

1. At a clear editing window, open Report 02.
2. Save the report with Save As and name it Ch 09, Ex 12.
3. Turn page numbering on and insert the number at the bottom right of the page with the accompanying text, *History of Telecommunications*, by completing the following steps:
   a. With the insertion point positioned anywhere on page 1, click Format, point to Page Numbering, then click Select.
   b. At the Select Page Numbering Format dialog box, click Position, then Bottom Right.
   c. Click Custom.
   d. At the Custom Page Numbering dialog box, press the left arrow key once (the insertion point is automatically positioned in the Insert text box), key **History of Telecommunications**, then press the space bar once.
   e. Click OK to close the Custom Page Numbering dialog box.
   f. At the Select Page Numbering Format dialog box, click OK.
4. Save the report again with the same name (Ch 09, Ex 12).
5. Print and then close Ch 09, Ex 12.

Inserting Page Formatting

Adding Additional Page Numbering

Four different page numbering options are available in WordPerfect. You can number pages as described earlier and you can also number another set of pages called *secondary numbers*. In addition, chapter and volume numbering are also available.

Secondary page numbering lets you add a second page numbering level. Periodicals or journals sometimes number every page consecutively for the year while also numbering each page within an issue. For this situation, you can use the regular numbering method for the consecutive numbering for the year and the secondary method for the numbering within the individual issue. Secondary page numbers operate exactly like page numbers. Page numbers and secondary page numbers increment automatically.

With chapter and volume numbering, you can include chapter or volume numbers in a document. For example, if a document contains three chapters, you can have the page numbering list the chapter number as well as the page number. Chapter and volume numbers do not increment automatically like page numbers and secondary page numbers. You must increment them manually. As an example of how to use these features, complete exercise 13.

EXERCISE

Using Different Levels of Page Numbering

1. At a clear editing window, open Report 03.
2. Save the report with Save As and name it Ch 09, Ex 13.
3. Insert a hard page break at the heading *CHAPTER 2: DEVELOPMENT OF TECHNOLOGY, 1850 - 1900*.
4. Turn page numbering on and insert the number at the bottom left of the page and add chapter numbering with the accompanying text, **Chapter** *x*, **Page** *y* (where *x* represents the chapter number and *y* represents the page number) by completing the following steps:
   a. Position the insertion point anywhere on page 1.
   b. Click Fo_r_mat, point to Page _N_umbering, then click _S_elect (or click the Page Numbering button on the Page Toolbar).
   c. At the Select Page Numbering Format dialog box, click _P_osition, then click _B_ottom Left.
   d. Click _C_ustom.
   e. At the Custom Page Numbering dialog box, complete the following steps:
      (1) Press the left arrow key once to move the insertion point to the left of the *[Page #]* code in the _I_nsert text box.
      (2) Key **Chapter** and then press the space bar.
      (3) Insert the chapter page numbering code. To do this, position the arrow pointer on the arabic numbers 1,2,3,... in the _C_hapter text box and click the left mouse button, then click the _I_nsert button.
      (4) After inserting the *[Chpt #]* code, complete the following steps:
         (a) Position the I-beam pointer between the *[Chpt #]* code and the *[Page #]* code and click the left mouse button.
         (b) Key a comma, then press the space bar.
         (c) Key **Page**.
         (d) Press the space bar.

>   (5) Click OK to close the Custom Page Numbering dialog box.
>   f. At the Select Page Numbering Format dialog box, click OK.
> 5. Change the number to *Chapter 2* in the document at page 3 by completing the following steps:
>   a. Position the insertion point anywhere on page 3. (This is the page where Chapter 2 begins.)
>   b. Click Format, point to Page Numbering, then click Select (or click the Page Numbering button on the Page Toolbar).
>   c. At the Select Page Numbering Format dialog box, click Value.
>   d. At the Values dialog box, click the Chapter tab.
>   e. Click the up-pointing triangle next to the Set chapter number text box once to change the number to **2**.
>   f. Click OK to close the Values dialog box.
>   g. At the Select Page Numbering Format dialog box, click OK.
> 6. Save the report again with the same name (Ch 09, Ex 13).
> 7. Print and then close Ch 09, Ex 13.

You would follow similar steps to add Supplemental page numbering or Volume page numbering to a document.

Page x of y Numbering

The Select Page Numbering Format dialog box has an option that will print the current page number along with the total numbers of pages in the document. For example page 3 of a document containing 10 pages would print *Page 3 of 10* at the page number position. To use this feature, complete exercise 14.

EXERCISE 14

> ### Page x of y Numbering
>
> 1. At a clear editing window, open Report 02.
> 2. Save the report with Save As and name it Ch 09, Ex 14.
> 3. With the insertion point positioned anywhere on page 1, make the following changes:
>   a. Change the top margin to 1.5 inches.
>   b. Turn on the Widow/Orphan feature.
>   c. Turn on page numbering so numbers print at the top right of each page.
>   d. Change the page numbering format by completing the following steps:
>   (1) Click Format, point to Page Numbering, then click Select (or click the Page Numbering button on the Page Toolbar).
>   (2) At the Select Page Numbering Format dialog box, change Page numbering format to *Page 1 of 3*. To do this, position the arrow pointer on the *Page 1 of 3* option in the Page numbering format list box and then click the left mouse button.
>   (3) Click OK or press Enter to close the dialog box.
> 4. Save the report again with the same name (Ch 09, Ex 14).
> 5. Print and then close Ch 09, Ex 14.

Inserting Page Number in Document

The Page Numbering menu has an Insert In Text option that will display the Insert Number in Text dialog box. Use this option to insert the current page number directly into the document at the insertion point.

Forcing Odd or Even Page Numbering

With the Force Page dialog box, shown in figure 9.9, you can force an even page number on a page that would otherwise be an odd number, or force an odd number on a page that would be even. If you force an even number on a page that would otherwise be odd, WordPerfect prints the even page number on the page with no other text. The text on the page is moved to the next page, which is odd. This might be useful in a situation where you want a page that is blank except for the page number where you can insert a diagram, photo, illustration, or other visual aid. This feature can also be useful in a document containing chapters, which should always begin with an odd number.

Figure 9.9

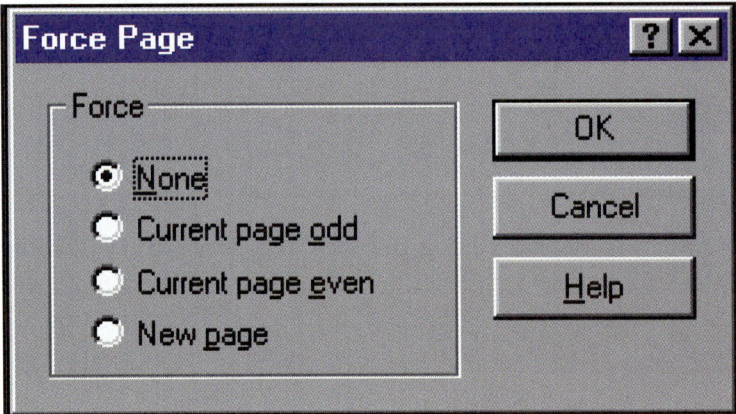

Force Page Dialog Box

EXERCISE 15

Forcing an Even Page Number

1. At a clear editing window, open Report 02.
2. Save the report with Save As and name it Ch 09, Ex 15.
3. With the insertion point positioned anywhere on page 1, make the following changes:
   a. Change the top margin to 1.5 inches.
   b. Turn on the Widow/Orphan feature.
   c. Change justification to full.
   d. Turn on page numbering and number pages at the top outside, alternating.
4. Force an even number on page 3 by completing the following steps:
   a. Position the insertion point at the beginning of page 3 and press the Enter key to insert a hard return code.
   b. Click Format, point to Page, then click Force Page (or click the Force Page button on the Page Toolbar).
   c. At the Force Page dialog box, click Current page even.
   d. Click OK or press Enter.
5. Save the report again with the same name (Ch 09, Ex 15).
6. Print and then close Ch 09, Ex 15. (Page 3 will be blank.)

Force Page

CHAPTER SUMMARY

- WordPerfect inserts a page break at approximately 10 inches from the top of the page. With the default 1-inch top and bottom margins, this allows a total of 9 inches of text to be printed on a standard page.

- The default 1-inch top and bottom margins can be changed at the Margins dialog box. No matter where the insertion point is positioned when the margins are changed, the top and bottom margin will appear in Reveal Codes at the top of that page. These codes will affect the remainder of the document unless a new code is inserted.

- In addition to the margin codes at the top of the page where the insertion point was located when margins were changed, a Delay code will appear at the beginning of the document as [Delay Codes: [Bot Mar][Top Mar]].

- The Keep Text Together dialog box contains three options you can use to keep a certain number of lines together on one page: Widow/Orphan, Block protect, and Conditional end of page.

- If an automatic page break (soft page break) occurs in an undesirable location, you can insert a page break. A page break you insert in a document is called a hard page break and appears in Draft mode as a double line across the screen.

- To center text vertically on one page or on all pages in a document, use the options at the Center Page(s) dialog box. The text will look centered in the Page and Two-Page viewing modes, but not the Draft mode.

- WordPerfect includes several options at the Select Page Numbering Format dialog box. The page numbers in a document can be placed in different locations on the page, turned on and off, or suppressed temporarily.

- These additional options are also available at the Select Page Numbering Format dialog box: changing the page number, changing from Arabic to Roman numerals, adding text to the page number, adding a secondary page number, numbering chapter and volume, and inserting a page number along with the total number of pages in the document.

COMMANDS REVIEW

	Mouse	**Keyboard**
Margins dialog box	Format, Margins; or click Page Margins button on Format Toolbar	Format, Margins
Keep Text Together dialog box	Format, Page, Keep Text Together; or click Keep Together button on Page Toolbar	Format, Page, Keep Text Together
Hard page break	Insert, Page Break	CTRL + ENTER
Center Page(s) dialog box	Format, Page, Center; or click Center Page button on Page Toolbar	Format, Page, Center
Select Page Numbering Format dialog box	Format, Page Numbering, Select; or click Page Numbering button on Page Toolbar	Format, Page Numbering, Select
Suppress dialog box	Format, Page, Suppress; or click Suppress button on Page Toolbar	Format, Page, Suppress

CHECK YOUR UNDERSTANDING

Matching: In the space provided at the left, indicate the correct letter that matches each description.

- (A) 1 inch
- (B) 8.5 inches
- (C) 9 inches
- (D) 11.5 inches
- (E) 7.5 inches
- (F) 10 inches
- (G) 11 inches
- (H) 9.5 inches
- (I) Block protect feature
- (J) Center Page(s) dialog box
- (K) Conditional end of page feature
- (L) Ctrl + Enter
- (M) Margins button
- (N) Orphan
- (O) Page Margins button
- (P) Shift + Enter
- (Q) Vertically Center Pages dialog box
- (R) Widow

_____ 1. Length of a standard piece of paper.
_____ 2. Width of a standard piece of paper.
_____ 3. Default top and bottom margins.
_____ 4. Total inches of printed vertical text on a page.
_____ 5. Click this button on the Format Toolbar to display the Margins dialog box.
_____ 6. Approximate measurement at which the automatic page break occurs on a page.
_____ 7. Press these keys on the keyboard to insert a hard page break in a document.
_____ 8. This is the term for the last line of a paragraph that appears at the top of a page.
_____ 9. This feature is used to tell WordPerfect to keep a certain number of lines together and not to insert a page break.
_____ 10. Center text vertically on a page with options at this dialog box.

SKILL ASSESSMENTS

Assessment 1

1. At a clear editing window, open Report 04.
2. Save the report with Save As and name it Ch 09, SA 01.
3. With the insertion point positioned at the beginning of the document, make the following changes:
   a. Change the top, left and right margins to 1.5 inches.
   b. Turn on the Widow/Orphan feature.
   c. Number pages at the bottom center of each page.
4. Insert a hard page break at the line that contains the heading *CHAPTER 4: DEVELOPMENT OF TECHNOLOGY, 1950 - 1960*.
5. Select the heading *World War II* (toward the end of the first page) and three lines of text below the heading and identify the lines as a block to be protected.
6. Save the report again with the same name (Ch 09, SA 01).
7. Print and then close Ch 09, SA 01.

Assessment 2

1. At a clear editing window, change the font to 14-point Arial Bold, then key the notice shown in figure 9.10 centered and bolded.
2. Center the notice vertically on the page.
3. Save the document and name it Ch 09, SA 02.
4. Print and then close Ch 09, SA 02.

Figure 9.10

DRYER ELEMENTARY SCHOOL

Winter Program

Performing Arts Center

Tuesday, December 8, 1998

7:30 p.m.

Assessment 3

1. At a clear editing window, open Report 04.
2. Save the report with Save As and name it Ch 09, SA 03.
3. With the insertion point positioned at the beginning of the document, make the following changes:
   a. Change the left margin to 1.5 inches.
   b. Turn on the Widow/Orphan feature.
   c. Insert a page break at the heading *CHAPTER 4: DEVELOPMENT OF TECHNOLOGY, 1950 - 1960*.
   d. Number pages at the bottom right corner of each page. Add chapter numbering with the accompanying text, **Chapter** *x*, **Page** *y* (where *x* represents the chapter number and *y* represents the page number). Change the number to *Chapter 3* in the document at page 1 and change the number to *Chapter 4* at page 3.
4. Check page breaks and, if necessary, insert your own.
5. Save the report again with the same name (Ch 09, SA 03).
6. Print and then close Ch 09, SA 03.

Reminder: You may want to delete outdated document files now.

10

MANIPULATING TABS

PERFORMANCE OBJECTIVE

Upon successful completion of chapter 10, you will be able to enhance business memos and letters and generate two- and three-column tables with tab settings including left, right, center, and decimal.

When you work with a document, WordPerfect offers a variety of default settings such as margins and line spacing. One WordPerfect default setting is tab settings every one-half inch. In some situations, these default tab settings are appropriate; in others, you may want to create your own tab settings. There are two methods for clearing and setting tabs. Tabs can be cleared and set at the Ruler Bar or at the Tab Set dialog box.

Manipulating Tabs with the Ruler Bar

The Ruler Bar can be used, together with the mouse, to clear, set, and move tabs. If the Ruler Bar is not displayed as shown in figure 10.1, click View, then Toolbars/Ruler. At the Toolbars dialog box, click the check box to the left of Ruler Bar, then click OK. You can also display the Ruler Bar by pressing Alt + Shift + F3.

Ruler Bar

Figure 10.1

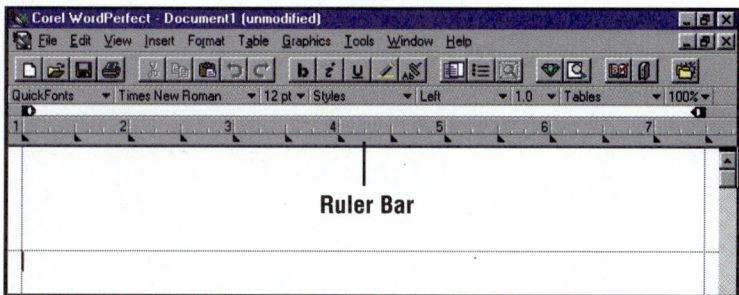

Manipulating Tabs *199*

The Ruler Bar, by default, contains left tabs every 0.5 inches. This is indicated by the left triangles below the numbers. At this setting, text aligns at the left edge of the tab setting. The other types of tabs that can be set are Center, Right, and Decimal. The columns displayed in figure 10.2 show text aligned at different tabs. Text in the first column was keyed at a left tab. The second column was keyed at a center tab, the third column at a right tab, and the fourth column at a decimal tab.

Figure 10.2

Types of Tabs

Ashe	Maine	Augusta	5.313
Ferdinand	New Hampshire	Concord	134.7
Kalinsky	Vermont	Montpelier	1,772.875

To display the types of tabs available, position the arrow pointer on any tab icon on the Ruler Bar, then click the *right* mouse button. This causes a drop-down menu to display as shown in figure 10.3.

Figure 10.3

Tab Drop-Down Menu

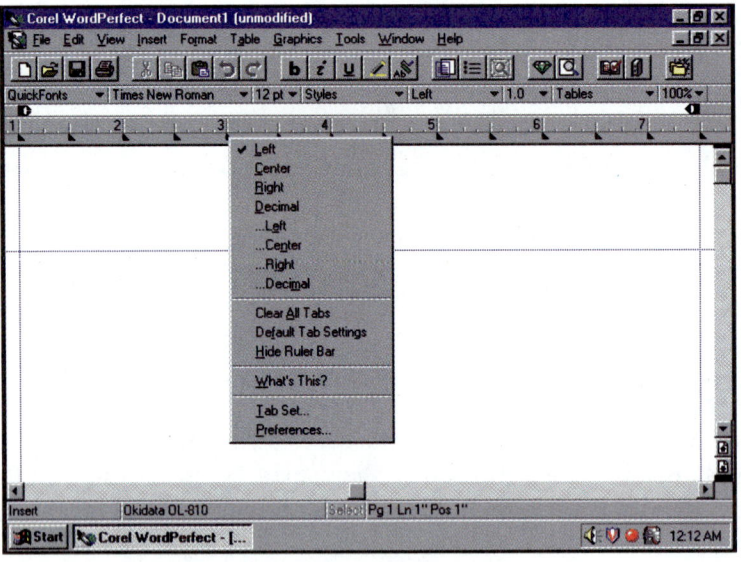

The four types of tabs can also be set with dot leaders. Leaders are useful in a table of contents or other material where you want to direct the reader's eyes across the page. Figure 10.4 shows an example of leaders. The text in the first column was keyed at a left tab. The text in the second column was keyed at a right tab with dot leaders.

200 Chapter 10

Figure 10.4

Leader Tabs

> British Columbia . . . . Victoria
> Alberta . . . . Edmonton
> Saskatchewan . . . . Regina
> Manitoba . . . . Winnipeg
> Ontario . . . . Toronto
> Quebec . . . . Montreal

Clearing Tabs

Before setting tabs, you will more than likely want to clear the default tabs. You can clear an individual tab, all tabs, or selected tabs. To clear one tab from the Ruler Bar, position the tip of the arrow pointer on the tab icon to be cleared, then hold down the left mouse button. (If the arrow pointer is in the proper position, a vertical dashed line will appear on the screen. This vertical dashed line is called the *ruler guide*.) Drag the tab icon down into the editing window, then release the mouse button.

To clear all tabs from the Ruler Bar, position the tip of the arrow pointer on a tab icon on the Ruler Bar, hold down the *right* mouse button, drag the arrow pointer to Clear All Tabs, then release the mouse button.

In addition to clearing one tab or all tabs, you can also clear selected tabs. To clear more than one (but not all) tabs, you must select the tab icons on the Ruler Bar. To do this, position the tip of the arrow pointer on the Ruler Bar in the gray area below the numbers and to the left of the first tab to be included. Hold down the Shift key on the keyboard, then hold down the left mouse button. Drag the arrow pointer to the right until all tabs to be cleared are selected, then release the mouse button and then the Shift key. (The selected area on the Ruler Bar will display with a white background rather than gray.) After the tabs are selected, the arrow pointer displays as a warning symbol ⊘ unless it is positioned in the selected area. This symbol indicates that you cannot complete another function with the mouse until you complete the tab function. Move the warning symbol back into the selected area (displays as an arrow pointer). Hold down the left mouse button, drag the arrow pointer into the editing window, then release the mouse button.

Setting Tabs

To set a left tab on the Ruler Bar, position the arrow pointer at the position on the Ruler Bar where you want the tab set, then click the left mouse button. To set a tab other than a left tab, you must change the type of tab. To do this, position the tip of the arrow pointer on a tab icon, then click the *right* mouse button. At the drop-down menu that displays, move the arrow pointer to the desired tab type, then click the left mouse button. After changing the tab type, set the tab on the Ruler Bar in the normal manner. If you change the type of tab at the Tab drop-down menu, the type stays changed until you change it again or until you exit WordPerfect.

EXERCISE

Setting Tabs on the Ruler Bar

1. At a clear editing window, create the directory shown in figure 10.5 by completing the following steps:
   a. Key the heading, **FINANCE DEPARTMENT**, centered and bolded.
   b. Press Enter two times.
   c. Set left tabs at the 2.5-inch mark on the Ruler Bar and the 4.75-inch mark by completing the following steps:
      (1) If the Ruler Bar is not displayed, click View, then Toolbars/Ruler. At the Toolbars dialog box, click the left mouse button in the check box next to Ruler Bar. Click OK to return to the document.
      (2) Position the arrow pointer on a tab icon on the Ruler Bar, click the *right* mouse button, move the arrow pointer to Clear All Tabs, then click the left mouse button. (This clears all tab icons from the Ruler Bar.)
      (3) Position the arrow pointer just below the 2.5-inch mark on the Ruler Bar, then click the left mouse button.
      (4) Position the arrow pointer just below the 4.75-inch mark on the Ruler Bar, then click the left mouse button.
   d. Key the text in columns as shown in figure 10.5. Press the Tab key before keying each column entry. (Make sure you press Tab before keying the text in the first and second columns.)
2. Save the document and name it Ch 10, Ex 01.
3. Print and then close Ch 10, Ex 01.

Figure 10.5

FINANCE DEPARTMENT

Patient Accounts	Julius Ramo
Admitting	Simone Watanabe
Medical Records	Marina Pasquale
Payroll	James Fairbanks

EXERCISE

Setting Tabs with Dot Leaders on the Ruler Bar

1. At a clear editing window, key the document shown in figure 10.6 by completing the following steps:
   a. Key the heading, **NURSING DEPARTMENT**, centered and bolded.
   b. Press Enter three times.

c. Change the line spacing to double (2).
   d. Set a left tab at the 2.5-inch mark on the Ruler Bar and a decimal tab with dot leaders at the 6-inch mark by completing the following steps:
      (1) If necessary, turn on the display of the Ruler Bar.
      (2) Position the tip of the arrow pointer on a tab icon, click the *right* mouse button, move the arrow pointer to Clear All Tabs, then click the left mouse button.
      (3) Position the arrow pointer just below the 2.5-inch mark on the Ruler Bar, then click the left mouse button.
      (4) Position the tip of the arrow pointer on the tab icon on the Ruler Bar, click the *right* mouse button, move the arrow pointer to ...*Right* in the drop-down menu, then click the left mouse button.
      (5) Position the arrow pointer just below the 6-inch mark on the Ruler Bar, then click the left mouse button.
   e. Key the text in columns as shown in figure 10.6. Press the Tab key before keying each column entry. (Make sure you press Tab before keying the text in the first and second columns.)
2. Save the document and name it Ch 10, Ex 02.
3. Print and then close Ch 10, Ex 02.

Figure 10.6

NURSING DEPARTMENT

Intensive Care Unit . . . . Terrie Mamaud

Emergency Room . . . . Kimberly Goetz

Labor and Delivery . . . . Ola Busching

Coronary Care Unit . . . . Thomas Heusers

Surgical Unit . . . . Bernice Light

Medical Services . . . . Bethany Mortensen

Pediatrics . . . . Tina Vitali

Moving Tabs

After a tab has been set on the Ruler Bar, it can be moved to a new location. To move a single tab, position the tip of the arrow pointer on the tab icon to be moved, hold down the left mouse button, drag the icon to the new location on the Ruler Bar, then release the mouse button. To move several tabs at once, select the tabs first, then move them in the same manner as a single tab.

Selected tabs can be moved on the Ruler Bar or copied to a new location. When tabs are moved to a new location, they no longer display in their original location. When tabs are copied, however, the tabs stay in their original location as copies are moved to the new location. To copy selected tabs to a new location on the Ruler Bar, select the tabs to be copied. Move the arrow pointer back into the selected area (turns into an arrow pointer), hold down the Ctrl key and then the left mouse button, drag the arrow pointer to the new location, then release the mouse button and then the Ctrl key.

EXERCISE 3

Moving Tabs to Create More Space between Columns

1. At a clear editing window, open Ch 10, Ex 02.
2. Save the document with Save As and name it Ch 10, Ex 03.
3. Move the tab settings so there is more space between the columns by completing the following steps:
   a. Move the insertion point to the line containing *Intensive Care Unit*.
   b. Position the insertion point on the left tab icon at the 2.5-inch mark, hold down the left mouse button, move the arrow pointer to the left until it is located below the 2-inch mark, then release the mouse button.
   c. Position the arrow pointer on the right tab icon with dot leaders at the 6-inch mark, hold down the left mouse button, drag the arrow pointer to the right until it is located below the 6.5-inch mark, then release the mouse button.
4. Center the document vertically on the page. (Use the Current page option from the Center Page(s) dialog box.)
5. Save the document again with the same name (Ch 10, Ex 03).
6. Print and then close Ch 10, Ex 03.

Using the Tab Bar

When you create custom tab settings in a document, an arrow pointing to a page icon appears in the far left margin as shown in figure 10.7. If you click this icon, a Tab Bar appears in the document right above the insertion point as shown in figure 10.8. The Tab Bar can be used to move, clear, set, and change tab types in the same manner as you would if you were using the Ruler Bar. You may prefer to use the Tab Bar because it is placed directly above the text affected.

Tab Bar Icon

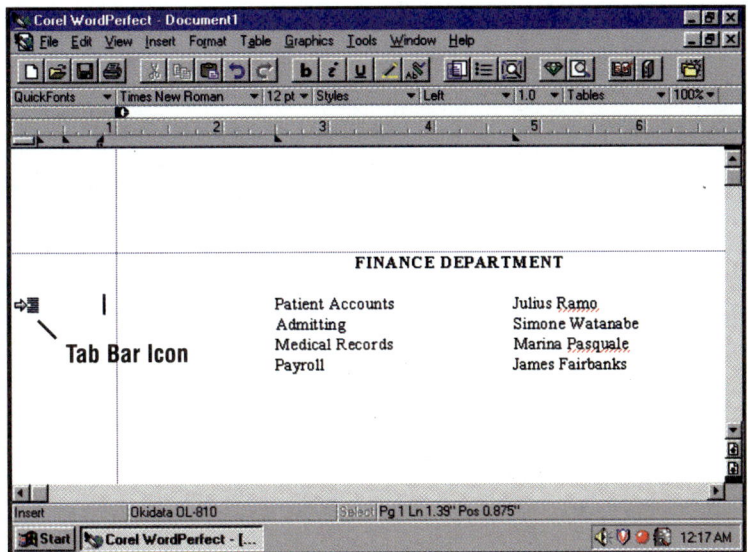

Figure 10.7

Tab Bar

Figure 10.8

EXERCISE 4

Moving Tabs Using the Tab Bar

1. At a clear editing window, open Ch 10, Ex 01.
2. Save the document with Save As and name it Ch 10, Ex 04.
3. Move the tab settings using the Tab Bar by completing the following steps:
   a. Position the arrow pointer on the left scroll arrow on the horizontal scroll bar and click the left mouse button until the Tab Bar icon displays.
   b. Click the left mouse button on the Tab Bar icon to display the Tab Bar.
   c. Position the arrow pointer on the left tab icon at the 2.5-inch mark on the Tab Bar and drag the icon to the left until the tab position box shows a relative left tab at the 2-inch position.
   d. Position the arrow pointer on the left tab icon at the 4.75-inch mark on the Tab Bar and drag the icon to the right until the tab position box shows a relative left tab at the 5.25-inch position.
   e. Click the left mouse button anywhere in a white portion of the screen to remove the Tab Bar.
4. Save the document again with the same name (Ch 10, Ex 04).
5. Print and then close Ch 10, Ex 04.

Manipulating Tabs   205

Manipulating Tabs with the Tab Set Dialog Box

The Tab Set dialog box shown in figure 10.9 can be used to complete such tasks as clearing a tab or tabs and setting a variety of tabs at precise measurements. There are several methods that can be used to display the Tab Set dialog box including:

- Click Format, point to Line, then click Tab Set.

- Position the arrow pointer anywhere on the Ruler Bar, click the *right* mouse button, then click Tab Set.

- Double-click a tab icon on the Ruler Bar.

- Double-click a tab icon on the Tab Bar.

- Double-click any tab code in Reveal Codes.

If the display of the Ruler Bar is on, the Ruler Bar can be seen above the Tab Set dialog box. This is helpful when determining tab settings.

Figure 10.9

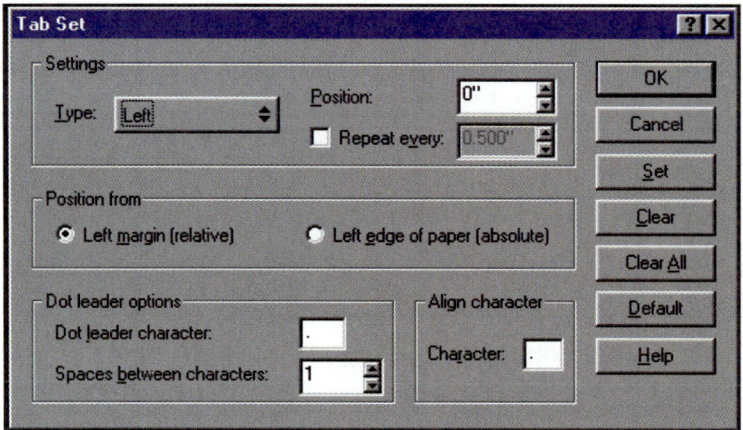

Tab Set Dialog Box

Clearing Tabs

At the Tab Set dialog box, you can clear an individual tab or all tabs. To clear all tabs from the Ruler Bar, click Clear All. To do this with the mouse, click the Clear All button in the dialog box. If you are using the keyboard, press Alt + A.

To clear an individual tab, display the Tab Set dialog box, click Position, then key the measurement of the tab to be cleared. You can also click the up-pointing triangle after Position until the desired measurement displays in the Position text box. Or, you can select the current measurement in the Position text box, then key the desired measurement. With the desired measurement displayed, click Clear.

Tabs in the Tab Set dialog box are, by default, relative tabs. Relative tabs are measured from the left margin. The Ruler Bar displays absolute tabs, which are measured from the left edge of the page. With tabs that are measured relative to the left margin, the left margin is 0 inches. Positions to the right of the left margin are positive numbers and positions to the left of the left margin are negative numbers. With relative tabs that are measured from the left margin, the distance between tab settings and the left margin remains the same regardless of what changes are made to the document.

Absolute tabs are measured from the left edge of the page. The left edge of the page is 0 inches. Tabs that are set from the left edge of the page remain at the fixed measurement regardless of what changes are made to the document.

Setting Tabs

All the tab types available with the Tab drop-down menu are available with the Type option from the Tab Set dialog box. To change the type of tab at the Tab Set dialog box, display the dialog box, click Type, then click the desired tab at the drop-down menu.

The Position option from the Tab Set dialog box is used to identify the specific measurement where the tab is to be set. To set a tab, click Position, key the desired measurement, then click Set. The measurement that you key is a relative measurement. For example, if you set a tab at 3 inches, the tab will appear at the 4-inch mark on the Ruler Bar (if the left margin is at the default setting of 1 inch). In Reveal Codes, the tab would display as *Tab Set: (Rel)+3" L*. As an example of how to clear and set tabs at the Tab Set dialog box, complete exercise 5.

EXERCISE 5

Clearing and Setting Tabs at the Tab Set Dialog Box

1. At a clear editing window, key the document shown in figure 10.10 by completing the following steps:
    a. Key the headings and the first paragraph of the memo, then center and bold the title, **TOP TEN CALORIE-BURNING EXERCISES.**
    b. With the insertion point a double space below the title, use the mouse and the Tab Set dialog box to set a left tab 1.25 inches from the left margin and a right tab 5.25 inches from the left margin by completing the following steps:
       (1) If necessary, display the Ruler Bar.
       (2) Double-click a tab icon on the Ruler Bar. (This displays the Tab Set dialog box.)
       (3) At the Tab Set dialog box, click the Clear All button.
       (4) Make sure the tab type is Left. (If not, position the arrow pointer in the Type text box, click the left mouse button, move the arrow pointer to *Left*, then click the left mouse button.)
       (5) Select the 0" in the Position text box.
       (6) Key **1.25**.
       (7) Click the Set button.
       (8) Position the arrow pointer in the Type text box, click the left mouse button, move the arrow pointer to *Right*, then click the left mouse button.
       (9) Select the *1.25"* in the Position text box.
       (10) Key **5.25**.
       (11) Click the Set button.
       (12) Click the OK button.
    c. Key the text in columns as shown in figure 10.10. Bold the text as indicated. Press the Tab key before keying each column entry. (Make sure you press Tab before keying the text in the first and second columns.)
2. Key the remaining text in the memo.
3. Save the memo and name it Ch 10, Ex 05.
4. Print and then close Ch 10, Ex 05.

Figure 10.10

DATE: February 9, 1998

TO: Paula Kerns, Editor, *Hospital Happenings*

FROM: Steve Ayala

SUBJECT: MARCH NEWSLETTER

At the last department meeting, you told us that the theme for the March *Hospital Happenings* newsletter was exercise. Just last week, I ran across this information about the efficiency of common exercises.

TOP TEN CALORIE-BURNING EXERCISES

Activity	Cal. per hr.
Skiing (cross-country)	1,000
Running	950
Bicycling (stationary)	850
Bicycling (12 mph)	650
Swimming	640
Rowing machine	600
Tennis	600
Handball/Racquetball	577
Jogging (12-minute mile)	570
Aerobic dance	525

I thought this information would be interesting to the readers of the newsletter. Let me know if you decide to publish it.

xx:Ch 10, Ex 05

When tabs are set, a tab set code is inserted in the document at the beginning of the paragraph where the insertion point is positioned. The tab set code displays the relative measurement of the tab as well as the type of tab. For example, if previous tabs were cleared and a left tab was set at 2.3 inches from the left margin, a center tab 4.5 inches from the left margin, and a right tab 6.4 inches from the left margin, the code `Tab Set: (Rel)+2.3"L, +4.5"C, +6.4"R` would display in Reveal Codes. Tab codes take effect from the location of the code to the end of the document or until another tab set code is encountered.

EXERCISE 6

Creating a Table of Contents with a Dot Leader Tab

1. At a clear editing window, create the document shown in figure 10.11 by completing the following steps:
   a. Change the font to 12-point Arrus BT (or a similar typeface).
   b. Change the line spacing to double (2).
   c. Center and bold the title, **TABLE OF CONTENTS**.
   d. With the insertion point a double space below *TABLE OF CONTENTS*, use the Tab Set dialog box to set a left tab 1 inch from the left margin and a right tab with dot leaders 5.5 inches from the left margin by completing the following steps:
      (1) Click Format, point to Line, then click Tab Set.
      (2) At the Tab Set dialog box, click the Clear All button.
      (3) Select the *0"* in the Position text box.
      (4) Key **1**.
      (5) Click the Set button.
      (6) Position the arrow pointer in the Type text box, click the left mouse button, move the arrow pointer to *Dot Right*, then click the left mouse button.
      (7) Select the *1"* in the Position text box.
      (8) Key **5.5**.
      (9) Click the Set button.
      (10) Click the OK button.
   e. Key the text in columns as shown in figure 10.11. Press the Tab key before keying each column entry. (Make sure you press Tab before keying the text in the first and second columns.)
2. Save the document and name it Ch 10, Ex 06.
3. Print and then close Ch 10, Ex 06.

Figure 10.11

TABLE OF CONTENTS

Administration of Employee Survey	2
Calendar of Events	5
Administrative Feedback	6
Clerical Support	7
Team Talk	8
Confidentiality	10
Team Leaders/Members	12
Summary	13
Exhibit A	14
Exhibit B	15
Exhibit C	16

Manipulating Tabs

Setting Evenly Spaced Tabs

With the Repeat every option from the Tab Set dialog box, you can set tabs at regular intervals. First clear all previous tabs, then click Position. With the insertion point in the Position text box, key the measurement where the first tab set is to occur, then click Set. Click Repeat every, key the measurement of the interval, then click OK to close the Tab Set dialog box.

Returning to Default Tabs

If you make changes to the tab settings, then want to return to the default tabs, use the Default button at the Tab Set dialog box. Clicking this button returns the tabs to the default of a tab set every 0.5 inches. Another method for returning to default tab settings is to position the arrow pointer on a tab icon on the Ruler Bar, click the *right* mouse button, then click Default Tab Settings at the drop-down menu.

Changing Tab Type

As mentioned earlier, tabs can be set that are measured from the left margin or the left edge of the page. Tabs that are measured from the left margin are called *relative tabs* and tabs set from the left edge of the page are called *absolute tabs*. By default, tabs are measured from the left margin.

The Tab Set dialog box contains a Left margin (relative) option and a Left edge of paper (absolute) option. The default option is Left margin (relative).

EXERCISE

Creating Columns with Absolute Tabs

1. At a clear editing window, key the document shown in figure 10.12 by completing the following steps:
   a. Turn on page numbering at the bottom right corner of all pages.
   b. Change the line spacing to double (2).
   c. Center and bold the title, **THE ROLE OF TRANSMISSION IN TELECOMMUNICATIONS**.
   d. Press Enter, then bold the heading, **Receiving**.
   e. Press Enter, then key the first paragraph.
   f. After keying the paragraph, press Enter once, then change the line spacing to single (1).
   g. Clear all tabs and set absolute left tabs at 2.8 and 4.5 by completing the following steps:
      (1) Display the Tab Set dialog box.
      (2) At the Tab Set dialog box, click the Clear All button.
      (3) Click in the circle before the Left edge of paper (absolute) option.
      (4) Select *0"* in the Position text box.
      (5) Key **2.8**.
      (6) Click Set.
      (7) Select *2.80"* in the Position text box.
      (8) Key **4.5**.
      (9) Click the Set button.
      (10) Click OK.

h. Key the text in columns. After keying the last entry in the second column, press Enter twice.
i. Change the line spacing to double.
j. Return the tabs to the default settings by completing the following steps:
  (1) Position the arrow pointer on a tab icon on the Ruler Bar, then click the *right* mouse button.
  (2) From the drop-down menu that displays, click De_f_ault Tab Settings.
k. Key the remaining text in the document.
2. Save the document and name it Ch 10, Ex 07.
3. Print and then close Ch 10, Ex 07.

Figure 10.12

THE ROLE OF TRANSMISSION IN TELECOMMUNICATIONS

Receiving

Information is sent through the atmosphere as an electromagnetic signal (a signal with magnetic properties resulting from being passed through electrical current). At the intended destination, the electromagnetic signal must be recognized and captured by an antenna system. Antenna systems must accept only those signals we want them to receive and ignore the rest. Some common receiving devices include:

TV Antenna	Satellite Dish
Tuner	Amplifier
Modem	VSAT

The typical home satellite earth station has a number of electromagnetic signals that may strike it. These signals may come from AM (amplitude modulation) or FM (frequency modulation) radio towers, a variety of television stations, ham radio operators, CB radio operators, or microwave signals used for telephone or other telecommunications services. One task of the antenna is to sort out which signal to accept and which to ignore.

Receiving Information Sent Through Physical Channels

If we look at the physical channels used for transmitting information, we can see the need to design devices that allow for the physical interconnection of the channel to the transmitter and receiver. This may take a simple form, such as fastening a copper wire to a screw on the back of the receiver, or a quite complicated form, such as splicing a fiber optic cable. Unfortunately, there is little standardization of the physical interconnection of channels to the receiving device. Whether voice, data, or video system, the methods for physical connection are numerous and varied.

Changing the Dot Leader Character

By default, WordPerfect uses a period as a dot leader. However, the dot leader can be changed to any character. In addition, the amount of spacing between dot leader characters can be increased or decreased. To change the dot leader character, display the Tab Set dialog box, then key the desired symbol in the Dot leader character text box. Clear and/or set desired tabs and then click OK to close the Tab Set dialog box.

EXERCISE

Changing the Dot Leader Character to a Hyphen

1. At a clear editing window, key the document shown in figure 10.13 by completing the following steps:
   a. Change the font to 12-point BernhardMod BT (or a similar serif typeface).
   b. Center and bold the title, **ACCOMMODATIONS**.
   c. Press Enter three times, then change the line spacing to double (2).
   d. Change the dot leader character to a hyphen, then set a left tab 0.6 inches from the left margin and a left tab with dot leaders 4.5 inches from the left margin by completing the following steps:
      (1) Display the Tab Set dialog box.
      (2) At the Tab Set dialog box, click Clear All.
      (3) Change the dot leader character to a hyphen. To do this, select the period in the Dot leader character text box, then key a hyphen (-).
      (4) Make sure the tab type is Left. (If not, position the arrow pointer in the Type text box, click the left mouse button, move the arrow pointer to *Left*, then click the left mouse button.)
      (5) Select *0"* in the Position text box.
      (6) Key **0.6**.
      (7) Click Set.
      (8) Position the arrow pointer in the Type text box, click the left mouse button, move the arrow pointer to *Dot Left*, then click the left mouse button.
      (9) Select the *0.600"* in the Position text box.
      (10) Key **4.5**.
      (11) Click Set.
      (12) Click OK to close the dialog box.
   e. Key the text in columns as shown in figure 10.13. Press the Tab key before keying each column entry. (Make sure you press Tab before keying the text in the first and second columns.)
   f. Center the document vertically on the page. (Use the Current page option from the Center Page(s) dialog box.)
2. Save the document and name it Ch 10, Ex 08.
3. Print and then close Ch 10, Ex 08.

Figure 10.13

ACCOMMODATIONS

Cedar Ridge Inn - (206) 555-0932

Snohomish Motor Inn - - - - - - - - - - - - - - - - - - - (206) 555-1988

Country Side Motel - (509) 555-3100

Twin Pines Motel - (206) 555-0998

Rainbow Falls Motel - - - - - - - - - - - - - - - - - - - (509) 555-3049

Visually Aligning Columns

Columns of text or data in a document are usually centered between the left and right margins to provide a balanced look. If you do not know the measurements for setting tabs for columns of text, try visually centering columns of text using the Ruler Bar. To do this, you would follow these basic steps:

1. Change to the Draft viewing mode.
2. Make sure the Ruler Bar is displayed.
3. Make sure the desired tab type is selected.
4. Clear all previous tabs from the Ruler Bar, then visually insert tabs on the Ruler Bar where you want columns aligned.
5. Key the text in columns, pressing the Tab key before keying each column entry.
6. After keying the column text, position the insertion point at the beginning of the first line of column text.
7. Drag each tab icon on the Ruler Bar until the text in columns displays visually centered between the left and right margins.

EXERCISE 9

Visually Setting Left Tabs on the Ruler Bar

1. At a clear document screen, key the document shown in figure 10.14 by completing the following steps:
   a. Key the title, **WORDPERFECT TRAINING LIST**, bolded and centered.
   b. Press the Enter key twice.
   c. Change to the Draft viewing mode.
   d. Make sure the Ruler Bar is displayed.
   e. Make sure the tab type is Left. To do this, position the arrow pointer on a tab icon on the Ruler Bar, click the *right* mouse button, then click Left at the drop-down menu that displays.
   f. Clear all previous tabs from the Ruler Bar.
   g. Position the arrow pointer on the bottom gray portion of the Ruler Bar at approximately the 2.5-inch mark, then click the left mouse button.

Manipulating Tabs

h. Position the arrow pointer on the bottom gray portion of the Ruler Bar at approximately the 4.5-inch mark, then click the left mouse button.
i. Key the text in columns as shown in figure 10.14. Press the Tab key before keying each column entry.
j. If the columns of text do not look balanced, position the insertion point at the beginning of the first line of column text, then drag each of the two left tab icons to a more desirable location.

2. Save the document and name it Ch 10, Ex 09.
3. Print and then close Ch 10, Ex 09.

Figure 10.14

WORDPERFECT TRAINING LIST

Alan Losch	Admitting
Christine Danzer	Clinical Labs
Charles Blaszak	Community Relations
Trisha Weiske	Central Processing
LaDonna Rudon	Human Resources
Manuel Montel	Human Resources
Joseph Kenville	Medical Records

EXERCISE 10

Visually Setting Left and Right Tabs on the Ruler Bar

1. At a clear editing window, key the document shown in figure 10.15 by completing the following steps:
   a. Center and bold the title, **WORD PROCESSING CLASS**.
   b. Press Enter twice.
   c. Change to the Draft viewing mode.
   d. Make sure the Ruler Bar is displayed.
   e. Make sure the tab type is Left. To do this, position the arrow pointer on a tab icon on the Ruler Bar, click the *right* mouse button, then click Left at the drop-down menu that displays.
   f. Clear all previous tabs from the Ruler Bar.
   g. Insert a left tab icon on the Ruler Bar at the approximate location where you want the first column of text to display. (You determine the location.)
   h. Change the tab type to Right and then set a right tab on the Ruler Bar at the approximate location where you want the second column of text to display.
   i. Set right tabs on the Ruler Bar for the third and fourth columns of text. (You determine the locations.)
   j. Key the text in columns as shown in figure 10.15. Press the Tab key before keying each column entry.

> k. If the columns of text do not look balanced, position the insertion point at the beginning of the first line of column text, then drag each of the tab icons to a more desirable location.
> 2. Save the document and name it Ch 10, Ex 10.
> 3. Print and then close Ch 10, Ex 10.

Figure 10.15

WORD PROCESSING CLASS

Name	#1	#2	#3
Colin Kernen	80	93	98
Vivian Ehlen	78	65	69
Yoeun Hang	88	93	89
Michelle Walder	100	94	98
Jerry Woodward	94	100	89
Louis Vorak	59	63	71
Shaun Shriner	97	99	100
Isabel Sahota	74	0	79
Cliff Oppelt	100	97	93

Keying Column Headings

Column headings that are shorter than the column entries can be visually centered above the entries. To do this, key the column entries first, leaving blank lines above the columns for the headings. After the column entries have been keyed, move the insertion point above the columns, visually determine the center of the columns, then key the headings.

If there is only one column, center the heading over the column as follows:

1. Key the column entries, then go back and insert blank lines above the column for the heading.
2. Move the insertion point to the first position of the column.
3. Press the space bar once for every two characters, spaces, and so on, in the longest entry in the column.
4. Click Format, point to Line, then click Center (or press Shift + F7).
5. Key the column heading.

Some businesses are accepting column headings aligned at the tab setting rather than centered because centering takes extra time.

EXERCISE 11

Centering Column Headings

1. At a clear editing window, open Column 01.
2. Save the document with Save As and name it Ch 10, Ex 11.
3. Center the heading *Department Directors* over the names and titles by completing the following steps:
    a. With the insertion point positioned at the beginning of the document, press the space bar until the insertion point is located at approximately position 2.69".
    b. Click Format, point to Line, then click Center (or press Shift + F7).
    c. Key **Department Directors**.
4. Save the document again with the same name (Ch 10, Ex 11).
5. Print and then close Ch 10, Ex 11.

CHAPTER SUMMARY

▼ By default, left tabs are set every 0.5 inches.

▼ At the Ruler Bar, Tab Bar, or the Tab Set dialog box, tabs can be deleted, reset, or moved.

▼ The four types of tabs are Left (the default), Center, Right, and Decimal. Any type of tab can be set with dot leaders (periods).

▼ To display the types of tabs available to set on the Ruler Bar, position the arrow pointer on any tab icon on the Ruler Bar, then click the right mouse button. The tab type can also be changed at the Tab Set dialog box.

▼ By default, the Tab Set dialog box displays relative tabs—tabs that are measured from the left margin. The Ruler Bar displays absolute tabs—tabs that are measured from the left edge of the page.

▼ When tabs are set, a tab set code is inserted in the document at the beginning of the paragraph where the insertion point is positioned. Tab codes take effect from the location of the code to the end of the document or until another tab set code is encountered.

▼ At the Tab Set dialog box you can set new tabs at regular intervals or return to the default tabs.

▼ If you do not know the measurements for setting tabs for columns of text, visually center columns of text using the Ruler Bar.

▼ Column headings can be aligned at the column tab settings or centered individually over each column.

COMMANDS REVIEW

Mouse/Keyboard

Ruler Bar — View, Toolbars/Ruler, click Ruler Bar, then click OK

Tab Set dialog box — Format, Line, Tab Set; position the arrow pointer anywhere on Ruler Bar, click the right mouse button, then click Tab Set; double-click any tab code in Reveal Codes

Tab Bar — Click the Tab Bar icon in the left margin area

CHECK YOUR UNDERSTANDING

Completion: In the space provided at the right, indicate the correct command, term, or number.

1. How many inches apart are tabs set by default?
2. What are the four types of tabs?
3. Which kind of tab is the default?
4. Tabs can be set on the Ruler Bar, at the Tab Set dialog box, and here.
5. Relative tabs are measured from here.
6. When tabs are set, a tab set code is inserted in the document at this position.
7. This is the name for the line of periods that can run between columns.
8. Do this to existing tabs before setting new ones.

SKILL ASSESSMENTS

Assessment 1

1. At a clear editing window, key the document shown in figure 10.16. Before keying the text in columns, clear all tabs, then set left tabs on the Ruler Bar at the 2-inch mark, the 4.25-inch mark, and the 5.5-inch mark.
2. Save the document and name it Ch 10, SA 01.
3. Print and then close Ch 10, SA 01.

Figure 10.16

WELLNESS CLASSES

Personal Wellness	02/07/95	4:30 - 6:30
Counting Calories	02/09/95	4:00 - 5:30
Healthy Exercises	02/14/95	1:30 - 3:30
The Dieting Cycle	02/16/95	2:00 - 4:00

Assessment 2

1. At a clear editing window, key the document shown in figure 10.17. Before keying the text in columns, display the Tab Set dialog box, clear all tabs, then set a left tab 0.5 inches from the left margin and a decimal tab with dot leaders 5.5 inches from the left margin.
2. Save the document and name it Ch 10, SA 02.
3. Print and then close Ch 10, SA 02.

Figure 10.17

DATE: February 6, 1998

TO: Maxine Paulson, Editor

FROM: Barbara Essex, Investment Coordinator

SUBJECT: PORTFOLIO INFORMATION

Several clients have indicated that the "sample portfolio" helps them understand how and where our company invests their money. Would you please include the following information in the next client newsletter:

PORTFOLIO ACCUMULATION

Direct loans to business .... $ 60,453.20
Public debt securities 87,540.00
Mortgage loans 108,540.32
Real estate investments 55,490.90
All others 9,904.50

If you want more information about this sample portfolio, call me at extension 564.

xx:Ch 10, SA 02

Assessment 3

1. At a clear editing window, key the table shown in figure 10.18. Set a left tab for the first and third columns and set a right tab for the second and fourth columns. You determine the location for the tabs.
2. Save the document and name it Ch 10, SA 03.
3. Print and then close Ch 10, SA 03.

Figure 10.18

COLOR CODES BY DEPARTMENT

IC Unit	Red	CC Unit	Purple
Surgical Unit	Green	Medical	White
Pediatrics	Blue	Finances	Gray
Payroll	Brown	Admitting	Beige

Assessment 4

1. At a clear editing window, open Ch 10, SA 03.
2. Save the document with Save As and name it Ch 10, SA 04.
3. Delete the right tab icons for the second and fourth columns, change the tab to a right tab with dot leaders, then reset the tabs for the second and fourth columns.
4. Center the document vertically on the page.
5. Save the document again with the same name (Ch 10, SA 04).
6. Print and then close Ch 10, SA 04. (Check the printing of the document and make sure there are several dot leaders between entries in the first and second columns and the third and fourth columns. If not, increase the amount of space between the first and second columns and the third and fourth columns.)

Assessment 5

1. At a clear editing window, key the table of contents shown in figure 10.19. You determine the tab settings for the text in columns.
2. Center the document vertically on the page.
3. Save the document and name it Ch 10, SA 05.
4. Print and then close Ch 10, SA 05.

Figure 10.19

TABLE OF CONTENTS

Telecommunications at Work 4

Factors for Evaluating Systems 7

Technology Defined 10

What Telecommunications Offers 12

Development of Technology 14

Contributions of Historical Events 19

Summary 27

Review 29

Assessment 6

1. At a clear editing window, key the document shown in figure 10.20 with the following specifications:
   a. Change the line spacing to double (2) for the body of the report and single (1) for the tabbed columns.
   b. Before keying the first set of text columns (*Microphone*, *Mouse*, etc.), set a left tab at the 2.5-inch mark on the Ruler Bar and another at the 4.25-inch mark.
   c. After keying the first set of text columns, return tab settings to the default.
   d. Before keying the second set of text columns (*Broadcast Radio*, *Computer Systems*, etc.), set a left tab at the 2.5-inch mark on the Ruler Bar and another at the 4.25-inch mark.
   e. After keying the second set of text columns, return tab settings to the default.
   f. After keying all the text in the document, move the insertion point back to the beginning of the document, then number pages at the bottom center of the page.
2. Save the document and name it Ch 10, SA 06.
3. Print and then close Ch 10, SA 06.

Figure 10.20

THE ROLE OF TRANSMISSION IN TELECOMMUNICATIONS

Transmitting

Transmitting is the process of conveying information from one location to another. A signal often is transmitted directly after the encoding process has been completed. Transmitting systems take many forms that we use daily, such as the wire that connects our telephone to a local telephone office. Other common examples are the radio tower transmitting antenna that launches electromagnetic signals to be picked up by the antenna systems of our cars, homes, and offices. More exotic systems include satellite networks and fiber optic networks. Some examples of common transmitting devices include:

Microphone	Mouse
35 mm Camera	8 mm Camera
Joystick	Keyboard
Television	Touch-Sensitive Screen

Regardless of the specific technology used, the transmitting system must move information from its origin to its intended destination quickly and efficiently. Transmitting is accomplished by putting the information either on or through the atmosphere or through a copper wire or optical fiber. Some common system applications for transmitting devices include:

Broadcast Radio	Computer Systems
Telephone	Broadcast Television
Still Photography	Manufacturing Process

Transmission channels are classified as atmospheric or physical. *Atmospheric channels* make use of transmission processes that cause electromagnetic energy to move through space. This method of transmission is also called *free space propagation*. There is no physical connection between the transmitter and the receiver.

Physical channels use copper wire, fiber optics, or wave guides to move electrical, electromagnetic, or light energy through a physical link that connects the transmitter to the receiver. Many different processes are used to move information.

Reminder: You may want to delete outdated document files now.

Unit Two

PERFORMANCE ASSESSMENTS

PROBLEM SOLVING AND DECISION MAKING

Assessment 1

1. At a clear editing window, change the font to 24-point Ribbon131 Bd BT (or a similar serif typeface), change the line spacing to 1.5, then key the document shown in figure U2.1.
2. Save the document and name it Unit 02, PA 01.
3. Print and then close Unit 02, PA 01.

Friends of the Hospital

Charity Dinner and Auction

Temple Theater

Wednesday, August 12, 1998

6:30 - 10:00 p.m.

Figure U2.1

Assessment 2

1. At a clear editing window, key the text shown in figure U2.2 in an appropriate business letter format with the following specifications:
    a. Change the font to 12-point Century Schoolbook.
    b. Indent the text after the enumerated items.
    c. Set tabs for the text columns.

2. Complete a spell check on the letter.
3. Proofread and correct any grammar errors.
4. Save the letter and name it Unit 02, PA 02.
5. Print and then close Unit 02, PA 02.

March 16, 1998

Mrs. Darlene Frye
Public Works Department
2105 South 42nd Street
Tampa, FL 33613

Dear Mrs. Frye:

The third meting of the members of the Outcomes Assesment Project (OAP) were held yesterday, march 15. The following items were discused:

1. **Survey:** Each member shared the current status of the section of the survey for which he or she is responsible.

2. **Survey Instruments**: Members modified and prioritized items on the first draft of the survey questionnaire.

3. **Meeting Dates and Times**: The next three meeting days and times were determined as follows:

Tuesday, April 7	3:00 p.m.	Room 420
Wenesday, April 29	11:30 a.m.	Room 100A
Tusday, May 12	3:00 p.m.	Room 420

Hopefully, these days and times are convenient for your. If you want to discuss this meeting farther, give me a call.

Very truly yours,

Dawn Perez, Coordinator
Outcomes Assesment Project

xx:Unit 02, PA 02

Figure U2.2

Assessment 3

1. At a clear editing window, key the text shown in figure U2.3 in an appropriate memo format with the following specifications:
    a. Insert the appropriate bullets as indicated.
    b. Set tabs for the text columns.
2. Complete a spell check on the memo.
3. Save the memo and name it Unit 02, PA 03.
4. Print and then close Unit 02, PA 03.

DATE: October 5, 1998

TO: All Parents

FROM: Pat Windslow, Superintendent

SUBJECT: EMERGENCY WEATHER SCHEDULE

Each family should have a plan covering what to do when children arrive home early due to an emergency situation. Consider the following questions:

- What is the best route home if your child cannot be delivered to the normal bus stop?
- Where could your child go if he or she needed help?
- Who would care for him or her until you arrive?
- Is there someone your child could call to calm any concerns he or she might have?

Please develop an emergency plan for your family and practice it with your child.

Listen to the radio between 6:00 a.m. and 8:00 a.m. if you feel the weather may create hazardous traveling conditions. Radio/TV stations will be announcing schedule changes by district name and number. If the Omaha City School District is not mentioned on the air, assume normal operations will prevail.

The following AM and FM radio stations will broadcast changes in school and bus operations:

KTC 520	KPLC 88.5
KCIT 730	KLCY 93.5
KICS 1100	KUTE 100.0
KJS 1220	KZOS 103.7
KMPS 1350	KVTS 105.5

When you hear "Schools Closed," it means schools will be closed for the day and all after-school and evening activities will be canceled unless otherwise announced.

xx:Unit 02, PA 03

Figure U2.3

Assessment 4

1. At a clear editing window, create the document shown in figure U2.4 with the following specifications:
   a. Bold and center text as indicated.
   b. Visually determine the tab settings.
   c. Center the document vertically on the page.
2. Save the document and name it Unit 02, PA 04.
3. Print and then close Unit 02, PA 04.

Optional: Write a summary interpreting what the data means.

OMAHA CITY SCHOOL DISTRICT

Enrollment Comparisons

School	1996	1997
Nylan Senior High	1,087	995
Cleveland Senior High	978	1,009
Grant Junior High	595	660
Washington Junior High	693	710
Roosevelt Junior High	655	701
Carr Elementary	423	410
Leland Elementary	457	428
Sahala Elementary	502	478
Armstrong Elementary	398	411

Figure U2.4

Assessment 5

1. At a clear editing window, open Report 06.
2. Save the document with Save As and name it Unit 02, PA 05.
3. Make the following changes to the report:
   a. Change the line spacing to double (2). Delete all extra lines in the report so there is only a double space between all lines.
   b. Turn on the Widow/Orphan feature.
   c. Use Thesaurus to find appropriate synonyms for the following words in the document:

   dominant in the first paragraph in the
   Continued Growth of Photonics (Fiber Optics) section

   backbone in the first paragraph in the
   Continued Growth of Photonics (Fiber Optics) section

   traverse in the second paragraph in the
   Continued Growth of Photonics (Fiber Optics) section

features in the fourth paragraph in the
Continued Growth of Photonics (Fiber Optics) section

method in the fourth paragraph in the
Continued Growth of Photonics (Fiber Optics) section

4. Save the document again with the same name (Unit 02, PA 05).
5. Print and then close Unit 02, PA 05.

Optional: Rewrite the report in one page or less, assuming you are writing for a nontechnical audience (parents and community members).

Assessment 6

1. Display the Open dialog box and then complete the following steps:
    a. Create a folder named *Unit 2* that branches off from the root folder on the student data disk.
    b. Copy the documents that begin *Unit 02* to the *Unit 2* folder.
    c. Print a list of the documents located in the *Unit 2* folder.
    d. Change back to the root folder and then delete the documents that begin *Unit 02* (located in the root folder on the student data disk).
2. Close the Open dialog box.

WRITING

The following activities give you the opportunity to practice your writing skills along with demonstrating an understanding of some of the important WordPerfect features you have mastered in this unit. In planning the documents, remember to shape the information according to the writing purpose and the audience. Use correct grammar, appropriate word choices, and clear sentence constructions.

Activity 1

Situation: You work in the Training and Development Department of a large business. One of your job responsibilities includes preparing notices for upcoming training sessions. Prepare a notice of an upcoming training session titled *Searching the Internet, Discovering Business Resources*. The training will be held Tuesday, March 17, 1998, in the Computer Resource Room, from 1:30 to 4:00 p.m. Anyone interested in attending this training must contact you before March 13 at extension 459. When preparing the notice, change the font and font size for the text and position the information attractively on the page. Save the notice and name it Unit 02, Act 01. Print and then close Unit 02, Act 01.

Performance Assessments   227

Activity 2

Situation: You are Jocelyn Cook, assistant superintendent for the Omaha City School District. Compose a memo to all elementary school principals informing them that the members of the site selection committee will be visiting their schools on the following dates and times:

Carr Elementary School	February 20	10:00 - 11:30 a.m.
Leland Elementary School	February 20	1:30 - 3:00 p.m.
Sahala Elementary School	February 24	9:30 - 11:00 a.m.
Young Elementary School	February 24	1:00 - 2:30 p.m.
Armstrong Elementary School	February 27	10:00 - 11:30 a.m.
Bothell Elementary School	February 27	1:30 - 3:00 p.m.

You determine the tab settings for the columns of text (this includes columns for the school names, days, and times). Save the memo and name it Unit 02, Act 02. Print and then close Unit 02, Act 02.

Unit *Three*

Preparing AND **ENHANCING** Multiple-Page **Documents**

In this unit, you will learn to create multiple-page documents with elements such as headers, footers, footnotes, and endnotes; move text within and between documents; enhance the readability of documents with Grammatik; and prepare form documents with personalized information.

11 CREATING HEADERS AND FOOTERS

PERFORMANCE OBJECTIVE

Upon successful completion of chapter 11, you will be able to finish multiple-page reports with specific page characteristics including headers and footers.

In a WordPerfect document, you can create headers and footers. Text that appears at the top of pages is called a *header*, and text that appears at the bottom of pages is called a *footer*. When text is identified as a header or footer, it needs to be keyed only one time. After that, WordPerfect prints the text on each page. Headers and footers are common in manuscripts, textbooks, reports, and other publications. Typically, they are used to identify the chapter or section number and/or title.

Creating Headers and Footers

A maximum of two headers and/or two footers can be created in a WordPerfect document. WordPerfect refers to them as Header A, Header B, Footer A, and Footer B. A header or footer can contain as many lines as needed, up to one page. Generally, however, most headers and footers are only a few lines in length.

Headers and footers can be created in various forms. They can appear on every page or can be identified as alternating headers or footers. With alternating headers or footers, text is printed only on even-numbered or odd-numbered pages.

A header or footer can be turned off or discontinued in a document. For example, you can have a header printed on the first and second pages of a document and not printed on the remaining pages. You can also turn a header or footer off on specific pages.

A header or footer can be created in any of the viewing modes. However, the Page and Two-Page viewing modes will display headers or footers in a document.

When a header or footer is created, the header or footer code is inserted at the beginning of the page where the insertion point is positioned. For example, if you want a header to begin printing on page 1, make sure the insertion point is positioned somewhere in the first page.

To create a header or footer, you would complete the following steps:

1. Position the insertion point anywhere in the page where you want the header or footer to begin.
2. Click Format, then Header/Footer.
3. At the Headers/Footers dialog box, shown in figure 11.1, select the header or footer desired, then click Create.
4. At the Header or Footer window, key the text for the header or footer. (Figure 11.2 displays a Header window.)
5. Click Close.

Figure 11.1

Headers/Footers Dialog Box

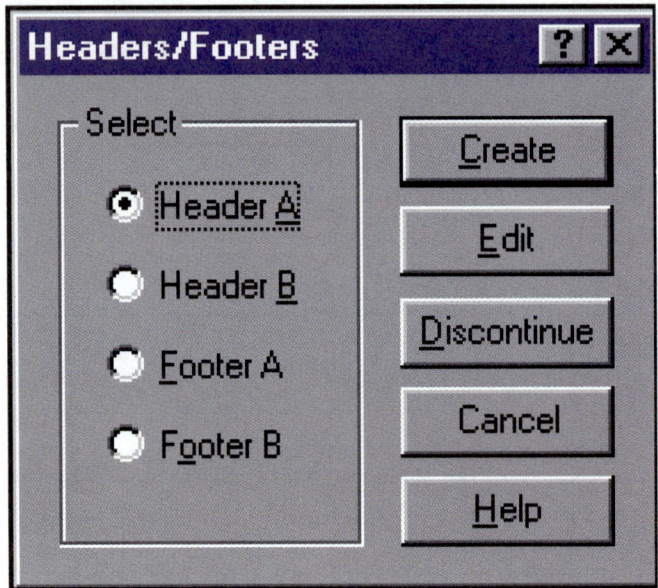

Figure 11.2

Header Window

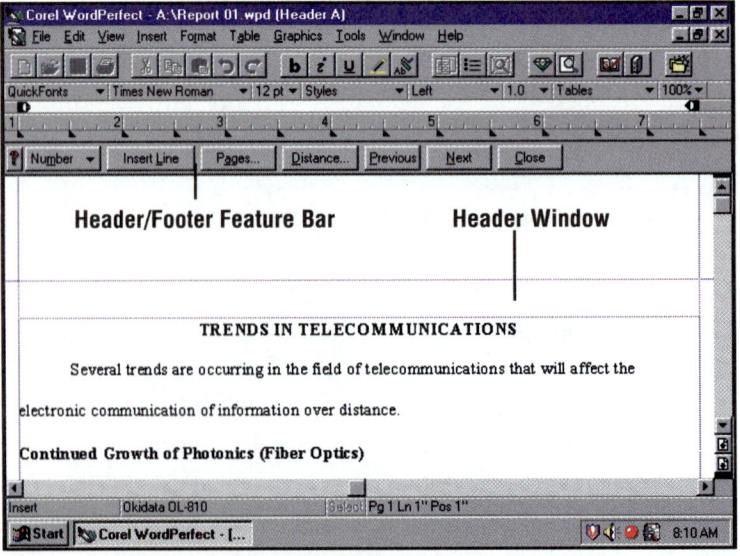

Chapter 11

The Header/Footer window area displays as a rectangular box surrounded by pink dotted lines in the Page viewing mode. When a Header or Footer window is displayed, a bar is inserted in the document window below the Power Bar (or the Ruler Bar). This bar is called the Header/Footer Feature Bar and is identified in figure 11.2. Use options on this feature bar to insert page numbering and specify the pages and location of headers or footers, and to close the Header or Footer window.

To choose options from the Header/Footer Feature Bar with the mouse, click the desired option. To choose options with the keyboard, hold down the Alt key, then the Shift key, then press the underlined letter of the desired option. For example, to choose the Close option on the Header/Footer Feature Bar, press Alt + Shift + C.

At the Header or Footer window, the options Next and Previous are available. For example, if you are creating Header A, you can view a previous Header A in the document by clicking Previous or pressing Alt + Shift + P. If there is no previous Header A in the document, WordPerfect displays this message. If you want to view a Header A that appears after the current Header A, click Next or press Alt + Shift + N. Again, if there is no Header A after the current Header A, WordPerfect will display this message.

EXERCISE 1

Creating a Footer

1. At a clear editing window, open Report 01.
2. Save the report with Save As and name it Ch 11, Ex 01.
3. Turn on the Widow/Orphan feature.
4. Create Footer A that prints at the bottom of every page, is bolded, and reads *Trends in Telecommunications* by completing the following steps:
    a. Position the insertion point anywhere in the first page of the report.
    b. Click Format, then Header/Footer.
    c. At the Headers/Footers dialog box, click Footer A.
    d. Click Create.
    e. At the Footer window, press Ctrl + B, then key **Trends in Telecommunications**.
    f. Click the Close button on the Header/Footer Feature Bar.
5. Save the report again with the same name (Ch 11, Ex 01).
6. Print and close Ch 11, Ex 01.

Beginning Headers or Footers on Specific Pages

If the insertion point is positioned in the first page when the header or footer is created, the header or footer code is inserted at the beginning of the document and the header or footer will print on every page.

To specify a different page for the header or footer to begin printing on, position the insertion point in that page, then create the header or footer. For example, if you want a header or footer to begin printing on page 2 of a document, position the insertion point anywhere in page 2, then create the header or footer.

You can also print headers or footers on only even-numbered or only odd-numbered pages. This option is available at the Pages dialog box.

Creating Headers and Footers   233

EXERCISE 2

Printing a Header on Even-Numbered Pages

1. At a clear editing window, open Report 02.
2. Save the report with Save As and name it Ch 11, Ex 02.
3. Turn on the Widow/Orphan feature.
4. Create Header A that prints at the top of all even-numbered pages, is bolded, and reads *Telecommunications Technology* by completing the following steps:
    a. Position the insertion point somewhere on the first line (the line containing the title of the report).
    b. Click Format, then Header/Footer.
    c. At the Headers/Footers dialog box, Header A should already be selected, so click Create.
    d. At the Header window, click the Pages button on the Header/Footer Feature Bar.
    e. At the Pages dialog box, click Even pages.
    f. Click OK or press Enter.
    g. Press Ctrl + B, then key **Telecommunications Technology**.
    h. Click the Close button on the Header/Footer Feature Bar.
5. Save the report again with the same name (Ch 11, Ex 02).
6. Print and then close Ch 11, Ex 02.

Printing Headers or Footers

A header in a document with default top and bottom margins will print an inch from the top of the page with a blank line separating the header from the text. Unless the bottom margin is changed, the last line of a footer prints an inch from the bottom of the page with a blank line separating the text in the document from the footer.

If you want a header or footer to print closer to the top or bottom of the page, change the top and/or bottom margins. For example, to have the header print 0.5 inches from the top of the page, change the top margin to 0.5 inches.

Headers and footers take the place of regular text lines. By default, 9 inches of text are printed on a standard piece of paper. WordPerfect automatically assigns a blank line after a header or a blank line before a footer. Therefore, if you create a header of two lines, WordPerfect prints the header (two lines), leaves one line blank, and then prints 8.5 inches of text. A footer prints in a similar manner.

EXERCISE 3

Printing a Footer One-Half Inch from Bottom of Page

1. At a clear editing window, open Report 01.
2. Save the report with Save As and name it Ch 11, Ex 03.
3. Make the following changes to the report:
    a. Change the bottom margin to 0.5 inches.

- **b.** Turn on the Widow/Orphan feature.
- **c.** Create Footer A that prints bolded and centered at the bottom of all pages and reads *Telecommunications Trends*.
4. Save the document again with the same name (Ch 11, Ex 03).
5. Print and then close Ch 11, Ex 03.

Changing the Distance Measurement

With the Distance button on the Header/Footer Feature Bar, you can specify the distance between the header and text or the text and the footer. By default the distance is 0.167" (approximately one blank line). This measurement can be decreased or increased. To change the distance between a header or footer and the text in a document, click Distance at the Header/Footer Feature Bar. At the Distance dialog box, increase or decrease the distance measurement. The measurement you enter at the Distance dialog box stays in effect for the entire document.

Keying Flush Right Text

When creating headers and/or footers in a document, you may want to key text that prints at the right margin. To create text at the right margin, use the Flush Right command. To do this, click Format, point to Line, then click Flush Right. You can also access the Flush Right command by pressing Alt + F7. The Flush Right command causes the insertion point to move to the right margin. As text is keyed, the insertion point moves to the left. The Flush Right command is ended when you press the Enter key. To align the next line at the right margin, click Format, point to Line, then click Flush Right; or press Alt + F7 again. (If you choose the Flush Right command twice in succession, the text you key will be preceded by dot leaders.)

EXERCISE 4

Changing the Distance between a Header and the Body Text

1. At a clear editing window, open Report 04.
2. Save the report with Save As and name it Ch 11, Ex 04.
3. Make the following changes to the report:
   - **a.** Turn on the Widow/Orphan feature.
   - **b.** Change the top margin to 0.5 inches.
   - **c.** Press the Enter key three times to move the report title to Line 1.68" (your measurement may vary slightly).
   - **d.** Insert a hard page break at the beginning of the line containing the title, *CHAPTER 4: DEVELOPMENT OF TECHNOLOGY, 1950 - 1960*.
   - **e.** Create Header A that prints at the right margin on every page except the first, is separated from the text in the document by 0.334 inches, is bolded, and reads *Technology, 1900 - 1950* by completing the following steps:
     - (1) Position the insertion point somewhere in the second page.
     - (2) Click Format, then Header/Footer.
     - (3) At the Headers/Footers dialog box, Header A should be selected, so click Create.

- (4) At the Header window, access the Flush Right command by clicking Format, Line, then Flush Right; or pressing Alt + F7.
- (5) Press Ctrl + B, then key **Technology, 1900 - 1950**.
- (6) Click the Distance button on the Header/Footer Feature Bar.
- (7) At the Distance dialog box, key **0.334**.
- (8) Click OK or press Enter.
- (9) Click the Close button on the Header/Footer Feature Bar.
4. Save the report again with the same name (Ch 11, Ex 04).
5. Print and then close Ch 11, Ex 04.

Creating Two Headers or Footers

If two headers or footers are created in the same document, you should separate them by either spaces or blank lines to ensure that they do not print on top of each other, or they should be printed on different pages. For example, you can create Header A at the left margin and Header B at the right margin; you can create Header A on the first line at the Header window and Header B on the second or third line; or, you can create Header A that prints on even-numbered pages and Header B that prints on odd-numbered pages.

EXERCISE

Creating Two Footers

1. At a clear editing window, open Report 03.
2. Save the report with Save As and name it Ch 11, Ex 05.
3. Make the following changes to the report:
   a. Change the bottom margin to 0.5 inches.
   b. Turn on the Widow/Orphan feature.
   c. Insert a hard page break at the beginning of the line containing the title, *CHAPTER 2: DEVELOPMENT OF TECHNOLOGY, 1850 - 1900*.
   d. Move the insertion point to the first page, then create Footer A that prints at the right margin of odd-numbered pages, is bolded, and reads *Development of Technology*.
   e. Create Footer B that prints at the left margin of all even-numbered pages, is bolded, and reads *Telecommunications*.
4. Save the report again with the same name (Ch 11, Ex 05).
5. Print and then close Ch 11, Ex 05.

Editing Headers or Footers

A header or footer can be edited at the Headers/Footers dialog box, or, if you are in the Page viewing mode, you can click the mouse inside the header/footer window and edit the text. In the Page viewing mode, the header/footer window is displayed as a rectangular box encased with pink dotted lines.

To edit using the Headers/Footers dialog box, click Format, then Header/Footer. At the Headers/Footers dialog box, select the header or footer (A or B) you want to change, then click Edit. Make any changes to the header/footer text and then click Close.

EXERCISE 6

Editing a Footer

1. At a clear editing window, open Ch 11, Ex 05.
2. Save the report with Save As and name it Ch 11, Ex 06.
3. Edit Footer A so that it reads *History from 1800 - 1900* by completing the following steps:
   a. Click Format, then Header/Footer.
   b. At the Headers/Footers dialog box, click Footer A, then click Edit.
   c. At the Footer window, delete the existing text, then key **History from 1800 - 1900** bolded.
   d. Click the Close button on the Header/Footer Feature Bar.
4. Save the report again with the same name (Ch 11, Ex 06).
5. Print and then close Ch 11, Ex 06.

Formatting Headers and Footers

A header or footer that is created in a document does not take on any formatting applied to the document. For example, if the margins and justification are changed in the document, the header or footer text does not conform to these changes. Header or footer text will print at default settings.

If you want formatting changes in a document to also affect header or footer text, insert the formatting codes at the Styles Editor dialog box. To display the Styles Editor dialog box, shown in figure 11.3, click Format, point to Document, then click Initial Codes Style. Insert formatting codes in this dialog box in the normal manner.

Figure 11.3

Styles Editor Dialog Box

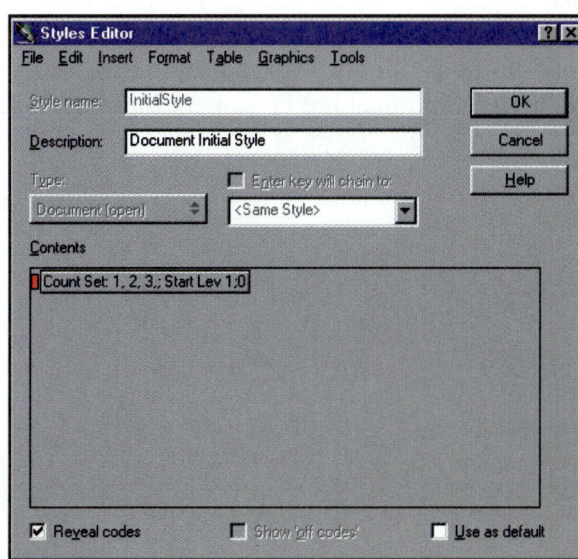

Creating Headers and Footers   237

EXERCISE 7

Changing Format at the Styles Editor Dialog Box

1. At a clear editing window, open Report 02.
2. Save the report with Save As and name it Ch 11, Ex 07.
3. Turn on the Widow/Orphan feature.
4. Change the left and right margins to 1.5 inches, the bottom margin to 0.5 inches, and the justification to Full at the Styles Editor dialog box by completing the following steps:
   a. Click Format, point to Document, then click Initial Codes Style.
   b. At the Styles Editor dialog box, complete the following steps to change the margins:
      (1) Click Format, then Margins. (Be sure to click the Format option at the top of the Styles Editor dialog box, not the Format option on the Menu Bar.)
      (2) At the Margins dialog box, change the left and right margins to 1.5" and the bottom margin to 0.5".
      (3) Click OK or press Enter to close the Margins dialog box.
      (4) Press Ctrl + J to change the justification to Full.
   c. Click OK to close the Styles Editor dialog box.
5. Create Footer A that prints at the right side of each page, is bolded, and reads *Telecommunications Development*. Change the distance between the footer and text to 0.334 inches.
6. Save the report again with the same name (Ch 11, Ex 07).
7. Print and then close Ch 11, Ex 07.

Including Font Changes in Headers and Footers

If you want to change the font for a document and you want the font to also affect header or footer text, select a new font at the Document Initial Font dialog box. To display this dialog box, shown in figure 11.4, click Format, point to Document, then click Initial Font. At the Document Initial Font dialog box, click the desired font in the Font face list box, then click OK or press Enter.

Any changes you make to the Styles Editor dialog box affect only the document in which you are working. Any changes you make at the Document Initial Font dialog box affect only the document in which you are working. If you want the font change to affect all new documents, select the Set as printer initial font option at the Document Initial Font dialog box.

Document Initial Font Dialog Box

Figure 11.4

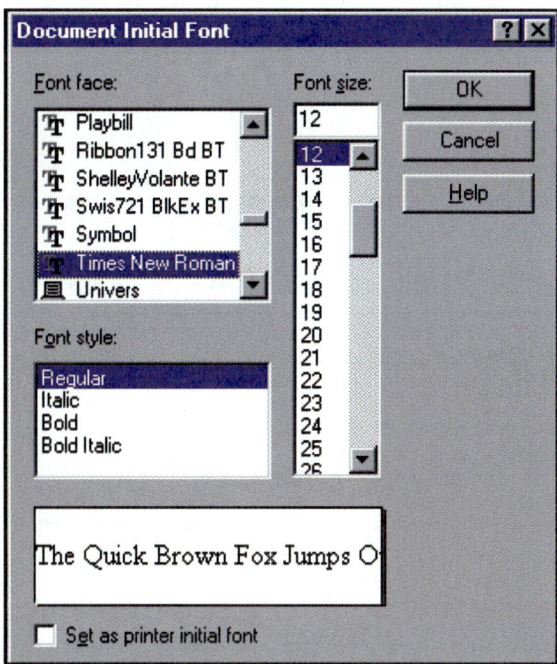

EXERCISE 8

Changing Formatting and Fonts for an Entire Document

1. At a clear editing window, open Report 02.
2. Save the report with Save As and name it Ch 11, Ex 08.
3. Turn on the Widow/Orphan feature.
4. Display the Styles Editor dialog box, change the left margin to 1.5 inches and the justification to Full, then close the dialog box.
5. Change the font for the entire document to 12-point Century Schoolbook by completing the following steps:
    a. Click Format, point to Document, then click Initial Font.
    b. At the Document Initial Font dialog box, click the Century Schoolbook font in the Font face list box (you will need to scroll up the list to display this font).
    c. Click OK or press Enter to close the Document Initial Font dialog box.
6. Create Footer A that prints at the left margin on every page, is bolded, and reads *Development of Telecommunications*.
7. Save the report again with the same name (Ch 11, Ex 08).
8. Print and then close Ch 11, Ex 08.

Inserting Page Numbering in Headers and Footers

Page numbering can be included in a header or footer with the Number button on the Header/Footer Feature Bar. When you click Number at the Header (or Footer) window, the drop-down menu shown in figure 11.5 displays.

Creating Headers and Footers   239

With the options from the drop-down menu, you can insert page numbers, secondary numbers, chapter numbers, volume numbers, or total pages numbers. For example, if you click Page Number at the Number drop-down menu, a *1* is inserted in the header or footer. This number will change on each subsequent page. (For example, a 2 will display in the header or footer on page 2.)

Figure 11.5

Header Window Number Drop-Down Menu

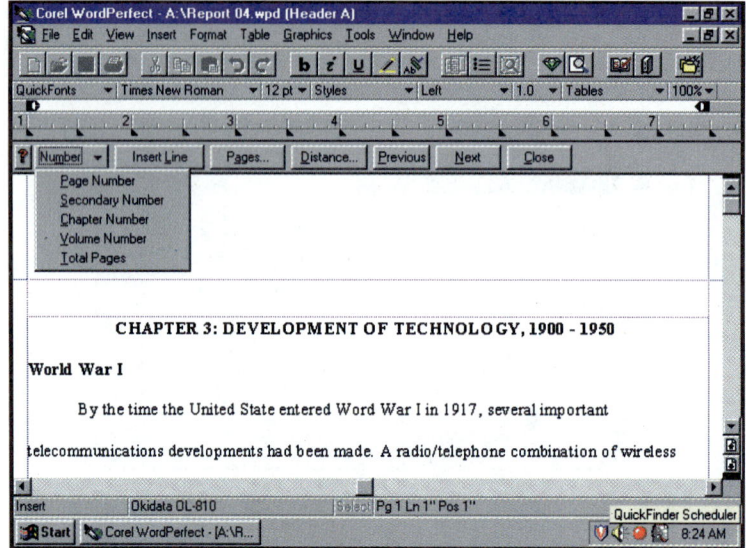

EXERCISE 9

Including Page Numbers in Footers

1. At a clear editing window, open Report 04.
2. Save the report with Save As and name it Ch 11, Ex 09.
3. Display the Styles Editor dialog box, then change the left and right margins to 1.25 inches.
4. Create Footer A that prints at the left margin of every page, is bolded, and reads *Development of Technology*.
5. Create Footer B that prints at the right margin of every page, is bolded, and reads *Page #* (where WordPerfect inserts the proper page number) by completing the following steps:
    a. Position the insertion point somewhere in the first page.
    b. Click Format, then Header/Footer.
    c. At the Headers/Footers dialog box, click Footer B, then Create.
    d. At the Footer window, click Format, point to Line, then click Flush Right (or press Alt + F7). (The previous footer text will disappear. The text, however, will display and print properly.)
    e. Press Ctrl + B, key **Page**, then press the space bar once.
    f. Click the Number button on the Header/Footer Feature Bar.
    g. At the Number drop-down list, click Page Number.
    h. Click the Close button on the Header/Footer Feature Bar.
6. Save the report again with the same name (Ch 11, Ex 09).
7. Print and then close Ch 11, Ex 09.

240 Chapter 11

Discontinuing Headers and Footers

Header or footer text can appear at the top or bottom of each page, or it can appear on certain pages and be turned off on others. For example, you can create Header A that prints on the first three pages of a document, then turn off Header A for the remaining pages of the document. You can do the same for footers. The Discontinue option at the Headers/Footers dialog box turns off the printing of the header or footer from the page where the insertion point is positioned to the end of the document.

EXERCISE 10

Turning Off the Printing of a Footer

1. At a clear editing window, open Ch 11, Ex 08.
2. Save the report with Save As and name it Ch 11, Ex 10.
3. Discontinue Footer A from page 3 to the end of the document by completing the following steps:
   a. Position the insertion point in page 3.
   b. Click Format, then Header/Footer.
   c. At the Headers/Footers dialog box, click Footer A, then Discontinue.
4. Save the report again with the same name (Ch 11, Ex 10).
5. Print and then close Ch 11, Ex 10.

Suppressing Headers and Footers

A header or footer can be suppressed on a specific page in a document. This might be useful for a page in a document such as a title page, copyright page, or opening page of a chapter. When a header or footer is discontinued, it is off for the remainder of the document (unless another header or footer is created). With options from the Suppress dialog box shown in figure 11.6, headers or footers can be suppressed on a specific page.

Figure 11.6

Suppress Dialog Box

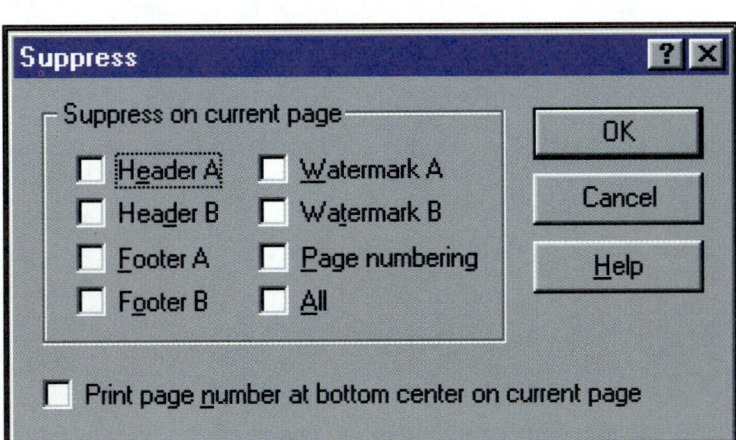

Creating Headers and Footers

EXERCISE 11

Suppressing a Footer on One Page

1. At a clear editing window, open Ch 11, Ex 08.
2. Save the report with Save As and name it Ch 11, Ex 11.
3. Suppress Footer A on page 3 by completing the following steps:
   a. Position the insertion point anywhere in page 3.
   b. Click Format, point to Page, then click Suppress.
   c. At the Suppress dialog box, click Footer A.
   d. Click OK or press Enter.
4. Save the report again with the same name (Ch 11, Ex 11).
5. Print and then close Ch 11, Ex 11.

CHAPTER SUMMARY

- Text that appears at the top of pages is called a header; text that appears at the bottom of pages is called a footer. Header/footer text will display on the screen in the Page and Two Page viewing modes but not the Draft mode.

- A maximum of two headers and/or two footers can be created in one document. WordPerfect calls them Header A, Header B, Footer A, and Footer B.

- A header or footer can contain up to one page of text.

- A header is created at a separate screen called the Header window and a footer is created at a separate screen called the Footer window.

- WordPerfect inserts a header or footer code at the beginning of the page where the insertion point is positioned. If the code is positioned in the first page of the document, the header/footer will print on every page.

- When the Header or Footer window is displayed, the Header/Footer Feature Bar is inserted in the document window below the Power Bar (or the Ruler Bar). Options on this bar include changing the distance measurement between the header/footer and the text and inserting page numbering in a header/footer.

- Use the Flush Right command to create text aligned at the right margin.

- A header/footer that is created in a document does not take on any formatting applied to the document. If you want formatting changes in a document to also affect header/footer text, insert the formatting codes at the Styles Editor dialog box.

- If you use a font in a document other than the default and want this font to apply to the headers/footers, change the font at the Document Initial Font dialog box.

- When a document is printed, header or footer text occupies the place of regular text lines. By default, a blank line separates the header or footer from the main text.

- Header or footer text can be edited by clicking Edit at the Headers/Footers dialog box.

- A header/footer can be discontinued at the Headers/Footers dialog box or suppressed at the Suppress dialog box.

COMMANDS REVIEW

	Mouse	Keyboard
Headers/Footers dialog box	Fo**r**mat, **H**eader/Footer	Fo**r**mat, **H**eader/Footer
Flush Right	Fo**r**mat, **L**ine, **F**lush Right	ALT + F7
Styles Editor dialog box	Fo**r**mat, **D**ocument, Initial Codes **S**tyle	Fo**r**mat, **D**ocument, Initial Codes **S**tyle
Document Initial Font dialog box	Fo**r**mat, **D**ocument, Initial **F**ont	Fo**r**mat, **D**ocument Initial **F**ont
Suppress dialog box	Fo**r**mat, **P**age, **S**uppress	Fo**r**mat, **P**age, **S**uppress

CHECK YOUR UNDERSTANDING

Completion: In the space provided at the right, indicate the correct term, command, or number.

1. Text that appears at the top of every page is referred to as this. _____

2. This is the maximum number of headers that can be created in the same document. _____

3. Text that appears at the bottom of every page is referred to as this. _____

4. A header or footer code will be inserted here when a header or footer is created in a document. _____

5. This is the shortcut command from the keyboard to align text at the right margin. _____

6. To print the header in a document on every page except page 3, place this code on page 3. _____

7. Headers and/or footers will not display in this viewing mode. _____

8. If you use a font in a document other than the default and want this font to apply to any headers or footers in the document, change the font at this dialog box. _____

9. If you want formatting changes in a document to affect any headers or footers in a document, insert the formatting codes at this dialog box. _____

10. Header text is separated from the main text in the document by this number of blank lines. _____

11. If you want a header to print one-half inch from the top of the page, change the top margin to this measurement. _____

SKILL ASSESSMENTS

Assessment 1

1. At a clear editing window, open Report 04.
2. Save the report with Save As and name it Ch 11, SA 01.

3. Make the following changes to the report:
   a. Turn on the Widow/Orphan feature.
   b. Insert a hard page break at the title, *CHAPTER 4: DEVELOPMENT OF TECHNOLOGY, 1950 - 1960*.
   c. Create Footer A that prints centered at the bottom of each page, is bolded, and reads *Telecommunications Trends*.
4. Save the report again with the same name (Ch 11, SA 01).
5. Print and then close Ch 11, SA 01.

Assessment 2

1. At a clear editing window, open Report 02.
2. Save the report with Save As and name it Ch 11, SA 02.
3. Make the following changes to the report:
   a. Turn on the Widow/Orphan feature.
   b. Change the top and bottom margins to 0.5 inches.
   c. Press the Enter key three times to move the title of the report down to approximately Line 1.68".
   d. Display the Styles Editor dialog box, then change the left and right margins to 1.25 inches and the justification to Full.
   e. Display the Document Initial Font dialog box, then change the font to 12-point Century Schoolbook.
   f. Create Footer A that prints centered and bolded at the bottom of every page and reads *Telecommunications*.
   g. Create Header A that prints at the right margin on every page except the first, is bolded, and reads *Development of Technology*.
4. Save the report again with the same name (Ch 11, SA 02).
5. Print and then close Ch 11, SA 02.

Assessment 3

1. At a clear editing window, open Report 03.
2. Save the report with Save As and name it Ch 11, SA 03.
3. Insert a page break in the second page at the line containing the title *CHAPTER 2: DEVELOPMENT OF TECHNOLOGY, 1850 - 1900*.
4. Move the insertion point back to the beginning of the document and make the following changes:
   a. Display the Styles Editor dialog box, change the left, right, and top margins to 1.5 inches, then close the Styles Editor dialog box.
   b. Display the Document Initial Font dialog box, then change the font to 12-point BernhardMod BT. (If BernhardMod BT is not available, choose Century Schoolbook.)
   c. Turn on the Widow/Orphan feature.
   d. Create Footer A that prints at the left margin of every page, is bolded, and reads *Chapter 1*.
   e. Create Footer B that prints at the right margin of every page, is bolded, and reads *Development of Technology*.
5. Position the insertion point in page 3, then discontinue Footer A.
6. With the insertion point still positioned in page 3, create a new Footer A, which prints at the left margin, is bolded, and reads *Chapter 2*.
7. Save the report again with the same name (Ch 11, SA 03).
8. Print and then close Ch 11, SA 03.

Reminder: You may want to delete outdated document files now.

CREATING FOOTNOTES AND ENDNOTES

PERFORMANCE OBJECTIVE

Upon successful completion of chapter 12, you will be able to amend a researched business report with properly formatted footnotes or endnotes.

A research paper or report contains information from a variety of sources. To give credit to those sources, a footnote can be inserted in the document. A *footnote* is an explanatory note or reference that is printed at the bottom of the page.

A footnote notation appears in the body of the document as a superscripted number. At the bottom of the page, this same number identifies the footnote containing information about the source. When footnotes are created in a document, WordPerfect determines the number of lines needed at the bottom of the page for the footnote information and adjusts the page endings accordingly.

An *endnote* is similar to a footnote, except that endnote reference information appears at the end of a document rather than on the page where the reference was made.

Creating Footnotes and Endnotes

Footnotes and endnotes are created in a similar manner with WordPerfect. To create a footnote in a document, move the insertion point to the location in the document where the notation is to appear, click Insert, point to Footnote, then click Create. At the Footnote window, shown in figure 12.1, key the footnote reference information, then click the Close button that displays toward the top of the screen. The Close button is located on the Footnote/Endnote Feature Bar that displays below the Ruler Bar as shown in figure 12.1.

To create an endnote, move the insertion point to the location in the document where the notation is to appear, click Insert, point to Endnote, then click Create. At the Endnote window, shown in figure 12.2, access the Indent command, key the endnote reference information, then click the Close button on the Footnote/Endnote Feature Bar.

After keying the footnote or endnote reference text, *do not* press the Enter key. By default, WordPerfect separates footnotes and endnotes by a blank line. If you press the Enter key after keying the footnote or endnote reference text, an extra blank line is inserted between the notes.

At the Footnote or Endnote window, choose options with the keyboard by holding down the Alt key, then the Shift key, then pressing the underlined letter of the desired option. For example, to close the Footnote window, press Alt + Shift + C for Close.

Figure 12.1

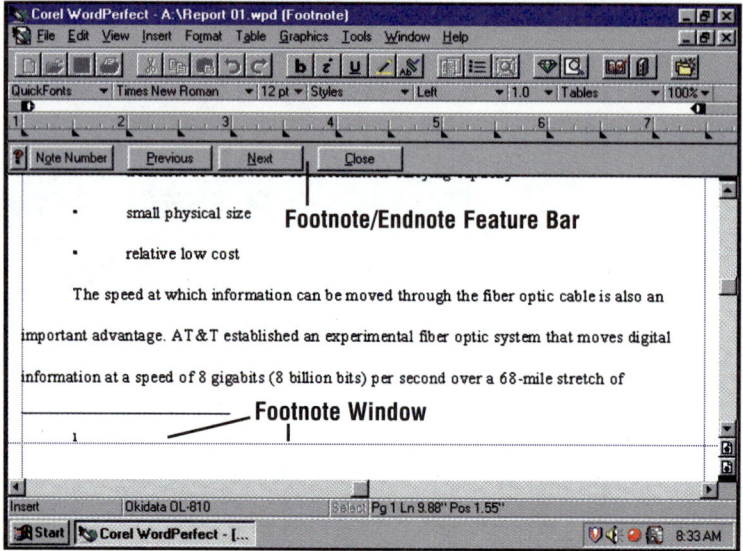

Footnote Window

Figure 12.2

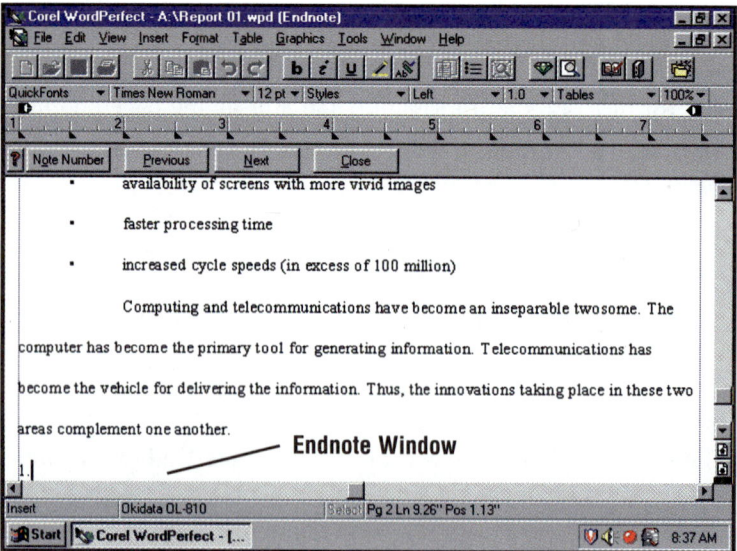

Endnote Window

EXERCISE 1

Creating Footnotes

1. At a clear editing window, open Report 01.
2. Save the report with Save As and name it Ch 12, Ex 01.
3. Turn on the Widow/Orphan feature.
4. Create the first footnote shown in figure 12.3 at the end of the first paragraph in the *Continued Growth of Photonics (Fiber Optics)* section by completing the following steps:
    a. Position the insertion point at the end of the first paragraph in the *Continued Growth of Photonics (Fiber Optics)* section.
    b. Click Insert, point to Footnote, then click Create.
    c. At the Footnote window, key the first footnote reference information shown in figure 12.3.
    d. Click the Close button on the Footnote/Endnote Feature Bar.
5. Move the insertion point to the end of the second paragraph in the *Continued Growth of Photonics (Fiber Optics)* section, then create the second footnote shown in figure 12.3 by completing steps similar to those in 4.
6. Move the insertion point to the end of the last paragraph in the *Continued Growth of Photonics (Fiber Optics)* section, then create the third footnote shown in figure 12.3 by completing steps similar to those in 4.
7. Move the insertion point to the end of the last paragraph in the report, then create the fourth footnote shown in figure 12.3 by completing steps similar to those in 4.
8. Check page breaks in the report and, if necessary, insert your own page breaks in more appropriate locations.
9. Save the report again with the same name (Ch 12, Ex 01).
10. Print and then close Ch 12, Ex 01.

Figure 12.3

[1]Mitchell, William, Robert Hendricks, and Leonard Sterry, *Telecommunications: Systems and Applications*, Paradigm Publishing, 1993, pages 39-41.

[2]Weik, Robert, "History of Light Wave Technology," *Computer Technologies*, May/June 1997, pages 9-12.

[3]Griffith, Kathleen, "The Importance of Fiber Optics," *Computing in the 90's*, April 1996, pages 2-6.

[4]McKenna, Kelly A., *Telecommunications Innovations*, Princetown Publishing, 1997, pages 44-48.

Printing Footnotes and Endnotes

When a document containing footnotes is printed, WordPerfect automatically reduces the number of text lines on a page by the number of lines in the footnote plus two lines for spacing between the text and the footnote. WordPerfect keeps at least 0.5 inches of footnote text together. If there is not enough room on the page for the 0.5 inches of footnote text, the footnote number and footnote are taken to the next page. WordPerfect separates the footnotes from the text with a 2-inch separator line that begins at the left margin. The footnote number in the document and the footnote number before the reference information print as superscripted numbers above the text line.

When endnotes are created in a document, WordPerfect prints all endnote references at the end of the document. If you want the endnotes printed on a separate page at the end of the document, move the insertion point to the end of the document, then insert a hard page break by clicking Insert, then Page Break; or by pressing Ctrl + Enter.

Endnotes can also be placed in other locations in the document. For example, in a document containing several sections, you can have the endnotes placed at the end of each section within the document. To position endnotes at a location other than the end of a document, access the Endnote Placement dialog box and click either Insert endnotes at insertion point or Insert endnotes at insertion point and restart numbering. To display the Endnote Placement dialog box, click Insert, point to Endnote, then click Placement.

EXERCISE

Creating Endnotes

1. At a clear editing window, open Report 02.
2. Save the report with Save As and name it Ch 12, Ex 02.
3. Make the following changes to the document:
   a. Turn on the Widow/Orphan feature.
   b. Move the insertion point to the end of the document, then insert a hard page break by clicking Insert, then Page Break; or pressing Ctrl + Enter.
   c. Key **ENDNOTES**, bolded and centered, then press the Enter key once. (This will cause the endnotes to print on a separate page with the heading *ENDNOTES*.)
   d. Create the first endnote shown in figure 12.4 by completing the following steps:
      (1) Position the insertion point at the end of the first paragraph in the report.
      (2) Click Insert, point to Endnote, then click Create.
      (3) At the Endnote window, press F7 to access the Indent command, then key the first endnote reference information shown in figure 12.4.
      (4) Click the Close button on the Footnote/Endnote Feature Bar.
   e. Move the insertion point to the end of the first paragraph in the *Contributions of Major Historical Events* section, then create the second endnote shown in figure 12.4 by completing steps similar to those in 3d.
   f. Move the insertion point to the end of the last paragraph in the *Contributions of Major Historical Events* section, then create the third endnote shown in figure 12.4 by completing steps similar to those in 3d.
   g. Move the insertion point to the end of the last paragraph in the document, then create the fourth endnote shown in figure 12.4 by completing steps similar to those in 3d.

4. Check page breaks in the report and, if necessary, insert your own page breaks in more appropriate locations.
5. Save the report with the same name (Ch 12, Ex 02).
6. Print and then close Ch 12, Ex 02.

Figure 12.4

1. Mitchell, William, Robert Hendricks, and Leonard Sterry, *Telecommunications: Systems and Applications*, Paradigm Publishing, 1993, pages 16-19.

2. Brewer, Ilene, *Industrialization in the U.S.*, City Publishing Services, 1995, pages 43-45.

3. Morrell, Ashley, *History of Computing*, G. Hardy Publishing, 1996, pages 12-20.

4. Pang, Yi, *Computing in the 1990s*, Pacific Coast Publishing, Inc., 1997, pages 7-13.

Formatting Footnotes and Endnotes

If you want formatting changes to affect footnotes or endnotes as well as the document, insert the formatting codes at the Styles Editor dialog box. If you also change the font in a document and want the new font to apply to footnotes or endnotes, change the font at the Document Initial Font dialog box. Otherwise, the footnotes or endnotes will print in the default font of the document.

Any changes you make at the Styles Editor dialog box or the Document Initial Font dialog box affect only the document in which you are working. When you begin a new document, the WordPerfect document defaults are in effect.

EXERCISE 3

Creating and Formatting Footnotes

1. At a clear editing window, open Ch 12, Ex 01.
2. Save the document with Save As and name it Ch 12, Ex 03.
3. Make the following changes to the document:
   a. Display the Styles Editor dialog box, change the left and right margins to 1.5 inches and the justification to Full, then close the dialog box.
   b. Display the Document Initial Font dialog box, change the font to 12-point Century Schoolbook, then close the dialog box.
   c. Select the title, *TRENDS IN TELECOMMUNICATIONS*, then change the font size to 14.
4. Check page breaks in the report and, if necessary, insert your own page breaks in more appropriate locations.
5. Save the document again with the same name (Ch 12, Ex 03).
6. Print and then close Ch 12, Ex 03.

Editing a Footnote or Endnote

Changes can be made to a footnote or endnote that was previously created in a document. These changes are made at the Edit Footnote dialog box shown in figure 12.5. The same options are offered at the Edit Endnote dialog box.

Figure 12.5

Edit Footnote Dialog Box

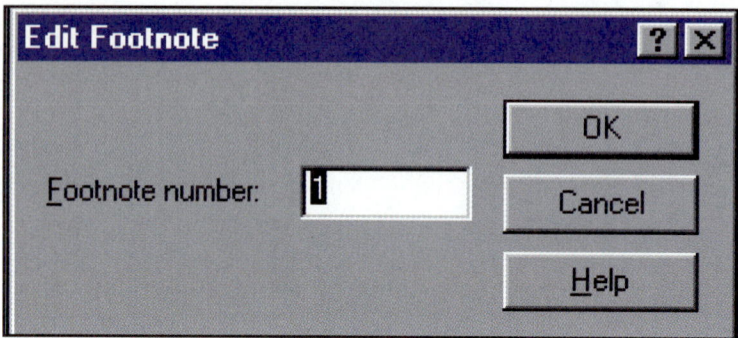

EXERCISE

Editing Endnotes

1. At a clear editing window, open Ch 12, Ex 02.
2. Save the document with Save As and name it Ch 12, Ex 04.
3. Make the following changes to the document:
   a. Display the Styles Editor dialog box, change the left and right margins to 1.25 inches, then close the dialog box.
   b. Display the Document Initial Font dialog box, change the font to 12-point Century Schoolbook, then close the dialog box.
   c. Number pages in the document at the bottom center of each page.
   d. Edit the second endnote, changing the year from *1995* to *1997* and changing the page numbers from *43-45* to *21-24*, by completing the following steps:
      (1) Click Insert, point to Endnote, then click Edit.
      (2) At the Edit Endnote dialog box, key **2**, then click OK or press Enter.
      (3) With the reference text for the endnote displayed in the Endnote window, change the year from *1995* to *1997* and the pages from *43-45* to *21-24*.
      (4) Click Close.
   e. Edit the fourth endnote, changing the title from *Computing in the 1990s* to *Perspectives in Telecommunications*.
4. Check page breaks in the report and, if necessary, insert your own page breaks in more appropriate locations.
5. Save the document again with the same name (Ch 12, Ex 04).
6. Print and then close Ch 12, Ex 04.

Deleting a Footnote or Endnote

A footnote or endnote can be deleted from a document by positioning the insertion point immediately to the left of the footnote or endnote number, then pressing the Delete key. You can also position the insertion point immediately to the right of the footnote or endnote number, then press the Backspace key. Or, you can use the mouse to drag the footnote or endnote code out of the Reveal Codes window. When a footnote or endnote is deleted from a document, WordPerfect automatically renumbers any remaining footnotes or endnotes.

EXERCISE 5

Editing and Deleting Footnotes

1. At a clear editing window, open Ch 12, Ex 01.
2. Save the document with Save As and name it Ch 12, Ex 05.
3. Make the following changes to the document:
   a. Display the Styles Editor dialog box, change the left and right margins to 1.25 inches and the justification to Full, then close the dialog box.
   b. Select the title, *TRENDS IN TELECOMMUNICATIONS*, then change the relative size to Very Large.
   c. Select the heading *Continued Growth of Photonics (Fiber Optics)*, then change the relative size to Large.
   d. Select the heading *Microcomputer Trends in the Nineties*, then change the relative size to Large.
   e. Move the insertion point to the end of the second paragraph in the *Continued Growth of Photonics (Fiber Optics)* section, then delete the footnote number.
4. Check page breaks in the report and, if necessary, insert your own page breaks in more appropriate locations.
5. Save the document again with the same name (Ch 12, Ex 05).
6. Print and then close Ch 12, Ex 05.

Changing the Beginning Number

When a footnote or endnote is created in a document, the numbering begins with 1 and continues sequentially. The beginning footnote or endnote number can be changed as well as the numbering style. For example, you can begin footnote numbering with 2 rather than 1. These kinds of changes are made at the Footnote Number dialog box, shown in figure 12.6. The Endnote Number dialog box contains the same options. Note that you can change the number by keying a new number or by clicking the Increase or Decrease option.

When a footnote or endnote number is changed, a code is inserted in the document at the location of the insertion point and can be seen in Reveal Codes.

Figure 12.6 Footnote Number Dialog Box

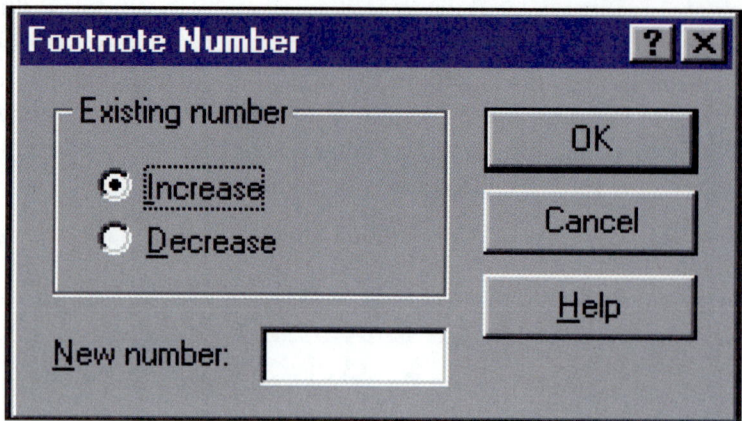

EXERCISE 6

Renumbering Footnotes

1. At a clear editing window, open Ch 12, Ex 01.
2. Save the document with Save As and name it Ch 12, Ex 06.
3. Make the following changes to the document:
    a. Change the top margin to 1.5 inches.
    b. With the insertion point located at the beginning of the document, change the beginning footnote number to 5 by completing the following steps:
        (1) Click Insert, point to Footnote, then click New Number.
        (2) At the Footnote Number dialog box, click in the New number text box.
        (3) Key 5.
        (4) Click OK or press Enter.
    c. Number each page except the first page in the top right corner of the page.
4. Check page breaks in the report and, if necessary, insert your own page breaks in more appropriate locations.
5. Save the document again with the same name (Ch 12, Ex 06).
6. Print and then close Ch 12, Ex 06.

Changing Footnote or Endnote Options

At the Footnote Options dialog box, shown in figure 12.7, changes can be made to the format of a footnote. To display the Footnote Options dialog box, click Insert, point to Footnote, then click Options. The Endnote Options dialog box contains many of the same options as the Footnote Options dialog box. To display the Endnote Options dialog box, click Insert, point to Endnote, then click Options.

Figure 12.7

Footnote Options Dialog Box

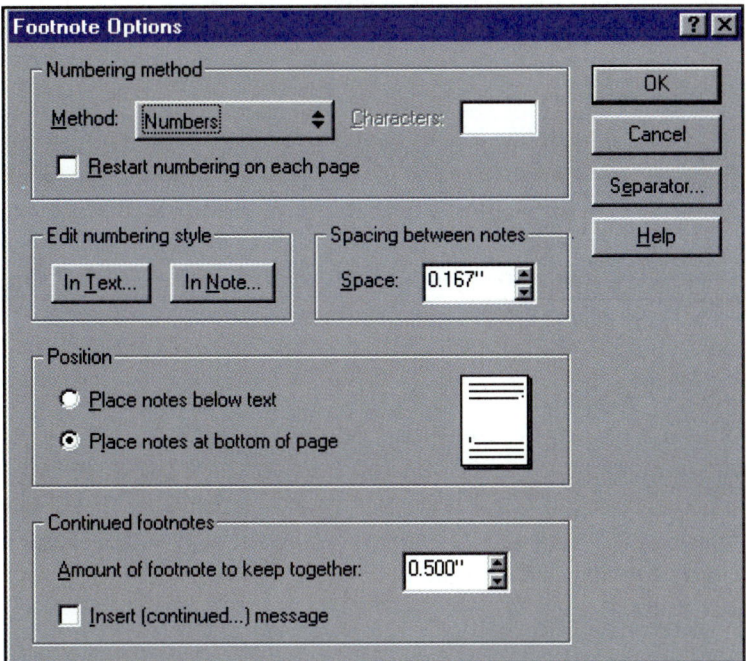

Numbering Method

The default numbering method for footnotes and endnotes is Numbers. This can be changed to Lowercase Letters, Uppercase Letters, Lowercase Roman, Uppercase Roman, or Characters. If you change the numbering method to Characters, the Characters option changes from dimmed to bright. In the Characters text box, you can identify the type of character you want to use for footnotes or endnotes. If you want to restart footnote numbering on each page, insert a check mark in the Restart numbering on each page check box. The Endnote Options dialog box does not contain this option.

Edit Numbering Style

The Edit numbering style section of the Footnote Options dialog box contains two options—In Text and In Note. If you click In Text, the Styles Editor dialog box displays showing the codes that are used for the footnote number in the text. If you click In Note, the Styles Editor dialog box displays showing codes that are used for the footnote number in the footnote. The Endnote Options dialog box contains the same options.

By default, a footnote or endnote number in the text appears as a superscripted number. In the Footnote window, a footnote appears as a superscripted number indented to the first tab setting. In the Endnote window, an endnote number appears as a number at the left margin followed by a period.

You can change how footnotes or endnotes appear in text or in the note at the Styles Editor dialog box. To change a footnote or endnote, insert or delete codes at the Styles Editor dialog box. For example, to include an indent code after the endnote number in the note, you would complete the following steps:

1. Click Insert, point to Endnote, then click Options.
2. At the Endnote Options dialog box, click In Note.
3. At the Styles Editor dialog box, use the right arrow key to move the insertion point past the *Endnote Num Disp: Lev: 1;0* code and the period.

Creating Footnotes and Endnotes

4. Press F7; or click Format, point to Paragraph, then click Indent.
5. Click OK.
6. At the Endnote Options dialog box, click OK.

Spacing between Notes

By default, a footnote or an endnote is single spaced and separated from the next footnote or endnote by a blank line (a double space). You can change the amount of space between footnotes or endnotes with the Space option at the Footnote Options dialog box or the Endnote Options dialog box. If you want more space to separate footnotes or endnotes, click Space, then increase the number. If you want less space to separate footnotes or endnotes, click Space, then decrease the number.

Position

The Footnote Options dialog box (but not the Endnote Options dialog box) contains a Position section. By default, a footnote is printed at the bottom of the page where the footnote was referenced. This can be changed to Place notes below text. This has an effect only on a page where the text ends before the end of the page. On a page where the text ends before the end of the page, the footnote prints after the text. When you make a change at the Position section, the page icon at the right reflects the change.

Continued and Continuous Notes

By default, WordPerfect prints a footnote at the bottom of the page where it was referenced. If the footnote is extremely long, all of the text may not fit at the bottom of the page. When that happens, WordPerfect prints at least 0.5 inches of the footnote on the page and wraps the remainder of the footnote to the next page.

When a footnote is wrapped to the next page, a continued message can be inserted at the location where the footnote ends (on the first page) and also at the beginning of the footnote on the next page. If you want the continued message inserted in a footnote, insert a check mark in the Insert (continued...) message check box at the Footnote Options dialog box. (This option is not available at the Endnote Options dialog box.)

The Amount of footnote to keep together option at the Footnote Options dialog box and the Endnote Options dialog box has a default setting of 0.500 inches. At this setting, WordPerfect keeps at least 0.5 inches of a footnote or endnote on a page before wrapping any remaining text to the next page. If you want more or less of a footnote or endnote to remain on the page, increase or decrease the measurement.

Separator

When a document containing footnotes is printed, the text is separated from the footnote references by a 2-inch line. This is the default setting at the Line Separator dialog box shown in figure 12.8. To display this dialog box, click the Separator button that displays at the right side of the Footnote Options dialog box. The Endnote Options dialog box does not contain this option.

With the Separation options—Space above line and Space below line—you can increase or decrease the amount of space above and/or below the separator line.

By default the separator line begins at the left margin. This can be changed to Full, Center, Right, or Set with drop-down options from the Line position option. If you change the Line position to Center, Right, Set, or leave it at the default of Left, you can set the line length with the Length of line option.

The default separator line is a single line. This can be changed to a variety of line types. To display the list of line choices using the mouse, position the arrow pointer on the line button to the right of the Line style option, then click the left mouse button. If you are using the keyboard, press Alt + N, then press the space bar.

To choose a line option with the mouse, position the arrow pointer on the desired option, then click the left mouse button. If you are using the keyboard, press the up, down, left, or right arrow key until the desired option is selected, then press Enter.

Figure 12.8

Line Separator Dialog Box

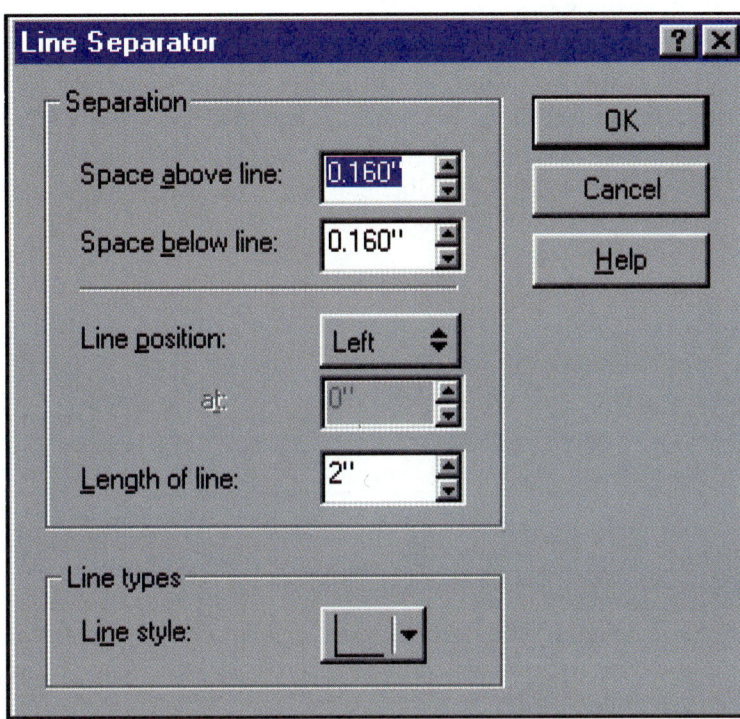

EXERCISE 7

Changing the Separator Line and Numbering Method

1. At a clear editing window, open Ch 12, Ex 06.
2. Save the document with Save As and name it Ch 12, Ex 07.
3. Make the following changes to the document:
   a. Change the numbering method to lowercase letters by completing the following steps:
      (1) Click Insert, point to Footnote, then click Options.
      (2) At the Footnote Options dialog box, change the Method option to Lowercase Letters. To do this, position the arrow pointer in the Method text box, click the left mouse button, then click Lowercase Letters that displays at the drop-down menu.
      (3) Click OK or press Enter to close the dialog box.

Creating Footnotes and Endnotes 255

    b. Change the spacing between footnotes to 0.084" by completing the following steps:
        (1) Click Insert, point to Footnote, then click Options.
        (2) At the Footnote Options dialog box, select the current measurement (0.167") that displays in the Space list box, then key **0.084**.
        (3) Click OK or press Enter to close the dialog box.
    c. Change the separator line to a double line that extends from the left to the right margin by completing the following steps:
        (1) Click Insert, point to Footnote, then click Options.
        (2) At the Footnote Options dialog box, click the Separator button.
        (3) At the Line Separator dialog box, click the Line position button, then click Full at the drop-down menu.
        (4) Display the list of line choices by positioning the arrow pointer on the line button that displays to the right of the Line style option, then clicking the left mouse button.
        (5) At the drop-down list of line choices, click the double line option (the second option from the left in the top row).
        (6) Click OK or press Enter.
        (7) At the Footnote Options dialog box, click OK or press Enter.
4. Check page breaks in the report and, if necessary, insert your own page breaks in more appropriate locations.
5. Save the document again with the same name (Ch 12, Ex 07).
6. Print and then close Ch 12, Ex 07.

Converting Footnotes and Endnotes

The WordPerfect program contains default macros that can be used to convert footnotes to endnotes or endnotes to footnotes. (For more information on macros, please refer to chapter 18.) To convert footnotes to endnotes using the WordPerfect macro, you would complete the following steps:

1. Open the document containing the footnotes.
2. Click Tools, point to Macro, then click Play.
3. At the Play Macro dialog box, double-click *Footend* that displays in the list box. (You can also click *Footend* once and then click the Play button.)

At the Play Macro dialog box, a list of WordPerfect macros is displayed in the list box. You can play a macro from the list box by double-clicking the macro name or clicking the macro and then clicking Play. To convert endnotes to footnotes, use the *Endfoot* WordPerfect macro. For the *Footend* and *Endfoot* macros to work, the macros must have been installed when WordPerfect 7 was installed, and WordPerfect must know where they are located.

Converting Footnotes to Endnotes

1. At a clear editing window, open Ch 12, Ex 06.
2. Save the document with Save As and name it Ch 12, Ex 08.
3. Move the insertion point to the end of the document, then complete the following steps:
   a. Insert a hard page break.
   b. Key **ENDNOTES** centered and bolded.
   c. Press Enter once.
4. Convert the footnotes to endnotes by completing the following steps:
   a. Click Tools, point to Macro, then click Play.
   b. At the Play Macro dialog box, double-click *Footend* in the list box.
5. Indent the reference text after endnote numbers by completing the following steps:
   a. Click Insert, point to Endnote, then click Edit.
   b. At the Edit Endnote dialog box, key **1**, then click OK or press Enter.
   c. With the reference text for the endnote displayed in the Endnote window and the insertion point positioned on the first character after 1., press F7.
   d. Click the Next button on the Footnote/Endnote Feature Bar. (This moves the insertion point to the first character after 2.)
   e. Press F7.
   f. Click the Next button on the Footnote/Endnote Feature Bar. (This moves the insertion point to the first character after 3.)
   g. Press F7.
   h. Click the Next button on the Footnote/Endnote Feature Bar. (This moves the insertion point to the first character after 4.)
   i. Press F7.
   j. Click the Close button on the Footnote/Endnote Feature Bar.
6. Check page breaks in the report and, if necessary, insert your own page breaks in more appropriate locations.
7. Save the document again with the same name (Ch 12, Ex 08).
8. Print and then close Ch 12, Ex 08.

CHAPTER SUMMARY

- A footnote is an explanatory note or reference that is printed at the bottom of a page. An endnote is a note or reference printed at the end of a document.
- When a footnote or endnote is created, a superscripted number is inserted in the document where the insertion point is located.
- Before the footnote/endnote is created at the Footnote/Endnote window, position the insertion point in the document where the notation (superscripted number) is to appear.
- A footnote prints at the bottom of the page where the text is referenced; footnotes are separated from the text by a 2-inch line that begins at the left margin.
- Endnotes print at the end of the last text in the document. To print endnotes on a separate page, insert a hard page break at the end of the document. Endnotes can be placed elsewhere at the Endnote Placement dialog box.
- A footnote/endnote that is created in a document does not take on any formatting applied to the document. If you want formatting changes in a document to also affect header/footer text, insert the formatting codes at the Styles Editor dialog box.
- If you use a font in a document other than the default and want this font applied to the footnotes/endnotes, change the font at the Document Initial Font dialog box.
- Footnotes/endnotes can be edited.
- A footnote/endnote can be removed by deleting the superscripted number in the document. WordPerfect will automatically renumber any remaining footnotes/endnotes.
- At the Footnote Options or Endnote Options dialog box, you can change the following: numbering method, numbering style, spacing between notes, positioning of footnotes/endnotes, including continued and continuous notes, and the separator line.
- WordPerfect contains default macros that can be used to convert footnotes to endnotes or vice versa. These are named *Footend* and *Endfoot*.

COMMANDS REVIEW

	Mouse/Keyboard
Footnote window	Insert, Footnote, Create
Endnote window	Insert, Endnote, Create
Styles Editor dialog box	Format, Document, Initial Codes Style
Document Initial Font dialog box	Format, Document, Initial Font
Edit Footnote dialog box	Insert, Footnote, Edit
Edit Endnote dialog box	Insert, Endnote, Edit

CHECK YOUR UNDERSTANDING

Completion: In the space provided at the right, indicate the correct term, command, or number.

1. So that the endnotes will print on a separate page, insert this at the end of the document. _____

2. If you want endnotes to print in a location other than the end of the document, display this dialog box. _____

3. When a footnote or endnote is created, this type of number is inserted in the document at the location of the insertion point. _____

4. By default, each footnote is single spaced and separated by this number of blank lines. _____

5. If you want formatting changes to affect footnotes or endnotes, insert the formatting codes here. _____

6. The footnote numbering style can be changed at this dialog box. _____

7. By default, WordPerfect separates footnotes from the text by this. _____

8. By default, footnotes are printed here. _____

9. If you use a font in a document other than the default and want this font applied to footnotes, change the font at this dialog box. _____

10. Use this macro to convert footnotes to endnotes. _____

SKILL ASSESSMENTS

Assessment 1

1. At a clear editing window, open Report 07.
2. Save the document with Save As and name it Ch 12, SA 01.
3. Make the following changes to the report:
   a. Turn on the Widow/Orphan feature.
   b. Change the line spacing to double (2).
   c. Number each page except the first page at the top right corner of the page.
   d. Create the first footnote shown in figure 12.9 at the end of the last paragraph in the *Industrialization* section of the report.
   e. Create the second footnote shown in figure 12.9 at the end of the last paragraph in the *Development of a World Market* section of the report.
   f. Create the third footnote shown in figure 12.9 at the end of the last paragraph in the report.
4. Check page breaks in the report and, if necessary, insert your own page breaks in more appropriate locations.
5. Save the document again with the same name (Ch 12, SA 01).
6. Print and then close Ch 12, SA 01.

Figure 12.9

[1]Mitchell, William, Robert Hendricks, and Leonard Sterry, "Contributions of Major Historical Events," *Telecommunications: Systems and Applications*, Paradigm Publishing, 1993, pages 16-17.

[2]Reynolds, Susan, "The World Market in the 1850s," *Communicating in the World Market*, Lowell & Howe Publishing, 1996, pages 25-28.

[3]Boronat, Walter, "Impact of the 1870s Depression on Technology," *Computer Technology*, Holstein/Mann Publishing, 1998, pages 55-78.

Assessment 2

1. At a clear editing window, open Ch 12, SA 01.
2. Save the document with Save As and name it Ch 12, SA 02.
3. Make the following changes to the report:
    a. Display the Document Initial Font dialog box, change the font to 12-point Century Schoolbook, then close the dialog box.
    b. Display the Styles Editor dialog box, change the left and right margins to 1.5 inches and the justification to Full, then close the dialog box.
    c. Select the title and then change the relative size to Large.
    d. Change the beginning footnote number to 4.
    e. Change the footnote separator line to a double line that is 3 inches long and centered on the page.
    f. Add the footnote shown in figure 12.10 at the end of the paragraph in the *Colonization* section of the report.
4. Check page breaks in the report and, if necessary, insert your own page breaks in more appropriate locations.
5. Save the document again with the same name (Ch 12, SA 02).
6. Print and then close Ch 12, SA 02.

Figure 12.10

[6]Champoux, Daniel, *Historical Perspectives in Computing*, Ashford Mountain Publishing Company, 1997, pages 75-87.

Assessment 3

1. At a clear editing window, open Ch 12, SA 01.
2. Save the document with Save As and name it Ch 12, SA 03.
3. Make the following changes to the report:
    a. Change the font to 12-point Garamond (or a similar serif typeface). (Make sure this affects all aspects of the report.)
    b. Delete the previous page numbering code and number all pages at the bottom center.
    c. Convert the footnotes to endnotes.
    d. Have all endnotes print at the end of the document on a separate page preceded by the title, *ENDNOTES*.
    e. Edit all the endnotes and indent the endnote reference text from the endnote number.
    f. Change the spacing between endnotes to 0.084".
    g. Edit endnote number 2 and change the date of the publication from *1996* to *1998* and change the pages from *25-28* to *41-54*.
4. Check page breaks in the report and, if necessary, insert your own page breaks in more appropriate locations.
5. Save the report again with the same name (Ch 12, SA 03).
6. Print and then close Ch 12, SA 03.

Reminder: You may want to delete outdated document files now.

13
MANIPULATING TEXT WITHIN AND BETWEEN DOCUMENTS

PERFORMANCE OBJECTIVE

Upon successful completion of chapter 13, you will be able to manipulate blocks and columns of text between areas of different business documents and create multiple windows to move or copy text between business documents.

Some documents may need to be heavily revised, and these revisions may include deleting, moving, or copying blocks of text. This kind of editing is generally referred to as *cut and paste*. In this chapter, you will learn to cut, copy, and paste text within and between documents.

WordPerfect 7 operates within the Windows 95 environment. When working in WordPerfect, a *window* refers to the editing window plus the scroll bars. Windows 95 creates an environment in which various software programs are used with menu bars, scroll bars, and icons to represent programs and files. With Windows 95, you can load several different software programs and move between them quickly. Similarly, using windows in WordPerfect, you can open several different documents and move between them quickly. In this chapter, you will learn to open multiple documents, tile and cascade documents, and move and copy text between open documents.

Working with Blocks of Text

When cutting and pasting, you work with blocks of text. A block of text is a portion of text that you have selected. (Chapter 2 explained the various methods for selecting text.) A block of text can be as small as one character or as large as an entire page or document.

Once a block of text has been selected, it can be:

- deleted,
- moved to a new location, or
- copied and placed in a certain location within a document.

The last two operations involve using WordPerfect's Cut, Copy, and Paste features.

Manipulating Text within and between Documents   *261*

Deleting a Block of Text

WordPerfect offers different methods for deleting text from a document. To delete a single character, you can use either the Delete key or the Backspace key. To delete more than a single character, select the portion of text to be deleted, then choose one of the following options:

- Press Delete.
- Press Shift + Delete.
- Click Edit, then Cut.
- Press Ctrl + X.
- Click the Cut button on the Toolbar.
- Click the right mouse button, then click Cut.

Cut

If you press Delete, the text is deleted permanently. (You can, however, restore deleted text with the Undo or Undelete options at the Edit menu.) Shift + Delete, Cut from the Edit menu, Ctrl + X, the Cut button on the Toolbar, and the Cut option from the shortcut menu accessed with the right mouse button will delete the selected text and store it in temporary memory. Text stored in temporary memory can be reinserted in a document at a later time.

EXERCISE

Selecting and Deleting Text

1. At a clear editing window, open Report 01.
2. Save the document with Save As and name it Ch 13, Ex 01.
3. Delete the following text in the report:
   a. Delete the sentence *The US Sprint network was the first to use a total fiber optic network to traverse the nation.* in the second paragraph of the *Continued Growth of Photonics (Fiber Optics)* section of the report by completing the following steps:
      (1) Select the sentence.
      (2) Press the Delete key.
   b. Delete the bulleted items on the first page and the line above the items by completing the following steps:
      (1) Select from *The advantages of light wave systems are many and include* through *relative low cost.*
      (2) Click Edit, then Cut.
   c. Delete the second bulleted item in the *Microcomputer Trends in the Nineties* section of the report.
   d. Delete the fifth bulleted item in the *Microcomputer Trends in the Nineties* section of the report.
4. Save the document again with the same name (Ch 13, Ex 01).
5. Print and then close Ch 13, Ex 01.

262 Chapter 13

Moving Blocks of Text

WordPerfect offers three methods for moving text within a document. After you have selected a block of text, you can press Shift + Delete to delete the selected text to temporary memory. You can then move the insertion point to the new location and press Shift + Insert to insert the selected text into the document at the location of the insertion point.

You can also use the Cut and Paste options from either the Edit drop-down menu or the shortcut menu, Ctrl + X to cut or Ctrl + V to paste, or the Cut and Paste buttons on the Toolbar to accomplish the same results. The Cut option from the Edit drop-down menu or the shortcut menu, Ctrl + X, or the Cut button on the Toolbar deletes text to temporary memory. The text in temporary memory can be inserted in a document with the Paste option from the Edit drop-down menu or the shortcut menu, Ctrl + V, or the Paste button on the Toolbar.

Paste

A block of selected text can also be moved with the mouse. To do this, you would complete the following steps:

1. Select the text.
2. Move the arrow pointer inside the selected text.
3. Hold down the left mouse button, drag the arrow pointer to the location where you want the selected text inserted, then release the button.
4. Turn off Select by clicking anywhere in the editing window (outside the selected text) or pressing F8.

When you hold down the left mouse button and drag the arrow pointer, the arrow pointer turns into an arrow connected to a box. The box represents the text that is being moved. When you move the arrow pointer to the desired location and release the mouse button, the selected text is removed from its original position and inserted in the new location.

Selecting and Moving Text

1. At a clear editing window, open Para 03.
2. Save the document with Save As and name it Ch 13, Ex 02.
3. Move the following text in the document:
   a. Move the second paragraph above the first paragraph by completing the following steps:
      (1) Select the second paragraph including the blank line below the paragraph.
      (2) Click Edit, then Cut.
      (3) Position the insertion point at the beginning of the first paragraph.
      (4) Click Edit, then Paste.
   b. Move the fourth paragraph above the third paragraph by completing the following steps:
      (1) Select the fourth paragraph including the blank line below the paragraph.
      (2) Click the Cut button on the Toolbar.
      (3) Position the insertion point at the beginning of the third paragraph.
      (4) Click the Paste button on the Toolbar.
   c. Move the fourth paragraph to the end of the document using the mouse by completing the following steps:

Manipulating Text within and between Documents   263

> (1) Select the fourth paragraph including the blank line below the paragraph.
> (2) Position the arrow pointer inside the selected text area.
> (3) Hold down the left mouse button, drag the arrow pointer a double space below the last paragraph, then release the mouse button.
> (4) Deselect the text.
> 4. Save the document again with the same name (Ch 13, Ex 02).
> 5. Print and then close Ch 13, Ex 02.

Copying a Block of Text

WordPerfect's Copy option can be useful in documents that contain repetitive portions of text. You can use this function to insert duplicate portions of text instead of rekeying the text. You can copy text in a document with one of the following methods:

- Click Edit, then Copy.
- Ctrl + Insert.
- Ctrl + C.

Copy

- The Copy button on the Toolbar.
- Click the right mouse button, then click Copy.

The mouse can also be used to copy a block of text in a document and insert the copy in a new location. To do this, you would complete the following steps:

1. Select the text.
2. Move the arrow pointer inside the selected text.
3. Hold down the left mouse button and the Ctrl key. Drag the arrow pointer to the location where a copy of the selected text is to be inserted.
4. Release the mouse button and then the Ctrl key.
5. Deselect the text.

With the Ctrl key down, the box with the arrow pointer displays with a page icon. There is a plus sign (+) in the middle of the page icon. When text is copied, the text remains in the editing window and a copy is inserted in temporary memory. Once text has been cut or copied to temporary memory, it can be inserted in a document any number of times without deleting or copying it again. The text will remain in temporary memory until other text is cut or copied to temporary memory or until you exit WordPerfect.

If you select a block of text and then decide you selected the wrong text or you do not want to do anything with the block, you can deselect it. If you are using the mouse, click the left mouse button outside the selected text. If you are using the keyboard, press F8 to turn Select off.

EXERCISE 3

Copying Selected Text

1. At a clear editing window, open Block 01.
2. Save the document with Save As and name it Ch 13, Ex 03.
3. Change the font to 18-point Brush738 BT (or a similar typeface).
4. Copy all the text to the end of the document by completing the following steps:
    a. Select the entire document (four lines of text plus two blank lines below the text by clicking Edit, pointing to Select, then clicking All).
    b. Click the Copy button on the Toolbar.
    c. Deselect the text.
    d. Move the insertion point to the end of the document.
    e. Click the Paste button on the Toolbar.
5. Insert the text again by pressing Ctrl + V.
6. Save the document with the same name (Ch 13, Ex 03).
7. Print and then close Ch 13, Ex 03.

Appending a Block of Text

Selected text in a document can be appended to Window's clipboard. This is useful in situations where you want to move or copy text to a document in another program. Text you append to the clipboard stays in the clipboard when you exit WordPerfect. It is deleted, however, when you exit Windows. For information on the clipboard, please refer to your Windows or WordPerfect reference documentation.

Working with Columns of Text

Text set up in columns and separated by tabs can be selected and then deleted, moved, or copied within the document. (Refer to chapter 10 for a review of setting tabs and entering text into columns.) To select a column of text, you would complete the following steps:

1. Move the insertion point or the arrow pointer to any character in the first entry of the column.
2. If you are using the mouse, hold down the left mouse button, drag the arrow pointer to the last entry of the column, then release the mouse button. (More than the one column will be selected, as shown in figure 13.1.) If you are using the keyboard, press F8 to turn on Select, then move the insertion point to any character in the last entry of the column.
3. To select just the column, click Edit, point to Select, then click Tabular Column. The column plus any tab code before or after the column is selected as shown in figure 13.2.

When you click Tabular Column, the selected text changes. The column and any tab before or after the column is selected. With the column selected, it can be deleted, moved, or copied.

Figure 13.1

Selecting Text in Columns

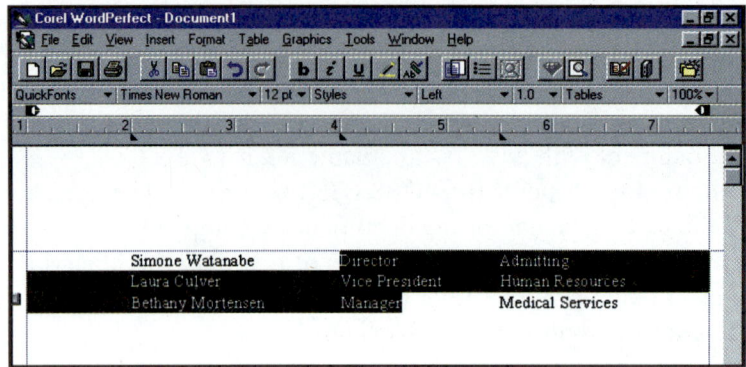

Figure 13.2

Selected Column

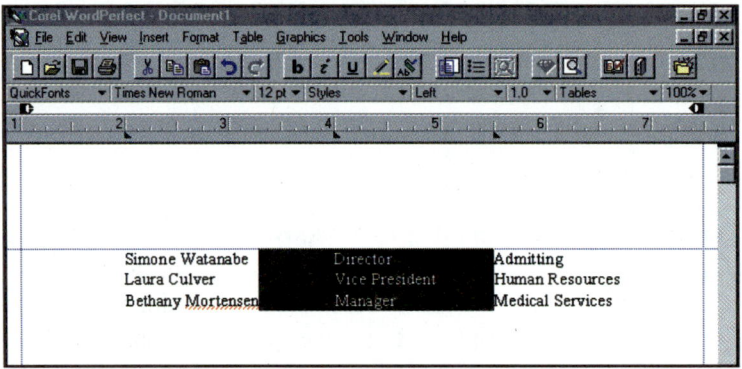

Moving Columns

To understand how to move a column, look at the columns shown in figure 13.3. The three columns were keyed with left tabs set at the 2-inch mark, the 3.75-inch mark, and the 5.5-inch mark on the Ruler. The Tab key was pressed to move from one column to the next when entering the text. To move the second column to the right of the third column, you would complete the following steps:

1. Move the insertion point or the arrow pointer to any character in the first entry of the second column (somewhere on *Director*).
2. If you are using the mouse, hold down the left mouse button, drag the arrow pointer to any character in the word *Manager*, then release the button. If you are using the keyboard, press F8 to turn on Select, then move the insertion point to any character in the word *Manager*.
3. Click Edit, Select, then Tabular Column.
4. Click the Cut button on the Toolbar.
5. Position the insertion point on the space immediately after the first column entry in the second column (*Admitting*).
6. Click the Paste button on the Toolbar. The columns will appear as shown in figure 13.4.

266 Chapter 13

Columns / Figure 13.3

Simone Watanabe	Director	Admitting
Laura Culver	Vice President	Human Resources
Bethany Mortensen	Manager	Medical Services

Moved Columns / Figure 13.4

Simone Watanabe	Admitting	Director
Laura Culver	Human Resources	Vice President
Bethany Mortensen	Medical Services	Manager

As with selected blocks of text, selected columns of text can be moved with the mouse. This capability is called "drag and drop" editing. You will practice using drag and drop to copy text in exercise 5.

EXERCISE 4

Moving Columns

1. At a clear editing window, open Tab 01.
2. Save the document with Save As and name it Ch 13, Ex 04.
3. Reverse the order of the columns by completing the following steps:
   a. Position the arrow pointer on any character in the column heading of the first column (somewhere on *California*).
   b. Hold down the left mouse button, drag the arrow pointer to any character in the words *Palm Springs*, then release the button.
   c. Click Edit, point to Se<u>l</u>ect, then click Tabular <u>C</u>olumn.
   d. Click the Cut button on the Toolbar.
   e. Position the insertion point at the space immediately following *Oregon*.
   f. Click the Paste button on the Toolbar.
4. Save the document again with the same name (Ch 13, Ex 04).
5. Print and then close Ch 13, Ex 04.

Copying a Column

Copying a column of text is very similar to moving a column. The main difference is that you click <u>C</u>opy (or click the Copy button) rather than Cu<u>t</u> at the <u>E</u>dit drop-down menu. You can also use the drag and drop feature to copy selected columns.

Manipulating Text within and between Documents 267

EXERCISE 5

Copying Columns

1. At a clear editing window, open Tab 02.
2. Save the document with Save As and name it Ch 13, Ex 05.
3. Make a copy of the text below *Pediatrics* and insert it below *Labor and Delivery* by completing the following steps:
   a. Change to the Draft viewing mode.
   b. Position the arrow pointer on any character in the words *Patient Records*, hold down the left mouse button, drag the arrow pointer to any character in the words *Insurance Forms*, then release the mouse button.
   c. Click Edit, point to Select, then click Tabular Column.
   d. Position the arrow pointer inside the selected column, then hold down the left mouse button and the Ctrl key. Drag the arrow pointer a double space below *Labor and Delivery*, at the left margin, release the mouse button, and then release the Ctrl key.
4. Key the following colors after the entries below *Labor and Delivery*. To do this, position the insertion point after the first entry, *Patient Records*. Press the Tab key, then key **Brown**. Press the down arrow key to move the insertion point down to the next line (do not press the Enter key). Press the Tab key, then key the next color, **White**. Continue in this manner until all colors have been keyed.

Patient Records	=	Brown
Supplies	=	White
Doctors' Reports	=	Red
Consultants' Reports	=	Yellow
Pharmacology	=	Purple
Insurance Forms	=	Blue

5. Save the document again with the same name (Ch 13, Ex 05).
6. Print and then close Ch 13, Ex 05.

Deleting a Column

To delete a column of text, select the column, then click Edit, then Cut; press Ctrl + X; press Shift + Delete; click the Cut button on the Toolbar; or click the right mouse button and then click Cut. When a column is removed from the editing window, any columns to the right move over to fill in the gap.

EXERCISE 6

Deleting Columns

1. At a clear editing window, open Tab 03.
2. Save the document with Save As and name it Ch 13, Ex 06.
3. Delete the second column by completing the following steps:
   a. Position the arrow pointer on any character in the word *Semi*.

      b. Hold down the left mouse button, drag the arrow pointer to any character in the number *42.00*, then release the mouse button.
      c. Click Edit, point to Select, then click Tabular Column.
      d. Click the Cut button on the Toolbar.
4. Display Reveal Codes, then move the insertion point to the line containing the Tab Set code.
5. Display the Tab Set dialog box, clear previous tabs, then set a left tab at position 1.5 and a right tab at position 4.9. Turn off the display of Reveal Codes.
6. Save the document again with the same name (Ch 13, Ex 06).
7. Print and then close Ch 13, Ex 06.

Working with Documents

Some documents may contain standard information—information that remains the same. For example, a legal document, such as a will, may contain text that is standard and appears in all wills. Repetitive text can be saved as a separate document and then retrieved into an existing document whenever needed.

There are two methods that can be used for saving text into a separate document. The first is to save a document just as you have been doing. The other method is to select standard text within a document and save it as a separate document.

Saving Standard Text

If you know in advance what information or text is standard and will be used again, you can save it as a separate document. You should determine how to break down the information based on how it will be used. After deciding how to break down the information, key the text at a clear editing window, then save it in the normal manner.

Saving Selected Text

When you create a document and then realize that a portion of the text in the document will be needed for future documents, you can save it as a separate document by selecting the text first. For example, to save a paragraph as a separate document, you would complete the following steps:

1. Select the paragraph.
2. Click File, then Save; or click the Save button on the Toolbar.
3. At the Save dialog box shown in figure 13.5, click Selected text, then click OK or press Enter.
4. At the Save As dialog box, key a name for the document.
5. Click Save or press Enter.

These steps save the paragraph as a separate document while retaining the paragraph in the original document.

Figure 13.5

Save Dialog Box When Text is Selected

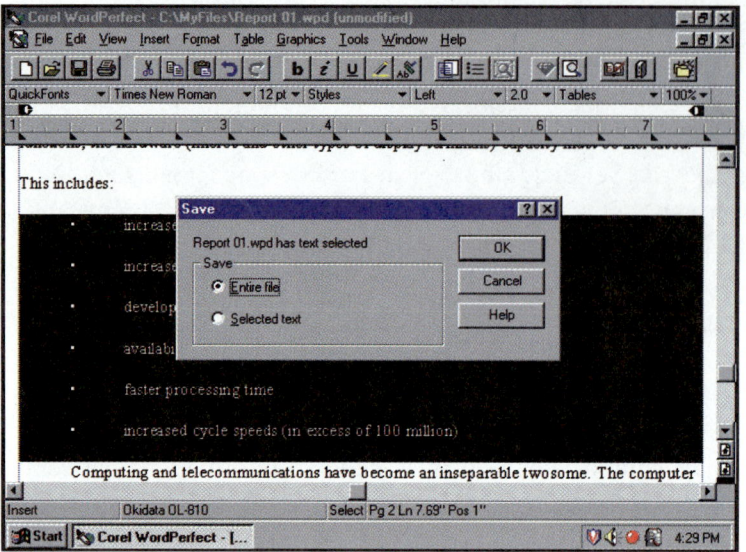

Inserting a Document

A document containing standard text can be inserted into an existing document with the File option from the Insert menu. For example, suppose you are keying a will and want to insert a standard document into the current will document. To do this, you would complete the following steps:

1. Position the insertion point in the will document at the location where you want the standard text.
2. Click Insert, then File.
3. At the Insert File dialog box, double-click the document name to be inserted, or key the document name, then press Enter or click Insert.

WordPerfect brings the entire document to the screen including any formatting codes. If you want standard text to conform to the formatting of the current document, do not insert any formatting codes in the standard document.

EXERCISE 7

Inserting a File into Another Document

1. At a clear editing window, open Report 01.
2. Select the bulleted items on the second page, then save them to a separate document named *Hardware* by completing the following steps:
    a. Select the six bulleted items on the second page.
    b. Click the Save button on the Toolbar.
    c. At the Save dialog box, click Selected text, then click OK or press Enter.
    d. At the Save As dialog box, key **Hardware**.
    e. Click Save or press Enter.
    f. Deselect the text.
3. Close Report 01.

4. At a clear editing window, key the memo headings and the first paragraph of the text shown in figure 13.6. Use an appropriate memo format. After keying the first paragraph, press Enter twice, then insert the *Hardware* document by completing the following steps:
    a. Click Insert, then File.
    b. At the Insert File dialog box, double-click *Hardware* in the list box.
5. Move the insertion point a double space below the bulleted items, then key the last paragraph. Include your initials and the document name a double space below the last line of the paragraph.
6. Save the memo and name it Ch 13, Ex 07.
7. Print and then close Ch 13, Ex 07.

Figure 13.6

DATE: March 25, 1998; TO: Heath Brewer; FROM: Sonya Roth; SUBJECT: HARDWARE

The microcomputers at the two high schools need to be upgraded or replaced. This past quarter, I completed a telecommunications class at the local community college. During this class, I learned that new hardware should include the following:

[Insert Hardware document here.]

We need to get together in the next week or so to put together our equipment request for the next school year. Please call me to schedule a meeting.

xx:Ch 13, Ex 07

Working with Windows

In WordPerfect, multiple documents can be open at the same time. With multiple documents open, you can move or copy information between documents or compare the contents of several documents.

Opening Windows

With multiple windows open, you can move the insertion point between them. You can move or copy information between documents or compare the contents of several documents. The maximum number of documents (windows) that you can have open at one time depends on the memory of your computer system and the amount of text in each document. When you open a new window, it is placed on top of the original window. Once multiple windows are opened, you can resize the windows to see all or a portion of them on the screen.

A document can be opened at the Open dialog box or a blank document can be opened by clicking the New Blank Document button on the Toolbar. You can also open multiple documents at the same time at the Open dialog box. To do this, display the Open dialog box, click the first document to be opened, then hold down the Ctrl key while clicking the remaining desired document names. Release the Ctrl key, then click the Open button. *(Note: Some virus protection software will let you open only one document at a time.)*

New Blank Document

When you are working in a document, the document fills the entire editing window. If you open another document without closing the first, the newly opened document will fill the editing window. The first document is still open, but it is covered by the new one. To see what documents are currently open, click the Window option on the Menu bar. When you click Window, the Window drop-down menu shown in figure 13.7 displays. (The number of documents and document names displayed at the bottom of the menu will vary.)

Figure 13.7

Window Drop-Down Menu

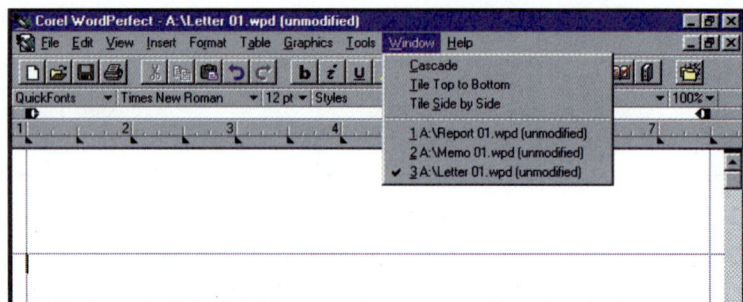

The open document names are displayed at the bottom of the menu. The document name with the check mark in front of it is the *active* document. The active document is the document containing the insertion point.

To make one of the other documents active, move the arrow pointer to the desired document, then click the left mouse button. If you are using the keyboard, key the number shown in front of the desired document. When you change the active document, the Window menu is removed from the screen and the new active document is displayed.

Closing Windows

To close an open document, make the document active, then click the Close button on the document Title bar (the last button at the right side of the Title bar containing the letter X). You can also close the active document by clicking File, then Close or pressing Ctrl + F4. To close the other open documents, repeat these steps.

EXERCISE

Opening Multiple Documents

1. At a clear editing window, open several documents at the same time by completing the following steps:
   a. Display the Open dialog box.
   b. Click the document named *Column 01*. (Be sure to click once and *not* double-click.)
   c. Hold down the Ctrl key, then click *Letter 01* and then *Memo 05*.
   d. Release the Ctrl key.
   e. Click the Open button.
2. Make Letter 01 the active document by clicking Window, then 2.

3. Make Column 01 the active document by clicking Window, then 1.
4. Close Column 01.
5. Close Letter 01.
6. Close Memo 05.

Cascading Windows

When you have more than one open document, you can use the Cascade option from the Window drop-down menu to view portions of all open documents. When open documents are cascaded, they overlap down the window, leaving the Title bar of each open document visible. For example, suppose you have the three following documents open: Letter 01, Memo 01, and Report 01. To cascade these three open documents, you would click Window, then Cascade. The documents are arranged and displayed as shown in figure 13.8.

By default, the document closest to the front is the active document. The document name (along with drive and path) is displayed at the top of each open document. The Title bar of the active document displays with a blue background. The Title bar of the inactive document displays with a gray background.

To change the active window with the mouse, position the arrow pointer on the Title bar, then click the left button. This causes the open document to move to the front and become active. If you are using the keyboard, click Window, then key the number of the desired document. You can also press Ctrl + F6 to make the next window active.

Figure 13.8

Cascaded Windows

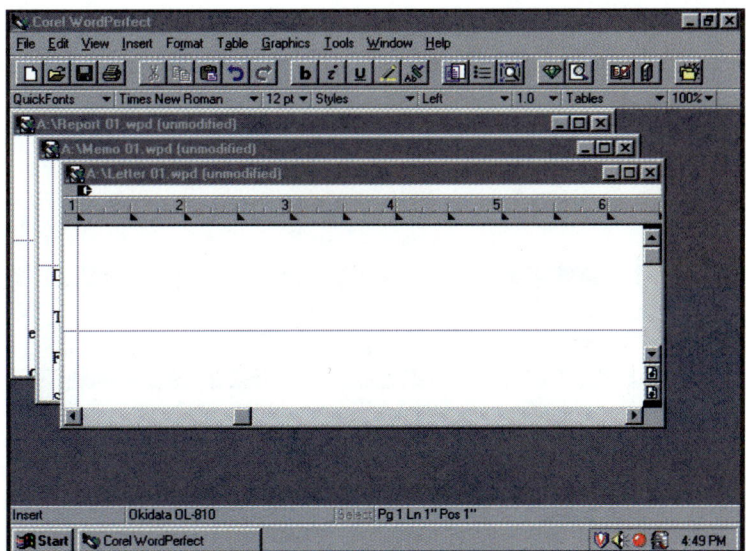

Manipulating Text within and between Documents   273

EXERCISE 9

Cascading Open Files

1. At a clear editing window, display the Open dialog box, then open Letter 01, Memo 01, Para 01, and Report 01.
2. Cascade the windows by clicking Window, then Cascade.
3. Make Para 01 the active document by positioning the arrow pointer on the Title bar for Para 01, then clicking the left mouse button.
4. Close Para 01.
5. Make Memo 01 active, then close it.
6. Make Letter 01 active, then close it.
7. Close Report 01.

Tiling Windows

The Tile Top to Bottom and Tile Side by Side options from the Window menu cause each open document to appear in a separate window with no windows overlapping. For example, suppose you have the following three documents open: Letter 01, Memo 01, and Report 01. To tile these three open documents vertically, click Window, then Tile Top to Bottom. The windows display as shown in figure 13.9. Documents can also be tiled horizontally as shown in figure 13.10 by clicking Window, then Tile Side by Side.

The Title bar in the active document displays with white characters on a blue background. The Title bar for inactive documents displays with light gray characters on a darker gray background. To change the active window, move the arrow pointer to the document you want active, then click the left button. If you are using the keyboard, click Window, then key the number of the desired document or press Ctrl + F6.

The ability to see more than one document on the screen at the same time can be useful in certain situations. For example, you can create an outline for a report in one window while you create the actual report in another.

Figure 13.9

Windows Tiled Top to Bottom

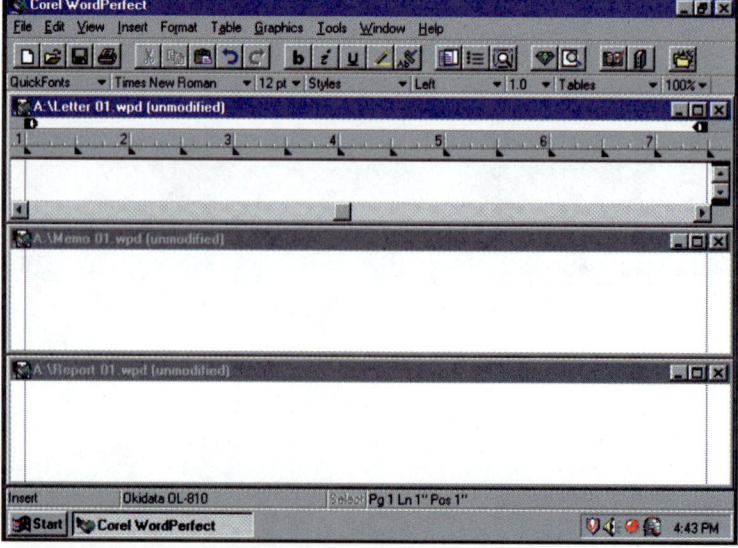

Windows Tiled Side by Side

Figure 13.10

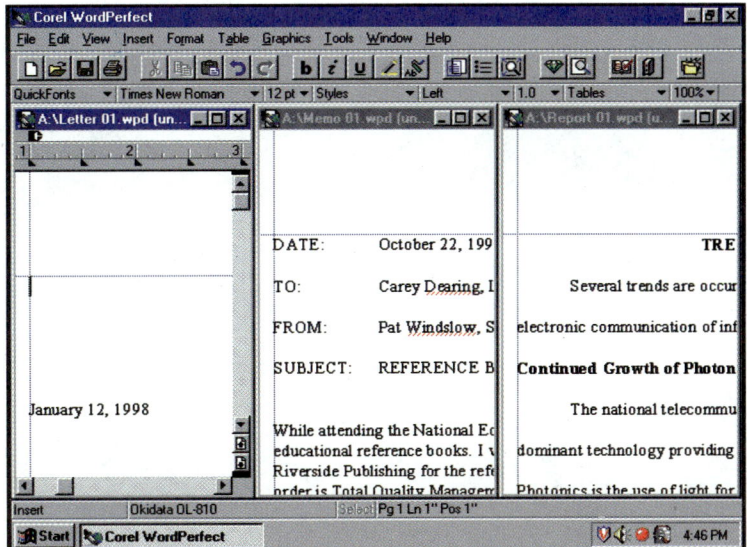

EXERCISE 10

Tiling Open Documents

1. At a clear editing window, display the Open dialog box, then open Block 01, Legal 01, Report 04, and Tab 01.
2. Tile the windows vertically by clicking Window, then Tile Top to Bottom.
3. Make Report 04 the active document.
4. Close Report 04.
5. Make Block 01 active, then close it.
6. Make Legal 01 active, then close it.
7. Close Tab 01.

Sizing Windows

You can use the Maximize and Minimize buttons at the right side of the Title bar to reduce or increase the size of the active window. The Maximize button is the button in the upper right corner of the Title bar of the active window with the icon of a square with a thick dark line across the top. The Minimize button is the button in the upper right corner with the icon of a thick underscore character. The Maximize and Minimize buttons display in a document that has been tiled or cascaded.

Maximize

Minimize

If you cascade or tile open documents, then click the Maximize button in the active document, the active document expands to fill the editing window. If you click the Minimize button in the active document, the document is reduced to a small Title bar that displays along the bottom of the screen. To restore a document that has been reduced to a Title bar, move the arrow pointer to the Title bar, then click the Restore button (formerly the Minimize button). Figure 13.11 shows an example of a document named Letter 01 that has been minimized to a Title bar along the bottom left corner of the screen. (Not all of the document name is visible in the Title bar in figure 13.11—only *Letter 0....*) Notice the Minimize button has changed to an icon of two squares with thick dark lines across the top. Clicking this button restores the document to its previous size.

Restore

Manipulating Text within and between Documents

Figure 13.11

Minimized Document

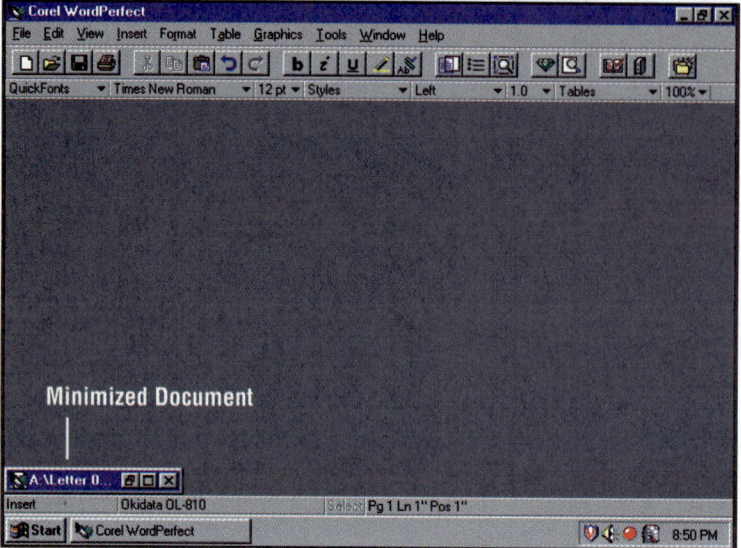

Application Control

Document Control

If only one document is open, two Corel WordPerfect icons display in the upper left corner of the document window. The top Corel WordPerfect icon is called the Application control button. It is used to change the size of the Windows application window. The second Corel WordPerfect icon is called the Document control button. The Document control button is used to change the size of the WordPerfect 7 application window. When documents are tiled or cascaded, the Document control button displays at the left side of the Title bar.

To minimize a document using the Document control button with the mouse, click the Document control button (the second one in the upper left corner of the screen), then at the Document control drop-down menu, click Mi*n*imize. To minimize a document using the Document control button with the keyboard, press Alt + hyphen (-), then at the Document control drop-down menu, key **N** for Mi*n*imize.

When a document has been minimized, it can be restored or maximized with the mouse or keyboard and the Document control button. To maximize a minimized document using the mouse, click the Maximize button on the Title bar. To maximize a document using the Document control button with the keyboard, make the icon the active document by pressing Ctrl + F6 until the Title bar for the minimized document displays with white letters on a blue background, then press Alt + hyphen (-). At the Document control drop-down menu, key **X** for Ma*x*imize or key **R** for *R*estore.

The difference between the Ma*x*imize and *R*estore options is that Ma*x*imize increases the size of the document to fill the entire editing window while *R*estore returns the document to its previous size.

The size of documents that have been cascaded or tiled can be increased or decreased using the mouse. To increase or decrease the width of the active window, move the arrow pointer to the border at the right or left side of the window until the arrow pointer becomes a left- and right-pointing arrow. Hold down the left mouse button, then drag the border to the right or left. When the window is the desired size, release the mouse button.

To increase or decrease the height of the active window, move the arrow pointer to the border at the top or bottom of the window until the arrow pointer becomes an up- and down-pointing arrow. Hold down the left mouse button, then drag the arrow pointer up or down to increase or decrease the size. When the window is the desired size, release the mouse button.

EXERCISE 11

Changing the Size of Open Documents

1. At a clear editing window, display the Open dialog box, then open Memo 02, Report 02, and Tab 02.
2. Tile the windows top to bottom.
3. Make Memo 02 the active window.
4. Minimize Memo 02 to an icon by clicking the Minimize button at the right side of the Title bar in the active window. (The Minimize button is the button with the thick underscore character.)
5. Make Report 02 the active document, then minimize Report 02 using the Document control button by completing the following steps:
   a. Click the Report 02 Title bar to make it active.
   b. Click the Document control button (the Corel WordPerfect icon at the left side of the Report 02 Title bar).
   c. At the Document control drop-down menu, click Mi<u>n</u>imize.
6. Restore the size of Report 02 using the mouse by clicking the Restore button on the Report 02 Title bar at the bottom of the screen.
7. Restore the size of Memo 02 by clicking the Restore button on the Memo 02 Title bar at the bottom of the screen.
8. Make Tab 02 the active document, then close it.
9. Close Report 02.
10. Close Memo 02.

Cutting and Pasting Text between Windows

With several documents open, you can easily move, copy, and/or paste text from one document to another. To move, copy, and/or paste text between documents, use the cutting and pasting commands you learned in this chapter together with the information about windows.

With WordPerfect 7, selected text can be "dragged" to a document in another window using the mouse. For example, to drag selected text from one document to another, you would complete the following steps:

1. Open the document you want to move text from and also the document you want to move text to.
2. Tile the documents.
3. Select the text to be moved.
4. Position the I-beam pointer inside the selected area until it turns into an arrow pointer, hold down the left mouse button, drag the arrow pointer to the location in the other window where the text is to be inserted, then release the mouse button.

You would complete similar steps to copy selected text except you would hold down the Ctrl key while dragging the arrow pointer.

Manipulating Text within and between Documents

EXERCISE 12

Moving Text between Documents

1. At a clear editing window, change to the Draft viewing mode, then key the memo shown in figure 13.12 in an appropriate memo format. (Press the Enter key four times after keying the first paragraph and before you key the second paragraph.)
2. Save the memo and name it Ch 13, Ex 12.
3. With Ch 13, Ex 12 still open on the screen, open Memo 02, then change the viewing mode to Draft.
4. Tile the windows side by side.
5. Copy the first three books listed in Memo 02 by completing the following steps:
   a. Select the three paragraphs containing the first three book titles (the paragraphs containing *The ABCs of Integrated Learning*, *Total Quality Management in the Education Environment*, and *Health Education for Today's Child*).
   b. Move the arrow pointer into the selected area until it turns into an arrow pointer.
   c. Hold down the Ctrl key and the left mouse button. Drag the arrow pointer a double space below the first paragraph in Ch 13, Ex 12, then release the left mouse button and then the Ctrl key.
   d. Maximize Ch 13, Ex 12.
   e. Deselect the text.
6. Save the memo again with the same name (Ch 13, Ex 12).
7. Print and then close Ch 13, Ex 12.
8. Close Memo 02.

Figure 13.12

DATE: October 26, 1998; TO: Carey Dearing, Librarian; FROM: Phillip Kainu, Assistant Librarian; SUBJECT: REFERENCE BOOKS

I found $62.40 in the library reference fund and $32.50 in the emergency fund. With these combined amounts, I was able to purchase the following books:

Not enough funds were available to purchase the *Grant Writing* book. I contacted Anissa Jackson in the Human Resources Department and suggested they purchase the book out of their budget. I asked her to contact you directly.

xx:Ch 13, Ex 12

CHAPTER SUMMARY

▼ Deleting, moving, or copying blocks of text within a document is generally referred to as cutting and pasting. A selected block of text can be as small as one character or as large as one page or one document.

▼ Selected text can be deleted permanently with the Delete key, or deleted and stored in temporary memory and reinserted later in a document.

▼ Selected text can be copied one or more times in a document. The text can be appended to the Window's clipboard if you want to move or copy text to a document in another program.

▼ Text that has been set up in columns and separated by tabs can be selected and then deleted, moved, or copied within a document.

▼ Standard blocks of text that will be used repeatedly can be saved as separate documents, then inserted into existing documents. These blocks can be keyed separately, then saved. Or, sections of text within other documents can be selected then saved as separate documents.

▼ When working in WordPerfect 7, a window refers to the editing window plus the scroll bars.

▼ With multiple documents open, you can copy or move text between documents or compare the contents of several documents.

▼ Each document you open will fill the entire editing window. Move among the open documents by clicking Window, then clicking the left mouse button on the desired document name or keying the number in front of that document name.

▼ Open documents can be cascaded, one over the top of the other; or they can be tiled top to bottom or side by side, each arranged next to the other.

▼ Use the Maximize, Minimize, and Close buttons in the upper right corner of the Title bar of the active window to reduce or increase the size of the window, or to close the document.

▼ The Minimize button will reduce the document to a small Title bar that displays at the bottom of the screen. A minimized document can be restored to a normal document by clicking the Maximize button of the Title bar; or to its previous size by clicking the Restore button on the minimized Title bar.

▼ The Application control button, the Corel WordPerfect icon in the upper left corner of the document window, is used to change the size of the Windows application window.

▼ The Document control button, the second Corel WordPerfect icon in the upper left corner of the document window, is used to change the size of the WordPerfect 7 application window.

▼ Use the mouse on the border of the window to increase or decrease the width or height of the window.

COMMANDS REVIEW

	Mouse	Keyboard
Delete text permanently		DEL
Delete text to temporary memory	Edit, Cut; or Cut button on Toolbar	SHIFT + DEL or CTRL + X
Insert cut text into document	Edit, Paste; or Paste button on Toolbar	SHIFT + INS or CTRL + V
Move selected text using mouse	With arrow pointer inside block of selected text, hold down the left mouse button, drag arrow pointer to desired location, release button	
Copy selected text	Edit, Copy; or Copy button on Toolbar	CTRL + INS or CTRL + C
Copy selected text using mouse	With arrow pointer inside block of selected text, hold down left mouse button and the Ctrl key, drag arrow pointer to desired location, release button and Ctrl key	
Select tabular columns	Use the arrow pointer to select the column from any point in the first line of the column to any point in the last line, then click Edit, Select, Tabular Column	Press F8, select text, then choose Edit, Select, Tabular Column
Move selected columns using mouse	With arrow pointer inside selected column of text, hold down left mouse button, drag arrow pointer, release button	
Copy selected columns using mouse	With arrow pointer inside selected column of text, hold down left mouse button and Ctrl key, drag arrow pointer, release button and Ctrl key	
Save selected text as separate document	File, Save; or click Save button on Toolbar	File, Save
Insert File dialog box	Insert, File	Insert, File
Open a new blank document	New Blank Document button on Toolbar	
Cascade windows	Window, Cascade	Window, Cascade
Tile windows vertically	Window, Tile Top to Bottom	Window, Tile Top to Bottom
Tile windows horizontally	Window, Tile Side by Side	Window, Tile Side by Side

Minimize a document	Click Minimize button; or click Document control icon, then click Mi<u>n</u>imize	ALT + −, Mi<u>n</u>imize
Maximize a document	Click Maximize button; or click Document control icon, then click Ma<u>x</u>imize	ALT + −, Ma<u>x</u>imize
Restore a document	Click Restore button; or click Document Control icon, then click <u>R</u>estore	ALT + −, <u>R</u>estore
Size a document using mouse	With arrow pointer on double line border at right/left or top/bottom, hold left mouse button, drag the border	

CHECK YOUR UNDERSTANDING

Completion: In the space provided at the right, indicate the correct term, command, or number.

1. Click this button on the Toolbar to remove selected text from the document and store it in temporary memory. _____

2. Click this button on the Toolbar to insert text that is stored in temporary memory into the document. _____

3. To copy, rather than move, selected text, hold down this key on the keyboard while dragging the selected text to the new location. _____

4. To display the Insert File dialog box, click this option at the <u>I</u>nsert drop-down menu. _____

5. This is the name of the feature that causes each open document to overlap down the window, leaving the Title bar of each document visible. _____

6. This is the word that describes the document where the insertion point is located. _____

7. Click this button if you want a previously minimized document to fill the editing window. _____

8. This is the name of the second Corel WordPerfect icon located in the upper left corner of the open document. _____

9. This is the name of the button containing a thick underscore located in the upper right corner of a tiled or cascaded window. _____

Manipulating Text within and between Documents

Look at the table shown below. Assume you wish to move the second column to the left of the first column. Answer the following questions related to moving the column in the space provided at the right.

Director	Rose Palermo	Room 130
Administrative Assistant	Steven Kingston	Room 130A
Assistant Director	Carol Kwan	Room 130B

1. On what word(s) should the insertion point be placed before selecting the text? _____

2. What word(s) would be at the end of the selected text? _____

3. When selecting text in #1 and #2 above, more than the second column will be highlighted. What are the next commands that will select only the column? _____

4. After cutting the second column to temporary memory, what will happen to the space it occupied? _____

5. On what word(s) must the insertion point be placed in order to insert the second column to the left of the first column? _____

SKILL ASSESSMENTS

Assessment 1

1. At a clear editing window, open Report 06.
2. Save the document with Save As and name it Ch 13, SA 01.
3. Make the following changes to the report:
   a. Move the section titled *Continued Growth of Photonics (Fiber Optics)* below the section titled *Microcomputer Trends in the Nineties*.
   b. Delete the first sentence of the last paragraph in the *Continued Growth of Photonics (Fiber Optics)* section (the sentence that begins *The growth of fiber optics has other...*).
   c. Change the relative size of the title to Large.
   d. Change the line spacing to double (2).
   e. Delete extra blank lines so there is only a double space between all lines in the document.
   f. Number pages at the bottom center of each page.
4. Save the document again with the same name (Ch 13, SA 01).
5. Print and then close Ch 13, SA 01.

Assessment 2

1. At a clear editing window, create the document shown in figure 13.13 with the following specifications:
    a. Change the font to 12-point Courier New (or a similar monospaced typeface).
    b. Key the text as shown in figure 13.13. Triple space after the last line in the document.
    c. Select and copy the text a triple space below the original text.
    d. Copy the text two more times. (There should be a total of four forms when you are done and they should fit on one page.)
2. Save the document and name it Ch 13, SA 02.
3. Print and then close Ch 13, SA 02.

Figure 13.13

```
                    COURSE REGISTRATION

Name:_____

Title:  _____  Department:_____

Course:_____

Days:  _____       Times:_____
```

Assessment 3

1. At a clear editing window, create the document shown in figure 13.14. You determine the tab settings for the columns.
2. Save the document and name it Ch 13, SA 03.
3. Print Ch 13, SA 03.
4. With Ch 13, SA 03 open in the editing window, reverse the second and third columns.
5. Save the document with the same name (Ch 13, SA 03).
6. Print Ch 13, SA 03.
7. Delete the second column (the *Non-Res* column).
8. Change the tab settings so the remaining columns are more balanced on the page.
9. Save the document with the same name (Ch 13, SA 03).
10. Print and then close Ch 13, SA 03.

Figure 13.14

	TUITION	
Credits	**Resident**	**Non-Res**
1 - 2	$ 77.00	$ 296.00
3	115.50	445.50
4	154.50	594.00
5	192.50	742.50
6	231.00	891.00
7	269.50	1,039.50
8	308.00	1,188.00
9	346.50	1,336.50
10 - 18	385.00	1,485.00
19 - 22	418.25	1,628.25

Assessment 4

1. At a clear editing window, create the document shown in figure 13.15. You determine the tab settings for the columns.
2. Select the first, second, and third columns below *Word Processing I* and copy them a double space below *Word Processing II*.
3. Insert the times, 7 - 9 p.m., after Sessions A, B, C, and D for *Word Processing II*.
4. Save the document and name it Ch 13, SA 04.
5. Print and then close Ch 13, SA 04.

Figure 13.15

WORD PROCESSING CLASS SCHEDULE

Word Processing I

Session A	M/W	May 4 - May 20	5 - 7 p.m.
Session B	T/Th	May 5 - May 21	5 - 7 p.m.
Session C	M/W	June 8 - June 24	5 - 7 p.m.
Session D	T/Th	June 9 - June 25	5 - 7 p.m.

Word Processing II

Assessment 5

1. At a clear editing window, open Policy 01.
2. Complete the following steps:
   a. Select all the text in the PERSONS INSURED section (including the title), then save it as a separate document named Pol 01.
   b. Select all the text in the LIMITS OF LIABILITY section (including the title), then save it as a separate document named Pol 02.

c. Select all the text in the UNINSURED MOTORISTS section (including the title), then save it as a separate document named Pol 03.
d. Select all the text in the PHYSICAL DAMAGE section (including the title), then save it as a separate document named Pol 04.
e. Select all the text in the second PHYSICAL DAMAGE section (including the title), then save it as a separate document named Pol 05.
f. Select all the text in the SUPPLEMENTAL PAYMENTS section (including the title), then save it as a separate document named Pol 06.
3. Close Policy 01.
4. At a clear editing window, make the following changes:
  a. Change the top margin to 1.5 inches.
  b. Change the line spacing to double (2).
5. Key the information shown in figure 13.16 with the following specifications:
  a. Key the document to the first bracketed item.
  b. Insert the documents as indicated in the brackets.
  c. After inserting Pol 06, move the insertion point to the end of the paragraph, make sure there is a double space after the paragraph, then change the line spacing back to single.
  d. Key the remaining text as indicated in figure 13.16.
  e. Move the insertion point to the beginning of the document, then create Footer A that prints Automobile Insurance Policy, Page # at the right side of each page (where the appropriate page number is inserted at the location of the # symbol).
6. Save the document and name it Ch 13, SA 05.
7. Print and then close Ch 13, SA 05.

Figure 13.16

AUTOMOBILE INSURANCE POLICY

Policy #: CR321-03

Name of Insured: Karen Heaberlin

Address of Insured: 1302 Second Street, Vancouver, BC V2Y 3X7

[Insert Pol 01 here.]

[Insert Pol 02 here.]

[Insert Pol 03 here.]

[Insert Pol 04 here.]

[Insert Pol 06 here.]

KAREN HEABERLIN, Insured

Authorized Representative

Assessment 6

1. Display the Open dialog box, then open Block 01, Memo 02, Para 03, and Tab 01.
2. Make Para 03 the active document.
3. Make Memo 02 the active document.
4. Cascade the windows.
5. Tile the windows side by side.
6. Make Para 03 the active document, then minimize it.
7. Minimize the remaining documents.
8. Make Memo 02 active, then restore it. (Be sure to restore the document and not maximize it.)
9. Restore Tab 01.
10. Restore Block 01.
11. Restore Para 03.
12. Close all documents.

Assessment 7

1. At a clear editing window, key the letter shown in figure 13.17 in an appropriate letter format through the first paragraph (to the location where the bolded message is displayed).
2. Save the partial letter and name it Ch 13, SA 07.
3. With Ch 13, SA 07 still open, open Report 01.
4. Tile the windows top to bottom.
5. With Report 01 the active document, copy the first paragraph below the heading *Microcomputer Trends in the Nineties* and the six bulleted items that follow and then paste the items and paragraph at the end of the first paragraph in the letter.
6. Make Report 01 the active document, then close it.
7. Maximize Ch 13, SA 07.
8. Key the remaining text in the letter.
9. Save the letter again with the same name (Ch 13, SA 07).
10. Print and then close Ch 13, SA 07.

Figure 13.17

June 9, 1998

Mr. Vance Petersen
Director of Computer Services
Denver Memorial Hospital
900 Colorado Boulevard
Denver, CO 86530

Dear Mr. Petersen:

At Quality Systems, we maintain computer hardware and software that keeps us on the cutting edge of technology. **[Insert copied text here.]**

Quality Systems is offering a free assessment of the computer systems operating at Denver Memorial Hospital. Please contact me at 555-3422 to schedule a time for a visitation.

Very truly yours,

QUALITY SYSTEMS

Megan MacDougal
System Analyst

xx:Ch 13, SA 07

14

REVISING AND PRINTING DOCUMENTS

PERFORMANCE OBJECTIVE

Upon successful completion of chapter 14, you will be able to revise text and codes in standard business letters and reports by using WordPerfect's Find and Replace feature and control printing of business documents.

In this chapter, you will learn to use WordPerfect's Find and Replace feature. With this feature you can look for specific words or codes within a document and then replace, edit, or delete the words or codes. You will also learn in this chapter to use the print options at the Print dialog box to customize a printing job.

Finding and Replacing Text

With WordPerfect's Find and Replace feature, you can look for a specific word(s) or code(s) within a document. When WordPerfect finds the word(s) or code(s), you can replace, edit, or delete the word(s) or code(s). With Find and Replace, you can:

- Correct a misspelled word by searching for it and replacing it throughout a document with the correct spelling.

- Use abbreviations for common phrases when entering text, then replace the abbreviations with the actual text later.

- Set up standard documents with generic names and replace them with other names to make personalized documents.

- Find and replace format codes.

This is just a short list of how the Find and Replace feature can make your keyboarding job easier. As you use the Find and Replace feature, you may find more ways that it can benefit you.

When you click Edit, then Find and Replace, the Find and Replace Text dialog box shown in figure 14.1 displays. In the text box below the Find option, enter the string for which you are searching. A search string can be up to 80 characters in length and can include spaces. After you have completed a find and replace, the Find text box will default to the previous search string. Alternatively, clicking the down-pointing triangle to the right of the Find text box will display a list of previously searched-for words and you can search for the same word again by clicking it in the drop-down list.

Figure 14.1

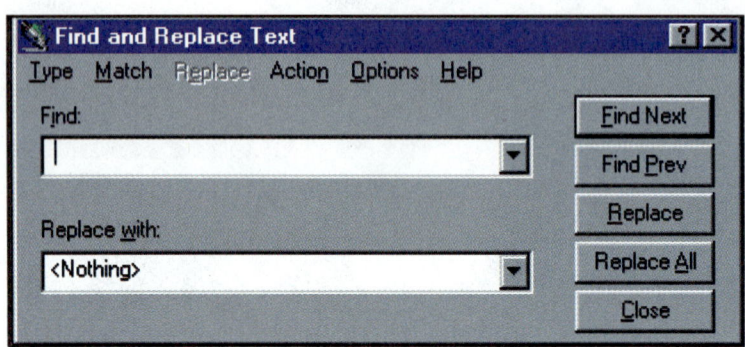

Find and Replace Text Dialog Box

Click Replace with to move the insertion point to the text box below the Replace with option. In this text box, enter the string with which you want the search string replaced. You can also click the down-pointing triangle to the right of the Replace with text box to display a list of words you have replaced previously. At the drop-down list, click the words you want inserted in the Replace with text box.

A find and replace begins at the position of the insertion point. You can find and replace a search string from the location of the insertion point to the beginning of the document or from the insertion point to the end of the document.

The Find and Replace Text dialog box contains five command buttons at the right side. Click the Find Next button to tell WordPerfect to find the next occurrence of the search string. Click the Find Prev button to search from the insertion point to the previous occurrence of the search string. Select Replace to replace the currently selected search string and find the next occurrence of the string. If you know that you want all occurrences of the search string replaced in the document, click Replace All. This replaces every occurrence of the search string from the location of the insertion point to the beginning or end of the document (depending on the search direction). Click Close to close the Find and Replace Text dialog box.

EXERCISE 1

Using Find and Replace

1. At a clear editing window, open Report 08.
2. Save the document with Save As and name it Ch 14, Ex 01.
3. Find all occurrences of SSL and replace with Space Systems Laboratory by completing the following steps:

> a. Position the insertion point at the beginning of the document.
> b. Click Edit, then Find and Replace.
> c. At the Find and Replace Text dialog box, key **SSL**.
> d. Press the Tab key to move the insertion point to the Replace with text box.
> e. Key **Space Systems Laboratory**.
> f. Click Replace All.
> g. Click Close to close the Find and Replace Text dialog box.
>
> 4. Save the document again with the same name (Ch 14, Ex 01).
> 5. Print and then close Ch 14, Ex 01.

In exercise 1, WordPerfect makes all replacements without getting confirmation from you. If you want to confirm each replacement before it is made, click Find Next or Find Prev. When WordPerfect stops at the first occurrence of the search string, click Replace if you want to replace the search string. Click Find Next or Find Prev if you want WordPerfect to find the next or the previous occurrence of the search string without replacing the current occurrence.

Customizing Find and Replace

The Find and Replace Text dialog box contains a menu bar with six options—Type, Match, Replace, Action, Options, and Help. Use options from this menu bar to customize a find and replace.

Changing Type Options

If you click Type from the Find and Replace Text dialog box, the options Text, Word Forms, and Specific Codes display in a drop-down menu. The default setting is Text. Use this setting when searching for text.

Click the Word Forms option to find and replace words based on the root form of the word. For example, you can search for the word form *buy* and WordPerfect will find words that match the root form such as *buys*, *buying*, and *bought* and replace them with the correct tense of the root form of the replace word.

EXERCISE 2

> **Using the Word Forms Option**
>
> 1. At a clear editing window, open Para 05.
> 2. Save the document with Save As and name it Ch 14, Ex 02.
> 3. Find all forms of *prepare* and replace with *create* by completing the following steps:
>   a. With the insertion point at the beginning of the document, click Edit, then Find and Replace.
>   b. Key **prepare** in the Find text box.
>   c. Press the Tab key to move the insertion point to the Replace with text box, then key **create**.
>   d. Click Type, then Word Forms.
>   e. Click Replace All.

>   **f.** Remove the check mark from the Word Forms option by clicking Type, then Word Forms.
>   **g.** Click Close to close the Find and Replace Text dialog box.
> **4.** Save the document again with the same name (Ch 14, Ex 02).
> **5.** Print and then close Ch 14, Ex 02.

Use the Specific Codes option from the Type drop-down menu to find a code that has been assigned a specific value. For example, instead of telling WordPerfect to search for a *Ln Spacing* code, which would find any line spacing code, you can specify a 1.5 line spacing code.

When you click Specific Codes, the Specific Codes dialog box shown in figure 14.2 displays. This dialog box contains a list of specific codes. To choose a specific code, click the desired code, then click OK or press Enter. When you make a choice from this dialog box, WordPerfect then displays a dialog box where you enter the value. For example, to find all 1.5 line spacing codes, you would complete the following steps:

1. Position the insertion point at the beginning of the document.
2. Click Edit, then Find and Replace.
3. At the Find and Replace Text dialog box, click Type, then Specific Codes.
4. At the Specific Codes dialog box, click the down-pointing arrow in the vertical scroll bar until *Ln Spacing* is visible, then click *Ln Spacing*.
5. Click OK or press Enter.
6. At the Find and Replace Line Spacing dialog box, key **1.5**.
7. Click Find Next.
8. Continue clicking Find Next until WordPerfect displays the Find Not Found dialog box. At this dialog box, click OK or press Enter.
9. Click Close to close the Find and Replace Line Spacing dialog box.

Figure 14.2

Specific Codes Dialog Box

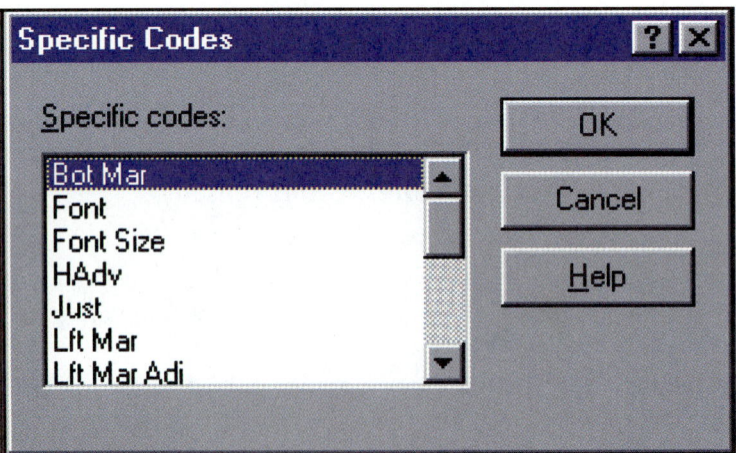

Changing Match Options

With the Match drop-down menu options shown in figure 14.3, you can specify what you want WordPerfect to match. When finding a search string, WordPerfect will stop at occurrences that match the search string. For example, if you enter the string *her* in the Find text box, WordPerfect stops at t*her*e, *her*s, rat*her*, and so on. If you want to find a specific word such as *her*, click Whole

Word at the Match drop-down menu. With this option selected, WordPerfect will stop at any occurrence of the word *her* as a whole word. This includes any occurrence of *her* that ends in punctuation. You can also tell WordPerfect to find a whole word by keying a space followed by the word, then another space in the Find text box. This, however, causes WordPerfect to skip any word that is followed by punctuation.

Figure 14.3

Match Drop-Down Menu

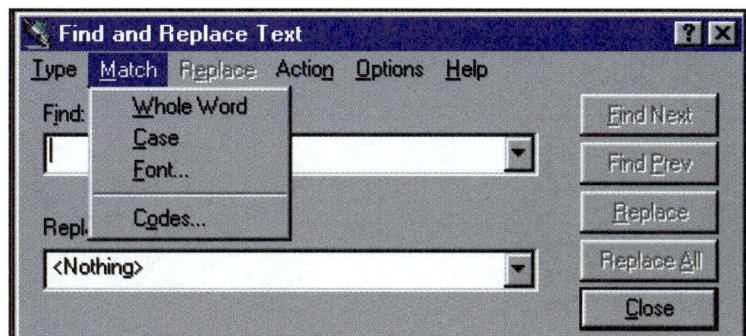

If you enter text as the search string, WordPerfect will match any case of the text. For example, if you enter *robin* as the search string, WordPerfect will find *robin*, *Robin*, or *ROBIN* (or any other combination of uppercase and/or lowercase letters). If you want WordPerfect to find only those occurrences that exactly match the search string, click Case at the Match drop-down menu.

With the Font option from the Match drop-down menu, you can find a specific typeface, type size, or type style. When you click Font from the Match drop-down menu, the Match Font dialog box shown in figure 14.4 displays.

Figure 14.4

Match Font Dialog Box

Revising and Printing Documents 293

At the Match Font dialog box, identify the font, font style, point size, and/or attributes, then click OK or press Enter.

With the Codes option from the Match drop-down menu, you can find codes within a document. When you click Codes, the Codes dialog box shown in figure 14.5 displays in the upper right corner of the editing window.

Figure 14.5

Codes Dialog Box

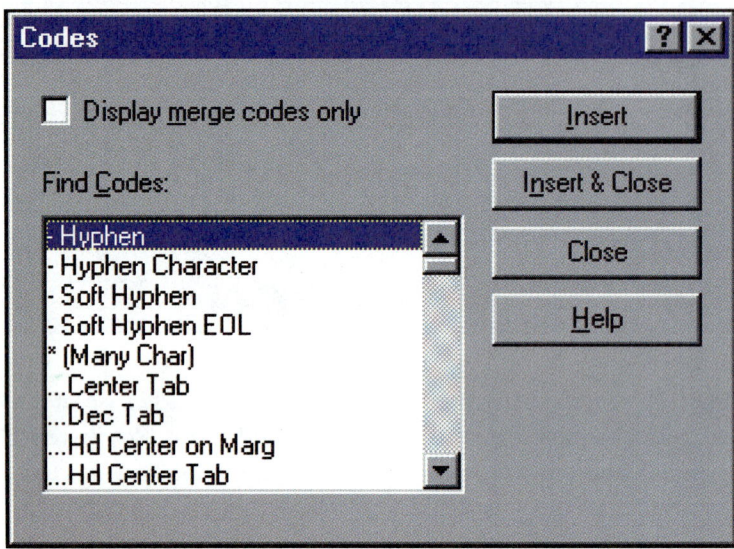

The Codes dialog box contains an extensive list of codes. Position the insertion point on the desired code, then click Insert. This inserts the code in the Find text box. If you are using the mouse, you can also position the arrow pointer on the desired code, then double-click the left mouse button. More than one code can be inserted in the Find text box. When the code or codes have been inserted in the Find text box, you can close the Codes dialog box by clicking the Close button or you can begin the search. (The Codes dialog box will disappear when the search begins.) As an example of how to search a document for codes, complete exercise 3.

EXERCISE 3

Searching a Document for Codes

1. At a clear editing window, open Report 03.
2. Save the document with Save As and name it Ch 14, Ex 03.
3. Find all bold codes, then delete them by completing the following steps:
   a. With the insertion point positioned at the beginning of the document, click Edit, then Find and Replace.
   b. At the Find and Replace Text dialog box, click Match, then Codes.
   c. At the Codes dialog box, click the down-pointing arrow in the vertical scroll bar until *Bold On* is visible, then click *Bold On*.
   d. Click the Insert & Close button.

e. Make sure there is nothing in the Replace with text box. If there is, select it, then delete it.
  f. At the Find and Replace Text dialog box, click Replace All.
  g. Click Close to close the Find and Replace Text dialog box. (The insertion point will be positioned in the document at the last occurrence of a bold code that was removed.)
4. Save the document again with the same name (Ch 14, Ex 03).
5. Print and then close Ch 14, Ex 03.

With the Find and Replace feature, you can also find codes and replace codes with other codes. For example, you can search for all double indent codes and replace them with hanging indent codes. For practice on finding and replacing codes, complete exercise 4.

EXERCISE 4

Finding and Replacing Codes

1. At a clear editing window, open Report 08.
2. Save the document with Save As and name it Ch 14, Ex 04.
3. Find all *Hd Left Ind* codes and replace with *Hd Left/Right Ind* codes by completing the following steps:
   a. Position the insertion point at the beginning of the document.
   b. Click Edit, then Find and Replace.
   c. At the Find and Replace Text dialog box, click Match, then Codes.
   d. At the Codes dialog box, position the insertion point on *Hd Left Ind*, then click Insert. (You must scroll down through the list to find the *Hd Left Ind* code.)
   e. Click in the Replace with text box. (Make sure that no text displays in the Replace with text box.)
   f. Position the insertion point on the *Hd Left/Right Ind* code in the Codes dialog box, then click the Insert & Close button.
   g. Click Replace All.
   h. Click Close to close the Find and Replace Text dialog box. (The insertion point will be positioned in the document at the last occurrence of a Hard Left Indent code that was replaced with a Hard Left/Right Indent code. Turn on the display of Reveal Codes to view the replacement code at the insertion point.)
4. Save the document again with the same name (Ch 14, Ex 04).
5. Print and then close Ch 14, Ex 04.

Changing Replace Options

When the Find and Replace Text dialog box is first displayed, the Replace option on the Menu bar is dimmed. This option will become available and display in black when the insertion point is positioned in the Replace with text box. When you click Replace, a drop-down menu displays with the options Case, Font, and Codes. These are the same options you have available at the Match drop-down menu.

Changing Action Options

When WordPerfect finds text, it selects text that matches the search string. This is because the default setting at the Action drop-down menu at the Find and Replace Text dialog box is Select Match.

If you click the Position Before option, WordPerfect will position the insertion point in front of the text. If you click the Position After option, WordPerfect will position the insertion point after the text. You can click Extend Selection to tell WordPerfect to select text from the insertion point to a specific word in the document.

EXERCISE 5

Using Find and Replace Options

1. At a clear editing window, open Report 04.
2. Move the insertion point to page 2 and then select the text from the title, *CHAPTER 4: DEVELOPMENT OF TECHNOLOGY, 1950 - 1960*, to the end of the document.
3. Find *telecommunications* in the selected text and tell WordPerfect to position the insertion point before the text (rather than selecting it) by completing the following steps:
   a. Click Edit, then Find and Replace.
   b. At the Find and Replace Text dialog box, key **telecommunications**.
   c. If there is any text in the Replace with text box, select it and then delete it.
   d. Click Action, then Position Before.
   e. Click Find Next. (WordPerfect will stop at the first occurrence of *telecommunications* in the selected text. The insertion point will blink quickly and then will not be visible. You may want to move the Find and Replace Text dialog box down toward the bottom of the editing window.)
   f. Continue clicking Find Next until WordPerfect displays the Find and Replace "telecommunications" Not Found dialog box. At this dialog box, click OK or press Enter.
   g. Click Close to close the Find and Replace Text dialog box.
4. Change Action back to the default of Select Match by completing the following steps:
   a. Click Edit, then Find and Replace.
   b. At the Find and Replace Text dialog box, click Action, then Select Match.
   c. Click Close.
5. Close Report 04.

Changing Options

If you click Options from the Menu bar, the drop-down menu shown in figure 14.6 displays. The default setting is Include Headers, Footers, etc. in Find. At this setting, WordPerfect searches all parts of a document for the search string including such features as headers, footers, footnotes, endnotes, and graphic elements.

Options Drop-Down Menu

Figure 14.6

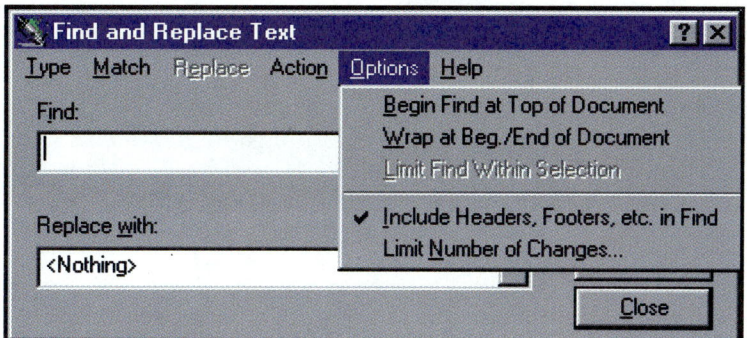

If you click Begin Find at Top of Document, WordPerfect will begin the search at the beginning of the document no matter where the insertion point is positioned.

At the Wrap at Beg./End of Document setting, WordPerfect will search from the position of the insertion point to the end of the document, then search from the beginning of the document to the position of the insertion point.

If you select text and then display the Find and Replace Text dialog box, the Limit Find Within Selection option is automatically selected. At this setting, WordPerfect will only search the selected text.

Use the Limit Number of Changes option to tell WordPerfect that you want only *x* number of changes made. For example, if you know you only want the first four occurrences of the search text replaced with the replacement text, you would click Options, then Limit Number of Changes. This causes the Limit Number of Changes dialog box to display. At this dialog box, you would key **4**, then click OK or press Enter. When you complete the find and replace, WordPerfect only replaces the first four occurrences.

EXERCISE

Conducting a Find and Replace

1. At a clear editing window, open Report 08.
2. Save the document with Save As and name it Ch 14, Ex 06.
3. Find the *Ln Spacing: 2.0* code and replace it with *Ln Spacing: 1.5* using the mouse by completing the following steps:
   a. Click Edit, then Find and Replace.
   b. At the Find and Replace Text dialog box, click Type, then Specific Codes.
   c. At the Specific Codes dialog box, click the down-pointing arrow at the right side of the Specific Codes list box until *Ln Spacing* is visible, then click *Ln Spacing*.
   d. Click OK.
   e. At the Find and Replace Line Spacing dialog box, click the down-pointing triangle after the Replace with option box until the number in the option box displays as *1.5*.
   f. Click Find Prev. (The line spacing code is positioned before the location of the insertion point.)

Revising and Printing Documents

  g. Click <u>R</u>eplace.
  h. At the Find and Replace Specific code not found dialog box, click OK.
  i. Click <u>C</u>lose. (Turn on the display of Reveal Codes and notice the insertion point is positioned in front of the new line spacing code.)
4. Find and delete all bold codes except the bold codes around the title, *IDENTIFICATION OF CI*, and the subheadings, *Requirements During Development* and *Requirements for Operations/Maintenance*, by completing the following steps:
  a. Position the insertion point at the beginning of the document.
  b. Click <u>E</u>dit, then <u>F</u>ind and Replace.
  c. At the Find and Replace Text dialog box, click <u>M</u>atch, then C<u>o</u>des.
  d. At the Codes dialog box, click *Bold On* in the Find <u>C</u>odes list box. (You will need to scroll through the list to display this code.)
  e. Click the <u>I</u>nsert & Close button.
  f. Make sure there is no text or codes in the text box below the Replace <u>w</u>ith option. If there is, select it, then delete it.
  g. Click <u>F</u>ind Next.
  h. WordPerfect stops at the first *Bold On* code at the beginning of the title. (You will not be able to see the insertion point.) You do not want to delete this code, so click <u>F</u>ind Next.
  i. WordPerfect stops at the next occurrence of the *Bold On* code (at the heading *Introduction*; you will not be able to see the insertion point). You want this code removed, so click <u>R</u>eplace.
  j. Continue finding *Bold On* codes. Click <u>F</u>ind Next if you do not want to delete the code or click <u>R</u>eplace if you do. (Remember, do not replace the Bold On code for the subheadings *Requirements During Development* and *Requirements for Operations/Maintenance*.)
  k. Click <u>C</u>lose to close the Find and Replace Text dialog box.
5. Save the document again with the same name (Ch 14, Ex 06).
6. Print and then close Ch 14, Ex 06.

Using the Print Dialog Box

In chapter 1, you learned to print documents with the Print button on the Toolbar or at the Print dialog box. You also learned to print document(s) in chapter 6 using the <u>P</u>rint option from the shortcut menu at the Open dialog box. In this chapter, you will learn to customize a print job with selections from the Print dialog box. To display the Print dialog box shown in figure 14.7, click <u>F</u>ile, then <u>P</u>rint or click the Print button on the Toolbar. You can also display the Print dialog box by pressing Ctrl + P.

Print Dialog Box

Figure 14.7

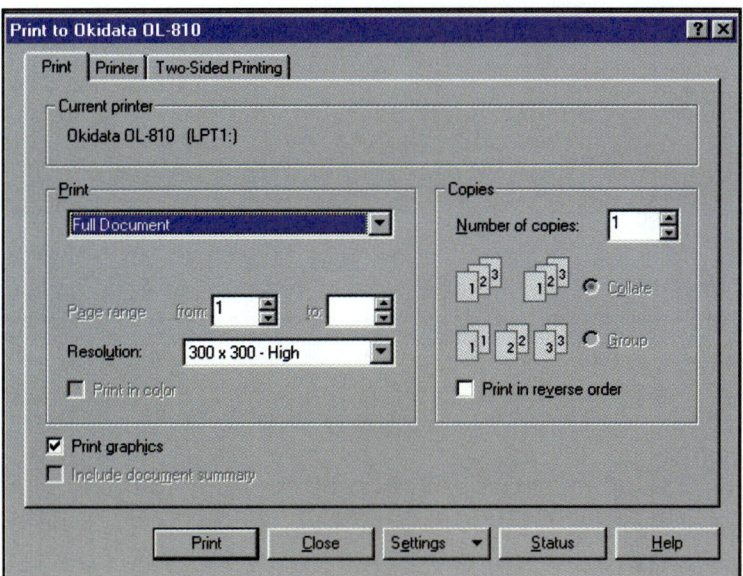

Current Printer

The Current printer section in the Print dialog box displays the name of the selected printer. When Corel WordPerfect 7 was installed on the hard drive or network, a printer was selected. The printer displayed in the Current printer section should be the printer you are using.

If more than one printer was selected during installation, you can select a different printer. To do this, click the Printer tab toward the top of the dialog box, then click the down-pointing triangle to the right of the Name list box. All of the installed printers will appear in a drop-down list. Click the desired printer name, then click the Close button to close the dialog box, the Print button to send the document to the printer, or the Print tab to return to the Print dialog box with the Print tab selected.

At the Print dialog box with the Printer tab selected, you can also change the initial font, edit the printer properties, add a printer, and access the system printer setup for Windows 95.

Print Selection

The Print list box at the Print dialog box with the Print tab selected contains five options to control printing. Click the down-pointing triangle below Print to view the options.

Full Document: Choose this option to print all pages of the open document. This is the default setting.

Current Page: Use this option to print the specific page where the insertion point is located. To print a specific page, position the insertion point on the page to be printed and then display the Print dialog box. At the Print dialog box, click the down-pointing triangle at the right side of the Print list box. At the drop-down list that displays, click *Current Page* and then click the Print button.

Revising and Printing Documents 299

Printing the Current Page

1. At a clear editing window, open Report 01.
2. Print page 2 by completing the following steps:
   a. Position the insertion point on page 2.
   b. Display the Print dialog box.
   c. At the Print dialog box, click the down-pointing triangle at the right side of the Print list box, then click *Current Page* at the drop-down list.
   d. Click the Print button.
3. Close Report 01.

Multiple Pages: The Multiple Pages option at the Print drop-down list is used to print a range of sequential pages, such as pages 1 through 3, of the document currently displayed in the editing window. To print a range of sequential multiple pages, click the up or down-pointing triangle next to the Page range from: text box to change the starting page number and then click the up or down-pointing triangle next to the Page range to: text box to change the ending page number. The Multiple Pages option will be automatically selected in the Print list box once you set a starting or ending page number. Click the Print button to print the range of pages.

Advanced Multiple Pages: To print nonsequential pages, click *Advanced Multiple Pages* at the Print drop-down list. An Edit button will appear just below the Print list box when you click Advanced Multiple Pages. When you click the Edit button, the Advanced Multiple Pages dialog box displays as shown in figure 14.8.

Figure 14.8

Advanced Multiple Pages Dialog Box

By default, the Page(s)/label(s) text box contains the word *all*. At this setting, all pages of the current document will be printed. If you want specific multiple pages printed, use a comma (,) to indicate *and* and use a hyphen (-) to indicate *through*. For example, to print pages 4 and 7, you would key **4,7** in the Page(s)/label(s) text box. To print pages 4 through 9, you would key **4-9**. The following table illustrates options for printing pages (X, Y, and Z denote page numbers):

Entry	Action
X	Page X printed
X,Y	Pages X and Y printed
X-	Pages X to end of document printed
X-Y	Pages X through Y printed
-X	Beginning of document through page X printed
X-Y,Z	Pages X through Y and page Z printed

As illustrated in the last entry, the hyphen and comma can be used in the same print job. Page numbers must be entered in numerical order. If you do not enter page numbers in numerical order, WordPerfect will print only the first page. For example, if you key **9,3,4** in the Page(s)/label(s) text box, WordPerfect will print only page 9.

EXERCISE 8

Printing Specific Pages

1. At a clear editing window, open Report 02.
2. Print pages 1 and 3 by completing the following steps:
   a. Display the Print dialog box.
   b. At the Print dialog box, click the down-pointing triangle at the right side of the Print list box, then click *Advanced Multiple Pages* at the drop-down list.
   c. Click the Edit button that displays just below the Print list box.
   d. At the Advanced Multiple Pages dialog box, key **1,3**. (The insertion point is automatically inserted in the Page(s)/label(s) text box.)
   e. Click OK to close the Advanced Multiple Pages dialog box.
   f. At the Print dialog box, click the Print button.
3. Close Report 02.

Document on Disk: If you click *Document on Disk* at the Print drop-down list, then click the Edit button, the Document on Disk dialog box, shown in figure 14.9, displays.

The Document on Disk dialog box is very similar to the Advanced Multiple Pages dialog box. The difference is that you can identify a specific document for printing with the Document name option at the Document on Disk dialog box.

Figure 14.9

Document on Disk Dialog Box

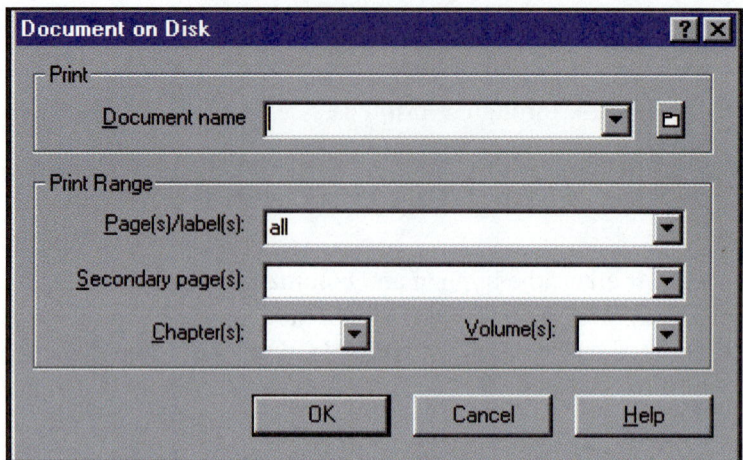

EXERCISE 9

Printing a File from the Disk

1. At a clear editing window, print Para 02 by completing the following steps:
    a. Display the Print dialog box.
    b. At the Print dialog box, click the down-pointing triangle at the right side of the Print list box, then click *Document on Disk* at the drop-down list.
    c. Click the Edit button that displays below the Print list box.
    d. At the Document on Disk dialog box, key **Para 02.wpd**. (Be sure to key the extension, *.wpd*. Depending on your system setup, you may also need to include the disk drive location. For example, if your student data disk is located in drive a:, you would key **a:\Para 02.wpd**.)
    e. Click OK to close the Document on Disk dialog box.
2. At the Print dialog box, click the Print button.

Copies

The Copies section of the Print dialog box contains four options for printing multiple copies of a document—Number of copies, Collate, Group, and Print in reverse order.

Number of copies: If you want to print more than one copy of a document or page(s), use the Number of copies option from the Print dialog box. To print multiple copies of a document, increase the number in the Number of copies text box. The number of copies will remain at the new setting until you change it or close the document.

EXERCISE 10

Printing Multiple Copies

1. At a clear editing window, open Notice 01.
2. Print three copies of this document by completing the following steps:
   a. Display the Print dialog box.
   b. Change the number in the Number of copies text box to 3 by moving the arrow pointer to the up-pointing triangle after Number of copies, then clicking the left mouse button until *3* displays in the box.
   c. Click the Print button.
3. Close Notice 01.

Collate and Group: When the number of copies has been increased to a value greater than one, the Collate and Group options become available. The default setting is Collate, which means that all pages of the document are printed in the correct order and then the process is repeated until the requested number of copies is complete. With the Group option, the printer assembles the pages by printing all copies of page 1, then all copies of page 2, and so on until the print job is complete. The Group option usually results in faster printing time, but then you have to collate the pages manually.

Print in reverse order: If your printer prints pages face up, select this option to start printing with the last page first.

Resolution

The Resolution option at the Print dialog box provides three settings that affect the quality of print—High, Medium, and Low. To display these options, click the down-pointing triangle at the right side of the Resolution text box. The resolution characters per inch (e.g., 300 x 300) displayed before the High, Medium, and Low settings will vary depending on which printer is installed. The higher the resolution, the longer it takes to print the document. The Low option causes a document to print the fastest and uses the least amount of printer memory.

Print Color: If you have a color printer and have selected it, you can instruct WordPerfect to print the colors by clicking the Print in color check box. The check box will be dimmed and not available if a color printer is not selected.

Print Graphics: If a document contains text as well as graphics, both the text and graphics will print by default. If you want only the text to print, click the check box before Print graphics to deselect it.

EXERCISE 11

Printing with Low Resolution

1. At a clear editing window, open Report 01.
2. Print the report with a print resolution of Low by completing the following steps:
   a. Display the Print dialog box.

Revising and Printing Documents *303*

>   **b.** Click the down-pointing triangle to the right of the Res<u>o</u>lution list box, then click *Low*.
>   **c.** Click the Print button.
> **3.** Close Report 01.

Include document summary: Click this check box to print a document summary. If a document does not contain a document summary, this option is dimmed.

Two-Sided Printing

The Print dialog box with the Two-Sided Printing tab selected contains options that affect printing on two sides of a page, binding width, or booklet printing. The Print dialog box with the Two-Sided Printing tab selected is shown in figure 14.10.

Figure 14.10

Print Dialog Box with Two-Sided Printing Tab Selected

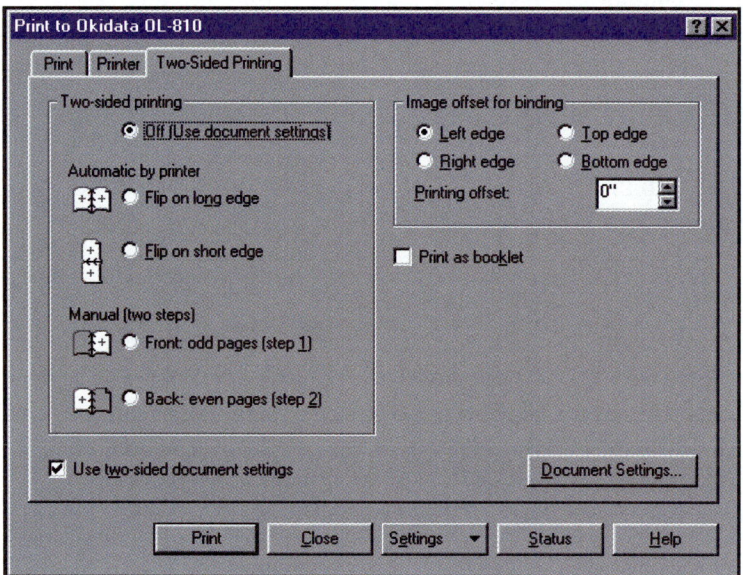

Two-Sided printing is off by default. If you are going to print on both sides of a page you can select an option in the *Automatic by printer* section or an option in the *Manual (two steps)* section. This depends on your printer's capabilities. If the printer you are using is capable of duplex printing, click either *Flip on lo<u>n</u>g edge* so that the pages can be bound like a book, or click *Flip on short edge*, to bind the pages on the top like a flip chart. These options will be dimmed if the printer you have selected is not capable of printing on both sides of the paper automatically.

You can manually print on two sides of the page by printing all of the odd pages first, then turning the pages over, and printing all of the even pages. To do this, click the radio button before *Front: odd pages (step 1)*, then click Print. Turn the pages over, reload them in the printer, click *Back: even pages (step 2)*, then click Print.

Image offset for binding: These options will vary depending on which two-sided printing options have been selected. Adjustment can be made for documents you want to bind by specifying a P<u>r</u>inting offset measurement in inches. This offset is added to the <u>L</u>eft edge, <u>R</u>ight edge, <u>T</u>op edge, or <u>B</u>ottom edge of the page in addition to the margin. Select which edge you want

Chapter 14

the offset added to by clicking the appropriate radio button, then specify the offset by clicking the up- or down-pointing triangles next to Printing offset to increase or decrease the measurement.

Print as booklet: Use the Print as booklet check box to automatically arrange pages of a document so they print as a booklet. In order for this option to work, the document has to be subdivided into logical pages versus physical pages. When the document is printed, you will see dialog boxes appear instructing you on which pages to insert into the printer so that they are printed in the correct order. When the printing is complete, you can staple or bind the pages into a booklet.

EXERCISE

Printing Even Pages and Adding a Binding Width

1. At a clear editing window, open Report 03.
2. Insert a hard page break at the beginning of the line on page 2 that reads, *CHAPTER 2: DEVELOPMENT OF TECHNOLOGY, 1850 - 1900*.
3. Number the pages at the bottom center of each page.
4. Print even-numbered pages and add a half-inch of extra space for a binding width by completing the following steps:
    a. Display the Print dialog box.
    b. Click the Two-Sided Printing tab.
    c. Click the radio button before *Back: even pages (step 2)*.
    d. Click the radio button before *Right edge* in the Image offset for binding section.
    e. Click the up-pointing triangle next to Printing offset until the number in the text box reaches *0.5* inches.
    f. Click the Print button.
5. Close Report 03 <u>without</u> saving the changes.

Printing Selected Text

Many print methods limit you to printing an entire document, a page, or specific pages. If you want to print a specific amount of text (such as two paragraphs, half a page, or a page and a half), select the text you want printed first, then display the Print dialog box. The option *Selected Text* will automatically appear in the Print list box. Clicking the Print button will send the selected text to the printer.

When selected text is printed, it is positioned on the page exactly where it would be if the entire page were printed. For example, if you select a paragraph at the bottom of a page, then print it, the paragraph will print at the bottom of the paper with blank space above it where the other text was that you did not select.

EXERCISE 13

Printing Selected Text

1. At a clear editing window, open Report 06.
2. Select and print the last six lines of text in the report by completing the following steps:
   a. Select the last six lines of text in the report.
   b. Display the Print dialog box.
   c. At the Print dialog box, click the Print button.
3. Close Report 06.

CHAPTER SUMMARY

- ▼ Use the Find and Replace feature to quickly locate a search string such as word(s) and/or code(s) and replace the search string with other words or codes.

- ▼ The text and/or codes you search for is called a search string and can be up to 80 characters in length.

- ▼ The Find and Replace Text dialog box contains a Menu bar with six options—Type, Match, Replace, Action, Options, and Help. Each option has a drop-down menu that allows you to customize your search.

- ▼ WordPerfect will search for specific formatting codes and replace them with other codes. Codes that are turned on and off, such as bold and underline, can be deleted in this manner but cannot be replaced with another code.

- ▼ If the search string is entered in lowercase letters, WordPerfect will find all occurrences of the string that contain lowercase or uppercase letters. If you want WordPerfect to find only those occurrences that exactly match the search string, click Case at the Match drop-down menu.

- ▼ To search for format codes, use the Codes option from the Match drop-down menu or the Specific Codes option from the Type drop-down menu.

- ▼ The options available at the Print dialog box can help to customize a print job.

- ▼ The printer displayed in the Current printer list box should be the printer you are using. If other printers were selected during the installation of Corel WordPerfect 7, a different printer can be selected at the Print dialog box with the Printer tab selected.

- ▼ Five options are available in the Print list box at the Print dialog box: Full Document, Current Page, Multiple Pages, Advanced Multiple Pages, and Document on Disk.

- ▼ Use the Number of copies option at the Print dialog box to print more than one copy of a document or page(s) of a document.

- ▼ The Resolution list box at the Print dialog box contains three options—High, Medium, and Low.

- ▼ The Print dialog box with the Two-Sided Printing tab selected contains options for printing on two sides of a page, binding width offsets, and printing a document as a booklet.

- ▼ Selected text can be printed by selecting the text first, displaying the Print dialog box, then clicking the Print button.

COMMANDS REVIEW

	Mouse/Keyboard
Find and Replace Text dialog box	Edit, Find and Replace
Codes dialog box	Edit, Find and Replace, Match, Codes
Specific Codes dialog box	Edit, Find and Replace, Type, Specific Codes
Print dialog box	File, Print; click Print button on Toolbar; or Ctrl + P

CHECK YOUR UNDERSTANDING

Completion: In the space provided at the right, indicate the correct term, command, or number.

1. This is the maximum length of a search string.

2. Click this option on the Menu bar to display a drop-down menu containing the Find and Replace option.

3. Click this button at the Find and Replace Text dialog box to replace all occurrences of the search string with the replacement text.

4. Click this button at the Find and Replace Text dialog box to search for the next occurrence of the search string without replacing the current text.

5. Enter the search string in this case and WordPerfect will find all occurrences of the string in uppercase and lowercase.

6. If you want WordPerfect to find only those occurrences that exactly match the search string, click this option at the Match drop-down menu.

7. To select a different printer, display the Print dialog box with this tab selected.

8. Choose this option from the Print drop-down list at the Print dialog box to print a range of sequential pages.

9. Choose this option from the Print drop-down list at the Print dialog box to print a range of nonsequential pages.

10. If you select text in a document and then display the Print dialog box, this option automatically displays in the Print list box.

In the space provided below, list the steps you would complete to find all occurrences of *dtp* and automatically replace them with *desktop publishing*.

_____

_____

_____

SKILL ASSESSMENTS

Assessment 1

1. At a clear editing window, open Report 08.
2. Save the document with Save As and name it Ch 14, SA 01.
3. Complete the following find and replaces:
   a. With the insertion point positioned at the beginning of the document, find all occurrences of *configuration item* and replace with *design unit*.
   b. Move the insertion point back to the beginning of the document, then complete a find and replace for all occurrences of *CI* and replace with *DU*.
4. Save the document again with the same name (Ch 14, SA 01).
5. Print and then close Ch 14, SA 01.

Assessment 2

1. At a clear editing window, open Legal 01.
2. Save the document with Save As and name it Ch 14, SA 02.
3. Complete the following find and replaces:
   a. Find all occurrences of NAME1 and replace with *ALAN C. HOLMES*.
   b. Find all occurrences of NAME2 and replace with *LOREN M. GUILL*.
   c. Find the one occurrence of NUMBER and replace with C-54327.
4. Find and delete all bold codes, except the bold codes around the document title (two lines of text) and the word DATED.
5. Save the document again with the same name (Ch 14, SA 02).
6. Print and then close Ch 14, SA 02.

Assessment 3

1. At a clear editing window, open Legal 02.
2. Save the document with Save As and name it Ch 14, SA 03.
3. Complete the following find and replaces:
   a. Find all occurrences of NAME1 and replace with *ELENA C. TREECE*.
   b. Fine the one occurrence of NUMBER and replace with D-4311.
   c. Find all *Bold On* codes and delete them *except* the following:
      (1) IN DISTRICT COURT NO. 4, PIERCE COUNTY, STATE OF WASHINGTON (displays on two lines)
      (2) DATED
      (3) LESLIE COBURN
   d. Find all *Hd Left/Right Ind* indent codes and replace with *Hd Left Ind* codes.
4. Save the document again with the same name (Ch 14, SA 03).
5. Print and then close Ch 14, SA 03.

Assessment 4

1. At a clear editing window, print two copies of Memo 01.
2. Change the number of copies back to 1.

Assessment 5

1. Open Report 03.
2. Select and print the heading *The American Civil War* and the paragraph below it.
3. Close Report 03.

Assessment 6

1. Open Report 02.
2. Change the top margin to 1.5 inches.
3. Print pages 1 and 4 of the document.
4. Close Report 02 without saving the changes.

Assessment 7

1. Open Report 09.
2. Insert page numbering at the top right of the page.
3. Print only the odd pages of the document.
4. Close Report 09 without saving the changes.

USING GRAMMATIK

PERFORMANCE OBJECTIVE
Upon successful completion of chapter 15, you will be able to use Grammatik to improve the grammar and style of written business documents.

WordPerfect includes a grammar-checking program called Grammatik (pronounced Gram•mat´•ik). The Grammatik program searches a document for incorrect grammar, style, punctuation, and word usage. Like Spell Checker, Grammatik does not find every error in a document and may stop at correct phrases. Grammatik can help you create a well-written document, but it does not replace the need for human proofreading.

Editing a Document with Grammatik

To check a document with Grammatik, you would open the document to be checked, then click Tools, then Grammatik or press Alt + Shift + F1. Grammatik automatically starts checking the document and stops at the first error. When Grammatik selects an error, you can correct it or skip the error. When Grammatik is done checking the document, a dialog box displays with the message *"Grammar check completed. Close Grammatik?"* At this message, click Yes.

When you are done checking the document with Grammatik, the open document is displayed on the screen. The changes made during the check are inserted in the document. You can save the document with the same name, overwriting the original; or, you can save the document with a different name, retaining the original.

When you click Tools, then Grammatik, a Writing Tools dialog box (with the Grammatik tab selected) like the one shown in figure 15.1 displays when an error is encountered. The error is selected in the document and the dialog box contents will vary depending on the type of error that Grammatik has found.

When Grammatik selects an error, possible replacement words may be displayed in the Replacements list box in the dialog box. These replacement words can be used to quickly correct the error.

In addition to the Replacements list box, Grammatik may also rewrite the sentence containing an error and place that sentence in the New sentence text box. If the rewritten sentence is correct, click Replace and Grammatik will replace the original sentence with the rewritten sentence, then continue searching for errors. If you want Grammatik to use a different word in the Replacements list box when writing the sentence, select the desired word. Grammatik then rewrites the sentence using the selected word and displays it in the New sentence text box.

When Grammatik selects an error in a document, the rule class for the error is displayed in the dialog box below the New sentence text box.

At the bottom of the Writing Tools dialog box with the Grammatik tab selected, the Checking style text box displays the current checking style. The default checking style is Quick Check. Later in this chapter, you will learn how to change the checking style.

Figure 15.1

Writing Tools Dialog Box with Grammatik Tab Selected

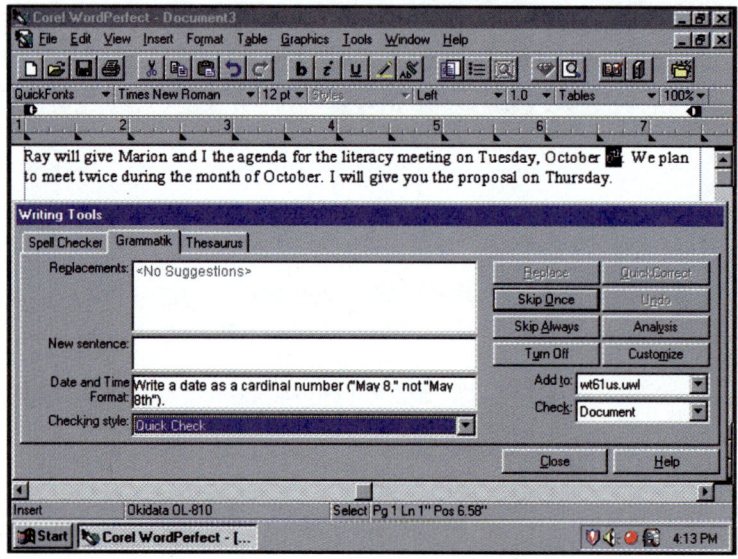

Making Replacements

When Grammatik detects an error, it tries to include replacement words in the Replacements list box and displays a rewritten sentence in the New sentence text box. If you want to replace the selected sentence with the suggested sentence, click Replace. If there is more than one replacement option in the Replacements list box, select the desired replacement option, then click Replace.

If you want to leave the text as written and not make a correction, click Skip Once or Skip Always. If you click Skip Once, Grammatik will ignore the selected phrase for the current occurrence only. If you click Skip Always, Grammatik will ignore the selected phrase for the rest of the document.

If Grammatik stops at an error and does not offer a replacement or the offered replacements are not acceptable, you can edit the error. To do this, position the arrow pointer in the editing window at the location of the error, then click the left mouse button. Make the necessary corrections, then click Resume to continue grammar checking.

Grammatik will check a document for spelling as it checks the grammar. Grammatik uses the same dictionaries that the Spell Checker uses. If Grammatik selects a word that is spelled correctly, you can click Add to add the selected word to the default user word list named *wt61us.uwl*.

EXERCISE 1

Checking for Errors with Grammatik

1. At a clear editing window, open Memo 08.
2. Save the document with Save As and name it Ch 15, Ex 01.
3. Complete a grammar check with Grammatik by completing the following steps:
   a. Click T̲ools, then G̲rammatik.
   b. Grammatik selects *Vanderburg*. This proper name is spelled correctly so click Skip A̲lways.
   c. Grammatik selects *likes* and displays the rule class *Incorrect Verb Form* with the advice, *Words like* would *require that the following verb be in the base verb form*. The word *like* is displayed in the Replacements list box, so click R̲eplace.
   d. Grammatik selects *a computer literacy programs* and displays the rule class *Noun Phrase* with the advice, *A is not usually used with a plural noun such as programs*. Grammatik suggests two possible corrections in the Replacements list box. Click *a computer literacy program* in the Replacements list box, then click R̲eplace.
   e. Grammatik selects *compare* and displays the rule class *Subject-Verb Agreement* with the advice, *If* it *is the subject of the verb compare, try making them agree in number*. The word *compares* is displayed in the Replacements list box, so click R̲eplace.
   f. Grammatik selects *08* and displays the rule class *Number Style* with the advice *Spell out whole numbers in this range, even as part of larger numbers ("eight million")*. Since this is the document identification in the initial line, click Skip O̲nce.
   g. At the *Grammar check completed. Close Grammatik?* question, click Y̲es.
4. Save the document again with the same name (Ch 15, Ex 01).
5. Print and then close Ch 15, Ex 01.

Changing Checking Style

At the bottom of the Writing Tools dialog box with the Grammatik tab selected, the Check̲ing style option has a default setting of *Quick Check*. Grammatik provides a number of checking styles for various documents. Some checking styles use all Grammatik rules of grammar when checking a document. Other checking styles are less formal and use fewer grammar rules when checking a document.

To change the checking style, position the tip of the arrow pointer on the down-pointing triangle to the right of the Check̲ing style list box, then click the left mouse button. This causes a pop-up menu to display as shown in figure 15.2. Move the arrow pointer to the desired style, then click the left mouse button.

The default checking style is *Quick Check*. This is appropriate for general correspondence targeted to a general population. If you are preparing a formal business letter, choose the *Formal Memo or Letter* style. If you are preparing a technical document, choose the *Technical or Scientific* style. Choose the checking style that matches your document.

Using Grammatik 313

Figure 15.2

Checking Style Pop-Up Menu

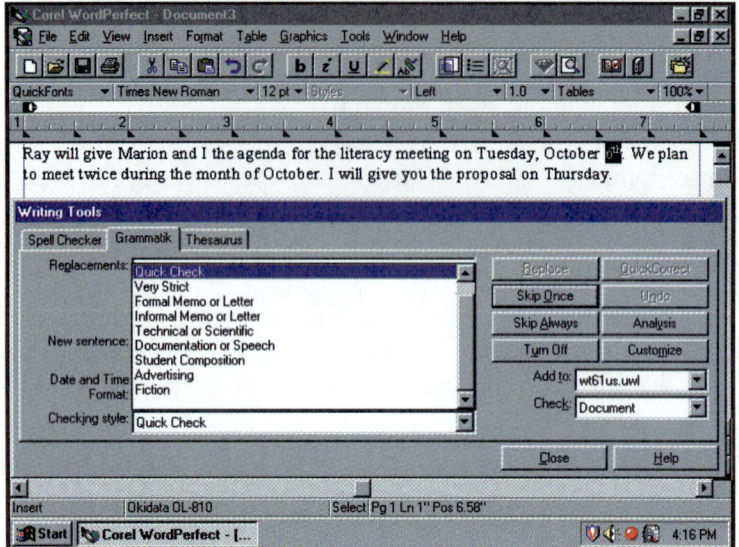

EXERCISE 2

Checking with the Technical or Scientific Style

1. At a clear editing window, open Report 08.
2. Save the document with Save As and name it Ch 15, Ex 02.
3. Change the checking style to *Technical or Scientific* and complete a grammar check on the document by completing the following steps:
   a. Click Tools, then Grammatik.
   b. When Grammatik selects *CIs*, change the checking style to *Technical or Scientific* by completing the following steps:
      (1) Click the down-pointing triangle to the right of the Checking style list box.
      (2) At the drop-down menu that displays, click *Technical or Scientific*.
   c. After changing the checking style, click Skip Always to tell Grammatik to skip all occurrences of *CIs*.
   d. Grammatik selects *For the purpose of*. (You may not be able to see the selected text in the document. You may want to move the dialog box toward the top of the editing window.) Change this to *For* by clicking Replace.
   e. Grammatik selects *Purpose and Scope*. Click Skip Always.
   f. Grammatik selects *SSL*. Click Skip Always.
   g. Grammatik selects *in order to*. Change this to *to* by clicking Replace.
   h. Grammatik selects *configuration*. Click Skip Always.
   i. Grammatik selects *utilization*. Change this to *use* by clicking Replace.
   j. Grammatik selects *and/or*. Click Skip Always.
   k. Grammatik selects the word *The*. Notice the rule class displayed in *Sentence Variety*. Grammatik provides the advice, *You have used* The *to begin the last 3 sentences*. Click Skip Always.
   l. Grammatik selects *There*. Click Skip Always.

m. Grammatik selects *Requirements During Development:*. Click Skip Always.
   n. Grammatik selects *a CI*. Click Skip Always.
   o. Grammatik selects *Requirements for Operations/Maintenance*. Click Skip Always.
   p. Grammatik selects *shall*. Change this to *will* by clicking Replace.
   q. Grammatik selects *shall* (again). Change this to *will* by clicking Replace.
   r. At the *Grammar check completed. Close Grammatik?* question, click No.
   s. Change the checking style back to *Quick Check* by following steps similar to those in 3b.
   t. Click Close.
4. Save the document again with the same name (Ch 15, Ex 02).
5. Print and then close Ch 15, Ex 02.

Viewing Rule Class Information

When an error is detected, the rule class for the problem is displayed. If you need further information about the problem or the rule class, move the arrow pointer over the rule class title at the left side of the rule class text box. When the arrow pointer displays with a question mark in a circle, click the left mouse button. The Grammatik Help on Grammar dialog box will open with information about the rule class and sample sentences to explain the rule as shown in figure 15.3. After reading the information, click the Close button on the Grammatik Help on Grammar Title bar.

You can also display help on key words displayed in green in the rule class text box by following the same steps. For example, in figure 15.3 the words *subject pronoun* are displayed in green. If you are not sure what a subject pronoun is, you can move the arrow pointer over the words *subject pronoun* in the help dialog box until the arrow pointer displays with a question mark attached, then click the left mouse button to read information on subject pronouns.

Figure 15.3

Grammatik Help on Grammar Dialog Box

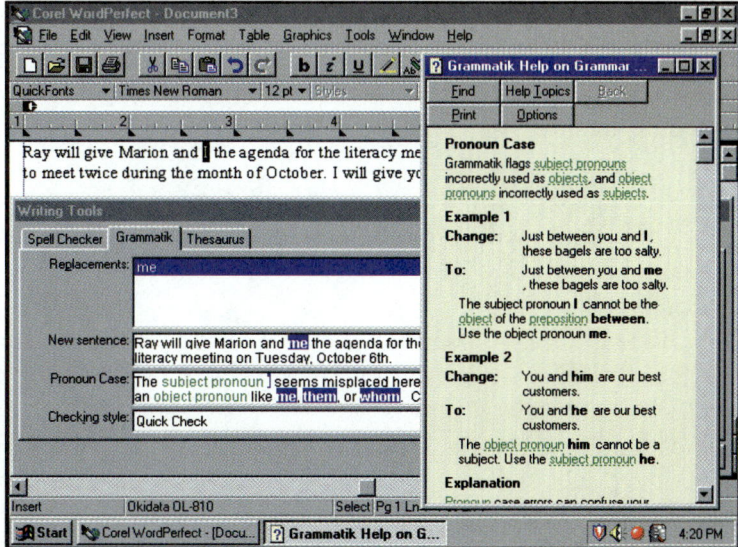

Using Grammatik 315

EXERCISE 3

Viewing Rule Class Information in Grammatik Help on Grammar

1. At a clear editing window, open Memo 01.
2. Save the document with Save As and name it Ch 15, Ex 03.
3. Change the checking style and complete a grammar check by completing the following steps:
   a. Click Tools, then Grammatik.
   b. When Grammatik selects *Dearing*, change the checking style to *Formal Memo or Letter*, then click Skip Always (to tell Grammatik to leave *Dearing* as written.)
   c. Grammatik selects *Windslow*. This name is correct, so click Skip Always.
   d. Grammatik selects *of Integrated Learning by Riverside Publishing for the reference section for teachers* and inserts the rule *Consecutive Elements* with the advice, *Avoid using too many prepositional phrases in a row. They can be confusing to follow and may deaden your writing*. View information about consecutive elements, then correct the error by completing the following steps:
      (1) Move the arrow pointer over the words *Consecutive Elements* until the arrow pointer displays with a question mark in a circle, then click the left mouse button.
      (2) Read the information and example sentences about Consecutive Elements that displays at the right side of the editing window. Click the down-pointing triangle in the vertical scroll bar to continue reading text until you reach the end. When you have finished reading the example sentences, click the Close button on the Grammatik Help on Grammar Title bar.
      (3) Edit the partial sentence so it reads, *of Integrated Learning by Riverside Publishing for the teachers' reference section*. To do this, position the arrow pointer inside the selected text in the document, then click the left mouse button. Delete and/or insert text as needed to edit the sentence.
      (4) After editing the sentence, click Resume.
   e. Grammatik selects *This book should be made* and inserts the rule, *Passive Voice* with the advice, *Consider revising using active voice*. View information about passive voice, then correct the error by completing the following steps:
      (1) Move the arrow pointer over the words *Passive Voice* until the arrow pointer displays with a question mark in a circle, then click the left mouse button. Click Passive Voice in the Topics Found dialog box, then click Display.
      (2) Read the information on Passive Voice. Click the down-pointing triangle in the vertical scroll bar until you have read all of the information and example sentences.
      (3) Click the Close button on the Grammatik Help on Grammar Title bar.
      (4) Edit the partial sentence so it reads, *This book will be available in the administrators' reference section*. Position the arrow pointer inside the selected text in the document, then click the left mouse button. Delete and/or insert text as needed to edit the sentence.

- (5) After editing the sentence, click Resume.
  - f. Grammatik selects *5*, inserts the rule *Number Style*, and displays the message *Spell out whole numbers in this range, even as part of larger numbers ("eight million"). If this is part of a fraction standing alone, spell out the fraction ("one-quarter of the class")*. The word *five* is displayed in the suggested Replacements text box, so click Replace.
  - g. Grammatik selects *A tour of the Washington High School library by the members of the Board of Education is planned*. Edit this sentence so it reads *The members of the Board of Education will be touring the Washington High School library next month*. After editing the sentence, click Resume.
  - h. Grammatik selects, *The tour is tentatively scheduled*. Leave this as written by clicking Skip Always.
  - i. Grammatik selects *01*. Click Skip Once since this is the document identification line.
  - j. At the *Grammar check completed. Close Grammatik?* question, click No.
4. Change the checking style back to *Quick Check*, then close the Grammatik dialog box.
5. Save the document again with the same name (Ch 15, Ex 03).
6. Print and then close Ch 15, Ex 03.

When Grammatik has selected an error and displayed the rule class violation, you can click Turn Off to instruct Grammatik to ignore any errors associated with that rule in the current document. For example, if you have written a document in the passive voice and do not want Grammatik to stop on all sentences with the passive voice style, click Turn Off when Grammatik stops on the first sentence. If a rule has been turned off, you can turn it back on by clicking the Customize button, then clicking Turn On Rules. Other options on the Customize menu are described in figure 15.4.

Figure 15.4

Customize Menu Options

Use this option	to...
Checking Styles	Edit or delete the predefined set of writing styles to adapt them to your style of writing.
Save Rules	Save the rules that have been turned off as a new checking style.
User Word Lists	Add, delete, or edit words in the default user word list, or select a different word list for Grammatik to use while proofreading your document.
Language	Select a different language to use for proofreading. The dictionary files for the other language must be installed for this option to work.
Auto start	Turn auto start off or back on after it has been turned off. Auto start is on by default, which means Grammatik starts proofreading the document as soon as you click Tools, then Grammatik.
Prompt before auto replacement	If QuickCorrect is activated, click this option if you want Grammatik to prompt you before it makes an automatic replacement.

Using Grammatik

Suggest spelling replacements	Turn suggest spelling replacements off or back on after it has been turned off. This option is on by default, so Grammatik will offer alternative words for the selected word in the Replacements list box.
Check headers, footers, footnotes in WordPerfect	Instruct Grammatik to proofread all headers, footers, and footnotes in the current document.

Checking Styles

When you click Customize, then Checking Styles, the Checking Styles dialog box shown in figure 15.5 displays. The Checking Styles dialog box shows the same checking style options as the Checking Style pop-up menu. Checking styles can be selected at this dialog box or with options from the Checking Style pop-up menu.

Figure 15.5

Checking Styles Dialog Box

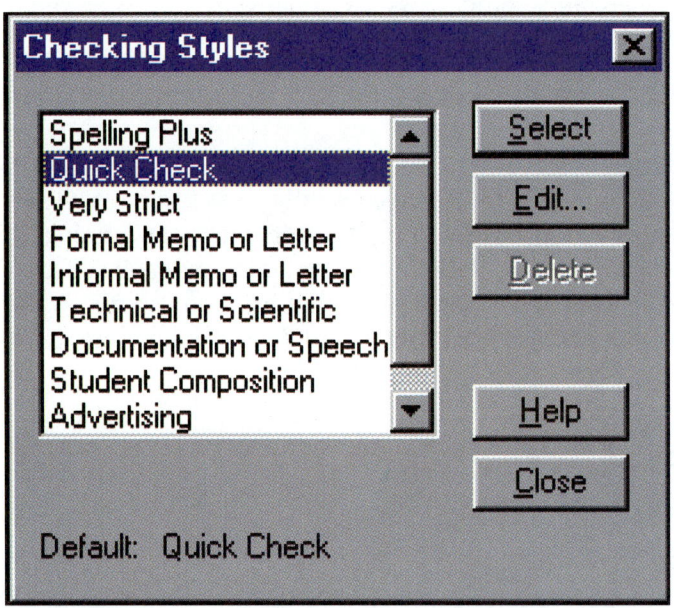

For the formal checking styles such as *Formal Memo or Letter*, *Technical or Scientific*, and *Documentation or Speech*, Grammatik checks a document using most rules of grammar. If you choose a less formal style such as *Informal Memo or Letter*, *Advertising*, or *Fiction*, Grammatik uses fewer grammar rules when checking a document.

To see the rules that Grammatik uses for each checking style, select the desired checking style at the Checking Styles dialog box, then click Edit. At the Edit Checking Styles dialog box, rules are displayed in the Rule classes list box. If the check box before the rule contains an X, the rule is used when checking the document. If there is no X in the check box, the rule is not used. For example, figure 15.6 displays the Edit Checking Styles - Quick Check dialog box showing the rules that are used with the default checking style of *Quick Check*.

Edit Checking Styles - Quick Check Dialog Box **Figure 15.6**

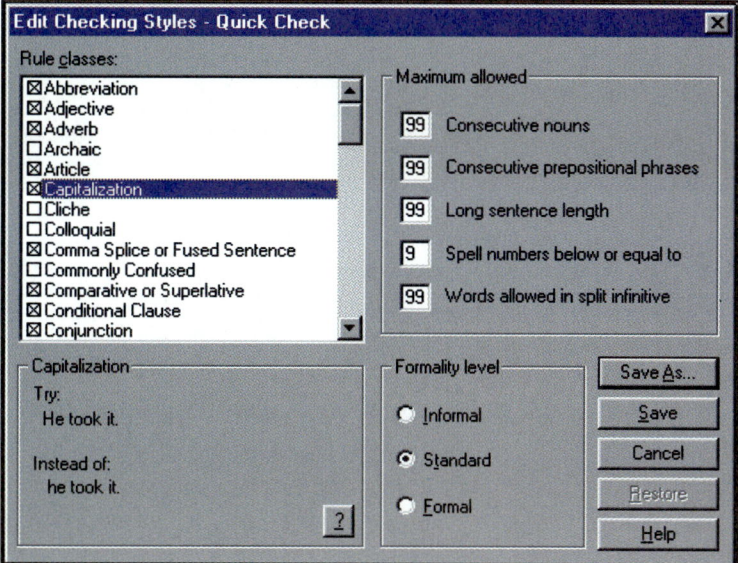

Changing Checking Options

If you click Chec<u>k</u> from the Grammatik dialog box, a drop-down menu displays with the following options: Document, To End of Document, and Selected Text. The default setting is Document. Choose one of the other options to control how much of the document you want to check with Grammatik.

EXERCISE 4

Customizing a Checking Style

1. Turn off automatic start and customize a Grammatik checking style by completing the following steps:
    a. At a clear editing window, click <u>T</u>ools, then <u>G</u>rammatik.
    b. At the *Grammar check completed. Close Grammatik?* question, click <u>N</u>o.
    c. At the Grammatik dialog box, click Custo<u>m</u>ize, then Chec<u>k</u>ing Styles.
    d. At the Checking Styles dialog box, select *Formal Memo or Letter* in the list box, then click <u>E</u>dit.
    e. At the Edit Checking Styles - Formal Memo or Letter dialog box, click *Capitalization* to remove the X from the Capitalization check box.
    f. Click *Doubled Word or Punctuation* to remove the check mark. (You will need to scroll down the list to see this option.)
    g. Click *Spelling* to remove the check mark. (You will need to scroll down the list to see this option.)
    h. Click <u>S</u>ave.
    i. At the Checking Styles dialog box, click <u>C</u>lose.
    j. At the Grammatik dialog box, click Custo<u>m</u>ize.
    k. At the Customize menu, remove the check mark beside *Auto start* by moving the arrow pointer to Auto <u>s</u>tart to select the option, then clicking the left mouse button.

Using Grammatik **319**

       l. Close the Grammatik dialog box.
    2. Open Letter 03.
    3. Save the document with Save As and name it Ch 15, Ex 04.
    4. Complete a grammar check by completing the following steps:
       a. Click Tools, then Grammatik.
       b. If necessary, change the checking style to *Formal Memo or Letter*.
       c. Click Start to begin checking.
       d. When Grammatik selects *in a thorough and efficient manner*, edit this by deleting the selected text and keying *efficiently*. Click Resume to resume grammar checking.
       e. When Grammatik selects *Your account is managed*, change this to *We manage your account*.
       f. When Grammatik selects *orders have been shipped*, leave it as written.
       g. When Grammatik selects *03*, click Skip Once.
       h. At the *Grammar check completed. Close Grammatik?* question, click Yes.
    5. The letter overuses the words *efficiently* and *manage*. Use Thesaurus to change one or more occurrences of *efficiently* and *manage* or *managing* to make the letter read better.
    6. Save the letter again with the same name (Ch 15, Ex 04).
    7. Print and then close Ch 15, Ex 04.
    8. At a clear editing window, return the checking style *Formal Memo or Letter* back to the default rule checking and turn automatic start back on by completing the following steps:
       a. Click Tools, then Grammatik.
       b. At the Grammatik dialog box, click Customize, then Checking Styles.
       c. At the Checking Styles dialog box, make sure *Formal Memo or Letter* is selected in the list box, then click Edit.
       d. At the Edit Checking Styles - Formal Memo or Letter dialog box, click Restore. (This returns the checking style rules back to the default.)
       e. Click Save.
       f. At the Checking Styles dialog box, select *Quick Check* in the list box, then click the Select button.
       g. At the Grammatik dialog box, turn automatic start back on by completing the following steps:
          (1) Click Customize.
          (2) At the Customize menu, move the arrow pointer to *Auto start*, then click the left mouse button to insert a check mark beside the option.
       h. Close the Grammatik dialog box.

Analyzing Elements of the Document

With options from the Analysis drop-down menu, you can view parts of speech, a parse tree, or statistics for the entire document.

During a grammar check, if you click Analysis, then Parts of Speech, Grammatik will display the Parts of Speech dialog box with the current line of text displayed and the parts of speech listed in green. Figure 15.7 shows a document being checked with Grammatik with the parts of speech displayed. After viewing the parts of speech, click Close to close the Parts of Speech dialog box. Click Close to close the Grammatik dialog box.

Parts of Speech Dialog Box

Figure 15.7

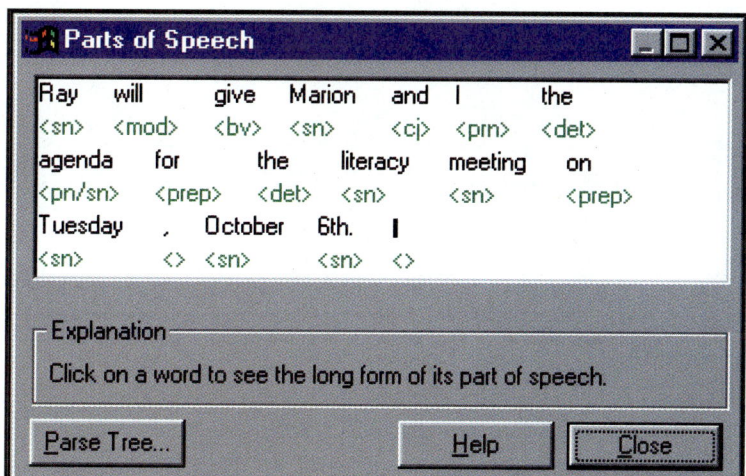

With the Parse Tree option from the Analysis drop-down menu, Grammatik will show whether a group of words in a sentence has been identified as a clause and, if so, what kind of clause. The word *parse* means to break a sentence into parts and to identify the parts of speech, the functions, and the interrelation of the parts. Figure 15.8 shows a parse tree for text in a document. At the Parse Tree dialog box, you can display parts of speech for text by clicking the Parts of Speech button at the bottom of the dialog box. Click Close to close the Parse Tree dialog box.

Parse Tree Dialog Box

Figure 15.8

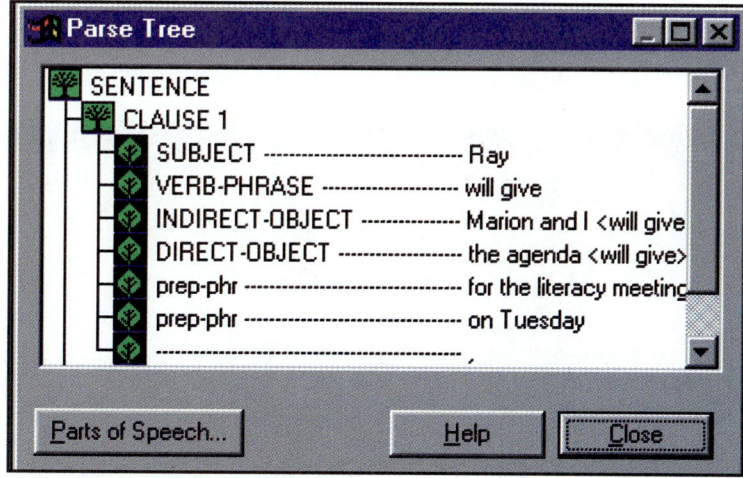

Use the Basic Counts option from the Analysis drop-down menu to find out specific information about the document. Grammatik will display the Basic Counts dialog box showing the number of syllables, words, sentences, and paragraphs. It will also show the number of short and long sentences, big words, and averages. Figure 15.9 shows the Basic Counts dialog box for the document Report 01 on your student data disk.

Figure 15.9

Basic Counts Dialog Box

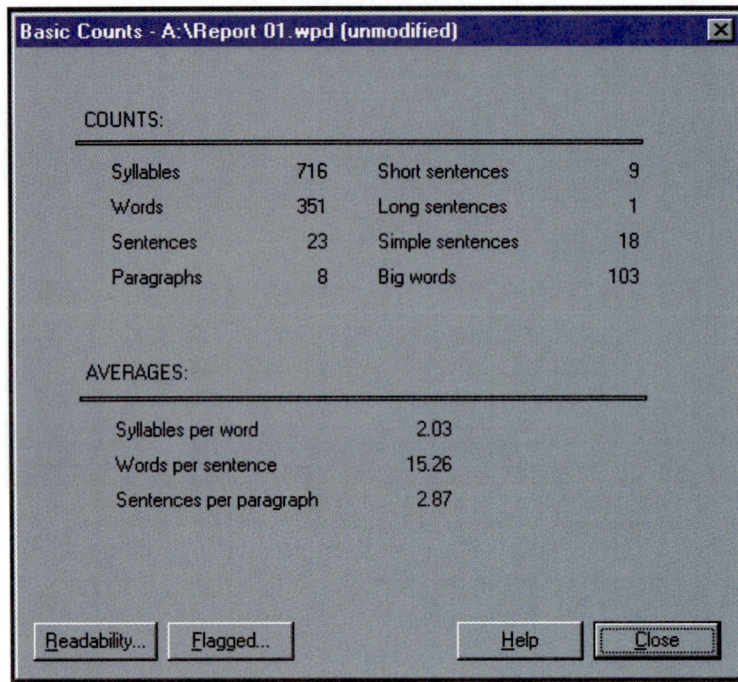

If you click Readability at the Basic Counts dialog box, or from the Analysis drop-down menu, Grammatik will display the Readability dialog box. At this dialog box, the open document is compared to three sample documents for complexity, readability, and use of passive voice. Figure 15.10 shows the Readability dialog box for the document Report 07 on your student data disk.

Figure 15.10

Readability Dialog Box

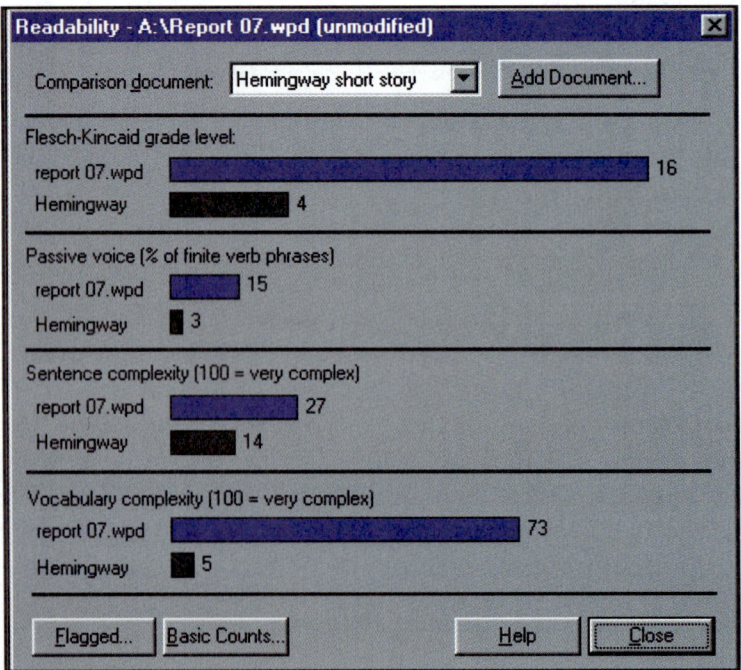

During grammar checking, Grammatik keeps track of the rule class errors in the document and the number of times an error occurred with the rule class. To view the rule class errors in a document, click Flagged at the Basic Counts dialog box, or at the Analysis drop-down menu. Figure 15.11 shows the Flagged dialog box for a document.

Figure 15.11

Flagged Dialog Box

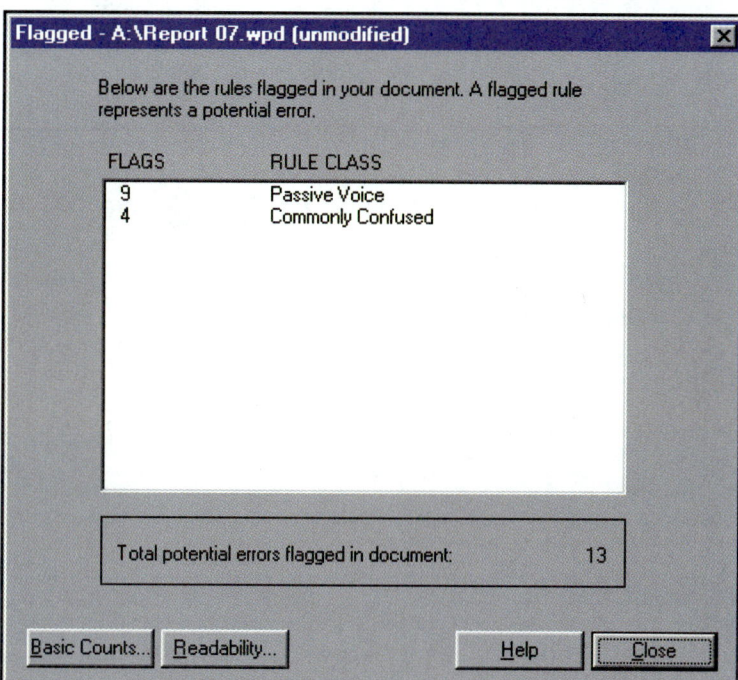

EXERCISE 5

Viewing Document Statistics during Checking

1. At a clear editing window, open Report 07.
2. Save the document with Save As and name it Ch 15, Ex 05.
3. Change the checking style and complete a grammar check by completing the following steps:
   a. Click Tools, then Grammatik.
   b. When Grammatik selects *Ohm's*, change the checking style to *Technical or Scientific*. After changing the checking style, click Skip Always to leave *Ohm's* as written.
   c. When Grammatik selects *a telegraph network spanning 8,000 feet*, click Skip Always.
   d. When Grammatik selects *Some of the*, change this to *Some*.
   e. When Grammatik selects *erected*, change this to *built*.
   f. When Grammatik selects *made use of*, change this to *used*.
   g. When Grammatik selects *By the 1850s*, click Skip Always to leave this as written.
   h. When Grammatik selects *phonautograph*, click Skip Always.

Using Grammatik

i. When Grammatik selects *communicate*, click Skip Always to leave this as written.
   j. When Grammatik selects *acquiring*, click Skip Always.
   k. When Grammatik selects *Elisha*, click Skip Always.
   l. When Grammatik selects *he*, click Skip Always.
   m. When Grammatik selects *advent*, change this to *arrival*.
   n. At the *Grammar check completed. Close Grammatik?* question, click No.
4. With the Grammatik dialog box still displayed in the editing window, view statistics about the document by completing the following steps:
   a. Click Analysis, then Basic Counts.
   b. Read the information displayed in the Basic Counts dialog box, then click Readability.
   c. Read the information displayed in the Readability dialog box, then click Flagged.
   d. Read the information displayed in the Flagged dialog box, then click Close.
5. With the Grammatik dialog box still displayed in the editing window, change the checking style back to *Quick Check*. After changing the checking style, click Close to close the Grammatik dialog box.
6. Save the document again with the same name (Ch 15, Ex 05).
7. Print and then close Ch 15, Ex 05.

User Word Lists

The first time you click Add during a grammar check, Grammatik adds the word to the default user word list, *wt61us.uwl*. To view the default user word list, click Customize, then User Word Lists. At the User Word List Editor dialog box, you can create, edit, and delete custom word lists. This is the same word list editor described in chapter 8. Refer to the section *Adding, Creating, or Removing User Word Lists* in chapter 8 for more information.

QuickCorrect

The QuickCorrect button in Grammatik operates the same way as it does during a Spell Check. If you key *teh*, QuickCorrect changes it to *the*. You can add misspelled words with the correct spelling in QuickCorrect. To do this, make sure the proper spelling is selected in the Replacements text box, then click QuickCorrect.

CHAPTER SUMMARY

- WordPerfect includes a grammar-checking program called Grammatik. With Grammatik you can check the grammar, style errors, and spelling errors in a document.

- When Grammatik detects an error, it tries to include replacement words or sentences in the Replacements list box. You can incorporate these replacements in the document, click Skip Once or Skip Always, or edit the document yourself.

- When an error is detected, the rule class for the problem is displayed along with advice on how to fix the error. If you need further information about the rule class, move the arrow pointer to the rule class words until it displays with an attached question mark in a circle, then click the left mouse button.

- Grammatik uses a default checking style of *Quick Check*. This can be changed with options from the Checking Style pop-up menu or at the Checking Styles dialog box.

- With Grammatik, you can view statistics about a document including basic counts, readability, and what errors have been flagged.

- During a grammar check, you can click Analysis, then Parts of Speech and Grammatik will display the current line of text with the parts of speech listed in green. Click Parse Tree to show whether a group of words in a sentence has been identified as a clause and, if so, what kind of clause.

- Grammatik scans the same user word list, *wt61us.uwl*, that is used when spell checking a document. Words can be added to or deleted from this user word list as described in chapter 8.

COMMANDS REVIEW

	Menu Bar/Keyboard
Grammatik dialog box	Tools, Grammatik

CHECK YOUR UNDERSTANDING

Completion: In the space provided at the right, indicate the correct word or words relating to the sentences below.

1. Click this button at the Grammatik dialog box to change the checking style. _____

2. The option *Auto start* is located at this drop-down menu. _____

3. Click the left mouse button when the arrow pointer displays with this icon attached to view information about the rule class. _____

4. This is the default checking style for Grammatik. _____

5. This word means to break a sentence into parts explaining the grammatical forms and clauses. _____

6. During a grammar check, click Analysis, then this to show whether a group of words in a sentence has been identified as a clause and, if so, what kind of clause. _____

7. Add words to this user word list that you want Grammatik to skip when grammar checking a document. _____

8. To view the rule class errors in a document, click this option at the Basic Counts dialog box. _____

9. If you are preparing a formal business letter, choose this checking style at the Writing Tools dialog box with the Grammatik tab selected. _____

10. If you are preparing a technical document, choose this checking style at the Writing Tools dialog box with the Grammatik tab selected. _____

SKILL ASSESSMENTS

Assessment 1

1. At a clear editing window, open Memo 09.
2. Save the document with Save As and name it Ch 15, SA 01.
3. Change the checking style and check the grammar of the document by completing the following steps:
    a. Click Tools, then Grammatik.
    b. When Grammatik stops at *Mortensen*, change the checking style to *Formal Memo or Letter*, then click Skip Always to leave *Mortensen* as written.
    c. When Grammatik selects *prevelance*, change it to the correct spelling.
    d. When Grammatik selects *have*, replace it with *has*.
    e. When Grammatik selects *a moderately high prevalence of latex allergies has been noted*, change it to *We have noted a moderately high prevalence of latex allergies*.
    f. When Grammatik selects *prevelance*, change it to the correct spelling.
    g. When Grammatik selects *rate for health care workers are*, change it to *rate for health care workers is*.
    h. When Grammatik selects *reason for this difference are*, change it to *reason for this difference is*.
    i. When Grammatik selects *09*, click Skip Once.
    j. At the *Grammar check completed. Close Grammatik?* question, click No.
    k. Change the checking style back to the default of *Quick Check*, then close the Grammatik dialog box.
4. Save the document again with the same name (Ch 15, SA 01).
5. Print and then close Ch 15, SA 01.

Assessment 2

1. At a clear editing window, complete the following steps:
   a. Display the Grammatik dialog box.
   b. Click the Customize button, then click Auto start at the drop-down menu. (This removes the check mark.)
   c. Close the Grammatik dialog box.
2. Open Report 09.
3. Save the document with Save As and name it Ch 15, SA 02.
4. Change the checking style and complete a grammar check by completing the following steps:
   a. Display the Grammatik dialog box.
   b. Change the checking style to *Technical or Scientific*.
   c. Start grammar checking.
   d. As Grammatik selects the following text, make the changes indicated:

wizzy-wig	Skip Always
is defined as	replace with *is*
(	Skip Once
utilizing	replace with *using*
you	Skip Always
it is easy to learn	replace with *learning it is easy*
there	Skip Always
But	replace with *However*
WYS	Skip Always
WYG	Skip Always
an	Skip Always
CPU	Skip Always
unit	Skip Always
input	Skip Always
inputting	replace with *entering*
Display monitor	Skip Always
Provides	Skip Always
Laser printer	Skip Always
to determine	replace with *to decide*

   e. When Grammatik has completed the grammar check, do not close the Grammatik dialog box.
   f. At the Grammatik dialog box, turn on automatic start of Grammatik and change the checking style back to *Quick Check*.
   g. Close the Grammatik dialog box.
5. Save the document again with the same name (Ch 15, SA 02).
6. Print and then close Ch 15, SA 02.

Assessment 3

1. At a clear editing window, open Memo 10.
2. Save the document with Save As and name it Ch 15, SA 03.
3. Begin grammar checking the document. When Grammatik stops at *Vitali*, change the checking style to *Formal Memo or Letter.* Click Skip Always to skip *Vitali*, then complete the grammar check. You determine what to leave as written and what to change. (Proper names are spelled correctly.)
4. Before closing the Grammatik dialog box, view statistics for the document. Change the checking style back to *Quick Check*, then close the Grammatik dialog box.
5. Save the document again with the same name (Ch 15, SA 03).
6. Print and then close Ch 15, SA 03.

MERGING DOCUMENTS

PERFORMANCE OBJECTIVE

Upon successful completion of chapter 16, you will be able to format and merge separate files to create a series of similar business documents, such as personalized form letters and envelopes.

WordPerfect includes a merge feature that you can use to create letters, envelopes, labels, and much more, all with personalized information. Generally, there are two documents that need to be created for merging. One document, which WordPerfect calls the *data file*, contains the variable information (information that changes). The second document contains the standard text along with identifiers showing where variable information is to be inserted. WordPerfect refers to this as the *form file*.

Creating a Data File

The data file and the form file required for a merge can be created in any order. However, creating the data file first and then the form file may be the easiest.

The data file contains the variable information that will be inserted in the form file. Before creating a data file, you need to determine into what type of correspondence you will be inserting the variable information. For example, suppose the sales manager of Sealine Products wants to introduce a new sales representative to all customers in the Spokane, Washington, area. The sales manager decides that a personal letter should be sent to all customers in the greater Spokane area. Figure 16.1 shows one way this letter can be written. The date, body of the letter, and the complimentary close are standard. The variable information—information that will change with each letter—includes the name, company name, address, city, state, ZIP Code, and salutation.

Merging Documents 329

Figure 16.1

Sample Letter

> June 8, 1998
>
> Name
> Company name
> Street address
> City, State ZIP
>
> Dear (Name):
>
> At Sealine Products, we are committed to providing quality products and services to our customers. To provide continuing service to you, a new sales representative has been hired. The new sales representative, Ms. Leanne Guile, began her employment with Sealine Products on May 1. She comes to our company with over 10 years' experience in the food industry.
>
> Ms. Guile will be in the Spokane area during the third week of June. She would like to schedule a time for a visit to your company, and will be contacting you by telephone next week.
>
> Sincerely,
>
>
> Mark Deveau, Manager
> Sales Department

Determining Fields

In the letter shown in figure 16.1, the variable information needs to be broken into sections called *fields*. To determine the variable fields, you need to decide how, and in what form, the information will be used. The following is a name and address of a customer of Sealine Products:

> Mr. Albert Rausch
> Lobster Shoppe
> 450 Marginal Way
> Spokane, WA 98012

The name, *Mr. Albert Rausch*, could be identified as an entire field. However, the salutation for this letter should read *Dear Mr. Rausch*. If the name is left as one field, the salutation will read *Dear Mr. Albert Rausch*. In this example, then, the name should be broken into three fields: title (Mr.), first name, and last name.

There is no need for the company name, *Lobster Shoppe*, to be broken into smaller parts. Therefore, it can be identified as one field. The street address, *450 Marginal Way*, can also remain as one field.

The city, state, and ZIP Code in this example can also be considered as one field. However, if you decide that you need the city, state, or ZIP Code separated, you need to make separate fields for each item.

After all fields have been determined, the next step is to determine field names. (This step is optional. If you do not include field names, WordPerfect numbers the fields.) There is no limit to the number of fields a data file can contain. The following list shows one way the fields can be named:

> title
> first name
> last name
> company name
> street address
> city, state ZIP

A field name can be up to 80 characters in length and can include spaces. You can use either uppercase or lowercase letters.

Variable information in a data file is saved as a *record*. A record contains all the information for one unit (for example, a person, family, customer, client, or business). A series of fields makes one record, and a series of records makes a data file.

In the data file for the example letter in figure 16.1, each record will contain six fields of information: title; first name; last name; company name; address; and the city, state ZIP. Each record in the data file must contain the same number of fields. If the number of fields is not consistent, information will not be inserted correctly during the merge.

WordPerfect offers two methods for creating a data file. You can create a data file as a normal text file, or you can create a data file in the Table format.

Keying a Data File

Remember that the data file contains the variable information that will be inserted into a form file. When you create a data file, name the fields consistent with the field names in the form file. To create a data file for the example letter in figure 16.1, you would complete the following steps:

1. At a clear editing window, display the Merge dialog box, shown in figure 16.2, by clicking Tools, then Merge.
2. At the Merge dialog box, click Data File.
3. At the Create Data File dialog box, shown in figure 16.3, key **title**, then press Enter. (This inserts *title* in the Field name list list box.)
4. Key **first name**, then press Enter.
5. Key the other field names—**last name**; **company name**; **street address**; and **city, state ZIP**. Press Enter after each field name.
6. When all field names have been keyed, click OK.
7. When you click OK at the Create Data File dialog box, the Quick Data Entry dialog box is displayed as shown in figure 16.4. Key the title of a customer to receive the letter, then press Enter. Continue keying the information in each of the fields in the dialog box.
8. After keying the last field for the last customer, click Close.
9. WordPerfect inserts the message *Save the changes to disk?* At this message, click Yes.
10. At the Save Data File As dialog box, key a name for the data file (such as **Sales rep**), then click Save.
11. Close the file. WordPerfect automatically assigns the filename extension *.dat* to your data files.

Figure 16.2

Merge Dialog Box

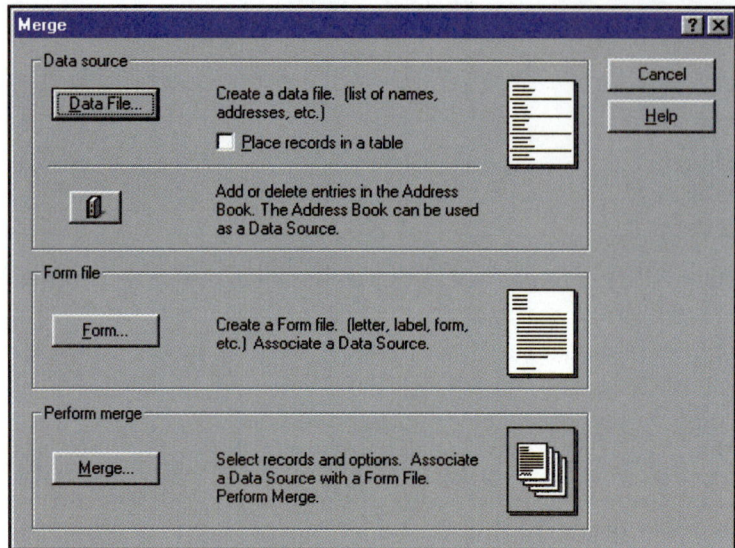

Figure 16.3

Create Data Dialog Box

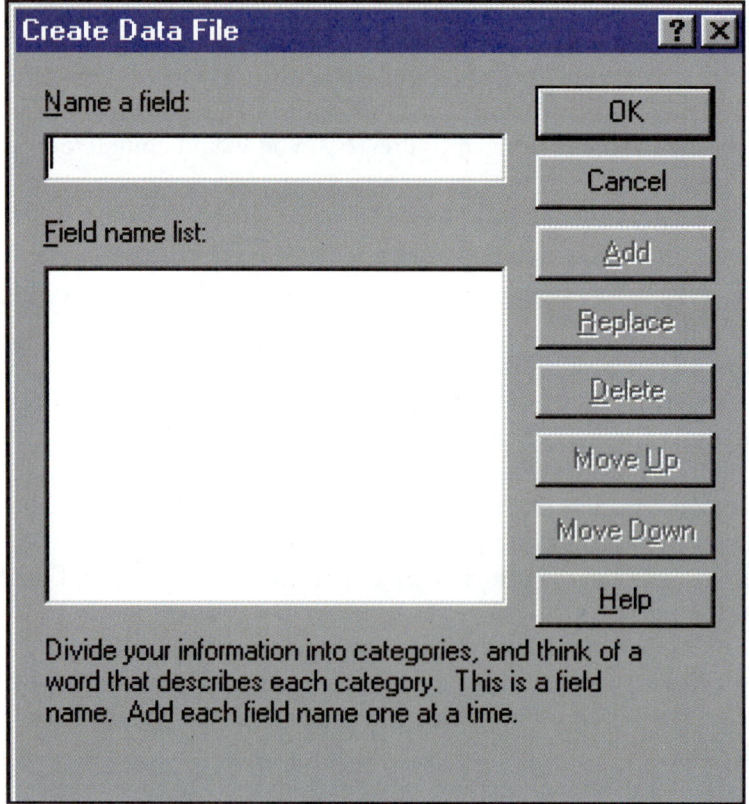

Figure 16.4

Quick Data Entry Dialog Box

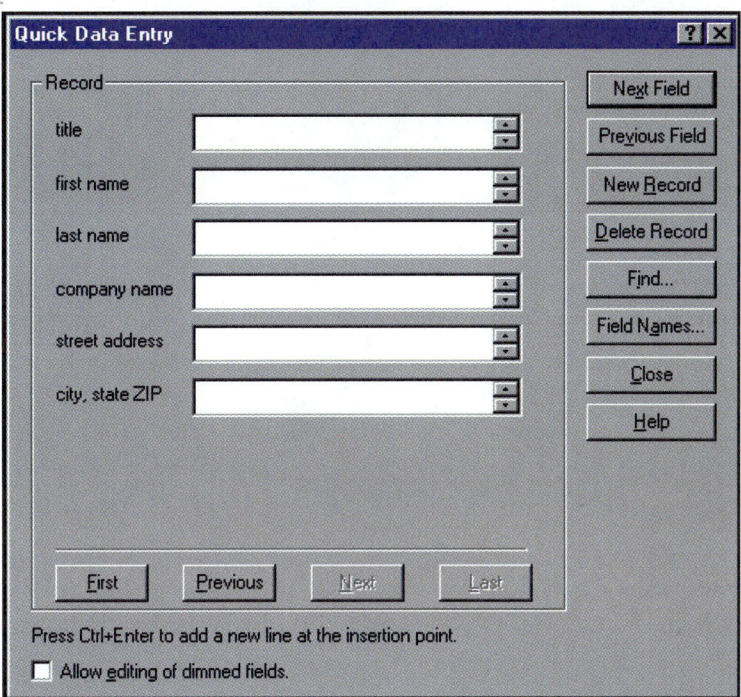

When entering text in the Quick Data Entry dialog box, you can use the Tab key to move the insertion point to the next field or press Shift + Tab to move the insertion point to the previous field. These commands are useful for editing text in the fields.

When you save the document in step 10, the data file displays in the editing window. The Data File Feature Bar displays below the Power Bar (or Ruler Bar). Figure 16.5 shows an example of how a data file might display for customers of Sealine Products.

Figure 16.5

Sample Text Data File

FIELDNAMES(title;first name;last name;company name; street address;city, state ZIP)**ENDRECORD**

Mr.**ENDFIELD**
Darren**ENDFIELD**
Judd**ENDFIELD**
Chips 'n Chowder**ENDFIELD**
2349 Lowell Drive**ENDFIELD**
Spokane, WA 98031**ENDFIELD**
ENDRECORD

Mrs.**ENDFIELD**
Kiley**ENDFIELD**

Merging Documents

Hostkins**ENDFIELD**
Kiley's Kitchen**ENDFIELD**
903 Fifth Street**ENDFIELD**
Spokane, WA 98036**ENDFIELD**
ENDRECORD

Mr. and Mrs.**ENDFIELD**
Tristin**ENDFIELD**
Keating**ENDFIELD**
The Salmon Cafe**ENDFIELD**
332 River Drive**ENDFIELD**
Spokane, WA 98031**ENDFIELD**
ENDRECORD

In the data file shown in figure 16.5 each field takes up only one line. A field can contain more than one line, however. For example, the record for Mr. and Mrs. Keating could include the following:

Mr. and Mrs.**ENDFIELD**
Tristin**ENDFIELD**
Keating**ENDFIELD**
The Salmon Cafe**ENDFIELD**
332 River Drive
Suite 210**ENDFIELD**
Spokane, WA 98031**ENDFIELD**

When entering the information in the street address field at the Quick Data Entry dialog box, key the first line (332 River Drive), then press Ctrl + Enter. This causes the first line to move up in the street address field and it does not display. Key the second line of the field, then press Enter. This moves the insertion point to the next field.

EXERCISE

Creating a Data File

1. At a clear editing window, create a data file containing the information shown in figure 16.6 by completing the following steps:
   a. Click Tools, then Merge.
   b. At the Merge dialog box, click Data File.
   c. At the Create Data File dialog box, key **title**, then press Enter. (This inserts *title* in the Field name list list box.)
   d. Key **first name**, then press Enter.
   e. Key the other field names—**last name**, **street address**, **city**, **state**, and **ZIP**. Press Enter after each field name.
   f. When all field names have been keyed, click OK.

g. At the Quick Data Entry dialog box, key **Mr. and Mrs.** in the title field, then press Enter.
h. Continue keying the information in figure 16.6 in the appropriate field.
i. After keying the last field of information for the last customer, click <u>C</u>lose.
j. WordPerfect inserts the message *Save the changes to disk?* At this question, click <u>Y</u>es.
k. At the Save Data File As dialog box, key **Fund df**, then click <u>S</u>ave (WordPerfect automatically assigns the filename extension *.dat* to your data file).

2. Print Fund df. (This may be optional. Check with your instructor to see if you should print this document. Each record will print on a separate page.)
3. Close the Fund df document.

Figure 16.6

title	=	Mr. and Mrs.
first name	=	Marcus
last name	=	Olsen
street address	=	408 Highland Drive
city	=	St. Louis
state	=	MO
ZIP	=	63409
title	=	Ms.
first name	=	Jeanne
last name	=	Hillesland
street address	=	1321 North Orchard
city	=	St. Louis
state	=	MO
ZIP	=	63401
title	=	Mr. and Mrs.
first name	=	Patrick
last name	=	Dusek
street address	=	3740 South Thompson
city	=	St. Charles
state	=	MO
ZIP	=	63306
title	=	Dr.
first name	=	Armen
last name	=	Rhoades
street address	=	17435 Zircon Drive
city	=	St. Louis
state	=	MO
ZIP	=	63409

Creating the Form File

When you have determined the fields and field names and created the data file, the next step is to create the form file. When the form letter for our example company, Sealine Products, is completed and the fields have been keyed in the proper locations, it will look like the letter in figure 16.7. Notice that there is a space between the fields. Spaces are inserted between fields as if there were text; then, when the variable information is inserted, it is spaced correctly. This is also true for punctuation. Insert punctuation in a form file as you would a normal file. For example, place the colon (:) immediately after *FIELD(last name)* in the salutation.

Figure 16.7

Example Form File

June 8, 1998

FIELD(title) **FIELD**(first name) **FIELD**(last name)
FIELD(company name)
FIELD(street address)
FIELD(city, state ZIP)

Dear **FIELD**(title) **FIELD**(last name):

At Sealine Products, we are committed to providing quality products and services to our customers. To provide continuing service to you, a new sales representative has been hired. The new sales representative, Ms. Leanne Guile, began her employment with Sealine Products on May 1. She comes to our company with over 10 years' experience in the food industry.

Ms. Guile will be in the Spokane area during the third week of June. She would like to schedule a time for a visit to your company, and will be contacting you by telephone next week.

Sincerely,

Mark Deveau, Manager
Sales Department

The title and last name field were used more than once in the form file in figure 16.7. Fields in a form file can be used as often as needed. Now you will create your own form file for the data file you created in exercise 1.

EXERCISE 2

Creating a Form File

1. At a clear editing window, create the form file shown in figure 16.8 by completing the following steps:
    a. Click Tools, then Merge.
    b. At the Merge dialog box, click Form.
    c. At the Create Form File dialog box, key **Fund df** in the Associate a data file text box (the name of the data file), then click OK.
    d. At the editing window with the Merge Feature Bar displayed, key the letter shown in figure 16.8 to the point where the first field code (the field for title) is to be inserted.
    e. Click Insert Field on the Merge Feature Bar. This causes the Insert Field Name or Number dialog box to display.
    f. At the Insert Field Name or Number dialog box, make sure *title* is selected in the Field Names list box, then click Insert. (This inserts *FIELD(title)* in the document.)
    g. Press the space bar once, click *first name* in the Insert Field Name or Number dialog box, then click Insert.
    h. Continue creating the fields and text shown in figure 16.8 following steps similar to those in steps 1f and 1g. (Leave on the display of the Insert Field Name or Number dialog box until you have inserted all fields in the form file.)
    i. After inserting the fields in the letter, close the Insert Field Name or Number dialog box, then key the remainder of the letter in figure 16.8.
2. When the form file is completed, save it in the normal manner and name it *Fund ltr*. (WordPerfect automatically assigns the filename extension *.frm* to your form files).
3. Print and then close Fund ltr.

Figure 16.8

September 21, 1998

FIELD(title) **FIELD**(first name) **FIELD**(last name)
FIELD(street address)
FIELD(city), **FIELD**(state) **FIELD**(ZIP)

Dear **FIELD**(title) **FIELD**(last name):

Thank you for your support of the financial aid and scholarship programs at Manorwood School District. Each year, we budget nearly $50,000 for deserving students needing financial assistance to attend school in the Manorwood School District. During the next school year, we will depend on people like you to help us raise that amount of money.

At present, over $30,000 has been pledged or given as a result of the Scholarship Fund Drive. Your scholarship investment will be a key part in the success of our ability to raise the necessary funds. Thank you for your support of the Manorwood School District.

Very truly yours,

MANORWOOD SCHOOL DISTRICT

Sharon Sibrel
Superintendent

xx:Fund ltr

Merging Files

Once the data file and the form file have been created and saved, they can be merged. To merge a form file with a data file, click Tools, then Merge. At the Merge dialog box, click Merge. At the Perform Merge dialog box, shown in figure 16.9, key the name of the form file in the Form file text box, then click OK.

When the merge is complete, the merged letters are displayed on the screen and the insertion point is positioned at the end of the last letter. The number of letters is determined by the number of records in the data file.

Figure 16.9

Perform Merge Dialog Box

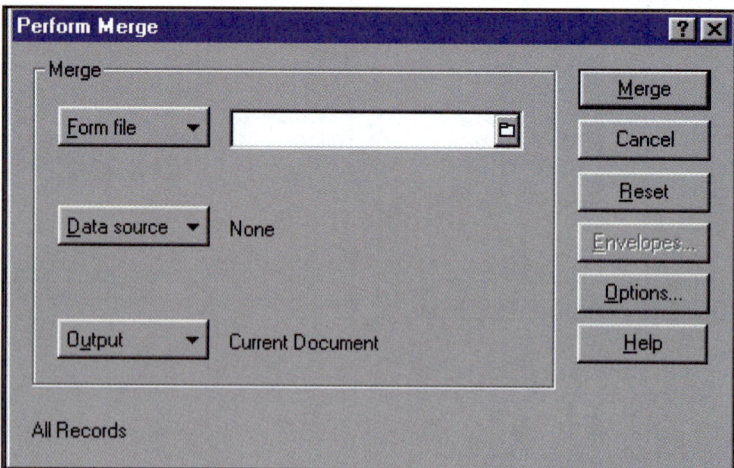

EXERCISE 3

Merging a Data File and a Form File

1. At a clear editing window, merge *Fund ltr* with *Fund df* by completing the following steps:
   a. Click Tools, then Merge.
   b. At the Merge dialog box, click Merge.
   c. At the Perform Merge dialog box, key **Fund ltr** in the Form file text box.
   d. Click Merge.
2. Save the merged document and name it Ch 16, Ex 03.
3. Print and then close Ch 16, Ex 03.

Changing the Merge Output

By default, WordPerfect merges the data file and the form file and inserts the merged documents into the current document. At the Perform Merge dialog box, you can control the output of the merged documents. If you click the down-pointing triangle in the Output button, a drop-down menu displays with the options Current Document, New Document, Printer, File on Disk, and E-mail.

Click New Document to merge files to a new document. The Printer choice sends the merged files directly to the printer without displaying them in the editing window. If you click File on Disk, the Select Output File dialog box displays. This dialog box is similar to the Open File dialog box. At this dialog box, choose a file from the list or key a name for the merged files, then press Enter. The E-mail option allows you to send the merged document by e-mail to the recipients. If you click E-mail, you will need to specify the field for the e-mail address and the subject line for the merged messages.

Changing Merge Options

By default, WordPerfect merges each record in the data file once with the form file and inserts a hard page break between records. You can change these default settings at the Perform Merge Options dialog box, shown in figure 16.10. To display this dialog box, click Options at the Perform Merge dialog box.

By default, a hard page break separates each merged document. If you do not want a hard page break between merged documents, remove the check mark from the Separate each merged document with a page break option.

If you want to merge each record in the data file more than once, click Number of copies for each record, then key a number. For example, if you want to merge each record in the data file twice with the form file, click Number of copies for each record, then key **2**.

The If empty field in data file option has a default setting of Remove Blank Line. At this setting, WordPerfect will remove the blank line if a record does not contain a field entry. For example, the records in the sample data file shown in figure 16.5 each include six fields. If one of the records did not include a company name, the **ENDFIELD** code for that field must still be included in the data file. This is because each record must contain the same number of fields. If one of the records does not contain a company name entry, leave the setting at Remove Blank Line. This will cause the street address to move up just below the title, first name, and last name. The If empty field in data file option can be changed to Leave Blank Line. At this setting WordPerfect will leave a blank line if the field is empty.

When records in a data file are merged with a form file, the merged documents display in the current document without merge codes. If you want merge codes to display in merged documents, click Display options at the Perform Merge Options dialog box. This causes a drop-down menu to display with the options Show Codes, Hide Codes (the default), and Show as Markers. At the default setting of Hide Codes, no merge codes display in the merged document. Click Show Codes if you want merge codes to display in the merged document. Or, click Show as Markers if you want the merge codes to display as markers in the merged document.

Figure 16.10

Perform Merge Options Dialog Box

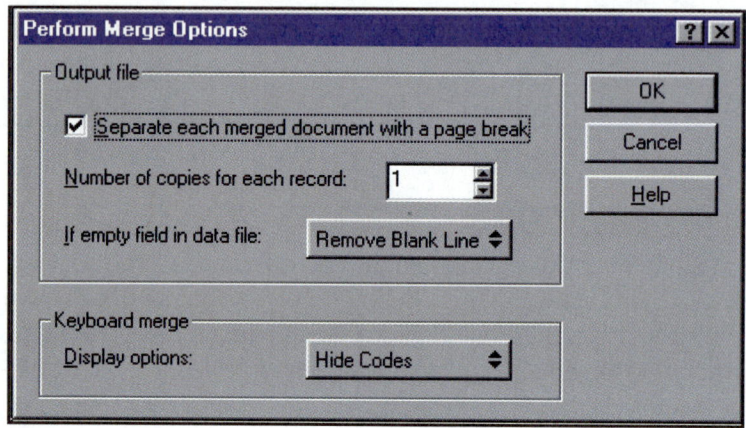

Creating a Table Data File

Fields in a data file can be entered in cells within a table. In this manner, each field in a cell is easily identified. To create a table data file, you would follow the same steps for creating a normal text data file, except that you click Place records in a table at the Merge dialog box. Figure 16.11 shows an example of a table data file containing the same records as the data file in figure 16.5. Notice that some of the cells in figure 16.11 show text wrapping to a second line. Do not worry when text wraps within a table data file since the spacing of the text is determined by the placement of the field codes in the form file. In exercises 4 and 5 you will create a similar table data file and merge it with the form file you created in exercise 2.

Figure 16.11

Sample Table Data File

title	first name	last name	company name	street address	city, state ZIP
Mr.	Darren	Judd	Chips 'n Chowder	2349 Lowell Drive	Spokane, WA 98031
Mrs.	Kiley	Hostkins	Kiley's Kitchen	903 Fifth Street	Spokane, WA 98036
Mr. and Mrs.	Tristin	Keating	The Salmon Cafe	332 River Drive	Spokane, WA 98031

EXERCISE 4

Creating a Table Data File

1. At a clear editing window, change the font to 10-point Times New Roman, then create the table data file shown in figure 16.12 by completing the following steps:
   a. Display the Merge dialog box.
   b. At the Merge dialog box shown, click Place records in a table.
   c. Click Data File.
   d. At the Create Merge File dialog box, click OK.
   e. At the Create Data File dialog box, key **title**, then press Enter. (This inserts *title* in the Field name list list box.)
   f. Key **first name**, then press Enter.
   g. Key the other field names—**last name**, **street address**, **city**, **state**, and **ZIP**. Press Enter after each field name.
   h. When all field names have been keyed, click OK.
   i. At the Quick Data Entry dialog box, key **Mr. and Mrs.** in the title field, then press Enter. Continue keying the information in each of the fields identified as shown in figure 16.12.
   j. After keying the last field of information for the last customer, click Close.
   k. WordPerfect inserts the message *Save the changes to disk?* At this question, click Yes.
2. At the Save Data File As dialog box, key **Fund2 df**, then click Save (WordPerfect automatically assigns the filename extension *.dat*).
3. Print and then close Fund2 df. (This may be optional. Check with your instructor.)

Figure 16.12

title	first name	last name	street address	city	state	ZIP
Mr. and Mrs.	James	Ricardo	16304 12th Avenue	St. Charles	MO	63306
Mr.	Glenn	Neigel	2223 East Wright	St. Louis	MO	63404
Ms.	Ruby	Marttala	4566 South Oakes	St. Charles	MO	63306
Mr. and Mrs.	Nicholas	Kobe	3348 34th Court East	St. Louis	MO	63402

EXERCISE 5

Merging Two Files

1. At a clear editing window, merge *Fund ltr* with *Fund2 df* to the printer by completing the following steps:
   a. Click Tools, then Merge.
   b. At the Merge dialog box, click Merge.
   c. At the Perform Merge dialog box, key **Fund ltr** in the Form file text box.
   d. Select the filename displayed in the Data source text box, then key **Fund2 df**.
   e. Change the Output option to Printer by clicking the Output button, then clicking Printer at the drop-down menu.
2. Click Merge and the merged documents are sent directly to the printer.

Canceling a Merge

If, during the merge, you want to stop it, press the Esc key or press Ctrl + Break. To begin the merge again, you will need to repeat the steps for completing a merge.

Formatting the Form File

Any formatting codes you want applied to the merged documents should be inserted at the Styles Editor dialog box in the form file. To display the Styles Editor dialog box, click Format, point to Document, then click Initial Codes Style. You can also use the Document Initial Font dialog box if you want to change the font for the merged documents.

EXERCISE 6

Editing the Format of a Form File

1. At a clear editing window, open Fund ltr.
2. Make the following changes to the document:
   a. Display the Styles Editor dialog box, then change the left and right margins to 1.5 inches.
   b. Display the Document Initial Font dialog box, then change the font to 12-point Century Schoolbook.
3. Save Fund ltr with the same name.
4. Close Fund ltr.
5. Merge Fund ltr with Fund df into the current document. (Make sure that the Output option at the Perform Merge dialog box is set at *Current Document*.)
6. Save the merged document and name it Ch 16, Ex 06.
7. Print and then close Ch 16, Ex 06.

Creating Envelopes

There are two methods you can use to create envelopes with a data file. You can create a form file to print envelopes, or you can create envelopes while merging a letter or other form file.

Merging Envelopes Only

You can create a form file for printing envelopes that you will merge with a data file. Exercise 7 shows you how to create the form file.

EXERCISE

Creating an Envelope Form File

1. At a clear editing window, create an envelope form file to be merged with the Fund df data file by completing the following steps:
   a. Display the Merge dialog box.
   b. At the Merge dialog box, click Form.
   c. At the Create Form File dialog box, key **Fund df** in the Associate a data file text box, then click OK.
   d. At the clear editing window (with the Merge Feature Bar displayed), click Format, then Envelope.
   e. At the Envelope dialog box, make sure the insertion point is positioned in the Mailing addresses section. If it is not, click inside the Mailing addresses text box.
   f. Click Field (located at the bottom of the dialog box). This causes the Insert Field Name or Number dialog box to display.
   g. At the Insert Field Name or Number dialog box, make sure the *title* is selected in the Field Names list box, then click Insert. (This inserts the title field in the Mailing addresses section of the Envelope dialog box.)
   h. Press the space bar once, then click Field.
   i. At the Insert Field Name or Number dialog box, double-click *first name* in the Field Names list box.
   j. Press the space bar once, then click Field.
   k. At the Insert Field Name or Number dialog box, double-click *last name* in the Field Names list box.
   l. Press the Enter key once, then click Field.
   m. At the Insert Field Name or Number dialog box, double-click *street address* in the Field Names list box.
   n. Continue inserting field names in the Mailing addresses section of the Envelope dialog box. Insert the field names in the appropriate location.
   o. After all field names have been entered in the Mailing addresses section of the dialog box, click Append to Doc.
   p. At the editing window containing the envelope fields, save the document in the normal manner and name it Env ff.
   q. Close Env ff.
2. Merge *Env ff* with *Fund df* to the current document.
3. Save the merged document and name it Ch 16, Ex 07.
4. Print and then close Ch 16, Ex 07.

Merging Documents

Creating Envelopes During Merging

Envelopes can be created for the form file during the merge. When you create envelopes during the merge, you do not have to create a separate form file. When the merge is completed, an envelope for each record in the data file is created and positioned at the end of the document separated by page breaks.

EXERCISE 8

Creating Envelopes during a Merge

1. At a clear editing window, create envelopes when merging *Fund ltr* with *Fund2 df* by completing the following steps:
   a. Display the Merge dialog box.
   b. At the Merge dialog box, click Merge.
   c. At the Perform Merge dialog box, key **Fund ltr** in the Form file text box.
   d. Select the filename displayed in the Data source text box, then key **Fund2 df**.
   e. Click Envelopes.
   f. At the Envelope dialog box, insert the fields in the Mailing addresses section as described in exercise 7.
   g. After all necessary fields have been inserted in the Mailing addresses section, click OK.
   h. At the Perform Merge dialog box, click Merge.
2. When the merge is completed, save the merged document and name it Ch 16, Ex 08.
3. Print and then close Ch 16, Ex 08. (Check with your instructor to see if you should print the entire document or just the envelopes.)

Merging at the Keyboard

WordPerfect's Merge feature contains a large number of merge codes and merge programming commands that can be inserted in a form file. One of the most commonly used merge codes is KEYBOARD. This merge code is included on the Merge Feature Bar that displays in a form file. Other merge codes are available by clicking Merge Codes at the Merge Feature Bar. This displays the Insert Merge Codes dialog box in the editing window with a list of all merge codes.

The steps to insert a KEYBOARD code are explained in the following section. For a detailed list of all the merge formatting commands, please refer to the help menu.

Situations may arise in which you do not need to keep variable information in a data file. WordPerfect lets you input variable information directly from the keyboard. You can create a form file with fields *and* keyboard entry, or you can create a document that requires just keyboard entry.

To insert a KEYBOARD code in a form file, display the Merge dialog box, then click Form. At the Create Form File dialog box, click No association, then click OK. This tells WordPerfect that there is no data file associated with the form file. At the editing window, key the text of the form file to the point of the first KEYBOARD code. To insert the KEYBOARD code, click Keyboard on the Merge Feature Bar. At the Insert Merge Code dialog box, key a message specifying what is to be entered at the keyboard, then click OK. Continue in this manner until all text and KEYBOARD codes have been inserted in the document, then save the document in the normal manner.

To merge a form file containing KEYBOARD codes, display the Merge dialog box, then click Merge. At the Perform Merge dialog box, key the form file document name in the Form file text box, then click OK. WordPerfect merges the form file to the first KEYBOARD code and inserts the message you entered at the bottom of the editing window. Key the required information, then click Continue. (The Continue button is located on the Merge Feature Bar.) WordPerfect continues the merge to the next KEYBOARD code and inserts the specified message. Continue inserting the required information and clicking Continue until all information has been entered in the merged document.

EXERCISE

Performing a Keyboard Merge

1. At a clear editing window, open Fund ltr.
2. Save the document with Save As and name it Donate ltr.
3. Position the insertion point on the space between *investment* and *will be* in the second sentence of the second paragraph, press the space bar once, key **of**, press the space bar once again, then insert a KEYBOARD merge code by completing the following steps:
   a. Click Keyboard on the Merge Feature Bar.
   b. At the Insert Merge Code dialog box, key **enter amount of donation**, then click OK.
4. Save the document again with the same name (Donate ltr).
5. Close Donate ltr.
6. At a clear editing window, merge *Donate ltr* with *Fund df* to the current document by completing the following steps:
   a. Display the Merge dialog box.
   b. At the Merge dialog box, click Merge.
   c. At the Perform Merge dialog box, key **Donate ltr** in the Form file text box.
   d. Click the Data source button, then click File on Disk at the drop-down menu. In the Select Data File dialog box, click *Fund df*, then click Select.
   e. At the Perform Merge dialog box, click Merge.
   f. WordPerfect merges the letter to the keyboard merge code and inserts the message *enter amount of donation* at the bottom of the editing window. Key **$200**, then click Continue.
   g. When WordPerfect stops at the keyboard merge code for the second record, key **$150**, then click Continue.
   h. When WordPerfect stops at the keyboard merge code for the third record, key **$300**, then click Continue.
   i. When WordPerfect stops at the keyboard merge code for the fourth record, key **$250**, then click Continue.
7. When the merge is completed, save the merged document and name it Ch 16, Ex 09.
8. Print and then close Ch 16, Ex 09.

Specifying Records for Merging

With options from the Select Records dialog box, you can specify what records you want merged. This might be useful, for example, to merge only those records containing a certain city or a certain ZIP Code. You can also specify a range of records to be merged. For example, you could specify that only records three through eight be merged.

Marking Records

You can mark specific records in a data file to be merged with the form file. When you specify certain records for merging, you can identify the records by field. To specify certain records for merging, display the Perform Merge dialog box. At the Perform Merge dialog box, key the name of the form file in the Form file text box, then click Select Records. At the Select Records dialog box shown in figure 16.13, click Mark records. This causes the Select Records dialog box to change as shown in figure 16.14. Click First field to display, then specify the field to be used for selecting records, then click Update Record List. This causes only the field information for each record to display in the Record list list box. At this list box, mark the desired records. Repeat this for any other desired records. When all desired records have been selected, click OK. At the Perform Merge dialog box, click Merge. When the data file is merged with the form file, only those records marked in the Record list list box are merged.

Figure 16.13

Select Records Dialog Box

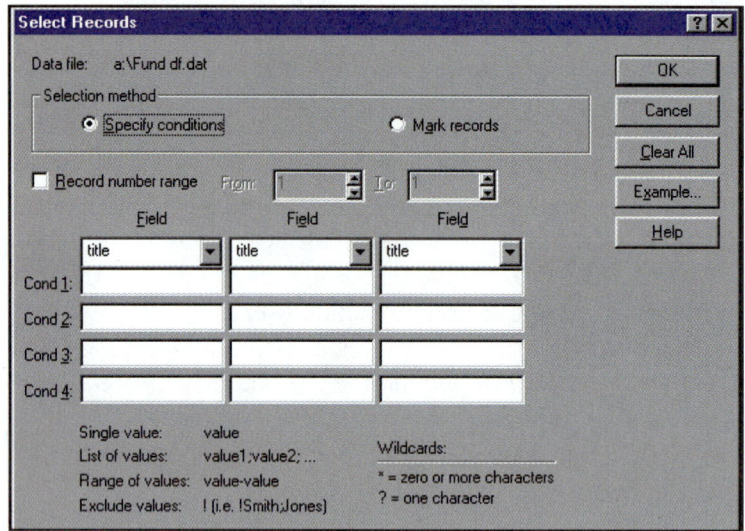

Select Records Dialog Box with Mark Records Selected

Figure 16.14

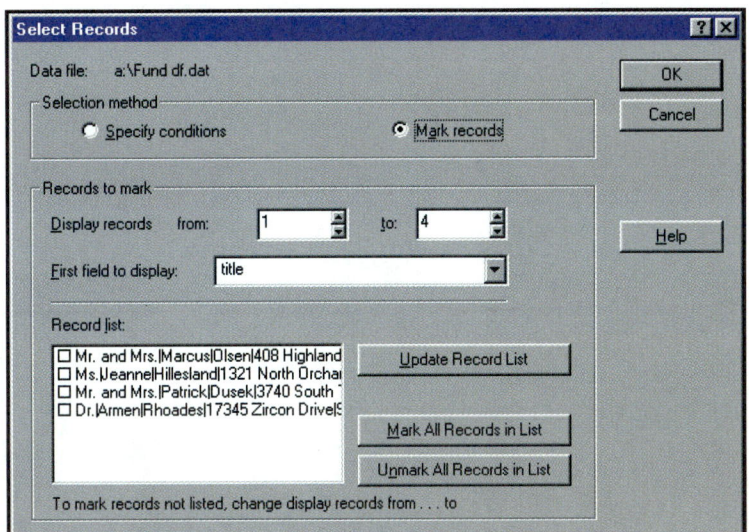

EXERCISE 10

Merging Selected Records

1. At a clear editing window, merge *Fund ltr* with only those records in *Fund df* containing St. Louis by completing the following steps:
   a. Display the Merge dialog box.
   b. At the Merge dialog box, click Merge.
   c. At the Perform Merge dialog box, key **Fund ltr** in the Form file text box.
   d. Select the filename displayed in the Data source text box, then key **Fund df**.
   e. Click Select Records.
   f. At the Select Records dialog box, click Mark records.
   g. Click the down-pointing arrow after the First field to display text box. At the drop-down list that displays, click the down-pointing arrow in the scroll bar until *city* displays, then click *city*.
   h. Click Update Record List and WordPerfect displays only the city for records in the Record list list box.
   i. Mark records with St. Louis as the city. To do this, click the check box before the first record with St. Louis as the city. Repeat the steps for any other records with St. Louis as the city. (This inserts an X in the check box before the record.)
   j. When all necessary records have been marked, click OK.
   k. At the Perform Merge dialog box, click Merge.
2. When the merge is completed, save the document and name it Ch 16, Ex 10.
3. Print and then close Ch 16, Ex 10. (Check with your instructor to see if you should print the entire document or just the letters.)

Merging Documents   *347*

Specifying a Range of Records

With the Record number range from the Select Records dialog box, you can identify a range of records to be merged. When the data file and form file are merged, a merged document is created only for the specified records.

EXERCISE 11

Merging a Range of Records

1. At a clear editing window, select records three and four in the *Fund2 df* data file and merge with *Fund ltr* by completing the following steps:
   a. Display the Merge dialog box.
   b. At the Merge dialog box, click Merge.
   c. At the Perform Merge dialog box, identify Fund ltr as the Form file and Fund2 df as the Data source.
   d. Click Select Records.
   e. At the Select Records dialog box make sure Specify conditions is selected. Click Record number range, then key **3** in the From text box and **4** in the To text box.
   f. Click OK.
   g. At the Perform Merge dialog box, click Merge.
2. Save the merged document and name it Ch 16, Ex 11.
3. Print and then close Ch 16, Ex 11. (Check with your instructor to see if you should print the entire document or only the letters.)

Defining Merge Conditions

With options from the Select Records dialog box, you can define conditions for the merge. For example, you may want to select only those records that contain a specific city name. Up to four conditions can be specified. A record is selected if it matches all the conditions.

To specify the first field for which you want to assign a condition, click Field, then display the desired field in the box below the option. Click Cond 1, then key the selection condition.

When specifying a condition, you can enter a value (text, amount, number, etc.) and WordPerfect will search for records that contain that value. For example, if you identify *city, state ZIP* as the field, then key **Spokane** in the Cond 1 text box, WordPerfect will only select those records containing Spokane in the *city, state ZIP* field in the data file. You can also use symbols in conjunction with a value. Figure 16.15 shows what the symbols will perform when used with a value.

Figure 16.15 Condition Symbols

Symbol	Condition
;	or
-	through
!	exclude
*	wildcard character meaning zero or more characters
?	one character wildcard

There are a variety of ways that selection conditions can be written. WordPerfect includes condition examples at the Example Select Records dialog box, shown in figure 16.16. To display this dialog box, click E‌xample from the Select Records dialog box.

WordPerfect will also display information about valid entries as shown in figure 16.17. To display this information, click M‌ore at the Example Select Records dialog box. This screen shows you a variety of ways that selection conditions can be written.

Figure 16.16

Example Select Records Dialog Box

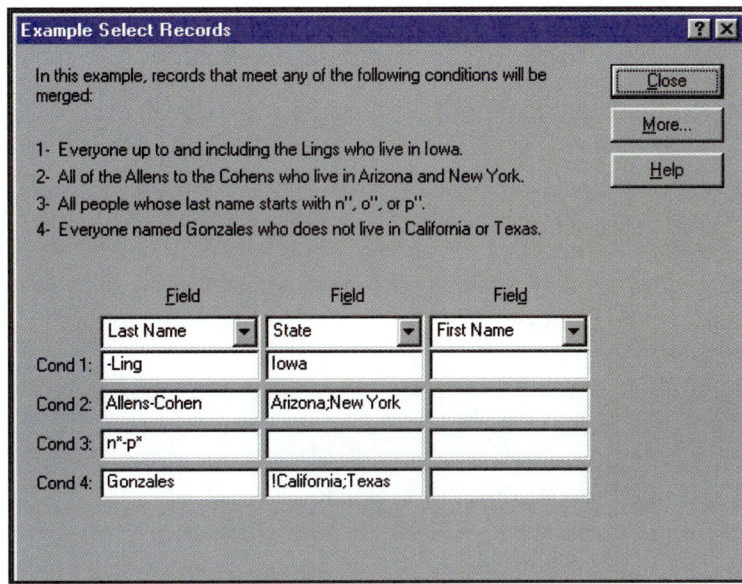

Figure 16.17

Valid Entry Examples

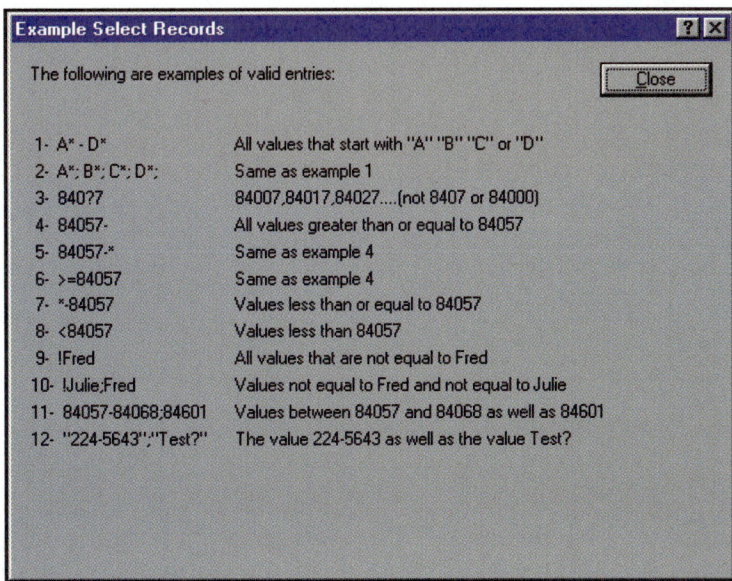

Clearing the Select Records Dialog Box

If you make changes to the Select Records dialog box, these changes remain in effect until you make other changes or you exit WordPerfect. If you want to perform a merge on a different document, you will need to clear any conditions established in the Select Records dialog box. To do this, click Clear All in the Select Records dialog box.

EXERCISE

Specifying Merge Conditions

1. At a clear editing window, select those records in *Fund df* with St. Louis as the city and 63409 as the ZIP Code, then merge with *Fund ltr* by completing the following steps:
    a. Display the Merge dialog box.
    b. At the Merge dialog box, click Merge.
    c. At the Perform Merge dialog box, identify Fund ltr as the Form file and Fund df as the Data source.
    d. Click Select Records.
    e. At the Select Records dialog box, click the down-pointing arrow to the right of the Field text box, then click *city* at the drop-down list.
    f. Click the down-pointing arrow to the right of the Field text box (the second field), then click *ZIP* at the drop-down list.
    g. Click inside the Cond 1 text box, then key **St. Louis**.
    h. Press the Tab key to move the insertion point into the text box below Field, then key **63409**.
    i. Click OK.
    j. At the Perform Merge dialog box, click Merge.
2. Save the merged document and name it Ch 16, Ex 12.
3. Print and then close Ch 16, Ex 12.
4. Clear the changes you made to the Select Records dialog box by completing the following steps:
    a. Display the Merge dialog box.
    b. At the Merge dialog box, click Merge.
    c. At the Perform Merge dialog box, click Select Records.
    d. At the Select Records dialog box, click Clear All.
    e. Click OK.
    f. Close the Perform Merge dialog box.

CHAPTER SUMMARY

- Personalized form documents, such as letters and envelopes, can be created with the Merge feature.
- The Merge feature generally requires two documents: the data file that contains the variable information and the form file that contains the standard text.
- A data file contains records. A record contains all the information for one unit (a person, family, or business). To be merged with the form file, the information in one record must be divided into fields.
- When you create a form file, name the fields consistent with the field names in the data file.
- You can create a data file at the Create Data File dialog box. The data for each record can then be entered at the Quick Data Entry dialog box.
- The form file includes standard text along with identifiers showing where variable information is to be inserted. The form file is created at the Create Form File dialog box.
- Once the data file and form file have been created and saved, they can be merged at the Perform Merge dialog box.
- When the merge is complete, the merged letters (or other documents) are displayed in the editing window. These merged letters can then be saved as a separate document.
- Control the output of the merged documents at the Perform Merge dialog box.
- Another way to create a data file is to enter the fields of the data file in cells within a table. To use this method, click Place records in a table, then click Data at the Merge dialog box.
- Any formatting codes you want applied to the merged documents should be inserted in the form file using the Styles Editor dialog box.
- Create a form file to print envelopes at the Envelope dialog box, or you can create envelopes while merging a letter or other form file.
- Data can be inserted directly from the keyboard during a merge if a KEYBOARD code is inserted in the form file. Other merge codes are available by clicking Merge Codes on the Merge Feature Bar.
- With options from the Select Records dialog box, you can mark specific records or a range of records in a data file to be merged with the form file.

COMMANDS REVIEW

	Mouse/Keyboard
Merge dialog box	Tools, Merge
Create Data File dialog box	Tools, Merge, Data
Create Form File dialog box	Tools, Merge, Form
Perform Merge dialog box	Choose Merge at the Merge dialog box
Perform Merge Options dialog box	Choose Options at the Perform Merge dialog box
Styles Editor dialog box	Format, Document, Initial Codes Style
Document Initial Font dialog box	Format, Document, Initial Font
Envelope dialog box	Format, Envelope
Select Records dialog box	Choose Select Records at the Perform Merge dialog box

CHECK YOUR UNDERSTANDING

Completion: In the space provided at the right, indicate the correct term, command, or number.

1. Creating a personalized form letter with WordPerfect's Merge feature usually requires this number of documents. _____

2. A data file can be created as a normal text file or in this format. _____

3. Once the data file and form file have been created and saved, they can be merged at this dialog box. _____

4. In the Quick Data Entry dialog box, press this key on the keyboard to move the insertion point to the next field. _____

5. This code will appear at the end of each field created in a data file. _____

6. This code will appear at the end of each record created in a data file. _____

7. Any formatting codes you want applied to the merged documents should be inserted in the form file at this dialog box. _____

8. You can control the output of merged documents at this dialog box. _____

9. When merging a document containing a keyboard merge code, key the required information, then click this button. _____

10. This code is required in the form file for keyboard entry during a merge. _____

11. When specifying a merge condition, key this symbol to indicate *or*. _____

12. When specifying a merge condition, key this symbol to indicate *exclude*. _____

Suppose you work for a car dealer and are responsible for sending a letter to customers congratulating them on the purchase of a new automobile. In the letter, you mention the specific type of automobile they purchased. In the future, you know you will need to send letters to customers in specific cities offering special discounts. Determine the fields you would use for the letter to customers who have purchased a new automobile. When determining the fields, consider the future use of the information. In the space provided below, write the field names you would use in the form file for this example.

_____

_____

SKILL ASSESSMENTS

Assessment 1

1. At a clear editing window, look at the letter in figure 16.19 and the records in figure 16.18. Determine the fields you need for the form file, then create a data file for the records in figure 16.18.
2. Save the data file and name it Customers df.
3. Print and then close Customers df. (Check with your instructor to see if you should complete this step.)

Figure 16.18

Ms. Gayle Waymire
14952 Pioneer Way
Toronto, ON M5W 3X9

Mr. and Mrs. LeRoy Huse
1450 Willow Street
Vancouver, BC V3R 2A7

Mr. Douglas Ichikawa
8509 Bayview Drive SW
Calgary, AB T2V 3M1

Mrs. Heather Casey
1409 Wyman Place
Ottawa, ON K1N 8M5

Dr. Holly Bartel
348 Castlegrove Blvd.
Toronto, ON M3A 1L6

Assessment 2

1. At a clear editing window, create the form file shown in figure 16.19 in an appropriate business letter format. (At the Create Form File dialog box, identify *Customers df* as the data file.)
2. Save the form file and name it Refinance ltr.
3. Print and then close Refinance ltr.

Figure 16.19

(current date)

name
address
city, state ZIP

Dear (name):

If you have considered buying a new home or refinancing your present home, then take a minute to read this letter. Interest rates have fallen and now is the time to refinance. In addition, real estate prices have appreciated tremendously.

The decline of interest rates lets you refinance your home loan at a lower interest rate, which could save you thousands of dollars or give you extra money to renovate or pay off debts.

Northwest Brokers is the largest mortgage broker in Canada. We specialize in portable, blended, and variable-rate loans. We have over 50 lenders to choose from to help find you the lowest rates at no extra cost to you.

If you are curious about the options available to you, the amount you qualify for in a new home, or the amount of equity that is accessible in your current home, then please call me at Northwest Brokers. The information is free and I guarantee the best rates and service available.

Sincerely,

NORTHWEST BROKERS

Anthony Masela
Loan Officer

xx:Refinance ltr

Assessment 3

1. At a clear editing window, merge *Refinance ltr* with *Customers df* to the current document.
2. Save the merged document and name it Ch 16, SA 03.
3. Print and then close Ch 16, SA 03.

Assessment 4

1. Create an envelope form file named Envelope2 with fields to create envelopes for the records in Customers df.
2. Merge *Envelope2* with *Customers df* to the current document.

3. Name the merged document Ch 16, SA 04.
4. Print and then close Ch 16, SA 04.

Assessment 5

1. At a clear editing window, create the memo shown in figure 16.20. Insert the KEYBOARD codes with messages after the codes as indicated.
2. Save the memo form file and name it Benefits memo.
3. Merge *Benefits* memo (there is no data file). When WordPerfect stops at the KEYBOARD merge codes, key the following information:

Name	=	**Eric Coster**
Retirement plan	=	**Key Retirement Plan**
Medical plan	=	**MedServices Plan**

4. Save the merged memo and name it Memo A.
5. Print and then close Memo A.
6. At a clear editing window, merge *Benefits* memo again and key the following information at the KEYBOARD merge codes:

Name	=	**Cheryl Bjork**
Retirement plan	=	**Monroe Retirement Plan**
Medical plan	=	**Health Plus Plan**

7. Save the merged memo and name it Memo B.
8. Print and then close Memo B.
9. At a clear editing window, merge *Benefits* memo again and key the following information at the KEYBOARD merge codes:

Name	=	**Brian Miyamoto**
Retirement plan	=	**Golden Retirement Plan**
Medical plan	=	**Health Plus Plan**

10. Save the merged memo and name it Memo C.
11. Print and then close Memo C.

Figure 16.20

DATE: (Insert the date as a code.)

TO: KEYBOARD(enter name of person receiving memo)

FROM: Shawna Kesler, Benefits Coordinator

SUBJECT: RETIREMENT AND MEDICAL BENEFITS

Next month, there will be an open enrollment period for retirement and medical plans. During this month, you are entitled to change plans. According to our records you are enrolled in the KEYBOARD(enter retirement plan) and the KEYBOARD(enter medical plan).

An open enrollment period occurs only once a year. Please take advantage of this opportunity to ensure that you have the best possible retirement and medical coverage.

Assessment 6

1. At a clear editing window, select those records in *Customers df* with Toronto as the city, then merge with *Refinance ltr*.
2. Save the merged document and name it Ch 16, SA 06.
3. Print and then close Ch 16, SA 06.

Unit Three

PERFORMANCE ASSESSMENTS

PROBLEM SOLVING AND DECISION MAKING

Assessment 1

1. At a clear editing window, open Loan doc.
2. Complete the following steps:
   a. Select the first paragraph and save it as a separate document named Loan Pr 01.
   b. Select the second paragraph and save it as a separate document named Loan Pr 02.
   c. Do the same with the other paragraphs and name them Loan Pr 03, Loan Pr 04, and Loan Pr 05.
3. Close Loan Doc.
4. At a clear editing window, create the document shown in figure U3.1 with the following specifications:
   a. Change the top margin to 1.5 inches.
   b. Turn on the Widow/Orphan feature.
   c. Change the line spacing to double (2) for the body of the document. Change the line spacing back to single (1) for the signature lines.
   d. Insert the documents as indicated by the bracketed items.
   e. After inserting the documents, renumber the paragraphs.
   f. Insert page numbering at the bottom center of each page.
5. Complete a spell check on the document.
6. Save the document and name it Unit 03, PA 01.
7. Print and then close Unit 03, PA 01.

Optional: Think of a different method for copying the paragraphs in step 2 to the new document you create. Use this method and then write a paragraph discussing which method is more efficient.

CONSUMER LOAN AGREEMENT

This Consumer Loan Agreement governs the open-end consumer loan plan issued through State Employees Credit Union. EDWARD G. WALLACE and TARA L. WALLACE, applicants, agree jointly to follow the terms and conditions and all other loan documents related to this Account including any Loan Advance Voucher, Loan Proceeds Check, Power of Attorney, if applicable, given when a loan is made, which collectively shall govern this account.

[Insert Loan Pr 03 here.]

[Insert Loan Pr 01 here.]

[Insert Loan Pr 04 here.]

[Insert Loan Pr 02 here.]

5. **Finance Charge.** When finance charges accrue, EDWARD G. WALLACE and TARA L. WALLACE will pay a finance charge calculated on the daily unpaid balance of all loans under this Account and any loan fee applicable to the Account. The finance charges will begin to accrue as of the date each loan advance is made. The finance charge is based on the outstanding balance.

_____
EDWARD G. WALLACE, Applicant

_____
TARA L. WALLACE, Applicant

Figure U3.1

Assessment 2

1. At a clear editing window, open Unit 03, PA 01.
2. Save the document with Save As and name it Unit 03, PA 02.
3. Make the following changes to the document:
    a. Delete the top margin code.
    b. Delete the page numbering code.
    c. Insert page numbering at the top right of every page except the first page with the accompanying text, *Loan Agreement, Page*. (Make sure the page number displays after the word Page.)
    d. Complete the following search and replaces:
        (1) Find *EDWARD G. WALLACE* and replace with *BARRY C. NOLLAN*.
        (2) Find *TARA L. WALLACE* and replace with *MELISSA A. NOLLAN*.
4. Save the document again with the same name (Unit 03, PA 02).
5. Print and then close Unit 03, PA 02.

Optional: Research and define these terms: Power of Attorney, accrue, overdraft, and deposit share account.

Assessment 3

1. At a clear editing window, change the left and right margins to 2 inches, then create the Loan Agreement Outline document shown in figure U3.2.
2. Save the outline and name it Unit 03 Outline.
3. With Unit 03 Outline still open, open Loan doc.
4. Save the Loan Doc document with Save As and name it Unit 03, PA 03.
5. Make the following changes to the document:
    a. Tile the windows horizontally
    b. With Unit 03, PA 03 the active window, select and move paragraphs so they are in the order shown in the outline.
    c. Renumber the paragraphs. (Make sure the spacing is correct between paragraphs.)
6. Save the Unit 03, PA 03 document again with the same name.
7. Print and then close Unit 03, PA 03.
8. With Unit 03 Outline the active document, print and then close Unit 03 Outline.

LOAN AGREEMENT OUTLINE

1. Payment
2. Minimum Payment
3. Paying Loans
4. Overdraft Protection
5. Limitations on Credit Advances

Figure U3.2

Assessment 4

1. At a clear editing window, key the document shown in figure U3.3 in an appropriate business letter format with the following specifications:
    a. Change the font to 12-point Garamond.
    b. Change the left and right margins to 1.5 inches.
2. After keying the letter, save it and name it Unit 03, PA 04.
3. Print Unit 03, PA 04.
4. Click Tools and then Grammatik, then complete the following steps:
    a. When Grammatik selects *Attorney*, change the checking style to *Formal Memo or Letter*.
    b. Complete a grammar check. You determine what to leave as written and what to change. (Proper names are spelled correctly.)
    c. View statistics for the document.
    d. Change the checking style back to *Quick Check*.
5. Save the document again with the same name (Unit 03, PA 04).
6. Print and then close Unit 03, PA 04.

Optional: Write a short memo summarizing the analysis provided by Grammatik.

> April 20, 1998
>
> Ms. Julia Carrick
> Attorney at Law
> 1322 Pine Street
> Denver, CO 86441
>
> Dear Ms. Carrick:
>
> Re: Hutton vs. Isham
>
> Enclosed please find the Complaint in the case of Hutton vs. Isham. The Complaint was filed by our legal aide on April 17, 1998, with the Superior Court. I represent the Plaintiff, Benjamin Hutton, in this court action.
>
> Your immediate response to this Complaint will be appreciated. Please respond to Rhonda Howell or I by the date of April 27, 1998. Mr. Hutton is interested in settling this situation as soon as possible.
>
> Very truly yours,
>
> PITTMAN & HOWELL
>
>
> Robert Pittman
> Attorney at Law
>
> xx:Unit 03, PA 04

Figure U3.3

Assessment 5

1. At a clear editing window, open Report 04.
2. Save the report with Save As and name it Unit 03, PA 05.
3. Insert a page break in the second page at the line containing the title *CHAPTER 4: DEVELOPMENT OF TECHNOLOGY, 1950 - 1960*.
4. Move the insertion point back to the beginning of the document, then make the following changes:
    a. Turn on the Widow/Orphan feature.
    b. Change the left and right margins to 1.5 inches. (Make sure this affects all aspects of the document.)
    c. Change the font to 12-point Century Schoolbook. (Make sure this affects all aspects of the document.)
    d. Create Header A that prints on every page except the first, is bolded, and reads *Trends in Telecommunications* at the left margin and inserts the page number at the right margin.

e. Create the first footnote shown in figure U3.4 at the end of the last paragraph in the *World War I* section of the report.
   f. Create the second footnote shown in figure U3.4 at the end of the last paragraph in the *World War II* section of the report.
   g. Create the third footnote shown in figure U3.4 at the end of the last paragraph in the report.
   h. Change the footnote separator line to a single line that prints from the left to the right margin.
5. Save the report again with the same name (Unit 03, PA 05).
6. Print and then close Unit 03, PA 05.

---

[1]Mitchell, William, Robert Hendricks, and Leonard Sterry, "A Brief History of Telecommunications," *Telecommunications: Systems and Applications*, Paradigm Publishing, 1993, pages 20-22.

[2]Rhoads, Katherine, "Technological Advances During World War II," *Communications in America*, TrueLine Publishing Services, 1994, pages 112-119.

[3]Junitti, Carl, "Satellite Technology," *Data Transmission*, Puget Sound Publishing, 1996, pages 43-51.

Figure U3.4

Assessment 6

1. At a clear editing window, open Unit 03, PA 05.
2. Save the document with Save As and name it Unit 03, PA 06.
3. Make the following changes to the report:
   a. Convert the footnotes to endnotes.
   b. Have all endnotes print at the end of the document on a separate page preceded by the title ENDNOTES.
   c. Edit all the endnotes and indent the endnote reference text from the endnote number.
   d. Edit endnote number 2 and change the spelling of the author's last name from *Rhoads* to *Rhodes* and change the date of the publication from *1994* to *1997*.
   e. Add the endnote shown in figure U3.5 at the end of the paragraph in the *Korean War* section of the report.
   f. Change the beginning endnote number to 8.
   g. Change the spacing between endnotes to 0.084".
   h. Add Footer A that prints bolded, is centered at the bottom of each page, and reads *Development of Technology*.
4. Save the report again with the same name (Unit 03, PA 06).
5. Print and then close Unit 03, PA 06.

---

3. Wong, Lynette, "Entertainment Innovations," *Evolution Broadcasting*, Los Altos Publishing, 1996, pages 25-29.

Figure U3.5

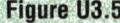

Performance Assessments *361*

Assessment 7

1. At a clear editing window, look at the letter in figure U3.7 and the records in figure U3.6. Determine the fields you need for the form file, then create a data file for the records in figure U3.6.
2. Save the data file and name it New Hope df.
3. Print and then close New Hope df. (Check with your instructor to see if you should complete this step.)

Mrs. Sheila Goldsmith
33 Rosemont Way
Petersburg, VA 23415

Mr. Thomas Dircks
2007 East Harris
Hopewell, VA 22459

Ms. Susan Benford
201 West Point Drive
Hopewell, VA 22459

Dr. Glen Davis
7843 90th Street
Petersburg, VA 23451

Mr. Robert Weisert
29044 East Graham
Hopewell, VA 22459

Mrs. Donna Rudman
4812 South 191st Place
Petersburg, VA 23415

Figure U3.6

Assessment 8

1. At a clear editing window, key the letter shown in figure U3.7 in an appropriate business letter format as a form file. (At the Create Form File dialog box, identify New Hope df as the data file.) You determine the fields and field names.
2. Save the letter and name it New Hope ltr.
3. Print and then close New Hope ltr.

Optional: Rewrite this letter in a more enthusiastic and positive tone.

February 12, 1998

(name)
(address)

Dear (salutation):

The Assisted Living Program and New Hope Retirement Center offer an independent and dignified lifestyle for senior adults with modest needs for physical assistance. There is assistance available to each resident at New Hope Retirement Center according to his or her individual needs. This assistance is provided 24 hours a day by trained staff members. The types of assistance provided include:

- storing prescribed medication
- reminders of medical schedule
- assistance with dressing and grooming
- assistance with bathing and hygiene
- supervision of nutritional intake
- arranging transportation for medical appointments

Assisted Living residents are provided three full meals a day plus snacks. Housekeeping is done weekly unless more frequency is required. There is a full schedule of social activities such as games and crafts to hold the interest of each resident.

New Hope Retirement Center is committed to providing a fulfilling lifestyle for each resident. If you would like an informational brochure on Assisted Living, please call 555-9093. A tour of the New Hope Retirement Center facilities can also be arranged.

Sincerely,

Antoinette Moreno
Director, Assisted Living

Figure U3.7

Assessment 9

1. At a clear editing window, merge *New Hope ltr* with *New Hope df*.
2. After the records are merged, save the document and name it Unit 03, PA 09.
3. Print and then close Unit 03, PA 09.

Assessment 10

1. At a clear editing window, open New Hope df.
2. Save the document with Save As and name it Hopewell df.
3. With Hopewell df open in the editing window, select only the records of those individuals living in the city of Hopewell.
4. Save Hopewell df again.
5. Close Hopewell df.
6. At a clear editing window, create a form file for printing envelopes and name it Envelopes ff.
7. Close Envelopes ff.
8. At a clear editing window, merge *Envelopes ff* with *Hopewell df*.
9. Save the merged document and name it Unit 03, PA 10.
10. Print, then close Unit 03, PA 10.

WRITING

The following activities give you the opportunity to practice your writing skills along with demonstrating an understanding of some of the important WordPerfect features you have mastered in this unit. In planning the documents, remember to shape the information according to the writing purpose and the audience. Use correct grammar, appropriate word choices, and clear sentence constructions.

Activity 1

Situation: You are responsible for creating an outline based on the information contained in *Report 03* and *Report 04* on your student data disk. The outline should contain the title and headings within each report. (*Hint: Try using multiple windows to complete this activity.*) Save the outline document and name it Unit 03, Act 01. Print and then close Unit 03, Act 01.

Activity 2

Situation: You are responsible for formatting the report in the document named *Report 11* on your student data disk. This report should include page numbers and headers and/or footers. Change to a serif typeface for the body of the report and a sans serif typeface for the title and headings. Correct the spelling in the document.

After formatting the report, create an appropriate title page for the report. Include your name as the author of the report. Save the document and name it Unit 03, Act 02. Print and then close Unit 03, Act 02.

Activity 3

Situation: You are Owen Lindal, administrative assistant for Jocelyn Cook, the assistant superintendent for the Omaha City School District. You have been asked by Ms. Cook to compose a letter to the individuals listed below with the following information. They have been selected by the principal of the school where their child or children attend to serve on the Facilities Planning Committee. This committee will be comprised of school district administrators, staff, and teachers, as well as people with a child or children attending school in the Omaha City School District. The committee will be responsible for establishing short- and long-term priorities for facilities planning for the district. The first meeting of the committee will be held from 7:00-9:30 p.m. on Tuesday, February 10, 1998, in room 106 at the school administration building. Approximately five additional meetings will be scheduled for the remainder of the school year.

Create a form file containing this information and create a data file for the names and addresses listed below. You determine the names for the form file and data file. After creating the data file and the form file, merge the documents. Save the merged document and name it Unit 03, Act 03. Print and then close Unit 03, Act 03.

Mr. Paul Jackson
302 East 40th Street
Omaha, NE 45056

Mrs. Elaine Natario
9932 Montgomery
Omaha, NE 45054

Ms. Josefina Valdes
14503 South Mildred
Omaha, NE 45054

Mr. Vance Blumenthal
3712 Del Monte Drive
Omaha, NE 45056

Ms. Vicki Cates
24113 Rembert Court
Omaha, NE 45054

Ms. Sung Lim
2033 Columbia Avenue
Omaha, NE 45056

RESEARCH

Review Chapter 11, "Creating Headers and Footers." Then outline the information on headers, adding additional points offered in the Help feature or appropriate facts from other sources.

Unit *Four*

ENHANCING THE *Visual Display* of **Documents**

In this unit, you will learn to add special features to documents and enhance the visual display of documents with macros, templates, graphic features, Draw, and TextArt.

17

FORMATTING DOCUMENTS WITH SPECIAL FEATURES

PERFORMANCE OBJECTIVE

Upon successful completion of chapter 17, you will be able to manipulate the height and length of lines in finished business documents, create documents more quickly with the date and abbreviations features, and improve the visual appeal of documents with hard spaces and insertion point advancement.

WordPerfect contains a variety of features that can affect the line endings of text in a document such as hyphenation and hard spaces. Additionally, you can use WordPerfect's abbreviations feature to simplify inserting commonly used words, names, or phrases in a document. You can improve the visual appeal of a document with special symbols, hard spaces, and insertion point advancement. The date can be inserted in a document as text or a code. Bookmarks can be inserted in specific locations in a document and you can move the insertion point quickly to these bookmarks. You will learn to use these features in this chapter.

Hyphenating Words

In some WordPerfect documents, especially documents with left and right margins wider than 1 inch, the right margin may appear quite ragged. If the justification of the paragraph is changed to Full, the right margin will appear even, but there will be gaps of extra space added throughout the line. In these situations, hyphenating long words that fall at the end of the text line provides the document with a more balanced look.

Changing the Hyphenation Zone

WordPerfect provides a left hyphenation zone and a right hyphenation zone. The default left hyphenation zone is 10% of the typing line before the right margin and the default right hyphenation zone is 4% of the typing line after the right margin. If a word begins after the left hyphenation zone and extends beyond the right hyphenation zone, WordPerfect wraps it to the next line. If a word begins at or before the left hyphenation zone and extends past the right hyphenation zone, it will be hyphenated (if it is located in the Spell Checking dictionary and if hyphenation is turned on). The illustration in figure 17.1 shows how the word *calculations* will be either wrapped to the next line or hyphenated.

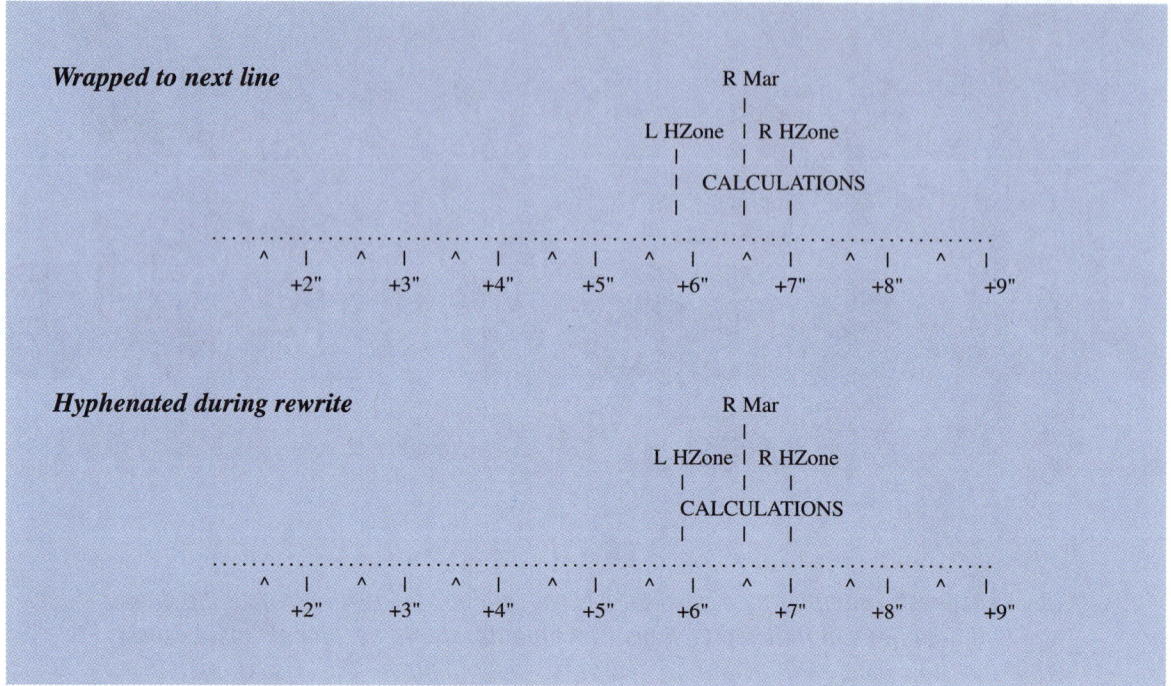

Figure 17.1 Word Wrap and Hyphenation

If the hyphenation zone is shortened, more words will be hyphenated. If the hyphenation zone is lengthened, fewer words will be hyphenated. The shorter the hyphenation zone, the more words that will begin at or before the left hyphenation zone and continue past the right hyphenation zone.

To change hyphenation zones, click Format, point to Line, then click Hyphenation. At the Line Hyphenation dialog box, click the up-pointing triangle at the right of the Percent left option to increase the hyphenation zone or click the down-pointing triangle to decrease the hyphenation zone. Complete the same steps to increase or decrease the percentage in the Percent right text box. You can also select the current percentage in the Percent left or Percent right text box and then key a new measurement.

When you change the hyphenation zones, codes are inserted in the document at the beginning of the paragraph where the insertion point is located. These codes can be seen in Reveal Codes. For example, if the left hyphenation zone is changed to 5% and the right hyphenation zone is changed to 2%, the codes *Lft Hzone: 5%* and *Rgt Hzone: 2%* appear in Reveal Codes. The percentage number will only appear if the insertion point is positioned immediately to the left of the code or you click the code. If you delete all hyphenation zone codes, WordPerfect returns to the default settings of 10% and 4%.

Turning Hyphenation On

By default, hyphenation is off. To turn on hyphenation, display the Line Hyphenation dialog box, then click Hyphenation on. To ensure that all text in a document is checked for possible hyphenations, move the insertion point to the end of the document.

If you would like total control over hyphenating words in a document, you can make a change at the Environment Preferences dialog box, shown in figure 17.2. To display the Environment Preferences dialog box, click Edit, then Preferences. At the Preferences dialog box, double-click Environment. At the Environment Preferences dialog box, click Hyphenation prompt. This causes a pop-up menu to appear with the choices Always, Never, and When Required. The default setting is When Required. At this setting, WordPerfect makes most hyphenation decisions. If you want WordPerfect to make all hyphenation decisions, click Never. If you want total control over hyphenating words, click Always. At this setting, WordPerfect prompts you to make all hyphenation decisions.

Figure 17.2

Environment Preferences Dialog Box

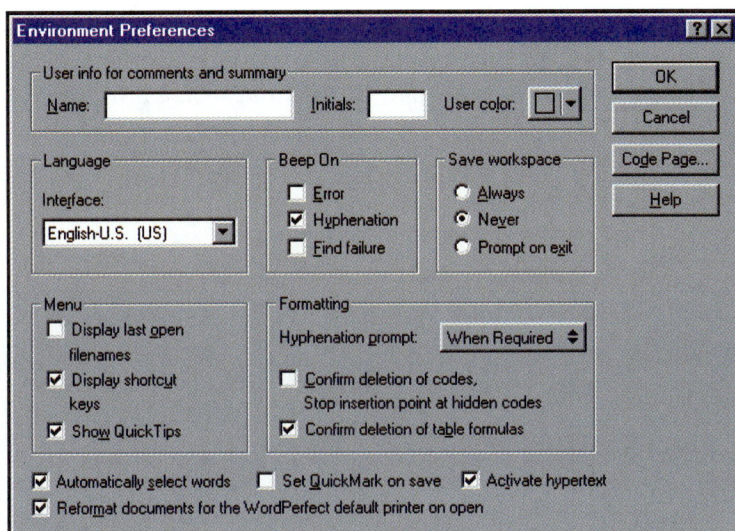

If the Hyphenation Prompt is set at When Required or Always, WordPerfect displays the Position Hyphen dialog box, shown in figure 17.3, during hyphenation.

Figure 17.3

Position Hyphen Dialog Box

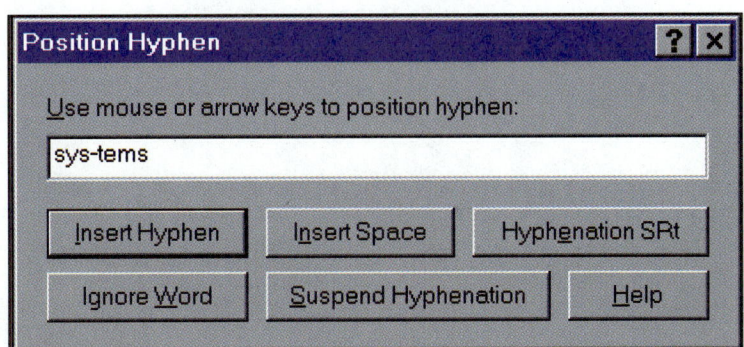

In the box at the top of the Position Hyphen dialog box, the word that WordPerfect wants help hyphenating is displayed. You can move the hyphen to a more desirable location if necessary by pressing the left or right arrow keys. When the hyphen is positioned in the desired location, click Insert Hyphen or press Enter. You can also move the hyphen with the mouse by positioning the arrow pointer on the word where you want the hyphen, then clicking the left mouse button.

Formatting Documents with Special Features 369

If you do not want to hyphenate the word displayed in the dialog box, click Ignore <u>W</u>ord. This causes WordPerfect to wrap the entire word to the next line and continue the hyphenation process. The code *Cancel Hyph* is inserted at the beginning of the word. This code tells WordPerfect not to present the word again for hyphenation.

With the I<u>n</u>sert Space option, you can insert a space between words. This is useful if you accidentally keyed two words together. During hyphenation, when WordPerfect stops and asks for a hyphenation decision, position the hyphen between the two words, then click I<u>n</u>sert Space.

With the Hyph<u>e</u>nation SRt option, you can insert a soft return in the middle of a word rather than a hyphen. This is useful in a situation where you have words divided by a slash, such as *problem/conflict*. When WordPerfect presents words with a slash, position the hyphen immediately to the right of the slash, then click Hyph<u>e</u>nation SRt. This divides the words after the slash if the words fall at the end of the line. If the words do not fall at the end of the line, the soft return is ignored. If you want to stop or suspend hyphenation, click <u>S</u>uspend Hyphenation. When hyphenating words, keep in mind the hyphenation guidelines shown in figure 17.4.

Figure 17.4 — Hyphenation Guidelines

> **Hyphenation Guidelines**
>
> Adapted from *The Paradigm Reference Manual* (Paradigm Publishing Inc., 1993)
>
> **One-Syllable Words:** Do not divide one-syllable words such as length, served, or thoughts.
>
> **Multiple-Syllable Words:** Divide multiple-syllable words between syllables, as in pub-lish.
>
> Note: Some divisions between syllables can confuse a reader, particularly if one or both parts may be read as words by themselves. Examples include coin-sure, reed-ucate, and reap-portion. In such cases, break the word at a different place (co-insure, re-educate, and re-apportion).
>
> **Prefixes, Suffixes:** Generally, divide *after* a prefix and *before* a suffix. If the root word ends in a double consonant, divide after the double consonant (example: bill-ing). If adding a suffix results in a double consonant, divide between the doubled letters, as in refer-ring.
>
> **Consecutive Line Ends:** Avoid dividing words at the ends of more than two consecutive lines.
>
> **Abbreviations, Numbers, Contractions:** Do not divide except for abbreviations already containing hyphens, as in MS-DOS.
>
> **Names of People:** Avoid dividing a person's name. But if it becomes necessary, hyphenate the name according to the guidelines for common words.
>
> **Dash:** Do not divide before a dash or between the hyphens if the dash consists of two hyphens.
>
> **Dates:** Divide date expressions between the day and the year, not between the month and day.
>
> **Address:** Do not separate the number and the street name. The city, state, and ZIP Code may be divided between the city and state or between the state and the ZIP Code.
>
> **Word Groups Used as Units:** Avoid divided word groups such as page and number, chapter and number, or number and unit of measure, as in page 311, chapter 6, and 29 inches.

EXERCISE 1

Changing Hyphenation Zones and Turning on Hyphenation

1. At a clear editing window, open Report 01.
2. Save the document with Save As and name it Ch 17, Ex 01.
3. With the insertion point positioned at the beginning of the document, change the hyphenation zones and turn on hyphenation by completing the following steps:
   a. Click Format, point to Line, then click Hyphenation.
   b. At the Line Hyphenation dialog box, click the down-pointing triangle at the right side of the Percent left option until *5%* displays.
   c. Click the down-pointing triangle at the right side of the Percent right option until *2%* displays.
   d. Click Hyphenation on.
   e. Click OK or press Enter. (Make hyphenation decisions, if required.)
   f. Move the insertion point to the end of the document to make sure that all necessary words are hyphenated.
4. Save the document again with the same name (Ch 17, Ex 01).
5. Print and then close Ch 17, Ex 01.

EXERCISE 2

Using Hyphenation Options

1. At a clear editing window, open Report 02.
2. Save the document with Save As and name it Ch 17, Ex 02.
3. With the insertion point positioned at the beginning of the report, make the following changes:
   a. Change the Hyphenation prompt to Always at the Environment Preferences dialog box by completing the following steps:
      (1) Click Edit, then Preferences.
      (2) At the Preferences dialog box, double-click the Environment option.
      (3) At the Environment Preferences dialog box, click the Hyphenation prompt button (contains the words *When Required*), then click Always at the pop-up menu.
      (4) Click OK to close the Environment Preferences dialog box.
      (5) Click Close to close the Preferences dialog box.
   b. Change the left hyphenation zone to 5%, the right hyphenation zone to 2%, and turn hyphenation on.
   c. Make hyphenation decisions as required. (Move the insertion point to the end of the document to make sure that all necessary words are hyphenated.)
4. Change the Hyphenation prompt back to When Required. (Refer to step 3a.)
5. Save the document again with the same name (Ch 17, Ex 02).
6. Print and then close Ch 17, Ex 02.

Formatting Documents with Special Features

Inserting Hyphens

There are several ways that a hyphen is inserted in a document. The type of hyphen in a word like *co-worker* is called a *regular* hyphen. This hyphen is inserted by keying the minus sign on the keyboard. During hyphenation, WordPerfect will break hyphenated words, if necessary, at the hyphen.

A hyphen that you or WordPerfect inserts during hyphenation is considered a *soft* hyphen. A soft hyphen appears in the editing window and prints only if the word falls at the end of the text line. If text is adjusted and the word no longer falls at the end of the line, the soft hyphen is removed from the editing window and will not print. A soft hyphen can be seen in Reveal Codes as *-Soft Hyphen*. A soft hyphen is inserted in a word during hyphenation. You can also insert your own soft hyphen in a word by pressing Ctrl + Shift + -. If a word containing a soft hyphen falls at the end of the line, WordPerfect automatically breaks the word at the soft hyphen. If the word does not fall at the end of the line, the hyphen will not be visible in the editing window and will not print.

In some text, such as telephone numbers and Social Security numbers, you may want to insert a *hard* hyphen rather than a regular hyphen. A hard hyphen tells WordPerfect that the text is to be considered a unit and not to break it between lines. A hard hyphen is inserted in text by pressing Ctrl + -.

Deleting Hyphens

A hyphen inserted automatically by WordPerfect displays in Reveal Codes as *Auto Hyphen EOL*. A hyphen you inserted during hyphenation is considered a soft hyphen and displays as *-Soft Hyphen*. A soft hyphen can be easily deleted by deleting the *-Soft Hyphen* code in Reveal Codes or by deleting the hyphen in the document.

A hyphen inserted automatically by WordPerfect cannot be individually deleted. You can, however, delete all *Auto Hyphen EOL* codes in a document by deleting the *Hyph: On* code in Reveal Codes. When this code is deleted, WordPerfect removes all *Auto Hyphen EOL* codes in the document.

EXERCISE 3

Deleting Hyphens

1. At a clear editing window, open Ch 17, Ex 02.
2. Save the document with Save As and name it Ch 17, Ex 03.
3. Display Reveal Codes, then delete the hyphenation on code. (Leave on the display of Reveal Codes.)
4. Delete the following hyphens:
   a. Delete the hyphen in the first hyphenated word at the end of a text line by completing the following steps:
      (1) Position the insertion point immediately to the left of the hyphen (and the *-Soft Hyphen* code) in the first hyphenated word at the end of a text line.
      (2) Press the Delete key. (If there is more than one soft hyphen code, delete all soft hyphen codes in the first word.)
   b. Delete the hyphen in the second hyphenated word at the end of a text line.
   c. Delete the hyphen in the third hyphenated word at the end of a text line.
5. Save the document again with the same name (Ch 17, Ex 03).
6. Print and then close Ch 17, Ex 03.

Deleting the *Hyph: On* code does not remove soft hyphens (hyphens you insert during hyphenation). If you want to delete all soft hyphens in a document, you would delete the hyphenation on code, then use the Find and Replace feature to find all soft hyphen codes.

Removing All Soft Hyphens

1. At a clear editing window, open Ch 17, Ex 02.
2. Save the document with Save As and name it Ch 17, Ex 04.
3. Delete all soft hyphens in the document by completing the following steps:
   a. Turn on the display of Reveal Codes, delete the hyphenation on code, then turn off the display of Reveal Codes.
   b. Click Edit, then Find and Replace.
   c. At the Find and Replace Text dialog box, click Match, then Codes.
   d. At the Codes dialog box, click *-Soft Hyphen* in the Find Codes list box.
   e. Click Insert & Close.
   f. At the Find and Replace Text dialog box make sure there is nothing in the Replace with text box (or the word *<Nothing>*), then click Replace All.
   g. Click Close to close the Find and Replace Text dialog box.
4. Save the document again with the same name (Ch 17, Ex 04).
5. Print and then close Ch 17, Ex 04.

Changing Line Height

WordPerfect provides a Line Height dialog box that can be used to specify the amount of space a line occupies. The default setting for the line height at the Line Height dialog box is Auto. At this setting, WordPerfect automatically adjusts the line height when changes are made to the font and/or type size of text.

The Auto setting can be changed to Fixed, which lets you control the amount of space occupied by a line. To change the line height in a document, click Format, point to Line, then click Height. At the Line Height dialog box, shown in figure 17.5, click Fixed. Click the up- or down-pointing triangle at the right side of the Fixed text box until the desired measurement displays; or, select the current measurement and then key the new line height measurement.

Figure 17.5

Line Height Dialog Box

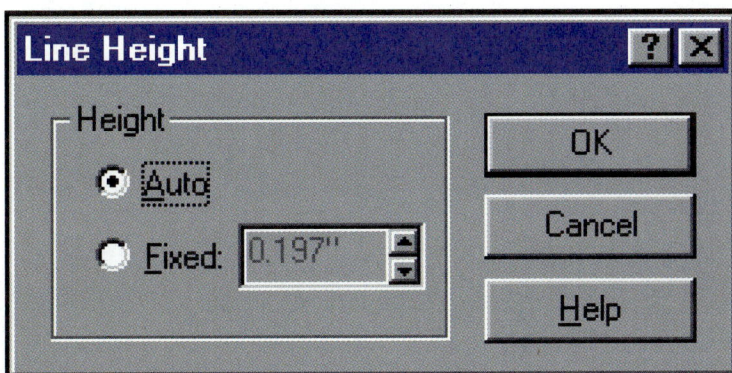

Formatting Documents with Special Features   373

By default, WordPerfect measures line height in inches. In typesetting, line height is referred to as *leading* (pronounced *ledding*) and is measured in points rather than inches. WordPerfect lets you enter a measurement as either inches, points, or centimeters. When entering a measurement, enter a number followed by the letter *p* to specify points or enter a number followed by the letter *c* to specify centimeters. WordPerfect automatically converts the point or centimeter measurement to inches.

EXERCISE 5

Changing Line Height and Hyphenation

1. At a clear editing window, open Letter 04.
2. Save the document with Save As and name it Ch 17, Ex 05.
3. With the insertion point positioned at the beginning of the document, make the following changes:
    a. Change the line height to 15 points by completing the following steps:
        (1) Click Format, point to Line, then click Height.
        (2) At the Line Height dialog box, click the radio button before Fixed.
        (3) Select the current numbers in the Fixed text box, then key **15p**.
        (4) Click OK or press Enter.
    b. Change the left hyphenation zone to 4% and the right hyphenation zone to 2%. Turn on hyphenation and make hyphenation decisions if requested. (Move the insertion point to the end of the document to ensure that all necessary words are hyphenated. More than likely, only one or two words will be hyphenated.)
4. Save the document again with the same name (Ch 17, Ex 05).
5. Print and then close Ch 17, Ex 05.

Turning on Line Numbering

With options at the Line Numbering dialog box, you can tell WordPerfect to number each line as it is being printed. This has practical applications for certain legal papers or for reference purposes. To turn on line numbering, click Format, point to Line, then click Numbering. At the Line Numbering dialog box shown in figure 17.6, click in the Turn line numbering on check box to insert a check mark.

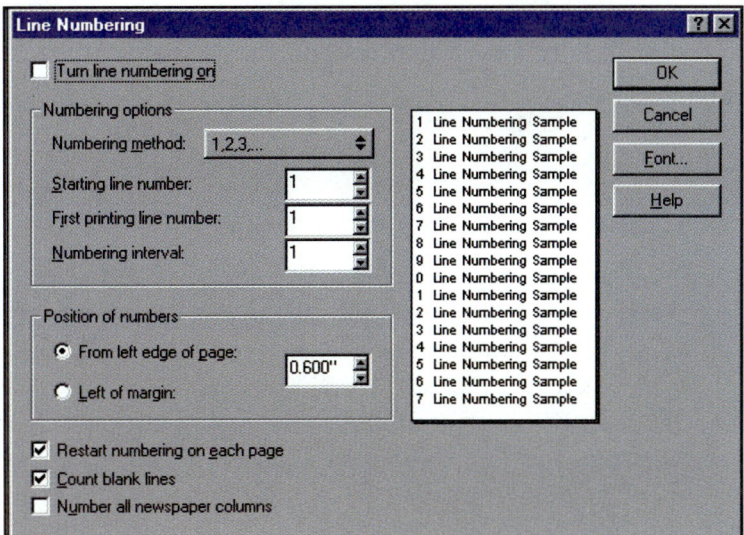

Figure 17.6
Line Numbering Dialog Box

At the right side of the dialog box, a sample page is displayed showing a visual representation of how line numbering will print on the page. The display changes as you make changes to the dialog box.

By default, WordPerfect numbers lines with Arabic numbers. With the Numbering method option, you can change this to abc; ABC; i,ii,iii; or I,II,III. To change the numbering method, click the Numbering method list box, then click the desired numbering method at the pop-up menu.

By default, WordPerfect begins line numbering with line number 1. With the Starting line number option, you can change to a different beginning number. You can do this by clicking the option, then keying the new beginning number, or you can click the up-pointing or down-pointing triangles after the option.

With the First printing line number option, you can specify the first line number to print. For example, if you do not want any line numbers to print until line 4, enter 4 at this option.

You can specify the interval between printed line numbers with the Numbering interval option. For example, if you want every second line numbered, you would enter 2 at this option.

The Position of numbers section contains two options—From left edge of page and Left of margin. By default, a line number will print 0.6 inches from the left edge of the page. This can be changed to any measurement desired, but you must make sure that the left margin is set to accommodate the line number. If you change to Left of margin, enter a measurement from the left margin to the line number.

WordPerfect starts numbering over at the beginning of each page. If you want to number lines in a document consecutively, remove the check mark in the Restart numbering on each page check box.

When WordPerfect numbers lines, blank lines are also numbered. If you do not want blank lines numbered, remove the check mark in the box before the Count blank lines option.

If a document includes newspaper columns, insert a check mark in the Number all newspaper columns option to number the lines in each column. (You will learn about newspaper columns in chapter 23.)

When line numbering is turned on, line numbers appear in the editing window. In Page or Draft viewing mode, you may need to scroll the text on the screen to the right to see the line numbers.

Formatting Documents with Special Features 375

EXERCISE 6

Adding Line Numbering to a Document

1. At a clear editing window, open Legal 01.
2. Save the document with Save As and name it Ch 17, Ex 06.
3. Complete the following find and replaces:
   a. Find *NAME1* and replace with *DAVID R. AMES*.
   b. Find *NAME2* and replace with *SALLY M. ROJAS*.
   c. Find *NUMBER* and replace with *C-7754*.
4. With the insertion point positioned at the beginning of the document, turn on line numbering by completing the following steps:
   a. Click Format, point to Line, then click Numbering.
   b. At the Line Numbering dialog box, click the Turn line numbering on option to insert a check mark.
   c. Click OK.
5. Save the document again with the same name (Ch 17, Ex 06).
6. Print Ch 17, Ex 06.
7. With Ch 17, Ex 06 still displayed in the editing window, display Reveal Codes, then delete the *Ln Num: On* code.
8. With the insertion point positioned at the beginning of the document, turn on line numbering with uppercase letters that are 0.3 inches from the left edge of the page by completing the following steps:
   a. Click Format, point to Line, then click Numbering.
   b. At the Line Numbering dialog box, click the Turn line numbering on option to insert a check mark.
   c. Click the Numbering method button (contains *1,2,3,...*), then click A,B,C,... at the drop-down list.
   d. Make sure the From left edge of page option is selected. (If not, click in the radio button preceding the option.) Click the down-pointing triangle at the right of the measurement text box until *0.300"* displays.
   e. Click OK.
9. Save the document again with the same name (Ch 17, Ex 06).
10. Print and then close Ch 17, Ex 06.

Using Abbreviations

WordPerfect contains an abbreviations feature that simplifies inserting commonly used words, names, or phrases. You can assign an abbreviation to a particular word or phrase, then use that abbreviation to insert the word or phrase into a document. When creating an abbreviation for a word or phrase, try to keep it as short as possible. This saves time when keying the abbreviation. Abbreviations are case sensitive. This means that you can use the abbreviation *IC* for the company *International Consultants* and use the abbreviation *ic* for *inventory control*.

Abbreviations are created by selecting the text to which you want to assign the abbreviation, then displaying the Abbreviations dialog box shown in figure 17.7. To display this dialog box, click Insert, then Abbreviations.

After an abbreviation has been created, it can be used in a document and expanded. To use an abbreviation in a document, key the abbreviation, then press Ctrl + Shift + A. The Ctrl + Shift + A command tells WordPerfect to expand the abbreviation to the full text. To expand an abbreviation, the insertion point must be positioned either immediately to the right of the abbreviation or on a character in the abbreviation. In addition to the shortcut command, Ctrl + Shift + A, you can also expand an abbreviation by keying the abbreviation, clicking Insert, then Abbreviations to display the Abbreviations dialog box, then clicking the Expand button.

Abbreviations you have created can be deleted with the Delete option at the Abbreviations dialog box. With the Replace option, you can replace the contents of an abbreviation. When you use Replace, the contents of the abbreviation are changed but not the abbreviation itself.

Figure 17.7

Abbreviations Dialog Box

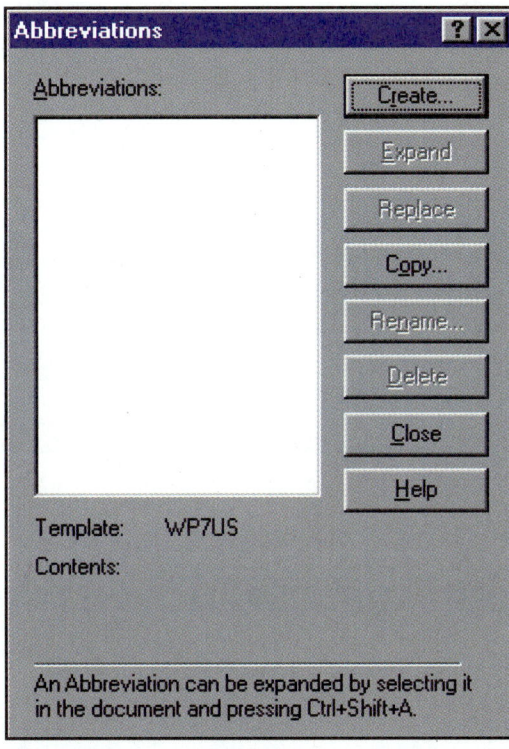

EXERCISE 7

Creating Abbreviations

1. At a clear editing window, create the abbreviation CHS for Cleveland High School by completing the following steps:
   a. Key **Cleveland High School**.
   b. Select *Cleveland High School*.
   c. Click Insert, then Abbreviations.
   d. At the Abbreviations dialog box, click Create.
   e. At the Create Abbreviation dialog box, key **CHS**.

Formatting Documents with Special Features 377

f. Click OK or press Enter.
   g. At the Abbreviations dialog box, click <u>C</u>lose.
2. Complete steps similar to those in step 1 to create abbreviations for the following text:

NHS	=	Nylan High School
GJHS	=	Grant Junior High School
WJHS	=	Washington Junior High School
RJHS	=	Roosevelt Junior High School
CES	=	Carr Elementary School
LES	=	Leland Elementary School
SES	=	Sahala Elementary School

3. Close the document without saving it.
4. At a clear editing window, key the memo shown in figure 17.8 in an appropriate memo format. Display the full text where you see the abbreviations in the document. To do this, key the abbreviation, then press Ctrl + Shift + A.
5. After completing the memo, delete the abbreviations by completing the following steps:
   a. Click <u>I</u>nsert, then <u>A</u>bbreviations.
   b. At the Abbreviations dialog box, click *CES* in the <u>A</u>bbreviations list box.
   c. Click the <u>D</u>elete button.
   d. At the *Delete Abbreviation from Template* question, click <u>Y</u>es.
   e. With the Abbreviations dialog box still open, delete the remaining abbreviations you created in step 2.
6. Save the document and name it Ch 17, Ex 07.
7. Print and then close Ch 17, Ex 07.

Figure 17.8

DATE: January 17, 1998
TO: All School Principals
FROM: William Cho
SUBJECT: SCHOOL VISITATIONS

The Computer Technology Study Team will be conducting on-site visits of all schools in the district. The purpose of this visit is to determine the current level of computer hardware and software and to determine immediate and long-term hardware and software needs.

The study team members will be visiting the high schools on the following days:

    02/17/98   NHS
    02/18/98   CHS

The study team members will be visiting the junior high schools on the following days:

    03/10/98   RJHS
    03/12/98   WJHS
    03/24/98   GJHS

> The study team members will be visiting the elementary schools on the following days:
>
> 04/01/98   SES
> 04/07/98   LES
> 04/14/98   CES
>
> The team members will try not to interrupt classes. They may, however, need to visit computer classrooms. If you have any concerns about the date of the visitation, contact me as soon as possible.
>
> xx:Ch 17, Ex 07

Displaying Symbols

When you press the space bar, Enter key, Tab key, or a variety of other keys, a symbol is inserted in the document. By default, these symbols are not displayed in the editing window. However, being able to see the symbols may be helpful when you need to insert special formatting elements such as hard spaces, which are not easy to judge with the eye. To turn on the display of symbols, click View, then Show ¶. When the display of symbols is turned on, the editing screen will look similar to the one shown in figure 17.9. To turn off the display of symbol, click View, then Show ¶ again.

Figure 17.9

Document with Symbols Displayed

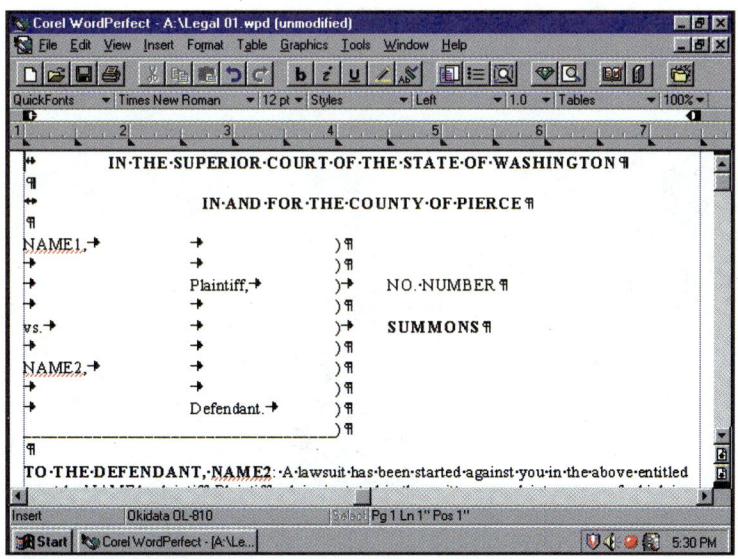

Inserting Hard Spaces

As you key text in a document, WordPerfect makes line-end decisions and automatically wraps text to the next line. Word wrap is a time-saving feature that can increase your keyboarding speed. Even though word wrap is helpful, there may be times when word wrap breaks up words or phrases that should remain together. For example, a name such as *Katherine L. Brynn* can be broken after, but should not be broken before, the initial *L*. The phrase *World War II* can be broken

Formatting Documents with Special Features   379

between *World* and *War*, but should not be broken between *War* and *II*. To control what text is wrapped to the next line, a hard space can be inserted between words. When a hard space is inserted, WordPerfect considers the words as one unit and will not divide them.

To insert a hard space, press Ctrl + space bar. This inserts a code in the document that can be seen in Reveal Codes as *HSpace*. A hard space can also be inserted in a document using the Other Codes dialog box. To do this, click Fo_r_mat, point to _L_ine, then click _O_ther Codes. At the Other Codes dialog box, click Hard s_p_ace [HSpace], then click _I_nsert.

EXERCISE

Displaying Symbols and Inserting Hard Spaces

1. At a clear editing window, complete the following steps:
   a. Turn on the display of symbols by clicking _V_iew, then _S_how ¶.
   b. Change the left and right margins to 1.5 inches.
   c. Key the memo shown in figure 17.10 in an appropriate memo format. Insert hard spaces between the commands in the memo (for example, between *Ctrl + B* and *Ctrl + I*). Insert a hard space by pressing Ctrl + space bar. Insert a hard space before and after the plus symbol in all the shortcut commands.
2. Save the memo and name it Ch 17, Ex 08.
3. Print and then close Ch 17, Ex 08.
4. Turn off the display of symbols by repeating step 1a.

Figure 17.10

DATE:		March 4, 1998

TO:		All Medical Transcribers

FROM:		Debra Wong

SUBJECT:	SHORTCUT COMMANDS

The transition from WordPerfect for DOS version 6.0 to Corel WordPerfect 7 is almost complete. I will continue offering helpful hints to all medical transcribers.

Character formatting can be applied at the Font dialog box. At this dialog box, you are offered a wide variety of formatting options. To apply formatting quickly, you can use shortcut commands rather than the Font dialog box. For example, use Ctrl + B to bold text. To italicize text such as book and magazine titles, press Ctrl + I. Additional shortcut commands include Ctrl + U to underline text and Ctrl + F to display the Font dialog box.

xx:Ch 17, Ex 08

Inserting the Date

The current date can be inserted in a document as text or a code. To insert the date as text, press Ctrl + D or click Insert, point to Date, then click Date Text. The date is inserted as month, day, and year. For example, if today's date is May 4, 1998, it will be inserted as *May 4, 1998*. When you insert the date as text, the date is considered text and can be edited.

If you insert the date as a code, the date the document is opened is inserted in the document. The date displays as text on the screen, but as a code in Reveal Codes. For example, if you insert the date code in a document created on April 21, 1998, that is the date that will appear. If you open the document on May 5, 1998, the date April 21, 1998, is replaced with May 5, 1998. To insert a date as a code in a document, press Ctrl + Shift + D or click Insert, point to Date, then click Date Code.

EXERCISE 9

Inserting the Date as Text

1. At a clear editing window, open Letter 04.
2. Save the document with Save As and name it Ch 17, Ex 09.
3. Complete the following steps:
   a. Delete the date, *September 15, 1998*, in the letter.
   b. Insert the date as text by pressing Ctrl + D.
4. Save the document again with the same name (Ch 17, Ex 09).
5. Print and then close Ch 17, Ex 09.

Changing the Date Format

The format for the date can be changed at the Document Date/Time Format dialog box, shown in figure 17.11. To display this dialog box, click Insert, point to Date, then click Date Format. The Date/Time formats list box in the dialog box displays a variety of options for inserting the date and/or time in a document. To make a choice, click the desired option, then click OK or double-click the desired option.

Figure 17.11

Document Date/Time Format Dialog Box

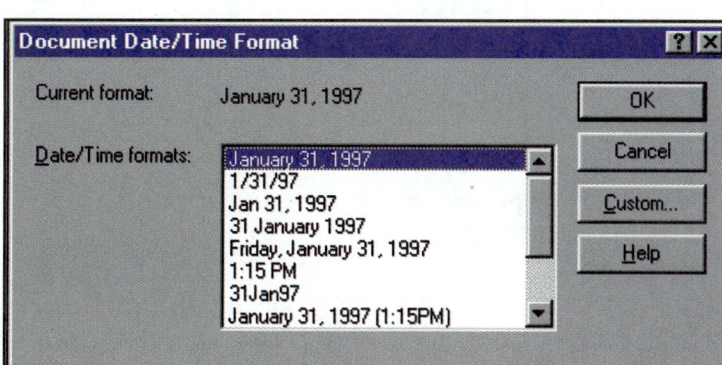

Formatting Documents with Special Features — 381

If the Document Date/Time Format dialog box does not contain the option you desire for displaying the date and/or time in a document, you can create your own custom display with the Custom Date/Time Format dialog box. To display this dialog box, shown in figure 17.12, click the Custom button in the Document Date/Time Format dialog box.

At the Custom Date/Time Format dialog box, you can choose the individual codes you want to use to display the date and/or the time. At the bottom of the dialog box, the Date/time sample section shows how the date will display with the codes currently displayed in the Edit date/time format text box. To change the display, add codes to or delete codes from the Edit date/time format text box. As you add or delete codes, the display after Date/time sample section changes.

To insert a date or time code in the Edit date/time format text box, click the desired tab for Year, Month, Day, or Time. With the desired tab selected, select the required code, then click the Insert button. When all codes have been added or deleted, click OK.

Figure 17.12

Custom Date/Time Format Dialog Box

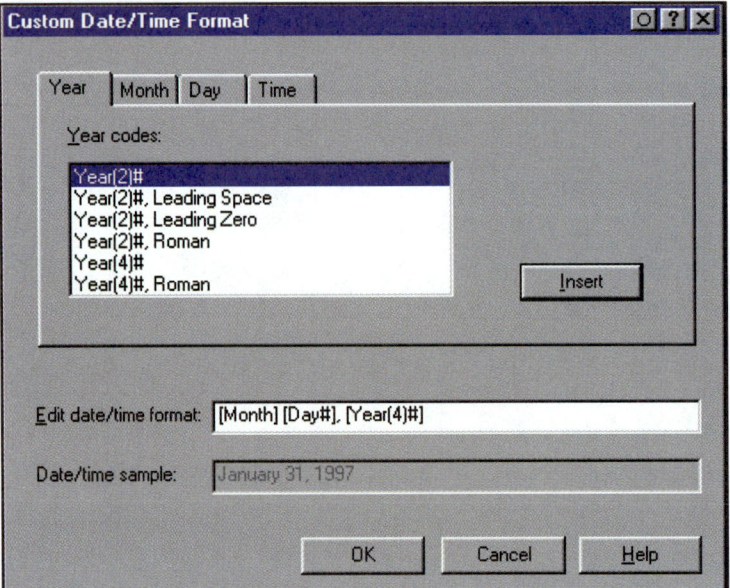

EXERCISE 10

Inserting a Date Code

1. At a clear editing window, open Memo 01.
2. Save the document with Save As and name it Ch 17, Ex 10.
3. Make the following changes:
   a. Delete the date, *October 22, 1998*.
   b. Insert the date as a code by pressing Ctrl + Shift + D.
4. Save the document again with the same name (Ch 17, Ex 10).
5. Print Ch 17, Ex 10.
6. With Ch 17, Ex 10 still open in the editing window, display Reveal Codes, then delete the *Date* code.
7. Insert the date in the military format by completing the following steps:
   a. Position the insertion point where the date is to be located.

> b. Click Insert, Date, then Date Format.
> c. At the Document Date/Time Format dialog box, position the arrow pointer on the date entry that displays the day in figures first, the month spelled out second, and the year in figures third. (The date that displays is the current date. For example, if today is February 17, 1998, the date displays as *17 February 1998*.) Double-click the left mouse button.
> d. Press Ctrl + Shift + D to insert the date as a code.
> 8. Save the document again with the same name (Ch 17, Ex 10).
> 9. Print and then close Ch 17, Ex 10.

Bookmarks

In long documents, you may find it useful to mark a location in the document so you can quickly move the insertion point to the location. You can mark just one location in a document with a QuickMark Bookmark code or you can mark several locations with Bookmark codes.

Using a QuickMark

You can insert one QuickMark code at a time. If you set another QuickMark code, the first one is removed from the document. Insert a QuickMark code in a location in the document that you want to be able to return to quickly. To insert a QuickMark code, position the insertion point at the location in the document where the QuickMark code is to appear, then press Ctrl + Shift + Q or click Insert, then Bookmark. At the Bookmark dialog box, click Set QuickMark. (This option displays at the bottom of the dialog box.)

When a QuickMark code is inserted in the document, it appears as *Bookmark: QuickMark* in Reveal Codes. The insertion point must be positioned immediately left of the code to display the entire code or you must click the code.

After a QuickMark bookmark has been inserted in a document, you can move the insertion point to the location of the code by pressing Ctrl + Q. You can also move the insertion point to a QuickMark by clicking Insert, then Bookmark to display the Bookmark dialog box and then clicking Find QuickMark. (This option displays at the bottom of the dialog box.)

Using Bookmarks

You can create bookmarks for locations in a document at the Bookmark dialog box. When you create bookmarks, you can insert as many as needed in a document. To create a bookmark, you would complete the following steps:

1. Position the insertion point at the location in the document where the bookmark code is to appear.
2. Click Insert, then Bookmark.
3. At the Bookmark dialog box, click Create.
4. At the Create Bookmark dialog box, key a name for the bookmark.
5. Click OK or press Enter.

Repeat these steps as many times as needed in a document to insert bookmarks. Make sure you give each bookmark a unique name. When you insert a bookmark in a document, the bookmark code is visible in Reveal Codes. For example, if you create a bookmark named Section 1, it displays as *Bookmark: Section 1* in Reveal Codes. (The insertion point must be positioned immediately left of the code to see the bookmark name or you must click the code.)

After bookmarks have been inserted in a document, you can move the insertion point to a specific bookmark. To do this, display the Bookmark dialog box, click the name of the desired bookmark in the Bookmark list box, then click Go To.

A bookmark can be inserted at the beginning of selected text. Then, when moving the insertion point to the bookmark, the text is automatically selected. To create a bookmark for selected text, select the text first, then follow the basic steps listed on the previous page.

After a bookmark has been created for selected text, you can find the bookmark and select the text with the Go To & Select option at the Bookmark dialog box. Other options allow you to delete, move, or rename a bookmark.

Creating Bookmarks

1. At a clear editing window, open Report 03.
2. Create a QuickMark bookmark by completing the following steps:
   a. Position the insertion point at the beginning of the line containing the heading *CHAPTER 2: DEVELOPMENT OF TECHNOLOGY, 1850 - 1900*. (This heading is located on page 2.)
   b. Press Ctrl + Shift + Q.
3. Position the insertion point at the beginning of the document, then move the insertion point to the location of the QuickMark code by pressing Ctrl + Q.
4. With the insertion point located at the QuickMark, display Reveal Codes, then delete the QuickMark code.
5. Create a bookmark named *Indust* by completing the following steps:
   a. Position the insertion point at the beginning of the line containing the subheading *Industrialization*. (This subheading is located below the Chapter 1 title.)
   b. Click Insert, then Bookmark.
   c. At the Bookmark dialog box, click Create.
   d. At the Create Bookmark dialog box, key **Indust**.
   e. Click OK or press Enter.
6. Create a bookmark named *World* at the beginning of the line containing the subheading *Development of a World Market* by completing steps similar to those in step 5. (The *Development of a World Market* subheading is located below the Chapter 2 title.)
7. Move the insertion point to the *Indust* bookmark by completing the following steps:
   a. Click Insert, then Bookmark.
   b. At the Bookmark dialog box, make sure *Indust* is selected in the Bookmark list box (if not, click *Indust*), then click Go To.
8. Move the insertion point to the *World* bookmark by completing steps similar to those in step 7.
9. Close the report without saving the changes.

Advancing the Insertion Point

With options from the Advance dialog box, shown in figure 17.13, you can move the insertion point horizontally or vertically relative to the position of the insertion point or an absolute distance from the top and left edges of the page. To advance the insertion point, you would complete the following steps:

1. Position the insertion point at the location where you want to begin advancing the insertion point.
2. Click Format, point to Typesetting, then click Advance.
3. At the Advance dialog box, choose the direction you want to move the insertion point.
4. Key the desired distance measurement.
5. Click OK or press Enter.

When entering a position measurement, you can enter the measurement in inches (the WordPerfect default) or you can enter a point measurement. If you want to advance the insertion point by points, enter the point measurement followed by the letter *p*. For example, to advance the insertion point down 6 points you would enter *6p* at the Advance dialog box.

Advance Dialog Box

Figure 17.13

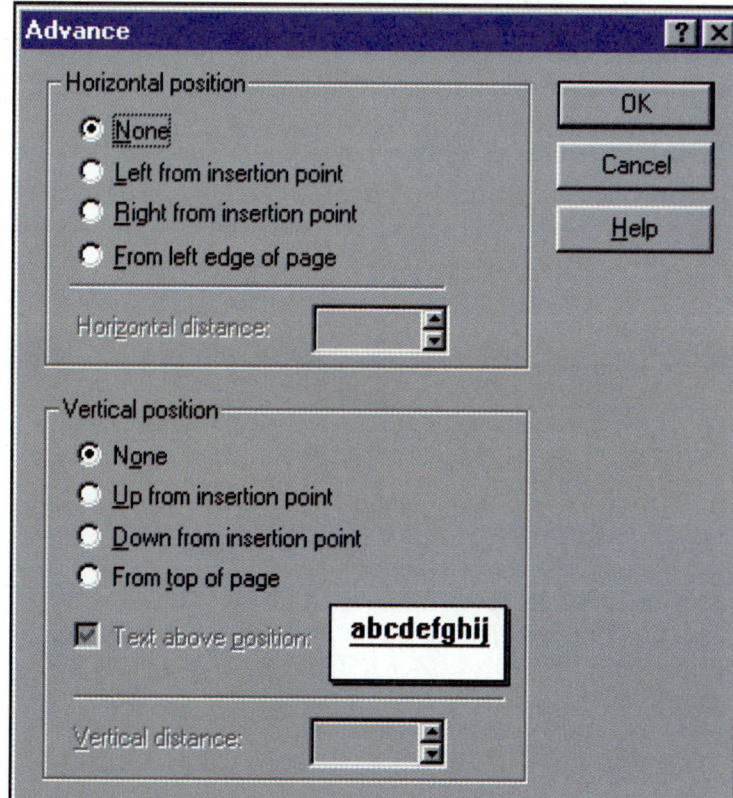

Formatting Documents with Special Features

EXERCISE 12

Using Advance Options

1. At a clear editing window, open Report 06.
2. Save the document with Save As and name it Ch 17, Ex 12.
3. Advance the line *The national telecommunications network will...* up from the insertion point 6 points by completing the following steps:
   a. Position the insertion point at the left margin of the line containing the text *The national telecommunications network will...*.
   b. Click Format, point to Typesetting, then click Advance.
   c. At the Advance dialog box, click Up from insertion point.
   d. Change the Vertical distance to 6 points. To do this, select the current numbers in the Vertical distance text box, then key **6p**.
   e. Click OK.
4. Complete steps similar to those in 3a through 3e to move the line *As more applications are done...* 6 points up from the insertion point.
5. Save the document again with the same name (Ch 17, Ex 12).
6. Print and then close Ch 17, Ex 12.

Converting the Case of Letters

With the Convert Case option from the Edit drop-down menu, you can convert the case of selected letters to uppercase, lowercase, or initial caps. When you click Lowercase, WordPerfect changes selected letters to lowercase except the word *I*, words starting with *I* followed by an apostrophe such as *I've* and *I'm*, and the first letter of the first word of a sentence.

WordPerfect also provides the shortcut command, Ctrl + K, to convert the case of selected text. If selected text displays in lowercase letters, pressing Ctrl + K changes the text to uppercase. If selected text displays in uppercase, pressing Ctrl + K changes the text to lowercase.

EXERCISE 13

Changing Case

1. At a clear editing window, open Report 04.
2. Save the document with Save As and name it Ch 17, Ex 13.
3. Make the following changes to the document:
   a. Change the font to 12-point Century Schoolbook.
   b. Turn on the Widow/Orphan feature.
   c. Convert the heading, *World War I*, to uppercase letters by completing the following steps:
      (1) Select *World War I*.
      (2) Click Edit, point to Convert Case, then click Uppercase.
      (3) Deselect the text.
   d. Convert the case of each of the following headings to uppercase:
      World War II
      Korean War
      Cold War and Vietnam
4. Save the document again with the same name (Ch 17, Ex 13).
5. Print and then close Ch 17, Ex 13.

386 Chapter 17

CHAPTER SUMMARY

- ▼ Use WordPerfect's hyphenation feature when the right margin of a left-justified document is particularly ragged, or when the lines in a full-justified document include large gaps of extra space.

- ▼ The default hyphenation zones of 10% and 4% can be changed. If the hyphenation zone is shortened, more words will be hyphenated. If the zone is lengthened, fewer words will be hyphenated.

- ▼ If the hyphenation zone is changed or if hyphenation is turned on, a code is inserted in the document at the beginning of the paragraph where the insertion point is located.

- ▼ Keying a minus sign in the document inserts a regular hyphen. A hyphen inserted by you during the hyphenation process is called a *soft* hyphen. Insert a *hard* hyphen in words or groups of numbers that should be kept together on one line.

- ▼ Line height (the amount of space a line of text occupies vertically) automatically adjusts when changes are made to the font and/or type size. At the Line Height dialog box, the Auto setting can be changed to Fixed and the line height can be changed manually.

- ▼ At the Line Numbering dialog box, you can tell WordPerfect to number each line as it is being printed.

- ▼ The abbreviations feature allows you to assign an abbreviation to a particular word or phrase. That text can then be inserted quickly into a document by keying the abbreviation, then pressing Ctrl + Shift + A.

- ▼ The display of symbols such as the space bar and Enter key can be turned on by clicking View, then Show ¶.

- ▼ When a *hard* space is inserted between words, WordPerfect considers the words to be one unit and will not divide them.

- ▼ The current date can be inserted in a document as text or a code. The date format can be changed at the Document Date/Time Format dialog box

- ▼ To mark one location in a document so you can quickly move the insertion point to it, use the QuickMark feature; to mark more than one location, create bookmarks at the Bookmark dialog box.

- ▼ With options from the Advance dialog box, you can move the insertion point horizontally or vertically relative to the position of the insertion point or an absolute distance from the top and left edges of the page.

- ▼ With the Convert Case option from the Edit drop-down menu, you have the options of converting the case of selected letters to uppercase, lowercase, or initial caps. Use the shortcut command, Ctrl + K, to convert the case of selected text.

COMMANDS REVIEW

	Mouse	Keyboard
Line Hyphenation dialog box	Format, Line, Hyphenation	Format, Line, Hyphenation
Display Preferences dialog box	Edit, Preferences, Display	Edit, Preferences, Display
Insert a soft hyphen manually		CTRL + SHIFT + -
Insert a hard hyphen		CTRL + -
Line Height dialog box	Format, Line, Height	Format, Line, Height
Line Numbering dialog box	Format, Line, Numbering	Format, Line, Numbering
Abbreviations dialog box	Insert, Abbreviations	Insert, Abbreviations
Expand abbreviation	Insert, Abbreviations, Expand	CTRL + A
Turn on/off display of symbols	View, Show ¶	View, Show ¶
Insert a hard space	Format, Line, Other Codes, Hard Space, Insert	CTRL + SPACE
Document Date/Time dialog box	Insert, Date, Date Format	Insert, Date, Date Format
Insert date as text	Insert, Date, Date Text	CTRL + D
Insert date as code	Insert, Date, Date Code	CTRL + SHIFT + D
Insert a QuickMark Bookmark code	Insert, Bookmark, Set QuickMark	CTRL + SHIFT + Q
Move insertion point to the QuickMark code	Insert, Bookmark, Find QuickMark	CTRL + Q
Insert a Bookmark code	Insert, Bookmark, Create	Insert, Bookmark, Create
Move insertion point to the Bookmark code	Insert, Bookmark, click name, Go To	Insert, Bookmark, select name, Go To
Advance dialog box	Format, Typesetting, Advance	Format, Typesetting, Advance
Convert case of letters	Edit, Convert Case	CTRL + K

CHECK YOUR UNDERSTANDING

Completion: In the space provided at the right, indicate the correct term, command, or number.

1. This is the default percentage for the left hyphenation zone. _____

2. This is the default percentage for the right hyphenation zone. _____

3. This is the command to insert a soft hyphen from the keyboard when hyphenation is off. _____

4. This is the command to insert a hard hyphen from the keyboard. _____

5. This is the command to insert a hard space from the keyboard. _____

6. Press this key to insert a regular hyphen. _____

7. This is the shortcut command to insert a QuickMark Bookmark code in a document. _____

8. You can simplify inserting commonly used words, names, or phrases with this feature. _____

9. Key this in the <u>V</u>ertical distance text box at the Advance dialog box to advance the insertion point 6 points. _____

10. With this option from the Edit drop-down menu, you can convert the case of selected letters to uppercase, lowercase, or initial caps. _____

In the space provided below, list the steps you would complete to advance up 9 points from the insertion point.

_____

_____

_____

SKILL ASSESSMENTS

Assessment 1

1. At a clear editing window, open Report 04.
2. Save the document with Save As and name it Ch 17, SA 01.
3. Make the following changes to the document:
    a. With the insertion point at the beginning of the document, display the Environment Preferences dialog box, then change the Hyphenation <u>p</u>rompt to <u>A</u>lways.
    b. Change the left hyphenation zone to 5%, the right hyphenation zone to 0%, and turn on hyphenation. Hyphenate words in the document as required. Move the insertion point to the end of the document to ensure that all necessary words are hyphenated.
4. Save the document again with the same name (Ch 17, SA 01).
5. Change the Hyphenation <u>p</u>rompt to <u>W</u>hen Required at the Environment Preferences dialog box.
6. Print and then close Ch 17, SA 01.

Assessment 2

1. At a clear editing window, open Legal 02.
2. Save the document with Save As and name it Ch 17, SA 02.
3. Complete the following find and replaces:
    a. Find *NAME1* and replace with *MARY J. SLATER*.
    b. Find *NUMBER* and replace with *C-0334*.
    c. Find *Hd Left/Right Indent* codes and replace with *Hd Left Ind* codes.
4. With the insertion point positioned at the beginning of the document, make the following changes:
    a. Turn on line numbering. (Use the default settings at the Line Numbering dialog box.)
    b. Change the left hyphenation zone to 4%, the right hyphenation zone to 0%, and turn on hyphenation. Move the insertion point to the end of the document to make sure any necessary words are hyphenated.

5. Save the document again with the same name (Ch 17, SA 02).
6. Print and then close Ch 17, SA 02.

Assessment 3

1. At a clear editing window, open Report 04.
2. Save the document with Save As and name it Ch 17, SA 03.
3. Make the following changes to the document:
    a. Change the font to 12-point Century Schoolbook.
    b. Change the left and right margins to 1.5 inches.
    c. Turn on line numbering and remove the check mark from the Restart numbering on each page option at the Line Numbering dialog box.
    d. Change the left hyphenation zone to 4%, the right hyphenation to 0%, and turn on hyphenation. (Make hyphenation decisions if required; move the insertion point to the end of the document to make sure all necessary words are hyphenated.)
4. Save the document again with the same name (Ch 17, SA 03).
5. Print and then close Ch 17, SA 03.

Assessment 4

1. At a clear editing window, create the memo shown in figure 17.14. Make the following changes:
    a. Change the left and right margins to 1.5 inches.
    b. Insert hard spaces within the keystroke commands to keep each command together.
    c. Insert the current date as text.
2. Save the memo and name it Ch 17, SA 04.
3. Print and then close Ch 17, SA 04.

Figure 17.14

DATE: (current date)

TO: Medical Transcribers

FROM: Debra Wong

SUBJECT: SHORTCUT COMMANDS

As you continue working with Corel WordPerfect 7, you can display dialog boxes with options from the menu bar or with shortcut commands. For example, you can insert the current date in a document with the command Ctrl + D or you can use the Date option from the Insert menu.

Text can be aligned at the right margin with the Flush Right feature. Pressing Alt + F7 moves the insertion point to the right margin. You can also click the Flush Right option from the Format Line drop-down menu. Use bookmarks in a long document to move the insertion point to a specific location in the document. Ctrl + Shift + Q is the shortcut command to set a QuickMark bookmark, and Ctrl + Q is the command to move the insertion point to a QuickMark bookmark.

xx:Ch 17, SA 04

FORMATTING WITH MACROS AND TEMPLATES

PERFORMANCE OBJECTIVE

Upon successful completion of chapter 18, you will be able to record keystrokes for commands, then play those keystrokes in many different business documents. You will also be able to create business documents such as a letter, sign, and calendar using WordPerfect templates.

In this chapter, you will learn about two time-saving features—macros and templates. In chapter 17, you learned about WordPerfect's abbreviations feature that simplifies inserting commonly used words, names, or phrases in a document. WordPerfect includes another time-saving feature called a *macro*. With macros, you can automate the formatting of a document. The word *macro* was coined by computer programmers for a collection of commands used to make a large programming job easier and to save time. A WordPerfect *macro* is a document containing recorded commands that can accomplish a task automatically and save time.

In this chapter, you will learn to record and play macros. WordPerfect's macro feature can also be used to write more complex macros. For more in-depth information on writing macros and macro programming techniques, refer to the help menus.

Every document created in WordPerfect is based on a template. When you create a document at a blank editing window, you are using the default template. This default template establishes the formatting for the document such as margins, tabs, font, etc. WordPerfect also includes a number of other templates that can be used to produce a variety of business documents such as memos, business letters, calendars, faxes, and much more.

Changing the Location of Macro Documents

Before learning about recording and playing macros, you may want to change the location of macro documents. By default, a macro document is saved in the *c:\Corel\Office7\Macros\WPWin* folder (the drive letter may vary depending on the system you are using). In some situations, you may want to change where WordPerfect saves macro documents. For example, in a school setting, you may want to change the location of macro documents to drive **a:** or drive **b:** (the drive that contains your student disk). This lets you record macros and save them on your disk. Change the location of macro documents at the Files Preferences dialog box. To do this, you would complete the following steps:

1. Click Edit, then Preferences.
2. At the Preferences dialog box, double-click the Files icon.
3. At the Files Preferences dialog box, click the Merge/Macro tab.
4. At the Files Preferences dialog box with the Merge/Macro tab selected, select the text displayed in the Default macro folder text box, then key **a:** (or **b:**). (Key the drive letter where your student data disk is located.)
5. Select any text that displays in the Supplemental macro folder text box (or click in the text box if no text is displayed), then key **c:\Corel\Office7\Macros\WPWin**.
6. Click OK to close the Files Preferences dialog box.
7. At the Preferences dialog box, click Close.

Changes made to the Files Preferences dialog box stay in effect even after you exit WordPerfect. Check with your instructor before completing any exercises in this chapter to see if you need to change the location of macro documents.

Creating Macros

In WordPerfect, creating a macro is referred to as *recording*. As a macro is being recorded, all the keys pressed and the menus and dialog boxes displayed are recorded and become part of the macro. For example, you can record a macro to change the left and right margins or insert page numbering in a document. Once a macro is recorded, it can be played back in a document. A macro can also be replaced, edited, paused, and deleted.

Recording a Macro

You can use the Macro option from the Tools drop-down menu to record a macro, or you can use a button on the Macro Tools Toolbar. To display the Macro Tools Toolbar, position the arrow pointer on the current Toolbar, click the right mouse button, then click Macro Tools. When you click Macro Tools, the Macro Tools Toolbar displays as shown in figure 18.1. Recording a macro involves four steps. They are:

1. Click Tools, point to Macro, then click Record; or click the Record button on the Macro Tools Toolbar (the fifth button from the right).
2. Key a name for the macro.
3. Complete the steps to be recorded in the macro.
4. End the recording of the macro by clicking Tools, pointing to Macro, then clicking Record; or by clicking the Record button on the Macro Tools Toolbar.

Figure 18.1

Macro Tools Toolbar

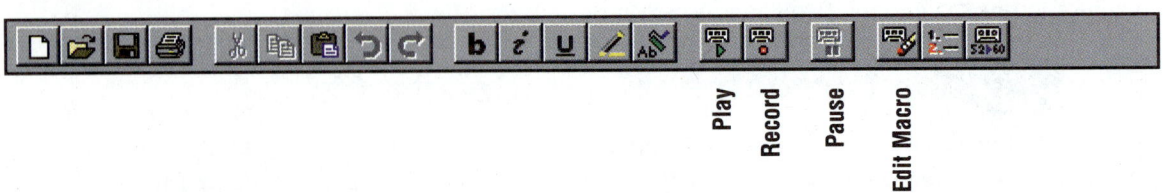

392 Chapter 18

When you click <u>T</u>ools, point to <u>M</u>acro, then click <u>R</u>ecord; or click the Record button on the Macro Tools Toolbar, the Record Macro dialog box shown in figure 18.2 displays on the screen.

Record

Record Macro Dialog Box **Figure 18.2**

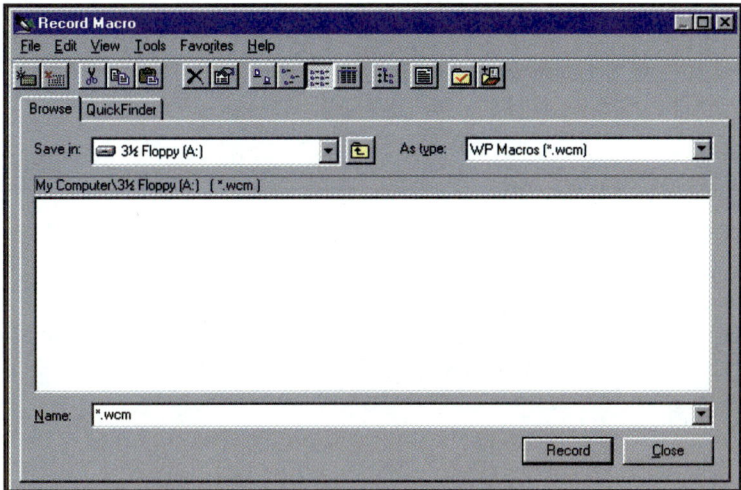

Naming a Macro

At the Record Macro dialog box, key a name for the macro. Macro names follow the same file naming rules as Windows 95. A macro name can be up to 255 characters in length, and can include any letter, number, or space. Avoid using the symbols + : , = [and]. Do not use the period when naming a macro. WordPerfect adds a period and the extension *.wcm* (for WordPerfect Corporation Macro) to the macro name. When you name a macro, name it something that is easy to remember and that gives you an idea of what is saved in the macro.

You can also name a macro with Ctrl + a letter, or Ctrl + Shift + a letter. Be careful not to name a macro with a Ctrl + letter or Ctrl + Shift + letter combination that is already in use by WordPerfect. The macro would be ignored by WordPerfect and the shortcut command assigned to the same keys would be executed instead. For example, if you create a macro and name it *Ctrlb*, pressing Ctrl + B would execute the Bold command instead of your macro keystrokes.

WordPerfect uses most of the letters for shortcuts to accessing features, leaving only the letter Y for naming macros with the Ctrl key, and the letters E, G, I, J, K, M, T, U, W, X, and Y for naming macros with the Ctrl + Shift keys. As an example of how to record a macro, complete exercise 1. (Before completing exercise 1, check with your instructor to see if the macro directory location should be changed.)

EXERCISE 1

Creating Macros

1. At a clear editing window, record a macro named *Sig* that includes the signature information shown in figure 18.3 by completing the following steps:
   a. Display the Macro Tools Toolbar by completing the following steps. (If the Macro Tools Toolbar is already displayed, skip this step.)
      (1) Position the arrow pointer on the current Toolbar, then click the right mouse button.

Formatting with Macros and Templates

(2) At the drop-down menu that displays, click Macro Tools.
- b. Click <u>T</u>ools, point to <u>M</u>acro, then click <u>R</u>ecord; or click the Record button on the Macro Tools Toolbar (the fifth button from the right).
- c. At the Record Macro dialog box, key **Sig**, then click the Record button or press Enter. (The Record button displays at the bottom right corner of the dialog box.)
- d. At the editing window, key the text shown in figure 18.3. (Be sure to include the blank lines between the complimentary close and the name as shown in the figure.)
- e. After keying the signature information, end the recording of the macro by clicking <u>T</u>ools, pointing to <u>M</u>acro, then clicking <u>R</u>ecord; or by clicking the Record button on the Macro Tools Toolbar.
- f. Close the document without saving it. (The document does not need to be saved since the keystrokes are now stored in a macro file.)

2. At a clear editing window, create a macro named with the Ctrl key, Shift key, and the letter M that changes the left and right margins to 1.5 inches by completing the following steps:
   - a. Click <u>T</u>ools, point to <u>M</u>acro, then click <u>R</u>ecord; or click the Record button on the Macro Tools Toolbar.
   - b. At the Record Macro dialog box, key **Ctrlsftm**, then click the Record button or press Enter.
   - c. At the editing window, execute the steps required to change the left and right margins to 1.5 inches.
   - d. At the editing window, end the recording of the macro by clicking <u>T</u>ools, pointing to <u>M</u>acro, then clicking <u>R</u>ecord; or by clicking the Record button on the Macro Tools Toolbar.
   - e. Close the document without saving it. (The margin change codes are inserted in the current document as the macro is recorded—closing the document will clear these codes.)

3. Record a macro named *Ls* that changes the line spacing to double. After creating the macro, close the document without saving it.

4. Use WordPerfect's abbreviation feature to create the abbreviation *CCH* for *Chicago Community Hospital*. (For a review of the abbreviations feature, refer to chapter 17.) After creating the abbreviation, close the document without saving it.

Figure 18.3

Sincerely yours,

ENERSEN & TALBOTT

Jeanette Enersen
Senior Partner

xx:

Once you begin recording a macro, the Macros Feature Bar appears in the editing window below the Power Bar (or Ruler Bar if it is displayed). This feature bar contains command buttons that can be used while creating or editing macros. The feature bar contains a stop button (the second button from the left) that can be used to end recording instead of using the Macro Tools Toolbar or the Tools drop-down menu.

Playing a Macro

After a macro has been recorded, it can be played back in a document. To play a macro, display the Play Macro dialog box shown in figure 18.4 by clicking Tools, pointing to Macro, then clicking Play; or, clicking the Play button on the Macro Tools Toolbar. At the dialog box, select the macro in the list box, then click Play. You can also play a macro by double-clicking the macro name in the list box at the Play Macro dialog box. To play a macro named with the Ctrl key, hold down the Ctrl key, then press the letter you assigned to the macro. To play a macro named with the Ctrl + Shift keys, hold down the Ctrl key and the Shift key simultaneously, then press the letter you assigned to the macro.

Figure 18.4

Play Macro Dialog Box

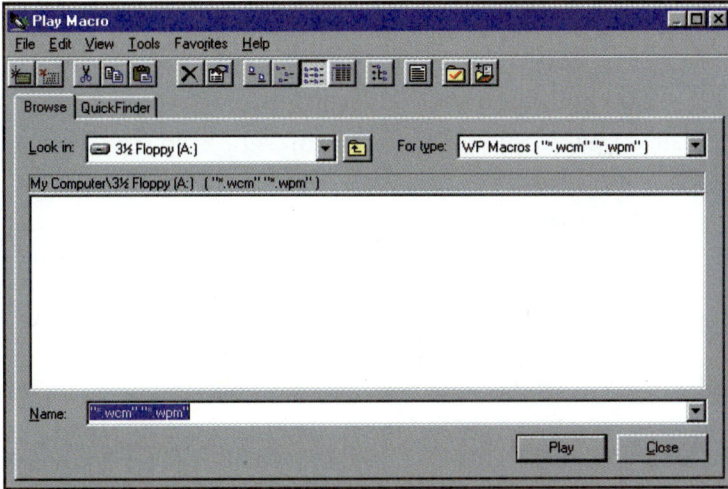

EXERCISE 2

Playing Macros within a Letter

1. At a clear editing window, complete the following steps:
   a. Play the *Ctrlsftm* macro by pressing Ctrl + Shift + M.
   b. Key the letter shown in figure 18.5. Insert the current date with the Date feature. Insert the full name where you see the abbreviation *CCH* (use Ctrl + Shift + A) Play the *Sig* macro where you see it in the letter by completing the following steps:
      (1) Click Tools, point to Macro, then click Play; or click the Play button on the Macro Tools Toolbar (the sixth button from the right).
      (2) At the Play Macro dialog box, double-click *Sig* in the list box.
   c. After you play the *Sig* macro, add the document name after your initials.
2. Save the letter and name it Ch 18, Ex 02.
3. Print and then close Ch 18, Ex 02.

Play

Formatting with Macros and Templates 395

Figure 18.5

(current date)

Mr. Charles Heinz
CCH
300 Midtown Drive
Chicago, IL 66732

Dear Mr. Heinz:

Re: Victoria Hunt vs. *CCH*

Thank you for sending the Complaint in the case of Victoria Hunt vs. *CCH*. I have reviewed the Complaint along with the list of allegations. There are some responses to questions that need your input. Please call my office to schedule an appointment.

At first glance, the Complaint seems to lack sufficient evidence for this to go to trial. I will have a clearer idea after I talk with you about the allegations in the Complaint.

Sig

Editing a Macro

If you have recorded a macro, then decide you want to change it, you can either replace it or edit it. If you replace the macro, you will need to re-record each keystroke. To replace a macro, display the Record Macro dialog box, select an existing macro in the Name list box, then click Record. WordPerfect inserts a box saying that the macro already exists and asks if you want to replace it. At this box, click Yes, then complete the steps to be recorded in the macro and end the recording.

There are two methods for opening a macro document for editing. You can open the document as you would a regular document. Or, you can edit a macro using the Edit option at the Edit Macro dialog box. In exercise 3, you will practice editing a macro.

EXERCISE

Changing Margins in a Macro

Edit Macro

1. At a clear editing window, edit the *Ctrlsftm* macro so it changes left and right margins to 1.25 inches (rather than 1.5 inches) by completing the following steps:
    a. Click Tools, point to Macro, then click Edit; or click the Edit Macro button on the Macro Tools Toolbar (third button from the right).
    b. At the Edit Macro dialog box, double-click *Ctrlsftm* in the list box.

396 Chapter 18

    c. At the macro document shown in figure 18.6, move the insertion point immediately to the left of the *5* in the line *MarginLeft (MarginWidth: 1.5")*, then key a **2**. (This should make the line display as *MarginLeft (MarginWidth: 1.25")*.)

    d. Move the insertion point immediately to the left of the *5* in the line *MarginRight (MarginWidth: 1.5")* then key a **2**. (This should make the line display as *MarginRight (MarginWidth: 1.25")*.)

    e. Click Save & Compile at the Macros Feature Bar.

    f. Close the macro by clicking Options on the Macros Feature Bar, then clicking Close Macro.

2. At a clear editing window, play the *Ctrlsftm* macro and the *Ls* macro.
3. Key the document shown in figure 18.7. Insert the full name where you see the abbreviation *CCH*. Change the line spacing back to single to key the signature line and the information below it.
4. Save the document and name it Ch 18, Ex 03.
5. Print and then close Ch 18, Ex 03.

Figure 18.6

Ctrlsftm Macro Document

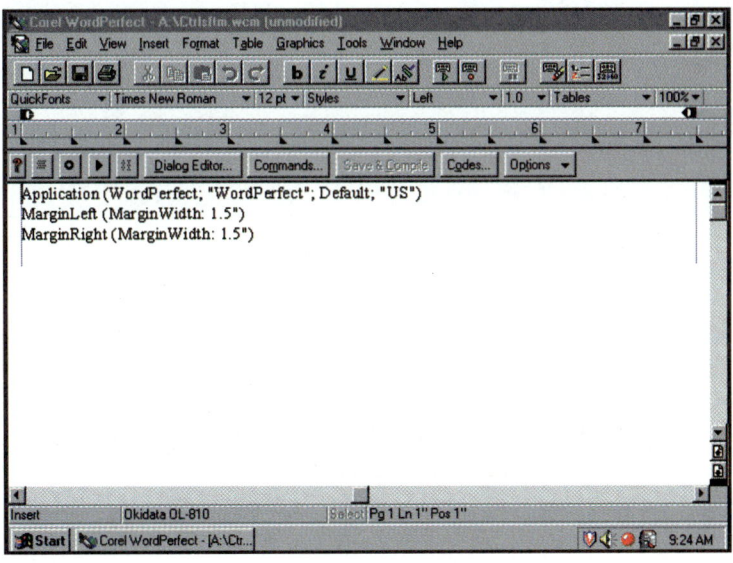

Formatting with Macros and Templates

Figure 18.7

> **CLAIM OF LIEN**
>
> *CCH*, Claimant vs. Ian Sands
>
> Notice is hereby given that the person named below claims a lien pursuant to Chapter 94.23 RCI. In support of this lien, the following information is submitted:
>
> 1. Name of Lien Claimant: *CCH*
>
>   Telephone Number: (215) 555-4300
>
>   Address: 300 Midtown Drive, Chicago, IL 66732
>
> 2. Date claimant performed services: October 15, 1998, through October 30, 1998
>
> 3. Name of person indebted to the claimant: Ian Sands
>
> 4. Principal amount claimed in the lien: $8,400
>
>   _____
>   JEANETTE ENERSEN
>   Attorney for Claimant

Pausing a Macro

Pause

When recording some macros, you may want to pause the macro to allow keyboard entry. The Pause button on the Macro Tools Toolbar or the Pause option from the Tools, Macro drop-down menu will pause a macro at a specific location. To create a macro with a pause, you would record the steps for the macro, clicking the Pause button twice wherever you want to insert a pause for keyboard entry. (These must be two separate clicks—not a double-click.) When the macro is played, the macro plays to the first pause. Key the required text, then press Enter. This continues playing the macro.

EXERCISE 4

Recording a Macro with Pauses

1. At a clear editing window, record a macro named *Notary* that contains pauses by completing the following steps:
   a. Click Tools, point to Macro, then click Record; or click the Record button on the Macro Tools Toolbar.
   b. At the Record Macro dialog box, key **Notary**, then click the Record button.

398 Chapter 18

    c. At the editing window, key the text shown in figure 18.8 to the location of the first *(pause)*, then insert a pause by clicking the Pause button on the Macro Tools Toolbar (fourth button from the right), then clicking the Pause button again. (You will not see anything identifying the pause in the editing window.)

    d. Press the space bar once, then continue keying the document. Insert pauses in the macro where you see *(pause)* in the figure. Do not key (pause) in the macro. This is only to identify where the pause is inserted.

    e. When you are done keying the text in figure 18.8, end the recording of the macro by clicking Tools, pointing to Macro, then clicking Record; or by clicking the Record button on the Macro Tools Toolbar.

    f. Close the document without saving it.

2. At a clear editing window, record a macro named *HeadA* (for Heading A) that selects a heading then changes the relative size to Very Large by completing the following steps:

    a. Key **This is a heading**. (This gives you some text to select when recording the macro.)

    b. Position the insertion point immediately to the left of the *T* in *This*.

    c. Click the Record button on the Macro Tools Toolbar.

    d. At the Record Macro dialog box, key **HeadA**, then click the Record button.

    e. At the editing window, complete the following steps:

       (1) Press F8 to turn on Select.
       (2) Press the End key to select text to the end of the line.
       (3) Double-click the Change the Font button on the Power Bar to display the Font dialog box.
       (4) At the Font dialog box, click Relative size, then Very Large.
       (5) Click OK to close the Font dialog box.
       (6) Press F8 to turn off Select.

    f. End the recording of the macro by clicking the Record button on the Macro Tools Toolbar.

3. Close the document without saving it.

Figure 18.8

STATE OF ILLINOIS   )
) ss.
COUNTY OF MADISON   )

I, the undersigned, duly swear that I am the *(pause)* in this case, have read the foregoing instrument, know the contents thereof, and believe the same to be true and correct.

    SUBSCRIBED AND SWORN to before me this *(pause)* day of *(pause)*, 1998.

                                              _____
                                              NOTARY PUBLIC in and for the State
                                              of Illinois, residing at Chicago

EXERCISE 5

Entering Text at Pauses

1. At a clear editing window, open Ch 18, Ex 03.
2. Save the document with Save As and name it Ch 18, Ex 05.
3. Position the insertion point just to the left of the *C* in *CLAIM OF LIEN*, then play the *HeadA* macro.
4. Move the insertion point to the end of the document (a triple space below the line *Attorney for Claimant*), then play the *Notary* macro. As the macro stops at a pause, enter the following text (press Enter after entering the text; this causes the macro to continue):

first pause	=	**Claimant**
second pause	=	**6th**
third pause	=	**November**

5. Save the document again with the same name (Ch 18, Ex 05).
6. Print and then close Ch 18, Ex 05.

Deleting a Macro

Delete a macro document in the same manner as a regular document. After selecting the macro name at the Open dialog box, position the arrow pointer over the selected name, click the right mouse button, then click Delete. At the question asking if you are sure you want to delete the macro, click Yes.

Using the WordPerfect Default Macros

WordPerfect includes a variety of prerecorded macros that can be used to automate certain features. These macros are located in the *c:\Corel\Office7\Macros\WPWin* folder (the drive letter and folder may vary depending on your system setup). You used the prerecorded macros *Endfoot* and *Footend* in chapter 12. With the Help feature, you can display a list of the WordPerfect macros along with a description of each. To display this information in Help, you would complete the following steps:

1. Click Help, then Help Topics.
2. At the Help Topics dialog box, click the Contents tab.
3. At the Help Topics dialog box with the Contents tab selected, double-click *Macros* that displays in the list box.
4. Double-click *Macro Programming* in the list box.
5. Double-click *Macros Included with WordPerfect* in the list box.
6. Double-click *Macros Included with WordPerfect* that displays in the list box preceded by an icon of a page containing a question mark.
7. Read the information about the WordPerfect macros that displays at the right side of the screen in the yellow box.
8. After reading about the macros, click the Close button (displays with an X) that displays at the right side of the WordPerfect Macros Help Title bar.

You can play any of these prerecorded macros in the same manner as a macro you record. Just remember to change the drive to the correct location. You might want to experiment with some of the prerecorded macros. For example, WordPerfect includes a macro that closes all open documents, a macro that inserts the document filename in a header, and a macro that inserts a watermark behind text. A watermark is a graphic that is dimmed and set behind text. You will learn how to create your own watermarks in chapter 19. In the next exercise you will play the prerecorded watermark macro to see how it works.

EXERCISE 6

Using the Watermark Macro

1. At a clear editing window, open Block 01.
2. Save the document with Save As and name it Ch 18, Ex 06.
3. Make the following changes to the document:
    a. Insert a code to center the text vertically on the current page.
    b. Change the font to 24-point BernhardMod BT (or a similar typeface).
4. Create a watermark behind the text using WordPerfect's prerecorded macro by completing the following steps:
    a. Click the Play button on the Macro Tools Toolbar.
    b. At the Play Macro dialog box, display the macros in the *c:\Corel\Office7\Macros\WPWin* folder. (This may vary, depending on your computer system.)
    c. Double-click *Watermrk* in the list box.
    d. At the Watermark Options dialog box, click OK to accept the default options.
    e. At the Graphic Watermarks dialog box, click *Important* in the list box, then click OK. (You will need to scroll down the list to display *Important*.)
5. Save the document again with the same name (Ch 18, Ex 06).
6. Click the Page/Zoom Full button (located on the WordPerfect 7 Toolbar) to display the entire page to see how the watermark fits on the page. After viewing the watermark on the page, click the Page/Zoom Full button again to return the view to the default.
7. Print and then close Ch 18, Ex 06.

Using Templates

WordPerfect has included a number of *template* documents that are formatted for specific uses. Each WordPerfect document is based on a template document with the main template document the default.

You can create a variety of documents using WordPerfect templates such as business documents, calendars, envelopes, faxes, legal documents, letters, memos, publication documents, reports, and résumés. To display the types of templates available, click File, then New; or click the New Document button on the Toolbar (the fifteenth button from the left).

The New Document button is different than the New Blank Document button. The New Blank Document button (the first button from the left) opens a new document based on the main template. The New Document button (the fifteenth button from the left) displays the Select New Document dialog box where you can choose the template on which you want the document based.

New Document

At the Select New Document dialog box shown in figure 18.9, types of templates are displayed in the Group list box. Select a type of template in the Group list box and WordPerfect displays specific templates in the Select template list box. For example, if you select *Business* in the Group list box, WordPerfect displays *Balance Sheet, Business Card - Contemporary, Business Card - Cosmopolitan*, and so on, in the Select template list box. To choose a template, double-click the desired template. You can also click the template once and then click the Select button. Depending on the template you choose, you will be presented with a screen or a dialog box requesting specific information.

Figure 18.9

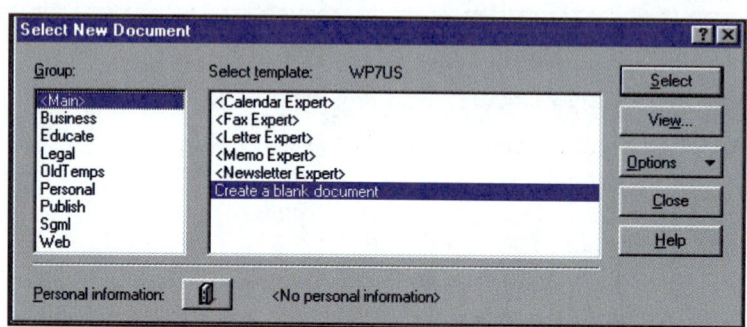

Select New Document Dialog Box

WordPerfect also includes a Calendar Expert, Fax Expert, Letter Expert, Memos Expert, and Newsletter Expert, which are listed in the *<Main>* group. These experts create business documents faster and easier than you can create them yourself. Depending on the expert you choose, you will be prompted for information needed to complete the document, then the expert will format the document for you and insert the required text. In many cases, you have the option of choosing from several pre-defined styles or formats that would take you hours to build on your own. In the next exercise you will use the Calendar Expert to create a full page calendar for the current month.

EXERCISE 7

Creating a Calendar

1. At a clear editing window, create a calendar for the current month using the Calendar Expert template by completing the following steps:
   a. Click File, then New; or click the New Document button on the Toolbar (fifteenth button from the left).
   b. At the Select New Document dialog box, double-click *<Calendar Expert>* in the Select template list box.
   c. At the Calendar Expert dialog box, make sure the current month and year display in the Starting month and Starting year text boxes, then click the Finished button (located at the upper right side of the dialog box).
2. When WordPerfect has completed building the calendar, make sure the default toolbar displays, then click the Page/Zoom Full button to view the calendar on the entire page. After viewing the calendar, click the Page/Zoom full button again to return the view to the default.
3. Save the document and name it Ch 18, Ex 07.
4. Print and then close Ch 18, Ex 07.

In exercise 7, you were able to create a calendar with minimal input. At the Calendar Expert dialog box you can alter the calendar's formatting with appearance and options settings at the Select element to modify drop-down list. Other templates, however, require considerable input from you. For example, in exercise 8, you will use a Letter Expert template to create a business letter that requires information from you.

The first time you create a document such as a business letter or memo, WordPerfect displays the Enter Your Personal Information dialog box. At this dialog box, you are prompted to enter information such as your name, title, organization, address, city, state, ZIP, telephone number, and fax number. This dialog box displays only the first time you create a document requiring personal information. After that, WordPerfect automatically uses the personal information. Because WordPerfect only prompts you for personal information the first time you create a document requiring it, the steps you take to complete exercise 8 may vary slightly from what is written.

EXERCISE 8

Creating a Business Letter with the Letter Expert Template

1. At a clear editing window, create a business letter with the text shown in figure 18.10 using a letter template by completing the following steps:
   a. Click File, then New; or click the New Document button on the Toolbar.
   b. At the Select New Document dialog box, double-click *Letter Expert* in the Select template list box.
   c. At the Personalize Your Templates dialog box, click OK.
   d. At the New Entry dialog box, make sure *Person* is selected in the Select entry type list box, then click OK.
   e. At the Properties for New Entry dialog box, key the following information. (After keying text in a text box, press the Tab key. This moves the insertion point to the next text box. If you want to skip a text box, press the Tab key. To enter the business and fax telephone numbers, select the telephone number you want to enter in the Phone #s list box by clicking the down-pointing triangle to the right of Phone #s, then clicking Business or Fax at the drop-down list. Click in the text box to the right of the Phone #s list and then key the number. If the following text already displays in the dialog box, skip to step g.)

First name	=	Cynthia
Last name	=	Wagner
Display name	=	(skip this)
Organization	=	Denver Memorial Hospital
E-mail address	=	(skip this)
E-mail type	=	(skip this)
Address	=	900 Colorado Boulevard
City	=	Denver
State	=	CO
ZIP code	=	86530
Country	=	U.S.A.
Department	=	Facilities
Title	=	Director of Facilities
Mailstop	=	(skip this)
Greeting	=	(skip this)
Phone #s - Business	=	(303) 555-4400
Phone #s - Fax	=	(303) 555-4110

   f. When all information is entered, click OK.

g. At the Corel Address Book dialog box with the My Addresses tab selected, make sure *Cynthia Wagner* is selected in the list box, then click OK.
h. At the Letter Expert dialog box, key the following information in the *To* text box:
   Ms. Rhea Hollis
   Consultant
   Rodelo & Associates
   4713 North Kelly Drive
   Denver, CO 86422
i. Click inside the *Greeting* text box, then key **Dear Ms. Hollis:**.
j. Click the down-pointing triangle to the right of the *To* in the text box below Select element to modify, then click *From* at the drop-down list. Make sure *Cynthia Wagner* displays in the From display box.
k. Click the down-pointing triangle to the right of the *From* in the text box below Select element to modify, then click *Appearance*.
l. In the Appearance section of the dialog box, click the down-pointing triangle at the right of the Letterhead style text box, then click *Contemporary* at the drop-down list.
m. Make sure *Full Block* displays in the Text format text box. If not, click the down-pointing triangle at the right of the Text format text box, then click *Full Block* at the drop-down list.
n. Click the Finished button that displays in the upper right corner of the Letter Expert dialog box.
o. With the insertion point positioned below the salutation, key the text shown in figure 18.10. (Press the Enter key once after each paragraph. The letter template contains a paragraph spacing code that will move the insertion point down almost a double space.)
p. Key the document identification after your initials at the bottom of the letter.
2. Save the completed letter and name it Ch 18, Ex 08.
3. Print and then close Ch 18, Ex 08.

Figure 18.10

Two copies of the Traffic Flow Study are attached for your review. After completion of the study, I recommend implementation of one of the following:

1. For a long-range plan, use a single, centrally located information desk with an adjacent area gift delivery.

2. Close the North entrance information desk and leave the West entrance information desk in its current location. Enhance the directional signs.

3. Retain both information desks, but reduce the hours of operation of the North entrance information desk to 12:00 noon to 5:00 p.m.

The first recommendation will be the most costly and will take the most time to implement. The second recommendation can be implemented within a six-month period and will require a modest financial outlay. The third recommendation does not require any financial outlay and could be a transitional step. Please call me at 555-4400 extension 767 to schedule a time to meet and discuss the analysis.

Changing Personal Information

The information displayed in the Address Book - Personal Information dialog box can be changed. To do this, display the Select New Document dialog box, then click the Personal information button that displays at the bottom of the dialog box. At the Address Book - Personal Information dialog box, select the person or organization you want to change then click the Edit button that displays in the bottom right corner of the dialog box. Select the field(s) that needs to be changed, then key the new text.

Viewing a Template

At the Select New Document dialog box, you can view a template to see how it is formatted before selecting the template. To do this, click the desired template type in the Group list box, click the desired template in the Select template list box, then click View. WordPerfect displays the template in the editing window. After viewing the template, close the Previewer window by clicking the Close button at the right side of the Previewer Title bar.

EXERCISE 9

Creating a Memo Using the Memo Expert

1. At a clear editing window, create a memo using the text shown in figure 18.11 using the Memo Expert template and change personal information by completing the following steps:
   a. Click File, then New; or click the New Document button on the Toolbar.
   b. Double click *Memo Expert* in the Select template list.
   c. At the Memo Expert dialog box, make the following changes:
      (1) Change the Memo style to *Cosmopolitan*.
      (2) Click in the To: text box and then key **All Directors and Managers**.
      (3) Select *Cynthia Wagner* in the From: text box and then key **Steven Ayala**.
      (4) Click in the Subject: text box and then key **Supervisory Education Series**.
      (5) Click OK to close the Memo Expert dialog box.
   d. With the insertion point positioned below the memo headings, key the text shown in figure 18.11.
2. After keying the body of the memo, save the memo and name it Ch 18, Ex 09.
3. Print and then close Ch 18, Ex 09.

Figure 18.11

The Leadership Series (LS) will begin in March. The series consists of 12 classes featuring information and exercises for managers and supervisors. Attendance at a minimum of 9 classes is required to be considered a graduate of the series.

Employees who want to gain leadership skills for future advancement and personal growth will be admitted on a space-available basis. The maximum number of participants will be 20.

xx:Ch 18, Ex 09

CHAPTER SUMMARY

- A *macro* is a document containing recorded commands. This document can be played back at any time to accomplish a task automatically.
- When creating a macro, known as *recording*, all commands and keystrokes pressed are stored in a macro document to be played back later.
- By default, a macro document is saved in the *c:\Corel\Office7\Macros\WPWin* folder. This can be changed at the Files Preferences dialog box.
- A macro name can be up to 255 characters. A macro can also be named with the Ctrl key plus a letter of the alphabet, or the Ctrl key and the Shift key plus a letter of the alphabet. The macro extension, *.wcm*, is added automatically.
- Macros can be played once or several times anywhere in a document from the Play Macro dialog box. To play a macro named with the Ctrl key, hold down the Ctrl key, then press the letter you assigned to the macro. To play a macro named with the Ctrl and Shift keys, hold down the Ctrl key and the Shift key and then press the letter you assigned to the macro.
- To change a macro, it must be either replaced or edited.
- While recording a macro, it can be paused to allow keyboard entry.
- A macro is deleted in the same manner as a regular document.
- WordPerfect includes a variety of prerecorded macros that can be used to automate certain features.
- A number of template documents are provided by WordPerfect that can be used to produce a variety of creative documents.
- The default template document is the main template.

COMMANDS REVIEW

	Mouse/Keyboard
Files Preferences dialog box	Edit, Preferences, Files
Macro Tools Toolbar	Position arrow pointer on current Toolbar, click the right mouse button, then click Macro Tools
Record Macro dialog box	Tools, Macro, Record; or click the Record button on the Macro Tools Toolbar
Play Macro dialog box	Tools, Macro, Play; or click the Play button on the Macro Tools Toolbar
Edit Macro dialog box	Tools, Macro, Edit; or click the Edit Macro button on the Macro Tools Toolbar
Pause during macro recording	Tools, Macro, Pause twice; or click twice on the Pause button on the Macro Tools Toolbar
New Document dialog box	File, New; or click the New Document button on the Toolbar

CHECK YOUR UNDERSTANDING

Completion: In the space provided at the right, indicate the correct term, command, or number.

1. This toolbar includes buttons for preparing macros such as the Record and the Play buttons. _____

2. A macro can be named with the Ctrl key plus a letter as well as the Ctrl key plus this key and a letter. _____

3. Change the location of macro documents at this dialog box with the Merge/Macro tab selected. _____

4. WordPerfect automatically adds this extension to a macro name. _____

5. Use this prerecorded WordPerfect macro to insert a watermark in a document. _____

6. Click this button on the Toolbar to display the Select New Document dialog box. _____

7. Select a type of template in this list box at the Select New Document dialog box. _____

8. This is the name of the default template document. _____

List the steps that are necessary to use the mouse to record a macro that changes the top margin to 2 inches. Name the macro *Top2*.

_____
_____
_____
_____
_____

List the steps that are necessary to use the mouse to play the *Top2* macro recorded above.

_____
_____
_____
_____
_____

Formatting with Macros and Templates 407

SKILL ASSESSMENTS

Assessment 1

1. At a clear editing window, record the following macros:
   a. Record a macro named *Pgnum* that numbers pages at the bottom center of the page.
   b. Record a macro named *HeadB* that selects text, then changes the Relative si<u>z</u>e to <u>L</u>arge.
   c. Record a macro named *Csb12* that changes the font to 12-point Century Schoolbook.
2. Close the document without saving it.

Assessment 2

1. At a clear editing window, open Report 01.
2. Save the document with Save As and name it Ch 18, SA 02.
3. With the insertion point positioned at the beginning of the document play the following macros:
   a. *Csb12*
   b. *Ctrlsftm*
   c. *Pgnum*
4. Position the insertion point on the *T* in TRENDS IN TELECOMMUNICATIONS, then play the *HeadA* macro.
5. Position the insertion point on the *C* in *Continued Growth of Photonics (Fiber Optics)*, then play the *HeadB* macro.
6. Position the insertion point on the *M* in *Microcomputer Trends in the Nineties*, then play the *HeadB* macro.
7. Save the document again with the same name (Ch 18, SA 02).
8. Print and then close Ch 18, SA 02.

Assessment 3

1. At a clear editing window, replace the *HeadA* macro so it selects text, changes the selected text to 16-point Arial, then turns off Select.
2. Replace the *HeadB* macro so it selects text, changes the selected text to 14-point Arial, then turns off Select.
3. Replace the *Pgnum* macro so page numbers are inserted at the bottom right corner of the page.
4. Close the document without saving it.

Assessment 4

1. At a clear editing window, open Report 08.
2. Save the document with Save As and name it Ch 18, SA 04.
3. With the insertion point positioned at the beginning of the document, play the following macros:
   a. *Csb12*
   b. *Ctrlsftm*
   c. *Pgnum*
4. Position the insertion point on the *I* in IDENTIFICATION OF CI, then play the *HeadA* macro.

5. Play the *HeadB* macro for each of the following headings:
    Introduction
    Purpose and Scope
    Application
    Requirements
6. Save the document again with the same name (Ch 18, SA 04).
7. Print and then close Ch 18, SA 04.

Assessment 5

1. At a clear editing window, create a sign using a template document by completing the following steps:
    a. Display the Select New Document dialog box.
    b. Click *Publish* in the Group list, then double-click *Sign - Seminar announcement* in the Select template list box.
    c. At the Template Information dialog box, key the following text in the specified field:

Title of seminar	=	Managing Stress on the Job
Sponsored by	=	Denver Memorial Hospital
Name of speaker	=	Jillian Youngblood
Speaker title	=	Trainer
Speaker organization	=	ROM Corporation
Date of seminar	=	Wednesday, March 18, 1998
Location of seminar	=	Room 234, East Wing
Telephone # for information	=	(303) 555-4428

    d. After keying the information at the Template Information dialog box, click OK.
2. When the sign is completed, save it and name it Ch 18, SA 05.
3. Print and then close Ch 18, SA 05.

19

INSERTING GRAPHICS IMAGES

PERFORMANCE OBJECTIVE

Upon successful completion of chapter 19, you will be able to insert graphics images in a document and insert tables, text, or art images inside boxes.

With WordPerfect's Graphics feature, you can insert graphics images into a document as well as create 10 different graphics boxes including text, figure, table, user, equation, button, watermark, inline equations, OLE 2.0 box, and inline text boxes. In each of these boxes, you can insert such items as graphics elements, equations, text, or statistical data. Each graphics box has a different border style.

You can insert what you want into any style of graphics box. Generally, however, insert text or quotes in a text box; images, logos, or drawings in a figure box; a table, spreadsheet, or statistical data in a table box; whatever is not addressed by the other seven in a user box; mathematical, scientific, or business equations in an equation box; a keystroke, function key, or icon in a button box; an image that is printed behind text in a watermark box; and an equation or expression in a line of text in an inline equation box. An inline text box is similar to an inline equation box in that text is inserted in a box in a line of text just like any other character in the line. Data from other programs can be inserted into an OLE box. OLE is an acronym for Object Linking and Embedding. When an object is inserted into WordPerfect using OLE, the data is linked to the original source. If the data is modified in the original source program, the object is updated automatically in WordPerfect.

In this chapter, you will learn how to create text, figure, table, user, and button boxes as well as watermark images. The equation and inline equation and text boxes are covered in the next chapter. For more information on OLE objects, refer to WordPerfect's help system.

Inserting an Image into a Document

The WordPerfect program includes several predesigned graphics images that are included when WordPerfect is installed. A partial display of these images and their names are included in Appendix C. You will be using some of these predesigned images in this chapter. You can insert one of the graphics images into a document, or you can retrieve a graphics image created in a different program. In this chapter, you will be using the images provided by WordPerfect.

WordPerfect provides a Graphics Toolbar that contains buttons for creating and editing graphics elements. To display the Graphics Toolbar, position the arrow pointer on the current Toolbar, click the right mouse button, then click Graphics at the drop-down menu.

An image can be inserted in a document. To do this, you would complete the following steps:

1. Position the insertion point where you want the image to appear.
2. Click Graphics, then Image; or click the Image button on the Graphics Toolbar.
3. At the Insert Image dialog box shown in figure 19.1, double-click the desired image in the list box.

Image

Figure 19.1

Insert Image Dialog Box

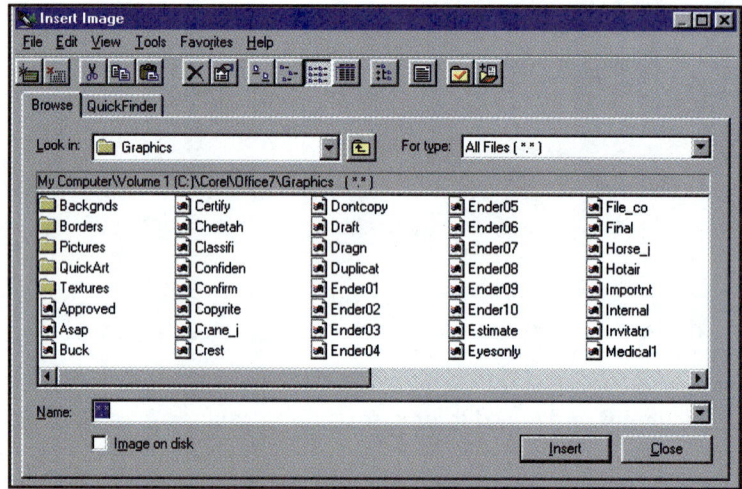

When a graphics image is inserted in a document, it displays at the left margin. The width and the height of the image will vary depending on the image. There is no border surrounding an image.

EXERCISE 1

Inserting a Predesigned Image

1. At a clear editing window, display the Graphics Toolbar by completing the following steps. (If the Graphics Toolbar is already displayed, skip this step.)
   a. Position the arrow pointer on the current Toolbar, then click the right mouse button.
   b. At the drop-down menu that displays, click Graphics.
2. At a clear editing window, insert the image named *Ender01* by completing the following steps:
   a. Click Graphics, then Image; or click the Image button on the Graphics Toolbar (ninth button from the right).
   b. At the Insert Image dialog box, double-click *Ender01* in the list box.
   c. Click in the editing window outside the image box to deselect it.
3. Save the document and name it Ch 19, Ex 01.
4. Print and then close Ch 19, Ex 01.

Chapter 19

Creating a Text Box

Generally, you create a text box for quotes or other special text to be set off from regular text in a document. When a text box is created, it displays with a thick top and bottom line and no left and right lines as a border. Graphics boxes display with different borders. For example, a figure box displays with a single line border on all sides while a user box displays with no border lines.

To create a text box, click Graphics, then Text Box; or click the Text Box button on the Graphics Toolbar. A text box is inserted in the document with the insertion point positioned inside the box as shown in figure 19.2.

Text Box

Figure 19.2

Text Box

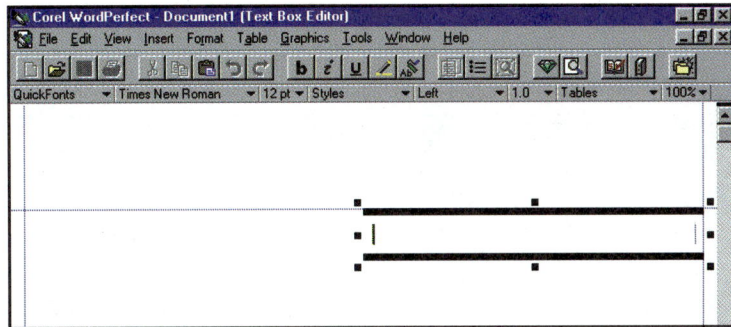

You can key up to one page of text in a text box and can format the text in the normal manner. For example, you can turn on bold or underlining, change the font, or change the justification of paragraphs.

A text box is inserted at the right margin at the location of the insertion point. The width of the text box is approximately one-half the distance between the left and right margins. If the left and right margins are set at the default of 1 inch, the text box width will be approximately 3.25 inches. The height of the text box depends on the amount of text entered in the box. The box expands to include the text (up to one page).

EXERCISE 2

Creating a Text Box

1. At a clear editing window, create a text box containing the text DENVER MEMORIAL HOSPITAL, bold and centered, by completing the following steps:
   a. Click Graphics, then Text Box; or click the Text Box button on the Graphics Toolbar (eighth button from the right).
   b. With the insertion point located inside the text box, complete the following steps:
      (1) Press Enter three times.
      (2) Press Shift + F7 to access the Center command.
      (3) Press Ctrl + B to turn on bold.
      (4) Key **DENVER MEMORIAL HOSPITAL**.
      (5) Press Ctrl + B to turn off bold.

Inserting Graphics Images

> (6) Press Enter three times.
> (7) Click in the editing window outside the text box to deselect it.
> 2. Save the document and name it Ch 19, Ex 02.
> 3. Print and then close Ch 19, Ex 02.

Creating a Figure Box

Custom Box

A figure box is generally created for an image, logo, or drawing. To create a figure box with a graphics image inside, you would click Graphics, then Custom Box; or click the Custom Box button on the Graphics Toolbar. At the Custom Box dialog box shown in figure 19.3, double-click *Figure* in the Style name list box.

Figure 19.3

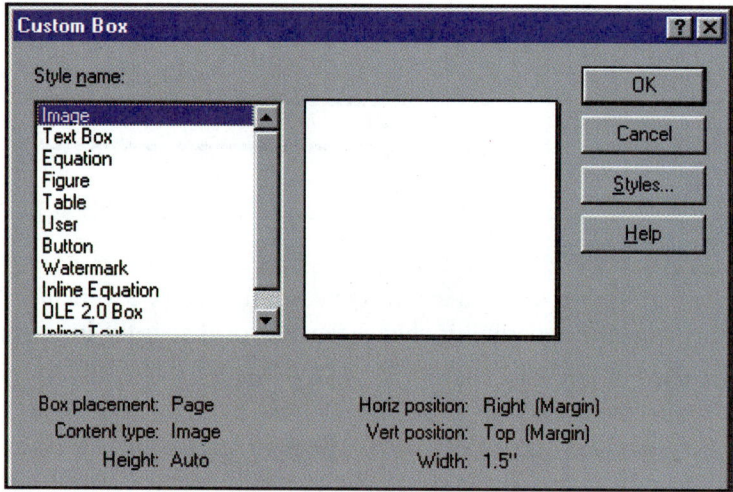

Custom Box Dialog Box

The default border for a figure box is a single line on each side of the box. The figure box is inserted in the document at the right margin and at the vertical location of the insertion point. If the left and right margins are set at the default of 1 inch, a figure box width will be approximately 3.25 inches. The height of the figure box will vary depending on what is inserted inside the box and how far down the page the insertion point is located.

Edit Box

To insert an image in a figure box, click the Edit Box button on the Graphics Toolbar. This causes the Edit Box dialog box to display as shown in figure 19.4. Another method for displaying the Edit Box dialog box is to click in the editing window outside the empty Figure box to deselect it, then move the arrow pointer over the empty figure box. This causes a QuickSpot button to display in the upper left corner of the figure box. Click the QuickSpot button and the Edit Box dialog box will display.

Figure 19.4
Edit Box Dialog Box

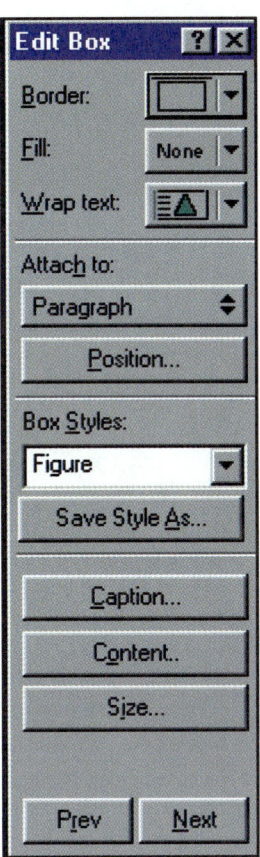

To insert a graphics image in the figure box, click the Content button on the Edit Box dialog box. This displays the Box Content dialog box. At this dialog box, click the folder icon to the right of the Filename text box. At the Insert Image dialog box that displays, double-click the desired image in the list box. Click OK to close the Box Content dialog box and then click the Close button at the right side of the Edit Box dialog box Title bar.

EXERCISE 3

Creating a Figure Box

1. At a clear editing window, insert the graphics image named *Crane_j* in a figure box by completing the following steps:
    a. Click Graphics, then Custom Box; or click the Custom Box button on the Graphics Toolbar.
    b. At the Custom Box dialog box, double-click *Figure* in the Style name list box.
    c. Click in the editing window outside the empty Figure box to deselect it.
    d. Move the arrow pointer over the empty figure box until the QuickSpot displays in the upper left corner of the figure box, then click the QuickSpot.
    e. At the Edit Box dialog box (see figure 19.4), click the Content button.

Inserting Graphics Images — **415**

      f. At the Box Content dialog box, click the folder icon to the right of the <u>F</u>ilename text box.
      g. At the Insert Image dialog box, double-click *Crane_j*.
      h. Click OK to close the Box Content dialog box.
      i. Click the Close button on the Edit Box dialog box Title bar. (Make sure the image is deselected. If not, click outside the image to deselect it.)
2. After the image is inserted in the document, press the Enter key until the insertion point reaches Line 3.75", then insert the graphics image named *Hotair* in a figure box by completing steps similar to those in steps 1a through 1i.
3. After the image is inserted in the document, press the Enter key until the insertion point reaches Line 6.51", then insert the graphics image named *Dragn* in a figure box by completing steps similar to those in steps 1a through 1i.
4. Click the Page/Zoom Full button to display the entire page. After viewing the images on the page, click the Page/Zoom Full button again to return to the default view. (The Page/Zoom Full button is located on the WordPerfect 7 Toolbar. If you have the Graphics Toolbar displayed, consider changing to the Two Page viewing mode instead of using the Page/Zoom Full button.)
5. Save the document and name it Ch 19, Ex 03.
6. Print and then close Ch 19, Ex 03.

Creating a Table Box

A table box is generally created for a table, spreadsheet, or statistical data. You can insert a previously created document into a table box or key text directly into the table box. To create a table box and insert the contents of a previously created document into the box, you would display the Custom Box dialog box, then double-click *Table* in the Style <u>n</u>ame list box. Display the Edit Box dialog box by clicking the Edit Box button on the Graphics Toolbar or clicking the QuickSpot button. At the Edit Box dialog box, click the C<u>o</u>ntent button. At the Box Content dialog box, key the name of the document you want inserted in the table box, and then click OK or press Enter.

EXERCISE 4

Inserting a Document into a Table Box

1. At a clear editing window, create a table box and insert the document *Block 01* into the box by completing the following steps:
    a. Click <u>G</u>raphics, then <u>C</u>ustom Box; or click the Custom Box button on the Graphics Toolbar.
    b. At the Custom Box dialog box, double-click *Table* in the Style <u>n</u>ame list box.
    c. Click the Edit Box button on the Graphics Toolbar. (If the Graphics Toolbar is not displayed, position the arrow pointer on the current toolbar, click the right mouse button, then click *Graphics* at the drop-down menu.)
    d. At the Edit Box dialog box, click the C<u>o</u>ntent button.
    e. At the Box Content dialog box, click in the <u>F</u>ilename text box, then key **Block 01.wpd** (you must include the file extension *.wpd*).
    f. Click OK or press Enter.

g. Click the Close button at the right side of the Edit Box Title bar to close the dialog box.
h. Click in the editing window outside the table box to deselect it.
2. Click the Page/Zoom Full button (or change to the Two Page viewing mode) to display the entire page. After viewing the table box on the page, return to the default view.
3. Save the document and name it Ch 19, Ex 04.
4. Print and then close Ch 19, Ex 04.

Like a text box, a table box has a thick top and bottom border and no left or right borders. A table box is one-half the distance between the left and right margins and is inserted at the right margin. If the left and right margins are set at the default of 1 inch, the table box width will be approximately 3.25 inches. The height of the table box depends on what is inserted in the table.

Creating a User Box

A variety of boxes can be created for different situations. It does not matter what you insert inside a box. You can insert text in a figure box or a graphics image in a text box. The reason WordPerfect offers the variety of boxes it does is to provide different border and fill styles. Additionally, you can use different boxes within the same document to keep information organized.

A user box can be created for any particular situation. A user box does not have any borders. It is inserted at the right margin and is approximately 3.25 inches wide. You can insert a previously created document into a user box or key text directly into the box. You can also insert a graphics image into a user box.

EXERCISE 5

Inserting a Document into a User Box

1. At a clear editing window, create a user box and insert the document *Notice 01* into the box by completing the following steps:
    a. Click Graphics, then Custom Box; or click the Custom Box button on the Graphics Toolbar.
    b. At the Custom Box dialog box, double-click *User* in the Style name list box.
    c. Click the Edit Box button on the Graphics Toolbar.
    d. At the Edit Box dialog box, click the Content button.
    e. At the Box Content dialog box, click in the Filename text box, then key **Notice 01.wpd** (you must include the file extension *.wpd*).
    f. Click OK or press Enter to close the dialog box.
    g. Click the Close button that displays at the right side of the Edit Box dialog box Title bar to close the dialog box.
    h. Click in the editing window outside the table box to deselect it.
2. Click the Page/Zoom Full button (or change to the Two Page viewing mode) to display the entire page. After viewing the user box on the page, return to the default view.
3. Save the document and name it Ch 19, Ex 05.
4. Print and then close Ch 19, Ex 05.

Inserting Graphics Images   417

Creating a Button Box

A button box can be created for items such as a keystroke, function key, or an icon. Unlike text, figure, table, and user boxes, a button box is inserted at the left margin at the location where the insertion point is positioned and is approximately 1 inch wide. Figure 19.5 displays a sample button box. This option is available at the Custom Box dialog box. Exercise 6 shows you how to add text to a button box.

Figure 19.5

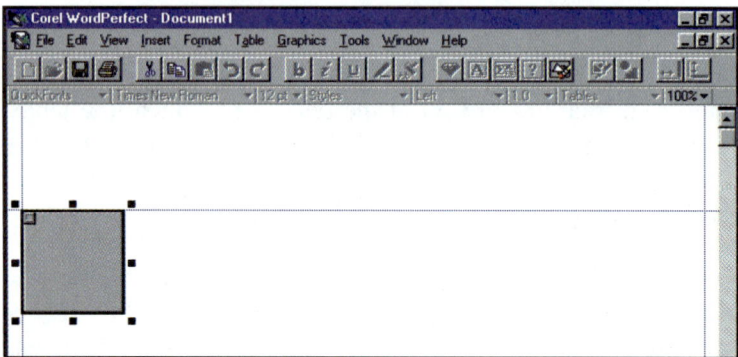

Button Box

EXERCISE 6

Adding Button Boxes to a Memo

1. At a clear editing window, key the top portion of the memo shown in figure 19.6 in an appropriate memo format. After keying the first paragraph of the memo, press Enter twice, then create the button boxes and text by completing the following steps:
    a. Press the Tab key once.
    b. Click Graphics, then Custom Box; or click the Custom Box button on the Graphics Toolbar.
    c. At the Custom Box dialog box, double-click *Button* in the Style name list box.
    d. Click the Edit Box button on the Graphics Toolbar to display the Edit Box dialog box.
    e. At the Edit Box dialog box, click the Content button.
    f. At the Box Content dialog box, click the Content box (displays with the word *Empty*), then click Text at the drop-down menu.
    g. Click the Edit button that displays at the right side of the Box Content dialog box. (This causes the insertion point to move into the button box.)
    h. With the insertion point positioned in the button box, complete the following steps:
        (1) Change the font size to 10 points.
        (2) Press Shift + F7 to move the insertion point to the horizontal center of the button box.
        (3) Key **Position**.
    i. Click the Close button that displays at the right side of the Edit Box dialog box Title bar to close the dialog box.

    j. Click in the editing window to the right of the button box to deselect it.

    k. Press the Tab key once, then key the equal sign (=). (The insertion point will display as large as the height of the button box. This is normal and does not mean that the text you key will be as large as the insertion point.)

    l. Press the Tab key once, then key the text after the Position button as shown in figure 19.6.

    m. Press Enter twice, then create the remaining buttons and text following steps similar to those in 1a through 1l.

2. After creating the last button box and the text after the button box, press Enter twice, then key the last paragraph and reference initials and document name for the memo.
3. When the memo is completed, save it and name it Ch 19, Ex 06.
4. Print and then close Ch 19, Ex 06.

Figure 19.6

DATE: April 3, 1998; TO: Newsletter Staff; FROM: Tonya Lowe, Editor; SUBJECT: GRAPHICS IN WORDPERFECT

One of the reasons we upgraded to Corel WordPerfect 7 was for the expanded graphics capabilities. As we learn to use this new version, I would encourage you all to experiment with buttons in the Edit Box dialog box. Some of the buttons available in the Edit Box dialog box include the following:

    [Position]   =   Position the box horizontally and vertically.

    [Caption]   =   Create a caption for the box.

    [Content]   =   Determine the contents of the box.

    [Size]   =   Determine width and height of the box.

A training session has been planned for early next month. I will contact all of you before the training to find out your specific needs.

xx:Ch 19, Ex 06

Inserting Graphics Images   **419**

Creating a Watermark

A watermark is a lightened image that displays on the entire page. Text can be inserted on top of the watermark creating a document with a foreground and a background. The foreground is the text and the background is the watermark image. Figure 19.7 shows an example of a document containing a watermark image. Watermark is another option available at the Custom Box dialog box. The steps to create a watermark are described in exercise 7.

Figure 19.7

Watermark Image

Important!!
All First-Year Residents
Operating Room Protocol
May 6, 1998
1:30 p.m. to 5:00 p.m.
Operating Room 3

EXERCISE 7

Inserting a Watermark Image

1. At a clear editing window, open Letter 04.
2. Save the document with Save As and name it Ch 19, Ex 07.
3. Create a watermark image with the document named *Tiger_j* by completing the following steps:
    a. Click Graphics, then Custom Box; or click the Custom Box button on the Graphics Toolbar.
    b. At the Custom Box dialog box, double-click *Watermark* in the Style name list box.
    c. Display the Edit Box dialog box.
    d. Click the Content button at the Edit Box dialog box.
    e. At the Box Content dialog box, click the file folder icon to the right of the Filename text box. This causes the Insert Image dialog box to display.
    f. At the Insert Image dialog box, double-click *Tiger_j*.
    g. At the Box Content dialog box, click OK.

    h. Close the Edit Box dialog box.
4. Save the document again with the same name (Ch 19, Ex 07).
5. Click the Page/Zoom Full button (or change to the Two Page viewing mode) to display the entire page. After viewing the watermark on the page, return to the default view.
6. Print and then close Ch 19, Ex 07.

Editing a Box

If you have closed the Edit Box dialog box and then want to redisplay it, simply move the arrow pointer over the box until the QuickSpot button appears, then click the button. The options available at the Edit Box dialog box can be used to edit the box. The same editing options are available when you click the *right* mouse button inside an image or a box.

Creating a Caption

A caption can be created for a box that displays information such as the box number and a description of the box contents. WordPerfect includes a default caption for each type of box as shown in figure 19.8.

Figure 19.8

Default Box Captions

Text box	=	1
Figure box	=	**Figure 1**
Table box	=	**Table 1**
User box	=	1
Button box	=	(Not applicable)
Watermark	=	(Not applicable)

    To create a caption, click the Caption button at the Edit Box dialog box. When you click the Caption button, the Box Caption dialog box shown in figure 19.9 displays. You can also display the Box Caption dialog box by positioning the arrow pointer on the graphics box, clicking the *right* mouse button, then clicking Caption at the shortcut menu.

Figure 19.9 Box Caption Dialog Box

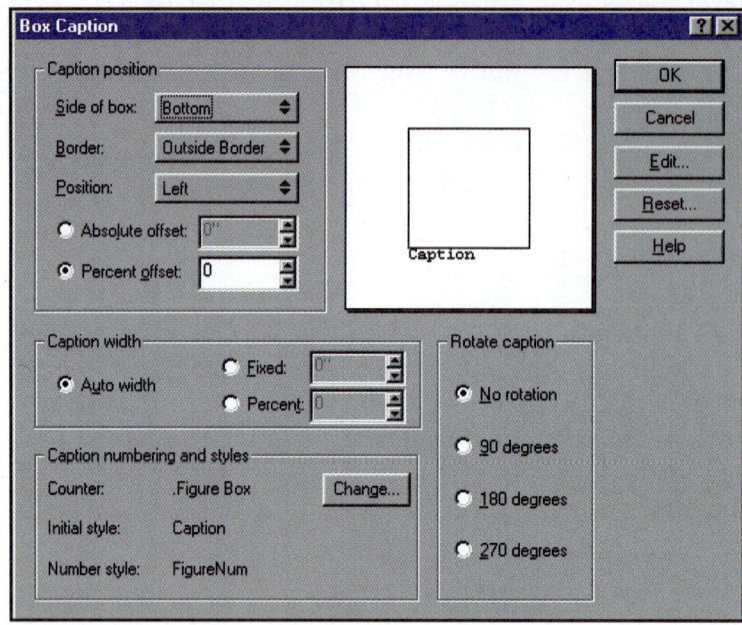

By default, a caption will display and print at the bottom of a figure box, outside the border, and at the left side. Default settings for text, table, and user boxes vary. These default settings for options in the Caption position section of the Box Caption dialog box can be changed.

With the Side of box option, you can insert the caption at the Left, Right, Top, or Bottom of the box. The Border option has a default setting of Outside Border. This can be changed to Inside Border. With the Position option, you can determine whether the caption is at the Left side of the border, the Right, or the Center.

The Absolute offset option from the Box Caption dialog box lets you specify the distance you want to shift the caption from its position. With the Percent offset option, you can specify the percentage distance (0 to 100) that you want to shift the caption text from its position.

WordPerfect automatically determines the width of the caption. If you want to specify the width of the caption, click Fixed to specify a measurement or click Percent to specify a percentage.

Each type of box has a different default caption. If you would like to use a different caption type for a box, click Change in the Caption numbering and styles section of the Box Caption dialog box.

With options in the Rotate caption section of the Box Caption dialog box, you can rotate a caption 90 degrees, 180 degrees, 270 degrees, or stay at the default setting of No rotation.

If you click the Edit command button at the right side of the Box Caption dialog box, the box in the document displays with the insertion point positioned in the caption. Edit the caption as desired. For example, you can add a descriptive name to the caption, turn on formatting such as italics or bold, and delete or change the caption.

If you make changes to options at the Box Caption dialog box and then want to return to the default settings, click Reset. When you click Reset, WordPerfect inserts the message, *Resetting caption to box style defaults will delete caption.* At this message, click OK.

EXERCISE 8

Creating Captions for Figure Boxes

1. At a clear editing window, open Ch 19, Ex 03.
2. Save the document with Save As and name it Ch 19, Ex 08.
3. Create a caption for the figure box containing the image of the crane and position the caption at the left side of the box and rotated 90 degrees by completing the following steps:
   a. Position the arrow pointer inside the figure box containing the image of the crane, click the *right* mouse button, then click Caption.
   b. At the Box Caption dialog box, click Side of box, then Left.
   c. Click 90 Degrees.
   d. Click Edit.
   e. At the caption editing window, complete the following steps:
      (1) Position the insertion point after the *1* in *Figure 1*.
      (2) Press Ctrl + B to turn on bold.
      (3) Key a colon (:).
      (4) Press the space bar once.
      (5) Key **Crane**.
      (6) Click Close.
4. Create a caption for the second figure box (the one containing the image of the hot air balloons) that reads *Balloons* by completing steps similar to those in steps 3a through 3e.
5. Create a caption for the third figure box (the one containing the image of the dragon) that reads *Dragon* by completing steps similar to those in steps 3a through 3e.
6. Save the document again with the same name (Ch 19, Ex 08).
7. Print and then close Ch 19, Ex 08.

Changing Content Options

If you click the Content button at the Edit Box dialog box or position the arrow pointer on a graphics box, click the *right* mouse button, then click Content at the shortcut menu, the Box Content dialog box shown in figure 19.10 displays. At this dialog box you can change the box contents.

Figure 19.10

Box Content Dialog Box

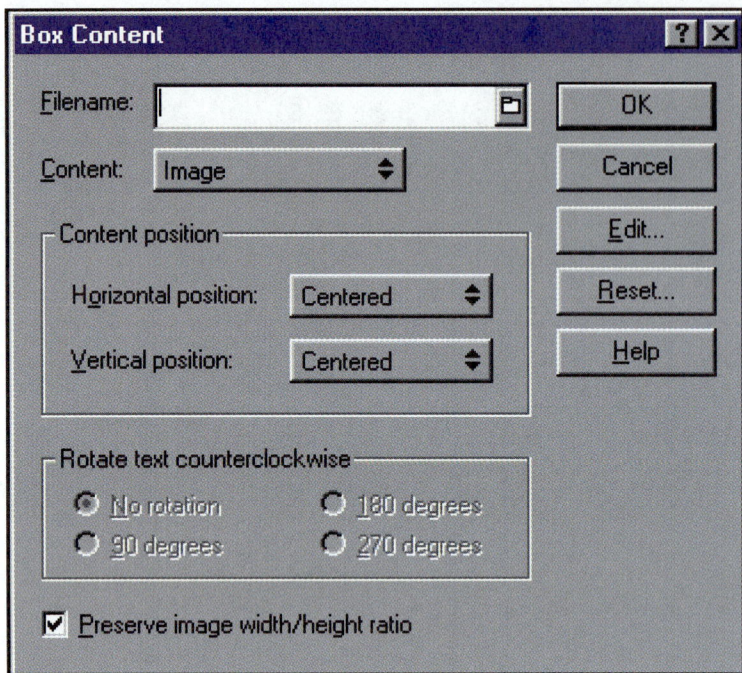

With the Filename option, you can key a document name to be inserted in the box or click the file folder icon at the right of the text box to display a list of graphics images. As mentioned earlier, WordPerfect provides several predesigned graphics images that can be inserted in a box.

When you click Content at the Box Content dialog box, a drop-down menu displays with the options Empty, Image, Text, Equation, and Image on Disk. If you have not inserted anything in the box, the word Empty displays in the Content text box. If you have inserted an image, the word Image displays in the text box. Click Text from the Content drop-down menu if you want to insert text inside a box, Equation if you want to insert an equation, or Image on Disk if you want to insert an image that is located on a disk.

With the Horizontal position option in the Content position section of the Box Content dialog box, you can move the contents of the box Left, Right, or leave it at the default of Centered. With the Vertical position option, you can move the contents of a box to the Top, Bottom, or leave it at the default of Centered.

With the options in the Rotate text counterclockwise section of the Box Content dialog box, you can rotate the contents of the box. At the default setting of No Rotation, the contents of the box display as normal. If you click 90 Degrees, the contents of the box rotate a quarter turn. Clicking 180 Degrees causes the contents of the box to turn upside down. The 270 Degree option causes the contents of the box to rotate three quarters of a turn. (If you rotate the contents of a box, the contents will print properly if you have a printer that can print landscape and portrait text on the same page. Check with your instructor or your printer manual to see if your printer is capable of this.)

Click Preserve image width/height ratio if you have made changes to the image within a box and want to preserve the width and height ratio of the image. Remove the check mark from this option if you do not want to preserve the ratio.

Use the Edit button at the right side of the Box Content dialog box to add text to a box or edit an image. If the box contains an image and you click Edit, WordPerfect's Draw screen is displayed. The Draw program is discussed in chapter 21.

If you click the Reset button at the right side of the box, WordPerfect will display the message *Resetting content to box style defaults will delete content.* At this message click OK or Cancel.

Changing the Box Position

If you click the Position button at the Edit Box dialog box or position the arrow pointer on a graphics box, click the *right* mouse button, then click Position, the Box Position dialog box shown in figure 19.11 displays.

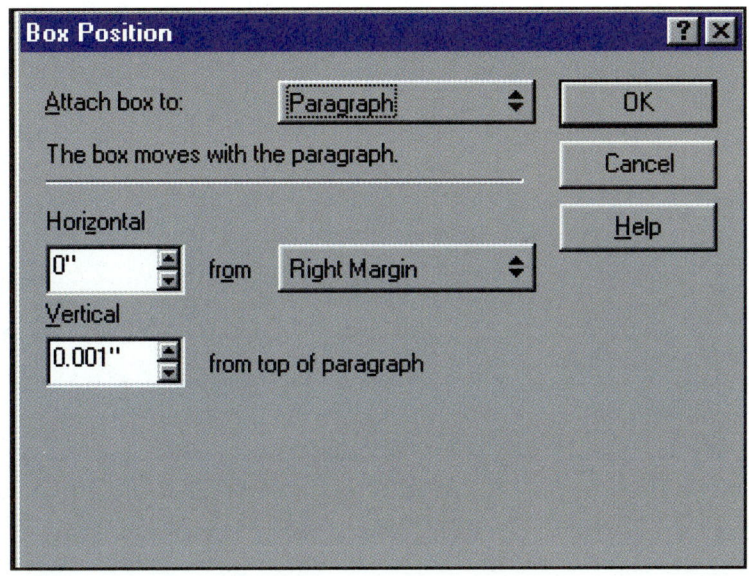

Figure 19.11

Box Position Dialog Box

With options in the Attach box to section of the Box Position dialog box, you can determine where the box is anchored. The default option is determined by the type of box. For example, a figure box is anchored in the current paragraph. The default setting for a figure box is Attach box to Paragraph. Table, text, and user boxes are also attached to the current paragraph.

The button box is attached to a character. The default setting for a button box is Attach box to Character. A watermark is attached to a page. The default setting for a watermark is Attach box to Page.

When a box is attached to a paragraph, the box stays with the paragraph even if text is inserted or deleted. The graphics box is positioned vertically relative to the beginning of the paragraph.

If a box is attached to a character, the box is anchored to a character position and the box is treated like a character in the text line. When text is added before the box, the box moves from left to right as any text character would.

The remaining options in the Box Position dialog box will change depending on the setting selected in the Attach box to option.

If a box is attached at the paragraph, you can specify the horizontal position of the box from the Left Edge of Page, Left Margin, Right Margin, or Center of Paragraph. You can also specify the vertical distance of the box from the top of the paragraph.

If a box is attached to a character, you can specify whether the box is anchored at the Top of the text line, Centered in the text line, at the Bottom of the text line, or at the Content Baseline. WordPerfect displays examples of each option. The character box, by default, will change the text line height. If you do not want the text line height changed, remove the check mark from the Box changes text line height check box.

If a box is attached to a page, you can specify the horizontal position of the box from the Left Edge of Page, Left Margin, Right Margin, Center of Margins, Left Column, Right Column, or Centered in Columns. You can also specify the vertical distance of the box from the Top of Page, Top Margin, Bottom Margin, or Center of Margins. Across columns allows you to span the box across columnar text. This option becomes available after you select a Horizontal position of Left Column, Right Column, or Centered in Columns. Use the Box stays on page option to specify whether the Box stays on that page or moves from page to page with surrounding text.

EXERCISE 9

Manipulating Text Box Elements

1. At a clear editing window, create a text box centered on the page by completing the following steps:
   a. Click the Text Box button on the Graphics Toolbar.
   b. Click outside the text box, move the arrow pointer back inside the text box, then click the QuickSpot button.
   c. Click the Content button at the Edit Box dialog box.
   d. At the Box Content dialog box, position the arrow pointer inside the Filename text box, then click the left mouse button.
   e. Key **Block 02.wpd**, then press the Enter key.
   f. At the *Insert file into box?* question, click Yes.
   g. Click the Position button at the Edit Box dialog box.
   h. At the Box Position dialog box, change the Attach box to setting to Page.
   i. Click the box below and to the right of the Horizontal option (the box containing the words *Right Margin*), then click Center of Margins at the pop-up list.
   j. Click the box below and to the right of the Vertical option (the box containing the words *Top Margin*), then click Center of Margins at the pop-up list.
   k. Click the OK button at the upper right side of the dialog box.
   l. Close the Edit Box dialog box.
2. Save the document and name it Ch 19, Ex 09.
3. Print and then close Ch 19, Ex 09.

Changing the Box Size

By default, figure, text, and table graphics boxes are one-half the width of the text line. For example, if the left and right margins are set at 1 inch, the graphics box is 3.25 inches wide (one-half the measurement of the text line). The height of the graphics box is automatically determined by WordPerfect. The height changes depending on what is inserted in the box.

The box size can be changed with options at the Box Size dialog box shown in figure 19.12. To display this dialog box, click the Size button at the Edit Box dialog box, or position the arrow pointer in a graphics box, click the *right* mouse button, then click Size at the shortcut menu.

Box Size Dialog Box

Figure 19.12

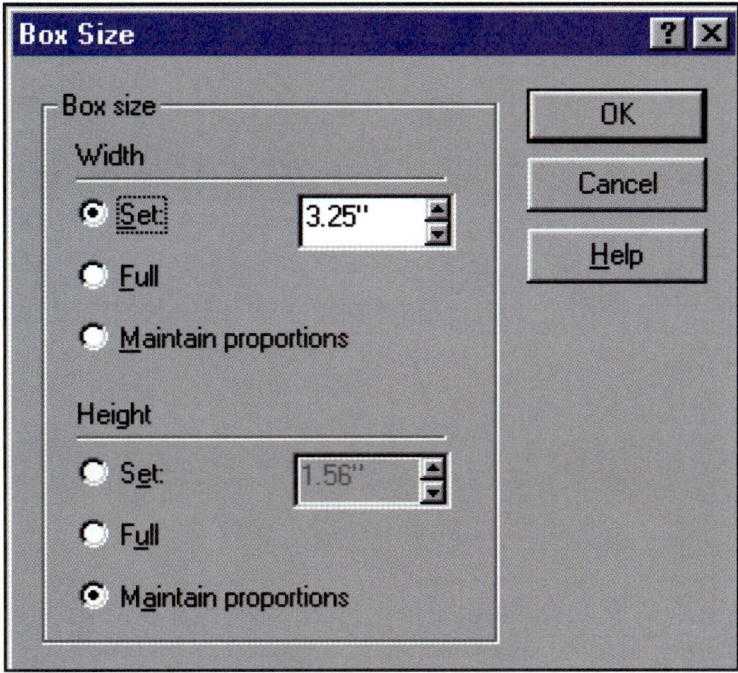

To change the width of a box, click Set, then key the width measurement. If you want the box to span the full width of the text line (from margin to margin) click Full. If you want WordPerfect to size the width of the box based on the height of the box, click Maintain proportions.

To change the height of a box, click Set, then key the height measurement. If you want the box to span the full length of the page (from top to bottom margin), click Full. If you want WordPerfect to size the height of the box based on the width of the box, click Maintain proportions.

EXERCISE

Editing a Figure Box and Adding a Caption

1. At a clear editing window, create a figure box with the image *Buck* inserted in the box, change the size of the box, and add a caption by completing the following steps:
   a. Click the Custom Box button on the Graphics Toolbar.
   b. At the Custom Box dialog box, double-click *Figure* in the Style name list box.
   c. Display the Edit Box dialog box.
   d. Click the Content button at the Edit Box dialog box.
   e. At the Box Content dialog box, click the file folder icon to the right of the Filename text box.
   f. At the Insert Image dialog box double-click *Buck*.
   g. Click OK at the Box Content dialog box.
   h. Click the Position button at the Edit Box dialog box.
   i. At the Box Position dialog box, change the Attach box to setting to Page.
   j. Click OK.

Inserting Graphics Images   427

k. Click the Size button at the Edit Box dialog box.
l. At the Box Size dialog box, click the Full option in the Width section.
m. Click the Full option in the Height section.
n. Click OK.
o. Click the Caption button at the Edit Box dialog box.
p. At the Box Caption dialog box, click Edit.
q. Key **Deer** bolded and separated from *Figure 1* by a colon and one space.
r. Close the Edit Box dialog box.
2. Save the document and name it Ch 19, Ex 10.
3. Print and then close Ch 19, Ex 10.

EXERCISE 11

Creating and Editing a User Box

1. At a clear editing window, create a user box with a border image, then change the box anchor and size by completing the following steps:
    a. Click the Custom Box button on the Graphics Toolbar.
    b. At the Custom Box dialog box, double-click *User* in the Style name list box.
    c. Display the Edit Box dialog box.
    d. Click the Content button at the Edit Box dialog box.
    e. Click the file folder icon to the right of the Filename text box.
    f. At the Insert Image dialog box, double-click the folder named *Borders* that displays toward the beginning of the list box.
    g. Double-click *Bord01p* in the list of border images.
    h. At the Box Content dialog box, click OK.
    i. Click the Position button at the Edit Box dialog box.
    j. At the Box Position dialog box, change the Attach box to setting to Page.
    k. Click OK.
    l. Click the Size button at the Edit Box dialog box.
    m. At the Box Size dialog box, click the Full option in the Width section.
    n. Click the Full option in the Height section.
    o. Click OK.
    p. Close the Edit Box dialog box.
2. Click the Page/Zoom Full button (or change to the Two Page viewing mode) to display the entire page. After viewing the user box on the page, return to the default view.
3. Save the document and name it Ch 19, Ex 11.
4. Print and then close Ch 19, Ex 11.

Changing Box Border and Fill Styles

Graphics boxes have varying borders. For example, a figure box has a border of a single line on all sides and a text box has a thick top and bottom border and no left or right border. If you click the Border button at the Edit Box dialog box, a palette of border styles appears to the right of the Edit Box dialog box. At this palette, click the desired border style. If you click the Fill button at the Edit Box dialog box, a palette of fill styles appears to the right of the Edit Box dialog box. At this palette, click the desired fill style.

You can also change border fill at the Box Border/Fill dialog box shown in figure 19.13. To display this dialog box, position the arrow pointer on a graphics box, then click the *right* mouse button. At the shortcut menu that displays, click Border/Fill. At the Box Border/Fill dialog box, you can customize the border and the fill of a box.

Figure 19.13

Box Border/Fill Dialog Box

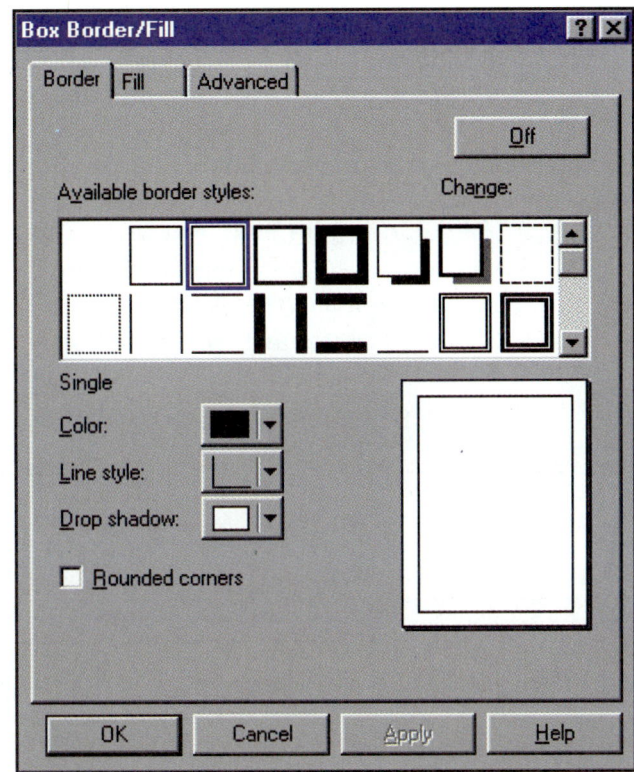

Changing Border Style: Click the Border tab at the Box Border/Fill dialog box and options display for changing the border style or using a customized style for the border. The Available border styles list box displays various border options such as double lines, dashed lines, and dotted lines. To choose an option, position the arrow pointer on the desired border option, then click the left mouse button. When you click an option, the name of the option displays immediately below the Available border styles list box.

When a change is made to the Available border styles option, the change is reflected in the Preview Box at the right side of the dialog box.

Adding Fill: Click the Fill tab at the Box Border/Fill dialog box and options will display for adding a fill to a box. WordPerfect provides a wide variety of fills including various shades of gray and designs and patterns such as Checkerboard, Chainlink, Fish Scale, Honeycomb, etc.

The Available fill styles list box contains a variety of fill styles. To choose an option, position the arrow pointer on the desired fill style, then click the left mouse button. When a fill style is selected, the Preview Box at the right side of the dialog box reflects the fill style.

Click the Advanced tab at the Box Border/Fill dialog box and options display for changing the color and spacing of lines in a border and adding a drop shadow.

Inserting Graphics Images   429

EXERCISE 12

Using Box Border and Fill Options

1. At a clear editing window, open Ch 19, Ex 03.
2. Save the document with Save As and name it Ch 19, Ex 12.
3. Change the border style to Double for the first figure box by completing the following steps:
   a. Position the arrow pointer inside the first figure box, click the *right* mouse button, then click Border/Fill at the shortcut menu.
   b. At the Box Border/Fill dialog box (with the Border tab selected), click the Double option that displays seventh from the left in the second row.
   c. Click OK.
4. Change the border style to a thick top and bottom line for the second figure box by completing steps similar to those in steps 3a through 3c. (Choose the Thick Top/Bottom option that displays fifth from the left in the second row.)
5. Change the border style to a shadow for the third figure box by completing steps similar to those in steps 3a through 3c. (Choose the Shadow option that displays sixth from the left in the first row [counting the first option, which is blank].)
6. Save the document again with the same name (Ch 19, Ex 12).
7. Print and then close Ch 19, Ex 12.

EXERCISE 13

More Practice with Borders and Fills

1. At a clear editing window, open Ch 19, Ex 10.
2. Save the document with Save As and name it Ch 19, Ex 13.
3. Change the border style to a thick/thin double line border and add fill by completing the following steps:
   a. Click the QuickSpot button that displays in the upper left corner of the box.
   b. At the Edit Box dialog box, click the Border button.
   c. At the palette of border choices, click the Thick/Thin 1 option that displays third from the left in the third row.
   d. At the Edit Box dialog box, click the Fill button.
   e. At the palette of fill choices, click the 10% Fill option that displays third from the left in the first row.
   f. Close the Edit Box dialog box.
4. Save the document with the same name (Ch 19, Ex 13).
5. Print and then close Ch 19, Ex 13.

Changing Foreground and Background Color

If fill has been added to a box, the foreground and/or background color of the box can be changed. When you add a fill, then click Foreground or Background, a box of color options displays. These options display in the Box Border/Fill dialog box with the Fill tab selected.

The foreground and background color will display in the editing window but will not print unless you are using a color printer. To display the Foreground box of color options, click the down-pointing triangle immediately to the right of the Foreground option at the Box Border/Fill dialog box with the Fill tab selected. Click the desired color in the palette of color choices. Change the Background color option by following steps similar to those used for changing the Foreground color.

When a change is made to the Foreground or Background options, the change is reflected in the Preview Box at the right side of the dialog box.

EXERCISE

Editing the Foreground Color

1. At a clear editing window, open Ch 19, Ex 11.
2. Save the document with Save As and name it Ch 19, Ex 14.
3. Change the foreground color of the user box to blue by completing the following steps:
    a. Position the arrow pointer inside the user box, click the *right* mouse button, then click Border/Fill at the shortcut menu.
    b. At the Box Border/Fill dialog box, click the Fill tab.
    c. Click the 10% Fill option that displays third from the left in the first row in the Available fill styles list box.
    d. Click the down-pointing triangle to the right of the Foreground option.
    e. At the palette of color choices, click the blue color (tenth option from the left in the first row).
    f. Click OK.
4. Save the document again with the same name (Ch 19, Ex 14).
5. Print Ch 19, Ex 14. (If you are not printing with a color printer, this step may be optional. Check with your instructor.)
6. Close Ch 19, Ex 14.

Wrapping Text Around a Box

WordPerfect provides two methods for specifying how text flows around a graphics box. One method is to use the Wrap text side menu shown in figure 19.14. To display this menu, click the Wrap text button at the Edit Box dialog box. This side menu provides a visual display of the choices for wrapping text as well as a short description of the wrapping method. Choose a wrapping method by clicking the desired option.

Figure 19.14

Wrap Text Side Menu

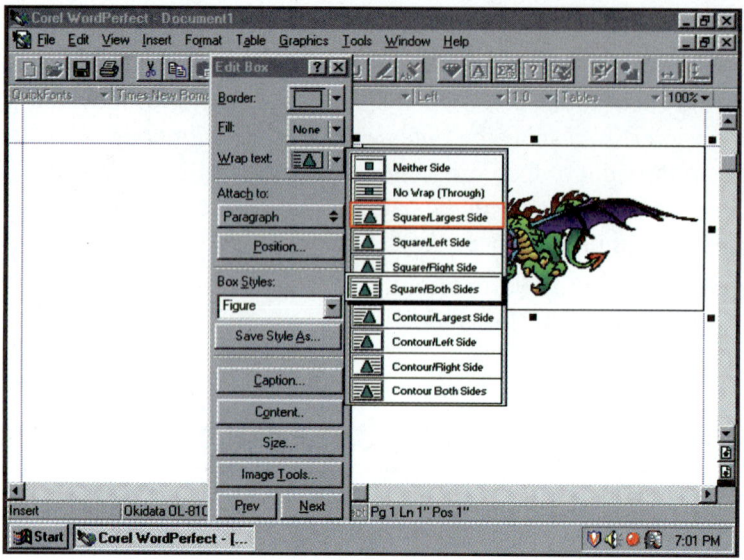

Specifying how text flows around a graphics box can also be accomplished at the Wrap Text dialog box shown in figure 19.15. To display this dialog box, position the arrow pointer in a graphics box, click the *right* mouse button, then click W*r*ap at the shortcut menu.

Figure 19.15

Wrap Text Dialog Box

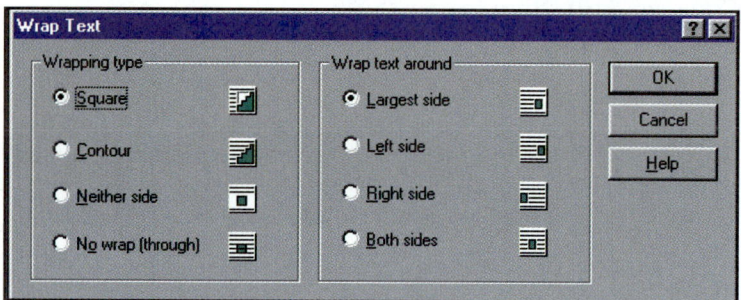

With the options in the Wrapping type section of the Wrap Text dialog box, you can specify whether text in a document wraps around the side of the box (*S*quare), wraps around the contours of the image (*C*ontour), does not wrap on either side of the box (*N*either side), or wraps through the box (N*o* wrap [through]). WordPerfect provides a visual representation of each of these options. Figure 19.16 also shows an example of wrapping text. The first image in the figure wraps text around the box border while the second image contours the text around the image.

Figure 19.16

Text Flow Around Graphics Images

This is a sample paragraph with a graphics image positioned within the paragraph. The first example displays with the text contoured around the borders of the box. The second example displays with text contoured around the image. With the Wrapping Type and Wrap Text Around options, you can also change the flow of text on the left side, right side, both sides, neither side, or through the box.

This is a sample paragraph with a graphics image positioned within the paragraph. The first example displays with the text contoured around the borders of the box. The second example displays with text contoured around the image. With the Wrapping Type and Wrap Text Around options, you can also change the flow of text on the left side, right side, both sides, neither side, or through the box.

The options in the Wrap text around section of the Wrap Text dialog box are used to specify where you want text wrapped in relation to the box. You can choose to wrap text around the largest side of the box, the left side, the right side, or both sides of the box. These options are also visually represented in the dialog box.

EXERCISE 15

Using the Wrap Text Option

1. At a clear editing window, open Ch 19, Ex 11.
2. Save the document with Save As and name it Ch 19, Ex 15.
3. Change the flow of text through the user box by completing the following steps:
   a. Position the arrow pointer inside the user box, click the *right* mouse button, then click W<u>r</u>ap.
   b. At the Wrap Text dialog box, click the radio button before the N<u>o</u> wrap (through) option.
   c. Click OK.
4. Key text that will print inside the border image by completing the following steps:
   a. Insert a code to center text vertically on the current page.
   b. Change the font to 30-point Ribbon131 Bd BT (or a similar decorative typeface).
   c. Select Center alignment from the Align text in document button on the Power Bar.
   d. Key **Denver Memorial Hospital Gift Shop**.
   e. Press Enter twice.
   f. Key **New Hours**.
   g. Press Enter twice.
   h. Key **8:00 a.m. to 8:30 p.m.**
   i. Press Enter twice.
   j. Key **Monday through Saturday**.
   k. Press Enter twice.
   l. Key **Stop by to see all of our new items!**
5. Save the document again with the same name (Ch 19, Ex 15).
6. Click the Page/Zoom Full button (or change to the Two Page viewing mode) to make sure the text is inside the border and centered on the page. After viewing the page, return to the default view.
7. Print and then close Ch 19, Ex 15.

Inserting Graphics Images

Changing the Box Style

As you have learned, WordPerfect provides a variety of box styles such as a text, table, figure, or user box. You can change the style of box with options at the Box Style dialog box or at the Box Styles drop-down menu at the Edit Box dialog box. To display the Box Style dialog box shown in figure 19.17, position the arrow pointer on a graphics box, click the *right* mouse button, then click Style at the shortcut menu.

Changing a box style changes the box border. For example, if you have a figure box displayed in the editing window, then change it to a text box, the top and bottom borders change to a thick line and the left and right border lines are removed.

Figure 19.17

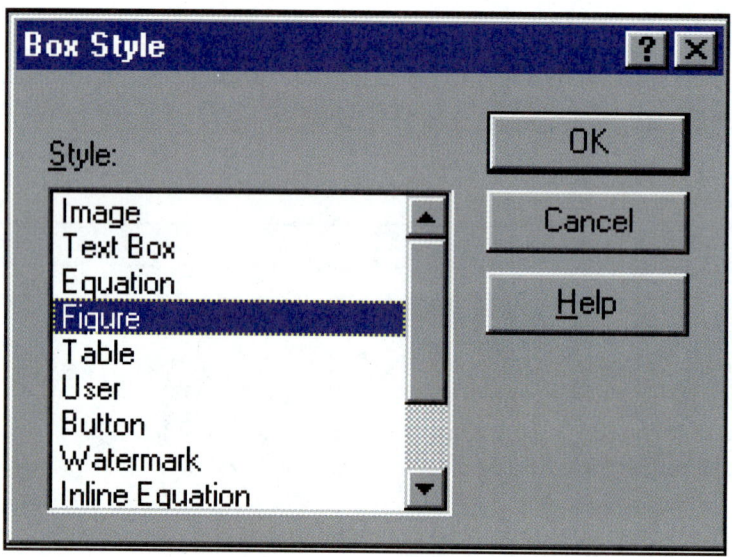

Box Style Dialog Box

Editing with the Image Tools Dialog Box

WordPerfect provides an Image Tools dialog box that contains a variety of tools you can use to edit or customize the contents of a figure box or a watermark image box. The Image Tools dialog box is not available for text, table, or button boxes. It is available for a watermark box and also for a figure box and user box containing a graphics image. To display the Image Tools dialog box as shown in figure 19.18, click the Image Tools button at the Edit Box dialog box. You can also display the Image Tools dialog box by positioning the arrow pointer on a graphics box, clicking the *right* mouse button, then clicking Image Tools at the shortcut menu. Figure 19.19 provides a brief description of the function of each button in the dialog box.

Figure 19.18

Image Tools Dialog Box

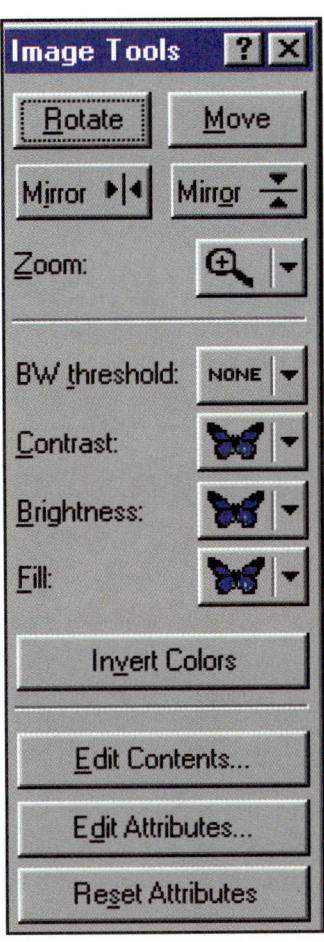

Figure 19.19

Image Tools Dialog Box Buttons

Name	Description
Rotate	Rotate the image around a selected point. To do this, click the button. This causes a point of rotation to display at the middle of the graphics box. Move the point of rotation by dragging it to a new location with the mouse.
Move	Move the image within the box. To do this, click the button. This causes the arrow pointer to turn into a hand. Position the hand on the box image, hold down the left mouse button, then drag the mouse.
Mirror ▶│◀	Mirror the image around its vertical axis.
Mirror ▼▲	Mirror the image around its horizontal axis.
Zoom	Zoom in or out on the image. This can also be used to display the image at its actual size.
BW threshold	Display the image in black & white only, and set threshold for blackness. When you click the button, a side menu of options displays. Use these options to set the blackness of the image. The darker the option, the darker the image.

Inserting Graphics Images   435

Name	Description
Contrast	Set the contrast level for the image. Use this button to change the appearance between light and dark areas of a color. When you click the **C**ontrast button, a side menu of contrast options displays. Choose one of the earlier options to decrease the contrast; choose one of the later options to increase the contrast.
Brightness	Set the brightness level for the image. When you click this button, a side menu of options displays. Choose one of the earlier options to increase the brightness; choose one of the later options to decrease the brightness.
F**i**ll	Select normal, no fill, or white fill. Use this button to make an image transparent or convert the image to an outline with a white fill. When you click the button, a side menu of options displays. The first option will maintain the normal fill. Click the second option to make the image transparent. Click the third to convert the image to an outline with white fill.
	Change the colors in the image to their complementary colors.
Edit Contents...	Edit the object with OLE server. Click this button to display the WordPerfect Draw program. (The Draw program is covered in chapter 21.)
Edit Attributes...	Display the Image Settings dialog box, which can be used to move, scale, rotate, set color and fill attributes, etc. At this dialog box, you can edit all image settings. The options available at this dialog box are the same options available with the buttons at the Image Tools dialog box.
Reset Attributes	Reset all image attributes. This returns the image to its original settings.

EXERCISE 16

Working with Contrast, Color, and Rotation

1. At a clear editing window, open Ch 19, Ex 03.
2. Save the document with Save As and name it Ch 19, Ex 16.
3. Flip the crane image on its vertical axis inside the first figure box and change the contrast of the image by completing the following steps:
    a. Position the arrow pointer inside the crane figure box, click the *right* mouse button, then click **I**mage Tools at the shortcut menu.
    b. Click the **C**ontrast button at the Image Tools dialog box.
    c. At the side menu that displays, click the last option (butterfly) in the bottom row.
    d. Click the M**i**rror button at the Image Tools dialog box.
    e. Close the Image Tools dialog box.
4. Change to the complementary colors for the hot air balloon image in the second figure box by completing the following steps:
    a. Position the arrow pointer inside the hot air balloon figure box, click the *right* mouse button, then click **I**mage Tools.
    b. Click the In**v**ert Colors button at the Image Tools dialog box.

c. Close the Image Tools dialog box.
5. Change the rotation of the dragon in the third figure box by completing the following steps:
   a. Position the arrow pointer inside the dragon figure box, click the *right* mouse button, then click Image Tools.
   b. Click the Rotate button at the Image Tools dialog box.
   c. Position the arrow pointer on the rotation handle in the upper left corner of the figure box until it turns into a double-headed arrow pointing diagonally. Hold down the left mouse button, drag the arrow pointer down, then release the mouse button. (The dragon should be angled down and to the left.)
   d. Close the Image Tools dialog box.
6. Save the document again with the same name (Ch 19, Ex 16).
7. Click the Page/Zoom Full button (or change to the Two Page viewing mode) to see how the images display on the page, then return to the default view.
8. Print and then close Ch 19, Ex 16.

Finding the Next or Previous Box

If you click the Next button at the Edit Box dialog box, WordPerfect will search and then display the next graphics box in the document. If there is no other graphics box, WordPerfect will display a not found message. Click the Prev button at the Edit Box dialog box to display the previous graphics box in the document.

Dragging a Box with the Mouse

When a graphics box is inserted in a document, the box can be moved to a different location using the mouse. To move a graphics box with the mouse, position the arrow pointer inside the graphics box, then click the left mouse button. This causes the mouse to turn into a four-headed arrow and sizing handles to appear as shown in figure 19.20.

Figure 19.20

Graphics Box with Sizing Handles

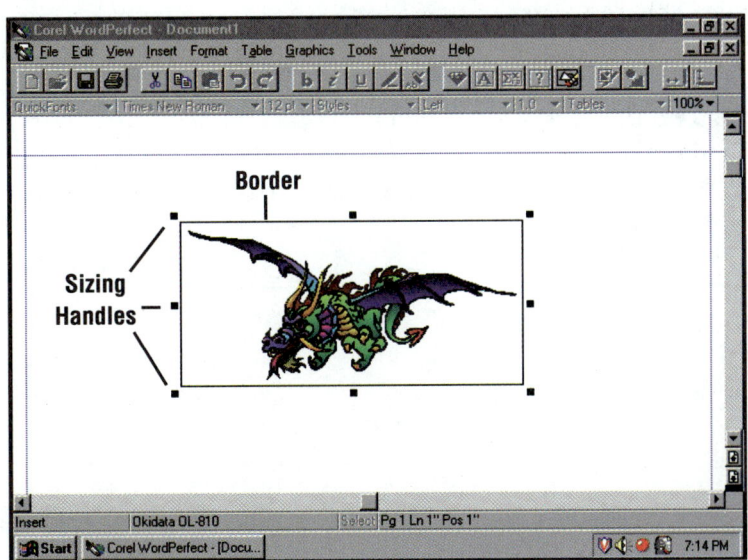

Inserting Graphics Images 437

To move the box, hold down the left mouse button, then drag the four-headed arrow. As you drag the four-headed arrow, an outline border of the box follows. When the outline border is in the desired position in the document, release the mouse button. This causes the graphics box to display in the location of the outline border.

Using the mouse with the sizing handles, you can change the size of the graphics box. For example, you can make the box wider or narrower. To do this, position the four-headed arrow on the sizing handle in the middle of the box at the left or right side of the box until it turns into a double-headed horizontal arrow. Hold down the left mouse button, drag the double-headed arrow to the left or right, then release the button.

To make the box taller or shorter, position the four-headed arrow on the sizing handle at the top or bottom of the box in the middle until the arrow pointer becomes a double-headed vertical arrow. Hold down the left mouse button, drag the double-headed arrow up or down, then release the mouse button.

If you position the four-headed arrow on any of the sizing handles at the corners of the border, the four-headed arrow becomes a double-headed arrow pointing diagonally. When it becomes a diagonally pointing double arrow, you can increase or decrease the width as well as the height of the box at the same time.

EXERCISE

Moving Figure Boxes

1. At a clear editing window, open Ch 19, Ex 03.
2. Save the document with Save As and name it Ch 19, Ex 17.
3. Move the first figure box to the middle of the screen by completing the following steps:
    a. Position the arrow pointer inside the first figure box (the one containing the crane), then click the left button.
    b. Hold down the left mouse button, drag the border outline to approximately the middle of the left and right margins, then release the mouse button.
    c. Move the arrow pointer outside the figure box, then click the left mouse button. This deselects the figure box.
4. Move the second figure box to the middle of the screen by completing steps similar to those in steps 3a through 3c.
5. Move the third figure box to the middle of the screen by completing steps similar to those in steps 3a through 3c.
6. Save the document again with the same name (Ch 19, Ex 17).
7. Print and then close Ch 19, Ex 17.

CHAPTER SUMMARY

- ▼ With WordPerfect's Graphics feature, you can insert a graphics image into a document and also have ten other graphics boxes available including text, figure, table, user, button, watermark, equation, inline equation, OLE 2.0 box, and inline text.

- ▼ The Graphics Toolbar contains buttons for creating and editing graphic elements.

- ▼ Insert a graphics image into a document by positioning the insertion point where the image is to display, then displaying the Insert Image dialog box. An image is inserted at the left margin of the document at the location of the insertion point.

- ▼ A text box is generally created for quotes or other special text. By default, it contains a thick top and bottom border, no side borders, is 3.25 inches wide, and is inserted at the right margin.

- ▼ A figure box is generally used for graphics images such as clip art, logos, drawings, or one of the images included in the WordPerfect program. A figure box, by default, contains a single line border on all sides, is 3.25 inches wide, and is inserted at the right margin. Create a figure box at the Custom Box dialog box.

- ▼ A table box is generally created for a table, spreadsheet, or statistical data. By default, it contains a thick top and bottom border, no side borders, is 3.25 inches wide, and is inserted at the right margin. Create a table box at the Custom Box dialog box.

- ▼ A user box can be created for any particular situation. By default, it does not have any borders, is 3.25 inches wide, and is inserted at the right margin. Create a user box at the Custom Box dialog box.

- ▼ A button box is created for items such as a keystroke, function key, or an icon. It is inserted at the left margin and is approximately 1 inch wide. Create a button box at the Custom Box dialog box.

- ▼ A watermark is a lightened image that displays on the entire page over which text can be inserted. Create a watermark at the Custom Box dialog box.

- ▼ The Edit Box dialog box provides options for editing a graphics box. Display the Edit Box dialog box by clicking the Edit Box button on the Graphics Toolbar or by clicking the QuickSpot button in the upper left corner of the graphics box. Options at the Edit Box dialog box include: creating a caption, changing content options, changing box position, changing box size, changing box border and fill styles, changing border style, changing foreground and background color, wrapping text around a box, and changing the box style.

- ▼ An Image Tools dialog box is provided that contains a variety of buttons you can use to edit or customize the contents of a watermark, figure, or user box.

- ▼ A graphics box can be moved to a different location by dragging the box with the mouse.

COMMANDS REVIEW

	Mouse/Keyboard
Graphics Toolbar	Position arrow pointer on current Toolbar, click right mouse button, click Graphics
Insert Image dialog box	Graphics, Image; or click Image button on the Graphics Toolbar
Create a Text Box	Graphics, Text Box; or click Text Box button on the Graphics Toolbar
Custom Box dialog box	Graphics, Custom Box; or click Custom Box button on the Graphics Toolbar
Edit Box dialog box	Click Edit Box button on Graphics Toolbar; or position arrow pointer on QuickSpot button in the upper left corner of the box, then click the left mouse button
Image Tools dialog box	Click Image Tools button at Edit Box dialog box; or click right mouse button in graphics box, then click Image Tools at shortcut menu

CHECK YOUR UNDERSTANDING

Matching: In the space provided at the left, indicate the correct *letter or letters* that match each description.

- **A** Figure
- **B** Table
- **C** Text
- **D** User
- **E** Equation
- **F** Button
- **G** Watermark
- **H** Inline

_____ 1. Default border style is a single line on all four sides.
_____ 2. Used for quotations.
_____ 3. Default border style is a thick line at the top and bottom.
_____ 4. Used for an image, logo, or drawing.
_____ 5. Used for whatever is not addressed in the other ten boxes.
_____ 6. Used for statistical data.
_____ 7. Used for an icon.
_____ 8. Approximately 1 inch wide by default.

Completion: In the space provided at the right, indicate the correct term, command, or number.

1. This is the default width of a figure box. _____

2. This is the term for a lightened image that displays on the entire page. _____

3. These two types of boxes display with a thick top and bottom line and no left and right lines as a border. _____

4. One method for displaying the Edit Box dialog box is to click this button that displays in the upper left corner of a graphics box. _____

5. This type of box does not have any borders, is inserted at the right margin, and is approximately 3.25 inches wide. _____

6. Add fill to a graphics box with options at this dialog box with the Fill tab selected. _____

7. Specifying how text flows around a graphics box can be accomplished at this dialog box. _____

8. Click this button at the Image Tools dialog box to change the colors in the image to their complementary colors. _____

SKILL ASSESSMENTS

Assessment 1

1. At a clear editing window, insert the graphics image named *Winrace* in a figure box. Make the following changes to the figure box:
    a. Change the box width to Full and the height to Maintain proportions.
    b. Create a caption that reads *Figure 1 Winner!*. Position the caption at the outside of the top border and at the right side.
2. Save the document and name it Ch 19, SA 01.
3. Print and then close Ch 19, SA 01.

Assessment 2

1. At a clear editing window, create the document shown in figure 19.21 by completing the following steps:
    a. Insert the graphics image named *Medical1* in a user box.
    b. Change the Horizontal position of the box to Left Margin at the Box Position dialog box.
    c. Deselect the image.
    d. At the editing window, complete the following steps:
        (1) Change the font to 12-point Arrus Blk BT (or a similar typeface).
        (2) Change the text alignment to Center.
        (3) Press Enter five times, then key **IMPORTANT!!**.
        (4) Press Enter three times, then key **ALL FIRST-YEAR RESIDENTS**.
        (5) Continue until all text has been keyed. (Press Enter three times between each line of text.)
2. Save the document and name it Ch 19, SA 02.
3. Print and then close Ch 19, SA 02.

Inserting Graphics Images

Figure 19.21

IMPORTANT!!

ALL FIRST-YEAR RESIDENTS

OPERATING ROOM PROTOCOL

MAY 6, 1998

1:00 p.m. to 4:30 p.m.

Operating Room 3

Assessment 3

1. At a clear editing window, key the memo shown in figure 19.22 in an appropriate memo format through the first paragraph. Create the text boxes by completing the following steps:
    a. Create a text box. Change the position of the text box to Center of Paragraph at the Box Position dialog box. Key the text in the text box as indicated in figure 19.22.
    b. After creating the first text box, press Enter eight times to move the insertion point below the first box.
    c. Create the second text box with the same specifications as the first box.
    d. After creating the second text box, press Enter seven times to move the insertion point below the second box.
    e. Create the third text box with the same specifications as the first box.
2. After creating the third text box, press Enter eight times to move the insertion point a double space below the third box, then key the remaining text in the memo.
3. Save the memo and name it Ch 19, SA 03.
4. Print and then close Ch 19, SA 03.

Figure 19.22

DATE: May 21, 1998; TO: Joni Paulsen; FROM: Anne Maeda; SUBJECT: NEW EMPLOYEE BOOKLET

Thank you for letting me know about the next printing date for the New Employee Booklet. I have received recommendations from various employees to include the following additional items in the Caring Actions section of the booklet.

Listen actively:

Take time to listen. Give the person your full attention.

Be timely:

Respond quickly. Explain delays.

Explain what you are doing:

Make explanations brief and easy to understand. Answer questions honestly and kindly.

The sample typeset pages of the New Employee Booklet look very professional. I look forward to using the new booklet at orientations.
xx:Ch 19, SA 03

Inserting Graphics Images

Assessment 4

1. At a clear editing window, create the *Dragn* image over the *Hotair* image by completing the following steps:
   a. Insert the image named *Hotair* into a user box. (Hint: To insert the *Hotair* image into the user box, create a user box, display the Box Content dialog box, display the filenames, then double-click *Hotair*.)
   b. Change the Attach box to setting to Page at the Box Position dialog box.
   c. Change the box width to Full and the height to Maintain proportions at the Box Size dialog box.
   d. Display the Wrap Text dialog box, then click No wrap (through).
   e. Click in the editing window outside the graphic to deselect it.
   f. Insert the graphics image named *Dragn* into a user box.
   g. Change the Attach box to setting to Page at the Box Position dialog box.
   h. Change the box width to 2 inches and the height to Maintain proportions.
   i. Display the Wrap Text dialog box, then click No wrap (through).
2. Save the document and name it Ch 19, SA 04.
3. Click the Page/Zoom Full button (or change to the Two Page viewing mode) to see how the images display on the entire page, then return to the default view.
4. Print and then close Ch 19, SA 04.

CREATING GRAPHIC ELEMENTS

PERFORMANCE OBJECTIVE

Upon successful completion of chapter 20, you will be able to create graphic elements such as equations, paragraph and page borders, graphics lines, reversed text, and drop caps to enhance standard business documents.

In the previous chapter you learned to create graphics boxes with a variety of contents. You learned to create graphics boxes with graphics images, text boxes, table boxes, user boxes, watermarks, and button boxes. In this chapter, you will learn to create equation boxes, inline equations, paragraph and page borders, reversed text, drop caps, and graphics lines.

Creating Equations

You can create a graphics box that contains mathematical and/or scientific equations. When you create an equation graphics box, you can display the Equation Editor screen where mathematical symbols and commands are created or inserted. WordPerfect uses conventions from the mathematic and scientific communities when creating equations. For example, numbers are printed in a normal font, and variables such as x and y are printed in italics.

The steps to create an equation box are similar to the steps you learned in chapter 19 for creating other types of boxes. To create an equation box containing an equation, you would complete the following steps:

1. Position the insertion point where you want the equation box and equation to appear.
2. Click Graphics, then Equation; or click the Equation button on the Graphics Toolbar.
3. At the Equation Editor shown in figure 20.1, key the equation.
4. View the equation by clicking View, then Redisplay; or by clicking the Redisplay button on the Equation Editor Toolbar.
5. Save the equation by clicking File, then Close; or by clicking the Close button on the Equation Editor Toolbar.

Equation

Redisplay

Creating Graphic Elements *445*

At the Equation Editor shown in figure 20.1, you can create or write an equation. The Equation Editor is divided into three sections: the editing window, the display window, and the equation palette.

Figure 20.1

Equation Editor

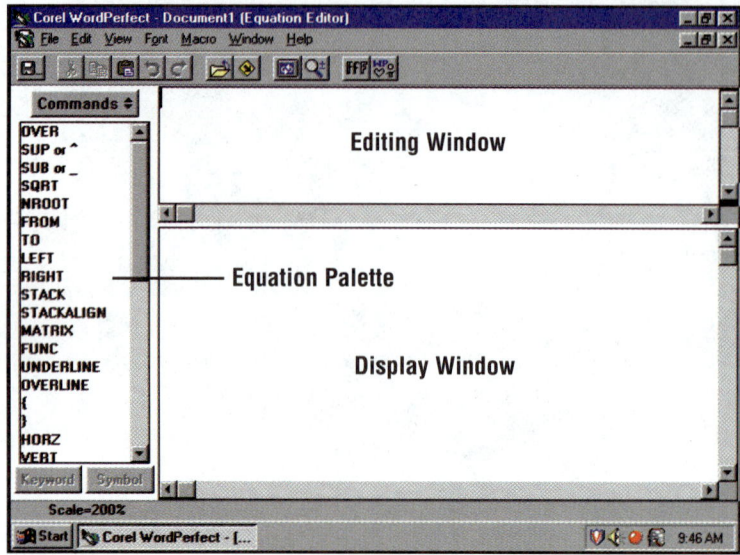

The top right portion of the window is the editing window and is the section where the equation is keyed. The display window is the bottom right portion of the window. This section displays equations as they will appear when inserted in the document and when printed. The section at the left side of the window is the equation palette. The palette contains a variety of commands and symbols that can be used when writing an equation.

Writing an Equation

To write an equation, key the equation using special commands and symbols. For example, to write the equation $a + b$ over c, you would key the following at the editing window:

{a~+~b} over c

Key the braces ({}) around $a + b$ to tell WordPerfect that both are to appear over the c. Key the tilde (~) to insert a space after the a and before the b.

To see how the equation will appear in the document and in print, click View, then Redisplay, or click the Redisplay button on the Equation Editor Toolbar. WordPerfect displays the equation in the display window as shown below.

$$\frac{a + b}{c}$$

When you press Enter in the editing window, the insertion point moves down to the next line, but a hard return is *not* inserted in the equation. To create multiple-line equations in the editing window, key the number symbol (#).

The space bar inserts a space in the editing window but does not add a space in the equation. To add a space to an equation, key a tilde (~) for a normal space or a backward accent (`) for a thin space. A thin space is equal to one-fourth of a normal space.

446 Chapter 20

To keep a section of an equation together as a unit, enclose the section in braces ({ }). Negative numbers (such as -100) should also be enclosed in braces. When a negative number is enclosed in braces, it tells WordPerfect that the minus symbol and the number are part of the same unit.

Moving between Windows

You can use the mouse to move the insertion point between the editing window and the equation palette. To move the insertion point with the mouse, position the arrow pointer in the editing window or the equation palette, then click the left mouse button.

Viewing the Equation

The display pane in the Equation Editor displays the equation as it appears in the document, except at 200% view. To display an equation at the Equation Editor, click View, then Redisplay; or click the Redisplay button on the Equation Editor Toolbar.

If you made a syntax error when writing the formula, the equation will not display in the display window. Instead, the message <<ERROR: Incorrect syntax>> appears at the bottom of the window in the Status bar, and the insertion point is positioned at the location in the equation where the error occurs.

Selecting from the Equation Palette

To make selections from the Equation palette, position the arrow pointer on the desired symbol then double-click the left mouse button. When you double-click the mouse button the command, symbol, or keyword is automatically inserted in the editing window.

Some commands can be displayed as keywords or as symbols. With the insertion point located on the desired command or symbol, check the two buttons—Keyword and Symbol—at the bottom of the palette. If the button is in normal display, you can choose to insert either the keyword or the symbol. If one of the buttons is dimmed, that choice is not available.

Using the Menu Bar

At the Equation Editor screen, a Menu bar displays at the top of the screen with the following options: File, Edit, View, Font, Macro, Window, and Help.

File: When you click File at the Equation Editor, a drop-down menu displays with the following options: Insert File, Save As, Cancel, and Close. If you save equations as separate documents, you can insert an equation document into the Equation Editor. To do this, click File, then Insert File. WordPerfect displays the Retrieve Equation Text dialog box. At this dialog box, key the name of the document equation to be inserted, then click OK or press Enter. With the Save As option, you can save the equation as a separate document. Click the Cancel option to leave the Equation Editor without saving an equation. WordPerfect will ask you for confirmation before closing the Equation Editor. Click the Close option from the File drop-down menu to close the Equation Editor, retaining any equations or changes made to equations.

Edit: When you click Edit at the Equation Editor, a drop-down menu displays. The options at the Edit drop-down menu from the Equation Editor are basically the same as the options from the Edit drop-down menu at the normal editing window. For example, you can undo or undelete; repeat the last command; cut, copy, or paste text; and perform a find and replace.

When you click Preferences from the Edit drop-down menu, the Preferences dialog box displays. At this dialog box, you can choose to change the preferences for the keyboard, display, etc.

View: When you click View at the Equation Editor, a drop-down menu displays with a variety of options. Click Redisplay to display the equation as it will appear when printed. Click the Zoom Display option and the Zoom Equation Display dialog box displays as shown in figure 20.2. With the options from the Zoom Equation Display dialog box, you can set a percentage for viewing the equation.

At the Equation Editor, the display of the Equation Editor Toolbar and the equation palette are on by default. Click View, then Palette from the Menu bar to turn off the display of the palette; click Toolbar to turn off the display of the Equation Editor Toolbar.

Figure 20.2

Zoom Equation Display Dialog Box

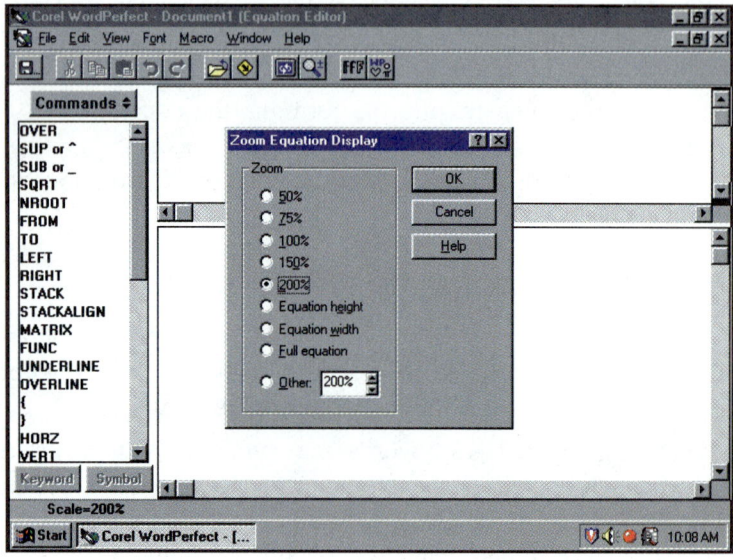

Font: If you click Font at the Equation Editor Menu Bar, two options display—Equation Font and Character. If you click Equation Font, the Equation Font dialog box displays on the screen. At this dialog box, you can choose a font face, font size, and font style for the equation. Click Character or press Ctrl + W and the WordPerfect Characters dialog box displays. At this dialog box, you can insert a WordPerfect character.

Macro: The options from the Macro drop-down menu can be used to create macros that are recorded and then placed inside the Equation Editor.

Window: When you click Window from the Equation Editor Menu Bar, a list displays showing the windows you currently have open.

Help: WordPerfect's Help feature is available to you at the Equation Editor with the Help option from the Menu Bar.

Using the Equation Editor Toolbar

Zoom Equation Display

WP Characters

You can use the Toolbar at the Equation Editor screen to quickly perform many of the functions available through the Equation Menu bar. For example, click the Redisplay button to display the equation in the display window. Click the Zoom Equation Display button to display the Zoom Equation Display dialog box, or click the WP Characters button to display the WordPerfect Characters dialog box.

Editing an Equation

After an equation has been created in a document, it can be edited. Editing might include changing the size and/or position of the equation box, customizing the equation box, adding a caption, or changing the caption number. The options for editing an equation box are the same as for editing a graphics box. Refer to chapter 19 for information on editing options.

EXERCISE 1

Creating an Equation

1. At a clear editing window, change the left and right margins to 1.5 inches.
2. Key the memo shown in figure 20.3 in an appropriate memo format. With the insertion point a double space below the first paragraph, complete the following steps to create the equation:
   a. Click the Equation button on the Graphics Toolbar.
   b. At the Equation Editor, key **SUM d^2~=~1 over N [N SUM X^2~-~(SUM X)^2]**. (The caret symbol (^) will cause the next character to be superscripted.)
   c. View the equation by clicking the Redisplay button on the Equation Editor Toolbar (fourth button from the right).
   d. Save the equation by clicking the Close button on the Equation Editor Toolbar. The equation is inserted into a graphics box in the memo.
3. Key the remaining text in the memo.
4. Save the memo and name it Ch 20, Ex 01.
5. Print and then close Ch 20, Ex 01.

Figure 20.3

DATE: May 5, 1998; TO: Allen Lavell; FROM: Lisa Bassett; SUBJECT: STATISTICAL ANALYSIS

Thank you for sending the statistical analysis on the lab blood draws so promptly. The mean and the range seem to be acceptable, but I would like the standard deviation computed using the following formula:

$$\sum d^2 = \frac{1}{N} [N \sum X^2 - (\sum X)^2]$$

Please have the computations to me by the end of next week. I will be presenting the statistics at the next department meeting.

xx:Ch 20, Ex 01

Creating Inline Equations

In the previous section of this chapter, you learned how to create equations in equation boxes. You can also create an equation as part of the text in a document by creating an inline equation box. Figure 20.4 shows an example of an inline equation. The steps to create an equation in an inline equation box are very similar to creating an equation in an equation box. You will practice the steps in exercise 2. After an inline equation has been created, it can be edited. The options for editing an equation box are the same as for editing a graphics box. Refer to chapter 19 for information on editing options.

Figure 20.4

Inline Equation

The equation can be included in a sentence within a document by inserting the equation in an inline equation box.

EXERCISE 2

Creating an Equation within a Sentence

1. At a clear editing window, key the memo shown in figure 20.5 in an appropriate memo format. Change the line spacing to 1.5 at the beginning of the first paragraph in the memo. Key the first paragraph to the location where the first equation is to appear, then complete the following steps:
    a. Click Graphics, then Custom Box; or click the Custom Box button on the Graphics Toolbar.
    b. At the Custom Box dialog box, double-click *Inline Equation* in the Style name list box.
    c. Display the Edit Box dialog box, then click the Content button.
    d. At the Box Content dialog box, click Edit.
    e. At the Equation Editor, key **C~=~Z_min over 3**. (The underscore character (_) causes the next characters to be subscripted.)
    f. View the equation by clicking View, then Redisplay; or by clicking the Redisplay button on the Equation Editor Toolbar.
    g. Close the Equation Editor by clicking File, then Close; or by clicking the Close button on the Equation Editor Toolbar.
2. Key the next sentence to the location of the second inline equation, then complete steps similar to those in steps 1a through 1g to create the second formula in the first paragraph. Key the following at the Equation Editor: **C_pk~=~Z_min over 3**.
3. Save the memo and name it Ch 20, Ex 02.
4. Print and then close Ch 20, Ex 02.

Figure 20.5

DATE: May 12, 1998; TO: Melissa Nobel; FROM: Danielle Curry; SUBJECT: SPECIFICATIONS MANUAL

A formula that appears on page 43 of Specifications Manual 14 is incorrect. The formula appears as $C = \dfrac{Z_{min}}{3}$. Please edit the formula so it appears as $C_{pk} = \dfrac{Z_{min}}{3}$.

Please let me know the printing date for the manual. I will be using the manual for a training session next month.

xx:Ch 20, Ex 02

Creating Borders

In this and the previous chapter, you have learned how to create graphics boxes in a document. These boxes contain a variety of borders including single lines, thick lines, and no lines. In addition to graphics boxes, you can surround text in a document with borders. The borders are similar to the borders of a graphics box. You can customize the border line style as well as the fill style. You can create a border for a paragraph, a page, or a column. Information on creating borders around columns is included in chapter 23.

Inserting a Paragraph Border

With the Paragraph border feature, you can insert a border around the paragraph where the insertion point is located or the current paragraph plus all subsequent paragraphs. Borders are created at the Paragraph Border/Fill dialog box shown in figure 20.6. You will practice the steps in exercise 3. The Paragraph Border/Fill dialog box contains the same options as the Box Border/Fill dialog box discussed in chapter 19.

Figure 20.6

Paragraph Border Dialog Box

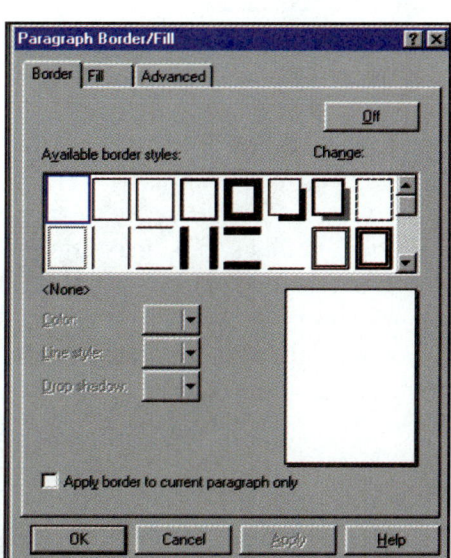

Creating Graphic Elements 451

EXERCISE 3

Inserting a Border Around a Paragraph

1. At a clear editing window, open Bibliography.
2. Save the document with Save As and name it Ch 20, Ex 03.
3. Insert a single line border around the first paragraph by completing the following steps:
   a. Position the insertion point on any character in the first paragraph.
   b. Click Format, point to Border/Fill, then click Paragraph.
   c. At the Paragraph Border/Fill dialog box, make sure the Border tab is selected.
   d. Click the Single option (third option from the left in the first row) in the Available border styles list box.
   e. Make sure there is a check mark in the Apply border to current paragraph only check box.
   f. Click OK.
4. Complete steps similar to those in 3a through 3f to insert a single line border around each of the remaining paragraphs.
5. Save the document again with the same name (Ch 20, Ex 03).
6. Print and then close Ch 20, Ex 03.

If you want to insert a paragraph border around all paragraphs in the document from the location of the insertion point to the end of the document, remove the check mark in the Apply border to current paragraph only check box. This check box is located at the bottom of the Paragraph Border/Fill dialog box.

EXERCISE 4

Creating a Border Around Multiple Paragraphs

1. At a clear editing window, open Report 06.
2. Save the document with Save As and name it Ch 20, Ex 04.
3. Change the bottom margin to 0.8".
4. Create a double line border with 10% fill around the last six lines at the end of the report by completing the following steps:
   a. Position the insertion point at the left margin of the line containing *increased random access memory* (toward the end of the document).
   b. Click Format, point to Border/Fill, then click Paragraph.
   c. At the Paragraph Border/Fill dialog box, make sure the Border tab is selected.
   d. Click the Double option (seventh option from the left in the second row) in the Available border styles list box.
   e. Remove the check mark in the Apply border to current paragraph only check box.
   f. Click the Fill tab.
   g. Click the 10% Fill option (third option from the left in the top row) at the Available fill styles list box.

h. Click OK.
5. Save the document again with the same name (Ch 20, Ex 04).
6. Print and then close Ch 20, Ex 04.

Inserting a Page Border

Inserting a page border is similar to inserting a paragraph border, except you click Page instead of Paragraph at the Border/Fill drop-down menu. A page border will surround the page and all subsequent pages in the document.

The Page Border/Fill dialog box, shown in figure 20.7, is similar to the Paragraph Border/Fill dialog box. The Available border styles list box will change depending on whether the Border type is set to Line or Fancy. Figure 20.7 shows the options available with the Fancy option for Border type. The check box at the bottom of the dialog box, Apply border to current page only, does not contain a check mark. At this setting, a page border will surround all pages in the document. If you want the page border for the current page only, insert a check mark in the Apply border to current page only option.

Figure 20.7

Page Border/Fill Dialog Box

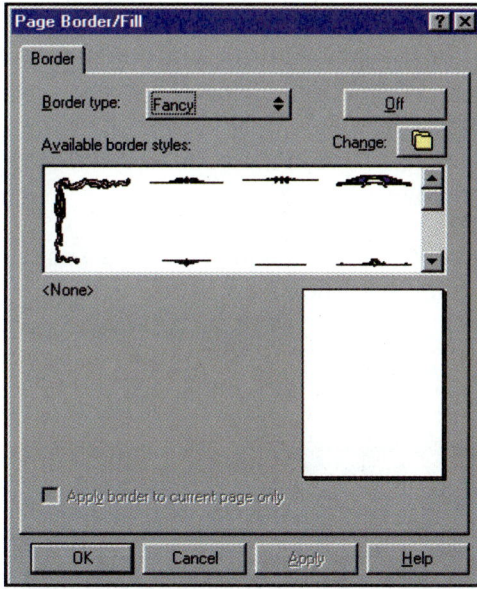

EXERCISE 5

Creating a Triple Line Page Border

1. At a clear editing window, open Block 01.
2. Save the document with Save As and name it Ch 20, Ex 05.
3. Make the following changes to the document:
    a. Insert a code to center the text vertically on the current page.
    b. Change the font to 24-point BernhardMod BT.
    c. Insert a triple line page border by completing the following steps:

Page Border

(1) Position the insertion point on any character in the page.
(2) Click Format, point to Border/Fill, then click Page; or click the Page Border button on the Page Toolbar.
(3) At the Page Border/Fill dialog box, make sure the Border tab is selected, then change the Border type to Line.
(4) Click the Triple option (fifth option from the left in the third row) at the Available border styles list box.
(5) Click OK.
4. Save the document again with the same name (Ch 20, Ex 05).
5. Click the Page/Zoom Full button (or change to the Two-Page viewing mode) to see how the border appears around the text, then return to the default view.
6. Print and then close Ch 20, Ex 05.

Customizing a Border

At the Paragraph Border/Fill or the Page Border/Fill dialog box with the Advanced tab selected, you can change the spacing inside and outside the border. You can also customize a graphics box by clicking the Advanced tab at the dialog box. To create and customize a paragraph border, you would complete the following steps:

1. Position the insertion point on any character in the paragraph where you want the border.
2. Click Format, point to Border/Fill, then click Paragraph.
3. At the Paragraph Border/Fill dialog box, make sure the Border tab is selected.
4. Click the desired option at the Available border styles list box.
5. Click the Advanced tab. This displays the dialog box as shown in figure 20.8.
6. Make any necessary changes to the Paragraph Border/Fill dialog box with the Advanced tab selected, then click OK.

If you want to customize a page border, complete steps similar to those listed above except click Format, point to Border/Fill, then click Page in step 2.

Figure 20.8

Paragraph Border/Fill Dialog Box with Advanced Tab Selected

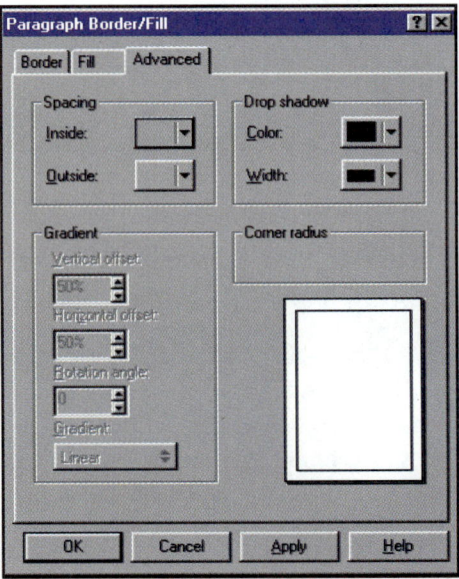

454 Chapter 20

Changing Border Spacing: By default, WordPerfect automatically determines the inside and outside spacing of a box. With the Inside and Outside options you can select from several predefined spacing settings or specify the measurement desired for the border.

Changing Corners: The corners of a page border and a box border can be rounded with the Corner radius Amount option. A paragraph border and column border cannot have rounded corners. To round the corners of a page border, increase the number in the Corner radius Amount text box. The higher the number, the more rounded the corner. The change to the radius is reflected in the Preview Box.

Modifying a Drop Shadow: With the options in the Drop shadow section of the Paragraph Border/Fill dialog box with the Advanced tab selected, you can add a drop shadow effect to a border. A drop shadow provides a three-dimensional look to a border. You can change the color of the drop shadow by clicking the Color button in the Drop shadow section. This causes a palette of color choices to display. At this palette, click the desired color. With the Width option, you can specify the width of the drop shadow. Click the Width button and a palette of width choices displays. Click the desired width option. You can also key a width measurement in the text box that displays at the bottom of the palette. The higher the number, the wider the drop shadow.

Gradient: The Gradient section options will be dimmed unless you have applied a fill selection to the Paragraph, Page, or Column border. With the Gradient section option, you can blend the background fill in a Linear style, Circular style, or Rectangular style. The Linear style will blend the color from one side of the border to the other. The Circular style will blend the color in a circular fashion from the center outward. The Rectangular style is similar to the circular style except that the image forms a rectangle instead of a circle.

Once you have selected a Gradient pattern, the Vertical and Horizontal offsets allow you to specify the percentage you want the gradient to offset from the top to the bottom of the border (Vertical), or from left to right in the border (Horizontal). The Rotation angle allows you to rotate the gradient inside the box. For example, if you select a Rectangular gradient, and then set the rotation angle to 45 degrees, the gradient will appear inside the border as a diamond shape.

EXERCISE 6

Customizing a Page Border

1. At a clear editing window, open Notice 01.
2. Save the document with Save As and name it Ch 20, Ex 06.
3. With the insertion point located at the beginning of the document, make the following changes:
    a. Insert a code to vertically center the current page.
    b. Change the font to 18-point BernhardMod BT.
4. Create a page border with a drop shadow by completing the following steps:
    a. Click Format, point to Border/Fill, then click Page.
    b. At the Page Border/Fill dialog box, make sure the Border tab is selected.
    c. Change the Border type to Line.
    d. Click the Single option (third option from the left in the first row) at the Available border styles list box.
    e. Click the down-pointing triangle to the right of Drop shadow, then click the second option from the top (with the shadow in the upper left corner of the box).
    f. Click the Advanced tab.

Creating Graphic Elements   455

g. At the Page Border/Fill dialog box with the Advanced tab selected, click the Width button in the Drop shadow section. (This causes a palette of width options to display.)
h. At the palette of width options, click the bottom option in the second column.
i. Click OK.
5. Click the Page/Zoom Full button (or change to the Two Page viewing mode) to see how the document will appear when printed, then return to the default view.
6. Save the document again with the same name (Ch 20, Ex 06).
7. Print and then close Ch 20, Ex 06.

EXERCISE 7

Customizing a Figure Box

1. At a clear editing window, insert the graphics image named *Dragn* in a figure box, then make the following changes to the figure box:
   a. Change the horizontal position to Center of Paragraph at the Box Position dialog box.
   b. Round the corners by completing the following steps:
      (1) Position the arrow pointer on the dragon image, then click the *right* mouse button.
      (2) At the shortcut menu that displays, click Border/Fill.
      (3) At the Box Border/Fill dialog box, click the Heavy border style option that displays fourth from the left in the first row (counting the first option, which is blank).
      (4) Click the Advanced tab.
      (5) At the Box Border/Fill dialog box with the Advanced tab selected, round the corners of the border. To do this, click the up-pointing triangle after the Corner radius Amount text box until *0.200"* displays in the text box.
      (6) Click OK.
   c. Create a caption that reads **Figure 1: Dragon**. Center the caption by changing the Position option to Center at the Box Caption dialog box.
2. Save the document and name it Ch 20, Ex 07.
3. Print and then close Ch 20, Ex 07.

Creating Horizontal and Vertical Lines

You can create horizontal and/or vertical lines in a document and adjust the width and shading of the lines. Horizontal and vertical lines can be used in a document to separate sections, create a focal point, separate columns, or add visual appeal.

Creating a Horizontal Line

Horizontal Line

To insert a horizontal line in a document, click Graphics, then Horizontal Line; or click the Horizontal Line button on the Graphics Toolbar. This inserts a horizontal line in the document at the location of the insertion point from the left margin to the right margin.

EXERCISE 8

Inserting Horizontal Lines

1. At a clear editing window, create the document shown in figure 20.9 by completing the following steps:
   a. Change the font to 12-point BernhardMod BT (or a similar typeface).
   b. Center and bold the title, *CARING ACTIONS*.
   c. Turn off bold and then press Enter three times.
   d. Key **reach out**.
   e. Press Enter once, then create a horizontal line by clicking Graphics, then Horizontal Line; or clicking the Horizontal Line button on the Graphics Toolbar.
   f. Press Enter twice, press F7 (the Indent command), then key the paragraph below *reach out*. (Space once after end-of-sentence punctuation.)
   g. Press Enter twice.
   h. Create the remaining headings and paragraphs following steps similar to those in 1d through 1g.
2. After keying the document, make the following changes:
   a. Select the title, *CARING ACTIONS*, then change the relative size to Very Large.
   b. Select *reach out*, then change the relative size to Very Large and the appearance to Bold and Italic.
   c. Select each of the remaining headings, *be friendly*, *show courtesy*, *demonstrate your competence*, *explain what you are doing*, and *look for an opportunity to serve* separately, then change the relative size to Very Large and the appearance to Bold and Italic. (Hint: Use the QuickFormat feature to do this.)
3. Save the document and name it Ch 20, Ex 08.
4. Print and then close Ch 20, Ex 08.

Figure 20.9

CARING ACTIONS

reach out

Welcome people immediately to your work area. Acknowledge their presence. Make eye contact and smile. Introduce yourself in a pleasant tone of voice. State your name and what job you perform. When the opportunity is available, use the person's name to address him/her. Be attentive, genuine, and positive.

be friendly

If you are unsure if someone needs help, ask him/her. Share information willingly and honestly. If you can't help, personally find someone who can. Know what services are available and how to get them.

show courtesy

Put yourself in the other person's place. Respond quickly. Allow others to go first. Be polite and helpful in person, or on the phone.

Creating Graphic Elements

demonstrate your competence

Confidence comes from competence in your job skills and knowledge. Stay current. Express confidence by performing tasks accurately and with ease. Be responsible. While knowing the limits of your practice (job), solve problems within your authority.

explain what you are doing

Make explanations brief and easy to understand. Answer questions honestly and kindly. Be willing to explain it again. Use language that the other person can understand.

look for an opportunity to serve

You represent the hospital to every person you encounter. Go out of your way to be helpful to others. Care enough to do your best.

Creating a Vertical Line

To insert a vertical line in a document, click Graphics, then Vertical Line; or click the Vertical Line button on the Graphics Toolbar. This inserts a vertical line in the document that extends from the top margin to the bottom margin and is positioned on the line at the insertion point location.

EXERCISE

Inserting Vertical Lines

Vertical Line

1. At a clear editing window, create the letterhead shown in figure 20.10 (the vertical line in your letterhead will extend to the bottom margin) by completing the following steps:
    a. Create a vertical line by clicking Graphics, then Vertical Line; or by clicking the Vertical Line button on the Graphics Toolbar (last button on the Toolbar).
    b. Change the font to 14-point Arrus Blk BT.
    c. Press Alt + F7 (the Flush Right command), then key **CARR ELEMENTARY SCHOOL**.
    d. Press Enter, press Alt + F7, then key **1098 South Linley**.
    e. Press Enter, press Alt + F7, then key **Omaha, NE 45034**.
    f. Press Enter, press Alt + F7, then key **(402) 555-3220**.
2. Save the document and name it Ch 20, Ex 09.
3. Click the Page/Zoom Full button to see how the letterhead appears on the page, then click Page/Zoom Full again.
4. Print and then close Ch 20, Ex 09.

Chapter 20

Figure 20.10

CARR ELEMENTARY SCHOOL
1098 South Linley
Omaha, NE 45034
(402) 555-3220

Creating Customized Lines

If you use the Horizontal Line or Vertical Line button on the Graphics Toolbar, or the Horizontal Line or Vertical Line option from the Graphics drop-down menu, a default line is inserted in the document. If you want to create a customized horizontal or vertical line, click Graphics, then Custom Line or click the Custom Line button on the Graphics Toolbar. This causes the Create Graphics Line dialog box shown in figure 20.11 to display.

Figure 20.11

Create Graphics Line Dialog Box

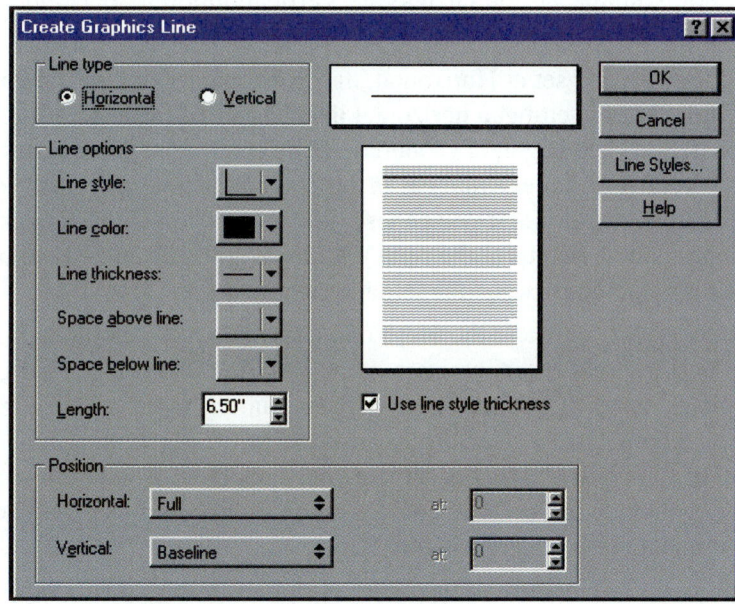

Line type: The Line type section of the Create Graphics Line dialog box contains two options—Horizontal and Vertical. The default setting is Horizontal. If you want to create a vertical line, click Vertical. This will change some of the options in the Line options and Position sections.

Line Style: Line style lets you select the style of line you want created. The default setting is Single. If you click the down-pointing triangle to the right of the Line style option, a box of line styles displays. These options are the same as the line style options available with graphics boxes and borders. For example, you can create a double line, thick and thin lines, shadow lines, and much more. To display the Line Styles dialog box, click Line Styles. (This command button is located at the right side of the dialog box.) The line style options available at this dialog box are the same as the ones available from the Line style option.

Creating Graphic Elements   459

Line color: The color of the line can be changed by clicking the down-pointing triangle to the right of Line color. A palette of color options will appear from which you can select the desired color.

Line thickness: When you click the down-pointing triangle to the right of Line thickness, a box of predefined lines with varying thicknesses will appear, or you can specify the exact measurement for the line in the text box at the bottom of the box.

Spacing: With the Space above line and Space below line options, you can specify the amount of white space you want between the line and the text above or below it. When you click the down-pointing triangle to the right of these options, a box of predefined spaces will appear, or you can specify a measurement in the text box at the bottom of the box.

If the Line type is set to Vertical, the Space above line and Space below line is replaced with Border offset. Use this option to specify the amount of white space on either side of the vertical line.

Length: If the Line type is set at Horizontal, the Length option in the Create Graphics Line dialog box has a default setting of 6.50 inches. If the Line Type is set at Vertical, the Length option has a default setting of 9 inches.

If you change the Horizontal option for a horizontal line, you can enter a different measurement in the Length option. For example, if you change the Horizontal option to Left rather than Full and you want a line drawn 3 inches beginning at the left margin, you would enter 3 in the Length text box.

If you change the Vertical option for a vertical line, you can enter a different measurement in the Length option. For example, if you change the Vertical option to Top and you want a 4-inch line beginning at the top margin, you would enter 4 in the Length text box.

Position: If the Line type is set at Horizontal, the Horizontal option in the Position section has a default setting of Full. At this setting, a horizontal line is inserted from the left to the right margin. This can be changed to Set, Left, Right, or Centered. If you choose the Set option, the insertion point is moved to the text box after *at*. Enter a number in this text box that represents the distance you want the line to appear from the left margin. If you choose Left, the horizontal line begins at the left margin and if you click Right, the line begins at the right margin. With the Centered option, you can create a horizontal line that is centered between the left and right margins.

If the Line type is set at Vertical, the Horizontal option has a default setting of Set. At this setting, a vertical line is inserted at the insertion point position. This can be changed to Left, Right, Centered, or Column Aligned. If you click the Left option, the vertical line is inserted at the left margin. If you click Right, the vertical line is inserted at the right margin. With the Centered option, you can create a vertical line that is centered between the top and bottom margins. The last option, Column Aligned, lets you insert a vertical line between columns in a document. (For more information on columns, please refer to chapter 23.)

If the Line type is set at Horizontal, the Vertical option in the Position section has a default setting of Baseline. At this setting, the bottom of the horizontal line is positioned along the text baseline. This can be changed to Set. At the Set option, you specify a distance in the *at* text box that represents the measurement from the top edge of the page.

If the Line type is set at Vertical, the Vertical option in the Position section has a default setting of Full. This causes the vertical line to extend from the top to the bottom margin. This can be changed to Set, Top, Bottom, or Centered. At the Set option, you can enter a measurement from the top edge of the page where you want the vertical line to begin. With the Top option, you can create a vertical line that begins at the top margin. Click Bottom to begin a vertical line at the bottom margin. Click Centered to center a vertical line between the top and bottom margins.

EXERCISE 10

Creating a Form with Horizontal Lines

1. At a clear editing window, create the form shown in figure 20.12 by completing the following steps:
   a. Key **PRINTING REQUISITION FORM**, centered and bold.
   b. Press Enter twice, key **Name:**, then press the space bar once.
   c. Create the horizontal line by completing the following steps:
      (1) Click Graphics, then Custom Line; or, click the Custom Line button on the Graphics Toolbar.
      (2) At the Create Graphics Line dialog box click Horizontal (located toward the bottom of the dialog box), then Set.
      (3) Click OK.
   d. Press Enter twice, key **Department:**, then press the space bar once.
   e. Create the horizontal line by completing the steps in 1c.
   f. Press Enter twice, key **Date Ordered:**, then press the space bar once.
   g. Create the horizontal line by completing the following steps:
      (1) Click Graphics, then Custom Line; or, click the Custom Line button on the Graphics Toolbar.
      (2) At the Create Graphics Line dialog box click Horizontal, then Set.
      (3) Select the current measurement in the Length text box, then key **2**.
      (4) Click OK.
   h. Press the Tab key until the insertion point is located on *Position 4.5"*.
   i. Key **Date Required:**, then press the space bar once.
   j. Create the horizontal line by completing the steps in 1c.
   k. Press Enter twice, key **Number of Copies:**, then press the space bar once.
   l. Create a horizontal line by completing the steps in 1c.
2. Save the form and name it Ch 20, Ex 10.
3. Print and then close Ch 20, Ex 10.

Figure 20.12

PRINTING REQUISITION FORM

Name: _____

Department: _____

Date Ordered: _____   Date Required: _____

Number of Copies: _____

Creating Graphic Elements

Customizing Existing Lines

When a horizontal or vertical line is created, a code is inserted in the document at the location of the insertion point. If you want to modify or change the existing line, you can delete the code, then recreate the line, or you can edit the line.

To edit a horizontal line, position the arrow pointer on the line to be edited, then click the left mouse button. This causes the line to be selected and sizing handles to display around the line. To edit the selected line, click Graphics, then Edit Line. This causes the Edit Graphics Line dialog box to display. This dialog box contains the same options as the Create Graphics Line dialog box shown in figure 20.11.

You can also display the Edit Graphics Line dialog box by positioning the insertion point *after* the line to be edited. (WordPerfect searches backward through a document.) Then click Graphics, then Edit Line.

Customizing a Line with the Mouse

After a horizontal or vertical line is created in a document, the length, thickness, and location of the line can be changed easily with the mouse. To make a change, position the arrow pointer on the horizontal or vertical line, then click the left mouse button. This causes the mouse to appear as a four-headed arrow and the line display to change as shown in figure 20.13.

Figure 20.13

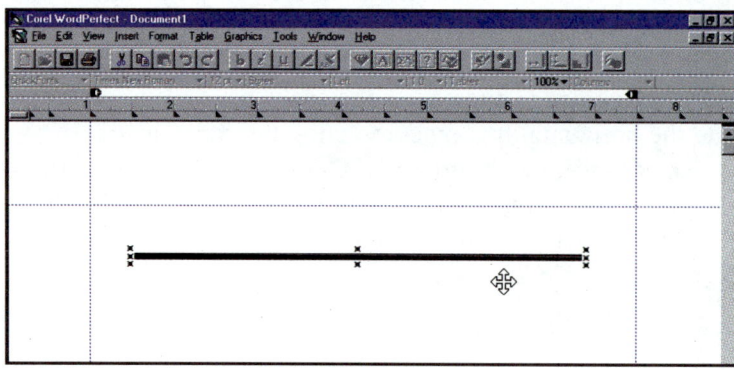

Graphics Line Edit Mode

The black boxes at the left, right, and center of the line borders are called *sizing handles.* You can use the sizing handles to shorten or lengthen the line as well as make it thinner or wider. To shorten or lengthen the line, position the arrow pointer on the middle sizing handle at the left or right side of the line until it turns into a double-headed arrow pointing left and right. Hold down the left mouse button, then drag the double-headed arrow to the left or right to lengthen or shorten the line. When the line is the desired length, release the mouse button.

To change the thickness of the horizontal line, position the arrow pointer on the middle sizing handle at the top or bottom of the line until it turns into a double-headed arrow pointing up and down. Hold down the left mouse button, then drag the double-headed arrow up or down to make the line wider or thinner. When the line is the desired width, release the mouse button.

You can change both the length and width of a graphics line with the sizing handles by using one of the sizing handles at the corners of the line.

EXERCISE 11

Creating Lines in a Letterhead

1. At a clear editing window, create the letterhead shown in figure 20.14 (the bottom line and the address and phone number will display in your document and print at the bottom of the page) by completing the following steps:
   a. Change the font to 18-point Arrus Blk BT.
   b. Create a user box with the image *Medical1* inserted with the following specifications:
      (1) Display the Box Position dialog box, change the Attach box to setting to Page, then close the dialog box.
      (2) Display the Box Size dialog box, change the width to Set at 1.5 inches, then close the dialog box.
   c. Press Enter once, then key **DENVER MEMORIAL HOSPITAL**.
   d. Press Enter once.
   e. Create a horizontal line with a thickness of 4 points by completing the following steps:
      (1) Click Graphics, then Custom Line.
      (2) At the Create Graphics Line dialog box, click the Line thickness button.
      (3) In the box containing line thickness options, select the measurement in the text box located at the bottom of the box, key **4p**, then press Enter.
      (4) Click OK to close the Create Graphics Line dialog box.
   f. Change the font to 12-point Arrus Blk BT.
   g. Press the Enter key until the insertion point is positioned on approximately Line 9.07".
   h. Create a horizontal line with a Line thickness of 2 points. (Refer to step 1e.)
   i. Press Enter once, press Alt + F7, then key **900 Colorado Boulevard**.
   j. Press Enter once, press Alt + F7, then key **Denver, CO 86530**.
   k. Press Enter once, press Alt + F7, then key **(303) 555-4400**.
2. Save the letterhead and name it Ch 20, Ex 11.
3. Print and then close Ch 20, Ex 11.

Figure 20.14

DENVER MEMORIAL HOSPITAL

900 Colorado Boulevard
Denver, CO 86530
(303) 555-4400

Creating Graphic Elements 463

EXERCISE 12

Editing Images and Lines with the Mouse

1. At a clear editing window, open Ch 20, Ex 11.
2. Save the document with Save As and name it Ch 20, Ex 12.
3. Move the graphics image to the left side of the page using the mouse by completing the following steps:
   a. Position the arrow pointer inside the user box, then hold down the left mouse button.
   b. Drag the user box outline to the left margin at the same vertical position, then release the mouse button.
4. Move the bottom horizontal line up slightly by completing the following steps:
   a. Position the arrow pointer on the bottom line, then hold down the left mouse button.
   b. Drag the line up slightly (about a tenth to an eighth of an inch), then release the mouse button.
5. Widen the top horizontal line by completing the following steps:
   a. Position the arrow pointer on the top horizontal line, then click the left mouse button.
   b. Move the arrow pointer to the middle sizing handle at the bottom of the line until it turns into a double-headed arrow pointing up and down, then hold down the left mouse button.
   c. Drag the double-headed arrow down until the line is about twice as wide, then release the button.
6. Widen the bottom horizontal line so it is twice as wide.
7. Save the document again with the same name (Ch 20, Ex 12).
8. Print and then close Ch 20, Ex 12.

Creating Drop Caps

In publications such as magazines, newsletters, or brochures, a graphics feature called "drop cap" can be used to enhance the appearance of the text. A drop cap is the first letter of the first word in a paragraph that is set into a paragraph and set in a larger font size. A drop cap identifies the beginning of major sections or parts of a document.

A drop cap looks best when set in a paragraph containing text set in a proportional font. It can be set in the same font as the paragraph text or it can be set in a complementary font. For example, a drop cap can be set in a sans serif font while the paragraph text is set in a serif font. Figure 20.15 shows a few examples of drop caps.

Figure 20.15

Drop Cap Examples

> In defending or prosecuting individuals, an attorney must research cases very extensively. This research is based on precedents established in cases having already been resolved before the courts. Many volumes of law books are available to search for the information needed. A number of companies have taken volumes of law manuals and recorded them electronically.
>
> In defending or prosecuting individuals, an attorney must research cases very extensively. This research is based on precedents established in cases having already been resolved before the courts. Many volumes of law books are available to search for the information needed. A number of companies have taken volumes of law manuals and recorded them electronically.
>
> In defending or prosecuting individuals, an attorney must research cases very extensively. This research is based on precedents established in cases having already been resolved before the courts. Many volumes of law books are available to search for the information needed. A number of companies have taken volumes of law manuals and recorded them electronically.
>
> In defending or prosecuting individuals, an attorney must research cases very extensively. This research is based on precedents established in cases having already been resolved before the courts. Many volumes of law books are available to search for the information needed. A number of companies have taken volumes of law manuals and recorded them electronically.

A drop cap can be one character, as shown in the first and fourth example, or the entire first word can be drop caps, as shown in the second and third examples. The four examples in figure 20.15 show only a few ways drop caps can be created. Many other formatting options are available for drop caps.

A drop cap can be created as you key text or a drop cap can be applied to existing text. To create a drop cap, display the Drop Cap Feature Bar shown in figure 20.16 by clicking Format, then Drop Cap. By default, a drop cap is created on the first letter of the paragraph and the letter is three lines high as shown in the first example in figure 20.15. After creating the drop cap, close the Drop Cap Feature Bar by clicking the Close button.

Figure 20.16

Drop Cap Feature Bar

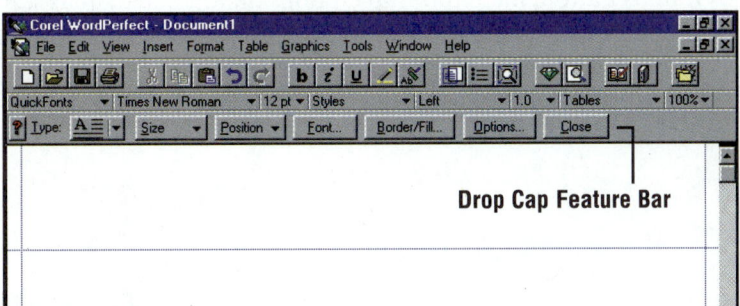

Creating Graphic Elements 465

EXERCISE 13

Inserting Drop Caps

1. At a clear editing window, open Para 01.
2. Save the document with Save As and name it Ch 20, Ex 13.
3. Create a drop cap for the first paragraph by completing the following steps:
   a. Position the insertion point anywhere in the first paragraph.
   b. Click Format, then Drop Cap.
   c. Click Close to close the Drop Cap Feature Bar.
4. Complete steps similar to those in 3a through 3c to create a drop cap for the second paragraph.
5. Save the document again with the same name (Ch 20, Ex 13).
6. Print and then close Ch 20, Ex 13.

Customizing a Drop Cap

The Drop Cap Feature Bar contains a variety of options for customizing a drop cap. You can change the size of the drop cap and the location of the drop cap in relation to the text by clicking Type. This causes a Drop Cap palette to display. This palette contains options for positioning the drop cap. For example, the drop cap can be positioned inside the paragraph, outside the paragraph, or partially above the paragraph. The drop cap can be two, three, or four lines tall. To choose an option from the palette, click the desired drop cap type.

The Drop Cap palette provides preformatted drop cap options. With the other buttons on the Drop Cap Feature Bar, you can format a drop cap with specific formatting.

With the Size button, you can choose to make the drop cap two to nine lines tall or enter a specific line number.

With the options from the Position button, you can specify whether the drop cap is positioned in the text with the In Text option or in the margin with the In Margin option. You can also click the Other option, which displays the Drop Cap Position dialog box where you can specify the number of lines the drop cap will occupy as well as the location of the drop cap in relation to the margin.

Use the Font button on the Drop Cap Feature Bar to change the font for the drop cap. When you click the Font button, the Drop Cap Font dialog box displays. This dialog box contains the same font choices as the Font dialog box.

Earlier in this chapter, you learned to create paragraph and page borders and border fill. A border or fill can also be added to a drop cap. To display the Drop Cap Border dialog box, click the Border/Fill button on the Drop Cap Feature Bar. The Drop Cap Border/Fill dialog box contains the same options as the Paragraph Border/Fill and Page Border/Fill dialog boxes.

If you click the Options button, the Drop Cap Options dialog box displays. Figure 20.17 shows the options available at this dialog box and what each option will perform.

Figure 20.17

Drop Cap Options

Choose this option...	to do this...
Number of characters in drop cap	specify the number of characters you want as the drop cap.
Make first whole word as drop cap	specify the first word of the paragraph as the drop cap.
Wrap text around drop cap	wrap paragraph text around the drop cap. If this option is deselected, paragraph text will flow through the drop cap.
Allow for descender	let paragraph text wrap around drop cap characters that extend below text baseline.
Allow for Diacritic	move drop cap down slightly for letters using diacritics such as the accent for the letter É.

After creating the drop cap, click the Close button on the Drop Cap Feature Bar to remove the feature bar from the document window.

Creating and Editing Drop Caps

1. At a clear editing window, open Para 02.
2. Save the document with Save As and name it Ch 20, Ex 14.
3. With the insertion point positioned at the beginning of the document, change the font to 12-point BernhardMod BT (or a similar typeface).
4. Create a drop cap for the first paragraph by completing the following steps:
    a. Position the insertion point anywhere in the first paragraph.
    b. Click Format, then Drop Cap.
    c. Change the height and font of the drop cap by completing the following steps:
        (1) Click the Type button on the Drop Cap Feature Bar (the button containing the letter A and several lines).
        (2) At the Drop Cap palette, click the first option in the bottom row. (This changes the drop cap height to two lines.)
        (3) Click the Font button on the Drop Cap Feature Bar.
        (4) At the Drop Cap Font dialog box, click Colonna MT (or a similar typeface) in the Font face list box, then click OK.
5. Create a drop cap for the second paragraph by completing steps similar to those in 4.
6. Click Close to close the Drop Cap Feature Bar.
7. Save the document again with the same name (Ch 20, Ex 14).
8. Print and then close Ch 20, Ex 14.

Creating Graphic Elements 467

Reversed Text

Reversed text is white text on a black background, as opposed to the normal black text on a white background. WordPerfect provides a macro called *Reverse* that will automatically format selected text to any color and background choice you select. Reversed text is often used in forms for titles and in newsletters for titles or pull quotes that you want to stand out. Complete exercise 15 to practice using the *Reverse* macro.

EXERCISE 15

Creating Reversed Text

1. At a clear editing window, create the text shown in figure 20.18 by completing the following steps:
    a. Change the font to 18-point Arial Bold
    b. Press Shift + F7, key **Denver Memorial Hospital**, then press Enter twice.
    c. Select the text, *Denver Memorial Hospital*.
    d. Click Tools, point to Macro, then click Play.
    e. At the Play Macro dialog box, make sure the folder that displays is *c:\Corel\Office7\Macros\WPWin*, then double-click the macro named *Reverse*.
    f. In the Reverse Text Options dialog box shown in figure 20.19, click OK.
    g. Press Ctrl + End to move the insertion point to the end of the document. (The end of the document is a double space below *Denver Memorial Hospital*.)
    h. Change the font to 14-point Arial Bold.
    i. Key the remaining text as shown in figure 20.18.
2. Save the document and name it Ch 20, Ex 15.
3. Print and then close Ch 20, Ex 15.

Figure 20.18

Denver Memorial Hospital

900 Colorado Boulevard   Denver, CO 86530
                                (303) 555-4400

Reverse Text Options Dialog Box

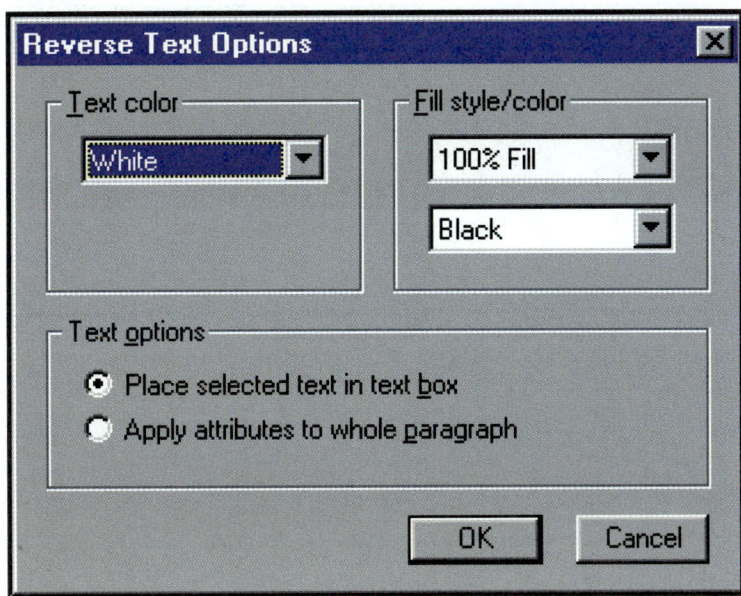

Figure 20.19

When the Reverse Text Options dialog box appears when playing the *Reverse* macro, you can select other colors for the text foreground and background. With the Text color option, you can select a variety of other colors for the text. In the Fill style/color section, the Fill text box defaults to 100% Fill. If you click the down-pointing triangle to the right of 100% Fill, you can select a range of percentages starting at 100% Fill (solid black) and progressing downward. As you decrease the percentage of the fill, the background will print in lighter shades of gray if the color option remains at Black. If you click the down-pointing triangle to the right of Black, you can select a variety of other colors from the drop-down list that displays.

In the Text options section, the default option is Place selected text in a text box. This can be changed to Apply attributes to whole paragraph.

Using Make It Fit

WordPerfect's Make It Fit feature will shrink or expand text in a document to fill a specified number of pages. For example, if a few lines of a business letter display at the beginning of the second page, Make It Fit can be used to shrink the text onto the first page.

To make text fit on a specified number of pages, Make It Fit automatically adjusts font size and line spacing. In addition, margins can be selected to help shrink or expand text in a document. To display the Make It Fit dialog box shown in figure 20.20, open a document containing text you want to shrink or expand, then click Format, then Make It Fit; or click the Make It Fit button on the Toolbar.

Make It Fit

Creating Graphic Elements 469

Figure 20.20　　　　　　　　　　　　　　　　　　　　　　　Make It Fit Dialog Box

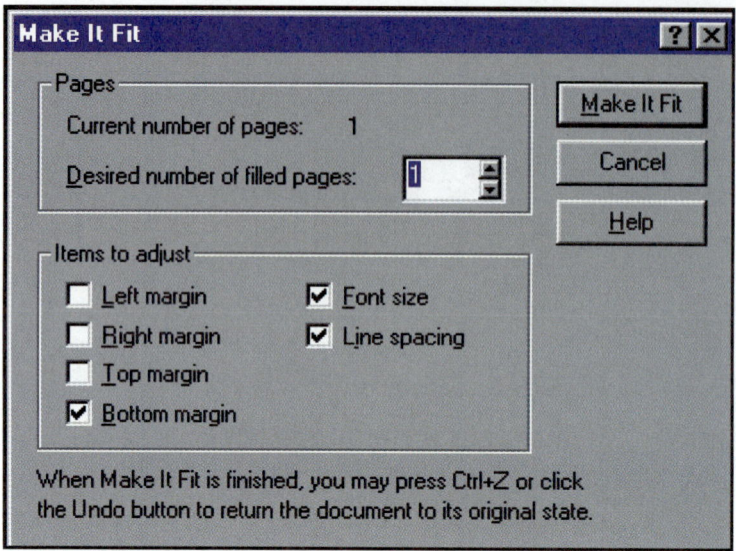

At the Make It Fit dialog box, the current number of pages in the open document is displayed after the Current number of pages option. Specify the number of pages desired in the Desired number of filled pages text box. By default, WordPerfect will change fonts and line spacing to shrink or expand text. If you do not want one of these features changed, remove the check mark from the check box before the option. You can also tell WordPerfect to use the left, right, top, or bottom margins to shrink or expand text by inserting a check mark in the check box before the option. When all changes have been made to the Make It Fit dialog box, click Make It Fit.

If you use Make It Fit on a document and do not like the changes, you can change the document back to its original state by clicking Edit, then Undo, or by clicking the Undo button on the Toolbar. (You must do this immediately after using Make It Fit.)

Making Text Fit

1. At a clear editing window, open Notice 01.
2. Save the document with Save As and name it Ch 20, Ex 16.
3. With the insertion point positioned at the beginning of the document, change the font to 14-point BernhardMod BT Bold.
4. Expand the document to fit the page by completing the following steps:
   a. Click Format, then Make It Fit; or click the Make It Fit button on the Toolbar.
   b. At the Make It Fit dialog box, make sure there is a check mark in the Font size check box and the Line spacing check box (and no check marks in the other check boxes), then click Make It Fit.
5. Save the document again with the same name (Ch 20, Ex 16).
6. Print and then close Ch 20, Ex 16.

470　Chapter 20

EXERCISE 17

More Practice with Make It Fit

1. At a clear editing window, open Policy 01.
2. Save the document with Save As and name it Ch 20, Ex 17.
3. With the insertion point at the beginning of the document, change the line spacing to 1.5.
4. Make the text fit on one page by completing the following steps:
    a. Click the Make It Fit button on the Toolbar.
    b. At the Make It Fit dialog box, change the number in the Desired number of filled pages to 1.
    c. Click Bottom margin. (This inserts a check mark in the check box.)
    d. Click Make It Fit.
5. Save the document again with the same name (Ch 20, Ex 17).
6. Print and then close Ch 20, Ex 17.

CHAPTER SUMMARY

▼ Mathematic and scientific equations can be created and edited with the Equation Editor.

▼ The three sections of the Equation Editor are the editing window where the equation is keyed; the display window, which shows how the equation will look in the document; and the equation palette, which contains the commands and symbols that can be used in the equation.

▼ Use an inline equation box to create an equation as part of the text in a document.

▼ Text in a document can be surrounded with borders at the Paragraph Border/Fill or Page Border/Fill dialog boxes.

▼ Create a horizontal or vertical line in a document with options from the Graphics drop-down menu or with buttons on the Graphics Toolbar. Create a customized horizontal or vertical line at the Create Graphics Line dialog box.

▼ The length, thickness, and location of a line can be changed easily with the mouse. To make a change, position the arrow pointer on the horizontal or vertical line, then click the left mouse button.

▼ A drop cap, used to enhance the appearance of text, can be created on the first letter or the first word of a paragraph using the Drop Cap feature.

▼ WordPerfect includes a macro named *Reverse* that will format selected text to a variety of foreground and background colors for visual emphasis in a document.

▼ The Make It Fit option will shrink or expand text in a document to fill a specified number of pages.

COMMANDS REVIEW

	Mouse/Keyboard
Equation Editor	Graphics, Equation; or click Equation button on Graphics Toolbar
Custom Box dialog box	Graphics, Custom Box; or click Custom Box button on Graphics Toolbar
Create Horizontal Line	Graphics, Horizontal Line; or click Horizontal Line button on Graphics Toolbar
Create Vertical Line	Graphics, Vertical Line; or click Vertical Line button on Graphics Toolbar
Create Graphics Line dialog box	Graphics, Custom Line; or click Custom Line button on Graphics Toolbar
Drop Cap Feature Bar	Format, Drop Cap
Reverse Text	Select text to be changed then click Tools, Macro, Play, double-click *Reverse*, then click OK in the Reverse Text Options dialog box
Make It Fit dialog box	Format, Make It Fit; or click Make It Fit button on Toolbar

CHECK YOUR UNDERSTANDING

Completion: In the space provided at the right, indicate the correct term, command, or number.

1. This section of the Equation Editor shows how the equation will look in the document.

2. This section of the Equation Editor contains the commands and symbols that can be used in the equation.

3. Use this type of equation box to create an equation as part of the text in a document.

4. Insert a page border in a document with options from this dialog box.

5. Click this option at the Graphics drop-down menu to display the Create Graphics Line dialog box.

6. Change the size of a drop cap and the location of a drop cap in relation to the text by clicking this button on the Drop Cap Feature Bar.

7. WordPerfect includes this macro that will format selected text to a variety of foreground and background colors.

8. Use this WordPerfect feature to expand or shrink text in a document to fill a specified number of pages.

In the space provided at the right, write each equation as you would key it at the Equation Editor.

1. $\dfrac{a}{b+c}$ _____

2. $\dfrac{a+c}{b}$ _____

3. $\dfrac{Q_2 + Q_3}{4}$ _____

SKILL ASSESSMENTS

Assessment 1

1. At a clear editing window, change the left and right margins to 1.5 inches. Key the memo shown in figure 20.21 in an appropriate memo format. When creating the equation, key the following at the Equation Editor:

    X^2~=~SUM {(O~-~3)^2} over E~=~6.908

2. Save the memo and name it Ch 20, SA 01.
3. Print and then close Ch 20, SA 01.

Figure 20.21

DATE: May 19, 1998; TO: Lisa Bassett; FROM: Allen Lavell; SUBJECT: STATISTICAL ANALYSIS

When I ran the statistical analysis on the lab blood draws, I used the following formula to determine the chi square by summing the resulting quotients:

$$X^2 = \sum \dfrac{(O-3)^2}{E} = 6.908$$

If you need anything further, please contact me by 5:00 p.m. tomorrow. I will be out of town the rest of the week.

xx:Ch 20, SA 01

Assessment 2

1. At a clear editing window, change the left and right margins to 1.5 inches. Key the memo shown in figure 20.22 in an appropriate memo format. Change the line spacing to 1.5 at the beginning of the first paragraph. Key the following when creating the first inline equation in the first paragraph:

    p~=~1 over 20~=~0.05

    Key the following when creating the second inline equation in the first paragraph:

    k_1 over k_2~=~5 over 25~=~0.20

Creating Graphic Elements   473

2. Save the memo and name it Ch 20, SA 02.
3. Print and then close Ch 20, SA 02.

Figure 20.22

DATE: May 5, 1998; TO: Melissa Nobel; FROM: Danielle Curry; SUBJECT: TRAINING MANUAL

Please add the equation $p = \frac{1}{20} = 0.05$ at the end of the second section on page 23 of Specifications Manual 14. In addition, I need the formula $\frac{k_1}{k_2} = \frac{5}{25} = 0.20$ added to the analysis section on page 52.

Thank you for your patience in getting this manual completed. Hopefully, there will be no further changes.

xx:Ch 20, SA 02

Assessment 3

1. At a clear editing window, open Block 02.
2. Save the document with Save As and name it Ch 20, SA 03.
3. Make the following changes:
    a. Change to a larger, serif font. (You determine the font.)
    b. Insert a code to center the text vertically on the current page.
    c. Create a page border (you determine the border and fill style).
4. Save the document again with the same name (Ch 20, SA 03).
5. Print and then close Ch 20, SA 03.

Assessment 4

1. At a clear editing window, create the document shown in figure 20.23 with the following specifications:
    a. Change to a larger and more formal font. (You determine the font.)
    b. Center the text vertically on the page.
    c. Insert bullets as shown in the figure.
2. Insert a double line page border.
3. Save the document and name it Ch 20, SA 04.
4. Print and then close Ch 20, SA 04.

Figure 20.23

TENETS FOR

COMPLIMENT/COMPLAINT SYSTEM

◆ We are paving our way to excellence with compliments and complaints.

◆ Compliments/complaints are encouraged by all employees.

◆ All customers are important, and their feelings are taken seriously and respected.

◆ Compliments/complaints are received and resolved at the lowest appropriate level of the organization.

◆ Customers are not given the impression that they are being "run around," either in registering their compliment/complaint or in the resolution.

◆ All compliments/complaints are dealt with in a timely manner.

◆ Guidelines for all employees and authority levels are defined.

Assessment 5

1. At a clear editing window, create the form shown in figure 20.24. Set the title *REGISTRATION FORM* in reversed text. Use the Create Graphics Line dialog box to create the horizontal lines in the form. (You determine the settings for the lines.)
2. Save the form and name it Ch 20, SA 05.
3. Print and then close Ch 20, SA 05.

Figure 20.24

REGISTRATION FORM

Name: _____ SSN: _____

Course Name: _____

Course Number: _____ Quarter: _____

Creating Graphic Elements

Assessment 6

1. At a clear editing window, create the letterhead shown in figure 20.25 by completing the following steps:
   a. Create a user box with the following specifications:
      (1) Insert the image named *Crest*.
      (2) Display the Box Position dialog box, change the Attach box to setting to Page, change the Horizontal setting to Left Margin, then close the dialog box.
      (3) Display the Box Size dialog box, change the width to Set at 1.5 inches, then close the dialog box.
   b. At the editing window, change the font to 14-point Humanst521 Lt BT. (If Humanst521 Lt BT is not available, use Arial.)
   c. Press Enter once, press Alt + F7, then key **BLUE RIBBON PRODUCTS**.
   d. Key the address and telephone number at the right margin as shown in the figure.
2. After keying the telephone number, press Enter, then create a horizontal line with a Line Thickness of 3 points.
3. Save the letterhead and name it Ch 20, SA 06.
4. Print and then close Ch 20, SA 06.

Figure 20.25

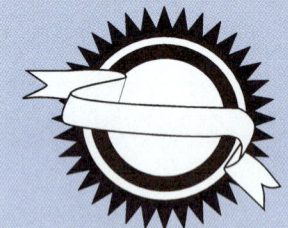

BLUE RIBBON PRODUCTS
4300 South Palm Drive
Mesa, AZ 85733
(602) 555-9776

Assessment 7

1. At a clear editing window, open Ch 20, SA 06.
2. Save the document with Save As and name it Ch 20, SA 07.
3. Make the following changes to the horizontal line:
   a. Move the horizontal line so it appears *above* the name *BLUE RIBBON PRODUCTS*.
   b. Widen the horizontal line so it is twice as wide.
   c. Customize the horizontal line so the color is a light shade of gray.
4. Save the document with the same name (Ch 20, SA 07).
5. Print and then close Ch 20, SA 07.

Assessment 8

1. At a clear editing window, open Para 03.
2. Save the document with Save As and name it Ch 20, SA 08.
3. Make the following changes to the document:
   a. With the insertion point at the beginning of the document, change the font to 13-point BernhardMod BT.
   b. Create a drop cap for the first letter of each paragraph. Make the drop cap two lines in height.
   c. Use the Make It Fit option to expand the document to fill the entire page.
4. Save the document again with the same name (Ch 20, SA 08).
5. Print and then close Ch 20, Ex 08.

21

USING DRAW AND TEXTART

PERFORMANCE OBJECTIVE

Upon completion of chapter 21, you will be able to enhance documents by creating shapes, images, or text in the Draw and TextArt programs.

Corel WordPerfect 7 provides many predesigned graphics images. You used some of these graphics images in exercises in chapters 19 and 20. When you installed WordPerfect, Corel Presentations was also installed. Presentations is a graphics program that allows you to create and edit your own graphics. Corel Presentations becomes the Draw module from within Corel WordPerfect. In this chapter, you will learn the basic functions of Draw. With Draw, you can draw shapes, draw free hand, insert graphics images, and create and customize text.

The TextArt program lets you distort and modify text so it conforms to a variety of shapes. You will practice using this program in this chapter.

Drawing Shapes

You can use the Draw program to draw a variety of shapes such as circles, squares, rectangles, ellipses, ovals, and much more. When using Draw to draw shapes, you will follow these basic steps:

1. Open Draw. To do this, click Graphics, then Draw; or click the Draw button on the Graphics Toolbar.
2. Draw the shape in the drawing area.
3. When you are done drawing, click the Close button on the Draw Toolbar or click in the editing window outside the drawing area.
4. Deselect the box containing the draw object(s). To do this, position the arrow pointer in the editing window outside the box, then click the left mouse button.

Draw

When you click the Close button on the Draw Toolbar, the shape you drew displays in the editing window and the Draw program is closed. What you drew is inserted in a box with no borders. This box is inserted at the left margin of the document and is approximately 3.5 inches wide and 3 inches tall. When you click Graphics, then Draw; or click the Draw button on the Graphics Toolbar, the Draw window shown in figure 21.1 displays.

Using Draw and TextArt 477

Figure 21.1

Draw Window

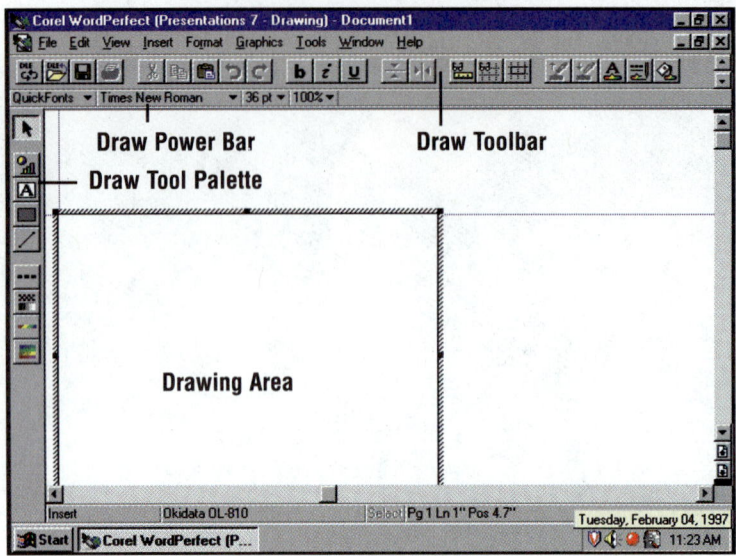

At the left side of the Draw window the Draw Tool palette is displayed. This palette includes a variety of tools for selecting, drawing, and changing the fill and attributes of objects. The names of the tools are shown in figure 21.2. Two tools on the Draw Tool palette, Closed Object Tools and Line Object Tools, contain options for drawing closed shapes and line shapes.

Figure 21.2

Draw Tool Palette Tools

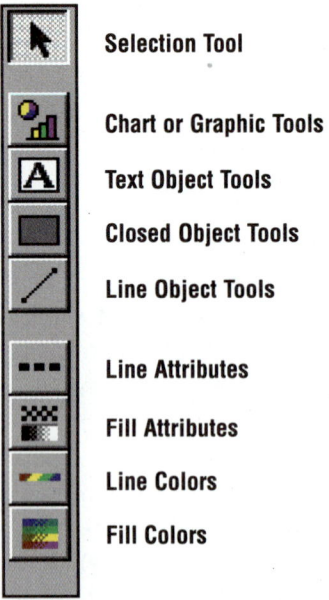

If you click Closed Object Tools, eight shape options display as shown in figure 21.3. With options from Closed Object Tools, you can draw closed shapes. The Draw program will fill a closed object with blue color. Click Line Object Tools and seven line options display as shown in figure 21.4. Use the options from Line Object Tools to draw lines. Shapes you draw with line tools are not considered closed objects and will not display with blue color.

Closed Object Tools Options

Figure 21.3

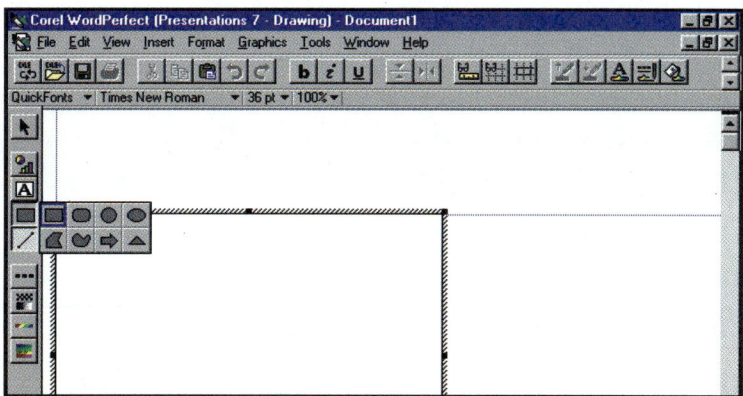

Line Object Tools Options

Figure 21.4

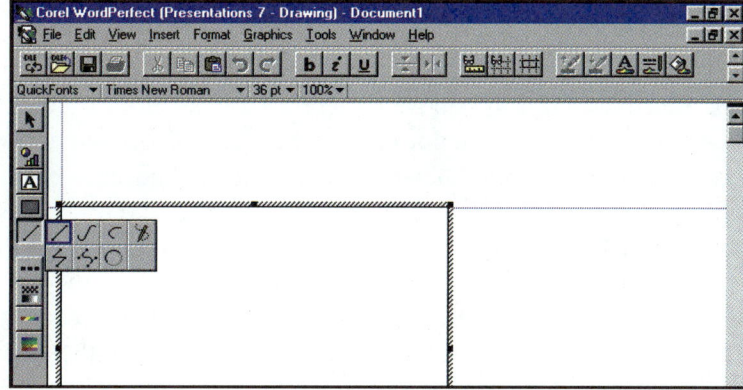

With the options from Closed Object Tools, you can draw a rectangle, a rectangle with rounded corners, a circle, an ellipse, a polygon, a closed curve, an arrow, and a regular polygon with equal sides. The shape is shown on the tool. Use options from Line Object Tools to draw a line, a curved line, sections of an ellipse, draw freehand, a line with one or more angles, a bezier curve, or a section of a circle. To draw a line drawing, you would complete the following steps:

1. Position the arrow pointer on Line Object Tools, hold down the left mouse button, drag the arrow pointer to the desired line tool, then release the mouse button.
2. Position the mouse pointer inside the drawing area. When the mouse pointer is positioned in the drawing area, it displays as a crosshairs.
3. Position the crosshairs at the location in the drawing area where the object is to begin, then click the left mouse button. Continue to click to add points, and double-click to end the drawing of the object. For some line tools, such as the freehand tool, you may need to hold down the left mouse button as you draw.

To draw a shape, you would complete the following steps:

1. Position the arrow pointer on Closed Object Tools, hold down the left mouse button, drag the arrow pointer to the desired shape tool, then release the mouse button.
2. Position the mouse pointer (crosshairs) inside the drawing area.
3. Position the crosshairs at the location where the object is to begin, hold down the left mouse button, drag the crosshairs up, down, left, or right to draw the shape, then release the mouse button when the desired shape displays.

Using Draw and TextArt

You can use the rectangle tool to draw a square. To draw a square, hold down the Shift key as you draw the shape in the drawing area.

EXERCISE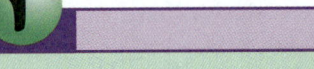

Creating a Circle and a Square

1. At a clear editing window, draw a circle and a square using Draw by completing the following steps:
    a. Open Draw. To do this, click Graphics, then Draw; or click the Draw button on the Graphics Toolbar.
    b. At the Draw window, position the arrow pointer on Closed Object Tools on the Draw Tool palette, hold down the left mouse button, drag the arrow pointer to the circle tool, then release the mouse button. (The circle tool is the third tool from the left in the top row.)
    c. Position the mouse pointer (crosshairs) in the drawing area. The crosshairs should be positioned slightly toward the bottom of where you want the circle to be in the drawing window. For example, as you drag the mouse down, the circle will form above the crosshairs position.
    d. Hold down the left mouse button, drag the crosshairs down until the outline image displays as a circle, then release the mouse button.
    e. Position the arrow pointer on Closed Object Tools, hold down the left mouse button, drag the arrow pointer to the rectangle tool, then release the mouse button. (The rectangle tool is the first tool from the left in the first row.)
    f. Position the crosshairs in the drawing area toward the right side.
    g. Hold down the Shift key and the left mouse button, drag the crosshairs down and to the right (or left) until the outline image displays as a square, then release the mouse button and the Shift key.
    h. Click the Close button on the Draw Toolbar (second button from the left); or click in the editing window outside the box containing the circle.
    i. Deselect the box containing the circle and square. To do this, click in the editing window outside the box.
2. Save the document and name it Ch 21, Ex 01.
3. Print and then close Ch 21, Ex 01.

Clearing a Shape

A shape you have drawn can be cleared from the drawing area. To clear a shape, click Edit, then Clear; or press Ctrl + Shift + F4 at the Draw window. Draw inserts a confirmation prompt asking if you want to delete ALL objects. At this box, click Yes. This clears the drawing area and keeps the Draw window open.

EXERCISE 2

Drawing a Diamond Shape

1. At a clear editing window, draw a diamond shape using Draw by completing the following steps:
    a. Open Draw.
    b. Position the arrow pointer on Line Object Tools, hold down the left mouse button, drag the arrow pointer to the line tool with angles (the first tool in the second row), then release the mouse button.
    c. Position the crosshairs approximately in the middle of the drawing area between the left and right edges and toward the top of the drawing area.
    d. Click the left mouse button once. This adds a point.
    e. Move the crosshairs down and to the right approximately 1 inch, then click the left mouse button. This adds another point.
    f. Move the crosshairs down and to the left approximately 1 inch, then click the left mouse button. This adds another point.
    g. Move the crosshairs up and to the left approximately 1 inch, then click the left mouse button. This adds another point.
    h. Position the arrow pointer on the first point, then double-click the left mouse button. This completes the diamond shape.
    i. If you are not satisfied with the way the diamond shape looks, you can clear the current shape, and redraw another by completing the following steps:
        (1) Click Edit, then Clear; or press Ctrl + Shift + F4.
        (2) At the confirmation prompt asking if you want to delete ALL objects, click Yes.
    j. When the diamond is the desired shape, click the Close button on the Draw Toolbar; or click in the editing window outside the drawing area.
    k. Deselect the box containing the diamond shape. To do this, click in the editing window outside the box.
2. Save the document and name it Ch 21, Ex 02.
3. Print and then close Ch 21, Ex 02.

Displaying the Ruler and Grid

The Draw program includes a ruler and grid that you can use to draw shapes or position images at specific locations in the drawing area. To turn on the display of the Ruler, click View, then Ruler; or click the Ruler button on the Draw Toolbar. This causes a horizontal ruler to display at the top of the drawing area and a vertical ruler to display at the left side of the drawing area as shown in figure 21.5. If you click View, point to Grid/Snap, then click Grid; or click the Grid button on the Draw Toolbar, a grid pattern displays in the drawing area as shown in figure 21.5.

With the Ruler displayed, a drawing tool selected, and the crosshairs positioned inside the drawing area, red marks display on the horizontal ruler and vertical ruler identifying the position of the crosshairs. If the crosshairs are positioned precisely on a whole number measurement, the red marker turns turquoise.

Ruler

Grid

Figure 21.5

Ruler and Grid in Draw

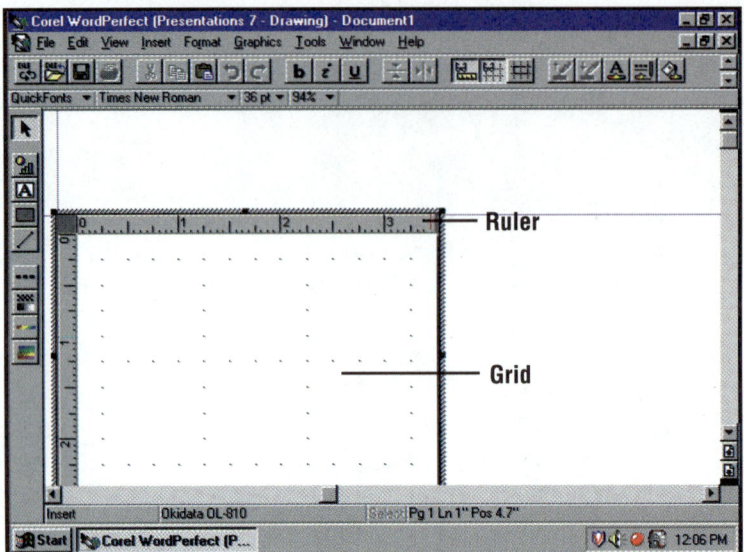

 EXERCISE

Drawing a Square on the Grid

1. At a clear editing window, create a square using Draw by completing the following steps:
   a. Open Draw.
   b. Click the Ruler button, then click the Grid button on the Draw Toolbar.
   c. Position the arrow pointer on Closed Object Tools, hold down the left mouse button, drag the arrow pointer to the rectangle tool, then release the mouse button.
   d. Position the crosshairs in the drawing area until the red markers are positioned on the 1-inch mark on the horizontal ruler and the 1-inch mark on the vertical ruler and the markers turn turquoise.
   e. Hold down the left mouse button, drag the crosshairs down and to the right until the red markers appear on the 2-inch mark on the horizontal and vertical rulers and the markers turn turquoise, then release the mouse button.
   f. Close Draw.
   g. At the editing window, deselect the box containing the square.
2. Save the document and name it Ch 21, Ex 03.
3. Print and then close Ch 21, Ex 03.

Editing a Box

When you close Draw, what you drew is inserted in a box with no borders. This box is inserted at the left margin of the document and is approximately 3.5 inches wide and 3 inches tall. The box that is inserted in the document when you close Draw is the same type of box you learned to create in chapter 19. All the same editing options are available.

482   Chapter 21

You can display the Edit Box dialog box for the box, then choose options from the dialog box. To display the Edit Box dialog box for a drawing box, position the arrow pointer on the QuickSpot button, then click the left mouse button. You can also click the Edit Box button on the Graphics Toolbar. Make changes to the box containing the drawn shapes just as you learned to edit graphics boxes in chapter 19.

You can also move the box containing the drawn shape with the mouse. To do this, position the arrow pointer on the shape, then click the left mouse button. This causes the box containing the shape to be selected. Position the arrow pointer (displays as a four-headed arrow) inside the selected area, hold down the left mouse button, drag the outline to the desired location, then release the mouse button.

EXERCISE 4

Editing a Drawing

1. At a clear editing window, open Ch 21, Ex 03.
2. Save the document with Save As and name it Ch 21, Ex 04.
3. Change the size of the box containing the square by completing the following steps:
   a. Position the arrow pointer on the QuickSpot button, then click the left mouse button.
   b. At the Edit Box dialog box, click the Size button.
   c. At the Box Size dialog box, change the box width to Full and the height to Maintain proportions.
   d. Click OK to close the Box Size dialog box.
   e. Close the Edit Box dialog box.
4. Display the full page to see how the box displays on the page, then change back to the default view.
5. Save the document again with the same name (Ch 21, Ex 04).
6. Print and then close Ch 21, Ex 04.

Deleting a Box

If you insert a box in the editing window, a Box code is inserted in the document. If you decide you want to delete the box from the editing window, display Reveal Codes, then delete the Box code. You can also delete the box by clicking the object to display the sizing handles around the box, then pressing the Delete key.

Drawing Freehand

Draw provides a variety of drawing tools to create many different shapes. If, however, you want to draw an object freehand, you can use the freehand tool. To select the freehand tool, position the arrow pointer on Line Object Tools, hold down the left mouse button, drag the arrow pointer to the last tool at the right in the first row (the one with the pencil), then release the mouse button. Position the crosshairs in the drawing area, hold down the left mouse button, then move the mouse as desired. When drawing with the freehand tool, you may find it difficult to draw smooth lines. It may take some practice to draw precise images.

Using Draw and TextArt 483

EXERCISE 5

Writing Your Name with Draw

1. At a clear editing window, write your first name using Draw by completing the following steps:
   a. Open Draw.
   b. Position the arrow pointer on Line Object Tools, hold down the left mouse button, drag the arrow pointer to the last tool at the right in the first row (the one with the pencil), then release the mouse button.
   c. Position the crosshairs in the drawing area.
   d. Hold down the left mouse button, then drag the crosshairs in the necessary directions to draw your first name. As you move the crosshairs, a line is drawn in the drawing area. When you release the left mouse button, the object is enclosed in sizing handles in the drawing window. You can then move the crosshairs to different areas without drawing a line. Resume drawing by selecting the freehand tool again on the Draw Tool palette.
   e. If you are not satisfied with the results, clear the drawing screen (Edit, Clear, then Yes, or Ctrl + Shift + F4, then Yes) and begin again.
   f. When the drawing is completed, close Draw.
   g. At the editing window, deselect the box containing your name.
2. Save the document and name it Ch 21, Ex 05.
3. Print and then close Ch 21, Ex 05.

Inserting Images

In chapter 19 you learned how to create a box and then insert a graphics image into the box. A variety of options can be used to customize the box and/or the image. A graphics image can also be inserted in the drawing area where it can be customized. The graphics image can then be inserted in the document.

EXERCISE

Inserting and Editing an Image

1. At a clear editing window, insert the graphics image named *Rose* in the drawing area, then into the document, by completing the following steps:
   a. Change to the Draft viewing mode.
   b. Open Draw.
   c. Position the arrow pointer on Chart or Graphic Tools, hold down the left mouse button, drag the arrow pointer to the QuickArt tool (last tool in second row; contains an image of a diamond); or click Insert, then QuickArt.
   d. Move the mouse pointer into the drawing area and it turns into a hand holding a square.
   e. Draw a box in the drawing area in which the image will be inserted. To do this, position the hand in the upper left corner of the drawing area, hold

down the left mouse button, drag the hand down and to the right to the lower right corner of the drawing area, then release the mouse button. This causes the QuickArt Browser dialog box to display.

    f. At the QuickArt Browser dialog box, click the Up One Level button to display the contents of the Graphics folder. Scroll down through the list of graphics images until *Rose* is visible, then double-click *Rose*. (This inserts the image inside the box you drew in the drawing area.)

    g. Change the color of the small unopened rose at the top left of the image to yellow, by completing the following steps.

        (1) Double-click the rose image. (This will cause a blue box to surround the entire rose image.)

        (2) With the Selection Tool selected, use the mouse and draw a dotted box around the small unopened rose at the top left of the image. (This selects all of the individual elements that the small rose contains.)

        (3) Click the Fill Colors tool on the Draw Tool palette.

        (4) Click a yellow shade in the Pattern/Gradient Color palette that displays.

    h. Close Draw.

2. At the editing window, change the position and size of the box by completing the following steps:

    a. Position the arrow pointer inside the box containing the rose, click the *right* mouse button, then click Size.

    b. At the Box Size dialog box, change the box width to Full and the height to Maintain proportions.

    c. Click OK to close the Box Size dialog box.

3. Display the full page to see how the box displays on the page, then change back to the default view.
4. Save the document and name it Ch 21, Ex 06.
5. Print and then close Ch 21, Ex 06.

Creating Text in Draw

In Draw, you can create, customize, and edit text. You can perform such activities as inserting text inside a graphics image, scaling text, contouring text, inserting text inside shapes, and much more. To insert text with Draw, you would complete the following steps:

1. Open Draw.
2. Position the arrow pointer on Text Object Tools, hold down the left mouse button, drag the arrow pointer to the first text tool (the one with an A on a white background), then release the mouse button.
3. Position the mouse pointer (hand holding a square) in the drawing area where you want the text to appear. Hold down the left mouse button, drag the mouse pointer (hand holding a square) down and to the right to draw a box for the text, then release the mouse button. This causes a blue box to appear in the drawing area as shown in figure 21.6.
4. Key the text in the blue box. If the text you key fills more than the first line in the box, the text wraps to the next line.
5. After keying the text, position the arrow pointer outside the blue box, then click the left mouse button.

Using Draw and TextArt   485

Figure 21.6

Text Box in Drawing Area

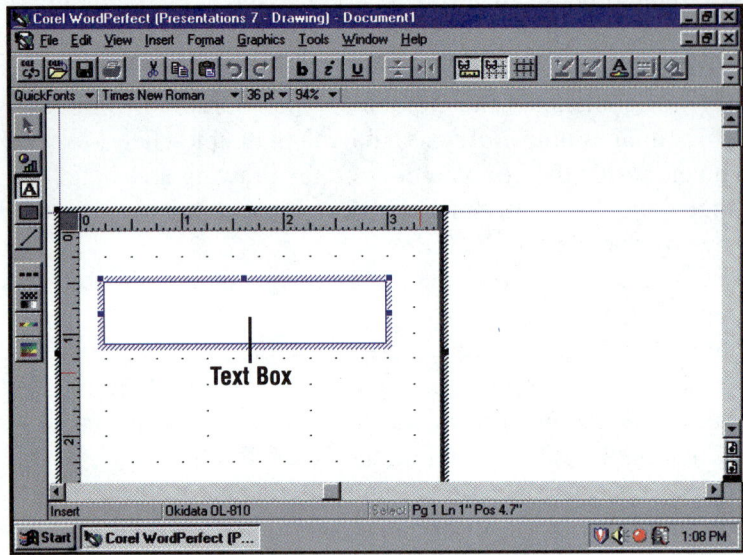

    You can also draw a box for text using the Insert option from the Draw Menu bar. To do this, click Insert, then Text Area. Position the mouse pointer in the drawing area and it turns into a hand holding a square. To draw an area for text and insert text, complete steps 3 through 5 listed above.

    You can also key text directly into the drawing area. To do this, position the arrow pointer on Text Object Tools, hold down the left mouse button, drag the arrow pointer to the second text tool (the A on a gray background), then release the mouse button. You can also click Insert, then Text Line. Move the crosshairs in the drawing area to the location where you want the text to appear, then click the left mouse button. This causes the insertion point to display in the drawing area.

    The third tool on Text Object Tools is used to create a bulleted list. Select this tool from Text Object Tools, then move the crosshairs in the drawing area to the location where you want the bulleted list to begin. Click the left mouse button, then drag the box to the right to make it as wide as you need for your text. When you release the left mouse button, a bullet automatically appears. Key the text for the first bulleted item, then press the Enter key. A second bullet is automatically inserted on the next line. Continue keying text using the Enter key to begin a new text line and to insert another bullet. When you are finished keying text, click outside the blue box surrounding the bulleted list.

Font Selection

Font Sizes

QuickFonts

    The default font for text in the drawing area is 36-point Times New Roman. This information displays on the Draw Power Bar. You can change the typeface by clicking the Font Selection button on the Draw Power Bar, then clicking the desired typeface at the drop-down menu. Use the Font Sizes button on the Draw Power Bar to change the size of text in the drawing area. You can also change the font for text in the drawing area at the Font Properties dialog box. To display the Font Properties dialog box, click Format, then Font. The QuickFonts button is available on the Draw Power Bar to display your most recently changed fonts.

EXERCISE 7

Creating a Shape Containing Text

1. At a clear editing window, create an oval with the words *Ramona Sampson* and *Vice Principal* inside using Draw by completing the following steps:
   a. Change to the Draft viewing mode.
   b. Open Draw.
   c. At the Draw window, turn on the display of the Ruler and the Grid.
   d. Position the arrow pointer on Closed Object Tools, hold down the left mouse button, drag the arrow pointer to the ellipse tool (the last tool at the right in the first row), then release the mouse button.
   e. Position the crosshairs in the drawing area until the red markers are positioned on the 0.5-inch mark on the horizontal and vertical ruler (the markers will turn turquoise when positioned properly).
   f. Hold down the left mouse button, drag the crosshairs down and to the right until the red markers display on the 3-inch mark on the horizontal ruler and the 2.5-inch mark on the vertical ruler. (When positioned properly, the red markers will turn turquoise.)
   g. Release the mouse button.
   h. Click in the drawing area outside the shape to deselect it.
   i. Change the font size to 14 points. To do this, click the Font Sizes button on the Draw Power Bar, then click 14. (You will need to scroll up the list to see 14.)
   j. Position the arrow pointer on Text Object Tools, hold down the left mouse button, drag the arrow pointer to the right to the first text tool (the one with the A on a white background), then release the mouse button.
   k. Position the crosshairs inside the oval until the red markers are positioned on the 0.75-inch mark on the horizontal ruler and the 1.25-inch mark on the vertical ruler (and the markers turn turquoise).
   l. Hold down the left mouse button, drag the mouse pointer (hand holding a square) down and to the right until the red markers are positioned on the 2.75-inch mark on the horizontal ruler and the 1.75-inch mark on the vertical ruler, then release the mouse button.
   m. Press Shift + F7, turn on bold, then key **Ramona Sampson**.
   n. Press Enter, press Shift + F7, then key **Vice Principal**.
   o. Click in the drawing area, outside of the oval. (This deselects the text box.)
   p. Close Draw.
   q. Deselect the box containing the oval.
2. Save the document and name it Ch 21, Ex 07.
3. Print and then close Ch 21, Ex 07.

Changing the Drawing Area Size

When you open the Draw program, the drawing area displays with sizing handles. Use these sizing handles to change the size of the drawing area. Use the sizing handles in the middle of the sides to change the width of the drawing area. Use the sizing handles in the middle at the top and bottom to change the height. The sizing handles in the corners are used to change both the width and height at the same time.

Zoom Options

The Draw Power Bar contains a Zoom Options button with options for changing the display of text in the drawing area. Click this button and a drop-down menu displays with options for changing the display area. These options include Zoom to Area, Margin Size, Screen Size, Full Page, Selected Objects, and various percentage sizes.

Use the Zoom To Area option to view a specific area. When you click Zoom To Area, the mouse pointer displays as a magnifying glass. Position the magnifying glass in the drawing area, hold down the mouse button, draw a box around the area you want to view, then release the mouse button. When you release the mouse button, the area inside the box fills the drawing area.

If you have zoomed in on an area, you can return to the default view by clicking the Zoom Options button, then clicking Margin Size. Use the percentages in the Zoom Options drop-down menu to change the percentage of the viewing size in the drawing area. Zoom options are also available by clicking View, then Zoom.

EXERCISE 8

Creating and Editing a Shape and Text

1. At a clear editing window, create a rounded rectangle with the words COMMITTED and CONCERNED inside by completing the following steps:
   a. Change to the Draft viewing mode.
   b. Open Draw.
   c. Turn on the display of the Ruler and the Grid.
   d. Change the size of the drawing area by completing the following steps:
      (1) Position the arrow pointer on the sizing handle in the middle of the bottom border until it turns into a double-headed arrow pointing up and down.
      (2) Hold down the left mouse button, drag the double-headed arrow down to the bottom of the editing window, then release the mouse button.
      (3) Position the arrow pointer on the sizing handle in the middle of the right border until it turns into a double-headed arrow pointing left and right.
      (4) Hold down the left mouse button, drag the double-headed arrow to the right side of the editing window, then release the mouse button.
   e. Position the arrow pointer on Closed Object Tools, hold down the left mouse button, drag the arrow pointer to the rounded rectangle tool, then release the mouse button.
   f. Draw a rounded rectangle from the 0.75-inch mark on the horizontal and vertical rulers to the 5-inch mark on the horizontal ruler and the 3-inch mark on the vertical ruler.
   g. Position the arrow pointer on Text Object Tools, hold down the left mouse button, drag the arrow pointer to the second tool (the A on a gray background), then release the mouse button.
   h. Position the crosshairs in the rounded rectangle at the 1.25-inch mark on the horizontal ruler and the 1.75-inch mark on the vertical ruler, then click the left mouse button.
   i. Key the word **COMMITTED**, then press the Enter key.
   j. Click Text Object Tool. (The A on the gray background should already be selected.)

    k. Position the crosshairs in the rounded rectangle at the 1.25-inch mark on the horizontal ruler and the 2.5-inch mark on the vertical ruler, then click the left mouse button.
    l. Key the word **CONCERNED**, then press the Enter key.
    m. Change the viewing area by completing the following steps:
        (1) Click the Zoom Options button on the Power Bar, then click 50%.
        (2) Click the Zoom Options button on the Power Bar, then click 150%.
        (3) Click View, point to Zoom, then click Margin Size. (This returns the view to the default.)
    n. Close Draw.
2. At the editing window, change the position and size of the box containing the shapes and text by completing the following steps:
    a. Position the arrow pointer on the rounded rectangle, click the *right* mouse button, then click Size.
    b. At the Box Size dialog box, change the box width to Full and the height to Maintain proportions.
    c. Click OK to close the Box Size dialog box.
3. Deselect the box. (To do this, click outside the selected box. You may need to scroll down the page to find a location where you can click outside the box.)
4. Display the full page to see how the rounded rectangle displays on the page, then return to the default view.
5. Save the document and name it Ch 21, Ex 08.
6. Print and then close Ch 21, Ex 08.

Editing an Object

Once you have inserted an object in the drawing area such as a shape or text, you may want to edit the object. For example, you may want to move, copy, or delete an object or sections of an object.

Selecting an Object

If you want to move, copy, or delete an object or a part of an object, it needs to be selected. To select an object in the drawing area, click Selection Tool on the Draw Tool palette. Position the arrow pointer on the object to be selected, then click the left mouse button. When you select an object in the drawing area, sizing handles surround the image as shown in figure 21.7.

Figure 21.7

Selected Object

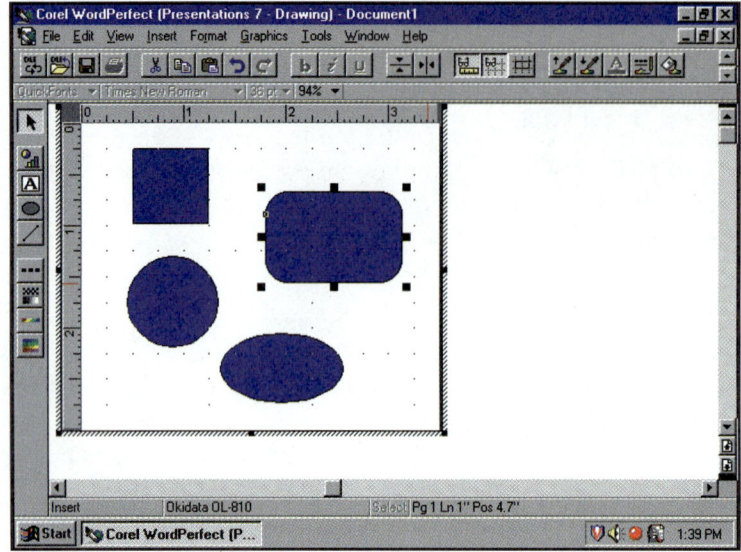

You can also select an object with the Edit menu option at the Draw window. To do this, click Edit, point to Select, then click Object(s). Position the arrow pointer on the item in the drawing area you want to select, then click the left mouse button.

The methods described above select just one image. You can also select several objects in the drawing area. To select several objects using the mouse, you would complete the following steps:

1. At the Draw window, click Selection Tool on the Draw Tool palette.
2. Position the arrow pointer on the object in the drawing area to be selected, hold down the Ctrl key, then click the left mouse button.
3. Position the arrow pointer on the next object to be selected, hold down the Ctrl key, then click the left mouse button.
4. Continue holding down the Ctrl key and clicking objects until you have selected all desired objects.

When you use the Ctrl key plus Selection Tool, the sizing handles include all selected images. For example, if you use the Ctrl key plus Selection Tool to select all the objects in figure 21.7, the sizing handles will appear as shown in figure 21.8.

All objects in the drawing area can be selected with options from the Edit menu. To select all objects in the drawing area, click Edit, point to Select, then click All.

Selected Objects

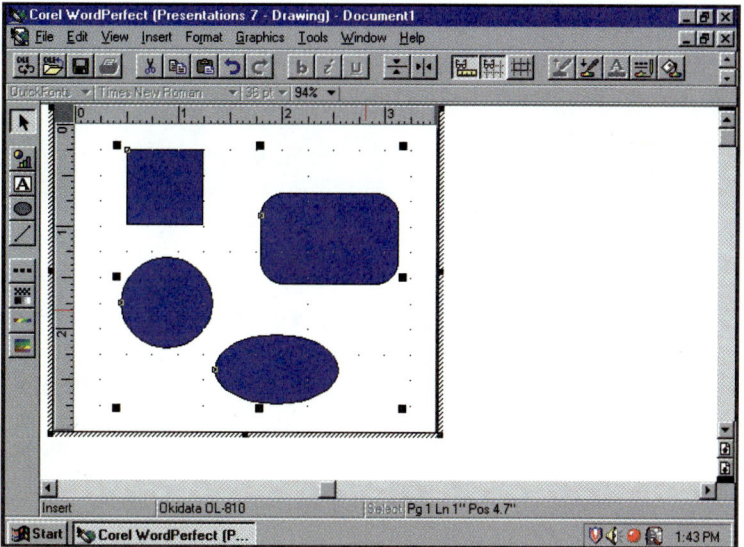

Figure 21.8

Moving a Selected Object

Once an object (or objects) has been selected, it can be moved. To do this, position the arrow pointer in the selected area, hold down the left mouse button, drag the outline of the object to the desired location in the drawing area, then release the mouse button. When you release the mouse button, the selected object(s) is inserted at the location of the outline.

EXERCISE 9

Editing a Selected Object

1. At a clear editing window, open Ch 21, Ex 01.
2. Save the document with Save As and name it Ch 21, Ex 09.
3. Change to the Draft viewing mode.
4. Position the arrow pointer on the circle shape, then double-click the left mouse button. This opens the Draw program.
5. At the Draw window, make the following changes:
   a. Position the arrow pointer on Closed Object Tools, hold down the left mouse button, drag the arrow pointer to the first tool from the left in the bottom row (the polygon tool).
   b. With the polygon drawing tool selected, draw a triangle in a free area of the drawing area.
   c. Select and move the circle you drew earlier by completing the following steps:
      (1) Click Selection Tool.
      (2) Position the arrow pointer on the circle, then click the left mouse button. (This selects the circle.)
      (3) Position the arrow pointer inside the selected area, hold down the left mouse button, drag the circle outline so it slightly overlaps the square, then release the button.

Using Draw and TextArt   **491**

(4) Select the triangle, then move it so it slightly overlaps the circle and the square.
  d. When all changes are made, close Draw.
  e. At the editing window, deselect the box containing the shapes.
6. Save the document again with the same name (Ch 21, Ex 09).
7. Print and then close Ch 21, Ex 09.

Copying a Selected Object

Moving a selected object removes the object from its original position and inserts it into a new location. You can also copy an object into a new location in the drawing area. To do this, position the arrow pointer in the selected area, hold down the Ctrl key and the left mouse button, drag the outline of the shape to the new location, then release the left mouse button and then the Ctrl key.

EXERCISE

Copying and Editing Squares

1. At a clear editing window, create the squares shown in figure 21.9 by completing the following steps:
   a. Change to the Draft viewing mode.
   b. Open Draw.
   c. Increase the size of the drawing area by completing the following steps:
      (1) Position the arrow pointer on the sizing handle at the bottom right corner of the drawing area until it turns into a diagonally pointing arrow.
      (2) Hold down the left mouse button, drag the outline of the drawing area down and to the right so the outline displays near the bottom of the editing window and near the right side of the editing window, then release the mouse button.
   d. Turn on the display of the Ruler and the Grid.
   e. Select the rectangle tool, then draw a square from the 2-inch mark on the horizontal ruler and the 1-inch mark on the vertical ruler to the 3-inch mark on the horizontal ruler and the 2-inch mark on the vertical ruler.
   f. Copy the square by completing the following steps:
      (1) Click Selection Tool.
      (2) Position the arrow pointer inside the square, then click the left mouse button.
      (3) With the arrow pointer still positioned inside the square, hold down the Ctrl key and the left mouse button.
      (4) Drag the outline of the square down and to the left so the left side is positioned at the 1.25-inch mark on the horizontal ruler and the 3-inch mark on the vertical ruler and the right side is positioned on the 2.25-inch mark on the horizontal ruler and the 3-inch mark on the vertical ruler.
      (5) When the outline is in the desired position, release the mouse button, then release the Ctrl key.

g. Copy the square again so that the left side of the square is positioned on the 2.75-inch mark on the horizontal ruler and the 3-inch mark on the vertical ruler and the right side is positioned at the 3.75-inch mark on the horizontal ruler and the 3-inch mark on the vertical ruler.
h. Position the arrow pointer on Text Object Tools, hold down the left mouse button, drag the arrow pointer to the second text tool (the A on a gray background), then release the mouse button.
i. Position the arrow pointer inside the top square, click the left mouse button, key the letter **A**, then press Enter.
j. Complete steps similar to those in 1h and 1i to insert the letter B in the square at the left and the letter C in the square at the right.
k. After keying the letters in the squares, you may need to adjust the letters so they are centered within the squares. To do this, complete the following steps:
   (1) Click Selection Tool.
   (2) Position the arrow pointer on the letter, then click the left mouse button.
   (3) Position the arrow pointer inside the selected area, hold down the left mouse button, drag the outline of the box containing the letter to the desired position in the square, then release the mouse button.
l. When the letters are in the correct position in the squares, close Draw.
m. At the editing window, change the position of the box containing the squares by completing the following steps:
   (1) Position the arrow pointer on one of the squares, click the right mouse button, then click Position.
   (2) At the Box Position dialog box, change the Horizontal option from Right Margin to Center of Margins.
   (3) Click OK to close the Box Position dialog box.
2. Deselect the box. (To do this, click outside the selected box. You may need to scroll down the page to find a location where you can click outside the box.)
3. Display the full page to see how the squares display on the page and then return to the default view.
4. Save the document and name it Ch 21, Ex 10.
5. Print and then close Ch 21, Ex 10.

Figure 21.9

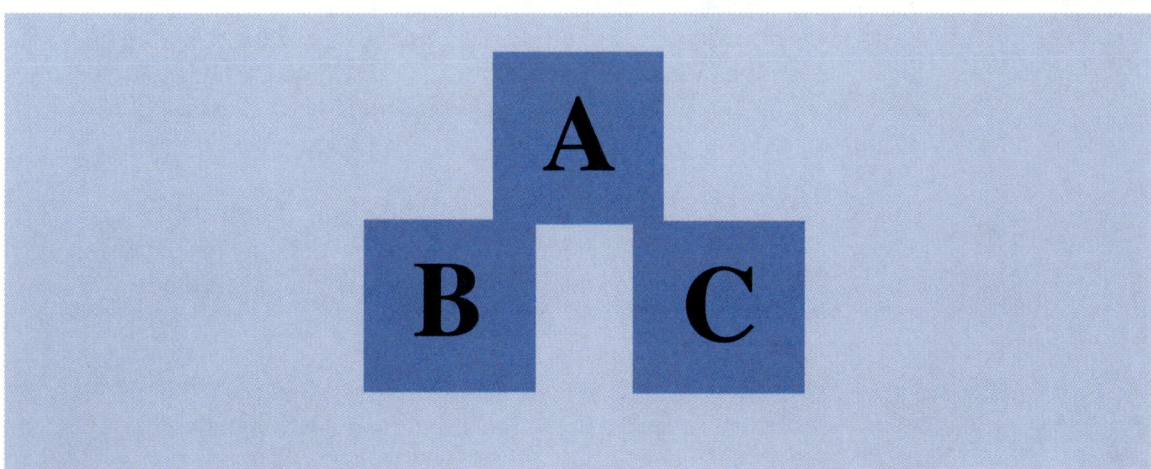

Deleting a Selected Object

After an object (or objects) has been selected, it can be deleted by pressing the Delete key. You can also delete everything in the drawing area by clicking Edit, then Clear; or by pressing Ctrl + Shift + F4. At the Clear Drawing dialog box, click Yes.

Changing the Size of a Selected Object

When an object (or objects) is selected, sizing handles display at the left, right, and middle of the image. Earlier you learned to use the sizing handles to change the size of the drawing area. Use them in the same way to change the size and/or shape of the selected object.

EXERCISE 11

Using the Sizing Handles

1. At a clear editing window, open Ch 21, Ex 03.
2. Save the document with Save As and name it Ch 21, Ex 11.
3. Make the following changes to the document:
   a. Change to the Draft viewing mode.
   b. Position the arrow pointer inside the square, then double-click the left mouse button. This opens the Draw program with the square displayed in the drawing area.
   c. Make sure the Ruler and the Grid are displayed. If not, click the Ruler button and the Grid button on the Draw Toolbar.
   d. Increase the size of the drawing area by completing the following steps:
      (1) Position the arrow pointer on the sizing handle at the bottom right corner of the drawing area until it turns into a diagonally pointing arrow.
      (2) Hold down the left mouse button, drag the outline of the drawing area down and to the right so the outline displays near the bottom of the editing window and near the right side of the editing window, then release the mouse button.
   e. Change the size of the square by completing the following steps:
      (1) Click Selection Tool, if it is not already selected.
      (2) Position the arrow pointer inside the square, then click the left mouse button. (This selects the square.)
      (3) Position the arrow pointer on the middle sizing handle at the right side of the square until it turns into a double-headed arrow pointing left and right.
      (4) Hold down the left mouse button, drag the double-headed arrow to the right to the 5-inch mark on the horizontal ruler, then release the mouse button.
      (5) Position the arrow pointer on the middle sizing handle at the bottom of the square until it turns into a double-headed arrow pointing up and down.
      (6) Hold down the left mouse button, then drag the double-headed arrow down to the 3-inch mark on the vertical ruler.
   f. Deselect the rectangle (previously a square).
   g. Draw a text box inside the rectangle from the 1.5-inch mark on the horizontal and vertical rulers to the 4.5-inch mark on the horizontal ruler.

- h. Change the font to 16-point Arial by completing the following steps:
    - (1) Click the Font Selection button on the Draw Power Bar.
    - (2) Click Arial at the drop-down menu. (You will need to scroll up the list to display Arial.)
    - (3) Click the Font Sizes button on the Draw Power Bar.
    - (4) Click 16 at the drop-down menu. (You may need to scroll up the list to display 16.)
- i. With the insertion point positioned inside the text box, press Shift + F7, then key **Word Processing**.
- j. Press Enter twice, press Shift + F7, then key **Room 244**.
- k. Click the Close button on the Draw Toolbar.
4. At the editing window, make the following changes:
    - a. Display the Edit Box dialog box.
    - b. Display the Box Size dialog box, change the box width to Full and the height to Maintain proportions, then close the Box Size dialog box.
    - c. Close the Edit Box dialog box.
5. Deselect the box. (To do this, click outside the selected box. You may need to scroll down the page to find a location where you can click outside the box.)
6. Save the document again with the same name (Ch 21, Ex 11).
7. Print and then close Ch 21, Ex 11.

Contouring Text

At the drawing area, you can insert text, draw a curved line, and then contour the text on the curved line. To do this, you would draw the curved line with the curved tool, access a text tool, key the text, and then select the curved line and text. When selected, the line and text display as shown in figure 21.10. Then use the Contour Text option from the Graphics drop-down menu to determine the text position in relation to the curve. If you do not change the settings at the Contour Text dialog box, the text will be contoured as shown in figure 21.11.

Figure 21.10

Selected Line and Text

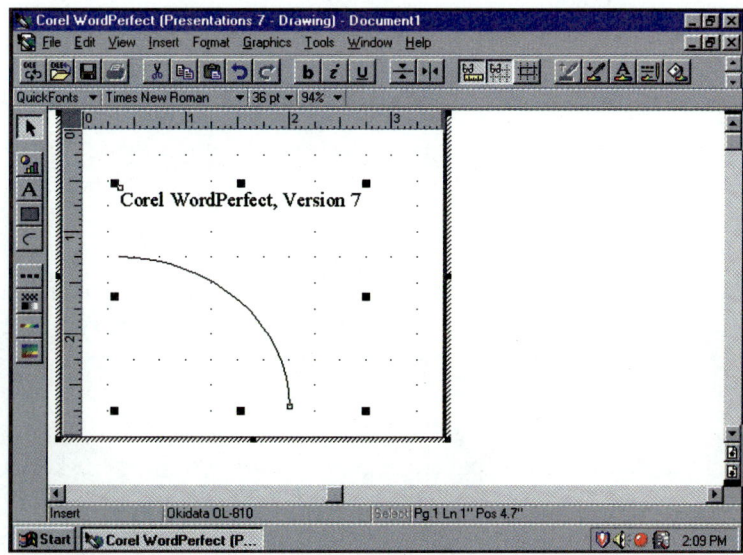

Using Draw and TextArt

Figure 21.11

Contoured Text

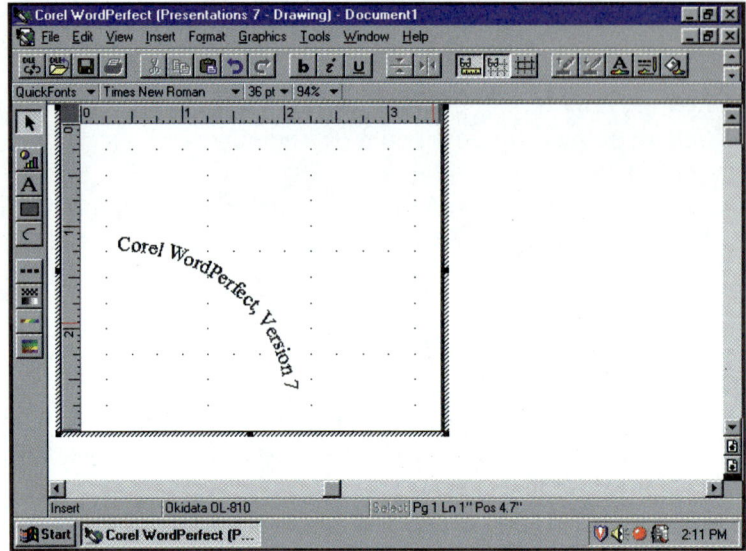

By default, Draw will contour text at the top left of the curved line. The Position option at the Contour Text dialog box lets you specify whether you want the text at the Top Left (the default), Top Center, Top Right, Bottom Left, Bottom Center, or Bottom Right of the curved line.

When text is contoured, the curved line does not display. If you want the contoured text and the curved line to display, remove the check mark from the Display text only check box at the Contour Text dialog box. If you contour text, then want to separate the text from the line, select the contoured text, then click Graphics, then Separate.

EXERCISE 12

Creating a Letterhead with Contoured Text

1. At a clear editing window, create the letterhead shown in figure 21.12 by completing the following steps:
    a. Change to the Draft viewing mode.
    b. Open Draw.
    c. Turn on the display of the Ruler and Grid.
    d. Expand the size of the drawing area so the 4.5-inch mark on the horizontal ruler is visible and the 3-inch mark on the vertical ruler is visible.
    e. Select the circle tool.
    f. Position the crosshairs at the 1-inch mark on the horizontal ruler and the 1.75-inch mark on the vertical ruler, hold down the left mouse button, drag the crosshairs down to the 2.5-inch mark on the vertical ruler (remain at the 1-inch mark on the horizontal ruler), then release the mouse button.
    g. Select the rectangle tool.
    h. Position the crosshairs at the 1.25-inch mark on the horizontal ruler and the 2-inch mark on the vertical ruler, then hold down the Shift key and the left mouse button. Drag the crosshairs to the 2.5-inch mark on the horizontal ruler and the 3.25-inch mark on the vertical ruler, then release the mouse button.

496 Chapter 21

i. Position the arrow pointer on Line Object Tools, hold down the left mouse button, drag the arrow pointer to the ellipse tool, then release the mouse button.
j. Position the crosshairs at the 0.75-inch mark on the horizontal and the vertical rulers, then hold down the left mouse button. Drag the crosshairs to the 3.25-inch mark on the horizontal and vertical rulers, then release the mouse button. (This causes a curved line to display.)
k. Position the arrow pointer on Text Object Tools, hold down the left mouse button, drag the arrow pointer to the second option (the A on a gray background), then release the mouse button.
l. Change the font to 30-point ShelleyVolante BT (or a similar decorative typeface).
m. Position the crosshairs at the 0.5-inch mark on the horizontal ruler and the 0.5-inch mark on the vertical ruler, then click the left mouse button.
n. Key **Shapes by Sarah and Sam**, then press Enter. (The text will remain selected.)
o. Click Selection Tool.
p. Position the arrow pointer on the curved line, hold down the Ctrl key, then click the left mouse button.
q. Click Graphics, then Contour Text.
r. At the Contour Text dialog box, click OK.
s. Click outside the selected area.
t. Close Draw.
2. At the editing window, display the Edit Box dialog box for the drawing objects, then make the following changes:
   a. Display the Box Position dialog box, change the horizontal position to Left Margin, then close the Box Position dialog box.
   b. Display the Box Size dialog box, change the width to 3 inches and the height to Maintain proportions, then close the Box Size dialog box.
   c. Close the Edit Box dialog box.
3. Deselect the box containing the shapes and the contoured text.
4. Save the document and name it Ch 21, Ex 12.
5. Print and then close Ch 21, Ex 12.

Figure 21.12

Changing Attributes

You can change attributes such as color and fill patterns. You can change the attribute, then draw the object, or you can draw the object, then select the object and change attributes. If you change attributes before drawing an object, these attributes will apply to all subsequent objects. If you want attributes to apply to only specific objects, draw the objects first, select the objects, then change attributes.

Changing Line Attributes

Draw uses a thin black line when drawing shapes. You can customize this line by clicking Line Attributes on the Draw Tool palette. This causes a list of options to display. Use these options to select a thicker or thinner line, turn off the border line, and change from a solid line to a line with varying patterns.

Line

Line attributes can also be changed at the Object Properties dialog box with the Line Width/Style tab selected. To display this dialog box, click the Line button on the Draw Toolbar. At the Object Properties dialog box with the Line Width/Style tab selected, you can specify a line width, style, and/or color. You can also add an arrowhead to a line.

Changing Fill Attributes

When you draw a shape, the shape is filled with a solid pattern. If you click Fill Attributes on the Draw Tool palette, a wide variety of fill patterns display. For example, you can choose a honeycomb pattern, diamond pattern, wave pattern, and much more. You can also choose a gradient pattern. A gradient pattern shades the object in varying degrees. For example, an object may be shaded darker at the left side and then gradually lighten toward the right side.

Object Properties

Fill attributes can also be changed at the Object Properties dialog box with the Fill Attributes tab selected. To display this dialog box, click the Object Properties button on the Draw Toolbar. At the Object Properties dialog box with the Fill Attributes tab selected, you can specify a fill pattern, a fill gradient, and specify a foreground and background color for the pattern.

Changing Line Color

In Draw, you can change the color of the line used to draw an object with Line Colors on the Draw Tool palette or with an option at the Object Properties dialog box with the Line Width/Style tab selected. To change the line color using the Draw Tool palette, click Line Colors, then click the desired color at the palette of colors that displays. The color you select will be used to draw the lines for shapes.

You can also change the line color at the Object Properties dialog box with the Line Width/Style tab selected. To display this dialog box, click the Line button on the Draw Toolbar.

Changing Fill Color

By default, WordPerfect fills a shape with the color blue. You can change this fill color by clicking Fill Colors on the Draw Tool palette or at the Object Properties dialog box with the Fill Attributes tab selected. When you click Fill Colors, a variety of color options displays. At this list of colors, click the desired color.

Fill color can also be changed at the Object Properties dialog box with the Fill Attributes tab selected. To display this dialog box, click the Object Properties button on the Draw Toolbar.

EXERCISE 13

Changing Shape Attributes

1. At a clear editing window, open Ch 21, Ex 10.
2. Save the document with Save As and name it Ch 21, Ex 13.
3. Change the border, fill, and pattern of the shapes by completing the following steps:
   a. Change to the Draft viewing mode.
   b. Position the arrow pointer on one of the shapes, then double-click the left mouse button. This causes the Draw window to display.
   c. Change the line, fill, and pattern of the top square by completing the following steps:
      (1) Select the square containing the A.
      (2) Click Line Attributes on the Draw Tool palette. From the line options that display, click the fourth line option from the top in the first column (a thick line).
      (3) Click Fill Colors on the Draw Tool palette. From the color options that display, click the bright pink color in the first row of the Pattern/Gradient Color palette.
      (4) Click Fill Attributes on the Draw Tool palette. From the pattern options that display, click the third pattern from the left in the third row (vertical lines).
   d. Change the line, fill, and pattern of the square containing the B by completing the following steps:
      (1) Select the square containing the B.
      (2) Click Line Attributes on the Draw Tool palette. From the line options that display, click the fourth line option from the top (a thick line).
      (3) Click Fill Colors on the Draw Tool palette. From the color options that display, click the yellow color in the first row of the Pattern/Gradient Color palette.
      (4) Click Fill Attributes on the Draw Tool palette. From the pattern options that display, click the fourth pattern from the left in the first row (diagonal lines).
   e. Change the line, fill, and pattern of the square containing the C by completing the following steps:
      (1) Select the square containing the C.
      (2) Click Line Attributes on the Draw Tool palette. From the line options that display, click the fourth line option from the top (a thick line).
      (3) Click Fill Colors on the Draw Tool palette. From the color options that display, click the green color in the first row of the Pattern/Gradient Color palette.
      (4) Click Fill Attributes on the Draw Tool palette. From the pattern options that display, click the fourth pattern from the left in the third row (diagonal lines).
   f. Close Draw.
4. Deselect the box. (To do this, click outside the selected box. You may need to scroll down the page to find a location where you can click outside the box.)
5. Save the document again with the same name (Ch 21, Ex 13).
6. Print and then close Ch 21, Ex 13. (Unless you are using a color printer, the colors will print in shades of gray.)

WordPerfect's Presentations program is a powerful application that contains tools for creating professional-looking graphics. You have learned many of the basic options in Draw. There are additional features you may want to try when creating graphics. When using some of the more advanced features in Draw, refer to the on-line help screens for information relating to specific features.

Using TextArt 7

With WordPerfect's TextArt 7 program, you can distort or modify text to conform to a variety of shapes. This is useful for creating company logos and headings. With TextArt, you can change the font, style, and justification of text. You can also add a shadow to the text, use different fills and outlines, and resize the text. To enter the TextArt 7 program, click Graphics, then TextArt. This causes the TextArt window with the TextArt 7 dialog box to display as shown in figure 21.13.

Figure 21.13

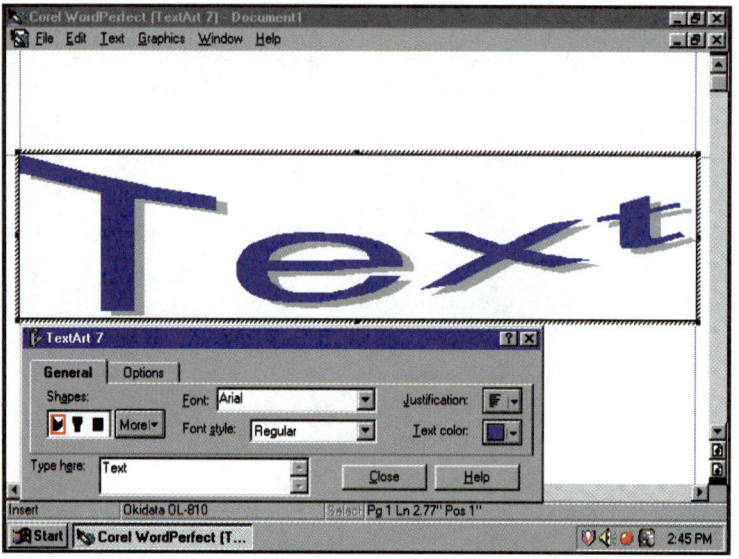

TextArt 7 Window

Entering Text

The word *Text* displays in blue toward the top of the TextArt window in a Preview box. The word *Text* also displays in the Type here text box in the lower left corner of the TextArt 7 dialog box. With the word *Text* selected in the Type here text box, key the text you want inserted as TextArt. The text you key is displayed in the Type here text box and also displayed in the Preview Box. The maximum number of characters that can be entered in TextArt varies depending on the size of the characters. Characters can be entered up to three lines. Press the Enter key to move the insertion point to the next line.

The Shapes option at the TextArt 7 dialog box with the General tab selected provides you with a variety of shapes to which you can conform the text. Only three shapes are visible below the Shapes option. To view more shapes, click the More button. A pop-up list of additional shapes will display as shown in figure 21.14. Choose a shape by clicking the desired shape and the text in the Preview Box will conform to the chosen shape.

More Shapes in TextArt 7

Figure 21.14

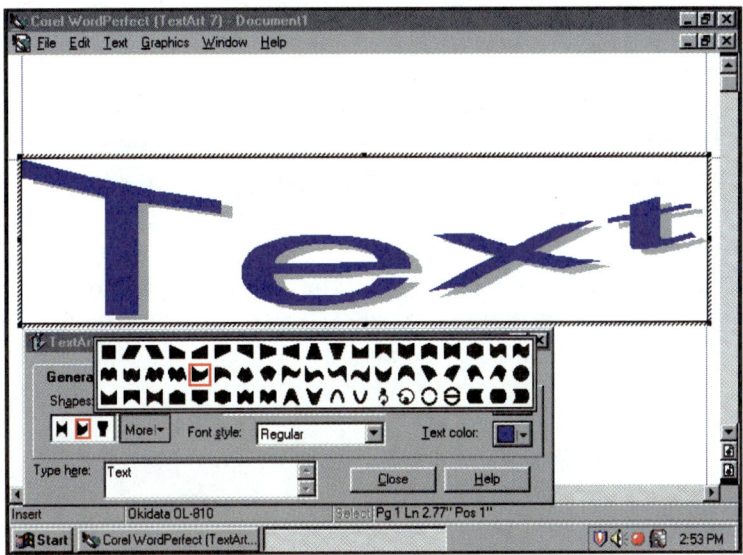

EXERCISE 14

Creating a Letterhead with TextArt

1. At a clear editing window, create the letterhead shown in figure 21.15 by completing the following steps:
   a. Create the NAN text using TextArt by completing the following steps:
      (1) Click Graphics, then TextArt.
      (2) At the TextArt window, make sure *Text* is selected in the Type here text box, then key **NAN**.
      (3) Click the More button that displays below and to the right of the Shapes option.
      (4) At the pop-up list of additional shapes, click the first shape in the first row (the square).
      (5) Position the arrow pointer anywhere in the editing window outside the TextArt window, then click the left mouse button. (This removes the TextArt window.)
   b. At the editing window, display the Edit Box dialog box for the box containing *NAN*. To do this, position the arrow pointer on the QuickSpot button in the box, then click the left mouse button.
   c. Display the Box Size dialog box, change the box width and height to 1 inch, then close the Box Size dialog box.
   d. Close the Edit Box dialog box.
   e. Change the font to 14-point Arial Bold.
   f. Key **NATIONAL ASSOCIATION OF NURSES**.
   g. Press Enter, then create a horizontal line by clicking Graphics, then Horizontal Line.
   h. Make the horizontal line thicker by completing the following steps:

Using Draw and TextArt *501*

(1) Position the arrow pointer on the horizontal line, then click the left mouse button. (This inserts sizing handles on the line.)
(2) Position the arrow pointer on the middle sizing handle at the bottom of the line until the arrow pointer turns into a double-headed arrow pointing up and down.
(3) Hold down the left mouse button, then drag the double-headed arrow down about an eighth of an inch, then release the mouse button.
(4) Deselect the horizontal line.
i. Advance the insertion point down 6 points by completing the following steps:
(1) Click Fo*r*mat, point to *T*ypesetting, then click *A*dvance.
(2) At the Advance dialog box, click *D*own from insertion point.
(3) Select the current measurement in the *V*ertical distance text box, then key **6p**.
(4) Click OK.
j. Key the address and telephone number as shown in figure 21.15.
2. Save the document and name it Ch 21, Ex 14.
3. Print and then close Ch 21, Ex 14.

Figure 21.15

NATIONAL ASSOCIATION OF NURSES

1211 Kinsington Drive
Kansas City, MO 84320
(314) 555-6700

Changing Fonts

By default, TextArt uses the Arial font (this may vary depending on the selected printer). You can change to a different font with options at the Font drop-down menu. To display this drop-down menu, click the down-pointing triangle to the right of the *F*ont text box that displays in the TextArt 7 dialog box. At the drop-down menu, click the desired font. When you change to a different font, the text in the Preview box reflects the new font.

Change the type style with options from the Font *s*tyle drop-down menu. To display this drop-down menu, click the down-pointing triangle to the right of the Font *s*tyle text box that displays in the TextArt 7 dialog box. The default font style is Regular. This will change depending on the font you have selected. For many fonts, you may have only one choice of style.

Modifying TextArt

The TextArt 7 dialog box contains options and buttons for modifying text. With options and buttons in the dialog box with the General tab selected, you can perform such actions as changing the font, font style, justification, and text color. Click the Options tab and you can further modify text with buttons that will change the text pattern, add a shadow, change the outline style of the text, and change the rotation and smoothness of the text. You can also insert special characters with the Insert Character button. Figure 21.16 displays the TextArt 7 dialog box with the Options tab selected. Figure 21.17 describes the functions of the options and buttons available at the TextArt 7 dialog box with the General tab selected and also with the Options tab selected.

Figure 21.16

TextArt 7 Dialog Box with Options Tab Selected

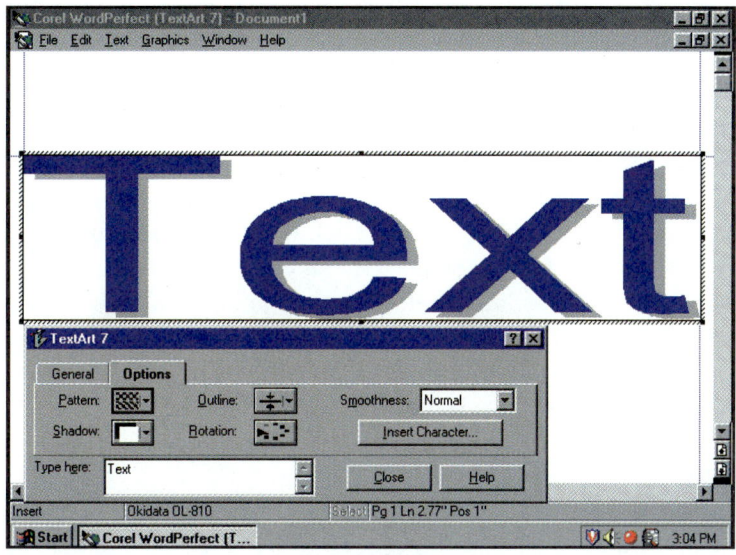

Figure 21.17

TextArt Options and Buttons

Choose this option/button	To do this...
TextArt 7 Dialog Box with General Tab Selected	
Shapes	Choose a shape to which the TextArt characters will conform.
Font	Choose a font for the TextArt characters.
Font style	Choose a font style for the TextArt characters.
Justification	Choose left, right, or center justification for the TextArt characters.
Text color	Choose the color for the TextArt characters.
TextArt 7 Dialog Box with Options Tab Selected	
Pattern	Choose a pattern for the TextArt characters.
Shadow	Choose a shadow type. Choosing the center box will turn off the shadow.
Outline	Choose the line width around characters. Choose the single line with the X through it to turn off the outline.
Insert Character	Display the Characters dialog box where a variety of characters display that can be inserted in TextArt.
Rotation	Drag a rotation handle to rotate TextArt.
Smoothness	Adjust the smoothness of the curves of the lines. You can select from Normal, High, and Very High. Choosing a higher smoothness greatly increases the size of the file.

Using Draw and TextArt   *503*

EXERCISE 15

Creating a Newsletter with TextArt

1. At a clear editing window, create the top part of a newsletter as shown in figure 21.18 by completing the following steps:
    a. Click Graphics, then TextArt.
    b. At the TextArt window, make sure *Text* is selected in the Type here text box, then key **THE ST. C**.
    c. Create Ô by completing the following steps:
        (1) Click the Options tab at the TextArt 7 dialog box, then click the Insert Character button.
        (2) At the Characters dialog box, click the down-pointing triangle in the vertical scroll bar in the Characters list box until Ô is visible, (the first character in the nineteenth row), then click Ô.
        (3) Click Insert and Close.
    d. Position the insertion point in the Type here text box (not the Preview Box) immediately after the Ô. To do this, position the I-beam pointer immediately to the right of the Ô, then click the left mouse button.
    e. Key **ME VOICE** (to complete the name).
    f. Click the General tab at the TextArt 7 dialog box.
    g. Click the More button that displays below and to the right of the Shapes option.
    h. At the pop-up list of additional shapes, click the last shape in the first row.
    i. Click the Options tab at the TextArt 7 dialog box.
    j. Change the text pattern by completing the following steps:
        (1) Click the Pattern button.
        (2) At the box containing pattern choices, click the first pattern in the third row.
        (3) With the pattern choices still displayed, change the text pattern foreground color by clicking the Pattern color button. At the palette of color choices, click the red color in the first row.
        (4) Click OK to close the box containing the pattern choices.
    k. Change the text outline width by completing the following steps:
        (1) Click the Outline button.
        (2) At the box containing outline choices, click the fourth option in the first column.
        (3) With the outline choices still displayed, change the outline color by clicking the Outline color button. At the palette of color choices, click the blue color in the first row.
        (4) Click OK to close the box containing the outline choices.
    l. Click in the editing window outside the TextArt window. (This removes the TextArt window.)
    m. Deselect the TextArt box.
2. Save the document and name it Ch 21, Ex 15.
3. Print and then close Ch 21, Ex 15.

Figure 21.18

THE ST. CÔME VOICE

EXERCISE 16

Changing the Shape of a Logo

1. At a clear editing window, create the logo shown in figure 21.19 by completing the following steps:
   a. Click Graphics, then TextArt.
   b. At the TextArt window, select *Text* in the Type here text box, then key **Visual Expressions**.
   c. Change the font to Arrus Blk BT (or a similar typeface).
   d. Change the shape by clicking the More button at the TextArt 7 dialog box with the General tab selected, then clicking the eleventh shape in the third row.
   e. Change the text pattern foreground color to light blue by clicking the Text color button. At the palette of color choices, click the light blue color in the first row.
   f. Click the Options tab.
   g. Add a shadow to the text by completing the following steps:
      (1) Click the Shadow button.
      (2) At the box containing shadow choices, click the last option in the last row.
      (3) With the shadow choices still displayed, change the shadow color by clicking the Shadow color button. At the palette of color choices, click the blue color in the first row.
      (4) Click OK to close the box of shadow choices.
   h. Change the text outline width by completing the following steps:
      (1) Click the Outline button.
      (2) At the box containing outline choices, click the fourth option in the first column.
      (3) Click OK to close the box of outline choices.
   i. Remove any pattern in the text by completing the following steps:
      (1) Click the Pattern button.
      (2) At the box containing pattern choices, click the *None* option (first option in the second row).
   j. Click in the editing window outside the TextArt window. (This removes the TextArt window.)
   k. Deselect the TextArt box.
2. Save the document and name it Ch 21, Ex 16.
3. Print and then close Ch 21, Ex 16.

Using Draw and TextArt

Figure 21.19

Editing a TextArt Image in the Editing Window

When a TextArt image is inserted in the document, it is inserted in a box. This box can be edited in the same manner as the graphics boxes you learned to create and edit in chapter 19. For example, you can select the box and then move it to a different location in the document, or change the size of the box. You can also display the Edit Box dialog box for the box containing the TextArt, then choose any of the editing options.

EXERCISE

Editing a TextArt Image Box

1. At a clear editing window, create the sign shown in figure 21.20 by completing the following steps:
    a. Click Graphics, then TextArt.
    b. At the TextArt window, select *Text* in the Type here text box, key **The Red Circle Restaurant**, then press the space bar once.
    c. Change the font to Arial.
    d. Change the shape by clicking the More button (below Shapes), then clicking the thirteenth shape from the left in the third row.
    e. Rotate the text 180 degrees by completing the following steps:
        (1) Click the Options tab.
        (2) Double-click the Rotation button.
        (3) At the Rotation dialog box, click in the radio button before 180 Degrees. (This rotates the text in the Preview Box.)
        (4) Click the Close button to close the Rotation dialog box.
    f. Change the smoothness to very high by completing the following steps:
        (1) Click the down-pointing triangle at the right side of the Smoothness text box.
        (2) At the Smoothness drop-down menu, click Very High.
    g. Change the shadow options by completing the following steps:
        (1) Click the Shadow button.
        (2) At the box of shadow choices, click the fourth option from the left in the first row.
        (3) With the box of shadow choices still displayed, click the Shadow color button.

506   Chapter 21

(4) At the palette of color choices, click the medium gray color in the first row.
(5) Click OK to close the box of shadow choices.
  h. Change the outline color by completing the following steps:
     (1) Click the Outline button.
     (2) At the box of outline options, click the Outline color button.
     (3) At the palette of outline color choices, click the light gray color in the first row.
     (4) Click OK to close the box of outline choices.
  i. Change the text color to red by completing the following steps:
     (1) Click the General tab.
     (2) Click the down-pointing triangle to the right of the Text color button.
     (3) At the palette of color choices, click the red color in the first row.
  j. Click in the editing window outside the TextArt window.
2. At the editing window (with TextArt closed), make the following changes:
  a. Deselect the TextArt image. To do this, position the arrow pointer in the editing window outside the image, then click the left mouse button.
  b. Click the Page/Zoom Full button on the Toolbar. (This displays the entire page.)
  c. Select the TextArt image by positioning the arrow pointer inside the image, then clicking the left mouse button.
  d. Increase the size of the TextArt image by completing the following steps:
     (1) Position the arrow pointer on the middle sizing handle at the bottom of the TextArt image box until it turns into a double-headed arrow pointing up and down. (The arrow pointer must be precisely positioned for it to turn into a double-headed arrow.)
     (2) Hold down the left mouse button, drag the outline down approximately 1 to 2 inches, then release the mouse button. (Drag the image down enough so the text appears in a more perfect circle.)
  e. Drag the image to the middle of the page by completing the following steps:
     (1) Position the arrow pointer inside the image (displays as a four-headed arrow).
     (2) Hold down the left mouse button, drag the outline of the TextArt image box to the middle of the page, then release the mouse button.
  f. Deselect the box containing the TextArt.
  g. Click the Page/Zoom Full button. (This returns the viewing mode back to Page.)
3. Save the document and name it Ch 21, Ex 17.
4. Print and then close Ch 21, Ex 17.

Figure 21.20

Using Draw and TextArt

CHAPTER SUMMARY

- With Corel WordPerfect's Presentations program, you can draw shapes, draw freehand, insert graphics images, and create and customize text.
- When Corel WordPerfect is installed, the Presentations program becomes the Draw module for WordPerfect.
- An object created in the drawing area can be cleared with the Clear option from the Edit drop-down menu or with Ctrl + Shift + F4.
- Whatever you create at the Draw window is inserted in the document in a box without borders that is approximately 3.5 inches wide and 3 inches tall.
- A graphics image can be inserted in the drawing area where it can be customized. The graphics image can then be inserted in the document.
- In Draw, you can create, customize, and edit text.
- The Draw program includes a ruler and grid that you can use to draw shapes or position objects at specific locations in the drawing area.
- A box containing drawn objects can be edited using options from the Edit Box dialog box. The box can also be sized and/or relocated in the document using the mouse.
- The Draw Tool palette is available at the Draw window and includes a variety of tools for selecting, drawing, and changing the fill and attributes of objects.
- At the Draw window, a drawn object can be moved, copied, or deleted. An object can also be made wider/narrower or taller/shorter.
- At the Draw window, you can create text, create a curved line, and then contour the text on the curved line.
- With WordPerfect's TextArt program, you can distort or modify characters of text to conform to a variety of shapes.
- Other options available with TextArt include the following: changing fonts, adding pattern, changing the foreground and background color, adding shadow, changing the outline width, changing the justification, and rotating text.

COMMANDS REVIEW

	Mouse/Keyboard
Draw	Graphics, Draw; or click the Draw button on the Graphics Toolbar
Edit Box dialog box	Position arrow pointer on drawn shape, then click the QuickSpot button; or click Edit Box button on Graphics Toolbar
TextArt	Graphics, TextArt

CHECK YOUR UNDERSTANDING

Completion: In the space provided at the right, indicate the correct term, command, or number.

1. Display the Draw window by clicking Graphics, then Draw or clicking the Draw button on this toolbar. _____

2. This displays at the left side of the Draw window and contains tools for selecting, drawing, and changing the fill and attributes of objects. _____

3. An object created in the drawing area can be cleared with the Clear option from this drop-down menu. _____

4. With this tool, you can draw closed shapes. _____

5. To draw a square, choose the rectangle tool, then hold down this key while drawing the square. _____

6. This is the default font at the drawing area. _____

7. Whatever you create at the Draw window is inserted in the document in a box without borders that is approximately this size. _____

8. A box containing drawn objects can be edited using options from this dialog box. _____

9. This button on the Draw Power Bar contains options for changing the display of text in the drawing area. _____

10. To select an object in the drawing area, click this tool on the Draw Tool palette, then click the object. _____

11. When an object is selected in the drawing area, these display around the object. _____

12. You can customize the black line used to draw shapes with this button on the Draw Tool palette. _____

13. By default, a shape is filled with this color. _____

14. Click this button in the TextArt dialog box to view more shapes to which you want the text to conform. _____

15. When the TextArt window is first displayed, the word *Text* displays in this text box that is located in the lower left corner of the TextArt 7 dialog box. _____

16. Change the font, font style, justification, and/or color of text in TextArt with options from the TextArt 7 dialog box with this tab selected. _____

17. To insert a WordPerfect character in TextArt, click the Insert Character button at the TextArt 7 dialog box with this tab selected. _____

Using Draw and TextArt

SKILL ASSESSMENTS

Assessment 1

1. At a clear editing window, use Draw to create the rounded rectangles containing text shown in figure 21.21 with the following specifications:
   a. Create the rounded rectangles at the Draw window. (Hint: Create the first rounded rectangle, then copy it.)
   b. After creating the rounded rectangles, select each one individually, then change the fill color to yellow.
   c. Close the Draw window.
   d. At the editing window, display the Edit Box dialog box for the box containing the rounded rectangles.
   e. Display the Box Position dialog box, change the horizontal position to Center of Margins, then close the dialog box.
   f. Close the Edit Box dialog box.
2. Save the document and name it Ch 21, SA 01.
3. Print and then close Ch 21, SA 01.

Figure 21.21

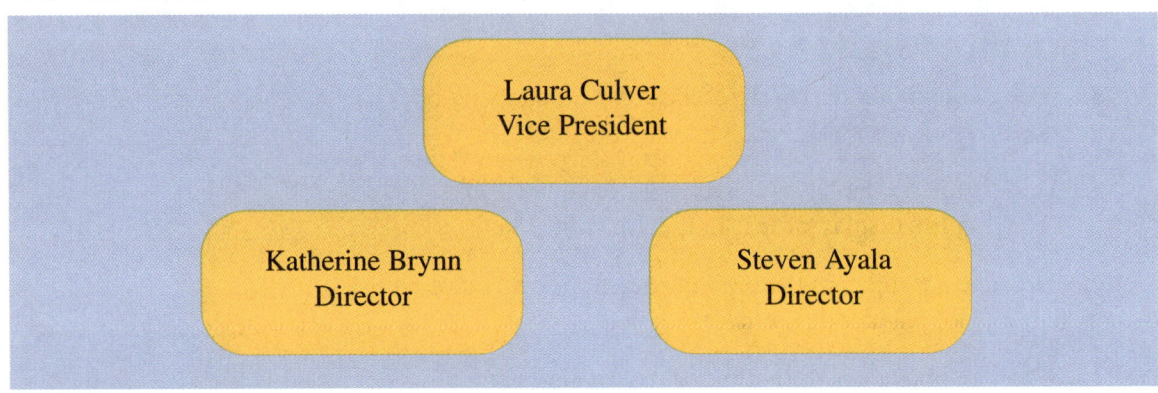

Assessment 2

1. At a clear editing window, create the letterhead shown in figure 21.22 using Draw with the following specifications:
   a. Create the five overlapping circles at the Draw window.
   b. At the editing window, display the Edit Box dialog box, then make the following changes:
      (1) Display the Box Position dialog box, change the horizontal position to Left Margin, then close the dialog box.
      (2) Display the Box Size dialog box, change the width to Set at 2 inches, the height to Maintain proportions, then close the Box Size dialog box. (Be sure to close the Edit Box dialog box when you are done.)
   c. Change the font to 18-point Arial Bold.
   d. Press Enter once, then key **FLOW SYSTEMS LIMITED**.
   e. Press Enter once, then create the horizontal line. Select the horizontal line, then change the thickness to approximately the thickness shown in figure 21.22.
2. Save the document and name it Ch 21, SA 02.
3. Print and then close Ch 21, SA 02.

Figure 21.22

Assessment 3

1. At a clear editing window, create the flow chart shown in figure 21.23 with the following specifications:
    a. Create the text, shapes, and lines at the Draw window. (Hint: If you draw a line in an incorrect location or the line is not straight, delete the line. To do this, click Selection Tool on the Draw Tools palette, click the line, then press the Delete key. Select the line tool from the Line Object Tools options, then try drawing the line again.)
    b. At the editing window, display the Edit Box dialog box, then make the following changes:
        (1) Display the Box Position dialog box, change the Attach box to setting to Page and the Horizontal placement to Center of Margins, then close the dialog box.
        (2) Display the Box Size dialog box, change the box width to Full and the height to Maintain proportions, then close the dialog box. (Be sure to close the Edit Box dialog box when you are done.)
2. Save the document and name it Ch 21, SA 03.
3. Print and then close Ch 21, SA 03. (Your document will appear larger than what you see in figure 21.23.)

Figure 21.23

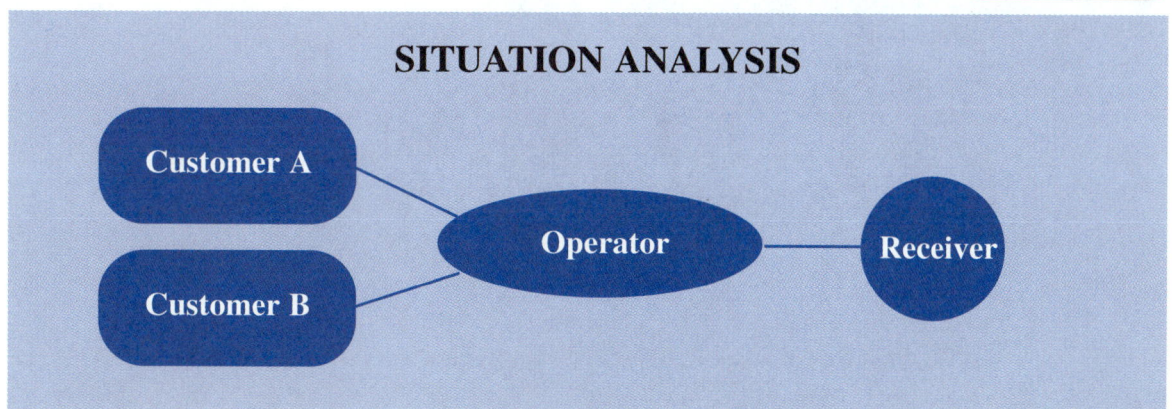

Assessment 4

1. At a clear editing window, create the document shown in figure 21.24 with the following specifications:
   a. At the Draw window, create the shapes, the curve, and the text. (Before keying the text, change the font to Impact (or a similar typeface). (You determine the point size.) Select the text and the curve, then contour the text around the curve.
   b. At the editing window, display the Edit Box dialog box, then make the following changes:
      (1) Display the Box Position dialog box, change the Attach box to setting to Page and the Horizontal placement to Center of Margins, then close the dialog box.
      (2) Display the Box Size dialog box, change the box width to Full and the height to Maintain proportions, then close the dialog box. (Be sure to close the Edit Box dialog box when you are done.)
2. Save the document and name it Ch 21, SA 04.
3. Print and then close Ch 21, SA 04. (Your document will print larger than what you see in figure 21.24.)

Figure 21.24

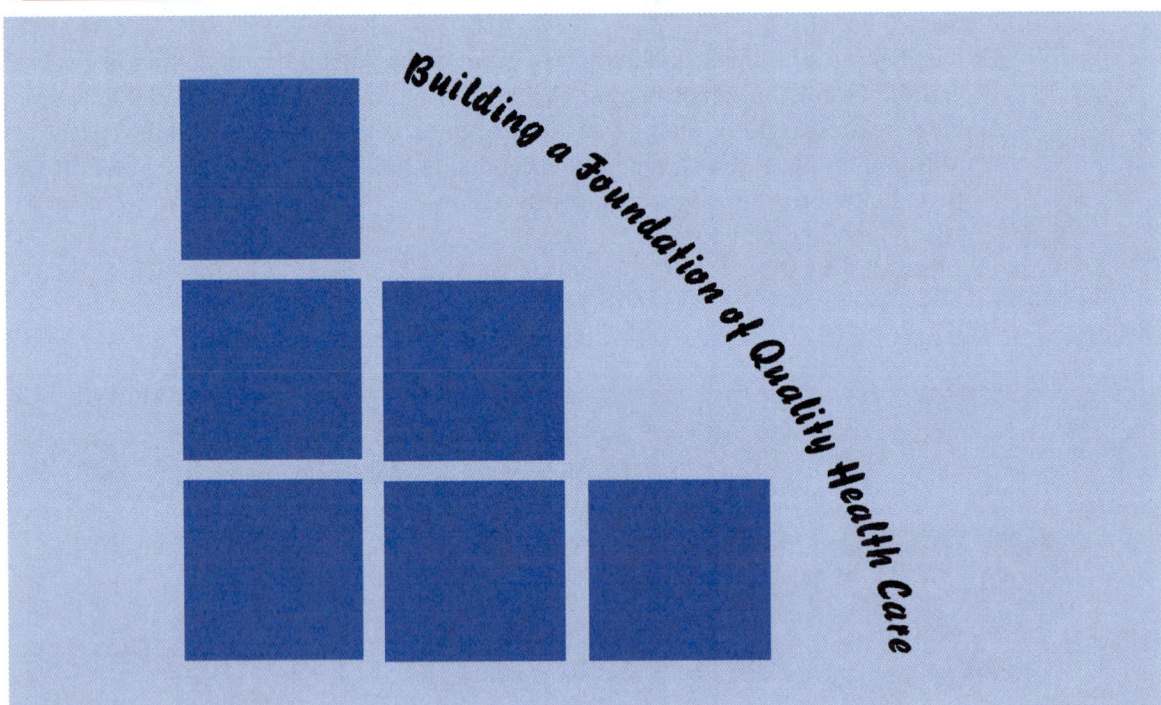

Assessment 5

1. At a clear editing window, create the sale notice shown in figure 21.25 at the TextArt window with the following specifications:
   a. At the TextArt window, change the font to Colonna MT (or a similar typeface).
   b. Select the word *Text* in the text box, then key **30% Off Sale!**.
   c. Change the shape to match what you see in the figure.
   d. Add a shadow to the lower right side of the text.
   e. Add a fill pattern and change the fill color. (You determine the fill and the color.)
   f. Close the TextArt window.
   g. At the editing window, display the Edit Box dialog box, then make the following changes:
      (1) Display the Box Position dialog box, change the Attach box to setting to Page and the Horizontal placement to Center of Margins, then close the dialog box.
      (2) Display the Box Size dialog box, change the box width to Full and the height to Maintain proportions, then close the dialog box. (Be sure to close the Edit Box dialog box when you are done.)
2. Save the document and name it Ch 21, SA 05.
3. Print and then close Ch 21, SA 05. (Your document will print larger than what you see in figure 21.25.)

Figure 21.25

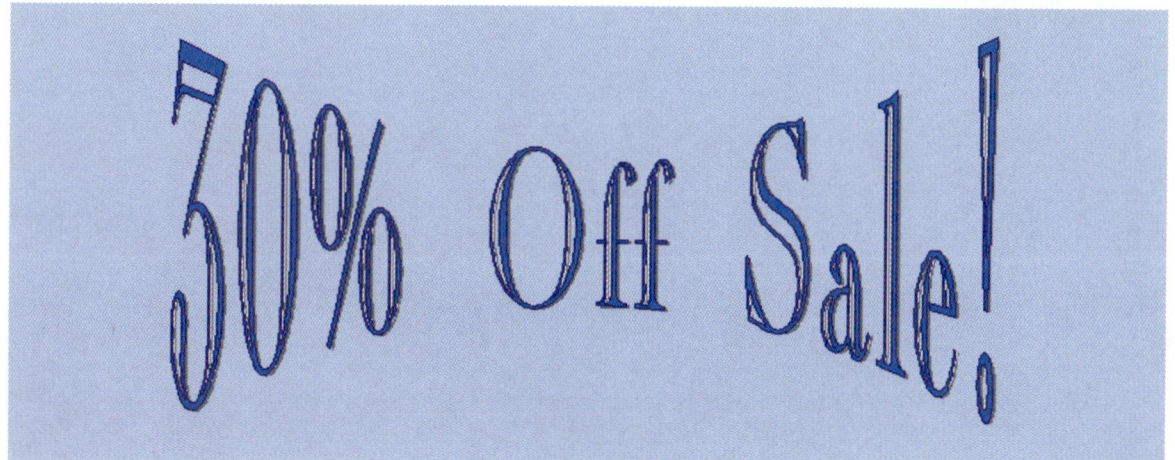

Unit Four

PERFORMANCE ASSESSMENTS

PROBLEM SOLVING AND DECISION MAKING

Assessment 1

1. At a clear editing window, open Report 06.
2. Save the document with Save As and name it Unit 04, PA 01.
3. Make the following changes to the document:
   a. Turn on the Widow/Orphan feature.
   b. Change the line spacing to double. Delete extra blank lines so there is only a double space between all lines in the document.
   c. Select the title and change the font to 14-point Arial. Select each of the following headings and change the font to 14-point Arial:
      Continued Growth of Photonics (Fiber Optics)
      Microcomputer Trends in the Nineties
   d. Display the Environment Preferences dialog box, then change the Hyphenation prompt to Always.
   e. Move the insertion point to the beginning of the document. Change the left hyphenation zone to 4% and the right hyphenation zone to 0%. Turn on hyphenation, then make hyphenation decisions as needed. (Move the insertion point to the end of the document to ensure that all necessary words are hyphenated.)
   f. Insert a double line page border in the document. (The page border will print on each page.)
4. Save the document again with the same name (Unit 04, PA 01).
5. Display the Environment Preferences dialog box, then change the Hyphenation prompt to When Required.
6. Print and then close Unit 04, PA 01.

Optional: Design a cover sheet consisting of at least two graphics images and the title of the report.

Assessment 2

1. At a clear editing window, create the abbreviations shown below for the text following the abbreviation:
   - TE = Training and Education Department
   - HR = Human Resources Department
   - KB = Katherine Brynn
   - SA = Steven Ayala
2. Close the document without saving it.
3. At a clear editing window, create a macro named *Memo* that includes the text shown in figure U4.1. Include pauses where you see (*pause*) in the figure. After keying *SUBJECT:*, then creating the pause, press Enter three times.
4. After creating the macro, close the document without saving it.
5. At a clear editing window, play the *Memo* macro. Insert the following text at the pauses:
   - DATE: (current date)
   - TO: KB, HR
   - FROM: SA, TE
   - SUBJECT: TRAINING CLASSES
6. After keying the text at the pauses, key the remaining text shown in figure U4.2. Insert the full name where you see the abbreviations.
7. Save the document and name it Unit 04, PA 02.
8. Delete the abbreviations created in step 1.
9. Print and then close Unit 04, PA 02.

Optional: Rewrite the document as a notice to employees inviting them to participate in some exciting new training classes.

DATE: (pause)

TO: (pause)

FROM: (pause)

SUBJECT: (pause)

Figure U4.1

The training classes for the HR have been scheduled for next month. Classes will be held on Monday and Wednesday from 3:30 to 5:00 p.m. The first class will focus on the new database management system used by the Hospital. The second class will focus on the electronic mail system.

There will be a $350 charge to the HR budget for training material. There will be material available for 30 people. If more than 30 will be attending, please contact me.

xx:Unit 04, PA 02

Figure U4.2

Unit 4

Assessment 3

1. At a clear editing window, create a certificate with the *Certificate of achievement* template (in the *Publish* group). Insert the following text at the Template Information dialog box:
    Name of recipient: **Rebecca Cook**
    Description of achievement: **Employee of the Month**
2. Save the certificate and name it Unit 04, PA 03.
3. Print and then close Unit 04, PA 03.

Assessment 4

1. At a clear editing window, open Report 07.
2. Save the document with Save As and name it Unit 04, PA 04.
3. Make the following changes to the document:
    a. Turn on the Widow/Orphan feature.
    b. Insert a hard return above and below the following headings:
        Industrialization
        Development of a World Market
        The American Civil War
        Colonization
        The 1870s Depression
    c. Insert the graphics image named *World* in a user box at the beginning of the second paragraph in the *Industrialization* section of the report. Display the Edit Box dialog box for the image, then make the following changes to the user box:
        (1) Display the Box Position dialog box, change the Attach box to option to Paragraph, change the horizontal position to Left Margin, then close the dialog box
        (2) Display the Box Size dialog box, change the width to Set at 2.5 inches, make sure the height is Maintain proportions, then close the dialog box.
        (3) Display the Wrap Text dialog box, contour the text around the image, then close the dialog box. (Be sure to close the Edit Box dialog box when you are done.)
4. Save the document again with the same name (Unit 04, PA 04).
5. Print and then close Unit 04, PA 04.

Assessment 5

1. At a clear editing window, insert the graphics image named *Horse_j* into a figure box with the following specifications:
    a. Display the Edit Box dialog box for the figure box.
    b. Display the Box Position dialog box, change the Attach box to setting to Page, then close the dialog box.
    c. Display the Box Size dialog box, change the box width to Full and the height to Maintain proportions, then close the dialog box.
    d. Change the figure box border style to a triple line of your choosing and add 10% fill.
    e. Close the Edit Box dialog box.
2. Save the document and name it Unit 04, PA 05.
3. Print and then close Unit 04, PA 05.

Optional: Experiment with different fill gradients and image sizes. Print your favorite variation.

Assessment 6

1. At a clear editing window, create the document shown in figure U4.3 by completing the following steps:
   a. Create a user box with the following specifications:
      (1) Insert the image named *Winrace* in the user box.
      (2) Display the Edit Box dialog box, then make the following changes:
         (a) Display the Box Position dialog box, change the horizontal position to Left <u>M</u>argin, then close the dialog box.
         (b) Display the Box Size dialog box, change the width to 2 inches, then close the dialog box.
      (3) Close the Edit Box dialog box.
   b. Deselect the user box.
   c. Change the font to 14-point Arrus Blk BT (or a similar typeface).
   d. Press Enter twice, then key the text shown in figure U4.3 centered.
   e. Change the font to 12-point Arrus Blk BT for the text *Sponsored by Denver Memorial Hospital*. (Press the Enter key twice after *Sponsored by Denver Memorial Hospital*.)
   f. Set the text *Sponsored by Denver Memorial Hospital* in reverse type.
2. Insert a double line paragraph border. (Make sure the insertion point is positioned at the beginning of the document before you create the border and that you remove the check mark from the Apply border to current paragraph only option.)
3. Save the document and name it Unit 04, PA 06.
4. Print and then close Unit 04, PA 06.

Figure U4.3

Optional: Recreate the document in a different font. Add information about the length of the race and where it starts and finishes.

Assessment 7

1. At a clear editing window, create the document shown in figure U4.4 with the following specifications:
   a. Change the font to 12-point Arrus Blk BT (or a similar typeface).
   b. Bold and center the title and subtitle.
   c. Use the graphics line feature to create the horizontal lines in the document. Create each horizontal line with the following settings:
      (1) Horizontal position at Set.
      (2) Length set at 3.5 inches.
   d. Insert a code to center the current document on the page.
2. Save the document and name it Unit 04, PA 07.
3. Print and then close Unit 04, PA 07.

Optional: Evaluate the design of the document you have created. Write a paragraph or two discussing ways you might want to change the design and why.

DENVER MEMORIAL HOSPITAL

Customer Service Satisfaction

Questionnaire Design
_____

- Survey questions were developed from behaviors identified by department managers and secondary research regarding factors influencing patient satisfaction.

- Two questionnaires will be developed using the same question content and format--one for the pediatric population and one for the adult population.

Sample Size
_____

- Approximately 1,300 patients discharged from Denver Memorial Hospital in April 1998, received questionnaires.

- This larger sample size will provide baseline information that is statistically valid to most department managers.

- On a routine quarterly basis, the sample size will be approximately 1,000.

Sample Design
_____

- Random sample design is based on discharges by the Pediatrics Unit and weighted to provide generalized responses to individual units.

- Independent variables such as age and residence zip code will be collected through data processing and correlated with patient responses.

Figure U4.4

Assessment 8

1. At a clear editing window, create a letterhead for the organization Wildlife Restoration League. Include the following information in the letterhead:

    Wildlife Restoration League
    P.O. Box 345
    Bismarck, ND 74523
    (701) 555-2309

    Include a user box in the letterhead with the image *Buck* inserted in the user box. Also, include at least one horizontal or vertical line.
2. Save the letterhead and name it Unit 04, PA 08.
3. Print and then close Unit 04, PA 08.

WRITING

The following activities give you the opportunity to practice your writing skills along with demonstrating an understanding of some of the important WordPerfect features you have mastered in this unit. In planning the documents, remember to shape the information according to the writing purpose and the audience. Use correct grammar, appropriate word choices, and clear sentence constructions.

Activity 1

Situation: You work for CYCLE CITY, a store that sells bicycles and bicycling gear. You have been asked to design a letterhead for the store. When designing this letterhead, include the image *Winrace* along with this information:

    CYCLE CITY
    2305 Benson Highway
    Kent, WA 98033
    (206) 555-4422

Save the letterhead and name it Unit 04, Act 01. Print and then close Unit 04, Act 01.

Activity 2

Situation: You are Cynthia Lakeland, assistant manager for CYCLE CITY. Write a letter to R & L Suppliers, 903 North Union Street, Seattle, WA 98049, using the letterhead you created in Activity 1. In the letter, request information on a new ultra light bicycling helmet you saw advertised in the R & L Suppliers catalog. Ask that a representative of the company visit the store and bring a sample of the helmet. You are also interested in any bicycling safety goggles manufactured by the company. Save the letter and name it Unit 04, Act 02. Print and then close Unit 04, Act 02.

Activity 3

Use TextArt to create a flier announcing that all bicycle helmets are 25% off on Saturday, April 18, 1998. Save the flier and name it Unit 04, Act 03. Print and then close Unit 04, Act 03.

Activity 4

Situation: You are Joni Kapshaw, editor of the Omaha City School District newsletter. You have been asked by Jocelyn Cook, assistant superintendent, to prepare a memo describing desktop publishing including the system components, input devices, and output devices. Use the information contained in *Report 09* on your student data disk to help you prepare the memo. Save the memo and name it Unit 04, Act 04. Print and then close Unit 04, Act 04.

Unit *Five*

ENHANCING THE Presentation OF Documents

In this unit, you will learn to enhance the presentation of text by formatting text into columns, tables, and charts.

22

CHANGING PAPER SIZE

PERFORMANCE OBJECTIVE

Upon successful completion of chapter 22, you will be able to change the page size to print text on a variety of stationery, including envelopes and labels.

When a printer is installed, a standard paper definition is included. This paper definition is used to print text on regular-sized stationery (8.5 x 11 inches). In addition to the standard paper definition, a definition may also be included for wide stationery (11 x 8.5 inches) and a definition for envelopes. Some printers can accept and print text on a variety of paper sizes, while others can print on only a few.

Inserting a Paper Definition Code

When a printer is selected, a few predesigned paper definitions are available that can be inserted in a document. For example, a wide stationery paper definition or an envelope paper definition can be inserted. To insert a paper definition code in a document, click Format, point to Page, then click Page Size. At the Page Size dialog box, shown in figure 22.1, click the down-pointing triangle to the right of the Name text box, then click the desired paper size from the drop-down list. Click OK to close the Page Size dialog box.

Figure 22.1

Page Size Dialog Box

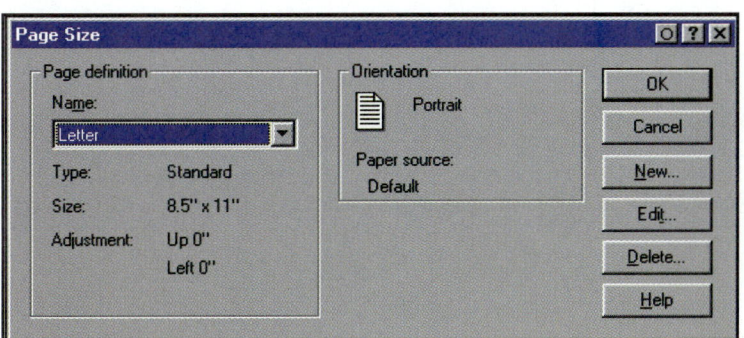

When the paper definition is changed, WordPerfect inserts the paper definition code at the beginning of the document. For example, if the paper definition is changed to Letter Landscape, the code [Paper Sz/Typ: 11" by 8.5": Letter Landscape] is inserted at the beginning of the document and can be seen in Reveal Codes. (The insertion point must be positioned immediately left of the code to view the entire code or you must click the code.)

EXERCISE 1

Inserting a Letter Landscape Code

1. At a clear editing window, open Report 01.
2. Save the document with Save As and name it Ch 22, Ex 01.
3. Insert the Letter Landscape paper definition code in the document by completing the following steps:
   a. Make sure the insertion point is positioned somewhere on the first page, then click Format, point to Page, then click Page Size.
   b. At the Page Size dialog box, click the down-pointing triangle to the right of the Name text box, then click Letter Landscape at the drop-down list.
   c. Click OK to close the dialog box.
4. Move the insertion point to the end of the document to adjust the soft page breaks. Check the location of page breaks to see if they are in desirable locations. If not, you may want to insert your own page break.
5. Save the document again with the same name (Ch 22, Ex 01).
6. Print and then close Ch 22, Ex 01. (Before printing, check with your instructor to determine whether the printer you are using is capable of landscape printing.)

Creating a Paper Definition

If you want to use a paper size not included in WordPerfect's list, you can create a paper definition with the New button at the Page Size dialog box. When you click the New button, the New Page Size dialog box shown in figure 22.2 displays. Key a name for the paper definition (this name must be unique), make any necessary changes to the options, then click OK.

The types of paper definitions you can create are only limited to the capabilities of your printer. A paper definition that you create is saved with the current printer and affects only the current printer. If you select another printer, the paper definition just created is not available.

New Page Size Dialog Box

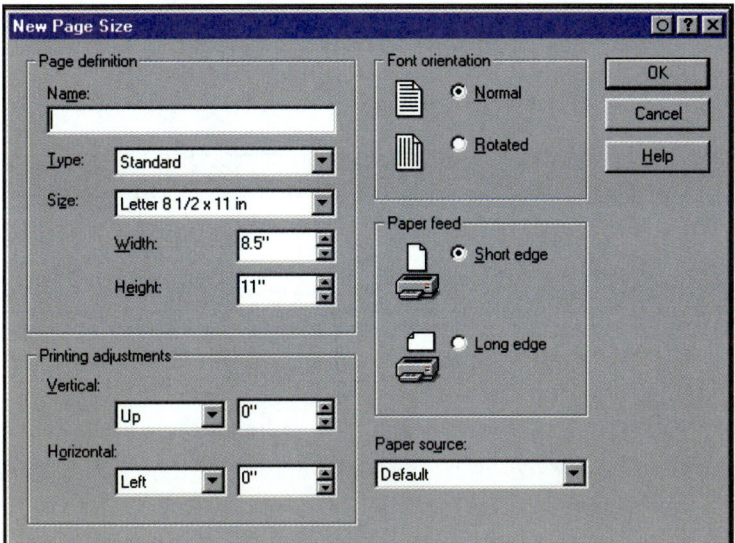

Figure 22.2

Making Changes to the New Page Size Dialog Box

The New Page Size dialog box contains a variety of options that can be used to create a specific paper definition.

Name: With the Name option, you can give the paper definition a unique name. The name can be a maximum of 35 characters and can include spaces. Name the paper definition something that describes it.

Type: Click the down-pointing triangle at the right of the Type text box and a drop-down list displays containing names for types of stationery. The options from this drop-down menu are meant as a description only of the type of stationery to be used.

Size: Clicking the down-pointing triangle at the right of the Size text box causes a drop-down menu to display with sizes available for the current printer. If the size you desire is not shown, you can enter your own width and height measurements. To do this, click *User Defined Size* at the Size drop-down list, then key the dimensions for the paper in the Width and Height text boxes.

Printing adjustments: Use the Vertical and Horizontal options from the Printing adjustments section if the text is not printing in the proper location on the page. For example, if you are using a dot-matrix printer that requires paper to be manually fed into the printer, you may want to adjust the page up about one inch. Choose Vertical to adjust printing up or down or choose Horizontal to adjust the printing to the left or right.

Font orientation: With the Font orientation options—Normal and Rotated—you can choose to print a wide or narrow form with either portrait or landscape fonts.

Paper feed: Depending on the printer you are using, you can either insert the Short edge of the paper into the printer or the Long edge. For most printers, WordPerfect can print on the paper in either portrait or landscape font orientation. At the portrait orientation, text comes out of the printer in the orientation that you read text. If you print with a landscape font, the text comes out of the printer rotated 90 degrees.

Paper source: If you click the down-pointing triangle at the right of the Paper source text box in the New Page Size dialog box, a drop-down menu displays with five options (depending on the printer selected)—Default, Upper tray, Manual feed, Envelope manual feed, and Envelope.

Changing Paper Size 525

These options describe how the paper is fed into the printer. Choose Manual feed if you are hand-feeding paper into the printer. The Continuous option is used for paper that is tractor-fed into the printer or for a printer that has a single sheet feeder bin. If the printer you have selected can pull paper from several sheet feeder bins, these bins are included in the drop-down menu.

Creating a Half-Size Paper Definition

1. At a clear editing window, create a half-size paper definition that measures 5.5 x 8.5 inches by completing the following steps:
    a. Click Format, point to Page, then click Page Size.
    b. At the Page Size dialog box, click New.
    c. At the New Page Size dialog box, key **Half Size**.
    d. Change the width size to 5.5 and the height size to 8.5 by completing the following steps:
        (1) Click the down-pointing triangle after the text box to the right of the Size option, then click User Defined Size at the drop-down list. (If *User Defined Size* is not available, choose *Custom Paper Size* or a similar size.)
        (2) Select the current measurement (*8.5"*) that displays in the Width text box and then key **5.5**.
        (3) Click the down-pointing triangle to the right of the Height text box until *8.5"* displays in the text box.
    e. Click OK to close the New Page Size dialog box.
    f. Click OK to close the Page Size dialog box.
2. Close the document without saving it.
3. Open Memo 09.
4. Save the document with Save As and name it Ch 22, Ex 02.
5. Change the page size to Half Size by completing the following steps:
    a. Click Format, point to Page, then click Page Size.
    b. At the Page Size dialog box, click the down-pointing triangle at the right of the Name text box, then click Half Size at the drop-down list.
    c. Click OK to close the dialog box.
6. Save the document again with the same name (Ch 22, Ex 02).
7. Print and then close Ch 22, Ex 02. (Before printing, check with your instructor to determine whether the printer you are using is capable of printing with this paper definition.)

Editing a Paper Definition

Any of the paper definitions can be edited with the Edit button at the Page Size dialog box. For example, you may want to change the width of the paper.

EXERCISE 3

Editing a Paper Definition

1. At a clear editing window, edit the Half Size page definition so that it prints in rotated orientation by completing the following steps:
    a. Display the Page Size dialog box.
    b. At the Page Size dialog box, change the Page Definition to *Half Size*, then click the Edit button.
    c. At the Edit Page Size dialog box, click Rotated in the Font orientation section.
    d. Click OK to close the Edit Page Size dialog box.
    e. At the Page Size dialog box, click OK.
2. Close the document without saving it.
3. At a clear editing window, open Memo 01.
4. Save the memo with Save As and name it Ch 22, Ex 03.
5. Display the Page Size dialog box, then change to the Half Size page definition.
6. Save the document again with the same name (Ch 22, Ex 03).
7. Print and then close Ch 22, Ex 03. (This document will print on two pages.)

Deleting a Paper Definition

A page definition can be deleted at the Page Size dialog box. To do this, display the desired page definition in the Name text box, then click the Delete button. At the question asking if you are sure you want to delete the highlighted page definition, click OK.

EXERCISE 4

Deleting a Paper Definition

1. At a clear editing window, delete the Half Size page definition by completing the following steps:
    a. Display the Page Size dialog box.
    b. At the Page Size dialog box, change the Page definition to the Half Size definition, then click the Delete button.
    c. At the Delete highlighted paper definition warning, click OK.
    d. Click Cancel to close the Page Size dialog box.

Printing Text on Envelopes

Text can be printed on envelopes with WordPerfect by selecting an envelope paper definition at the Page Size dialog box. If an envelope paper definition is available, select it as described earlier.

Once an envelope definition is selected, the margins should be changed. If you are using letterhead envelopes (with a preprinted company address in the upper left corner), change the top margin to approximately 2.25 inches and the left margin to approximately 4 inches. You might also want to change the bottom margin to something less than 1 inch to allow enough room for long addresses.

If you want to print an address in the upper left corner of the envelope, change the top and bottom margins to approximately 0.3 inches. Key the return address in the upper left corner of the envelope. After keying the return address, press the Enter key until the insertion point is positioned on approximately line 2.25". Press the Tab key until the insertion point is positioned on approximately position 4", then key the address.

After the address(es) has been keyed, print the envelope in the same manner as any other document. If the envelope is to be manually fed into the printer, insert the envelope, then perform the action required by WordPerfect. Before printing text on the envelope, you may want to change the viewing mode to Two Page or click the Page/Zoom Full button to see where text will print on the envelope.

Using WordPerfect's Envelope Feature

You can use WordPerfect's Envelope feature to create an envelope in the current document or using a return address and mailing address that you have specified.

Creating an Envelope at a Clear Editing Window

To create an envelope document at a clear editing window using the Envelope feature, click Format, then Envelope. At the Envelope dialog box, shown in figure 22.3, make sure the correct envelope definition is displayed in the Envelope definitions text box, key the return address, then key the mailing address. Print the envelope or click the Append to Doc button to insert the envelope definition code and the return and mailing addresses in the document.

Figure 22.3

Envelope Dialog Box

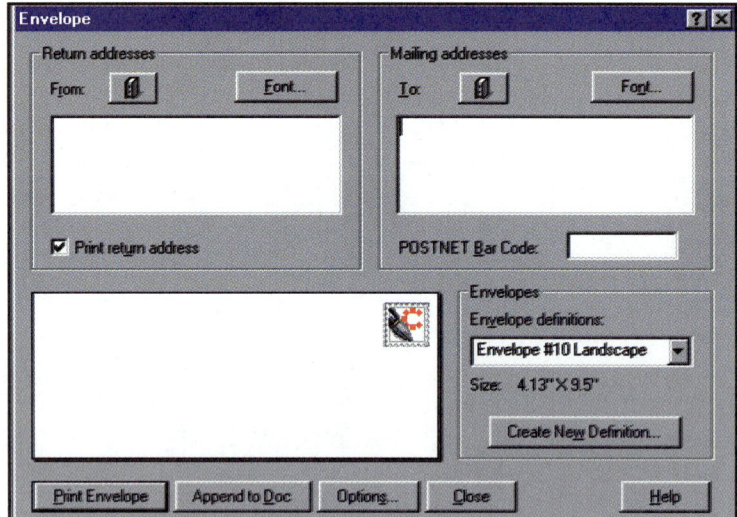

EXERCISE 5

Creating an Envelope

1. At a clear editing window, create an envelope using WordPerfect's Envelope feature by completing the following steps:
   a. Click Format, then Envelope.

528   Chapter 22

> b. At the Envelope dialog box, the insertion point should be positioned in the Mailing addresses text box. If it is not, click inside the Mailing addresses text box.
> c. Key the mailing address shown in figure 22.4. (This is the name and address for Mr. Scott Ingram.)
> d. Click inside the Return addresses text box.
> e. Key the return address shown in figure 22.4. (This is the name and address for Michelle Ching.)
> f. Click the Append to Doc button to insert the envelope definition code and the return and mailing addresses on the envelope.
> 2. Save the document and name it Ch 22, Ex 05.
> 3. Print and then close Ch 22, Ex 05.

Figure 22.4

Michelle Ching
3320 Westside Drive
San Diego, CA 99432

                              Mr. Scott Ingram
                              860 South 52nd Street
                              San Diego, CA 99567

Creating an Envelope in an Existing Document

If you open the Envelope dialog box in a document containing a letter, the inside address in the letter is automatically inserted in the Mailing addresses section of the Envelope dialog box. The mailing address in the letter must be located at the left margin and there must be two hard returns following the address.

Click the Append to Doc button to insert the envelope at the end of the document. WordPerfect automatically inserts a page break separating the envelope from the document. If you want to send the envelope directly to the printer without inserting it in the document, click the Print Envelope button instead of Append to Doc. When you click the Print Envelope button, the envelope (but not the letter) is sent directly to the printer.

Making Changes at the Envelope Dialog Box

The Envelope dialog box contains options for turning off the printing of the return address, changing the font of the return and mailing addresses, inserting a USPS Bar Code, and changing the envelope size.

Adding/Deleting Addresses: When you display the Envelope dialog box, WordPerfect inserts the last return address used to create an envelope. If you use several return addresses, you can add a return address to the address list. To do this, click the Address Book button to the right of From in the Return addresses section. This opens the Corel Address Book dialog box. Select an existing return address by double-clicking the address you want to insert.

A new entry that you will use frequently can be entered using the Add button. To add an entry, click Add, click *Person* or *Organization* in the Select entry type list box, then click OK. This displays the Properties for New Entry dialog box where information can be keyed for the new return address. Click OK when you have completed entering the data. This returns you to the Corel Address Book dialog box where you can insert the new address by double-clicking the entry line.

The Mailing addresses section includes an Address Book button located to the right of To. Click this button and the Corel Address Book dialog box displays. Include frequently used mailing addresses in the same manner as including frequently used return addresses.

Addresses that have been added to the Corel Address Book dialog box can be edited or deleted. To edit a return or mailing address, click the entry in the Corel Address Book dialog box, then click Edit. This opens the Properties dialog box for the entry. At this dialog box, edit fields as needed. Entries can be deleted by clicking the entry and then clicking Remove. A message will appear asking *Are you sure you want to delete the selected address book item?* Click Yes to remove the entry from the Corel Address Book.

Font: The Font button in the Return addresses section and the Font button in the Mailing addresses section allow you to change the font of the return address and/or the mailing address.

Print return address: By default, WordPerfect will print the return address on the envelope. If you do not wish the return address printed, remove the check mark from the Print return address check box.

Selecting and Creating Envelope Definitions: If your printer has more than one envelope definition, you can select a different envelope. To do this, click the down-pointing triangle at the right of the Envelope definitions text box, then click the desired definition at the drop-down list.

If there are no envelope definitions listed, you can create your own by clicking Create New Definition. This causes the New Page Size dialog box to display. This is the same dialog box described in the Creating a Paper Size Definition section.

Changing Options: WordPerfect includes default horizontal and vertical measurements for the return address and mailing address for each envelope definition. If you want to change these default measurements, click Options at the Envelope dialog box. This causes the Envelope Options dialog box shown in figure 22.5 to display. At this dialog box, make changes as desired.

Including a USPS Bar Code: You can include a USPS Bar Code in the mailing address at the Envelope dialog box. The bar code speeds mail sorting, increases the accuracy of delivery, and reduces postage costs. To create a USPS Bar Code, click Options, then click Include and position above address or Include and position below address in the USPS Bar Code options section. WordPerfect automatically converts the ZIP Code into short and tall lines that create the bar code.

Envelope Options Dialog Box

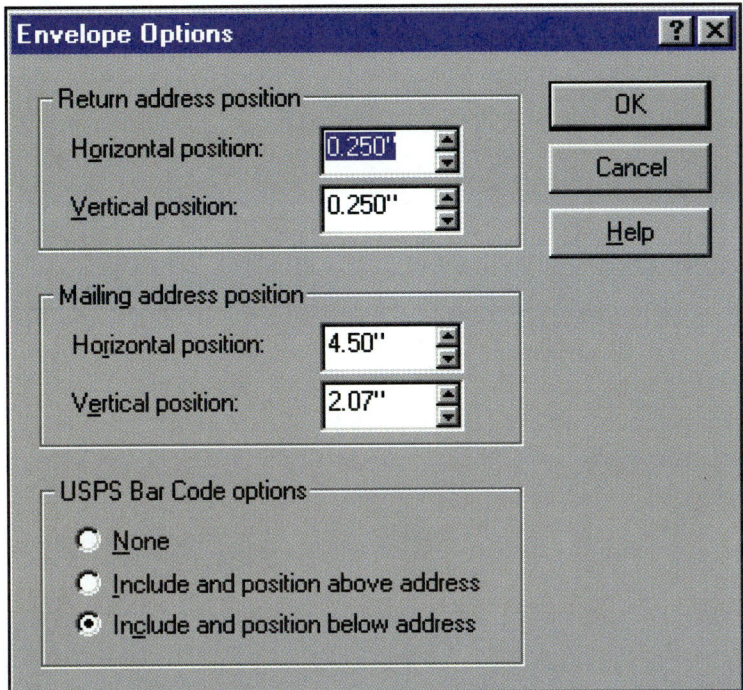

Figure 22.5

Creating an Envelope with a USPS Bar Code

1. At a clear editing window, open Letter 01.
2. Save the document with Save As and name it Ch 22, Ex 06.
3. Create an envelope for this letter with a USPS Bar Code using WordPerfect's Envelope feature by completing the following steps:
   a. Click Format, then Envelope.
   b. At the Envelope dialog box, make sure the mailing address is inserted properly in the Mailing addresses section.
   c. If there is an address in the Return addresses section, delete it.
   d. Click Options.
   e. At the Envelope Options dialog box, click Include and position below address in the USPS Bar Code options section.
   f. Click OK.
   g. Click Append to Doc.
4. WordPerfect inserts a hard page break at the end of the letter, then inserts the envelope definition, name, address, and the USPS Bar Code. Click the Page/Zoom Full button to see how the address will print on the envelope and then click the button again.
5. Save the document with the same name (Ch 22, Ex 06).
6. Print only the page containing the envelope.
7. Close Ch 22, Ex 06.

EXERCISE 6

Changing Paper Size **531**

Creating Labels

Use WordPerfect's Labels feature to print text on mailing labels, file labels, disk labels, or other types of labels. WordPerfect includes approximately 130 definitions for labels that can be purchased at an office supply store. If none of the predefined label definitions meet your requirements, you can create your own label definition.

Using a Predefined Label Definition

To use a predefined label definition in a document, click Format, then Labels. At the Labels dialog box, shown in figure 22.6, click the desired label type in the Labels list box, then click Select. As you click different label forms in the Labels list box, details of the label form appear below the Labels list box. The Label details section includes the Sheet size, Label size, Number of labels, and the Label type.

Figure 22.6

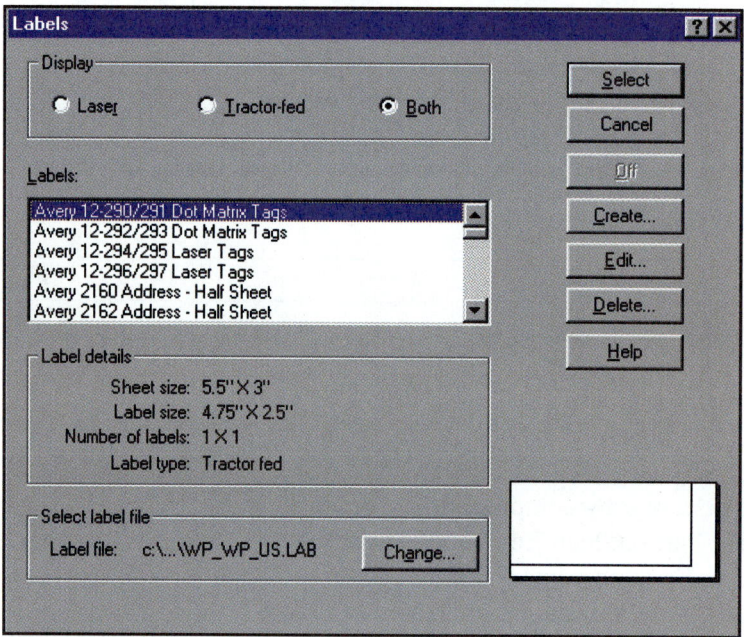

Labels Dialog Box

Entering Text in Labels

After inserting a label definition in a document, key the information for the labels. When entering information for labels, use the keys shown in figure 22.7 to perform the actions described.

Figure 22.7

Keys for Entering Label Information

CTRL + ENTER	=	Ends text of current label and moves insertion point to next label.
ENTER	=	Ends a line within a label.
ALT + PG DN	=	Moves insertion point to next label.
ALT + PG UP	=	Moves insertion point to previous label.
Edit, Go To, #	=	Moves insertion point to label number entered.

When entering text in a label, press Ctrl + Enter to insert a hard page break. The hard page break tells WordPerfect to move to the next label. In a labels form, a page created with Ctrl + Enter is called a *logical page*, while the entire sheet is called the *physical page*. Each label is considered a separate page. Formatting features that affect a page such as page numbering or headers and footers will print on each label.

In a labels document, you may want to change the font to a smaller point size to ensure that all information fits on the label. You may also want to insert a code to center text on the current page and subsequent pages. This will center the text of the label in the middle of the label vertically.

At the Page viewing mode, you will see the label in the editing window. When you press Ctrl + Enter, the insertion point is moved to the next label. The labels are outlined in a single blue line. At the Draft viewing mode, you will not see the label. When you press Ctrl + Enter, a double line is inserted in the editing window, and the insertion point is moved below the double line. Change to the Two Page viewing mode or click the Page/Zoom Full button to see how the labels will print on the page.

EXERCISE

Creating Labels

1. At a clear editing window, create mailing addresses using a predefined labels definition by completing the following steps:
   a. Click Format, then Labels.
   b. At the Labels dialog box, click the down-pointing triangle at the right of the Labels list box until *Avery 5160 Address* is visible, then click it. (This label is quite a ways down the labels list. Check with your instructor to see whether your printer will print this label form size. If not, use a different label form size.)
   c. Click Edit.
   d. At the Edit Labels dialog box, click the up-pointing triangle to the right of the Left option in the Labels margin section until *0.500"* displays.
   e. Click the up-pointing triangle to the right of the Top option in the Labels margin once (this displays *0.100"*).
   f. Click OK to close the Edit Labels dialog box.
   g. At the Labels dialog box, click Select.
2. At the editing window, key the addresses shown in figure 22.8. Press Ctrl + Enter to end a label and move the insertion point to the next label.
3. After keying all the label addresses, press Ctrl + Home to move the insertion point to the beginning of the document and then insert a code to center current and subsequent pages.
4. Save the document and name it Ch 22, Ex 07.
5. Print and then close Ch 22, Ex 07. (Before printing, check with your instructor to make sure that the printer you are using can print a document with this label definition.)

Changing Paper Size 533

Figure 22.8

Mr. Tony Brewster 903 North Academy Tampa, FL 33543	Dr. Dione Teague Madison Clinic 100 Madison Avenue Tampa, FL 33512	Ms. Lona Schauffer Southside Shipping 9873 Parker Road Tampa, FL 33422
Mrs. Elana Steffan 15403 South 42nd Street Tampa, FL 33541	Mr. Rodney Marlow 6320 South 32nd Tampa, FL 33453	Professor Lea Steele Bayside Community College 2300 North 51st Tampa, FL 33422

Printing Specific Labels

When you print a label page, the entire page is printed. You can, however, print individual labels. In chapter 14, you learned how to print individual pages in a document or a range of pages. You can do the same with labels.

To print specific labels, display the Print dialog box. At the Print dialog box, click the down-pointing triangle at the right side of the Print list box. At the drop-down list that displays, click *Advanced Multiple Pages*, then click Edit. At the Advanced Multiple Pages dialog box, key the number (or numbers) of the label (or labels) to be printed, (use a comma to indicate *and*; use a hyphen to indicate *through*), then click OK. Click Print to begin printing the labels. For example, to print labels 1, 4, 7, and 10, you would key **1,4,7,10** at the Advanced Multiple Pages dialog box. To print labels 14 through 22 and label 26, you would key **14-22,26**. For more information on printing ranges, please refer to chapter 14.

EXERCISE 8

Printing Individual Labels

1. At a clear editing window, open Ch 22, Ex 07.
2. Print labels 1 through 3 and label 5 by completing the following steps:
    a. Display the Print dialog box.
    b. At the Print dialog box, click the down-pointing triangle at the right of the Print list box, then click *Advanced Multiple Pages* at the drop-down list.
    c. Click the Edit button.
    d. At the Advanced Multiple Pages dialog box, key **1-3,5** and then click OK.
    e. Click Print.
3. Close the document without saving it.

Creating a Form File for Labels

A form file can be created for labels and can then be merged with a data file to create the labels. To create a labels form file, you would complete these basic steps:

1. Click Format, then Labels.
2. At the Labels dialog box, select the desired label in the Labels list box, then click Select.
3. At the editing window, display the Merge dialog box.
4. At the Merge dialog box, click Form.
5. At the Create Merge File dialog box, click OK.
6. At the Create Form File dialog box, key the name of the data form in the Associate a data file text box, then click OK.
7. At the editing window, click Insert Field from the Merge Feature Bar.
8. With the Insert Field Name or Number dialog box, insert fields in the appropriate location in the label.
9. When all fields have been inserted, close the Insert Field Name or Number dialog box and then save the labels form in the normal manner.

EXERCISE 9

Creating a Label Form File

1. At a clear editing window, create a label form file for printing mailing labels by completing the following steps:
    a. Click Format, then Labels.
    b. At the Labels dialog box, click *Avery 5160 Address* in the Labels list box. (You will need to scroll down the list to display this label form. Check with your instructor to see whether your printer will print this label form size. If not, use a different label form size.)
    c. Click Edit.
    d. At the Edit Labels dialog box, click the up- or down-pointing triangle at the right of the Left option in the Label margins section until *0.400"* displays. (Skip this step if this measurement already displays in the Left text box.)
    e. Click the up-pointing triangle at the right of the Top option in the Label margins section until *0.100"* displays. (Skip this step if the measurement already displays as *0.100"*.)
    f. Click OK.
    g. At the Labels dialog box, click Select.
    h. At the editing window, click Tools, then Merge.
    i. At the Merge dialog box, click Form.
    j. At the Create Merge File dialog box, make sure Use file in active window is selected, then click OK.
    k. At the Create Form File dialog box, key **Customer df** in the Associate a data file text box, then click OK.
    l. At the editing window, click Insert Field from the Merge Feature Bar.
    m. At the Insert Field Name or Number dialog box, double-click *title* in the Field Names list box.

n. Continue inserting field names in the appropriate location in the label. (The fields may wrap down a line and to the next label; this is okay. The *address* field contains the street address as well as the city, state, and ZIP Code.)
   o. When all field names have been inserted, click Close to close the Insert Field Name or Number dialog box.
   p. Save the labels form in the regular manner and name it Labels ff.
2. Close the Labels ff document.
3. At a clear editing window, merge Labels ff with Customer df to the printer.

CHAPTER SUMMARY

▼ When a printer is installed with WordPerfect, a standard paper definition is generally included in the printer definition menu.

▼ The standard paper definition is used to print text on stationery that is 8.5 x 11 inches. A paper definition for printing on wide stationery (11 x 8.5 inches) and a paper definition for envelopes might also be included.

▼ To change the page size, insert a paper definition code in the document at the Page Size dialog box.

▼ If the desired page size is not listed in the Page Size dialog box, another size can be added at the New Page Size dialog box. These customized page sizes are limited to the capabilities of your printer.

▼ A paper definition that you create is saved with the current printer. If you select another printer, the paper definition just created is not available.

▼ In addition to changing the page size, options for changing the following attributes are also available at the New Page Size dialog box: paper name, paper type, paper location, orientation, and text adjustments.

▼ Any of the paper definitions can be edited at the Edit Page Size dialog box. A paper definition can be deleted at the Page Size dialog box.

▼ Use the Envelope feature to create an envelope at a clear editing window or in an existing document. In an existing document, the address is automatically inserted in the Mailing addresses section of the Envelope dialog box.

▼ The Envelope dialog box contains options for turning off the printing of the return address, changing the font of the return and mailing addresses, inserting a USPS Bar Code, and changing the envelope size.

▼ Use the Labels feature to print text on mailing labels, file labels, disk labels, etc. To use a predefined label definition, display the Labels dialog box.

▼ A form file can be created for labels at the Labels dialog box and then merged with a data file to create the labels.

COMMANDS REVIEW

	Mouse/Keyboard
Page Size dialog box	Format, Page, Page Size
New Page Size dialog box	Format, Page, Page Size; choose New
Edit Page Size dialog box	Format, Page, Page Size; position insertion point on definition to be edited, then choose Edit
Envelope dialog box	Format, Envelope
Labels dialog box	Format, Labels
Create Labels dialog box	Format, Labels, Create
Edit Labels dialog box	Format, Labels, Edit
Labels dialog box	Format, Labels

CHECK YOUR UNDERSTANDING

Completion: In the space provided at the right, indicate the correct term, command, or number.

1. This is the width and length, in inches, of standard-sized stationery. _____

2. This orientation causes text to be rotated 90 degrees. _____

3. The location where printing begins on the paper can be changed with this option at the New Page Size dialog box. _____

4. If you display the Envelope dialog box in a document containing a letter, the address is automatically inserted here. _____

5. Click this option at the Envelope dialog box to insert the envelope definition code and the return and mailing addresses in the document. _____

6. This bar code speeds mail sorting, increases the accuracy of delivery, and reduces postage costs. _____

7. Press these keys on the keyboard to move the insertion point to the next label. _____

8. To print specific labels, not the entire page, display this dialog box. _____

9. An entire sheet of labels is called this kind of page. _____

10. One label on a full sheet of labels is this kind of page. _____

SKILL ASSESSMENTS

Assessment 1

1. At a clear editing window, open Report 02.
2. Save the document with Save As and name it Ch 22, SA 01.

3. Insert the Letter Landscape paper definition in the document.
4. Check the page break in the document. Make any necessary adjustments.
5. Save the document again with the same name (Ch 22, SA 01).
6. Print and then close Ch 22, SA 01.

Assessment 2

1. At a clear editing window, open Letter 04.
2. Save the document with Save As and name it Ch 22, SA 02.
3. Use WordPerfect's Envelope feature to create an envelope for this letter. Include a USPS bar code below the mailing address.
4. Save the document again with the same name (Ch 22, SA 02).
5. Print only the page containing the envelope.
6. Close Ch 22, SA 02.

Assessment 3

1. At a clear editing window, create mailing addresses using a predefined labels definition. Choose a labels definition that can be used by your printer. Depending on the label size, you may need to change the font to a smaller point size to ensure that the text fits on each line.
2. At the editing window, key the addresses shown in figure 22.9. Press Ctrl + Enter to end a label and move the insertion point to the next label.
3. Save the document and name it Ch 22, SA 03.
4. Print and then close Ch 22, SA 03.

Figure 22.9

Mr. Karl Erwin 320 McCutcheon Road Sante Fe, NM 88932	Ms. Patricia Paterno 1008 Valley Avenue Sante Fe, NM 88934	Doug Miyasaki, M.D. Miyasaki & Associates 1102 Lakeridge Drive Sante Fe, NM 88930
Ms. LaDonna Ferraro After-Five Flowers 4302 Third Avenue Sante Fe, NM 88432	Mr. Lloyd Catlin Atwood Fencing 4039 Ridge Street Sante Fe, NM 88043	Mrs. Tamara Butler 9803 Deer Road Sante Fe, NM 88032

Assessment 4

1. Using the Clients df data file (located on your student data disk), create a label form file using the Avery 5160 or Avery 5161 Address label definition. Save the label form file and name it Mail Labels ff. (The last field in the form file may wrap to the next label. When the form file is merged with the data file, the information will display in the correct location on the label.)
2. Merge *Mail Labels ff* with *Clients df*.
3. Name the merged document Ch 22, SA 04.
4. Print and then close Ch 22, SA 04.

23

CREATING NEWSPAPER & PARALLEL COLUMNS

PERFORMANCE OBJECTIVE

Upon successful completion of chapter 23, you will be able to create business documents, such as newsletters, agendas, and résumés, with different column styles.

When creating some business documents, you may want to establish the text in columns. In WordPerfect, you can create newspaper columns and parallel columns. Newspaper columns contain text that flows up and down in the document. When the first column on the page is filled with text, the insertion point moves to the top of the next column on the same page. When the last column on the page is filled with text, the insertion point moves to the beginning of the first column on the next page.

Creating Newspaper Columns with the Columns Dialog Box

Figure 23.1 shows text formatted in newspaper columns. Newspaper columns can be created with options at the Columns dialog box shown in figure 23.2. The Columns dialog box can be used to create newspaper columns that are evenly or unevenly spaced. To display the Columns dialog box, click Format, point to Columns, then click Define.

Figure 23.1

Newspaper Columns

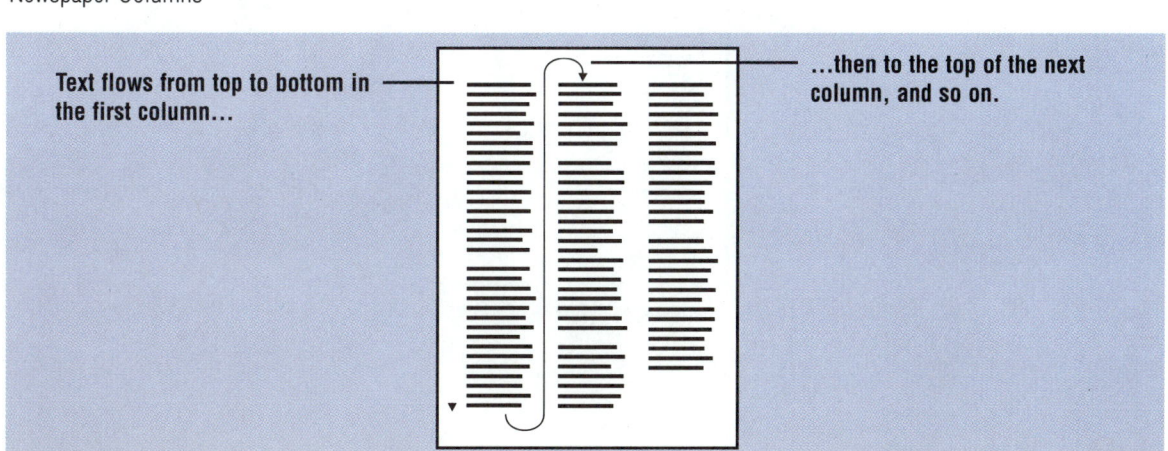

Text flows from top to bottom in the first column...

...then to the top of the next column, and so on.

Creating Newspaper & Parallel Columns 539

Figure 23.2

Columns Dialog Box

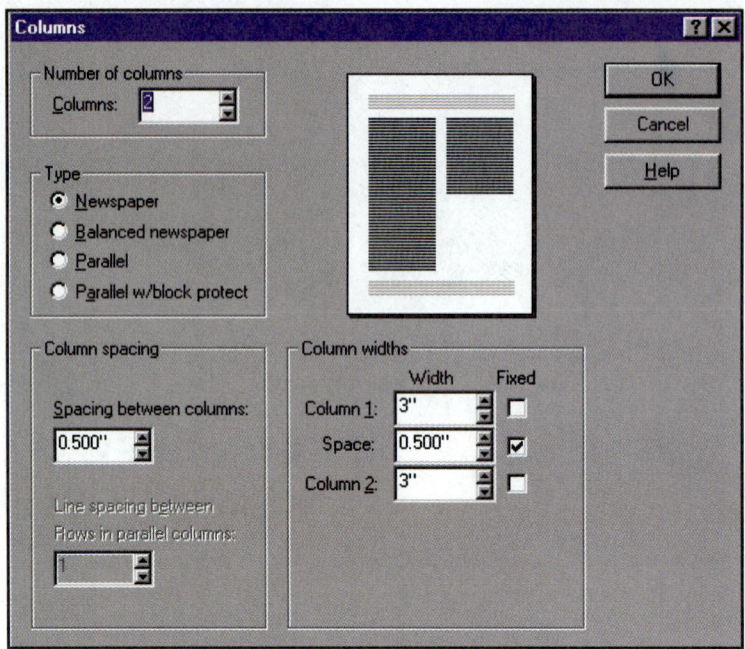

The Columns option in the Number of columns section has a default setting of 2. This number can be changed by keying a new number or by clicking the up- or down-pointing triangle after the Columns text box. The number of columns is only limited to the space available on the page.

The Type section of the dialog box contains four options, Newspaper, Balanced newspaper, Parallel, and Parallel w/block protect. The default setting is Newspaper. The Balanced newspaper option is like the Newspaper option, except each column is adjusted on the page to be as equal in length as possible as shown in figure 23.3. To change the Type, click the radio button preceding the desired option.

Figure 23.3

Balanced Newspaper Columns

By default, columns are separated by 0.5 inches of space. This space between columns is referred to as the *gutter*. The amount of space between columns can be increased or decreased with the Spacing between columns option. At this option, you can key a new measurement for the spacing or you can click the up- or down-pointing triangle after the text box.

If you create parallel columns, WordPerfect automatically inserts a blank line between the longest entry in a row and the first entry of the next row. With the Line spacing between rows in parallel columns option, you can increase or decrease this number. You will be creating parallel columns later in this chapter.

WordPerfect automatically determines column widths for the number of columns specified. By default, column widths are the same. If you want to enter your own column widths or change the amount of space between columns, choose the desired column, then key a measurement in the text box or click the up- or down-pointing triangle after the column text box.

Fixed check boxes are located to the right of the Column widths options. Insert a check mark in a Fixed check box if you want the width of the columns or space between columns to remain fixed regardless of what changes are made to the document margins or other column widths.

When columns are defined, a dashed red line border surrounds columns. This dashed border expands as text is keyed in the columns. If columns are defined in a document with existing text, a dashed red line border surrounds the text in columns.

Columns that have been defined in a document can be turned off or on as many times as needed in a document. To turn off columns, position the insertion point where columns are to be turned off, click Format, point to Columns, then click Off. If columns have been turned off in a document, they can be turned back on. To do this, position the insertion point where columns are to be turned on again, click Format, point to Columns, then click Define. At the Columns dialog box, click OK.

Newspaper columns can be defined before keying the text, or the columns can be defined in existing text. If you are defining newspaper columns in existing text, position the insertion point at the location where the columns are to begin, then define the columns.

If you want to end a newspaper column before the end of the page, insert a hard page break by pressing Ctrl + Enter or by clicking Format, pointing to Columns, then clicking Column Break. When a hard page break or column break is inserted, the insertion point moves to the beginning of the next column on the same page. If the hard page break is inserted in the last column on the page, the insertion point moves to the first column on the next page. When the insertion point is located in a newspaper column, the column number displays at the left side of the Status bar.

EXERCISE

Formatting Text into Two Newspaper Columns

1. At a clear editing window, open Report 07.
2. Save the document with Save As and name it Ch 23, Ex 01.
3. Turn on the Widow/Orphan feature.
4. Insert a hard return (by pressing Enter) above and below the following headings in the document:
    Industrialization
    Development of a World Market
    The American Civil War

Creating Newspaper & Parallel Columns

Colonization
The 1870s Depression
5. Position the insertion point at the beginning of the line containing the heading *Industrialization*, then define two evenly spaced newspaper columns by completing the following steps:
    a. Click Fo**r**mat, point to **C**olumns, then click **D**efine.
    b. At the Columns dialog box click OK.
6. Save the document again with the same name (Ch 23, Ex 01).
7. Check the column breaks in the document and make adjustments if needed. (To break the column at a different location, position the insertion point at the beginning of the line where you want the break to occur, then press Ctrl + Enter.)
8. Print and then close Ch 23, Ex 01.

EXERCISE 2

Creating Balanced Newspaper Columns

1. At a clear editing window, open Report 08.
2. Save the document with Save As and name it Ch 23, Ex 02.
3. Make the following changes to the document:
    a. Display Reveal Codes, then delete the *Ln Spacing: 2.0* code.
    b. Insert a hard return (by pressing Enter) above and below the following headings in the document:
        Introduction
        Purpose and Scope
        Application
        Requirements
    c. Move the insertion point to the beginning of the document, make sure the Ruler Bar is displayed, then add a left tab at the 1.25-inch mark.
    d. Position the insertion point at the left margin of the line containing *Introduction*, then define three balanced newspaper columns by completing the following steps:
        (1) Click Fo**r**mat, point to **C**olumns, then click **D**efine.
        (2) At the Columns dialog box, key **3**. (The insertion point is automatically positioned in the **C**olumns text box.)
        (3) Click **B**alanced newspaper.
        (4) Change the measurement in the **S**pacing between columns text box to 0.300" by clicking the down-pointing triangle after the **S**pacing between columns text box until *0.300"* displays.
        (5) Click OK.
    e. Change the left hyphenation zone to 4% and the right hyphenation zone to 0%, then turn on hyphenation. (Move the insertion point to the end of the document to ensure that all necessary words are hyphenated.)
    f. Select the title, *IDENTIFICATION OF CI*, then change the relative size to Large.
4. Save the document again with the same name (Ch 23, Ex 02).
5. Print and then close Ch 23, Ex 02.

Editing Text in Columns

To edit text established in columns, move the insertion point with the mouse or insertion point movement keys and commands either within columns or between columns.

Moving the Insertion Point within Columns

To move the insertion point in a document using the mouse, position the arrow pointer where desired, then click the left button. If you are using the keyboard, the insertion point movement keys—up, down, left, and right arrows—cause the insertion point to move in the direction indicated. If you press the up or down arrow key, the insertion point moves up or down within the column. If the insertion point is located on the last line of a column on a page, the down arrow will cause the insertion point to move to the beginning of the same column on the next page. If the insertion point is located on the first line of text in a column, pressing the up arrow key will cause the insertion point to move to the end of the same column on the previous page.

The left and right arrow keys move the insertion point in the direction indicated within the column. When the insertion point gets to the end of the line within the column, it moves down to the beginning of the next line within the same column.

Moving the Insertion Point between Columns

You can use the mouse or the keyboard to move the insertion point between columns. If you are using the mouse, position the arrow pointer where desired, then click the left button. If you are using the keyboard, use the insertion point movement commands shown in figure 23.4.

Figure 23.4

Insertion Point Movement between Columns

Move insertion point to next column	ALT + →
Move insertion point to previous column	ALT + ←
Move insertion point to last line of column	ALT + END
Move insertion point to top of column	ALT + HOME

The Go To dialog box can also be used to move the insertion point within and between columns. To display the Go To dialog box, shown in figure 23.5, position the insertion point in a column of text, click Edit, then Go To; or press Ctrl + G.

With the options in the Position list box, you can move the insertion point to the last position, top of column, bottom of column, previous column, next column, first column, or last column. To make a choice in the Position list box, double-click the desired option.

Creating Newspaper & Parallel Columns

Figure 23.5

Go To Dialog Box

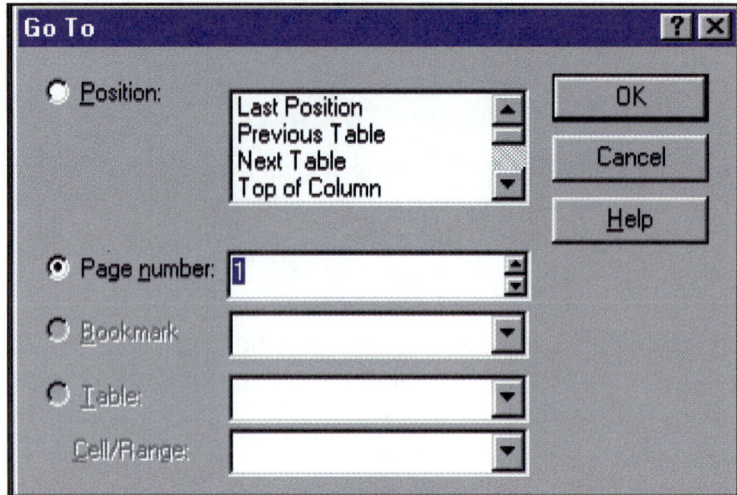

EXERCISE 3

Creating a Newsletter with Two Columns

1. At a clear editing window, create the heading shown in figure 23.6 for a newsletter by completing the following steps:
   a. Change the font to 14-point Arial bold.
   b. Key **DISTRICT HAPPENINGS**.
   c. Change the font size to 12 points.
   d. Press Enter.
   e. Create a horizontal line at the Create Graphics Line dialog box. Change the thickness by clicking the Line thickness button, then, at the pop-up list that displays, clicking the last option in the first column.
   f. Press Enter.
   g. Access the Flush Right command, then key **April Newsletter**.
   h. Press Enter, access the Flush Right command, then key **Joni Kapshaw, Editor**.
   i. Change the font to 11.8-point Century Schoolbook. (You will need to change the font at the Font dialog box. To change the point size to 11.8, key **11.8** in the Font size list box located toward the top of the dialog box.)
   j. Press the Enter key twice.
2. Insert the document News 01 into the current document. (Use the File command from the Insert menu.)
3. Bold the headings, *Recreation Program*, *Sixth Grade Camp*, and *Library News*.
4. Position the insertion point at the left margin of the line containing *Recreation Program*, then define two newspaper columns using the Columns dialog box by completing the following steps:
   a. Click Format, point to Columns, then click Define.
   b. At the Columns dialog box, make sure the Newspaper option is selected in the Type section and the number of columns is 2.
   c. Click OK.

544 Chapter 23

5. With the insertion point still positioned on the line containing *Recreation Program*, add a left tab at the 1.25-inch mark on the Ruler Bar.
6. Insert the graphics image named *World* in the document by completing the following steps:
   a. Position the insertion point at the left margin of the line containing the words *Young people are invited to...*(below the heading *Library News*).
   b. Create a user box with the following specifications:
      (1) Insert the image named *World*.
      (2) Display the Box Position dialog box, change the horizontal position to Left Margin, then close the dialog box.
      (3) Display the Box Size dialog box, change the width to Set at 1.2 inches, then close the dialog box.
      (4) Display the Wrap Text dialog box, change the Wrapping type to Contour with the text wrapping around the Largest side, then close the dialog box.
7. Save the newsletter and name it Ch 23, Ex 03.
8. Print and then close Ch 23, Ex 03.

Figure 23.6

DISTRICT HAPPENINGS

April Newsletter
Joni Kapshaw, Editor

Creating Parallel Columns

Parallel columns contain text that is grouped across the page in rows as shown in figure 23.7. The next row begins a double space below the longest column of the previous row. Parallel columns can be used to create documents such as an agenda, itinerary, résumé, or address list.

Figure 23.7

Parallel Columns

Creating Newspaper & Parallel Columns   545

To create parallel columns, display the Columns dialog box, click Parallel in the Type section, specify the number of columns, then click OK or press Enter.

After parallel columns have been defined, key the text for the first column, then insert a hard page or column break. The hard page or column break moves the insertion point to the next column. To insert a hard page break, press Ctrl + Enter. To insert a column break, click Format, point to Column, then click Column Break. When a hard page or column break is inserted in the last column in a document, the insertion point moves to the left margin a double space below the longest column entry. When you key text in columns, the word wrap feature will wrap text to the next line within the column.

At the Columns dialog box, parallel columns can be created with block protect. If you click Parallel w/block protect at the Columns dialog box, WordPerfect keeps all columns in a row together. If one column is too long to fit on a page, all the columns in the row are moved to the next page. If you define parallel columns without block protect, a row of columns may be divided between two pages.

As with newspaper columns, the parallel column number where the insertion point is located displays at the left side of the Status bar.

EXERCISE 4

Creating Parallel Columns

1. At a clear editing window, create the document shown in figure 23.8 by completing the following steps:
   a. Key the title, **PATIENT SATISFACTION**, then press the Enter key twice.
   b. Define three parallel columns by completing the following steps:
      (1) Click Format, point to Columns, then click Define.
      (2) At the Columns dialog box, key **3**. (This changes the number of columns to three.)
      (3) Click Parallel.
      (4) Click OK.
   c. Key the text in columns by completing the following steps:
      (1) Center and bold the heading *VALUE* and then press Ctrl + Enter to move the insertion point to the next column.
      (2) Center and bold the heading *ATTITUDE* and then press Ctrl + Enter to move the insertion point to the next column.
      (3) Center and bold the heading *BEHAVIOR* and then press Ctrl + Enter to move the insertion point to the first column, below *VALUE*.
      (4) Key the text **Individualized patient care** and then press Ctrl + Enter.
      (5) Continue keying the text in columns as shown in figure 23.8. Press Ctrl + Enter to move from column to column. Let the word wrap feature wrap text within columns (do not press Enter).
   d. After keying the text in columns, select the title, *PATIENT SATISFACTION*, then change the relative size to Very Large.
   e. Select the following text then change the relative size to Large:
      VALUE
      ATTITUDE
      BEHAVIOR

f. Position the insertion point at the beginning of the document, change the left hyphenation zone to 4%, the right hyphenation zone to 0%, then turn on hyphenation. (Move the insertion point to the end of the document to ensure that all necessary words are hyphenated.)
2. Save the document and name it Ch 23, Ex 04.
3. Print and then close Ch 23, Ex 04.

Figure 23.8

PATIENT SATISFACTION

VALUE	ATTITUDE	BEHAVIOR
Individualized patient care	Concern for the person; recognize that everyone is a unique person; recognize importance of patient's problem	Use patient's name; remember details about the patient's routine; provide personalized service
Respect for individual	Acceptance of physical disabilities, personalities, and cultural differences; tolerance and appreciation of differences	Handle patient situations with respect and tact; prepare personalized care plan; make sure they know you and you know them; provide for patient's individual needs for privacy and respect
Need for control and freedom of choice	Respect for patient competence; understanding; patients can take care of themselves	Explain environment; give choices, explain what is happening; involve patient in scheduling when possible
Being treated as a guest	Understand and respect that patient has fear; care for the whole person; treat people as guests	Respond to nonverbal cues, talk about fears; ask patient's opinion; do not rush treatment; maintain respect for family interaction; take time to allow patient to adjust

Changing Column Widths with the Ruler Bar

The options in the Column widths section of the Columns dialog box can be used to change the width of columns as well as determine the space between columns. You can also make these changes using the Ruler Bar. To display the Ruler Bar, click View, then Toolbars/Ruler. At the Toolbars dialog box, click Ruler Bar in the list box, then click OK. When the Ruler Bar is displayed in a document set in newspaper or parallel columns, column width and column markers display as shown in figure 23.9.

Figure 23.9

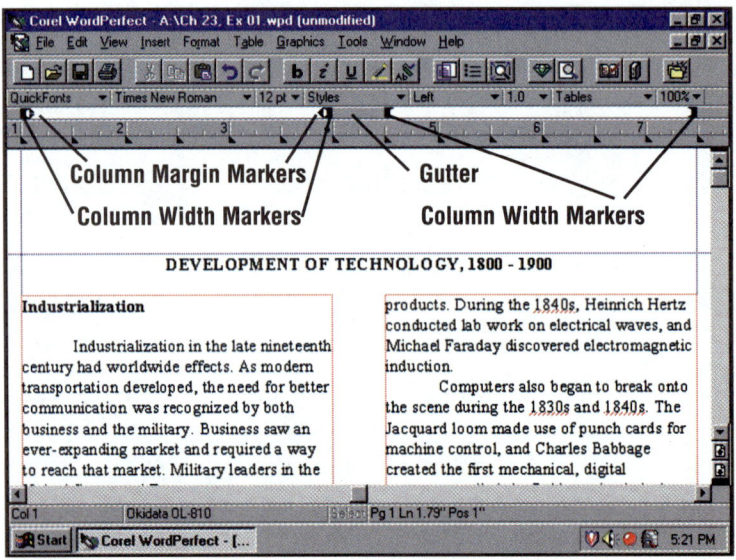

Column Markers on the Ruler Bar

Use the column margin markers shown in figure 23.9 to change left and right column margins. Use the column width markers to change column width. When changing column margins or widths, position the insertion point on the line where the column definition code is located because the change will affect the code. Position the arrow pointer on the desired marker, hold down the left mouse button, drag the marker to the desired position, then release the mouse button.

When you position the arrow pointer on a column marker and then hold down the left mouse button, a dashed vertical line displays down the editing window. This dashed vertical line is referred to as the Ruler Bar Guide. This guide can help you visually determine the correct position for the marker.

The gray space on the Ruler Bar between column markers is referred to as the *gutter*. You can move the gutter along the Ruler Bar. To move a gutter, position the arrow pointer in the gutter, hold down the left mouse button, drag the gutter to the desired position, then release the mouse button. The tab markers on the Ruler Bar can also be dragged to a new location with the mouse.

EXERCISE 5

Changing Column Widths

1. At a clear editing window, open Ch 23, Ex 01.
2. Save the document with Save As and name it Ch 23, Ex 05.
3. With the insertion point positioned at the beginning of the document, add a left tab at the 1.25-inch mark on the Ruler Bar.
4. Change the widths of the columns by completing the following steps:
   a. Position the insertion point at the left margin of the line containing *Industrialization*. (The insertion point must be positioned *after* the column definition code. If necessary, display Reveal Codes to determine if the insertion point is in the correct location.)
   b. Move the left column marker for the first column on the Ruler Bar by completing the following steps:
      (1) Position the arrow pointer on the left column marker for the first column (located at the 1-inch mark on the Ruler Bar).
      (2) Hold down the left mouse button, drag the arrow pointer to the 1.5-inch mark, then release the mouse button.
   c. Move the right column marker for the first column to the 4 1/8-inch mark by completing steps similar to those in 4b.
   d. Move the left column marker for the second column to the 4 3/8-inch mark.
   e. Move the right column marker for the second column to the 7-inch mark. (You may need to move the scroll box to the right on the horizontal scroll bar to be able to see the right column marker for the second column.)
5. Save the document again with the same name (Ch 23, Ex 05).
6. Print and then close Ch 23, Ex 05.

Creating Column Lines and Borders

Text in columns can be separated by a vertical line, or you can insert column borders around all columns in a document. A vertical line can be inserted between columns with options at the Create Graphics dialog box. This inserts a solid line from the location of the insertion point to the end of the page. Vertical lines can also be inserted between columns with options from the Column Border/Fill dialog box. When you use this dialog box to insert vertical lines, the lines are solid for newspaper columns but broken for parallel columns.

Figure 23.10 shows a document containing newspaper columns with a vertical line between columns created with options at the Create Graphics dialog box. Figure 23.11 shows the same document with a column border around and between the columns. Figure 23.12 shows a document containing parallel columns with vertical lines inserted between columns using options from the Column Border/Fill dialog box.

Figures 23.10, 23.11, and 23.12 show a single line between and/or around the columns. The border can be changed to a variety of other styles.

Figure 23.10 Newspaper Columns with Vertical Lines

Figure 23.11 Newspaper Columns with Borders

Figure 23.12 Parallel Columns with Vertical Lines

Inserting a Vertical Graphics Line

A vertical graphics line is inserted at the Create Graphics Line dialog box. The vertical graphics line begins at the position of the insertion point and continues down the page to the bottom margin. This vertical line is inserted between the first and second columns by default. Lines between columns two and three or three and four must be created separately.

EXERCISE 6

Creating Vertical Lines between Columns

1. At a clear editing window, open Ch 23, Ex 02.
2. Save the document with Save As and name it Ch 23, Ex 06.
3. Insert a vertical graphics line between the first and second columns by completing the following steps:
   a. Position the insertion point at the left margin of the line containing *Introduction*. (Make sure the insertion point is to the right of the Column Definition code.)
   b. Click Graphics, then Custom Line.
   c. At the Create Graphics Line dialog box, click Vertical in the Line type section.
   d. Click Horizontal in the Position section, then click Column Aligned.
   e. Click Vertical in the Position section, then click Set.
   f. Click OK.
4. Insert a vertical graphics line between the second and third columns by completing the following steps:
   a. With the insertion point still positioned at the left margin of the line containing *Introduction*, click Graphics, then Custom Line.
   b. At the Create Graphics Line dialog box, click Vertical in the Line type section.
   c. Click Horizontal in the Position section, then click Column Aligned.
   d. Key 2 in the After Column text box.
   e. Click Vertical in the Position section, then click Set.
   f. Click OK.
5. Save the document again with the same name (Ch 23, Ex 06).
6. Print and then close Ch 23, Ex 06.

Inserting Lines with the Column Border Dialog Box

The Column Border/Fill dialog box, shown in figure 23.13, contains the same options as the Page Border/Fill and Paragraph Border/Fill dialog boxes plus two additional border styles—Column Between and Column All. These border choices display in the Available border styles list box. The Column Between option is the seventh option from the left in the third row. The Column All option is the fifth option from the left in the fourth row. Use the Column Between border style to insert lines between columns. The lines can be customized with different line styles using the Line style option or with different colors with the Color option. This is the same dialog box that was explained in chapter 20.

Figure 23.13 Column Border/Fill Dialog Box

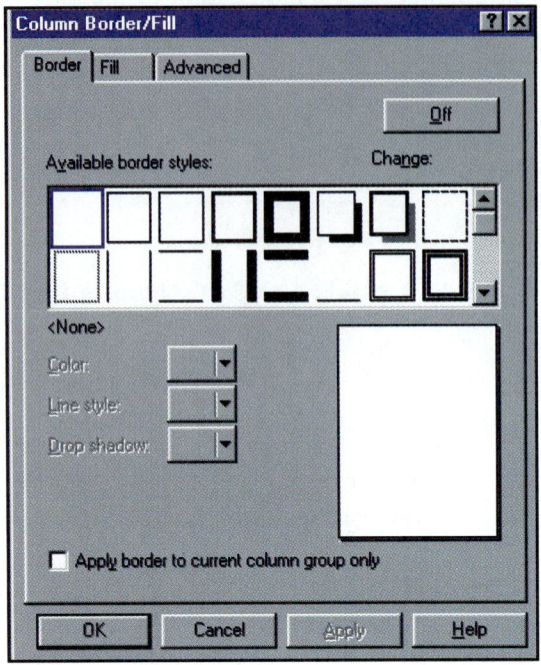

If you are inserting lines between newspaper columns, the lines will continue down the page to the end of the columns on the page. If you are inserting lines between parallel columns, the lines will be inserted between only one row of columns. If you want the lines inserted between each row of columns, make sure there is no check mark in the Apply border to current column group only option.

Inserting a Border

A border can be inserted around columns of text with the Available border styles option from the Column Border/Fill dialog box. The border option will insert a border around columns but not between columns. You will practice inserting different kinds of borders in exercises 7 and 8.

EXERCISE 7

Inserting a Line Border

1. At a clear editing window, open Ch 23, Ex 04.
2. Save the document with Save As and name it Ch 23, Ex 07.
3. Insert a border between the parallel columns by completing the following steps:
   a. Position the insertion point on the line containing *Individualized patient care*.
   b. Click Format, point to Border/Fill, then click Column.
   c. At the Column Border/Fill dialog box, click the Column Between option in the Available border styles list box (seventh option from the left in the third row).
   d. If there is a check mark in the Apply border to current column group only check box, click this option to remove the check mark.
   e. Click OK.
4. Save the document again with the same name (Ch 23, Ex 07).
5. Print and then close Ch 23, Ex 07.

552   Chapter 23

EXERCISE 8

Inserting a Dotted Line Border

1. At a clear editing window, open Ch 23, Ex 02.
2. Save the document with Save As and name it Ch 23, Ex 08.
3. Insert a double line border around the newspaper columns by completing the following steps:
   a. Position the insertion point at the left margin of the line containing *Introduction*.
   b. Click Format, point to Border/Fill, then click Column.
   c. At the Column Border/Fill dialog box, click the Dotted option in the Available border styles list box (first option from the left in the second row).
   d. Click OK.
4. Save the document again with the same name (Ch 23, Ex 08).
5. Print and then close Ch 23, Ex 08.

If you want a border around columns as well as in between columns, click the Column All option in the Available border styles list box at the Column Border/Fill dialog box. All the options available with paragraph and page borders are available for column borders. Chapter 20 covered the border and fill options available.

EXERCISE 9

Adding a Customized Border

1. At a clear editing window, open Ch 23, Ex 04.
2. Save the document with Save As and name it Ch 23, Ex 09.
3. Create a border around and between columns and add 10% fill by completing the following steps:
   a. Position the insertion point at the left margin of the line containing *VALUE*, *ATTITUDE*, and *BEHAVIOR*.
   b. Click Format, point to Border/Fill, then click Column.
   c. At the Column Border/Fill dialog box, click Column All in the Available border styles list box (fifth option from the left in the fourth row).
   d. Click the down-pointing triangle to the right of Line style.
   e. At the palette of line style choices that displays, click Double (second option in the first row).
   f. Click the Fill tab located toward the top of the dialog box.
   g. Click 10% Fill in the Available fill styles list box (third option from the left in the first row).
   h. Click OK.
4. Save the document again with the same name (Ch 23, Ex 09).
5. Print and then close Ch 23, Ex 09.

Creating Newspaper & Parallel Columns

CHAPTER SUMMARY

▼ Two types of text columns can be created with WordPerfect's column feature—newspaper and parallel.

▼ Newspaper columns contain text that flows up and down in the document.

▼ Text keyed into parallel columns flows horizontally across the page in rows.

▼ Create any number of newspaper or parallel columns at the Columns dialog box.

▼ The space between columns or rows and the column width can be customized at the Columns dialog box or on the Ruler Bar.

▼ The Type section of the Columns dialog box contains four options: Newspaper, Balanced newspaper, Parallel, and Parallel w/block protect. The last option keeps all columns in a row together on one page.

▼ Newspaper columns can be defined before keying the text, or the columns can be defined in existing text.

▼ Text in columns can be separated by a vertical line, or you can insert column borders around all columns in a document. Insert these lines and borders at the Create Graphics dialog box or the Column Border/Fill dialog box.

COMMANDS REVIEW

	Mouse	Keyboard
Columns dialog box	Format, Columns, Define	Format, Columns, Define
End a newspaper column	Format, Columns, Column Break	CTRL + ENTER
Move insertion point between columns	Position arrow pointer where desired, click left mouse button	
Move insertion point to		
—next column		ALT + →
—previous column		ALT + ←
—last line of column		ALT + END
—top of column		ALT + HOME
Go To dialog box	Edit, Go To	CTRL + G
Ruler Bar	View, Toolbars/Ruler, Ruler Bar	View, Toolbars/Ruler, Ruler Bar
Create Graphics Line dialog box	Graphics, Custom Line	Graphics, Custom Line
Column Border/Fill dialog box	Format, Border/Fill, Column	Format, Border/Fill, Column

CHECK YOUR UNDERSTANDING

Completion: In the space provided at the right, indicate the correct term, command, or number.

1. This type of column is best suited for creating an agenda, an itinerary, a résumé, or an address list. _____

2. To ensure that all columns in a row are kept together and not divided between two pages, choose this type of column. _____

3. This is the term that refers to the space between columns. _____

4. When creating parallel columns, press these keys to end the column and move the insertion point to the next column. _____

5. To create newspaper columns that are approximately equal in length, choose this type at the Columns dialog box. _____

6. Columns are separated by this amount of space by default. _____

7. Insert a vertical graphics line between columns with options at the Column Border/Fill dialog box or with options at this dialog box. _____

In the space provided below, write the steps you would complete to define two evenly spaced parallel columns and then the steps to insert a vertical line between the two columns.

_____

_____

_____

SKILL ASSESSMENTS

Assessment 1

1. At a clear editing window, open Report 02.
2. Save the document with Save As and name it Ch 23, SA 01.
3. Make the following changes to the document:
    a. Delete the *Ln Spacing: 2.0* code.
    b. Insert a hard return (by pressing Enter) above the first paragraph in the document. (This separates the title from the first paragraph by a double space.)
    c. Insert a hard return above and below the headings in the document (*Contributions of Major Historical Events, Development of a World Market, The American Civil War, Colonization,* and *The 1870s Depression*).
    d. Select the title and change the relative size to Large.
    e. Position the insertion point at the left margin of the line that begins *Most of the major developments...*, then define two evenly spaced newspaper columns.
    f. Position the insertion point at the beginning of the document, change the left hyphenation zone to 5%, the right hyphenation zone to 0%, then turn on hyphenation.
4. Save the document again with the same name (Ch 23, SA 01).
5. Print and then close Ch 23, SA 01.

Assessment 2

1. At a clear editing window, create the document shown in figure 23.14 by completing the following steps:
   a. Change the font to 12-point Century Schoolbook.
   b. Key the title *PROJECT TIMELINES* centered and bolded.
   c. Press Enter three times, then define three evenly spaced parallel columns.
   d. Key the text in columns as shown in figure 23.14. Center and bold the column headings as shown.
   e. Change the relative size of the title *PROJECT TIMELINES* to Very Large.
   f. Change the relative size of the headings *Project*, *Completion*, and *Update* to Large.
2. Save the document and name it Ch 23, SA 02.
3. Print and then close Ch 23, SA 02.

Figure 23.14

PROJECT TIMELINES

Project	**Completion**	**Update**
Engineering building	September - December 1998	Framing underway, roofing begun, masonry going up
Administration annex	October 1998	Expected bid date early spring, permit hearing scheduled
Remodeling of personnel offices	June - September 1999	Mechanical and electrical beginning
East parking lot	September 1999	Soil testing completed, preliminary plans completed

Assessment 3

1. At a clear editing window, create the résumé shown in figure 23.15 by completing the following steps:
   a. Change the font to 18-point Arrus BT, then key **ANDREA BOWEN**.
   b. Press Enter once, then create a horizontal line at the Create Graphics Line dialog box. Use the default settings, except change the line thickness to 0.060".
   c. Press Enter once, then change the font to 14-point Arrus BT.
   d. Key the address and telephone number as shown in figure 23.15 using the Flush Right command to align the text at the right margin.
   e. After keying the telephone number, change the font to 12-point Times New Roman.
   f. Press Enter twice, then define two parallel columns. Set the width for the first column at 1.5 inches and the width for the second column at 4.5 inches.

g. Key the remainder of the résumé shown in figure 23.15. Bold the headings *OBJECTIVE, EDUCATION, SKILLS, EMPLOYMENT*, and *ORGANIZATIONS*. Press Ctrl + Enter to end a column and move the insertion point to the next column.
h. After keying the last column entry, turn columns off.
i. Press Enter once, then create a horizontal line at the Create Graphics Line dialog box. Use the default settings, except change the line thickness to 0.037".
2. Save the résumé and name it Ch 23, SA 03.
3. Print and then close Ch 23, SA 03.

Figure 23.15

ANDREA BOWEN

1302 South 43rd Street
Tampa, FL 33643
(813) 555-9604

OBJECTIVE   A position as a legal secretary in a company that provides opportunity for growth and advancement.

EDUCATION   Bayside Community College—Associates of Arts and Sciences, Legal Secretary, June 1998

Wallace High School—Honor Graduate, 1996

SKILLS   Keyboarding (70+ wpm)   Legal theory
Legal terminology   Word processing
Desktop publishing   Machine transcription
Accounting   10-key calculator
Database management   Spreadsheet
Employee training   Supervision

EMPLOYMENT   Legal Secretary, Galvin & Jacobs, 833 Riverside Drive, Tampa, FL 33641. Duties include answering the telephone, taking messages, scheduling appointments, filing manually and electronically, and transcribing and preparing legal documents.

Assistant Manager, Sportland, 1200 East 32nd, Tampa, FL 33460. Duties included supervising employees, training new employees, taking inventory, customer service, sales, and operating and cashing out till.

Food Server, Bluewater's, 220 North Second, Tampa, FL 33659. Duties included customer service, hosting birthday parties, cooking, operating cash registers and drive-through window, and taking and filling customer orders.

ORGANIZATIONS   Treasurer, Student Government, Wallace High School, 1995-96
Member, Phi Beta Lambda, 1993-96

Assessment 4

1. At a clear editing window, open Ch 23, SA 01.
2. Save the document and name it Ch 23, SA 04.
3. Position the insertion point at the left margin of the line beginning *Most of the major developments...*, then use the Column Border/Fill dialog box to insert a line between the columns.
4. Save the document again with the same name (Ch 23, SA 04).
5. Print and then close Ch 23, SA 04.

Assessment 5

1. At a clear editing window, open Ch 23, SA 02.
2. Save the document with Save As and name it Ch 23, SA 05.
3. Create a double line border around and between the columns and add 10% fill.
4. Save the document again with the same name (Ch 23, SA 05).
5. Print and then close Ch 23, SA 05.

24

CREATING TABLES

PERFORMANCE OBJECTIVE

Upon successful completion of chapter 24, you will be able to define and adjust structures for business tables according to a variety of format and size considerations.

WordPerfect's Tables feature can be used to create columns and rows of information that are enclosed with horizontal and vertical lines. The boxes that are created by the intersection of rows and columns are called *cells*. A cell can contain text, characters, numbers, data, or formulas. Text within a cell can be formatted to display left, right, center, or decimal aligned and can include character formatting such as bold, italics, and underlining. The formatting choices available with Tables are quite extensive and allow flexibility in creating a variety of tables, including business forms and spreadsheets.

Creating a Table

A table can be created with the Tables button on the Power Bar or with the Table option from the Menu Bar. To create a table with the Tables button on the Power Bar, you would complete these steps:

Tables

1. Position the arrow pointer on the Tables button.
2. Hold down the left mouse button. This causes a grid to appear as shown in figure 24.1.
3. Drag the arrow pointer down and to the right until the correct number of rows and columns displays above the grid, then release the mouse button.

Creating Tables 559

Figure 24.1

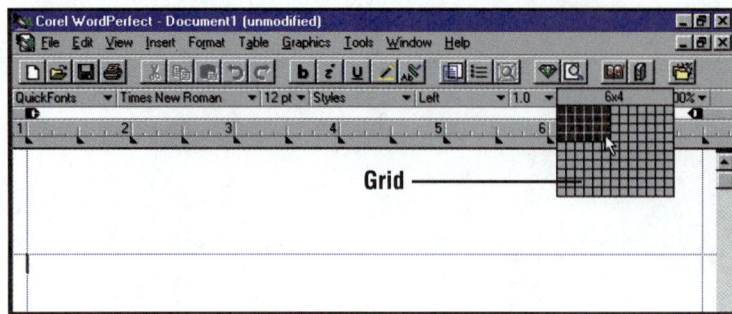

Table Grid

As you drag the arrow pointer, selected columns and rows are displayed in black, and the number of rows and columns displays above the grid.

A table can also be created at the Create Table dialog box, shown in figure 24.2. To create a table at the Create Table dialog box, follow these basic steps:

1. Click Table, then Create.
2. At the Create Table dialog box, key a number in the Columns text box.
3. Press the Tab key and then key a number in the Rows text box.
4. Click OK.

Figure 24.2

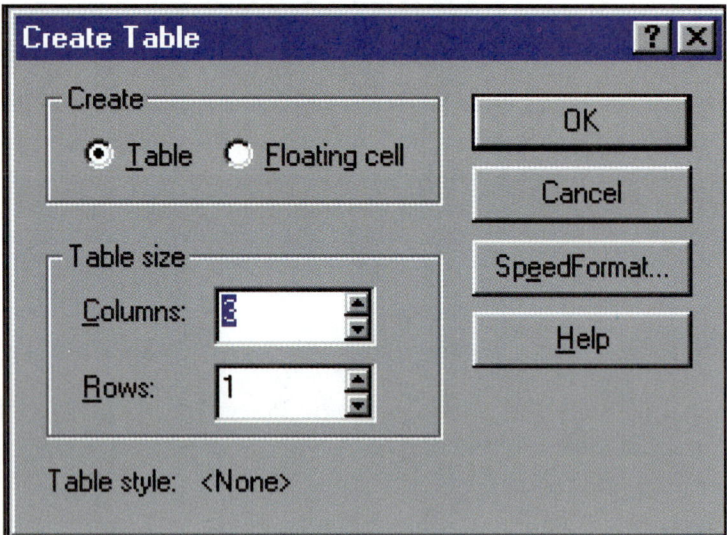

Create Table Dialog Box

When you click OK at the Create Table dialog box, a table similar to the one shown in figure 24.3 is inserted in the document at the location of the insertion point.

Table

Figure 24.3

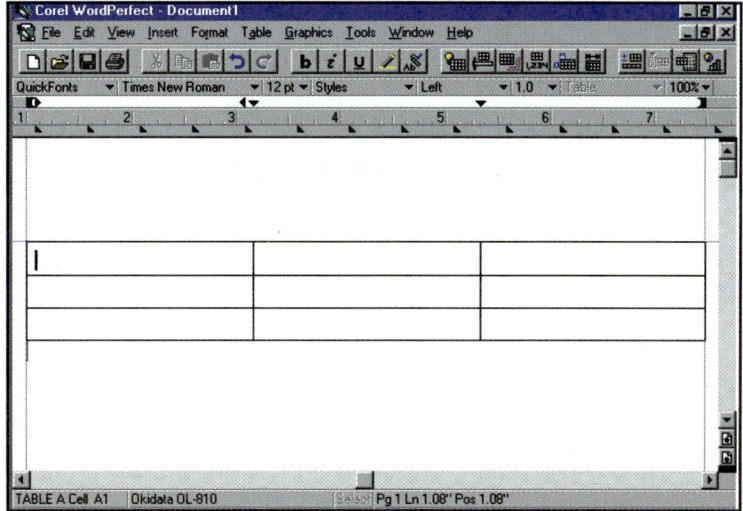

When the columns are displayed, the insertion point is located in the upper left corner of the table in cell A1. Columns are lettered from left to right, beginning with A. The cell to the right of A1 is B1, the cell to the right of B1 is C1, and so on. Rows in a table are numbered. The cell below A1 is A2, the cell below A2 is A3, and so on.

WordPerfect provides a Tables Toolbar containing buttons for formatting and customizing a table. To display the Tables Toolbar, position the arrow pointer on the current toolbar, click the right mouse button, then click Tables. If the insertion point is located within a table, the Tables Toolbar automatically displays. The Tables Toolbar contains a button that will identify columns and rows. To display column letters and row numbers, click the Row/Column Indicators button on the Tables Toolbar. This causes the column letters and row numbers to display as shown in figure 24.4. The cell name in which the insertion point is located is displayed at the left side of the Status Bar.

Row/Column Indicators

Table with Row/Column Indicators

Figure 24.4

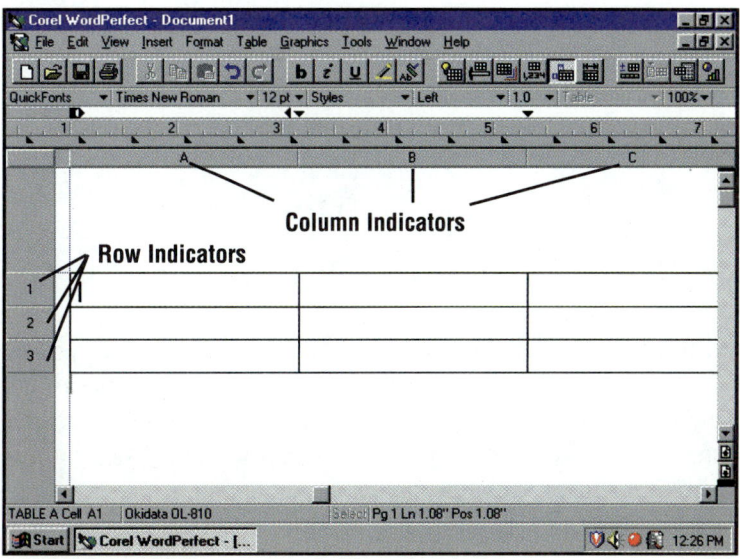

Creating Tables 561

When the insertion point is positioned in a table, the Tables button on the Power Bar and the Create option from the Table drop-down menu are grayed (dimmed) because a table cannot be created within a table. When a table is created, codes are inserted in the document that can be seen in Reveal Codes. For example, the codes for the table shown in figure 24.4 will display as shown in figure 24.5.

Figure 24.5

Table Codes in Reveal Codes

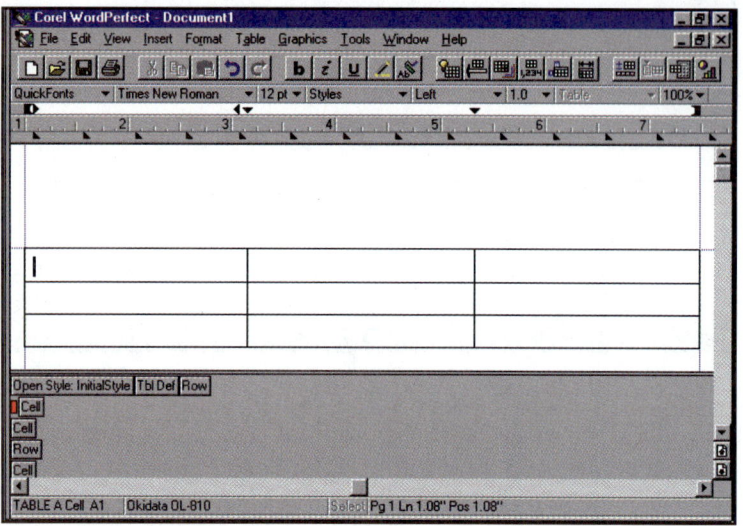

Entering Text in Cells

With the insertion point positioned in a cell, key or edit text as you would normal text. Move the insertion point to other cells with the mouse by positioning the arrow pointer in the desired cell, then clicking the left mouse button. If you are using the keyboard, press Tab to move the insertion point to the next cell or press Shift + Tab to move the insertion point to the previous cell.

If the text you key does not fit on one line, it wraps to the next line within the same cell. Or, if you press Enter within a cell, the insertion point is moved to the next line within the same cell. The cell vertically lengthens to accommodate the text, and all cells in that row also lengthen.

Pressing the Tab key in a table causes the insertion point to move to the next cell in the table. If you want to insert a tab within a cell, use one of the commands shown in figure 24.6.

Figure 24.6

Commands to Insert Tabs in Cells

Insert left tab in cell	CTRL + Tab
Insert decimal tab in cell	ALT + SHIFT + F7
Insert back tab (margin release)	CTRL + SHIFT + Tab

If the insertion point is located in the last cell of the table and you press the Tab key, WordPerfect adds another row to the table. To avoid this situation, make sure you do not press the Tab key after entering text in the last cell. You can insert a page break within a table by pressing Ctrl + Enter. The page break is inserted between rows, not within. When all information has been entered in the cells, move the insertion point below the table and, if necessary, continue keying the document, or save the document in the normal manner.

562 Chapter 24

Moving the Insertion Point within a Table

To move the insertion point to different cells within the table using the mouse, position the arrow pointer in the desired cell, then click the left button. To move the insertion point to different cells within the table using the keyboard, refer to the information shown in figure 24.7.

Figure 24.7

Insertion Point Movement within a Table

Move insertion point within cell in direction indicated	[↑], [←], [↓], and [→]
Move insertion point to next cell	[Tab]
Move insertion point to previous cell	[SHIFT] + [Tab]
Move insertion point one cell down	[ALT] + [↓]
Move insertion point one cell up	[ALT] + [↑]
Move insertion point to first cell in row	[HOME], [HOME]
Move insertion point to last cell in row	[END], [END]
Move insertion point to top line of multi-line cell	[ALT] + [HOME]
Move insertion point to bottom line of multi-line cell	[ALT] + [END]

EXERCISE 1

Creating a Table with the Table Button

1. At a clear editing window, create the table shown in figure 24.8 by completing the following steps:
   a. Center and bold the title, *WORDPERFECT CLASS*.
   b. Turn off bold and then press Enter twice.
   c. Create the table by completing the following steps:
      (1) Position the arrow pointer on the Tables button on the Power Bar.
      (2) Hold down the left mouse button. (This causes a grid to appear.)
      (3) Drag the arrow pointer down and to the right until the number above the grid displays as *2x10*, then release the mouse button.
   d. Key the heading *Employee* in cell A1 by completing the following steps:
      (1) Make sure the insertion point is positioned in cell A1.
      (2) Press Shift + F7.
      (3) Click the Bold button on the Toolbar; or press Ctrl + B.
      (4) Key **Employee**.
      (5) Press the Tab key to move the insertion point to cell B1.
      (6) Complete similar steps to insert *Department* in cell B1.
2. Save the document and name it Ch 24, Ex 01.
3. Print and then close Ch 24, Ex 01.

Creating Tables 563

Figure 24.8

WORDPERFECT CLASS

Employee	Department

EXERCISE 2

Creating a Table at the Create Table Dialog Box

1. At a clear editing window, create the table shown in figure 24.9 by completing the following steps:
   a. Center and bold *DENVER MEMORIAL HOSPITAL.*
   b. Press Enter twice, then center and bold *Executive Officers*.
   c. Turn off bold, press Enter three times, then create a table with two columns and five rows by completing the following steps:
      (1) Click T<u>a</u>ble, then <u>C</u>reate.
      (2) At the Create Table dialog box, key **2**.
      (3) Press the Tab key. (This moves the insertion point to the <u>R</u>ows text box.)
      (4) Key **5**.
      (5) Click OK.
   d. Key the text in the cells as shown in figure 24.9. To indent the text within cells, press Ctrl + Tab to insert a tab within the cell. (Do this for each cell.)
2. Save the document and name it Ch 24, Ex 02.
3. Print and then close Ch 24, Ex 02.

Figure 24.9

DENVER MEMORIAL HOSPITAL

Executive Officers

President	Chris Hedegaard
Vice President	Robert Freitas
Vice President	Richard Dudley
Vice President	Glenna Wykoff
Vice President	Laura Culver

Changing the Column Width of a Table

When a table is created, the columns are the same width. The width of the columns depends on the number of columns as well as the document margins. In some tables, you may want to change the width of certain columns to accommodate more or less text. You can change the width of columns using the mouse, the Ruler Bar, or the Properties for Table Format dialog box.

Changing Column Width with the Mouse

To change column widths using the mouse, position the pointer on the line separating columns until it turns into a left- and right-pointing arrow with a vertical line between. Hold down the left mouse button, drag the column line to the desired location, then release the mouse button. This moves only the column line where the double-headed arrow is positioned. If you hold down the Shift key while you drag a column line, all columns to the right are also moved.

Changing Column Width with the Ruler Bar

When the insertion point is positioned in a table, the column widths are displayed on the Ruler Bar above the ruler numbers as down-pointing triangles. (To display the Ruler Bar, click View, Toolbars/Ruler, click Ruler Bar, then click OK.) These down-pointing triangles are called *column width markers*. Other table markers display on the Ruler Bar, including the *table sizing marker*, the *right column margins marker*, and the *left column margins marker*. These markers are identified in figure 24.10. To change the column width with the Ruler Bar, you would complete the following steps:

1. Position the arrow pointer on the column width marker to be moved.
2. Hold down the left mouse button.
3. Drag the marker to widen or narrow the columns. (As you drag the marker, the column width marker in the original location displays in gray, and the column marker being moved displays in black, with a vertical guide showing the position.)
4. When the column width marker is in the new position, release the mouse button.

Creating Tables

Figure 24.10

Table Markers on the Ruler Bar

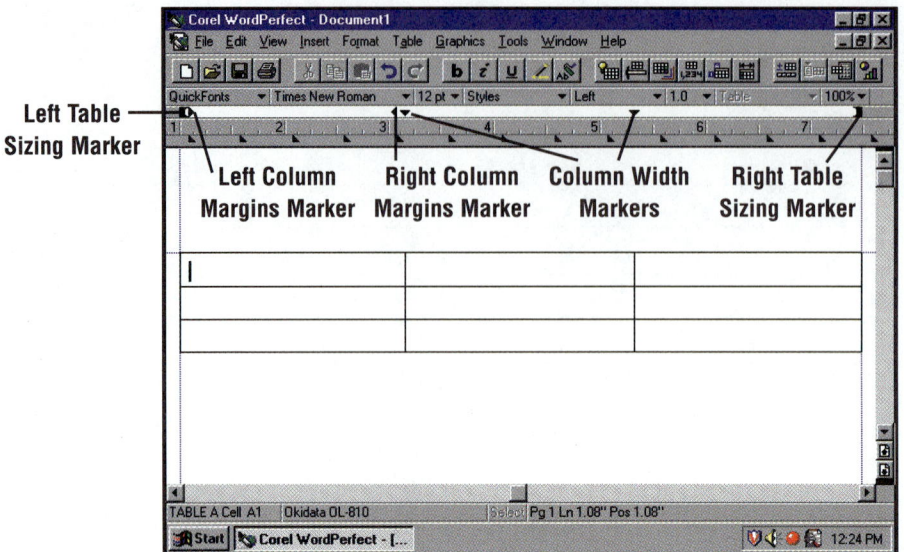

When you move a column width marker in this manner, only the column width marker on which the arrow pointer is positioned is moved. Any other column width markers in the table stay in their original position. If you want to move a column width marker and any other column width markers to the right the same distance, hold down the Shift key when dragging the mouse.

When you are dragging the column width marker, the Status Bar displays the position of the marker on the Ruler Bar. Use this position measurement to move the column width marker to the desired measurement on the Ruler Bar.

The left column margins marker and the right column margins marker can be used to adjust the left or right column margins in all columns. To do this, position the arrow pointer on the left or right column margins marker, drag the arrow pointer to the left or right, then release the mouse button. When you change the left or right margin in this manner, the margin is changed for all cells in the column and all columns in the table.

Use the table sizing marker to increase or decrease the overall size of a table. This does not affect the number of columns or rows; it only affects the width of the table. Position the arrow pointer on the left or right table sizing marker, hold down the left mouse button, drag the marker to the new position, then release the button.

EXERCISE

Creating and Editing a Table

1. At a clear editing window, create the memo shown in figure 24.11 by completing the following steps:
   a. Change the font to 12-point Courier New.
   b. Key the headings and the first paragraph of the memo. (Since this memo is set in a monospaced font, space twice after end-of-sentence punctuation.)
   c. With the insertion point a double space below the first paragraph, create a table that contains three columns and eight rows.
   d. Change the width of the first column by completing the following steps:

566 Chapter 24

- (1) Make sure the Ruler Bar is displayed.
- (2) Position the arrow pointer on the column width marker between the 3-inch and the 3.25-inch marks on the Ruler Bar.
- (3) Hold down the left mouse button.
- (4) Drag the marker to the 4.5-inch mark on the Ruler Bar, then release the mouse button. (Check the right side of the Status Bar. The position measurement should display as *4.5"* before the left mouse button is released.)

e. Change the width of the second column by completing the following steps:
- (1) Position the arrow pointer on the column width marker between the 5-inch and the 5.5-inch marks on the Ruler Bar.
- (2) Hold down the left mouse button.
- (3) Drag the marker to the 6-inch mark on the Ruler Bar, then release the mouse button. (The position measurement in the Status Bar should display as *6"* before the left mouse button is released.)

f. Key the text in the cells as indicated in figure 24.11. Center the text in cells A1, B1, and C1. Use Ctrl + Tab to indent the text in cells A2 through A8.

g. Move the insertion point below the table, then key the last paragraph and reference line shown in figure 24.11.

2. Save the memo and name it Ch 24, Ex 03.
3. Print and then close Ch 24, Ex 03.

Figure 24.11

```
DATE:       February 2, 1998
TO:         Paula Kerns
FROM:       Steven Ayala
SUBJECT:    WORDPERFECT CLASS
```

The deadline for enrolling in the WordPerfect class was January 30. A total of seven employees registered for the class. The list of employees and their status is displayed below.

Name	Hospital #	Department
Arnold Koch	523-44-0944	Med. Records
Margaret Williamson	312-33-0393	Finances
Karyn Thomas-Briggs	128-03-3372	Pediatrics
Lillian Smith	329-55-4964	Payroll
Raymond Ottmar	543-34-7751	Med. Records
Leonard Strickertz	243-09-5943	Finances
Elizabeth Landes	423-43-2009	Payroll

I have reserved Room 102 for the class. Please let me know what special equipment you will need. There will be eight computers available in the room.

xx:Ch 24, Ex 03

Changing Column Width with the Properties for Table Format Dialog Box

If you know the exact measurements for columns in a table, you can change column widths at the Properties for Table Format dialog box with the Column tab selected. This dialog box is displayed in figure 24.12. To display the dialog box, position the insertion point in any cell in a table, then click T<u>a</u>ble, then F<u>o</u>rmat. At the Properties for Table Format dialog box, click the Column tab. You can also display the Properties for Table Format dialog box with a QuickMenu. To display the Tables QuickMenu, position the insertion point in any cell in the table, then click the right mouse button. At the QuickMenu that displays, click F<u>o</u>rmat. At the Properties for Table Format dialog box, click the Column tab.

As you move the arrow pointer over cells within a table, a QuickSpot button will appear in the cells. If you rest the arrow pointer on one of the QuickSpots in the column for which you want to change the width, the Edit Table tip appears. Click the QuickSpot button to display the Tools dialog box. Click the For<u>m</u>at button at the Tools dialog box and the Properties for Table Format dialog box displays. At this dialog box, click the Column tab, then change the column width in the Wid<u>t</u>h text box. To do this, select the existing number and then key the new width, or click the up- or down-pointing triangles to the right of the Wid<u>t</u>h text box until the correct measurement displays.

Figure 24.12

Properties for Table Format Dialog Box with Column Tab Selected

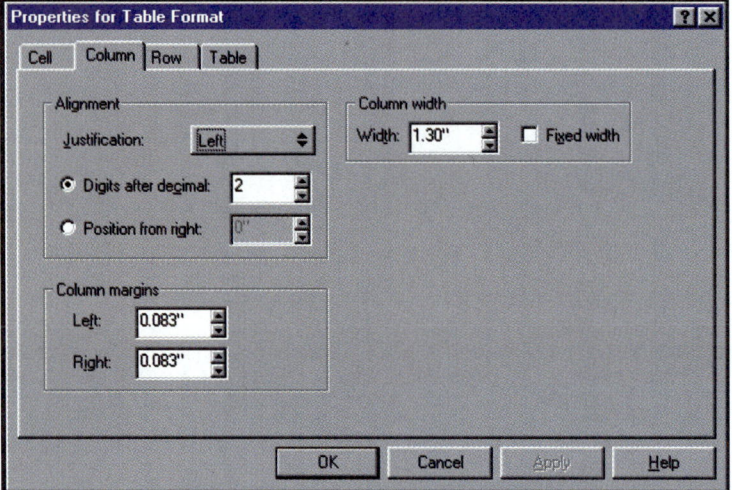

EXERCISE 4

Changing Column Widths

1. At a clear editing window, create the table shown in figure 24.13 by completing the following steps:
    a. Change the font to 14-point Century Schoolbook.
    b. Center and bold *CARIBBEAN CRUISE*.
    c. Change the font size to 12 points and then press Enter twice.
    d. Center and bold *Dining Room Reservations*.
    e. Press Enter three times, then create a table with three columns and five rows.

- **f.** Change the width of the first column to 2.5 inches by completing the following steps:
    - **(1)** Position the insertion point in any cell in the first column.
    - **(2)** Click T**a**ble, then F**o**rmat.
    - **(3)** At the Properties for Table Format dialog box, click the Column tab.
    - **(4)** Select the current number displayed in the Wid**t**h text box in the Column width section and then key **2.5**.
    - **(5)** Click OK.
- **g.** Change the width of the second column to 1.5 inches by completing steps similar to those in 1f.
- **h.** Change the width of the third column to 1.5 inches by completing steps similar to those in 1f.
- **i.** Key the text in the cells as indicated in figure 24.13. Center the text in the second and third columns. Bold the text in cells B1 and C1.

2. Change the size of the table with the table sizing marker by completing the following steps:
    - **a.** Position the insertion point inside the table.
    - **b.** Make sure the Ruler Bar is displayed.
    - **c.** Position the arrow pointer on the left table sizing marker.
    - **d.** Hold down the Shift key, then hold down the left mouse button.
    - **e.** Drag the arrow pointer to the 2-inch mark on the Ruler Bar. (Check the Status Bar for the position measurement.)
    - **f.** Release the mouse button and then the Shift key.
3. Save the table and name it Ch 24, Ex 04.
4. Print and then close Ch 24, Ex 04.

Figure 24.13

CARIBBEAN CRUISE

Dining Room Reservations

	Early	**Late**
Breakfast (in port)	6:45 a.m.	8:00 a.m.
Breakfast (at sea)	7:45 a.m.	9:00 a.m.
Luncheon	12:00 noon	1:30 p.m.
Dinner	6:00 p.m.	8:00 p.m.

Creating Tables

Selecting Cells

A table can be formatted in special ways. For example, the alignment or margins of text in cells or rows can be changed or character formatting can be added. To identify the cells that are to be affected by the formatting, the specific cells need to be selected.

Selecting Cells with the Mouse

The mouse pointer can be used to select a cell, row, column, or an entire table. The table selection arrows are used to select specific cells in a table. There is a left-pointing arrow called the *horizontal selection arrow* and an up-pointing arrow called the *vertical selection arrow*. To display the horizontal selection arrow, move the arrow pointer to the left border of any cell until it turns into a left-pointing arrow. This arrow is the horizontal selection arrow. To display the vertical selection arrow, move the arrow pointer to the top border of any cell until it turns into an up-pointing arrow. This arrow is the vertical selection arrow.

To select one cell in a table, position the arrow pointer in the cell to be selected so that either the horizontal or the vertical selection arrow is displayed, then click the left mouse button. When you click the left mouse button, the selected cell displays in black and any text within the cell displays in white. To select a row in a table, position the arrow pointer in any cell in the row until the horizontal selection arrow is displayed, then double-click the left mouse button. To select a column in a table, position the arrow pointer in any cell in the column at the top border of the cell until the vertical selection arrow is displayed, then double-click the left mouse button. To select all cells within a table, position the arrow pointer in any cell in the table until either the horizontal or the vertical selection arrow is displayed, then click the left mouse button quickly three times. If you want to select the text within a cell rather than the entire cell, select the text in the normal manner.

If you click the Row/Column Indicators button on the Tables Toolbar, letters display identifying columns and numbers display identifying rows. These column and row indicators can be used to select cells within a table. To select a row, click the row indicator number next to the row to be selected. To select a column, click the column letter above the column to be selected. When column and row indicators are displayed, a square displays in the top left corner of the row and column indicators. Click this button to select the entire table.

Selecting Text with the Keyboard

The keyboard can be used to select specific cells within a table. Figure 24.14 displays the commands for selecting specific amounts of a table.

Figure 24.14

Selecting Commands

Amount of the Table	Command
Current cell	SHIFT + F8
Current row	SHIFT + CTRL + →
Current column	SHIFT + CTRL + ↑
One cell, row, or column at a time	SHIFT + →
Beginning of current row	SHIFT + HOME
End of current row	SHIFT + END
Current table to beginning of document	SHIFT + CTRL + HOME
Current table to end of document	SHIFT + CTRL + END

If you want to select only text within cells, rather than the entire cell, press F8 to turn on the Select mode, then move the insertion point with the insertion point movement commands. When a cell is selected, the entire cell is changed to black. When text within a cell is selected, only those lines containing text are selected.

EXERCISE 5

Selecting Cells and Changing the Text Appearance

1. At a clear editing window, open Ch 24, Ex 03.
2. Save the document with Save As and name it Ch 24, Ex 05.
3. Select and bold cells A1, B1, and C1 using the mouse by completing the following steps:
   a. Position the arrow pointer in cell A1 at the left border of the cell until the horizontal selection arrow displays.
   b. Double-click the left mouse button.
   c. With the first row selected, click the Bold button on the Toolbar.
   d. Turn off Select by clicking the arrow pointer anywhere outside the selected area.
4. Select and italicize the text in cells B2 through B8 using the keyboard by completing the following steps:
   a. Position the insertion point in cell B2.
   b. Hold down the Shift key and press the down arrow key until the insertion point reaches cell B8, then release the Shift key.
   c. With cells B2 through B8 selected, press Ctrl + I.
   d. Press F8 to turn off Select.
5. Select and italicize the text in cells C2 through C8 by completing steps similar to those in 4.
6. Save the document again with the same name (Ch 24, Ex 05).
7. Print and then close Ch 24, Ex 05.

Editing a Table

A table that has been created with the Tables feature can be edited in a variety of ways. For example, text within cells can be inserted or deleted; columns or rows can be copied or moved; or rows and columns can be inserted or deleted.

Inserting Rows or Columns

With the Insert option from the Table drop-down menu or the Insert option from the Tables QuickMenu, you can insert rows or columns in a table. By default, a row is inserted above the row where the insertion point is positioned and a column is inserted to the left of the column where the insertion point is positioned. Figure 24.15 shows the Insert Columns/Rows dialog box. More than one column or row can be inserted at the Insert Columns/Rows dialog box. To insert more than one, click Columns or click Rows, then key the number to be inserted.

Figure 24.15

Insert Columns/Rows Dialog Box

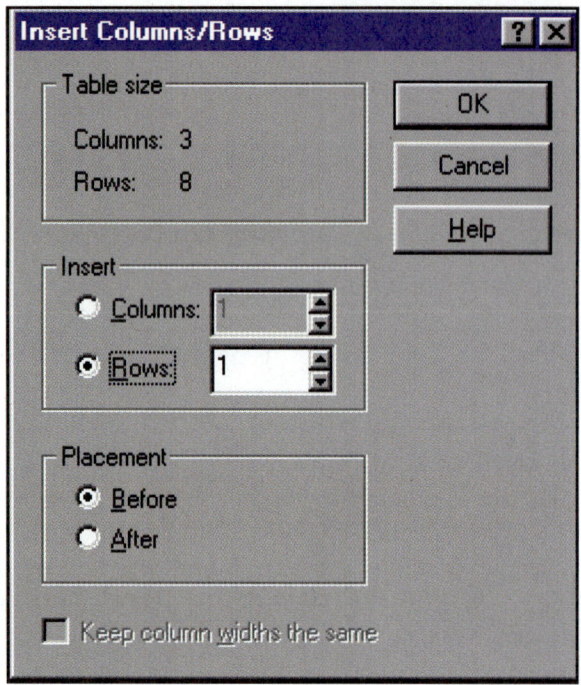

The Insert Columns/Rows dialog box contains a Placement section with two options—Before and After. The Before option is selected by default. This causes a row to be inserted above the position of the insertion point or a column to be inserted to the left of the position of the insertion point. If you click After, a row is inserted below the position of the insertion point and a column is inserted to the right of the position of the insertion point.

EXERCISE 6

Inserting a Row in a Table

1. At a clear editing window, open Ch 24, Ex 03.
2. Save the document with Save As and name it Ch 24, Ex 06.
3. Select cells A1 through C1 and then turn on bold.
4. Add a row in the table between Lillian Smith and Raymond Ottmar by completing the following steps:
    a. Position the insertion point in any cell in the row for Raymond Ottmar.
    b. Click Table, then Insert.
    c. At the Insert Columns/Rows dialog box, click OK.
5. Key the following text in the new cells:
    A6 = **Lena McCaw**
    B6 = **423-07-4534**
    C6 = **Finances**
6. Save the document again with the same name (Ch 24, Ex 06).
7. Print and then close Ch 24, Ex 06.

Deleting Rows or Columns

Rows or columns in a document can be deleted with the Delete option from the Table drop-down menu, or the Delete option from the Tables QuickMenu. At the Delete dialog box, shown in figure 24.16, follow steps similar to those used for inserting rows or columns. As with inserting, you can delete more than one column or row. Text in cells can also be deleted without removing the table structure. You can delete text within one cell or you can select several cells, then delete all the text in the selected cells with the Cell contents option.

Figure 24.16

Delete Dialog Box

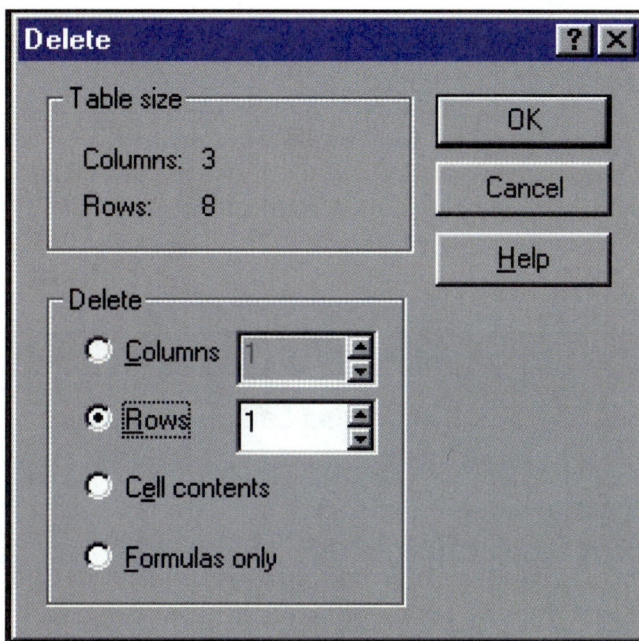

EXERCISE 7

Inserting and Deleting Rows

1. At a clear editing window, open Ch 24, Ex 03.
2. Save the document with Save As and name it Ch 24, Ex 07.
3. Delete rows 3 and 4 by completing the following steps:
    a. Position the arrow pointer in cell A3 (contains the name *Margaret Williamson*).
    b. Click the right mouse button, then click Delete at the Tables QuickMenu.
    c. At the Delete dialog box, click the up-pointing triangle at the right side of the Rows text box (this displays *2* in the text box).
    d. Click OK.
4. Insert two rows above the sixth row by completing the following steps:
    a. Position the arrow pointer in cell A6 (contains the name *Elizabeth Landes*). Position the arrow pointer on the name *Elizabeth*, not the name *Landes*.
    b. Click Table, then Insert.
    c. At the Insert Columns/Rows dialog box, select the *1* in the Rows text box, then key **2**.

Creating Tables

d. Click OK.
5. Key the following text in the identified cells:
   - A6 = **Jon LaMarr**
   - B6 = **542-20-5483**
   - C6 = **Med. Records**
   - A7 = **Marcia O'Neill**
   - B7 = **231-29-3827**
   - C7 = **Payroll**
6. Save the document again with the same name (Ch 24, Ex 07).
7. Print and then close Ch 24, Ex 07.

Joining Cells

Cells can be joined with the Join option from the Table drop-down menu. First, select the cells and then click Table, point to Join, then click Cell. You can also use the Tables QuickMenu to join cells. To do this, select the cells, click the right mouse button, then click Join Cells at the QuickMenu.

EXERCISE

Joining Cells

1. At a clear editing window, create the table shown in figure 24.17 by completing the following steps:
   a. Create a table with 3 columns and 10 rows.
   b. Join cells A1 through C1 by completing the following steps:
      (1) Select cells A1 through C1.
      (2) Click Table, point to Join, then click Cell.
   c. Join cells A2 through C2 by completing steps similar to those in 1b.
   d. Key the text in the table as shown in figure 24.17. Center and bold the text as indicated. (Press Enter once after keying **ACTIVITY LOG**. Press Enter once after keying **Training and Education Department**.)
2. Save the document and name it Ch 24, Ex 08.
3. Print and then close Ch 24, Ex 08.

Figure 24.17

	ACTIVITY LOG	
	Training and Education Department	
Client	Activity	Date

Splitting Cells

With the <u>S</u>plit option from the T<u>a</u>ble drop-down menu, you can split a cell or a row or column of cells. To split a cell, position the insertion point in the cell to be split, click T<u>a</u>ble, point to <u>S</u>plit, then click <u>C</u>ell. At the Split Cell dialog box, shown in figure 24.18, click <u>R</u>ows or <u>C</u>olumns, specify how many rows or columns, then click OK.

Figure 24.18

Split Cell Dialog Box

EXERCISE 9

Splitting Cells into Two Columns

1. At a clear editing window, open Ch 24, Ex 08.
2. Save the document with Save As and name it Ch 24, Ex 09.
3. Split cells C3 through C10 into two columns by completing the following steps:
   a. Select cells C3 through C10.

Creating Tables 575

b. Click T<u>a</u>ble, point to <u>S</u>plit, then click <u>C</u>ell.
   c. At the Split Cell dialog box, click OK.
4. Bold and center the word *Time* in cell D3.
5. Save the document again with the same name (Ch 24, Ex 09).
6. Print and then close Ch 24, Ex 09.

Deleting Text

After text has been inserted in a cell, it can be deleted in the normal manner with the Delete or Backspace keys. You can delete an entire row or column by selecting the row or column, then pressing Backspace. When you press Backspace, the Delete dialog box, shown in figure 24.16, displays on the screen. If you want to delete the row or column, click OK. If you want to delete the text in a column or row (but not the cells), click C<u>e</u>ll contents. If you want to delete the text within the cell as well as the cell in the column, make sure <u>C</u>olumns is selected at the Delete dialog box, then click OK.

EXERCISE

Deleting Cell Contents

1. At a clear editing window, open Ch 24, Ex 03.
2. Save the document with Save As and name it Ch 24, Ex 10.
3. Delete the contents of cells A4 through C5 by completing the following steps:
   a. Select cells A4 through C5.
   b. Press Backspace.
   c. At the Delete dialog box, click C<u>e</u>ll contents.
   d. Click OK.
4. Key the following text in the identified cell:
   A4 = **Toni Velluci**
   B4 = **490-43-9283**
   C4 = **Payroll**
   A5 = **Kenneth Barret**
   B5 = **865-04-3822**
   C5 = **Finances**
5. Save the document again with the same name (Ch 24, Ex 10).
6. Print and then close Ch 24, Ex 10.

Cutting and Pasting

In a table, columns and/or rows can be moved or copied to a different location within the table. To copy or move a row or column, select the row or column first, click <u>E</u>dit from the Menu Bar, then click Cu<u>t</u> or <u>C</u>opy; or click the Cut or Copy button on the Toolbar. At the Table Cut/Copy dialog box, shown in figure 24.19, click <u>C</u>olumn or <u>R</u>ow, then click OK. Move the insertion point to the column or row where you want the column or row pasted, then click <u>E</u>dit, then <u>P</u>aste; or click the Paste button on the Toolbar. (A column will be inserted to the left of the column where the insertion point is positioned, and a row will be inserted above the row where the insertion point is positioned.) You can also use the Tables QuickMenu to cut, copy, and paste text in a table.

576 Chapter 24

Figure 24.19

Table Cut/Copy Dialog Box

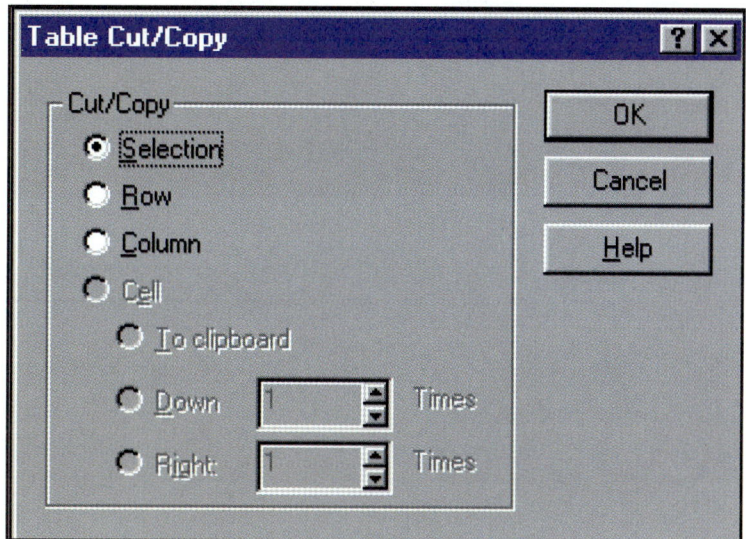

EXERCISE 11

Moving Columns

1. At a clear editing window, open Ch 24, Ex 02.
2. Save the document with Save As and name it Ch 24, Ex 11.
3. Reverse the columns by completing the following steps:
    a. Select the second column.
    b. Click the Cut button on the Toolbar.
    c. At the Table Cut/Copy dialog box, click Column.
    d. Click OK.
    e. Click the Paste button on the Toolbar.
4. Save the document again with the same name (Ch 24, Ex 11).
5. Print and then close Ch 24, Ex 11.

Deleting a Table

An entire table, including cell entries, can be deleted; you can delete the structure of the table, leaving the cell entries; or you can delete the cell entries, leaving the table structure. To delete the entire table, including cell entries, select the entire table, click the right mouse button, then click Delete; or press the Backspace key. At the Delete Table dialog box, shown in figure 24.20, make sure Entire table is selected, then click OK.

To delete only the table contents, leaving the table structure, click Table contents. If you want to delete the table structure and leave the text within cells, click Table structure (leave text) at the Delete Table dialog box.

Another method for displaying the Delete Table dialog box is to display Reveal Codes, position the insertion point immediately to the left of the table definition code, then press the Delete key. This displays the Delete Table dialog box where you can choose to delete the entire table, the cell contents only, or just the table structure, leaving the cell contents.

Creating Tables 577

Figure 24.20 Delete Table Dialog Box

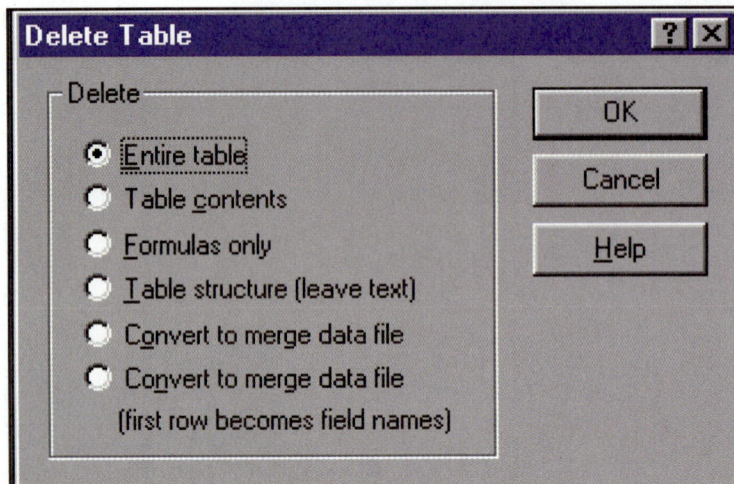

Deleting a Table Structure

1. At a clear editing window, open Ch 24, Ex 02.
2. Save the document with Save As and name it Ch 24, Ex 12.
3. Delete the table structure but leave the text by completing the following steps:
   a. Select the entire table.
   b. Press the Backspace key.
   c. At the Delete Table dialog box, click Table structure (leave text).
   d. Click OK.
4. With the insertion point positioned on the line containing *President* and *Chris Hedegaard*, use the mouse on the Ruler Bar to clear all tabs, then set left tabs at the 2.5-inch mark, the 4-inch mark, and the 4.75-inch mark.
5. Save the document again with the same name (Ch 24, Ex 12).
6. Print and then close Ch 24, Ex 12.

CHAPTER SUMMARY

▼ With WordPerfect's Tables feature, a form can be created that has boxes of information, called *cells*, with customized lines surrounding each cell.

▼ A table can be created with the Tables button on the Power Bar, or at the Create Table dialog box.

▼ Columns in a table are lettered from left to right, beginning with A. Rows in a table are numbered from top to bottom beginning with 1.

▼ Change the width of columns with the mouse in the table, the Ruler Bar, or with options at the Properties for Table Format dialog box with the Column tab selected.

▼ The arrow pointer or the keyboard can be used to select a cell, a row, a column, or an entire table. After cells are selected, alignment or margins can be changed or character formatting can be added.

▼ Insert rows or columns in a table with the Insert option from the Table drop-down menu, or the Insert option from the Tables QuickMenu.

▼ Delete rows or columns in a table with the Delete option from the Table drop-down menu, or the Delete option from the Tables QuickMenu.

▼ Two or more cells can be joined with the Join option from the Table drop-down menu. Or, a cell or a row or column of cells can be split with the Split option from the Table drop-down menu.

▼ At the Table Cut/Copy dialog box, columns and/or rows can be moved or copied to a different location within the table.

▼ An entire table, including cell entries, can be deleted; you can delete the structure of the table, leaving the cell entries; or you can delete the cell entries, leaving the table structure.

COMMANDS REVIEW

	Mouse	Keyboard
Create table with Tables button	With arrow pointer on Tables button on Power Bar, hold down left mouse button, drag arrow pointer down and right until desired number of rows and columns displays, then release mouse button	
Create Table dialog box	Table, Create	Table, Create
Format dialog box	Table, Format	Table, Format
Tables QuickMenu	With pointer inside table, click *right* mouse button	
Table Cut/Copy dialog box	Edit, Cut or Copy; or click Cut or Copy button on Toolbar	Edit, Cut or Copy
Move insertion point to next cell	With arrow pointer in desired cell, click left mouse button	

Move insertion point to previous cell	With arrow pointer in desired cell, click left mouse button	SHIFT + TAB
Insert left tab in cell		CTRL + TAB
Insert decimal tab in cell		ALT + SHIFT + F7
Insert back tab (margin release)		CTRL + SHIFT + TAB

CHECK YOUR UNDERSTANDING

Completion: In the space provided at the right, indicate the correct term, command, or number.

1. Press this key on the keyboard to move the insertion point to the next cell. _____

2. Press these keys on the keyboard to move the insertion point to the previous cell. _____

3. A table can be created with this button on the Power Bar. _____

4. Before joining cells, you need to first do this. _____

5. This is the cell that is located immediately to the right of cell C4. _____

6. This is the cell that is located immediately below cell D7. _____

7. Press these keys on the keyboard to move the insertion point to a tab setting within the cell. _____

8. Use this dialog box to copy or move a row or column. _____

9. Change the width of columns using the mouse, the Ruler Bar, or with options at this dialog box. _____

10. If you want to move a column width marker and any other column width markers to the right the same distance, hold down this key when dragging the mouse. _____

11. To delete the table structure and leave the text within cells, click this at the Delete Table dialog box. _____

SKILL ASSESSMENTS

Assessment 1

1. At a clear editing window, create the document shown in figure 24.21.
2. Save the document and name it Ch 24, SA 01.
3. Print and then close Ch 24, SA 01.

Figure 24.21

BUILDING A NETWORK

Contact six people working in the field of interest to you. Find out what they like about their job, what they do not like, how they obtained their position, and the skills and qualifications required for the position. Fill in the form below.

Name	Phone Number	Company	Comments

Assessment 2

1. At a clear editing window, create the letter shown in figure 24.22.
2. Save the document and name it Ch 24, SA 02.
3. Print and then close Ch 24, SA 02.

Creating Tables

Figure 24.22

January 10, 1998

Mr. and Mrs. Phillip Hunter
3120 South 32nd Avenue
Seattle, WA 98104

Dear Mr. and Mrs. Hunter:

The final arrangements have been made for your cruise to the Caribbean. The airfare has been charged to your account. A receipt of this transaction is included in your travel packet. Your itinerary for the cruise is described below:

Day	Port	Arrive	Depart
Saturday, 03/07/98	Miami		4:00 p.m.
Sunday, 03/08/98	At sea		
Monday, 03/09/98	San Juan	6:00 p.m.	
Tuesday, 03/10/98	San Juan		2:00 a.m.
Tuesday, 03/10/98	St. Thomas	8:00 a.m.	5:30 p.m.
Wednesday, 03/11/98	St. Maarten	7:00 a.m.	5:00 p.m.
Thursday, 03/12/98	At sea		
Friday, 03/13/98	At sea		
Saturday, 03/14/98	Miami	8:00 a.m.	

I am sure you will have a wonderful time on the cruise. Please stop by our office to pick up your travel packet before the end of the week.

Sincerely,

Judy Peterson

xx:Ch 24, SA 02

Assessment 3

1. At a clear editing window, open Ch 24, SA 02.
2. Save the document with Save As and name it Ch 24, SA 03.
3. Select cells B2 through B10, then access the Center command.
4. Select and center the text in cells C2 through C10.
5. Select and center the text in cells D2 through D10.
6. Save the document again with the same name (Ch 24, SA 03).
7. Print and then close Ch 24, SA 03.

Assessment 4

1. At a clear editing window, create the table shown in figure 24.23 with the following specifications:
    a. Create a table with three columns and eight rows.
    b. Change the width of the first column to 3.5 inches.
    c. Join cells A1 through C1.
    d. Join cells A2 through C2.
    e. Key the text in the cells as indicated. Bold and center text as shown. Use the Indent feature to indent the text after the numbers in the first column. When keying the text in the cells in the first column, do not press Enter. Let word wrap take text to the next line within the cell.
2. Save the table and name it Ch 24, SA 04.
3. Print and then close Ch 24, SA 04.

Figure 24.23

ACTIVITY DIRECTOR		
Rating Form for Candidates		
Rating Category	**Pts. Allowed**	**Pts. Awarded**
1. Experience managing a program designed to provide services for unemployed.	25	
2. Experience working with others as the chair of a committee or other group.	25	
3. Experience developing, maintaining, and evaluating adult education program.	15	
4. Communicates experience working with multiple agencies.	10	
5. Experience developing and maintaining budgets.	10	

Assessment 5

1. At a clear editing window, create the table shown in figure 24.24 with the following specifications:
    a. Create a table with 3 columns and 10 rows.
    b. Change the width of the second column to 3 inches.
    c. Join cells A1 through C1.
    d. Join cells A2 through C2.
    e. Bold and center the text as indicated.
2. Save the table and name it Ch 24, SA 05.
3. Print and then close Ch 24, SA 05.

Figure 24.24

EMERGENCY PREPAREDNESS COMMITTEE MEMBERS		
STEERING COMMITTEE		
Employee	**Position**	**Extension**
Sally Chapman	Chair, Emergency Preparedness	3410
Charlene Knudtsen	Medical Director	1023
Suzanna Childers	Associate Administrator	4311
Joseph Washington	Pharmacy Services	2019
Benjamin Lindler	Administrative Services	9422
Judith Krandall	Head Nurse, Emergency Room	6223
Montgomery Brooks	Director, Ambulatory Care	3492

Assessment 6

1. At a clear editing window, open Ch 24, SA 05.
2. Save the document with Save As and name it Ch 24, SA 06.
3. Delete rows 5 and 6.
4. Add two rows between the third and fourth rows.
5. Key the text in the identified cells.

    A4 = **Tina Boyer**
    B4 = **Safety Services**
    C4 = **3055**
    A5 = **Glen Maloney**
    B5 = **Nurse Manager**
    C5 = **8430**

6. Save the document again with the same name (Ch 24, SA 06).
7. Print and then close Ch 24, SA 06.

Assessment 7

1. At a clear editing window, create the table shown in figure 24.25 with the following specifications:
    a. Change the font to 12-point Century Schoolbook.
    b. Key the title and subtitle as shown in the figure.
    c. With the insertion point positioned a triple space below the subtitle, create a table with three columns and nine rows.
    d. Key the text in the cells as shown. Bold and center the text in cells A1, B1, and C1. (The columns will be wider than what appears in figure 24.25. This will be changed in the next step.)
    e. Move the left table sizing marker to the 2-inch mark on the Ruler Bar.
    f. Move the column width marker for the second column (displays at approximately the 3 1/8-inch mark) to the 4-inch mark on the Ruler Bar.
    g. Move the column width marker for the third column (displays at approximately the 5 3/8-inch mark) to the 5.5-inch mark on the Ruler Bar.
    h. Move the right table sizing marker to the 6.5-inch mark on the Ruler Bar.
2. Save the table and name it Ch 24, SA 07.
3. Print and then close Ch 24, SA 07.

Figure 24.25

FINANCES DEPARTMENT

Database Training Schedule

Name	**Date**	**Time**
VanGelder, Jake	02/03 and 02/05	4-6 p.m.
Herschel, Patricia	02/03 and 02/05	4-6 p.m.
Boesenberg, Anne	02/11 and 02/13	3-5 p.m.
Payne, Margaret	02/11 and 02/13	3-5 p.m.
Lyons, Virginia	02/17 and 02/19	1-3 p.m.
Auger, Kimberly	02/17 and 02/19	1-3 p.m.
Page, William	03/03 and 03/05	4-6 p.m.
Burdick, Sandra	03/03 and 03/05	4-6 p.m.

Assessment 8

1. At a clear editing window, open Ch 24, SA 07.
2. Save the document with Save As and name it Ch 24, SA 08.
3. Reverse the second and third columns.
4. Save the document again with the same name (Ch 24, SA 08).
5. Print and then close Ch 24, SA 08.

25

FORMATTING TABLES

PERFORMANCE OBJECTIVE

Upon successful completion of chapter 25, you will be able to customize tables you have created to illustrate different business situations, including mathematical analyses.

You learned to use WordPerfect's Tables feature in chapter 24 to create and edit tables. In this chapter, you will learn more about the formatting options available at the Table drop-down menu, shown in figure 25.1. The following options were discussed in chapter 24—Create, Insert, Delete, Join, and Split. In this chapter, you will learn about the Format, Numeric Format, SpeedFormat, Lines/Fill, Formula Bar, Copy Formula, Calculate, and QuickSum options.

Figure 25.1

Table Drop-Down Menu

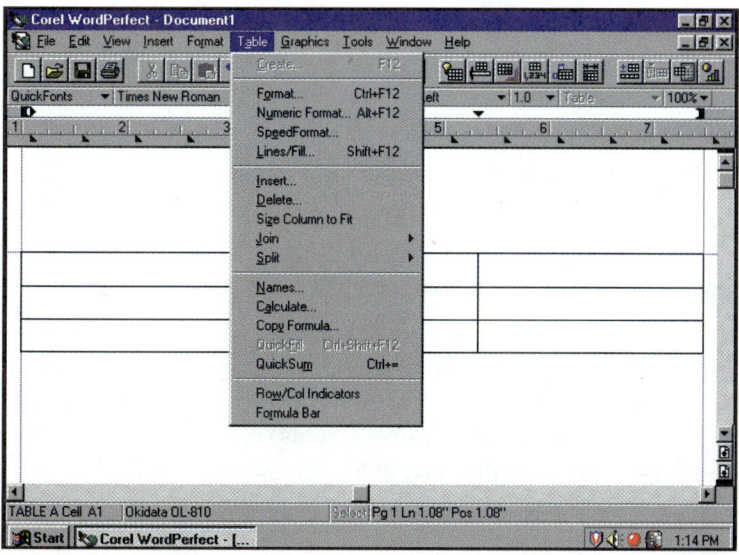

Formatting Tables 587

Clicking the F<u>o</u>rmat option at the T<u>a</u>ble drop-down menu causes the Properties for Table Format dialog box to display as shown in figure 25.2. The options in this dialog box change depending on the tab that is selected toward the top of the dialog box.

Figure 25.2 Properties for Table Format Dialog Box with Cell Tab Selected

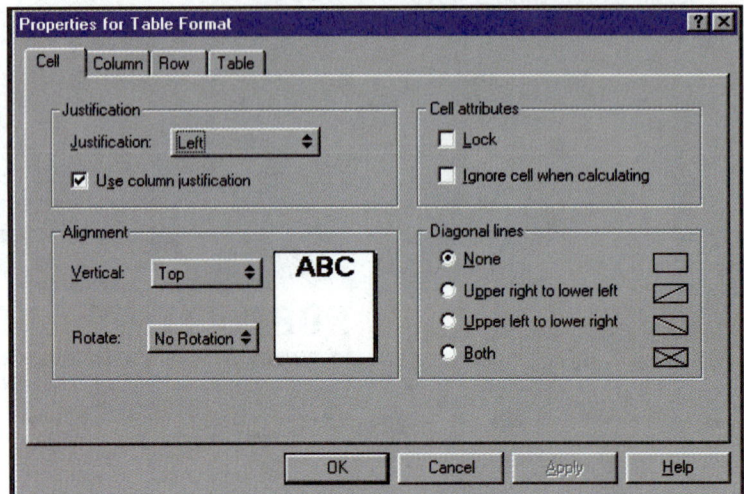

Formatting Cells

By default, the Cell tab is selected at the Properties for Table Format dialog box. This dialog box contains options for formatting a cell or selected cells.

Justification: By default, text in a cell is aligned at the left margin of the cell. This can be changed to <u>R</u>ight, <u>C</u>enter, <u>F</u>ull, <u>A</u>ll, or <u>D</u>ecimal Align. Note that all of the justification options concern the margins of the cell, not the document.

When you display the <u>J</u>ustification options, the last option is <u>M</u>ixed. This setting is dimmed if the cell or selected cells contain the same justification options. If, however, you select cells with varying justification options, the <u>M</u>ixed option displays in black.

Use Column Justification: By default, WordPerfect applies the current column's justification settings to a cell. If you do not want this to occur, remove the check mark from the U<u>s</u>e column justification option.

Changing Alignment

The Alignment section of the Format dialog box contains options that affect the alignment of text in cells.

Vertical: At the default setting of <u>T</u>op, text in a cell is aligned at the top. This can be changed to <u>B</u>ottom, <u>C</u>enter, or <u>M</u>ixed. The <u>M</u>ixed setting is dimmed if the cell or selected cells contain the same alignment options. If, however, you select cells with varying alignment options, the <u>M</u>ixed setting displays in black.

Rotate: Text within the cell can be rotated <u>9</u>0 degrees, <u>1</u>80 degrees, or <u>2</u>70 degrees with the Rotate button. The default setting is <u>N</u>o Rotation. The <u>M</u>ixed setting is dimmed if the cell or selected cells contain the same rotation options. If you select cells with varying rotation option, the <u>M</u>ixed setting displays in black when you select the Rotate button.

If you change the <u>V</u>ertical and/or Rotate options, the Preview box displays how the text will appear within the cell.

EXERCISE 1

Change Cell Justification

1. At a clear editing window, create the table shown in figure 25.3 by completing the following steps:
    a. Create a table with 3 columns and 10 rows.
    b. Change the column width of the second column to 3 inches.
    c. Join cells A1 through C1.
    d. Join cells A2 through C2.
    e. Change the justification to Center for cell A1 by completing the following steps:
        (1) Position the insertion point in cell A1 (do not select the cell).
        (2) Click Table, then Format.
        (3) At the Properties for Table Format dialog box, make sure the Cell tab is selected, then click the Justification button.
        (4) At the drop-down list that displays, click Center.
        (5) Click OK.
    f. Change the justification to Center for cell A2 by completing steps similar to those in 1e.
    g. Change the justification to Center for cells A3 through C3 by completing the following steps:
        (1) Select cells A3 through C3.
        (2) Click Table, then Format.
        (3) At the Properties for Table Format dialog box, select the Cell tab. (By default, WordPerfect displays the Properties for Table Format dialog box with the Row tab selected.)
        (4) Change the Justification to Center.
        (5) Click OK.
    h. Select cells C4 through C10, then change the Justification to Center by completing steps similar to those in 1g.
    i. Key the text in the cells as shown in figure 25.3. Bold the text as indicated.
2. Save the document and name it Ch 25, Ex 01.
3. Print and then close Ch 25, Ex 01.

Figure 25.3

OMAHA CITY SCHOOL DISTRICT		
Technology Advisory Committee		
Name	**Organization**	**Phone**
Barry Vialle	Horizon Broadcasting Company	555-3209
Colonel Gerry Lund	Satler Air Force Base	555-3321
Dr. Jeremy Needham	Omaha Community College	555-4332
Arlene Tommaney	Midwest Banking Institution	555-0091
Kathy Hemphill	Omaha Economic Development	555-8327
Lyle McKeller	Nebraska Health Council	555-1225
Roberta Hughes	Sampson/Kraft Corporation	555-3123

Changing Appearance

You can format text within a cell with a button on the Toolbar or with shortcut commands. When you format text with buttons on the Toolbar or shortcut commands, the codes are inserted in the cell and can be seen in Reveal Codes. To format text with more than one option at a time, select options at the Font dialog box. For example, you can select Bold, Underline, and Small caps as formatting to be applied to selected cells.

In some situations, you may see gray shading in the check boxes before Appearance options at the Font dialog box. This shading indicates that the appearance option is on for some, but not all, of the selected cells. This will happen, for example, if you select 12 cells that have been formatted with bold, but only 6 of the 12 have been formatted with italics. When you display the Format dialog box, the Bold check box will contain a check mark but the Italic check box will contain gray shading.

Changing Cell Attributes

The Cell attributes section of the Properties for Table Format dialog box contains two options—Lock and Ignore cell when calculating. In some tables you may want to lock certain cells so that text cannot be changed. Clicking Lock places a check mark in the check box. Click it again to unlock the cell.

Later in this chapter, you will learn how to insert formulas in cells. If you do not want the cell contents to be included in the calculation of the formula, click Ignore cell when calculating at the Properties for Table Format dialog box.

Diagonal Lines

The Diagonal lines section of the Properties for Table Format dialog box can be used to insert a line in the cell drawn from the Upper right to lower left, Upper left to lower right, or Both. These options are useful if you are using the Tables feature to create forms.

EXERCISE 2

Bolding and Italicizing Selected Cell Contents

1. At a clear editing window, open Ch 25, Ex 01.
2. Save the document with Save As and name it Ch 25, Ex 02.
3. Change the appearance of cells A4 to A10 to Bold by completing the following steps:
    a. Select cells A4 through A10.
    b. Click the Bold button on the Toolbar.
4. Change the appearance of cells B4 through B10 to Italics.
5. Save the document again with the same name (Ch 25, Ex 02).
6. Print and then close Ch 25, Ex 02.

Changing Size

The Position and Relative size buttons at the Font dialog box can be used to alter the size of text within cells in a table. When you click the Position button at the Font dialog box, a drop-down menu displays with the options Normal, Superscript, Subscript, and Mixed. Click the Superscript option to raise text above the text line, or click Subscript to lower text below the text line.

If you click Relative size at the Font dialog box, a drop-down menu displays with the options Normal (the default), Fine, Small, Large, Very Large, Extra Large, and Mixed. Choose one of these options to change the size of the text in the cell or selected cells. Depending on the printer you are using, all or only a portion of the options at the Relative size drop-down menu will be available.

EXERCISE

Making Multiple Formatting Changes

1. At a clear editing window, create the table shown in figure 25.4 by completing the following steps:
   a. Create a table with 4 columns and 11 rows.
   b. Change the width of the first column to 4 inches.
   c. Join cells A1 through D1.
   d. Join cells A2 through D2.
   e. Selects cells A1 and A2, then change the justification to Center and the appearance to Bold.
   f. Select cells B3 through D3, then change the justification to Center and the appearance to Bold.
   g. Select cells B4 through D11, then change the justification to Center.
   h. Key the text in the cells as indicated in figure 25.4.
2. Change the size of the text in cell A1 to Large by completing the following steps:
   a. Select the text in cell A1 (*OMAHA CITY SCHOOL DISTRICT*).
   b. Click Format, then Font.
   c. At the Font dialog box, click the Relative size button and then click Large at the drop-down list.
   d. Click OK.
3. Save the document and name it Ch 25, Ex 03.
4. Print and then close Ch 25, Ex 03.

Figure 25.4

OMAHA CITY SCHOOL DISTRICT			
Technology Study Question #4			
What technology would improve your job?	**H.S.**	**J.H.S.**	**E.S.**
1. Networking of computers.	3	2	2
2. Computers in the classroom for student use.	2	1	1
3. Adequate access to phone, intercoms, and FAX.	1	5	4
4. Systematic upgrading of hardware/software.	6	4	7
5. Computer in every classroom for teacher use.	4	9	5
6. Improved access to student information.	7	7	4
7. District-wide technology plan.	9	5	3
8. More frequent maintenance cycles.	3	5	3

Formatting Tables 591

Formatting Columns

If you click the Column tab at the Properties for Table Format dialog box, the dialog box displays as shown in figure 25.5.

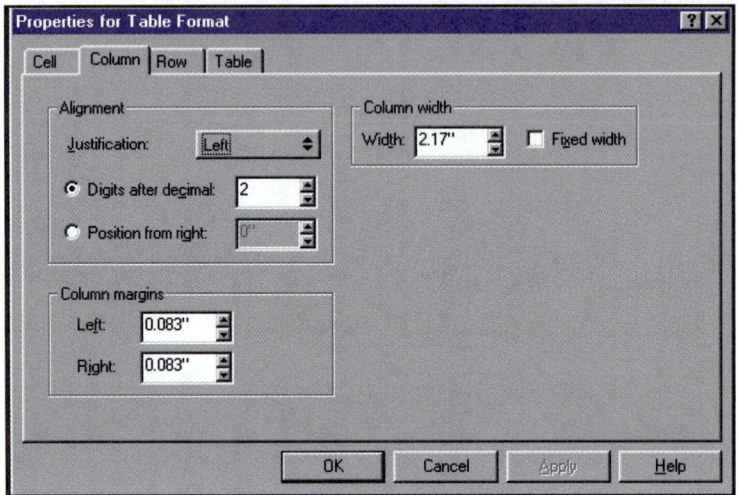

Figure 25.5 Properties for Table Format Dialog Box with Column Tab Selected

Changing Alignment

The Justification option in the Alignment section of the Properties for Table Format dialog box is used to change the alignment of text within cells in a column. By default, text in a cell is aligned at the left margin of the cell. The Justification options are the same as those available at the Properties for Table Format dialog box with the Cell tab selected.

By default, numbers within cells align two digits from the right edge of the cell. This can be changed with the Digits after decimal option. This option does not specify how many digits are displayed after the decimal but how far from the right edge of the cell the number will display. Increase the number to move text away from the right edge of cells or decrease the number to move text closer to the right edge.

You can also use the Position from right option to determine how far text displays from the right margin. Increasing the measurement moves the text away from the right margin; decreasing the measurement moves the text closer.

Changing Column Margins

Each cell contains a default left and right margin of 0.083" (about 1/12th of an inch). Increase the number to move text away from the left or right edge of the column; decrease the number to move text closer to the left or right edge of the column.

Changing Column Width

Use the Width option at the Properties for Table Format dialog box with the Column tab selected to change the column width. You learned about this option in chapter 24.

EXERCISE 4

Changing Column Width and Justification

1. At a clear editing window, create the memo shown in figure 25.6 by completing the following steps:
   a. Change the font to 12-point GeoSlab703 Lt BT (or a similar serif typeface).
   b. Key the headings and the first paragraph in the memo.
   c. With the insertion point a double space below the first paragraph, create the table by completing the following steps:
      (1) Create a table with three columns and six rows.
      (2) Change the width of the first column to 2.5 inches, the width of the second column to 1.8 inches, and the width of the third column to 2.2 inches.
      (3) Change the justification of the second column to Center by completing the following steps:
         (a) Position the insertion point in any cell in the second column.
         (b) Click Table, then Format.
         (c) At the Properties for Table Format dialog box, click the Column tab.
         (d) Click the Justification button, then click Center at the drop-down menu.
         (e) Click OK.
      (4) Change the justification of the third column to Right by completing steps similar to those in 1c(3).
      (5) Key the text in the columns as indicated.
      (6) After keying the text in the columns, position the insertion point a double space below the table, then key the remainder of the memo.
2. Save the document and name it Ch 25, Ex 04.
3. Print and then close Ch 25, Ex 04.

Formatting Tables

Figure 25.6

DATE: February 9, 1998

TO: Jack Eismann

FROM: Joni Kapshaw

SUBJECT: MARCH NEWSLETTER

The following information needs to be included in the March newsletter under the heading, "Newsletter Resources."

Superintendent	Pat Windslow	Administrative Offices
Assistant Superintendent	Jocelyn Cook	Administrative Offices
Director, Human Resources	Cheryl Woodburn	District Headquarters
Director, Curriculum Develop.	William Cho	District Headquarters
Newsletter Editor	Joni Kapshaw	Nyland High School
Newsletter Assistant Editor	Jack Eismann	Leland Elementary School

Please include how employees can submit articles or items of interest to be published in the newsletter.

xx:Ch 25, Ex 04

Formatting Rows

With options at the Properties for Table Format dialog box with the Row tab selected, shown in figure 25.7, you can specify the number of lines in a row, the height of the row, and the row top and bottom margins.

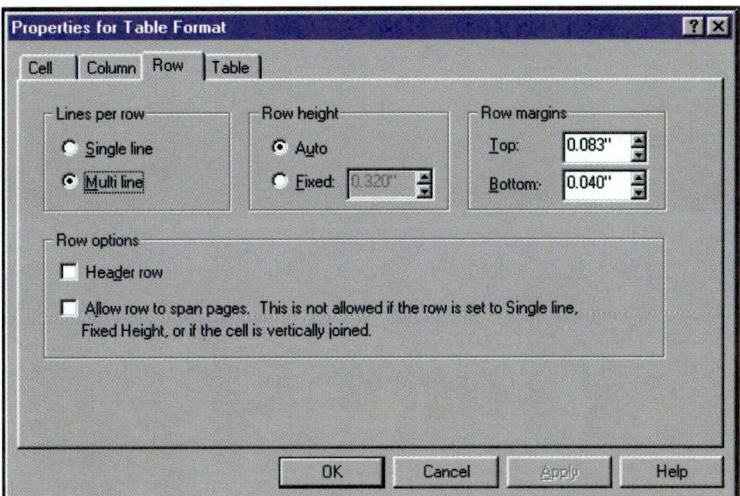

Figure 25.7 Properties for Table Format Dialog Box with Row Tab Selected

By default, WordPerfect determines the amount of vertical space in a row by the amount of text in the cells. The cell with the most lines of text sets the height for the entire row. You can use the options at the Properties for Table Format dialog box with the Row tab selected to limit the amount of text that can be entered into cells within the row, or to specify a minimum amount of space, regardless of what the cell contains. Changes made at the dialog box affect all cells in the row in which the insertion point is positioned.

The Lines per row section contains two options—Single line and Multi line—and the Row height section also contains two options—Auto and Fixed. The default is Multi line and Auto. At these settings, the row height automatically adjusts to accommodate any number of lines entered in a cell.

If you change the Row height to Fixed and retain the Lines per row at Multi line, you can enter multiple lines up to a specific height. You will use this combination when creating the calendar in exercise 5.

If you change the Lines per row to Single line and leave the Row height at Auto, WordPerfect will automatically adjust the row height to accommodate a single line of text regardless of the height of the text (size). At these settings, pressing the Enter key within a cell causes the insertion point to move to the next cell.

Changing the Lines per row to Single line and the Row height to Fixed maintains a fixed height and allows you to enter only one line of text.

The default top margin for cells is 0.083" and the default bottom margin is 0.040". You can decrease these numbers to allow text closer to the top and/or bottom of the cell, or increase the numbers to move text further away.

EXERCISE 5

Changing Row Height in a Calendar

1. At a clear editing window, create the calendar shown in figure 25.8 by completing the following steps:
   a. Key the title, **MAY 1998**, centered and bolded, then press the Enter key three times.
   b. Create a table that contains seven columns and six rows.
   c. Change the row height to 1 inch for each row by completing the following steps:
      (1) Select cells A1 through A6.
      (2) Click Table, then Format.
      (3) At the Properties for Table Format dialog box, click the Row tab.
      (4) At the Properties for Table Format dialog box with the Row tab selected, click the radio button before the Fixed option, then key **1**.
      (5) Click OK.
   d. Move the insertion point to cell F1 then key **1**. Move the insertion point to each of the cells, and key the remaining numbers as displayed in figure 25.8.
2. Save the calendar and name it Ch 25, Ex 05.
3. Print and then close Ch 25, Ex 05.

Figure 25.8

MAY 1998

					1	2
3	4	5	6	7	8	9
10	11	12	13	14	15	16
17	18	19	20	21	22	23
24	25	26	27	28	29	30
31						

Creating a Header Row

The Hea<u>d</u>er row option at the Properties for Table Format dialog box with the Row tab selected is useful in a table that spans more than one page. A header row may contain multiple rows, if necessary, and the header will display at the beginning of the second page. The header row on the second page displays in the Page and Two Page viewing modes but not the Draft mode. In the Status Bar, the header row cell(s) displays with an asterisk (for example, Cell A1*, Cell B1*, Cell C1*, etc.).

EXERCISE 6

Creating a Header Row

1. At a clear editing window, open Report 05.
2. Save the report with Save As and name it Ch 25, Ex 06.
3. Create a header row for the table at the end of the first page by completing the following steps:
   a. Position the insertion point in any cell in the first row of the table (toward the end of the first page).
   b. Click T<u>a</u>ble, then F<u>o</u>rmat.
   c. At the Properties for Table Format dialog box, click the Row tab.
   d. At the Properties for Table Format dialog box with the Row tab selected, click Hea<u>d</u>er row.
   e. Click OK.
4. Save the report again with the same name (Ch 25, Ex 06).
5. Print and then close Ch 25, Ex 06.

Formatting a Table

When formatting a table, you can format a specific cell, selected cells, columns of cells, or the entire table. When you click the Table tab at the Properties for Table Format dialog box, the dialog box displays as shown in figure 25.9.

Figure 25.9

Properties for Table Format Dialog Box with Table Tab Selected

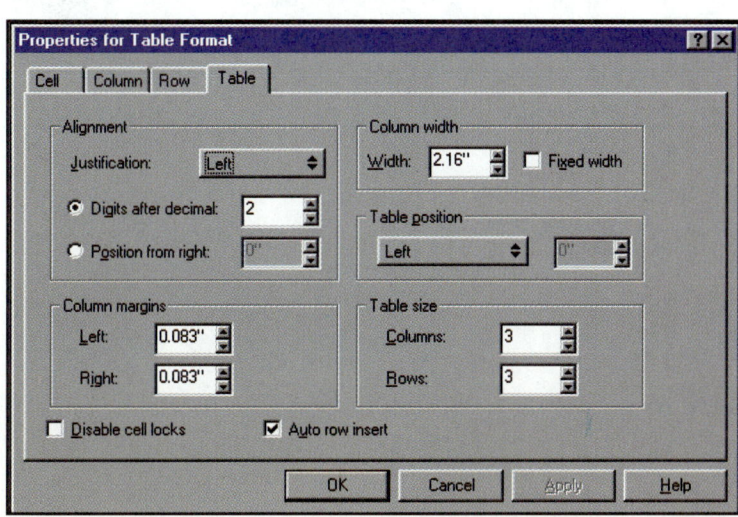

Formatting Tables 597

The options at this dialog box are basically the same as the options found in the Properties for Table Format dialog box with the Column tab selected. The Properties for Table Format dialog box with the Table tab selected contains two options that apply only to the entire table—Disable cell locks and Table position. Use the Disable cell locks to disable any cells that you have locked.

Use the Table position option to change the position of the table on the page. By default, the table aligns at the left margin of the document. This can be changed to Right, Center, Full, or From Left Edge. Click the Right option to align the table at the right margin of the document. The Center option will center the table between the left and right margins of the document. Click Full to align the table at the left and right margins of the document. Use the From Left Edge option to specify the distance from the left margin where you want the table positioned.

EXERCISE

Changing Column and Table Formatting

1. At a clear editing window, key the memo shown in figure 25.10 by completing the following steps:
   a. Key the headings and the first paragraph of the memo.
   b. With the insertion point a double space below the first paragraph, create a table that contains three columns and three rows.
   c. Change the width of each column to 1.5 inches.
   d. Change the justification of the second column to Center.
   e. Change the justification of the third column to Right.
   f. Change the position of the table to Center by completing the following steps:
      (1) Position the insertion point in any cell in the table.
      (2) Click Table, then Format.
      (3) At the Properties for Table Format dialog box, click the Table tab.
      (4) At the Properties for Table Format dialog box with the Table tab selected, click the Table position button, then click Center at the drop-down list.
      (5) Click OK.
   g. Key the text in the cells as indicated in the figure.
   h. After keying the text in the table cells, move the insertion point a double space below the table, then key the remaining text in the memo.
2. Save the memo and name it Ch 25, Ex 07.
3. Print and then close Ch 25, Ex 07.

Figure 25.10

DATE: February 6, 1998

TO: Steven Ayala

FROM: Paula Kerns

SUBJECT: DATABASE TRAINING

Three departments have requested training on the new database program. I spoke with Mandy Pitkin in Computer Services about the availability of the computer training center. After our discussion, I established this tentative schedule.

Medical Services	February 19	9:30 - 11:30 a.m.
Admitting	March 3	3:00 - 5:00 p.m.
Emergency Room	March 18	9:00 - 11:00 a.m.

Please check these days and times to see if they conflict with other training offered by our department. If the times are convenient, I will prepare an informational memo for each department.

xx:Ch 25, Ex 07

Changing Numeric Format

With the Numeric Format option at the Table drop-down menu, you can specify how numbers are used (such as values or text), how numbers are displayed, and how numbers are printed in a table. When you click Table, then Numeric Format, the Properties for Table Numeric Format dialog box displays as shown in figure 25.11. You can also display this dialog box by clicking the Numeric Format button on the Tables Toolbar or by clicking the right mouse button, then clicking Numeric Format.

Numeric Format

Figure 25.11

Properties for Table Numeric Format Dialog Box

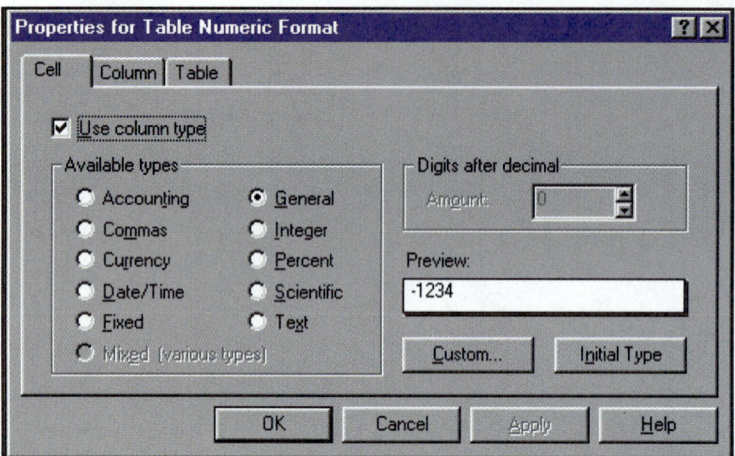

At this dialog box, you can specify numbering type for the current cell, all cells in a column, or all cells in a table. To specify which cells are to be affected, click the appropriate tab at the top of the dialog box. By default, the Cell tab is selected.

The Use column type option is on by default. At this setting, the number type already defined for the current column will be applied to the current cell. Remove the check mark from this check box if you do not want the column number type applied to the current cell.

The Available types section displays the variety of methods that can be used for displaying numbers. The default numbering type is General. At this setting, numbers display without a thousands separator and no trailing zeroes to the right of the decimal point. The other types are explained in figure 25.12. As you select different numbering types, the Preview box at the right side of the dialog box reflects the numbering type.

Figure 25.12

Numeric Formats

Accounting	Up to 15 decimal places display in a number, along with the currency symbol, thousands separator, and the decimal align character. The currency symbol displays at the edge of the column.
Commas	Up to 15 decimal places display in a number along with the thousands separator. Negative numbers are displayed within parentheses.
Currency	Up to 15 decimal places display in a number, the currency symbol, the thousands separator, and a decimal align character.
Date/Time	Converts numbers into the current date and time format.
Fixed	Up to 15 decimal places display in a number. The thousands separator does not display.
Integer	No trailing zeroes are displayed to the right of the decimal point. Numbers display without the thousands separator.
Percent	Numbers are displayed as percent values (multiplied by 100) with the percent symbol (%) included.
Scientific	Numbers display in scientific notation up to 15 decimal places.
Text	Designates the contents of the cell as text and will not use any numbers in calculations.

Chapter 25

EXERCISE 8

Changing Numeric Format

1. At a clear editing window, create the table shown in figure 25.13 by completing the following steps:
   a. Create a table with 3 columns and 10 rows.
   b. Change the width of each column to 1.5 inches.
   c. Change the position of the table to Center. (For assistance, refer to exercise 7, step 1f.)
   d. Join cells A1 through C1.
   e. Join cells A2 through C2.
   f. Select cell A1, then change the justification to Center, the appearance to Bold, and the relative size to Large.
   g. Select cell A2, then change the justification to Center and the appearance to Bold.
   h. Select cells A3 through C3, then change the justification to Center and the appearance to Bold.
   i. Change the numbering type to Currency for cells B4 through C10 and change the alignment to Decimal Align by completing the following steps:
      (1) Select cells B4 through C10.
      (2) Click Table, then Numeric Format.
      (3) At the Properties for Table Numeric Format dialog box with the Cell tab selected, click Currency in the Available types section.
      (4) Click OK to close the dialog box.
      (5) With the cells still selected, click Table, then Format.
      (6) At the Properties for Table Format dialog box with the Cell tab selected, click the Justification button, then click Decimal Align.
      (7) Click OK to close the dialog box.
   j. Key the text in the cells as indicated in figure 25.13. Do not key the dollar signs ($) or commas (but do key the decimal points). WordPerfect automatically adds a dollar sign and a comma because the number type is Currency.
2. Save the document and name it Ch 25, Ex 08.
3. Print and then close Ch 25, Ex 08.

Figure 25.13

UNITED DISTRIBUTION CENTER		
Sales in Selected States		
State	Last Year	This Year
Arkansas	$1,204,392.50	$1,139,302.59
California	$3,459,034.20	$3,545,209.65
Delaware	$995,302.85	$1,109,384.22
Florida	$893,410.47	$943,120.87
Montana	$558,390.21	$522,503.40
North Dakota	$421,329.84	$483,204.80
Pennsylvania	$2,298,432.58	$2,103,438.59

Changing Cell Lines and Fill

When a table is created, all lines around cells are single lines. These lines can be customized with options from the Properties for Table Lines/Fill dialog box, shown in figure 25.14. To display this dialog box, click T<u>a</u>ble, then click <u>L</u>ines/Fill. You can also display this dialog box by clicking the Lines/Fill button on the Tables Toolbar or clicking <u>L</u>ines/Fill at the QuickMenu.

Lines/Fill

With options from the Properties for Table Lines/Fill dialog box, you can specify the type of lines used to form cells in the table. You can also create a border around a table. By default, a table does not contain a border. At the Properties for Table Lines/Fill dialog box you can create a border for a table. By default, a cell contains a white background. You can fill cells in a table with shaded fill, insert a background color, and/or change the foreground color.

602 Chapter 25

Figure 25.14

Properties for Table Lines/Fill Dialog Box

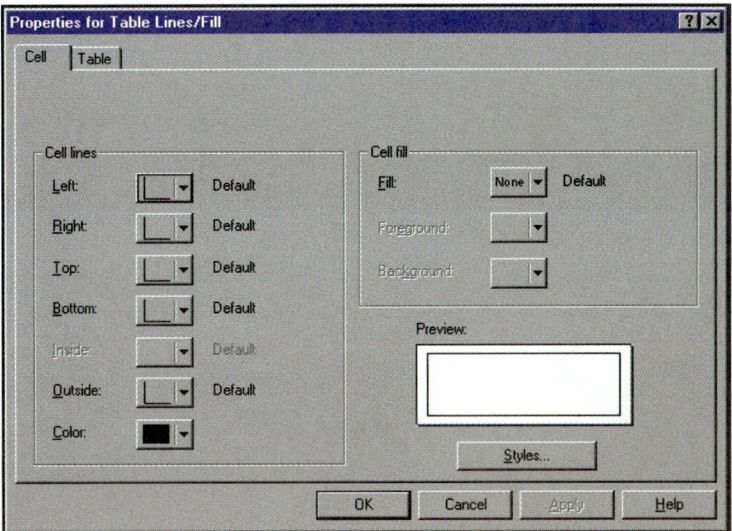

Changing Cell Lines

A table consists of two elements—lines and a border. Lines make up the columns, rows, and cells. The border surrounds the table and masks the outer table lines. These are two distinct elements and can be customized separately.

Table lines or border lines can be customized with the Cell lines options at the Properties for Table Lines/Fill dialog box. You can customize all cell lines within a table, border lines, specific lines within a cell, all lines within selected cells, or all lines outside selected cells.

To customize a line within a cell, click one of the Cell lines options at the Properties for Table Lines/Fill dialog box. For example, click the arrow pointer on the button to the right of the Left option and the box shown in figure 25.15 displays.

Figure 25.15

Cell Lines Options

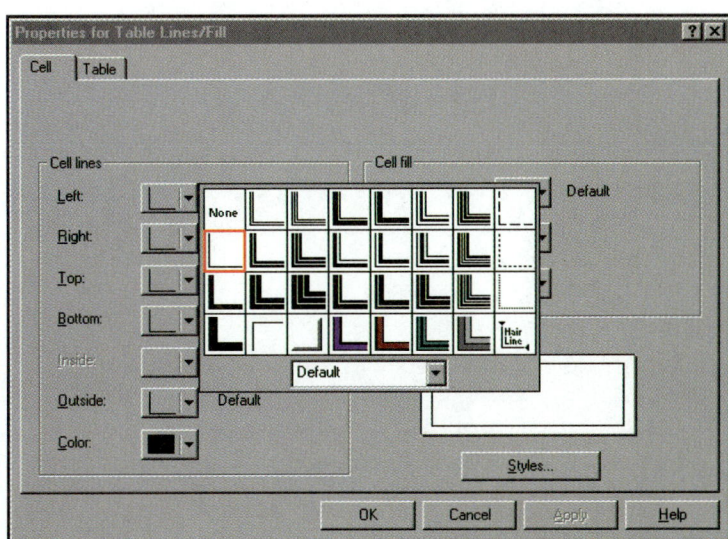

Formatting Tables 603

The box contains a variety of line options such as double lines, triple lines, quadruple lines, dashed lines, and dotted lines. The same options will display if you click the buttons immediately to the right of the Right, Top, Bottom, Inside, or Outside options.

You can also change cell lines with drop-down menus. To display a cell line option drop-down menu, position the arrow pointer on the Left, Right, Top, Bottom, Inside, or Outside button, click the left mouse button, then click the down-pointing triangle to the right of the text box containing the word *Default*. The options at this drop-down menu are the same as the visual icons displayed above it.

When changes are made to Cell lines options, the change is reflected in the Preview box at the right side of the dialog box.

EXERCISE

Changing Line Styles

1. At a clear editing window, open Ch 25, Ex 01.
2. Save the document with Save As and name it Ch 25, Ex 09.
3. Change the top lines of cells A3 through C3 to Double by completing the following steps:
   a. Select cells A3 through C3.
   b. Click Table, then Lines/Fill.
   c. At the Properties for Table Lines/Fill dialog box, display the box of Top options by clicking the Top button.
   d. At the box of options, click the Double option (second option from the left in the top row).
   e. Click OK.
4. Change the top lines of cells A4 through C4 to Double by completing steps similar to those in 3.
5. Save the document again with the same name (Ch 25, Ex 09).
6. Print and then close Ch 25, Ex 09.

EXERCISE

More Practice with Changing Line Styles

1. At a clear editing window, open Ch 25, Ex 07.
2. Save the document with Save As and name it Ch 25, Ex 10.
3. Remove the inside lines of the table by completing the following steps:
   a. Select all cells in the table.
   b. Position the arrow pointer anywhere in the table, click the right mouse button, then click Lines/Fill.
   c. At the Properties for Table Lines/Fill dialog box, click the Inside button in the Cell lines section. (This causes a palette of line choices to display.)
   d. At the palette of line choices, click the None option (first option in the first row).
   e. Click OK.
4. Save the document again with the same name (Ch 25, Ex 10).
5. Print and then close Ch 25, Ex 10.

Changing Line Color

By default, lines in a table are black. You can change the color of table lines with the Color option at the Properties for Table Lines/Fill dialog box. You can change the line color of an individual cell or you can select a group of cells and then change the line color. The line color will display in the editing window but will not print unless you are using a color printer.

EXERCISE

Changing Line Color

1. At a clear editing window, open Ch 25, Ex 08.
2. Save the document with Save As and name it Ch 25, Ex 11.
3. Change the cell lines in cell C4 to bright red by completing the following steps:
    a. Position the insertion point in cell C4.
    b. Click the Lines/Fill button on the Tables Toolbar.
    c. At the Properties for Table Lines/Fill dialog box, display the box of color options by clicking the Color button.
    d. At the box of color options, click the bright red option (fourth option from the right in the top row).
    e. Click OK.
4. Change the cell lines in cell C8 to bright red by completing steps similar to those in 3.
5. Change the cell lines in cell C10 to bright red by completing steps similar to those in 3.
6. Save the document again with the same name (Ch 25, Ex 11).
7. Print Ch 25, Ex 11. (Complete this step only if you have a color printer; if not, skip this step.)
8. Close Ch 25, Ex 11.

Adding Fill

With the Fill option in the Cell fill section of the Properties for Table Lines/Fill dialog box, you can add a fill to a cell, selected cells, or all cells in a table. WordPerfect provides a variety of fills including various shades of gray and designs and patterns such as Checkerboard, Chainlink, Fish Scale, and Honeycomb.

You can also add fill with the Fill drop-down menu. To display this drop-down menu, click the Fill button, move the arrow pointer to the down-pointing triangle to the right of the text box containing the word *Default*, then click the left mouse button.

When changes are made to the Fill option, the change is reflected in the Preview box at the right side of the dialog box.

EXERCISE 12

Changing Cell Fill

1. At a clear editing window, open Ch 25, Ex 01.
2. Save the document with Save As and name it Ch 25, Ex 12.
3. Change the fill to Button Fill for cells A3 through C3 by completing the following steps:
   a. Select cells A3 through C3.
   b. Click T<u>a</u>ble, then <u>L</u>ines/Fill.
   c. At the Properties for Table Lines/Fill dialog box, display the box of fill options by clicking the <u>F</u>ill button.
   d. At the box of fill options, click the Button Fill option (first option in the third row).
   e. Click OK.
4. Save the document again with the same name (Ch 25, Ex 12).
5. Print and then close Ch 25, Ex 12.

Changing Foreground and Background Color

If fill has been added to a cell, selected cells, or all cells in the table, the foreground and/or background color of the cell can be changed. When you add a fill, then click For<u>e</u>ground or <u>B</u>ackground, a box of color options displays. This box of color options is the same as the box that displays at the <u>C</u>olor option.

EXERCISE 13

Adding Fill and Changing Colors

1. At a clear editing window, open Ch 25, Ex 08.
2. Save the document with Save As and name it Ch 25, Ex 13.
3. Add 10% Fill and change the foreground color to light blue for cells C4 through C10 by completing the following steps:
   a. Select cells C4 through C10.
   b. Click the Lines/Fill button on the Tables Toolbar.
   c. At the Properties for Table Lines/Fill dialog box, click the <u>F</u>ill button.
   d. At the box of fill options, click the down-pointing triangle at the right side of the text box that displays at the bottom of the fill options box.
   e. At the pop-up menu that displays, click *10% Fill*. (You may need to scroll up the list to display *10% Fill*.)
   f. Click the For<u>e</u>ground color button, then click the light blue color (fifth color from the right in the first row).
   g. Click OK.
4. Save the document again with the same name (Ch 25, Ex 13).
5. Print Ch 25, Ex 13. (Complete this step only if you have a color printer; if not, skip this step.)
6. Close Ch 25, Ex 13.

606 Chapter 25

Changing Table Border Lines and Fill

The Properties for Table Lines/Fill dialog box contains two tabs—Cell and Table. When the Table tab is selected, the options change as shown in figure 25.16. At the Properties for Table Lines/Fill dialog box with the Table tab selected, you can change the Default cell lines for all lines in the table or just the Table border; add fill; and change the foreground and background colors.

Changing Default Cell Lines

With the Line option in the Properties for Table Lines/Fill dialog box with the Table tab selected, you can customize all lines within a table at one time. The line choices are the same as those from cell lines for individual cells. You can also remove all lines by clicking <None>.

Figure 25.16

Properties for Table Lines/Fill Dialog Box with Table Tab Selected

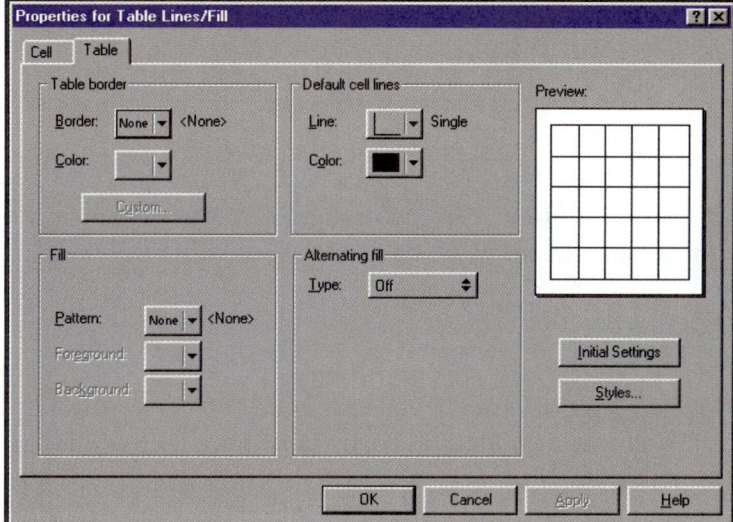

Customizing All Lines in a Table

1. At a clear editing window, open Ch 25, Ex 07.
2. Save the document with Save As and name it Ch 25, Ex 14.
3. Change all lines in the table to Button Bottom/Right by completing the following steps:
    a. Position the insertion point in any cell within the table.
    b. Click Table, then Lines/Fill.
    c. At the Table Lines/Fill dialog box, click the Table tab.
    d. At the Properties for Table Lines/Fill dialog box with the Table tab selected, display the box of Line options by clicking the Line button.
    e. At the box of options, click the Button Bottom/Right option (third option from the left in the bottom row).
    f. Click OK.
4. Save the document again with the same name (Ch 25, Ex 14).
5. Print and then close Ch 25, Ex 14.

Formatting Tables

EXERCISE 15

Removing All Lines in a Table

1. At a clear editing window, open Ch 25, Ex 07.
2. Save the document with Save As and name it Ch 25, Ex 15.
3. Remove all lines from the table by completing the following steps:
   a. Position the insertion point in any cell within the table.
   b. Click the Lines/Fill button on the Tables Toolbar.
   c. At the Table Lines/Fill dialog box, click the Table tab.
   d. At the Properties for Table Lines/Fill dialog box with the Table tab selected, click the Line button.
   e. At the box of options, click the <None> option (first option in the first row).
   f. Click OK.
4. Save the document again with the same name (Ch 25, Ex 15).
5. Print and then close Ch 25, Ex 15.

Changing Line Color

By default, lines in a table are black. You can change the color of all lines in the table with the Color option. The line color will display on the screen but will not print unless you are using a color printer.

Adding Border Lines

As mentioned earlier, a table consists of lines and a border. The table lines form the cells and rows. A border surrounds the table and overlays the outer table lines. The Border options available are the same as the Line options.

EXERCISE 16

Adding a Thick/Thin Border

1. At a clear editing window, open Ch 25, Ex 08.
2. Save the document with Save As and name it Ch 25, Ex 16.
3. Add a Thick/Thin 2 border around the table by completing the following steps:
   a. Position the insertion point in any cell within the table.
   b. Click the Lines/Fill button on the Tables Toolbar.
   c. At the Table Lines/Fill dialog box, click the Table tab.
   d. At the Properties for Table Lines/Fill dialog box with the Table tab selected, click the Border button.
   e. At the box of options, click the Thick/Thin 2 option (fourth option from the left in the third row).
   f. Click OK.
4. Save the document again with the same name (Ch 25, Ex 16).
5. Print and then close Ch 25, Ex 16.

608 Chapter 25

Adding Fill

A fill can be added to all cells within a table with the Pattern option in the Fill section of the Properties for Table Lines/Fill dialog box with the Table tab selected. To add a fill, complete steps similar to those described earlier for adding fill to individual cells.

EXERCISE 17

Adding Fill to All Cells

1. At a clear editing window, open Ch 25, Ex 04.
2. Save the document with Save As and name it Ch 25, Ex 17.
3. Add a double line border to the table in the memo.
4. Add 10% Fill to all cells in the table by completing the following steps:
    a. Position the insertion point in any cell within the table.
    b. Click the Lines/Fill button on the Tables Toolbar.
    c. At the Properties for Table Lines/Fill dialog box, click the Table tab.
    d. At the Table Lines/Fill dialog box with the Table tab selected, click the Pattern button.
    e. At the box of pattern options, click the 10% Fill option (third option from the left in the first row).
    f. Click OK.
5. Save the document again with the same name (Ch 25, Ex 17).
6. Print and then close Ch 25, Ex 17.

Changing Foreground and Background Color

Foreground and background color can be changed for all cells in a table. The color options available are the same as the foreground and background color options for individual cells. To change foreground or background color, complete steps similar to those described earlier for individual cells.

Changing Default

If you customize table lines, border, fill, or color and want to use these changes for the current session and future sessions, click Initial Settings. This button is located at the bottom right of the Properties for Table Lines/Fill dialog box with the Table tab selected.

Inserting Formulas in a Table

WordPerfect contains options that can be used to create a spreadsheet with the Tables feature. In this chapter, you will learn steps to create, insert, and calculate basic formulas in a table. For more information on formulas and functions, please refer to the WordPerfect Help system.

Inserting Formulas

A formula that will calculate numbers in rows or columns can be inserted in a cell. To insert a formula, display the Formula Bar shown in figure 25.17. To display the Formula Bar, click Table, then Formula; click the Formula Bar button on the Tables Toolbar; or position the arrow pointer in the table, click the right mouse button, then click Formula Bar. With the Formula Bar displayed, you can enter a formula in a specific cell. If changes are made to cells affected by the formula, the value of the formula can be recalculated.

Formula Bar

Formatting Tables 609

Figure 25.17

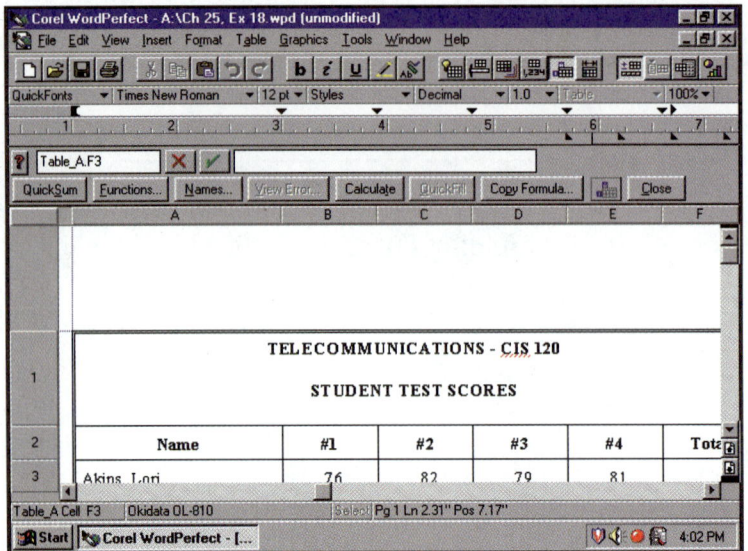

Formula Bar

Four basic operators can be used when writing formulas: the plus sign for addition, the minus sign (hyphen) for subtraction, the asterisk for multiplication, and the forward slash (/) for division. Examples of how formulas can be written are shown in figure 25.18.

Figure 25.18

Example Formulas

Cell E4 is the total price of items.
Cell B4 contains the quantity of items, and cell D4 contains the unit price. The formula for cell E4 is B4*D4. (This formula multiplies the quantity of items in cell B4 by the unit price in cell D4.)

Cell D3 is the percentage of increase of sales from the previous year.
Cell B3 contains the amount of sales for the previous year, and cell C3 contains the amount of sales for the current year. The formula for cell D3 is (C3-B3)/C3*100. (This formula subtracts the amount of sales last year from the amount of sales this year. The remaining amount is divided by the amount of sales this year and then multiplied by 100 to display the product as a percentage.)

Cell E1 is the average of test scores.
Cells A1 through D1 contain test scores. The formula to calculate the average score is (A1+B1+C1+D1)/4. (This formula adds the scores from cells A1 through D1, then divides that sum by 4.) You can also enter the formula as ave(A1:D1). The word "ave" tells WordPerfect to average all entries in cells A1 through D1. The colon is used to indicate a range.

If there are two or more operators in a calculation, WordPerfect calculates from left to right. If you want to change the order of calculation, use parentheses around the part of the calculation to be performed first.

A cell entry can be identified as a formula in the Formula Bar. With the insertion point positioned in the cell where the formula is to be inserted, position the arrow pointer in the Formula Bar edit box, then click the left mouse button. (This edit box is immediately to the right of the green check mark.) Key the formula, then click the green check mark in the Formula Bar or press Enter.

If you want to cancel a formula as you are writing it, click the red X on the Formula Bar. This removes any formula you have entered so far. If you want to write another formula, position the arrow pointer in the Formula Bar edit box, click the left mouse button, then key the formula.

Copying Formulas

Once a formula has been entered in a cell, use options at the Copy Formula dialog box to copy the formula to another cell or to copy a relative version of the formula down or across to other cells. To display the Copy Formula dialog box, shown in figure 25.19, click Table, then Copy Formula; or click Copy Formula at the Formula Bar.

The Copy Formula dialog box contains three options—To Cell, Down, and Right. Use the To Cell option to copy a formula to another cell. When you use this option, the formula is copied exactly to the specified cell. Use the Down and Right options if you want to copy a relative version of the formula to other cells. With either option, you would key the number of times the formula is to be copied, then click OK. When a formula is copied, it is copied relatively. For example, if the formula A1 + B1 +C1 in cell D1 is copied down, the formula changes to A2 + B2 + C2 in cell D2.

Figure 25.19

Copy Formula Dialog Box

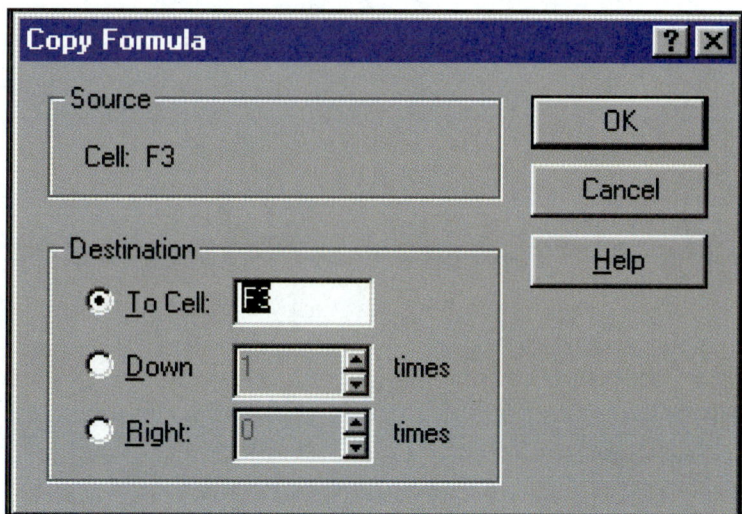

Calculating Numbers in a Table

When a formula is inserted in a table that contains numbers, the formula is automatically calculated and the answer is inserted in the cell (this default may vary). If changes are made to the numbers in cells, the formula is automatically recalculated. You can control whether recalculation occurs automatically or not at the Calculate dialog box, shown in figure 25.20. Display the Calculate dialog box by clicking Table, then Calculate; or by clicking Calculate at the Formula Bar. To turn off automatic calculation, click Off, then click OK. If you want WordPerfect to automatically calculate any formulas in a table, click Calculate table. Click Calculate document to calculate all formulas in a document.

Figure 25.20

Calculate Dialog Box

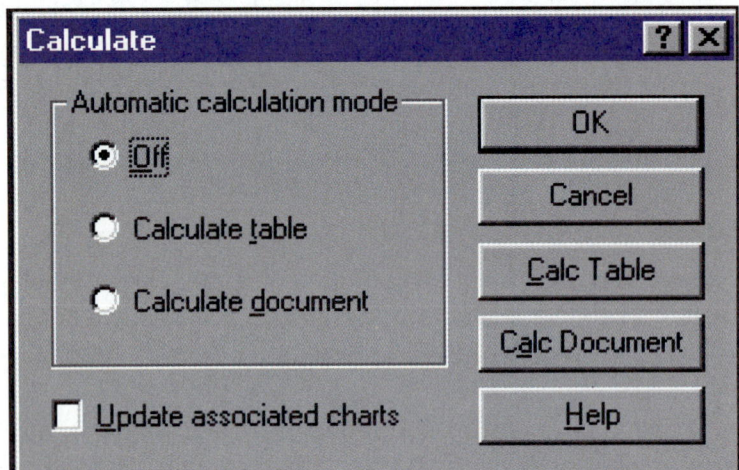

Inserting a Test Score Formula

1. At a clear editing window, open Table 01.
2. Save the document with Save As and name it Ch 25, Ex 18.
3. Turn on automatic calculation of formulas in the table by completing the following steps:
   a. With the insertion point positioned in any cell in the table, click T<u>a</u>ble, then C<u>a</u>lculate.
   b. At the Calculate dialog box, click Calculate <u>t</u>able.
   c. Click OK.
4. Insert a formula to calculate test scores in cell F3 by completing the following steps:
   a. Position the insertion point in cell F3.
   b. Turn on the display of the Formula Bar by clicking the Formula Bar button on the Tables Toolbar.
   c. Click the left mouse button in the Formula Bar edit box. (This box is located to the right of the green check mark.)
   d. Key **(B3+C3+D3+E3)/4**. (You can also enter **ave(B3:E3)**.)
   e. Click the green check mark to accept the formula and calculate the result in cell F3.
5. Copy the formula down five rows by completing the following steps:
   a. With the insertion point still positioned in cell F3 (this cell contains the formula), click the Copy Formula button on the Formula Bar.
   b. At the Copy Formula dialog box, click <u>D</u>own.
   c. Key **5**.
   d. Click OK.
6. Save the document again with the same name (Ch 25, Ex 18).
7. Print Ch 25, Ex 18.
8. Make the following changes to the test scores:

> Devries, Suzanne   #1, change *57* to *70*
> #4, change *58* to *75*
> Gaudette, Nicolas   #3, change *62* to *74*
> #4, change *60* to *76*
>
> 9. Press the Tab key to move the insertion point to a different cell. This recalculates the average.
> 10. Save the document again with the same name (Ch 25, Ex 18).
> 11. Print and then close Ch 25, Ex 18.

EXERCISE

Editing Cell Format and Inserting a Formula

1. At a clear editing window, create the memo shown in figure 25.21 by completing the following steps:
   a. Key the headings and first paragraph in an appropriate memo format.
   b. With the insertion point a double space below the first paragraph, create a table with four columns and seven rows.
   c. Change the width of the first column to 2.5 inches.
   d. Select cells A1 through D1, then change the justification to Center and the appearance to Bold.
   e. Select cells B2 through D7, then change the justification to Decimal Align.
   f. With cells B2 through D7 still selected, change the number type to Accounting.
   g. Add a double line border to the table.
   h. Add 10% Fill to cells A1 through D1.
   i. Key the information in the cells as shown in figure 25.21. Use Ctrl + Tab to indent the text in cells A2 through A7. When keying the numbers, do not key the dollar signs or the commas (but do key the decimal points). WordPerfect automatically inserts them because the number type was changed to Accounting.
   j. Key the remaining text in the memo.
2. Save the document and name it Ch 25, Ex 19.
3. Print Ch 25, Ex 19.
4. Position the insertion point in cell D2, then insert the formula *C2-B2* with the Formula Bar by completing the following steps:
   a. With the insertion point positioned in cell D2, click the Formula Bar button on the Tables Toolbar.
   b. Click the left mouse button in the Formula Bar edit box. (This is the box to the right of the green check mark.)
   c. Key **C2-B2**.
   d. Click the green check mark in the Formula Bar.
   e. With the insertion point still positioned in cell D2, copy the formula down five rows.
   f. Click Close to close the Formula Bar.
5. Save the memo again with the same name (Ch 25, Ex 19).
6. Print and then close Ch 25, Ex 19.

Formatting Tables

Figure 25.21

DATE: June 7, 1998; TO: Stanley Lucas, Principal; FROM: Mildred Hansen, PTO President; SUBJECT: FUND-RAISING
The fund-raising efforts this school year have been very successful because of the high number of parent volunteers. The following chart shows the expenditures and profit for each event.

Event	Costs	Profit	Net Profit
Book Fair	$ 1,785.10	$ 2,233.87	
Gift Wrap	$ 1,074.30	$ 2,209.55	
Fall Carnival	$ 644.75	$ 1,492.50	
T-shirts	$ 126.50	$ 799.10	
Popcorn	$ 126.50	$ 432.00	
Walk-a-thon	$ 125.30	$ 2,743.50	

Many of the volunteers have agreed to be involved in the same activities next school year. Next year we can anticipate even bigger profits!
xx:Ch 25, Ex 19

Using the Sum Option

QuickSum

The QuickSum option from the Table drop-down menu or the QuickSum button on the Formula Bar adds numbers in a column or row, then inserts the answer (sum) in the cell. For example, to add all numbers in a row and then insert the sum, position the insertion point in the cell where the sum is to be inserted, then click Table, then QuickSum. You can also click the QuickSum button on the Formula Bar or press Ctrl + =. The formula can be copied down or to the right. If numbers are changed, the sum is automatically recalculated.

EXERCISE 20

Using the QuickSum Option

1. At a clear editing window, open Ch 25, Ex 08.
2. Save the document with Save As and name it Ch 25, Ex 20.
3. Add a row at the end of the table.
4. Key the word **Total** in cell A11.
5. Add the numbers in the second column and insert the total in cell B11 by completing the following steps:
    a. Position the insertion point in cell B11.
    b. Click Table, then QuickSum.
6. Add the numbers in the third column and insert the total in cell C11 by completing steps similar to those in 5a and 5b.
7. Save the document again with the same name (Ch 25, Ex 20).
8. Print and then close Ch 25, Ex 20.

Formatting with SpeedFormat

WordPerfect has created a variety of table formatting options that can be applied to a table. This table formatting feature is called *SpeedFormat*. The various formatting options available at the Table SpeedFormat dialog box are shown in figure 25.22. To display this dialog box, position the insertion point in a table, then click T<u>a</u>ble, then Sp<u>e</u>edFormat. The dialog box can also be displayed by clicking the Table SpeedFormat button on the Tables Toolbar or by clicking the right mouse button, then clicking SpeedFormat.

Table SpeedFormat

The list of formatting options displays in the A<u>v</u>ailable styles list box. Click an option from this list and the preview table in the middle of the dialog box will display the formatting contained in the option. In this way, you can view the various options to find the one that suits you.

If you want to apply formatting to an individual cell, insert a check mark in the Apply <u>s</u>tyle on a cell by cell basis check box. Insert a check mark in the C<u>l</u>ear current table settings before applying check box if you want any previous formatting contained by the table to be removed.

Figure 25.22

Table SpeedFormat Dialog Box

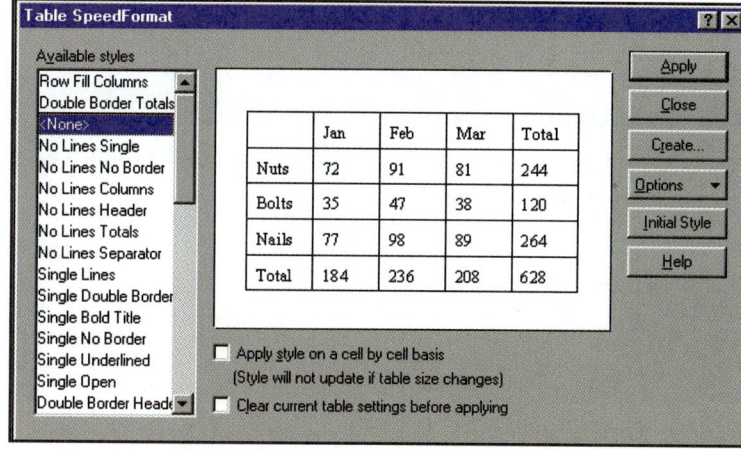

EXERCISE 21

Using Table SpeedFormat

1. At a clear editing window, open Table 01.
2. Save the document with Save As and name it Ch 25, Ex 21.
3. Apply formatting to the table at the Table SpeedFormat dialog box by completing the following steps:
   a. With the insertion point positioned in any cell in the table, click T<u>a</u>ble, then SpeedFormat.
   b. At the Table SpeedFormat dialog box, click *Double Border Totals* in the A<u>v</u>ailable styles list box. (You will need to scroll down the list of styles to display *Double Border Totals*.)
   c. Click the <u>A</u>pply button.
4. Save the document again with the same name (Ch 25, Ex 21).
5. Print and then close Ch 25, Ex 21.

Formatting Tables 615

EXERCISE 22

More Practice with Table SpeedFormat

1. At a clear editing window, open Table 01.
2. Save the document with Save As and name it Ch 25, Ex 22.
3. Apply formatting to the table at the Table SpeedFormat dialog box by completing the following steps:
   a. With the insertion point positioned in any cell in the table, click the Table SpeedFormat button on the Tables Toolbar.
   b. At the Table SpeedFormat dialog box, click *Row Fill Columns* in the Available styles list box. (You will need to scroll down the list of styles to display *Row Fill Columns*.)
   c. Click the Apply button.
4. Save the document again with the same name (Ch 25, Ex 22).
5. Print and then close Ch 25, Ex 22.

CHAPTER SUMMARY

- ▼ Additional formatting options available at the Table drop-down menu are Format, Numeric Format, SpeedFormat, Lines/Fill, Formula Bar, Copy Formula, Calculate, and QuickSum.

- ▼ At the Properties for Table Format dialog box, tabs for Cell, Column, Row, or Table expand the options available for making changes.

- ▼ With the Numeric Format option from the Table drop-down menu, you can specify how numbers are used, how numbers are displayed, and how numbers are printed in a table.

- ▼ When a table is created, all lines around cells are single lines. These lines can be customized with options from the Properties for Table Lines/Fill dialog box.

- ▼ WordPerfect contains a wide variety of options that can be used to create a spreadsheet with the Table feature. This chapter includes steps to create, insert, and calculate basic formulas in a table.

- ▼ With the Formula Bar, you can insert a formula in a cell that will calculate numbers in rows or columns.

- ▼ When a formula is inserted in a table containing numbers, the formula is automatically calculated and the answer is inserted in the cell. If changes are made to the numbers in cells, the formula is automatically recalculated.

- ▼ Use the QuickSum feature to add numbers in a column or row.

- ▼ Use the SpeedFormat feature to apply a variety of formatting options to a table.

COMMANDS REVIEW

	Mouse/Keyboard
Properties for Table Format dialog box	Table, Format; or with arrow pointer inside a table, click the right mouse button
Formula Bar	Table, Formula Bar
Calculate dialog box	Table, Calculate; or choose Calculate at the Formula Bar
Table SpeedFormat dialog box	Table, SpeedFormat

CHECK YOUR UNDERSTANDING

Completion: In the space provided at the right, indicate the correct term, command, or number.

1. The Properties for Table Format dialog box with this tab selected includes options for formatting a cell or selected cells. _____

2. By default, text in a cell is aligned at this margin in a cell. _____

3. Click this option at the Position drop-down menu at the Font dialog box to raise text above the text line. _____

4. By default, a table aligns at this margin in a document. _____

5. Add fill to cells in a table at this dialog box. _____

6. Specify how numbers are used in a table, how numbers are displayed, and how numbers are printed in a table with this option at the Table drop-down menu. _____

7. This is the default numbering type at the Properties for Table Numeric Format dialog box. _____

8. A table consists of two elements—lines and this. _____

9. The Copy Formula dialog box contains three options—To Cell, Down, and this. _____

10. Add numbers in a column or row and insert the answer (sum) in the cell by clicking this button on the Formula Bar. _____

11. This WordPerfect feature contains a variety of formatting options that can be applied to a table. _____

Write the formula that would bring about the correct calculation for each instance below.

1. In D4, calculate the difference between D2 and D3.

   _____

Formatting Tables

2. In B5, calculate the average of the scores in cells B2, B3, and B4.

3. In E1, calculate the total number of items in A1, B1, C1, and D1.

4. In D4, calculate the net pay by adding the regular salary in A4 to the overtime pay in B4 and then subtracting the tax in C4.

SKILL ASSESSMENTS

Assessment 1

1. At a clear editing window, create the document shown in figure 25.23 by completing the following steps:
   a. Create a table with four columns and eight rows.
   b. Change the width of the first column to 3.5 inches. (This should cause the other column widths to change to 1 inch.)
   c. Join cells A1 through D1.
   d. Select cells A1, A2, B2, C2, and D2, then change the justification to Center and the appearance to Bold.
   e. Select cells B3 through D8, then change the number type to Percent.
   f. With cells B3 through D8 still selected, change the justification to Center.
   g. Key the text in the cells as indicated in figure 25.23. Press Ctrl + Tab to indent the text in cells A3 through A8. When entering the percent number, key only the numbers before the decimal (i.e., 89, 67, 57, etc.). WordPerfect will automatically add the decimal, the zeros after the decimal, and the percent sign.
2. Save the table and name it Ch 25, SA 01.
3. Print and then close Ch 25, SA 01.

Figure 25.23

DENVER MEMORIAL HOSPITAL				

Percentage of Nursing Staff Participating in Continuing Education Units				
	R.N.	L.P.N.	C.N.A.
Intensive Care Unit	89.00%	67.00%	57.00%
Coronary Care Unit	75.00%	93.00%	41.00%
Labor and Delivery Unit	65.00%	71.00%	33.00%
Surgical Unit	58.00%	43.00%	39.00%
Pediatric Unit	86.00%	71.00%	57.00%
Emergency Room	56.00%	45.00%	30.00%

Assessment 2

1. At a clear editing window, create the table shown in figure 25.24 with the following specifications:
   a. Change the font to 10-point Humanst521 Lt BT (or a similar sans serif typeface).
   b. Create a table with 4 columns and 10 rows.
   c. Change the width of the first column to 4 inches.
   d. Join the cells as indicated.
   e. Change the justification of cells to Center and the appearance to Bold as indicated in the figure.
   f. Key the text in the cells as indicated in figure 25.24.
   g. Select the text in cell A1, then change the relative size to Very Large.
   h. Select the text in cell A2, then change the relative size to Large.
2. Save the document and name it Ch 25, SA 02.
3. Print and then close Ch 25, SA 02.

Figure 25.24

OMAHA CITY SCHOOL DISTRICT
Technology Study Question #5

What training do you need to utilize technology?	H.S.	J.H.S.	E.S.
1. Time for hands-on practice and exploration.	4	2	3
2. On-site technical resources to help with problems.	7	3	5
3. Updating of software/hardware.	5	2	6
4. Paid training (money, clock hours, college credits).	3	7	8
5. Training tied to curriculum.	8	4	6
6. Standardized software adoption process.	3	4	2
7. Technical training required for all staff.	2	5	4

Assessment 3

1. At a clear editing window, open Ch 25, Ex 07.
2. Save the document with Save As and name it Ch 25, SA 03.
3. Make the following changes to the table:
   a. Add 10% Fill to all cells in the table.
   b. Add a Shadow border to the table.
4. Save the document again with the same name (Ch 25, SA 03).
5. Print and then close Ch 25, SA 03.

Assessment 4

1. At a clear editing window, open Ch 25, Ex 05.
2. Save the calendar with Save As and name it Ch 25, SA 04.
3. Edit the calendar so it appears as shown in figure 25.25 by completing the following steps:

a. Select cells A1 through E1, then change the top, left, and inside lines to None.
   b. Select cells B6 through G6, then change the bottom, right, and inside lines to None.
   c. Key the text in the appropriate cells as indicated in figure 25.25.
   d. Add 10% Fill to cell D2.
   e. Add Diagonal Lines 2 fill to cells B5 and F5.
4. Save the calendar again with the same name (Ch 25, SA 04).
5. Print and then close Ch 25, SA 04.

Figure 25.25

MAY 1998

					1	2
3	4	5 Swim Meet	6 Half-Day School	7	8 Varsity Baseball	9
10	11	12 Swim Meet	13	14	15 Varsity Baseball	16
17	18	19	20 Spring Play	21	22 Varsity Baseball	23
24	25 No School	26 Swim Meet	27	28	29 No School	30
31						

Assessment 5

1. At a clear editing window, open Ch 25, Ex 08.
2. Save the document with Save As and name it Ch 25, SA 05.
3. Make the following changes to the document:
   a. Add a fourth column at the right side of the table.
   b. Change the column width to 1.5 inches for all columns.
   c. Join cells A1 and D1.
   d. Join cells A2 and D2.
   e. Key the word **Difference** in cell D3.

- f. With the insertion point still positioned in cell D3, change the Digits after decimal setting to 3 at the Properties for Table Format dialog box with the Column tab selected.
- g. Insert a formula in cell D4 that subtracts last year's sales from this year's sales.
- h. Copy the formula down six times.
4. Save the document again with the same name (Ch 25, SA 05).
5. Print and then close Ch 25, SA 05.

Assessment 6

1. At a clear editing window, create the purchase requisition form shown in figure 25.26 by completing the following steps:
   - a. Create a table with 5 columns and 11 rows.
   - b. Change the width of the first column to 0.5 inches and the second column to 2.5 inches.
   - c. Join cells A1 through E1.
   - d. Position the insertion point in cell A1, then change the row height to 2.75 inches.
   - e. Select cells A3 through A11, then change the justification to Center.
   - f. Select cells D3 through E11, then change the number type to Currency.
   - g. Select cells C3 through E11, then change the justification to Decimal Align.
   - h. Select cells A3 through E3, then change the lines at the top of the cells to Double.
   - i. Select cells A2 through E2, then change the lines at the top of the cells to Double.
   - j. With cells A2 through E2 still selected, change the justification to Center and the appearance to Bold.
   - k. With cells A2 through E2 still selected, insert 20% Fill.
   - l. Insert a double line border around the table.
   - m. Select cells A3 through A11, then change the inside lines to None.
   - n. Select cells B3 through B11, then change the inside lines to None.
   - o. Select cells C3 through C11, then change the inside lines to None.
   - p. Select cells D3 through D11, then change the inside lines to None.
   - q. Select cells E3 through E11, then change the inside lines to None.
   - r. Key the information in the table as shown in figure 25.26. Bold the text in cell A1 as indicated. Press Ctrl + Tab to indent the text in cell A1.
2. Save the table and name it Ch 25, SA 06.
3. Print and then close Ch 25, SA 06.

Figure 25.26

```
         DENVER MEMORIAL HOSPITAL
         900 Colorado Boulevard
         Denver, CO 86530
         (303) 555-4400

         Purchase Requisition

         Name _____  Dept. _____

         Purpose of Request _____

         Budget Account No. _____
```

#	Item	Qty.	Price	Total

Assessment 7

1. At a clear editing window, open Ch 25, SA 06.
2. Save the document with Save As and name it Ch 25, SA 07.
3. Key the following information in the table below the listed headings:

#	=	1		#	=	2
Item	=	**Syringes**		Item	=	**Compresses**
Qty.	=	**500**		Qty.	=	**750**
Price	=	**0.35**		Price	=	**0.30**

#	=	3		#	=	4
Item	=	**Suture Kits**		Item	=	**Stethoscopes**
Qty.	=	**50**		Qty.	=	**8**
Price	=	**2.25**		Price	=	**79.50**

4. Insert the formula **C3*D3** in cell E3.
5. Copy the formula in cell E3 down three rows.
6. Save the document again with the same name (Ch 25, SA 07).
7. Print and then close Ch 25, SA 07.

26

CREATING CHARTS

PERFORMANCE OBJECTIVE

Upon successful completion of chapter 26, you will be able to enhance and improve the clarity of data by presenting the data in a chart.

In chapters 24 and 25 you learned to create data in tables. While tables do an adequate job of displaying data, a chart created from data provides an even stronger visual presentation. A chart, sometimes referred to as a *graph*, is a picture of numeric data. A chart can be created in the Chart Editor or from data in a table. In this chapter you will learn how to create a chart from data in a table. For information on how to create charts in the Chart Editor, please refer to the WordPerfect on-screen help guide.

Creating a Chart from Table Data

A chart is created using data in a table. For example, the data shown in the table in figure 26.1 can be created as a chart.

Figure 26.1

Table

Salesperson	January	February	March
T. Landford	$54,540	$48,300	$59,800
S. Eckhardt	45,200	39,780	48,550
G. Lowenstein	35,100	29,480	41,320

Creating Charts 623

Chart

Close

To insert the data shown in the table in figure 26.1 into a Bar chart (the default), position the insertion point in any cell in the table, then click Graphics, then Chart; or click the Chart button on the Tables Toolbar (the Chart button is the last button on the Tables Toolbar). At the Chart Editor shown in figure 26.2, click the Close button on the Chart Toolbar (the second button from the left) or click in the editing window outside the chart area. This action inserts the chart into the document at the left margin as shown in figure 26.3. Like other graphics boxes, a box containing a chart is inserted at the left margin and is approximately 3.25 inches wide. A box containing a chart contains no border lines.

Figure 26.2

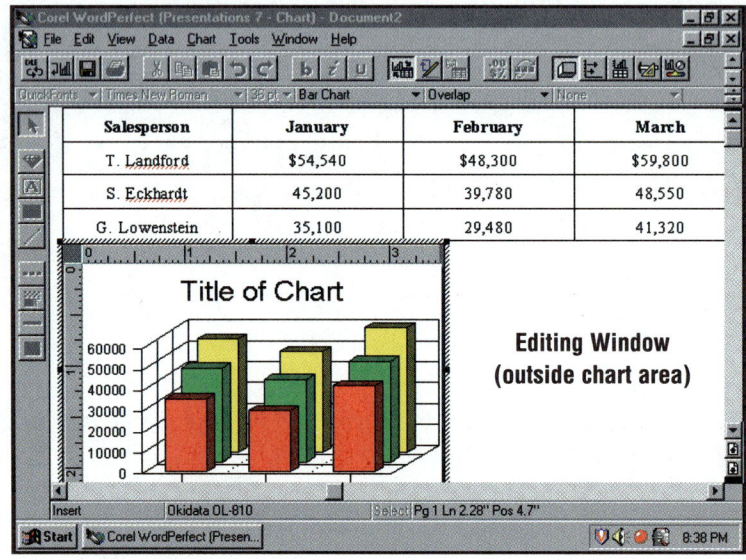

Chart Editor

Figure 26.3

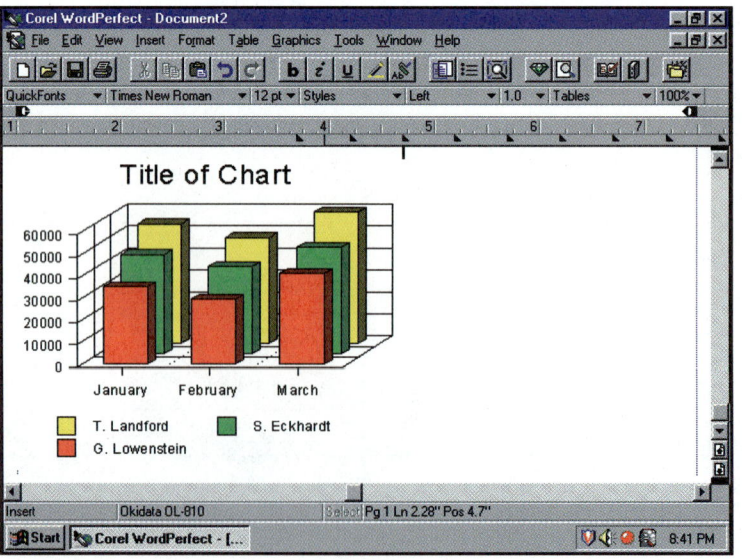

Chart Based on Table

624   Chapter 26

The left side of a chart is the vertical y-axis. The y-axis is marked like a ruler and is broken into units by marks called *ticks*. Next to each tick mark is the amount of the value at that particular point on the axis. In figure 26.3, the y-axis is displayed in numbers by ten thousands beginning with zero and continuing to 60,000.

The x-axis is the bottom of the chart. The names of items in the chart generally display along the x-axis. In the chart shown in figure 26.3, the bars are identified along the x-axis as *January*, *February*, and *March*.

EXERCISE

Creating a Bar Chart

1. At a clear editing window, open Table 02.
2. Save the document with Save As and name it Ch 26, Ex 01.
3. Create a Bar chart for the table by completing the following steps:
    a. Position the insertion point in any cell in the table.
    b. Click Graphics, then Chart.
    c. At the Chart Editor, click the Close button on the Chart Toolbar (the second button from the left).
    d. At the editing window, click outside the chart to deselect it.
4. Save the document again with the same name (Ch 26, Ex 01).
5. Print and then close Ch 26, Ex 01.

Creating a Title

The chart shown in figure 26.3 displays with the default title of *Title of Chart*. A title can be added to a chart at the Chart Editor. To create a title, you must display the chart in the Chart Editor. To display the Chart Editor for an existing chart, double-click the chart.

To create a title in the Chart Editor, click Chart, then Title or double-click the default title. This causes the Title Properties dialog box to display as shown in figure 26.4. At the Title Properties dialog box, you can create a title for a chart. You can further customize the title by choosing other tabs that display toward the top of the dialog box. The Title Font tab is selected by default. With this tab selected, you can change the Font face, Font style, Font size, and appearance of the chart title. The text of the title can be further customized by clicking the Text Fill and/or Text Outline tabs. Use options from the dialog box with these tabs selected to enhance the title by adding fill patterns to the letters, changing the outline of the characters with different line styles, and adding color to the text fill and outline.

Figure 26.4

Title Properties Dialog Box

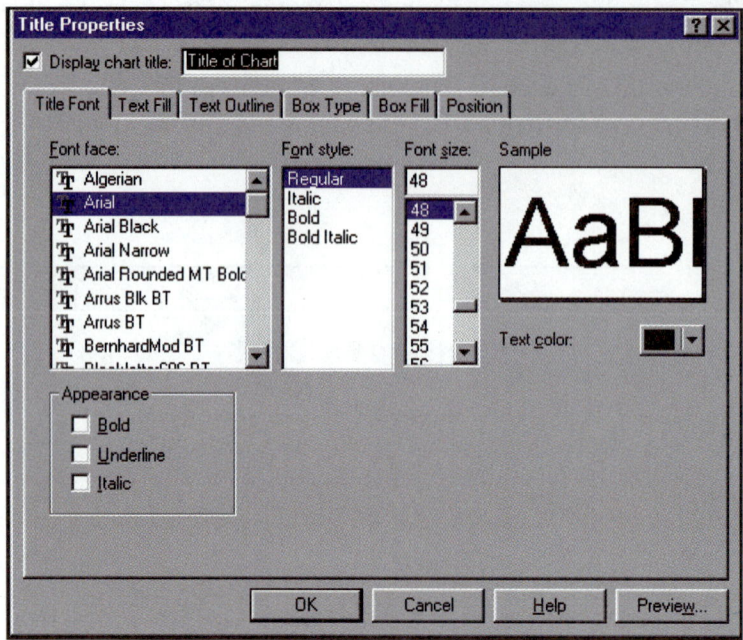

If you click the Box Type tab at the Title Properties dialog box, then remove the check mark from the No box check box, the Title Properties dialog box displays as shown in figure 26.5. Choose a style for the box surrounding the title by clicking the desired box type. The color of the border can be changed with the Border color button. As you make changes, the Sample box displays how the border will appear.

Figure 26.5

Title Properties Dialog Box with Box Type Tab Selected

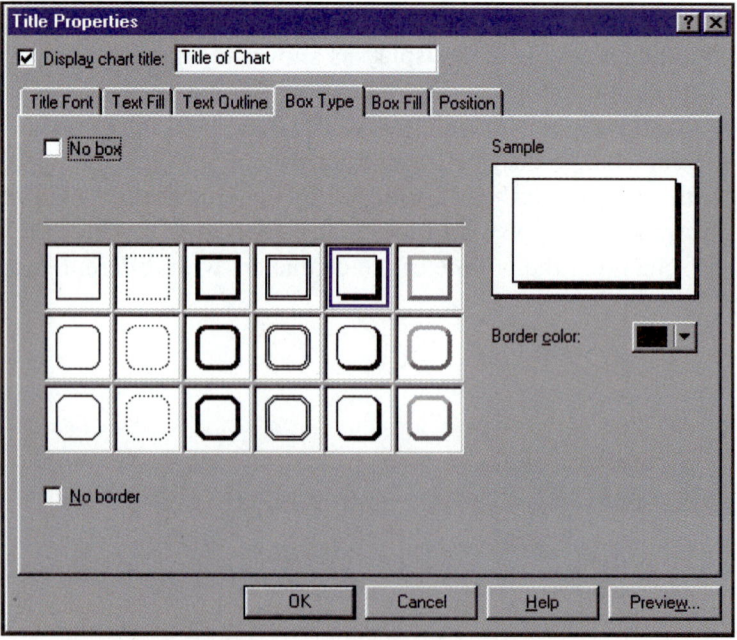

626 Chapter 26

Change the fill color of the box for the title with options at the Title Properties dialog box with the Box Fill tab selected. The Fill style can be changed to Pattern, Gradient, Texture, or Picture. If you click Texture or Picture at the Fill style drop-down list, the Category text box becomes available. The Category text box options change depending on whether Texture or Picture is selected. With the Texture and Picture fill styles, there are different categories from which to choose a fill style. For example, if you choose Picture as the fill style, the Category text box lists options such as: *Business*, *Commodit*, *Finance*, *Foodprod*, *Governme*, and *Nature*. As you select different categories, various pictures display in the selection area for you to add to the background of the title box.

By default, the title of a chart is centered at the top of the chart. This can be changed to the left or right side of the chart with options at the Title Properties dialog box with the Position tab selected.

EXERCISE 2

Adding a Title and Formatting a Chart

1. At a clear editing window, open Ch 26, Ex 01.
2. Save the document with Save As and name it Ch 26, Ex 02.
3. Create a title for the chart, add a double line border around the title, and change the font of the title by completing the following steps:
   a. Open the Chart Editor by double-clicking the chart.
   b. At the Chart Editor, click Chart, then Title.
   c. At the Title Properties dialog box, key **UNITED FOODS**.
   d. Click *Arrus BT* in the Font face list box.
   e. Click the Box Type tab.
   f. Click the No box check box to remove the check mark.
   g. Click the double line rectangle style (fourth box from the left in the first row).
   h. Click OK.
   i. Click the Close button on the Chart Toolbar or click in the editing window outside the chart.
   j. At the editing window, click outside the chart to deselect it.
4. Save the document again with the same name (Ch 26, Ex 02).
5. Print and then close Ch 26, Ex 02.

Creating a Subtitle

A subtitle can be added to a chart at the Chart Editor. To create a subtitle, you must display the Chart Editor, click Chart, then click Subtitle. This displays the Subtitle Properties dialog box. Click the Display chart subtitle check box to insert a check mark, then key the subtitle in the text box at the top of the dialog box. The Subtitle Properties dialog box contains the same options to enhance the subtitle as the Title Properties dialog box.

Customizing a Legend

When a chart is created from data in a table, a legend is automatically created. A legend identifies the bars in the chart. For example, the legend in figure 26.3 specifies the salesperson for each bar in the chart. The legend displays outside and below the chart. This can be changed at the Legend Properties dialog box shown in figure 26.6. To display the Legend Properties dialog box, click Chart, then Legend.

Creating Charts 627

Figure 26.6 Legend Properties Dialog Box

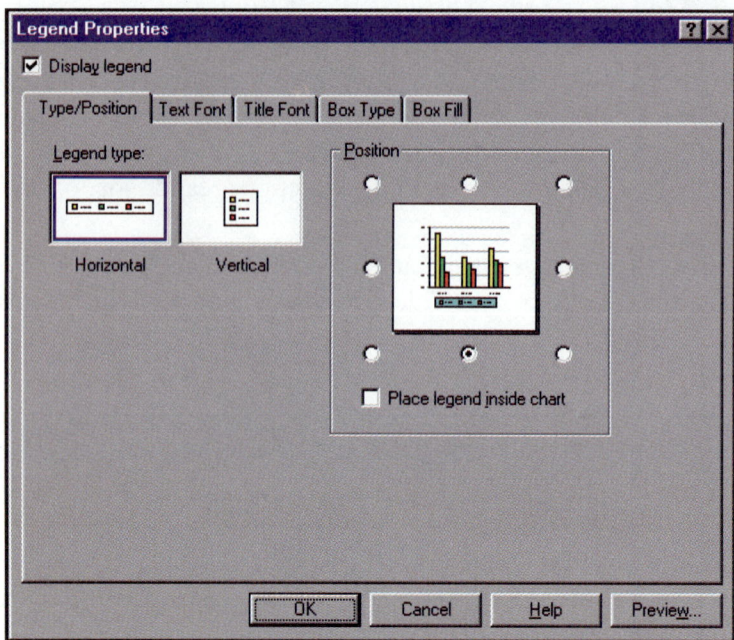

By default, a legend is displayed with the chart. If you do not want a legend displayed, remove the check mark from the Display legend check box. If the check mark is removed, many of the options at the dialog box become dimmed.

The Type/Position tab is selected by default at the Legend Properties dialog box. By default, a legend displays outside and at the bottom of the chart. The legend can be placed inside the chart by clicking Place legend inside chart. The legend position is bottom center. In the Position section, you can choose to place the legend at the top left, top center, top right, middle left, middle right, bottom left, or bottom right. To do this, click the radio button that displays around the sample legend where you want the legend to appear. The Legend type can be either Horizontal or Vertical.

Click the Text Font tab and options display to change the Font face, Font style, Font size, and Text color of the legend text. Bold, Underline, and Italic appearance attributes can also be applied to the legend text.

At the Legend Properties dialog box with the Title Font tab selected, insert a check mark in the Display title check box if you want a title to appear above the legend text. With options at this dialog box, you can also specify the Font face, Font style, Font size, and Text color of the legend text. In addition, appearance attributes such as Bold, Underline, and Italics can be applied to legend text.

If you click the Box Type tab at the Legend Properties dialog box, options display that are the same as options in the Title Properties dialog box with the Box Type tab selected as shown in figure 26.5. At this dialog box, you can create a border for the legend and add color to the border.

The Legend Properties dialog box with the Box Fill tab selected contains the same options as described for the Title Properties dialog box with the Box Fill tab selected.

EXERCISE 3

Formatting a Chart Legend

1. At a clear editing window, open Ch 26, Ex 02.
2. Save the document with Save As and name it Ch 26, Ex 03.
3. Customize the legend for the chart by completing the following steps:
    a. Open the Chart Editor by double-clicking the chart.
    b. At the Chart Editor, click Chart, then Legend.
    c. At the Legend Properties dialog box with the Type/Position tab selected, click the bottom left radio button in the Position section.
    d. Click the Box Type tab.
    e. Click the No box check box to remove the check mark.
    f. Click the double line octagon box style (fourth option from the left in the bottom row).
    g. Click OK.
    h. Click the Close button on the Chart Toolbar or click in the editing window, outside the chart area.
    i. At the editing window, deselect the chart.
4. Save the document again with the same name (Ch 26, Ex 03).
5. Print and then close Ch 26, Ex 03.

Deleting a Chart

When a chart is inserted in the editing window, a Box code is inserted in the document. To delete the chart, display Reveal Codes, then delete the Box code. You can also delete the chart by clicking the chart (this causes sizing handles to display around the chart), then pressing the Delete key.

As mentioned at the beginning of this chapter, you are learning how to create charts based on a table. If you create a chart based on a table, and then make changes to the data in the table, you must delete the first chart and then create another chart based on the edited table. You cannot update a chart that was created from a table.

EXERCISE 4

Deleting a Chart and Creating a New Chart

1. At a clear editing window, open Ch 26, Ex 03.
2. Save the document with Save As and name it Ch 26, Ex 04.
3. Delete the chart by completing the following steps:
    a. Click the chart (this causes sizing handles to display around the chart).
    b. Press the Delete key.
4. Make the following changes to the data in the table:
    a. Change the number in cell B2 from 120205 to 100500.
    b. Change the number in cell C3 from 115460 to 97800.
5. Create a chart based on the table by completing the following steps:

Creating Charts **629**

> a. Position the insertion point in any cell in the table, then click the Chart button on the Tables Toolbar.
> b. At the Chart Editor, click the Close button on the Chart Toolbar.
> 6. Save the document with the same name (Ch 26, Ex 04).
> 7. Print and then close Ch 26, Ex 04.

Editing a Chart Box

When a chart is inserted in a document, it is inserted in a graphics box. This is the same type of box you learned to create and edit in chapter 19. All the same editing options are available to you. For example, you can display the Edit Box dialog box for a chart box and then change the contents, size, position, and much more. The shortcut menu displayed by clicking the right mouse button on the chart also contains the same options as the Edit Box dialog box. To display the Edit Box dialog box, click the QuickSpot button that displays at the top left corner of the chart.

A box containing a chart can be moved and sized. To move a box containing a chart, position the arrow pointer inside the chart, then click the left mouse button. This selects the box and inserts sizing handles around the box. Position the arrow pointer inside the chart and it turns into a four-headed arrow. Hold down the left mouse button, drag the outline of the box to the desired location, then release the mouse button.

A selected box containing a chart can also be sized. To size the box, use the sizing handles that display in the corners and in the middle of the box surrounding the chart. Size the box in the same manner as you learned to size graphics boxes in chapter 19.

EXERCISE 5

> **Sizing and Positioning a Chart**
>
> 1. At a clear editing window, open Ch 26, Ex 03.
> 2. Save the document with Save As and name it Ch 26, Ex 05.
> 3. Delete the table in the document (not the chart) by completing the following steps:
>   a. Position the arrow pointer in any cell in the table until it turns into the horizontal or vertical selection arrow, then triple-click the left mouse button. (Make sure all cells in the table are selected.)
>   b. Press the Delete key.
>   c. At the Delete Table dialog box, make sure Entire table is selected, then click OK.
> 4. Click the Page/Zoom Full button on the Toolbar.
> 5. Change the position and size of the chart by completing the following steps:
>   a. Select the chart. To do this, position the arrow pointer inside the chart, then click the left mouse button.
>   b. Position the arrow pointer inside the chart and it turns into a four-headed arrow. With the four-headed arrow inside the chart, hold down the left mouse button, drag the outline of the box to the middle of the page, then release the mouse button.
>   c. Increase the height of the chart box by approximately one-half inch. To do this, position the arrow pointer on the middle sizing handle at the top of the

box until it turns into a double-headed arrow pointing up and down. Hold down the left mouse button, drag up approximately one-half inch, then release the mouse button.

   d. Increase the width of the chart box by approximately one-half inch. To do this, position the arrow pointer on the middle sizing handle at the right side of the box until it turns into a double-headed arrow pointing left and right. Hold down the left mouse button, drag to the right approximately one-half inch, then release the mouse button.
   e. If necessary, reposition the chart box so it is in the middle of the page.
   f. Click in the editing window outside the chart to deselect the chart box.
6. Save the document with the same name (Ch 26, Ex 05).
7. Print Ch 26, Ex 05.
8. With the chart still open in the editing window, change the size of the chart by completing the following steps:
   a. Display the Box Size dialog box by clicking the *right* mouse button inside the chart, then clicking Size at the drop-down menu.
   b. Change the box width to Full and the height to Maintain proportions.
   c. Click OK to close the Box Size dialog box.
   d. Click outside the chart to deselect it.
   e. Click the Page/Zoom Full button on the Toolbar.
9. Save the document again with the same name (Ch 26, Ex 05).
10. Print and then close Ch 26, Ex 05.

Changing Chart Layout and Type

In the Chart Editor, you can create eight different types of charts. Figure 26.7 shows an illustration and explanation of each type.

Figure 26.7

Types of Charts

Area	An Area chart shows trends and the amount of change over time.	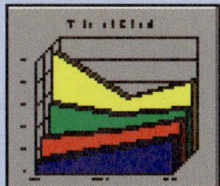
Bar	A Bar chart shows variations between components but not in relationship to the whole. Horizontal and Vertical Bar charts are available.	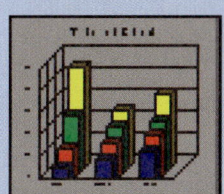

Creating Charts 631

High/Low   A High/Low chart shows the high, low, open, and close quotes for a stock.

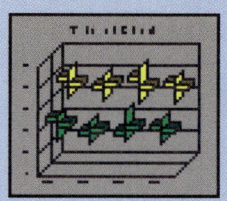

Line   A Line chart shows trends and change over time.

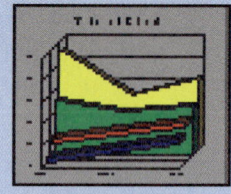

Pie   A Pie chart shows proportions and relationships of parts to the whole.

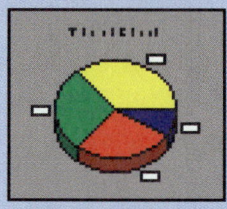

Radar   A Radar chart shows data over time and displays variations and trends.

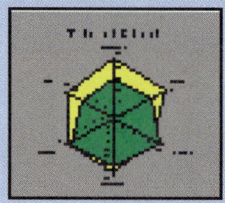

Scatter   A Scatter chart shows the interception points between x and y values.

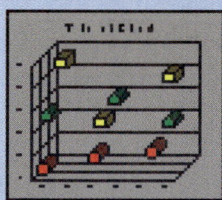

Surface   A Surface chart shows the data in a 3-D area that expands and dips in peaks and valleys like a landscape as it connects the data points.

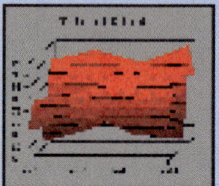

To change to a different chart type, click Chart, then Layout/Type. This displays the Layout/Type Properties dialog box. Click the down-pointing triangle at the right side of the Chart type text box and a drop-down list of chart types displays. At this drop-down list, click the desired chart type. The chart type can also be changed at the Data Chart Gallery dialog box shown in figure 26.8. To display this dialog box, click Chart, then Gallery.

Figure 26.8

Data Chart Gallery Dialog Box

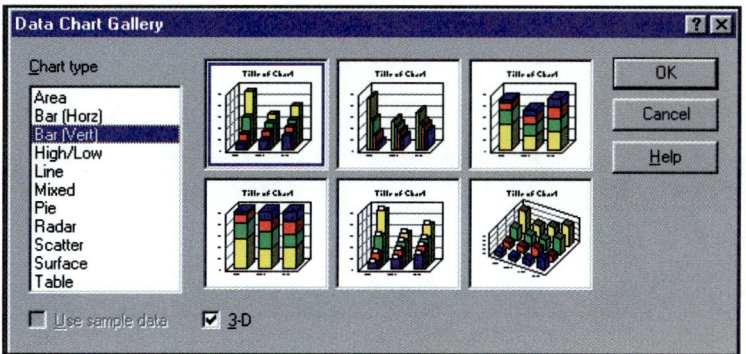

The eight chart types are displayed in the Chart type list box. To the right, the formatting for the selected chart displays. For each chart, WordPerfect provides variations containing different combinations of enhancements. You can choose a variation without having to customize the chart yourself. In exercises 6 through 9 you will create various types of charts.

EXERCISE 6

Creating a Pie Chart

1. At a clear editing window, create the table shown in figure 26.9. (The middle column must be blank for the data to display in the proper locations in the chart.)
2. Create a Pie chart for the table by completing the following steps:
   a. Position the insertion point inside the table, then display the Chart Editor.
   b. At the Chart Editor, click Chart, then Layout/Type.
   c. At the Layout/Type Properties dialog box, click the down-pointing triangle at the right side of the Chart type text box, then click *Pie* at the drop-down list.
   d. Click OK to close the Layout/Type Properties dialog box.
   e. Create the title, *VISION ASSOCIATION*.
   f. Close the Chart Editor.
3. At the editing window, delete the table.
4. Display the Edit Box dialog box for the chart, then change the box width to Full and the height to Maintain proportions at the Box Size dialog box.
5. Save the document and name it Ch 26, Ex 06.
6. Print and then close Ch 26, Ex 06.

Creating Charts 633

Figure 26.9

Category	Percentage
Research	37.5
Community Service	24.7
Management	5.5
Fund Raising	15
Education	17.3

EXERCISE 7

Creating a Line Chart

1. At a clear editing window, create the table shown in figure 26.10.
2. Create a Line chart for the table by completing the following steps:
    a. Position the insertion point inside the table, then display the Chart Editor.
    b. At the Chart Editor, click Chart, then Layout/Type.
    c. At the Layout/Type Properties dialog box, click the down-pointing triangle at the right side of the Chart type text box, then click *Line* at the drop-down list. Click OK to close the dialog box.
    d. Create a title for the chart and change the font size for the title by completing the following steps:
        (1) Click Chart, then Title.
        (2) At the Title Properties dialog box, key **Benefit of Tax-Free Compounding**.
        (3) Change the Font size to 36.
        (4) Click OK.
    e. Close the Chart Editor.
3. At the editing window, delete the table.
4. Display the Edit Box dialog box for the chart, then change the box width to Set at 5 inches and the height to Set at 4.5 inches at the Box Size dialog box.
5. Move the chart to the middle of the page by completing the following steps:
    a. Deselect the chart.
    b. Click the Page/Zoom Full button on the Toolbar.
    c. Click the chart to select it.
    d. Position the arrow pointer (four-headed arrow) inside the chart, hold down the left mouse button, drag the outline of the chart box to the middle of the page, then release the mouse button.
    e. Deselect the chart.
    f. Click the Page/Zoom Full button.
6. Save the document and name it Ch 26, Ex 07.
7. Print and then close Ch 26, Ex 07.

Figure 26.10

Years	10	20	30
Taxable Account	15000	22000	34000
Tax-Free Account	17000	32000	58000

EXERCISE 8

Creating a High/Low Chart

1. At a clear editing window, create the table shown in figure 26.11.
2. Create a High/Low chart for the table by completing the following steps:
    a. Position the insertion point inside the table, then display the Chart Editor.
    b. At the Chart Editor, click Chart, then Layout/Type.
    c. At the Layout/Type Properties dialog box, click the down-pointing triangle at the right side of the Chart type text box, then click *High/Low* at the drop-down list. Click OK to close the dialog box.
    d. Create the title, *STOCKS*, for the chart.
    e. Close the Chart Editor.
3. At the editing window, delete the table.
4. Display the Edit Box dialog box for the chart, then change the box width to Full and the height to Maintain proportions.
5. Save the document and name it Ch 26, Ex 08.
6. Print and then close Ch 26, Ex 08.

Figure 26.11

Stock	High	Low	Open	Close
United Foods	48	22.5	33.5	34
Milton Electric	74	45	71	70.25
SL Products	14	5	11.5	9.5
Lanson, Inc.	22	9	19.5	19.25

Creating Charts 635

EXERCISE 9

Changing the Line Chart Type

1. At a clear editing window, open Ch 26, Ex 07.
2. Save the document with Save As and name it Ch 26, Ex 09.
3. Change the type of Line chart by completing the following steps:
    a. Position the insertion point inside the chart, then display the Chart Editor.
    b. Click Chart, then Gallery.
    c. At the Data Chart Gallery dialog box, click the last Line chart option in the first row of the dialog box.
    d. Click OK.
4. Close the Chart Editor.
5. Save the document again with the same name (Ch 26, Ex 09).
6. Print and then close Ch 26, Ex 09.

Changing a Series

In a chart, a *series* is a row of data in the table. For example, in the chart in figure 26.3, a series would be all cell entries in row 1; another series would be all cell entries in row 2, and so on. In the chart in figure 26.3, a series is represented by the various colored bars. To select a series, position the arrow pointer on a bar that represents the series, then click the left mouse button. For example, if you want to customize the yellow bars in the chart in figure 26.3, click any yellow bar. This selects the yellow bars and causes selection markers to display at the top of the bars.

When the Chart Editor is displayed, the Draw Tool palette displays at the left side of the window. The tools on this tool palette are dimmed by default. The last four tools can be used to customize a series. These four tools were described in chapter 21. They provide the same options for a chart series. When a series is selected, these four tools become available.

The first tool, Line Attributes, provides a variety of line options. From the options that display when you click this tool, you can change the width of the line surrounding the series, change to a patterned line, or choose no line. With options from the Fill Attributes tool, you can change the pattern that fills the selected series. For example, you can add horizontal, vertical, or diagonal lines, or add a pattern such as Honeycomb or Chainlink. Choose the Line Colors tool to change the color of the line that surrounds the series. With the Fill Colors tool, you can change the color that fills the series.

EXERCISE 10

Customizing the Display of a Series

1. At a clear editing window, open Ch 26, Ex 05.
2. Save the document with Save As and name it Ch 26, Ex 10.
3. Open the Chart Editor for the chart.
4. Change the pattern and color of the yellow bars by completing the following steps:
    a. Click any yellow bar in the chart. (This selects all the yellow bars.)
    b. Click the Fill Attributes tool on the Draw Tool palette.

c. From the list of options that displays, click the last option in the second row.
   d. With the yellow bars still selected, click the Fill Colors button on the Draw Tool palette.
   e. Click the blue color in the first row in the Pattern/Gradient Color palette.
5. Change the pattern of the green bars by completing the following steps:
   a. Click any green bar in the chart. (This selects all the green bars.)
   b. Click the Fill Attributes tool on the Draw Tool palette.
   c. From the list of options that displays, click the fifth option in the third row.
6. Change the pattern and color of the red bars by completing the following steps:
   a. Click any red bar in the chart. (This selects all the red bars.)
   b. Click the Fill Attributes tool on the Draw Tool palette.
   c. From the list of options that displays, click the fifth option in the second row.
   d. With the red bars still selected, click the Fill Colors button on the Draw Tool palette.
   e. Click the fuchsia (bright pink) color in the first row of the Pattern/Gradient Color palette.
7. Close the Chart Editor.
8. At the editing window, save the document again with the same name (Ch 26, Ex 10).
9. Print and then close Ch 26, Ex 10.

Using Series Options

The options that are available with the tools on the Draw Tools palette are also available at the Series Properties dialog box shown in figure 26.12. To display this dialog box, click Chart, then Series; or click the Series button on the Chart Toolbar.

Series

Figure 26.12

Series Properties Dialog Box

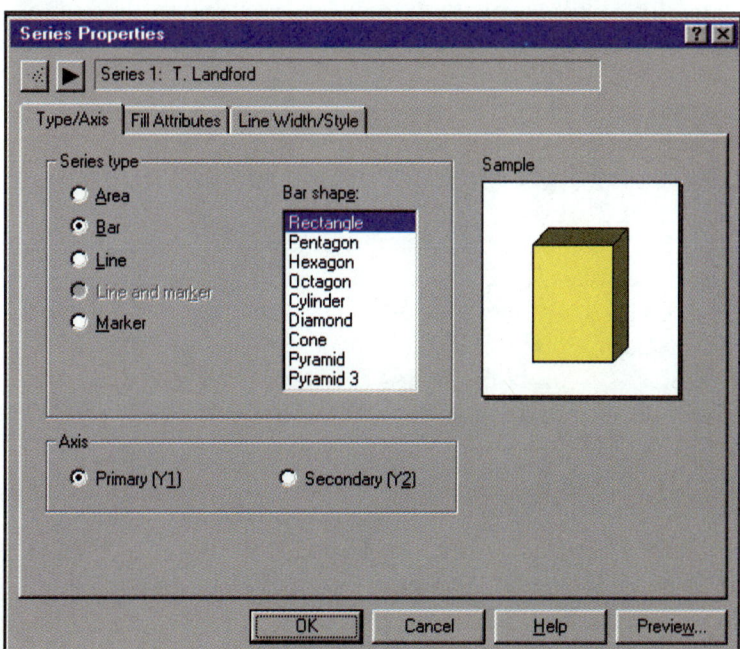

A Y2-axis can be created in a document and is generally used to chart one or more components on a different scale from the other components. For example, in the chart in figure 26.3, you can add a Y2-axis that displays the total sales over the months of January, February, and March.

To create a Y2-axis for the total sales, a row must be added to the table with formulas in the cells to calculate the total. When changes such as this are made to the table, delete the original chart, make changes to the table, then create a new chart.

In the Series Properties dialog box, different shapes can be chosen for each bar in the Bar shape list box. Each series can display a different shape. Display a different series toward the top of the dialog box by clicking the button that displays in the upper left corner of the dialog box and contains the image of a right-pointing triangle. With the desired series selected, click the desired shape in the Bar shape list box that displays in the middle of the dialog box. Repeat this process for any remaining series in the chart.

EXERCISE

Changing Series Options

1. At a clear editing window, open Ch 26, Ex 01.
2. Save the document with Save As and name it Ch 26, Ex 11.
3. Delete the chart (<u>not</u> the table). (One method for doing this is to display Reveal Codes, then delete the box code.)
4. Create the formula for calculating the totals of 1996, 1997, and 1998 and add a Y2-axis series that displays as a line by completing the following steps:
   a. Position the insertion point inside the table, then add a row to the bottom of the table.
   b. Insert a formula in cell B5 that adds B2, B3, and B4. (Copy this formula to the right twice [to cells C5 and D5].)
   c. With the insertion point positioned in the table, display the Chart Editor.
   d. At the Chart Editor, click any blue bar in the chart. (This selects all the blue bars.)
   e. Click Chart, then Series.
   f. At the Series Options dialog box, make the following changes:
      (1) Click Line in the Series type section. (This changes the totals from a bar to a line.)
      (2) Click Secondary (Y2) in the Axis section.
      (3) Click the left-pointing triangle at the top of the Series Properties dialog box until you see *Series 1: Washington* displayed, then click *Cone* in the Bar shape list box.
      (4) Click the right-pointing triangle at the top of the Series Properties dialog box to display *Series 2: Oregon*, then click *Cone* in the Bar shape list box.
      (5) Click the right-pointing triangle at the top of the Series Properties dialog box to display *Series 3: Idaho*, then click *Pyramid 3* in the Bar shape list box.
      (6) Click OK to close the Series Properties dialog box.
   g. At the Chart Editor, display the Titles dialog box, then create the title, *UNITED FOODS*.
   h. Close the Chart Editor.
5. At the editing window delete the table (not the chart).
6. Display the Edit Box dialog box for the chart, then change the width of the chart box to Full and the height to Maintain proportions.
7. Save the document again with the same name (Ch 26, Ex 11).
8. Print and then close Ch 26, Ex 11.

Changing Chart Layouts

The arrangement, appearance, shape, and size of chart elements can be changed with layout options. The Layout/Type Properties dialog boxes for Bar, Line, Area, and Scatter charts contain basically the same layout options. The Layout/Type Properties dialog boxes for Pie, High/Low, and Radar charts contain different options. To display the Layout/Type Properties dialog box for a Bar chart as shown in figure 26.13, click Chart, then Layout/Type or click the Layout button on the Chart Toolbar.

Layout

Figure 26.13

Layout/Type Properties Dialog Box

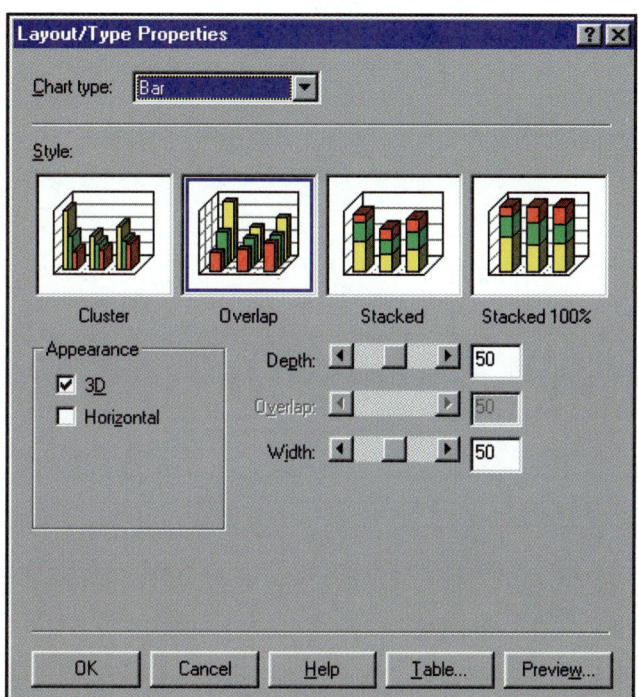

Style: This section contains options for changing the display of the chart elements. The Cluster option will cluster bars according to the column of data they represent. The Overlap option is the default and overlaps bars, lines, or areas. Choose the Stacked option if you want to stack bars, lines, or areas vertically. The Stacked 100% option will stack bars, lines, or areas vertically so that they appear as a percentage of a whole. Make a selection in the Style section of the dialog box, then click the Preview button to see what the style looks like.

3D: With this option, you can switch from a three-dimensional look for the chart to a two-dimensional look. You can also click the 3D Chart button on the Chart Toolbar to switch between a three-dimensional and a two-dimensional chart.

3D Chart

Horizontal: Choose Horizontal to display the chart horizontally. You can also click the Horizontal Chart button on the Chart Toolbar to switch between a horizontal and a vertical orientation for the chart.

Horizontal Chart

Sizes: You can change the Width, Depth, or Overlap of a series of elements depending on the Type selected.

Creating Charts 639

EXERCISE 12

Changing Chart Type

1. At a clear editing window, open Ch 26, Ex 05.
2. Save the document with Save As and name it Ch 26, Ex 12.
3. Change the Bar chart to a horizontal two-dimensional chart by completing the following steps:
   a. Display the Chart Editor for the chart.
   b. Click the Layout button on the Chart Toolbar.
   c. At the Layout/Type Properties dialog box, make the following changes:
      (1) Click 3D. (This removes the check mark from the check box.)
      (2) Click Cluster.
      (3) Click OK.
   d. Close the Chart Editor.
4. Save the document again with the same name (Ch 26, Ex 12).
5. Print and then close Ch 26, Ex 12.

Using Pie Chart Options

If a Pie chart is displayed at the Chart Editor and you click Chart, then Layout/Type; or click the Layout button on the Chart Toolbar, the Layout/Type Properties dialog box shown in figure 26.14 displays.

Figure 26.14 Layout/Type Properties Dialog Box for Pie Charts

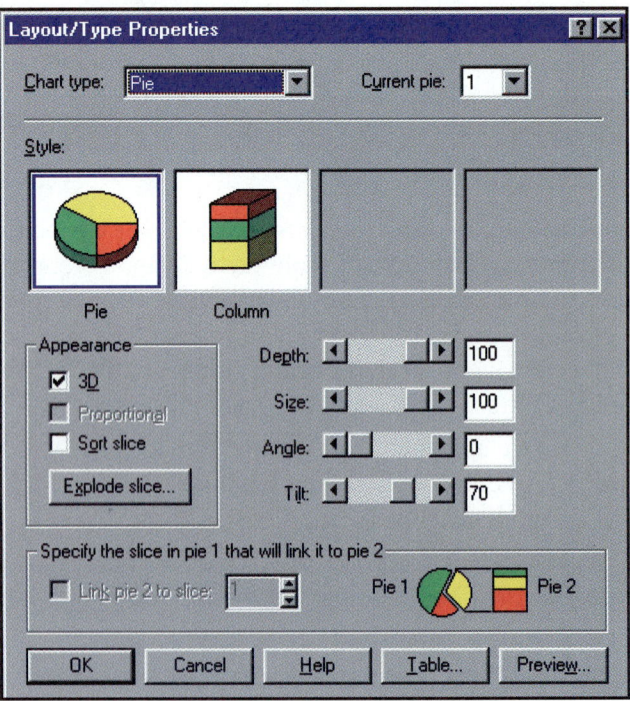

Current Pie: This displays the number of the pie currently selected. If there are two or more columns of data, change the Current pie number by clicking the down-pointing triangle to choose the column for which you want to change options.

3D: With the 3D option, you can display a pie with a three-dimensional look or a two-dimensional look. You can also click the 3D Chart button on the Chart Toolbar to switch to a three- or two-dimensional pie.

Proportional: This option is available only if you are working with two or more pies. With this option, you can show a ratio by size. For example, if the values in Pie 1 are two times those in Pie 2, Pie 1 displays twice as large.

Sort slice: The order of the slices of the pie can be sorted by clicking the Sort slice check box.

Explode slice: If you click the Explode slice button, the Explode Slice dialog box displays with Slice and Distance options. You can move a specified slice away from the other slices a specific distance. More than one slice can be exploded. At a distance setting of 0, the pie is whole. A quicker way to explode a slice of a pie chart is to click the left mouse button over the slice you want to explode to select it, then drag the slice away from the rest of the pie.

Depth: With the Depth option, you can change the height of a 3D pie.

Size: Choose Size to make the pie smaller or larger.

Angle: With the Angle option, you can change the starting point for the first pie slice.

Tilt: Change the pie viewpoint with the Tilt option.

If there are two pie charts in the chart editor, you can choose to link a slice in the Pie 1 chart to a slice in the Pie 2 chart.

EXERCISE 13

Changing Pie Chart Options

1. At a clear editing window, open Ch 26, Ex 06.
2. Save the document with Save As and name it Ch 26, Ex 13.
3. Explode a piece of the pie and change the angle and tilt of the pie by completing the following steps:
    a. Display the Chart Editor for the chart.
    b. Click the red slice of the pie. (This selects the red slice.)
    c. Click Chart, then Layout/Type.
    d. At the Layout/Type Properties dialog box, make the following changes:
        (1) Click the Explode slice button.
        (2) At the Explode Slice dialog box, select the *0* that displays in the Distance text box, then key **30**.
        (3) Click OK to close the Explode Slice dialog box.
        (4) Change the number in the Angle text box to *50*.
        (5) Change the number in the Tilt text box to *60*.
        (6) Click OK.
    e. Close the Chart Editor.
4. Save the document again with the same name (Ch 26, Ex 13).
5. Print and then close Ch 26, Ex 13.

Using High/Low Chart Options

If a High/Low chart is displayed at the Chart Editor and you click Chart, then Layout/Type; or click the Layout button on the Chart Toolbar, the Layout/Type Properties dialog box shown in figure 26.15 displays.

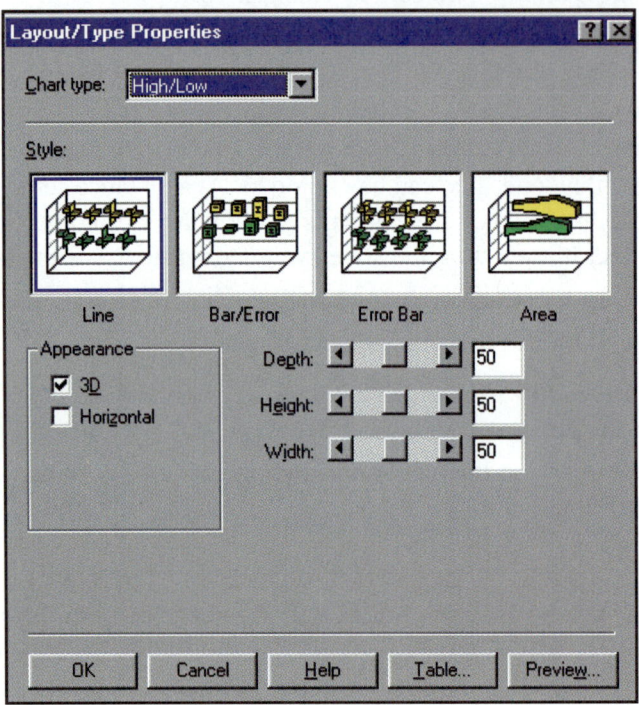

Figure 26.15 Layout/Type Properties Dialog Box for High/Low Charts

Styles: The Styles section of the Layout/Type Properties dialog box for High/Low charts displays several types of charts. You can choose a Line, Bar/Error, Error Bar, or Area chart.

3D: With this option, you can change the display of a High/Low chart from a three-dimensional look to a two-dimensional look.

Horizontal: Choose the Horizontal option to display the chart horizontally.

You can change the Depth, Height, or Width of a series of elements depending on the Type selected.

Labeling a Chart

When creating a chart from a table, WordPerfect uses column headings to label the chart. For example, the table in figure 26.1 contains the headings *January*, *February*, and *March*. When the chart is created as shown in figure 26.3, these headings are inserted below the bar that corresponds to the heading. The *Salesperson* heading is not included in the chart. You can use options from the Data Labels dialog box to further identify parts of a chart. If you click Chart, then Data Labels, the Data Labels dialog box shown in figure 26.16 displays.

Figure 26.16

Data Labels Dialog Box

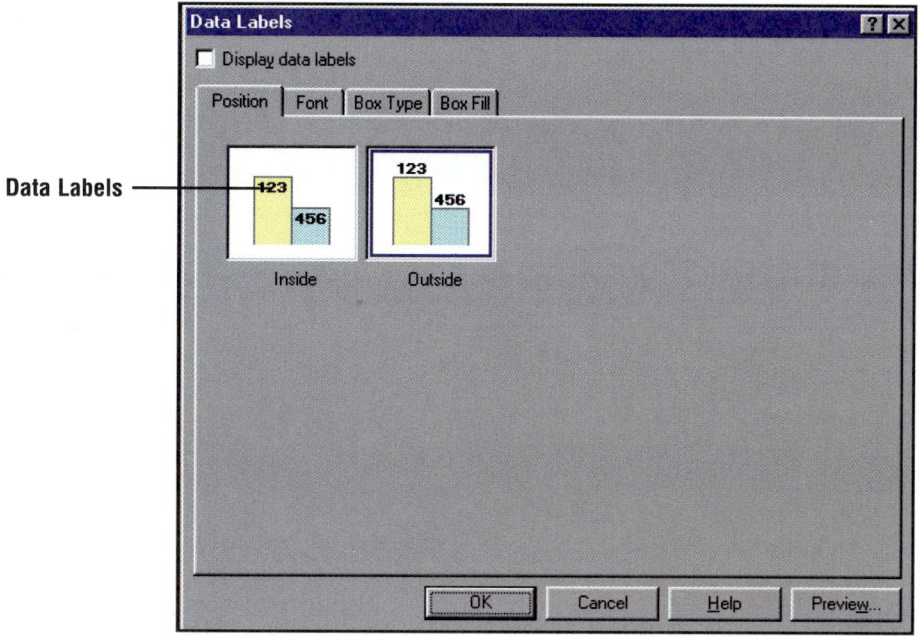

Data Labels

Data labels can be attached to specific data elements in the chart. For example, in a Bar chart, labels can be attached to each bar specifying the number. When data labels are added to a chart, you can specify whether you want the data labels Outside the chart element (above the bar) or Inside the chart element.

The Font, Box Type, and Box Fill tabs in the Data Labels dialog box contain the same options as described earlier in the chapter for Titles.

EXERCISE 14

Adding Data Labels

1. At a clear editing window, open Ch 26, Ex 05.
2. Save the document with Save As and name it Ch 26, Ex 14.
3. Add data labels to the bars in the chart by completing the following steps:
   a. Display the Chart Editor for the chart.
   b. At the Chart Editor, click Chart, then Data Labels.
   c. At the Data Labels dialog box, click the Display data labels check box. (This inserts a check mark.)
   d. Click OK.
   e. Close the Chart Editor.
4. Save the document again with the same name (Ch 26, Ex 14).
5. Print and then close Ch 26, Ex 14.

Creating Charts 643

X-Axis and Y-Axis Options

By default, the labels for the x-axis and the y-axis display in the chart. In the chart in figure 26.3, the x-axis labels are *January*, *February*, and *March*. The y-axis labels in the chart are the numbers along the left side. The display of these labels can be turned off. For example, if you do not want the x-axis labels displayed, click Chart, point to Axis, then click X. This displays the X-Axis Properties dialog box shown in figure 26.17. At this dialog box, click Display labels. This removes the check mark from the check box.

Figure 26.17

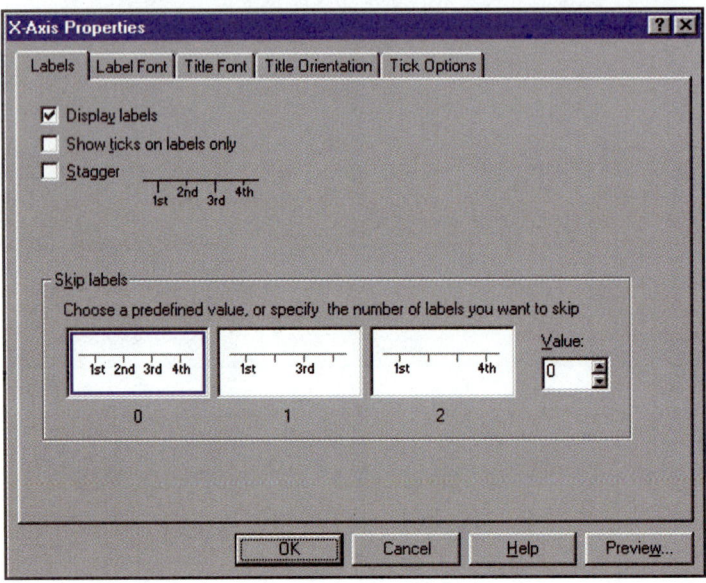

X-Axis Properties Dialog Box

Click Chart, point to Axis, then click Primary Y and the Primary Y Axis Properties dialog box displays as shown in figure 26.18. Follow similar steps as described above to turn off the display of y-axis labels.

Figure 26.18

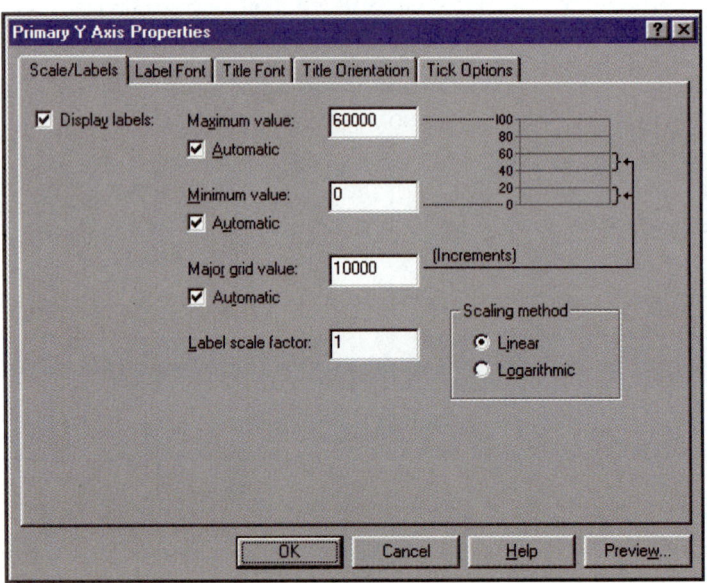

Primary Y Axis Properties Dialog Box

644 Chapter 26

At the X-Axis Properties dialog box, you can also specify whether you want to show tick marks on labels only, to stagger labels, or to change the tick interval. If you select stagger, the labels along the bottom of the chart will display staggered (one higher, one lower, etc.). In the Skip labels section you can choose to label the tick intervals by choosing a predefined value, or enter your own interval in the Value text box. The number you enter at this text box determines how often x-axis labels display. For example, if you change this to 2, only every other chart element along the x-axis will be labeled.

In the Primary Y Axis Properties dialog box, you can customize the scaling of the y-axis. By default, WordPerfect automatically scales the y-axis according to the data entered in the table used to generate the chart. You can choose to enter your own Maximum value, Minimum value, and Major grid values.

The X-Axis Properties and the Primary Y Axis Properties dialog boxes contain tabs to change the label fonts, title fonts, title orientations, and tick options. To add a title to the x-axis or y-axis, select the Title Font tab, then key the title in the text box at the top of the dialog box. The Title Orientation tab allows you to select a horizontal or vertical orientation for the title. The Tick Options tab contains selections to alter the display of the tick marks in the chart.

Labeling a Pie Chart

If you click Chart, then Data Labels when a Pie chart is displayed, the Data Labels (Pie) dialog box shown in figure 26.19 displays.

Orientation: With these options, you can position text labels in One line or Stacked in the chart. These options are only available if two of the same positions are selected (two outside or two inside).

Value: By default, no values will be displayed in the Pie chart. With the Value option, you can display values inside or outside the Pie chart.

Percent: The Percent option has a default setting of None. If you want to display percentages, you can change this to inside or outside the pie.

Label: A label for a Pie chart can be displayed inside or outside the pie with the Label option. The default setting for this option is None.

Leader: With the Leader option, you can select the length of line to connect a label to the corresponding pie slice.

The Data Labels (Pie) dialog box contains tabs for Font, Box Type, and Box Fill. These tabs contain the same options as described earlier in the chapter for Titles.

Figure 26.19 Data Labels (Pie) Dialog Box

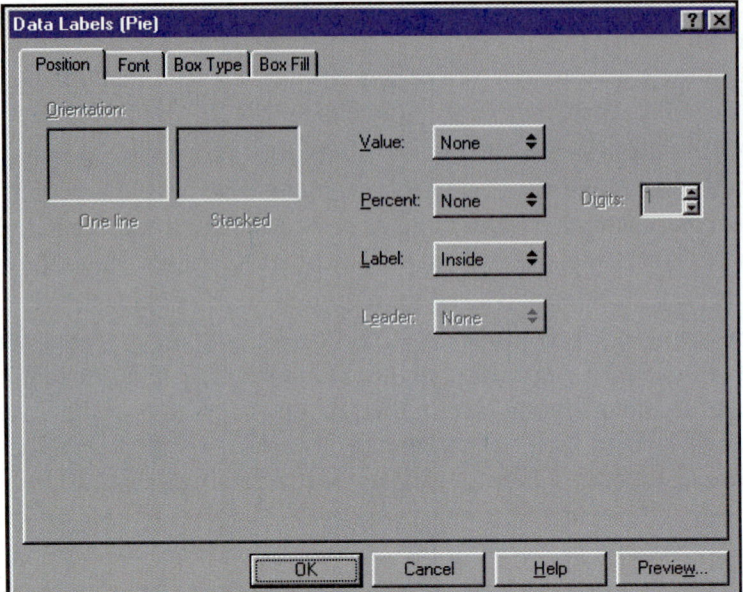

EXERCISE 15

Labeling a Pie Chart

1. At a clear editing window, open Ch 26, Ex 06.
2. Save the document with Save As and name it Ch 26, Ex 15.
3. Label the Pie chart by completing the following steps:
    a. Display the Chart Editor for the chart.
    b. Click Chart, then Data Labels.
    c. At the Data Labels (Pie) dialog box, click the Value button, then click Inside at the pop-up list.
    d. Click OK.
    e. Close the Chart Editor.
4. Save the document again with the same name (Ch 26, Ex 15).
5. Print and then close Ch 26, Ex 15.

CHAPTER SUMMARY

- A chart, sometimes referred to as a *graph*, can be created from data in a table. A chart provides a more visual presentation of the data.
- A Bar chart is the default style and is created at the Chart Editor.
- By default, a chart is approximately 3.25 inches wide and is inserted in a box with no border lines at the left margin.
- In a chart, the left side of the chart is the vertical y-axis while the bottom of the chart is the x-axis.
- A title and subtitle can be added to a chart at the Title and Subtitle Properties dialog boxes.
- At the Edit Box dialog box, you can make changes to the box containing the chart just as you can for other graphics boxes. You can also use the mouse to drag the chart in the document.
- The types of charts available include Area, Bar, High/Low, Line, Pie, Radar, Scatter, and Surface. Change the type of chart by clicking Chart, then Layout/Type at the Chart Editor.
- Tools on the Draw Tool palette at the Chart Editor can be used to change the appearance of the chart, add pattern and fill, and change line colors and line styles.
- The arrangement, appearance, shape, and size of chart elements can be changed with layout options. The Layout/Type Properties dialog box for a Bar, Line, Area, or Scatter chart contains the same layout options. The Layout/Type Properties dialog box for a Pie, High/Low, or Radar chart contains different options.
- You can use options from the Data Labels dialog box to identify parts of a chart. Options for labeling parts of a pie chart are different from the other types of charts.
- Titles for the x-axis or y-axis can be added at the X-Axis Properties or Primary Y Axis Properties dialog boxes.

COMMANDS REVIEW

	Mouse/Keyboard
Chart Editor	With insertion point in any cell in a table, choose Graphics, then Chart; or click the Chart button on the Tables Toolbar
Close Chart Editor	Click Close button on Chart Toolbar; or click in the editing window, outside the chart
Title Properties dialog box	Chart, Title
Subtitle Properties dialog box	Chart, Subtitle
Legend Properties dialog box	Chart, Legend
Series Properties dialog box	Chart, Series; or click Series button on Chart Toolbar
Layout/Type dialog box	Chart, Layout/Type; or click Layout button on Chart Toolbar
Data Labels dialog box	Chart, Data Labels
X-Axis Properties dialog box	Chart, Axis, X
Primary Y Axis Properties dialog box	Chart, Axis, Primary Y

CHECK YOUR UNDERSTANDING

Completion: In the space provided at the right, indicate the correct term, command, or number.

1. This is the default chart type. _____
2. This axis displays along the left side of the chart. _____
3. This axis displays along the bottom of the chart. _____
4. The y-axis is marked like a ruler and is broken into units by marks called these. _____
5. To create a title, the chart must be displayed here. _____
6. Create a subtitle for a chart at this dialog box. _____
7. One method for deleting a chart is to display Reveal Codes and then delete this code. _____
8. In a chart, this term refers to a row of data in the table. _____
9. This appears in a chart and shows which colors correspond with which series of data. _____
10. This type of chart shows proportions and relationship of parts to the whole. _____
11. This type of chart shows the interception points between x and y values. _____
12. This type of chart shows trends and the amount of change over time. _____

SKILL ASSESSMENTS

Assessment 1

1. At a clear editing window, create the table shown in figure 26.20.
2. Create a Bar chart with the table and add the title *RETIREMENT EXPENSES*. Set the title in 24 points.
3. At the editing window, delete the table.
4. Display the Edit Box dialog box for the chart, change the box width to Full and the height to Maintain proportions at the Box Size dialog box.
5. Save the document and name it Ch 26, SA 01.
6. Print and then close Ch 26, SA 01.

Figure 26.20

Expense	Current Cost	Retirement Cost
Housing	14080	4570
Food	5800	4000
Clothing	2800	1800
Medical and Dental	2360	2700
Entertainment	3920	6750

Assessment 2

1. At a clear editing window, create the table shown in figure 26.21.
2. Create a Line chart with the table with the following elements:
   a. At the Chart Editor, click Chart, then Gallery to display the Data Chart Gallery dialog box.
   b. At the Data Chart Gallery dialog box, change the Chart type to Line, then click the fifth line chart in the middle of the dialog box.
   c. Click OK to close the dialog box.
   d. Create the title, *CITY OF WESTON*.
   e. Create the subtitle, *Population Growth*.
3. At the editing window, delete the table.
4. Display the Edit Box dialog box for the chart, change the box width to Full and the height to Maintain proportions.
5. Save the document and name it Ch 26, SA 02.
6. Print and then close Ch 26, SA 02.

Figure 26.21

Year	1950	1960	1970	1980	1990
Population	9073	15218	28122	43932	48309

Assessment 3

1. At a clear editing window, key the headings and first paragraph of the memo in figure 26.22 in an appropriate memo format.
2. Create the table as shown in figure 26.22. After creating the table, select the third column, then change the Numeric Format to Currency.
3. Create a Pie chart with the table with the following specifications:
   a. At the Chart Editor, change the type of chart to Pie.
   b. Create the title, *PTO Fund Raising Events*.
   c. Create labels for the Pie chart that display the money amounts inside the pie. (*Hint:* Click the Value option at the Data Labels (Pie) dialog box.)
4. At the editing window, delete the table.
5. Move and/or size the Pie chart so it appears centered below the first paragraph of the memo.

6. Press Enter until the insertion point is positioned below the chart, then key the remaining text of the memo as shown in figure 26.22.
7. Save the document and name it Ch 26, SA 03.
8. Print and then close Ch 26, SA 03.

Figure 26.22

DATE: June 8, 1998

TO: Elizabeth White

FROM: Michelle Wong

SUBJECT: PTO FUNDS

The treasurer of the PTO, Leigh Gantz, presented the following information at the meeting on how the yearly PTO funds were raised.

Activity		Net Profit
Walk-a-thon		5800
Gift wrap		1130
Candy sale		570
Spring carnival		1450
Bake sale		150

The activity that provided the largest amount of money was one of the least time-consuming. After careful consideration of the various fund-raising activities, the PTO members voted to discontinue the bake sale and gift wrap for next year. Members will invest more time helping students get sponsors for the Walk-a-thon.

xx:Ch 26, SA 03

Assessment 4

1. At a clear editing window, create a High/Low chart with the information shown in figure 26.23. (*Hint:* Create a table for the information but do not include the title in the table. Create the title in the Chart Editor.) You determine the following:
   a. Elements to include in the chart.
   b. Position and size of the chart in the editing window. (Delete the table at the editing window after creating the chart.)
2. Save the document and name it Ch 26, SA 04.
3. Print and then close Ch 26, SA 04.

Figure 26.23

MAINLINE STOCKS

	High	Low	Open	Close
Calform Corporation	46	21	45.5	46.25
Packston Printing	14	6	11.5	10
Ehli Electronics	70	38	65.5	66
Meyers, Inc.	25	11	22	24.5

Unit Five

PERFORMANCE ASSESSMENTS

PROBLEM SOLVING AND DECISION MAKING

Assessment 1

1. At a clear editing window, open Report 01.
2. Save the document with Save As and name it Unit 05, PA 01.
3. Make the following changes to the document:
    a. Delete the *Ln Spacing: 2.0* code.
    b. Insert a hard return (by pressing Enter) below the title, *TRENDS IN TELECOMMUNICATIONS*.
    c. Change the first heading in the document so it displays as *Continued Growth of Photonics* rather than *Continued Growth of Photonics (Fiber Optics)*.
    d. Change the second heading in the document so it displays as *Microcomputer Trends* rather than *Microcomputer Trends in the Nineties*.
    e. Insert a hard return above and below the headings *Continued Growth of Photonics* and *Microcomputer Trends*.
    f. Select the title and then change the relative size to Large.
    g. Position the insertion point at the beginning of the document, then change the paper definition to Letter Landscape.
    h. Position the insertion point at the left margin of the line that begins *Several trends are occurring in the field...*, then define three balanced newspaper columns with 0.3 inches of space between columns.
    i. Position the insertion point at the beginning of the document, change the left hyphenation zone to 5%, the right hyphenation zone to 0%, then turn on hyphenation. Make hyphenation decisions as required.
4. Save the document again with the same name (Unit 05, PA 01).
5. Print and then close Unit 05, PA 01.

Assessment 2

1. At a clear editing window, create the list of medical suppliers shown in figure U5.1 with the following specifications:
    a. With the insertion point a triple space below the title, define three parallel columns with 0.4 inches of space between the columns.
    b. Change the relative size of the title to Large.
2. Save the document and name it Unit 05, PA 02.
3. Print and then close Unit 05, PA 02.

MEDICAL EQUIPMENT SUPPLIERS

Arthur Perella Office Manager	International Autoclave 32445 Ninth Avenue Denver, CO 86431	(303) 555-3049 Extension 43
Debra Faaborg Director of Personnel	Ryan Pharmaceuticals 2119 Mountain Avenue Denver, CO 86320	(303) 555-5544
Randy O'Connor Vice President	Bennett Medical 4032 North Fourth Street Denver, CO 86402	(303) 555-0098 Extension 122
Janet Zenor District Manager	A-1 Medical Suppliers 535 Pontiac Boulevard Denver, CO 86332	(303) 555-6675 Extension 20
Elena Torres-Wheeler Manager	Quality Care Products 12914 South 56th Denver, CO 86553	(303) 555-2200

Figure U5.1

Optional: Redesign the document by adding bolded column headings and by using a different font for the first column.

Assessment 3

1. At a clear editing window, create the table shown in figure U5.2.
2. Save the table and name it Unit 05, PA 03.
3. Print and then close Unit 05, PA 03.

ARMSTRONG ELEMENTARY SCHOOL			
READING INCENTIVE PROGRAM			
NAME:		GRADE:	ROOM:
Min.	Book Title	Min.	Book Title

Figure U5.2

Assessment 4

1. At a clear editing window, create the table shown in figure U5.3 with the following specifications:
    a. Change the appearance to Bold and the alignment to Center for cells A1, A2, A3, B3, and C3.
    b. Insert 10% Fill in cells A3 through C3 and cells A11 through C11.
    c. Change the numeric format to Accounting and the alignment to Decimal Align for cells B4 through C11.
    d. After entering the text in the cells, calculate the totals of columns B and C.
2. Save the table and name it Unit 05, PA 04.
3. Print, then close Unit 05, PA 04.

Optional: Create a balance sheet for your personal finances.

SCHOOL EMPLOYEES ANNUITY ASSOCIATION			
BALANCE SHEET			
Asset	1997		1998
Bonds	$ 42,334,655.00	$	44,569,345.00
Stocks	$ 2,345,600.00	$	3,214,748.00
Mortgages	$ 38,543,187.00	$	43,256,780.00
Real estate	$ 8,543,675.00	$	9,564,328.00
Other long-term investments	$ 954,367.00	$	1,284,660.00
Cash, short-term investments	$ 1,456,322.00	$	1,675,896.00
Other assets	$ 342,564.00	$	453,234.00
Total Liabilities			

Figure U5.3

Assessment 5

1. At a clear editing window, create the table shown in figure U5.4 with the following specifications:
   a. Change the appearance to Bold, the relative size to Large, and the justification to Center for cell A1.
   b. Change the appearance to Bold and the justification to Center for cells A2, A3, B3, C3, D3, and E3.
   c. Change the justification to Center for cells B4 through E10, the numeric format to Percent, and the Digits after decimal Amount to 0.
   d. Insert 10% Fill in cells A3 through E3.
   e. Insert a formula in cell E4 to average the test scores. Copy this formula down to the other cells in the column.
   f. Insert a double line around the table.
2. Save the table and name it Unit 05, PA 05.
3. Print and then close Unit 05, PA 05.

Optional: Write a summary explaining this chart and the trends you find in these data.

HUMAN RESOURCES DEPARTMENT

FIRST AID AND CPR TRAINING COURSE

Participant	Test 1	Test 2	Test 3	Aver.
Laura Culver	89%	95%	87%	
Katherine Brynn	97%	98%	99%	
Glenn Pruitt	74%	83%	86%	
Scott Wagner	83%	90%	87%	
Janet Zachary-Conn	94%	89%	93%	
Mark Hiebert	75%	85%	82%	
Judy Goebel	93%	95%	89%	

Figure U5.4

Assessment 6

1. At a clear editing window, create the table shown in figure U5.5.
2. Create a Line chart with the table and include the following:
   a. At the Chart Editor, display the Data Chart Gallery dialog box, click *Line* in the Chart type list box, then click the second line chart in the bottom row.
   b. Add the title *EFFECT OF 5% INFLATION*. Change the font size of the title to 24 points.
   c. Add the subtitle *ON $100,000 POLICY*.
   d. After creating the chart, delete the table from the editing window.
   e. Change the width of the box containing the chart to <u>F</u>ull and the height to <u>M</u>aintain proportions.
3. Save the chart and name it Unit 05, PA 06.
4. Print and then close Unit 05, PA 06.

Year	0	5	10	15	20
Amount	100,000	78,350	61,390	48,100	37,690

Figure U5.5

Assessment 7

1. At a clear editing window, create the table shown in figure U5.6.
2. Create a Pie chart with the table and include the following:
    a. Add the title *SOURCES OF*. Change the font size to 24 points.
    b. Add the subtitle *RETIREMENT INCOME*.
    c. Add percentage labels to the chart inside the pie.
    d. After creating the chart, delete the table from the editing window.
    e. Change the width of the box containing the chart to Full and the height to Maintain proportions.
3. Save the chart and name it Unit 05, PA 07.
4. Print and then close Unit 05, PA 07.

Optional: Personalize this chart for your anticipated or planned retirement source.

Income Source	Percentage
Social Security	32.5
Retirement Plan	24.4
SRAs, IRAs, etc.	17.6
Interest, Dividends	16.3
Savings	9.2

Figure U5.6

WRITING

The following activities give you the opportunity to practice your writing skills along with demonstrating an understanding of some of the important WordPerfect features you have mastered in this unit. In planning the documents, remember to shape the information according to the writing purpose and the audience. Use correct grammar, appropriate word choices, and clear sentence constructions.

Activity 1

Situation: Check the career center at your school, the Employment Security Department in your city, or the local newspaper for a job announcement that interests you. Using the job announcement and the résumé you created for assessment 3 in chapter 23 as an example, design a résumé for yourself. Save the résumé and name it Unit 05, Act 01. Print and then close Unit 05, Act 01.

Activity 2

Situation: You are Jenna McCormick, financial advisor for the Omaha City School District. You have been asked by Pat Windslow, the superintendent for the school district, to prepare a table showing computer expenditures for each school using the data that follows:

OMAHA CITY SCHOOL DISTRICT

Computer Expenditures, 1997-98

School	Amount
Leland Elementary School	$59,060
Carr Elementary School	43,230
Sahala Elementary School	15,304
Young Elementary School	20,430
Armstrong Elementary School	39,390
Grant Junior High School	68,405
Washington Junior High School	55,304
Roosevelt Junior High School	49,300
Nylan High School	89,000
Cleveland High School	100,230
Total Amount	(calculate total)

Create a table with the data and insert a formula to calculate the total. Save this document and name it Unit 05, Act 02. Print and then close Unit 05, Act 02.

Activity 3

Situation: You work for Northwest Planners and your supervisor has asked you to create a document that shows customers the types and percentages of industries in the Growth Account. Include the following information:

Northwest Planners Growth Account

The Northwest Planners Growth Account seeks favorable long-term returns from a diversified portfolio of common stocks with exceptional growth potential. The account invests in companies of all sizes, as long as they have the potential for significant capital appreciation.

Scott Evanston, the portfolio manager for the Growth Account, expects that the account will have substantial holdings of small or medium-sized companies in new and emerging areas of domestic and foreign markets. Mr. Evanston said that Northwest Planners will look for smaller, less-seasoned companies with above-average growth potential.

The pie chart below shows the type of industry and the percent that is contributed by that industry to the Growth Account.

Include this information in the pie chart:

Growth Account
Composition by Industry

Industry	Percentage
Products & Services	41%
Manufacturing	22%

Technology	17%
Financial	12%
Energy	8%

The Growth Account can invest in companies that may benefit from prospective acquisitions, reorganizations or corporate restructurings, or other special situations. Mr. Evanston states, "We look for companies we believe will have potential for strong earnings or sales growth, or that appear to be undervalued based on current earnings, assets, or growth prospects."

When creating the document, consider what typeface you will use, where you will place elements on the page, and how you will create the pie chart. Save the document and name it Unit 05, Act 03. Print and then close Unit 05, Act 03.

RESEARCH

Review Assessment 6. Then research the meaning of these terms: annuity, bonds, stocks, asset, and liability. Write the definitions and format your findings as a one-page report. Include a title.

Unit Six

Organizing Text in Documents

In this unit, you will learn to organize text with the outline, sort, and select features; automate the formatting of text using styles; and create tables of contents, indexes, and tables of authorities.

27 OUTLINING

PERFORMANCE OBJECTIVE

Upon successful completion of chapter 27, you will be able to enhance the organization of business reports and outlines with automatic outlining.

An outline usually contains general ideas in main headings followed by related topics indented below. These general ideas and related topics can be automatically numbered using WordPerfect's Outline feature. The advantage to using the Outline feature is that if ideas or topics are added or deleted, the remaining ideas or topics are automatically renumbered.

In chapter 7, you learned about the Bullets & Numbers dialog box. At this dialog box, you can automatically number paragraphs or insert bullets before paragraphs. This feature is probably best used for simple lists. For outlines or more complex lists, you may find the Outline feature offers the options you need.

Creating an Outline

Paragraphs can be automatically numbered with the command Ctrl + H or with the Outline feature. To create an outline, turn on the display of the Outline Feature Bar by clicking Tools, then Outline. This causes the Outline Feature Bar, shown in figure 27.1, to display below the Power Bar.

Figure 27.1

Outline Feature Bar

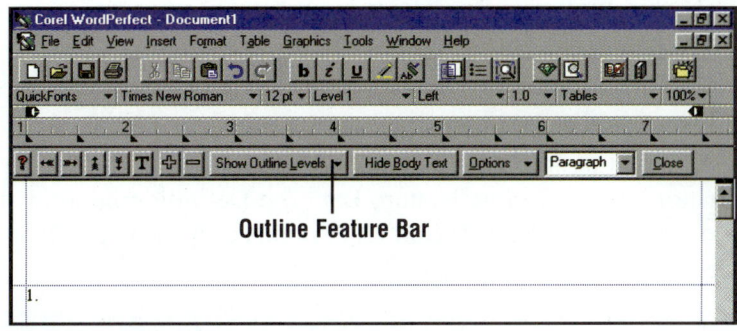

You can access the features provided on the Outline Feature Bar by clicking the desired button. Figure 27.2 shows the buttons available on the Outline Feature Bar, how you can access a feature using the keyboard, and the purpose of each feature.

Figure 27.2

Outline Feature Bar Buttons

Button	Keyboard	Action
?	ALT + SHIFT + F10	Displays features on the Outline Feature Bar and the keystroke. Also lets you access the Help feature.
←«	ALT + SHIFT + P	Moves insertion point to the previous level and inserts the previous level numbering style. Shift + Tab accomplishes the same thing.
»→	ALT + SHIFT + N	Moves insertion point to the next level and inserts the next level numbering style. The Tab key accomplishes the same thing.
↑	ALT + SHIFT + M	Moves outline item up one item without changing the level numbering.
↓	ALT + SHIFT + W	Moves outline item down one item without changing the level numbering.
T	ALT + SHIFT + T	Changes outline item to body text or body text to outline item.
+	ALT + SHIFT + S	Turns on or off the display of an outline family that has been collapsed.
−	ALT + SHIFT + I	Hides or collapses the outline family under the current outline item.
Show Outline Levels ▼	ALT + SHIFT + L	Displays specified number of levels.
Hide Body Text	ALT + SHIFT + B	Hides body text in an outline. When body text is hidden, this button changes to Show **B**ody Text.
Options ▼	ALT + SHIFT + O	Causes the Options drop-down menu to display where you can perform a variety of outlining functions.
Paragraph ▼	ALT + SHIFT + D	Definition button that lets you define the outline style for each level.
Close	ALT + SHIFT + C	Turns off the display of the Outline Feature Bar.

When you turn on the display of the Outline Feature Bar, you are in the *outlining mode*. A number 1 followed by a period is automatically inserted in the document at the left margin. The insertion point is automatically indented to the first tab setting. In addition, a 1 appears to the left of the left margin. If you cannot see this number, you may need to move the scroll box in the horizontal scroll bar to the left until it becomes visible. The icons outside the left margin identify the level of the outline as well as text lines.

By default, WordPerfect uses a Paragraph numbering style. This numbering style is displayed on the Definition button on the Outline Feature Bar. The Definition button is the second button from the right side on the Outline Feature Bar. Later in this chapter, you will learn how to change the numbering style.

Paragraph ▼
Definition

664 Chapter 27

The Paragraph numbering style automatically inserts numbers or letters based on the location of the insertion point. Figure 27.3 shows what style of numbering is used if the insertion point is positioned at a specific location.

Figure 27.3

Paragraph Numbering Styles

Insertion Point Location	Numbering Style
Left margin	1.
First tab	a.
Second tab	i.
Third tab	(1)
Fourth tab	(a)
Fifth tab	(i)
Sixth tab	1)
Seventh tab	a)

Entering Text

With the Outline Feature Bar displayed, the Enter key, Tab key, Shift + Tab, and Indent and Double Indent features will perform the actions described in figure 27.4.

Figure 27.4

Outline Actions

ENTER	=	Moves the insertion point down a line to the left margin or the tab setting of the previous level, and inserts the appropriate level numbering.
TAB	=	Moves the insertion point to the next tab setting and inserts the level numbering for that tab setting.
SHIFT + TAB	=	Moves the insertion point to the previous tab setting and inserts the level numbering for that tab setting.
Indent and Double Indent	=	Moves the insertion point to the next tab setting without changing the level numbering.

Ending Outlines

Automatic outlining can be turned off at any location in a document. This is useful if you want to continue keying text that is not part of the outline. To turn outlining off, click Options, then End Outline. To turn off the display of the Outline Feature Bar, click the Close button.

Outlining **665**

EXERCISE 1

Creating an Outline

1. At a clear editing window, create the document shown in figure 27.5 using the Outline feature by completing the following steps:
   a. Change the font to 12-point Century Schoolbook.
   b. Bold and center the title, *TEAM PARTICIPATION*.
   c. Press the Enter key twice.
   d. Click Tools, then Outline to turn on the Outline Feature Bar. (This inserts a *1.* at the left margin and indents the insertion point to the first tab setting.)
   e. Key the text of the first paragraph.
   f. Press the Enter key.
   g. Press the Tab key to move the insertion point to the next tab setting. (This changes the paragraph numbering to an *a.*)
   h. Key the text of the paragraph.
   i. Press Enter, then key the text of the next paragraph.
   j. Press Enter twice.
   k. Press Shift + Tab to move the insertion point back to the left margin. This changes the numbering to *2*.
   l. Continue keying the text of the paragraphs. Use Tab to indent the insertion point to a tab setting. Use Shift + Tab to move the insertion point to a previous tab setting.
2. Save the document and name it Ch 27, Ex 01.
3. Print and then close Ch 27, Ex 01.

Figure 27.5

TEAM PARTICIPATION

1. Present client survey process at all monthly staff meetings. Target departments that have not previously participated.
   a. Identify target departments for collection information at director and manager meetings.
   b. Schedule visits by the education office staff to coordinate the availability of audiovisual material.

2. Develop public relations brochure on client survey process.
   a. Design brochure for review by team leaders.
   b. Print brochure.
   c. Distribute brochure to team leaders.

3. Develop slide presentation with script on client survey process.
   a. Draft script for slides.
   b. Review script and make slides.
   c. Complete final printing of script and slides.

Numbering Paragraphs with Ctrl + H

In addition to the Outline feature, you can use Ctrl + H to turn on automatic paragraph numbering. The Outline Feature Bar does not need to be displayed for this command. The command Ctrl + H turns on automatic paragraph numbering and uses the Paragraph numbering styles as shown in figure 27.3. Automatic paragraph numbering operates similarly to outline numbering. Pressing the Tab key moves the insertion point to the next tab setting and inserts that level of numbering.

EXERCISE

Creating an Outline with Paragraph Numbering

1. At a clear editing window, create the document shown in figure 27.6 using the Ctrl + H command by completing the following steps:
    a. Change the left and right margins to 2 inches.
    b. Bold and center the title, *COMPUTER TRAINING*.
    c. Press Enter twice, then bold and center the subtitle, *Power Plus Software*.
    d. Press Enter three times.
    e. Press Ctrl + H to turn on automatic paragraph numbering.
    f. Key the text after *1*.
    g. Press the Enter key, then press the Tab key.
    h. Key the text after *a*.
    i. Continue keying text as shown in figure 27.6. Press Tab to indent the insertion point to the next tab setting and change the paragraph numbering or press Shift + Tab to move the insertion point to the previous tab setting and change the paragraph numbering. (Press Enter once after the last item.)
    j. When all text is entered, press Ctrl + H to turn off automatic paragraph numbering.
2. Save the document and name it Ch 27, Ex 02.
3. Print and then close Ch 27, Ex 02.

Figure 27.6

COMPUTER TRAINING

Power Plus Software

1. Introduction to Power Plus
    a. Manual spreadsheet
    b. Electronic spreadsheet
    c. Power Plus software
        i. Types of information
        ii. Mathematical operators

2. Range commands
    a. Command menu
        i. Worksheet commands

Outlining 667

     ii. Copy and move commands
   b. Range commands
     i. Range formatting
     ii. Range erase

3. Print and file commands
   a. Print commands
   b. Advanced file commands

4. Graph features
   a. Graph commands
     i. Data ranges
     ii. Type
     iii. View
   b. Graph options
     i. Titles
     ii. Legends

Changing the Numbering Definition

WordPerfect uses the Paragraph numbering definition by default. The numbers used at each level are described in figure 27.3. You can change the numbering definition with the Definition button on the Outline Feature Bar (the one containing the word *Paragraph*). For example, you might want to change the numbering definition to create legal numbers in a document or identify paragraphs with different types of bullets.

 Position the arrow pointer on the Definition button on the Outline Feature Bar, then click the left mouse button. This causes a drop-down list to display with the following options: *Bullets*, *Definitions*, *Headings*, *Legal*, *Legal 2*, *Numbers*, *Outline*, *Paragraph*, and *Quotations*. To change the numbering definition, position the arrow pointer on the desired definition, then click the left mouse button.

 Use the Bullets definition to insert bullets before paragraphs. The Headings definition is useful for identifying headings in a document. With the Headings definition, a heading is marked for a table of contents. (For more information on tables of contents, refer to chapter 30.) The Legal and Legal 2 definitions can be used to number paragraphs in legal documents. The Numbers definition inserts a paragraph number only for the current paragraph. You must use this style for each paragraph. The Outline definition can be used to number outlines in a document using Roman numerals. Paragraph is the default definition. Definitions and Quotations can be used to identify text as a definition or a quotation that is not numbered but can be collapsed, expanded, or otherwise manipulated as an outline family.

 If you change the numbering definition to Numbers, you can insert a number at the beginning of text by clicking the T button on the Outline Feature Bar. If you use the T button, you must insert an Indent code to indent the paragraph. You need to complete these steps for each paragraph you want numbered.

EXERCISE 3

Changing the Numbering Style

1. At a clear editing window, create the document shown in figure 27.7 by completing the following steps:
    a. Center and bold the title, *DENVER MEMORIAL HOSPITAL*.
    b. Press Enter twice, then bold and center the subtitle, *Training and Development Department*.
    c. Press Enter twice, then bold and center the heading, *AGENDA*.
    d. Press Enter three times.
    e. Click Tools, then Outline to turn on the display of the Outline Feature Bar.
    f. Change the numbering definition to Outline by completing the following steps:
        (1) Click the down-pointing triangle at the right side of the Definition button on the Outline Feature Bar.
        (2) Click *Outline* at the drop-down list.
    g. Key the remaining text as shown in figure 27.7. Use the Tab key and Shift + Tab to move the insertion point to the appropriate tab setting.
2. Save the document and name it Ch 27, Ex 03.
3. Print and then close Ch 27, Ex 03.

Figure 27.7

DENVER MEMORIAL HOSPITAL

Training and Development Department

AGENDA

I.   Approval of minutes from meeting of November 17, 1998

II. Introduction of new staff members

III. Division reports

    A. Training and Education, Steven Ayala
    B. Employee Relations, Katherine Brynn
        1. Compensations, Todd Japhet
        2. Benefits, Tanya Leigh
            a. Open enrollment period
            b. Dental programs

IV. Update on changes in policies and procedures

V.   Leadership series for 1999
    A. Development of schedule, Steven Ayala

Outlining

        B.   Equipment requirements, Julie Moceri
        C.   Employment outlook

VI.   Report on department productivity

VII.   Adjournment

EXERCISE 4

Using the Headings Numbering Definition

1. At a clear editing window, open Report 08.
2. Save the document with Save As and name it Ch 27, Ex 04.
3. Turn on outlining, change the numbering definition to Headings, and mark the headings in the document by completing the following steps:
   a. Turn on the Outline Feature Bar.
   b. Change the numbering definition to Headings.
   c. Position the insertion point at the left margin of the line containing *IDENTIFICATION OF CI*, then click the button on the Outline Feature Bar containing the T.
   d. Position the insertion point at the left margin of the line containing *Introduction*, then click the button on the Outline Feature Bar containing the T. (This will increase the size of the text and center it.)
   e. Complete steps similar to those in 3d for the following headings:
      Purpose and Scope
      Application
      Requirements
4. Save the document again with the same name (Ch 27, Ex 04).
5. Print and then close Ch 27, Ex 04.

Changing Levels

There are several methods you can use to change the level of automatic numbering in a document. To move an automatic number and the text following it to the next tab setting, choose one of the following methods:

- Press the Tab key.
- Click the button on the Outline Feature Bar containing the right-pointing arrow.

To move an automatic number and the text following it to the previous tab setting, choose one of the following methods:

- Press Shift + Tab key.
- Click the button on the Outline Feature Bar containing the left-pointing arrow.

In addition to the methods described above, you can change the numbering level at the Change Outline Level dialog box. To display this dialog box, click the O‌ptions button on the Outline Feature Bar, then click C‌hange Level at the drop-down menu. At the Change Outline Level dialog box, key the number of the desired level, then click OK or press Enter.

EXERCISE 5

Changing Numbering Levels

1. At a clear editing window, open Ch 27, Ex 03.
2. Save the document with Save As and name it Ch 27, Ex 05.
3. Change the numbering level for a few of the items in the document by completing the following steps:
   a. Change item III. B. 1. to the previous level by completing the following steps:
      (1) Position the insertion point on the *C* in *Compensations* in paragraph III. B. 1.
      (2) Press Shift + Tab.
   b. Change item III. C. 1. to the previous level by completing the following steps:
      (1) Position the insertion point on the *B* in *Benefits* in paragraph III. C. 1.
      (2) Click T‌ools, then O‌utline to display the Outline Feature Bar.
      (3) Click the button on the Outline Feature Bar containing the left-pointing arrow.
   c. Change item III. D. a. to the previous level.
   d. Change item III. D. 1. a. to the previous level.
   e. Change item V. C. to the previous level, then press Enter to create a blank line.
   f. Click C‌lose to turn off the Outline Feature Bar.
4. Save the document again with the same name (Ch 27, Ex 05).
5. Print and then close Ch 27, Ex 05.

Showing and Hiding Outline Families

If you are working in an outline containing many levels, you can collapse the outline by hiding subordinate levels in large outline families. An outline family is the current level where the insertion point is located, plus any sublevels within the level. Figure 27.8 shows examples of family outlines. If an outline has been collapsed, it can be expanded back to its original size. When an outline is collapsed, you can easily perform such actions as viewing, moving, copying, or deleting portions of the outline.

Outlining 671

Figure 27.8

Outline Families

```
                   I.    Evaluation

 Body              ┌The governing body, administration, medical staff, and training department will
 Text              └annually reappraise the employee evaluation program in the following areas:

                      ┌A.   Assignment of authority
                      │        1.    Non-medical employees
 Outline ─────────────┤        2.    Medical employees
 Family               │        3.    Administration
                      │  B.   Integration of information
                      │        1.    Internally
                      └        2.    Externally

                   II.   Follow-up

 Body              ┌As stated in the goals, when problems are identified or areas of improvement are
 Text              │noted, action and follow-up must be taken to ensure patient care is provided. Steps
                   └to take for improvement include the following:

                      ┌A.   Education/training
 Outline              │ B.   Department changes
 Family               │        1.    Personnel
                      │        2.    Equipment
                      └ C.   Revised policies and procedures
```

You can hide sublevels of an outline family with the button on the Outline Feature Bar containing the minus sign. For example, to hide the outline levels below *I. Evaluation* in the outline in figure 27.8 using the Outline Feature Bar, position the insertion point anywhere on the line containing *I. Evaluation*. Position the insertion point on the button containing the minus sign, then click the left mouse button.

When you click the button containing the minus sign, all levels below the heading *I. Evaluation* are removed from the screen. The number *1* that displays to the left of the left margin displays with a minus sign. This minus sign indicates that not all levels of the outline family are displayed.

After hiding an outline family, display the family again by clicking the button on the Outline Feature Bar containing the plus sign.

Displaying Specific Outline Levels

 With the Show Outline Levels button on the Outline Feature Bar, you can specify the number of levels you want displayed in an outline. For example, to display only the first level of an outline, you would click the Show Outline Levels button on the Outline Feature Bar, then click 1 at the drop-down menu.

Hiding/Displaying Body Text

If you want to hide just the body text in a document, click the Hide Body Text button on the Outline Feature Bar. This hides body text but leaves all levels of numbering. To redisplay the body text, click the Show Body Text button on the Outline Feature Bar.

EXERCISE 6

Showing and Hiding Outline Parts

1. At a clear editing window, create the outline shown in figure 27.9 by completing the following steps:
   a. Center and bold the title, *EMPLOYEE EVALUATION RECOMMENDATIONS*.
   b. Press Enter three times.
   c. Turn on the Outline Feature Bar.
   d. Change the numbering Definition to Outline.
   e. Key the text in item I.
   f. Press Enter twice. Change this to a text paragraph by clicking the button on the Outline Feature Bar containing the T.
   g. Key the paragraph below I.
   h. Press Enter twice.
   i. Change back to outlining by clicking the button on the Outline Feature Bar containing the T.
   j. Key the text in item II.
   k. Continue keying the text of the document following similar steps.
2. After keying the outline, complete the following steps:
   a. Hide all outline levels below *III. Team Expectations* by completing the following steps:
      (1) Position the insertion point anywhere on the line containing *III. Team Expectations*.
      (2) Position the insertion point on the button containing the minus sign, then click the left mouse button.
   b. Hide all outline levels below *IV. Team Training*, by completing steps similar to those in 2a.
   c. Show all outline levels below *III. Team Expectations* by completing the following steps:
      (1) Position the insertion point anywhere on the line containing *III. Team Expectations*.
      (2) Position the insertion point on the button containing the plus sign, then click the left mouse button.
   d. Show all outline levels below *IV. Team Training*.
   e. Display only the first level of the outline by clicking the Show Outline Levels button on the Outline Feature Bar, then clicking on 1.
   f. Display all levels of the outline by clicking the Show Outline Levels button on the Outline Feature Bar, then clicking 2.
   g. Hide the body text in the outline by clicking the Hide Body Text button on the Outline Feature Bar.
   h. Redisplay the body text in the outline by clicking the Show Body Text button on the Outline Feature Bar.
3. Save the outline and name it Ch 27, Ex 06.
4. Print and then close Ch 27, Ex 06.

Figure 27.9

EMPLOYEE EVALUATION RECOMMENDATIONS

    I.   Administration of Employee Evaluation

Based on employee comments from the original evaluation process, employees strongly objected to the amount of money spent on evaluations. Employee evaluations will be performed every year instead of every six months.

    II.   Number of Teams and Members

Employees are a strong force within an organization and capable of creating positive and negative results. The mechanism for participative management is in place through the employee evaluation teams and can encourage employees to work with management to influence excellence in the organization.

        A.   The number of teams will be five.
        B.   Membership on each team will be nine.

    III.   Team Expectations

All team members will be made aware of certain expectations that govern the employee evaluation process.

        A.   Regular team meetings will be held.
        B.   Both technical and analytical skills will be used.
        C.   Specific time frames will exist for each team meeting and management presentation.
        D.   All management presentations will be videotaped.
        E.   All members will participate in management presentations.

    IV.   Team Training

All team members and team leaders will be provided with specific training opportunities to help them be more effective in the employee evaluation process. Training topics include:

        A.   Brainstorming
        B.   Problem solving
        C.   Group dynamics
        D.   Data gathering

Editing Outline Families

With the Outline Feature Bar displayed, you can move, copy, cut, and/or paste an outline family. Before cutting or copying an outline family, it must be selected. To select an outline family, position the pointer to the left of the first line of the outline family until it turns into a double-headed arrow pointing up and down, then click the left mouse button. You may need to scroll the text to the right on the screen to view the area between the number outside the left margin and the outline number. After selecting the outline family, use the normal methods for cutting, copying, deleting, and/or pasting selected text.

EXERCISE 7

Moving and Deleting Outline Parts

1. At a clear editing window, open Ch 27, Ex 03.
2. Save the document with Save As and name it Ch 27, Ex 07.
3. Move *III. Division reports* and all sublevel paragraphs below *IV. Update on changes in policies and procedures* by completing the following steps:
    a. Turn on the Outline Feature Bar.
    b. Make sure the outline symbols are visible at the left side of the document window. If not, position the arrow pointer on the left scroll arrow on the horizontal scroll bar and click the left mouse button until the symbols are visible.
    c. Position the pointer to the left of the line containing *III. Division reports* until it turns into a double-headed arrow pointing up and down.
    d. Click the left mouse button.
    e. Click the Cut button on the Toolbar.
    f. Turn on Reveal Codes, then move the insertion point left of the [Style] code and the [Para Style: Level 1] code on the line containing *V. Leadership series for 1999*.
    g. Click the Paste button on the Toolbar.
4. Delete the outline family beginning with *V. Leadership series for 1999* by completing the following steps:
    a. Position the arrow pointer to the left of the line containing *V. Leadership series for 1999* until it turns into a double-headed arrow pointing up and down.
    b. Click the left mouse button.
    c. Press the Delete key.
5. Save the document again with the same name (Ch 27, Ex 07).
6. Print and then close Ch 27, Ex 07.

You can also use the mouse to drag a selected outline family to a different location in the outline. Display the Outline Feature Bar, then position the pointer to the left of the line containing the outline family to be moved until it turns into a double-headed arrow pointing up and down. Hold down the left mouse button and drag the double-headed arrow up or down. This causes a thin horizontal line to display. Continue dragging the double-headed arrow up or down until the thin horizontal line is positioned in the desired location, then release the mouse button.

EXERCISE 8

Dragging Outline Families to New Locations

1. At a clear editing window, open Ch 27, Ex 06.
2. Save the document with Save As and name it Ch 27, Ex 08.
3. Move *II.* below *III.* by completing the following steps:
    a. Turn on the Outline Feature Bar.
    b. Make sure the outline symbols are visible at the left side of the document window. If not, position the arrow pointer on the left scroll arrow on the horizontal scroll bar and click the left mouse button until the symbols are visible.

Outlining

c. Click the Show Outline Levels button on the Outline Feature Bar, then click 1. (This hides all levels except level 1.)
   d. Position the pointer to the left of the line containing *II. Number of Teams and Members* until it turns into a double-headed arrow pointing up and down.
   e. Hold down the left mouse button, drag the double-headed arrow down until the thin horizontal line displays below *III. Team Expectations* and above *IV. Team Training*, then release the mouse button.
4. Follow steps similar to those in step 3 to move *IV. Team Training* below *II. Team Expectations* and above *III. Number of Teams and Members*.
5. Click the Show Outline Levels button on the Outline Feature Bar, then click 2 to display all levels of the outline.
6. Save the document again with the same name (Ch 27, Ex 08).
7. Print and then close Ch 27, Ex 08.

Changing Outline Number

By default, outlining begins with number 1 and is incremented from there. If necessary, you can specify a different number by clicking the Options button on the Outline Feature Bar and then clicking Set Number at the drop-down list. If you specify a new number, succeeding outline numbers are incremented from this new number.

EXERCISE

Changing an Outline Number

1. At a clear editing window, open Ch 27, Ex 01.
2. Save the document with Save As and name it Ch 27, Ex 09.
3. Change the outlining number by completing the following steps:
   a. Turn on the Outline Feature Bar.
   b. Position the insertion point on the line containing *1. Present client survey process....*
   c. Click Options, then Set Number.
   d. At the Set Paragraph Number dialog box, key **4**.
   e. Click OK or press Enter.
4. Save the document again with the same name (Ch 27, Ex 09).
5. Print and then close Ch 27, Ex 09.

Defining Outlines

The numbering definitions such as Paragraph, Outline, Numbers, and Legal are predefined styles. If you click the Options button on the Outline Feature Bar, then click Define Outline at the drop-down menu, the Outline Define dialog box displays. At this dialog box, you can create and edit numbering definitions. For more information on creating customized numbering definitions, refer to the WordPerfect help system.

CHAPTER SUMMARY

▼ Paragraphs can be numbered automatically with the command Ctrl + H (Paragraph numbering definition only) or with the Outline feature.

▼ To create an outline, turn on the display of the Outline Feature Bar.

▼ By default, WordPerfect uses a Paragraph numbering style. When the Outline Feature Bar is first displayed, a number 1 followed by a period is automatically inserted in the document at the left margin.

▼ Change the numbering definition with the Definition button on the Outline Feature Bar.

▼ Use the Tab key, Shift + Tab, or the Outline Feature Bar to change the level of automatic numbering in a document.

▼ At the Outline Feature Bar, an outline family can be collapsed (hidden), then viewed, moved, copied, or deleted. The outline family can then be expanded again.

▼ At the Outline Feature Bar, you can also display specific outline levels, hide just the body text in an outline, or move, copy, cut, and/or paste an outline family.

COMMANDS REVIEW

	Mouse	Keyboard
Number paragraphs automatically		CTRL + H
Outline Feature Bar	Tools, Outline	Tools, Outline
Turn outlining off	Options, End Outline	ALT + SHIFT + O, End Outline
Turn off display of Outline Feature Bar	Close	ALT + SHIFT + C
Change automatic numbering level to next setting	Click right-pointing arrow button on Outline Feature Bar; or Options, Change Level	ALT + SHIFT + N
Change automatic numbering level to previous setting	Click left-pointing arrow button on Outline Feature Bar; or Options, Change Level	ALT + SHIFT + P
Hide outline family	With insertion point on first line of family, click left mouse button on minus sign on Outline Feature Bar	With insertion point on first line of family, press ALT + SHIFT + I
Expand hidden outline family	Click left mouse button on plus sign on Outline Feature Bar	ALT + SHIFT + S

CHECK YOUR UNDERSTANDING

Completion: In the space provided at the right, indicate the correct term, command, or number.

1. When you display the Outline Feature Bar, you are automatically in this mode. _____

2. To display the Outline Feature Bar, click this option on the Menu bar, then click <u>O</u>utline at the drop-down menu. _____

3. To number paragraphs without turning on the Outline Feature Bar, use this command. _____

4. Press this key on the keyboard to move the insertion point to the next tab setting and insert the level numbering for that tab setting. _____

5. This is the second level numbering for the default numbering style. _____

6. This is the third level numbering for the default numbering style. _____

7. Use this keyboard command to move the insertion point to the previous tab setting and insert the appropriate level numbering. _____

8. Press this key to move the insertion point down to the next line and insert the appropriate level numbering. _____

9. Click this button on the Outline Feature Bar to change the numbering method. _____

10. This refers to the current level in an outline where the insertion point is located plus any sublevels within the level. _____

SKILL ASSESSMENTS

Assessment 1

1. At a clear editing window, create the document shown in figure 27.10 using the Outline feature. (Make sure the numbering definition is Paragraph.)
2. Save the document and name it Ch 27, SA 01.
3. Print and then close Ch 27, SA 01.

Figure 27.10

LOAN AGREEMENT OUTLINE

1. Finance charge
   a. Accrual of finance charges
   b. Determining finance charges

2. Annual percentage rate
   a. Variable rate loans
      i. Personal line of credit
      ii. Shared secured loans
   b. Fixed rate loans
      i. Certificate secured loans
      ii. Other fixed rate loans

3. Other costs and charges
   a. Closing costs
   b. Late charges
   c. Return check fees
   d. Annual fees
   e. Attorney and collection costs

4. Amendments

5. Delay in enforcement

6. Credit Information/Financial Statements

Assessment 2

1. At a clear editing window, create the outline shown in figure 27.11 using the Outline feature. (Be sure to change the numbering definition to Outline.)
2. Save the outline and name it Ch 27, SA 02.
3. Print and then close Ch 27, SA 02.

Figure 27.11

TECHNICIAN COUNCIL AGENDA

I. Approval of minutes from March 10, 1998 meeting

II. Job Code Description

    A. Marty Smythe, job description draft
        1. JCAH recommendations
        2. New job descriptions
    B. Juliette Okada, draft clarification and corrections

III. Communication Task Force

    A. Distribution of information to LPNs
    B. LPN forum
    C. Letter to Berrington Vocational Technical Institute

IV. Education Task Force

    A. Education forum for hospital staff
    B. Time line for meetings

V. Nurse Governance Committee

    A. Representation from hospital
    B. Congress session

Assessment 3

1. At a clear editing window, open Ch 27, SA 01.
2. Save the document with Save As and name it Ch 27, SA 03.
3. Move the outline family beginning with *b. Fixed rate loans* above the outline family beginning with *a. Variable rate loans*.
4. Move the outline family beginning with *2. Annual percentage rate* above the outline family beginning with *1. Finance charge*.
5. Delete 3e and then 3c.
6. Save the document again with the same name (Ch 27, SA 03).
7. Print and then close Ch 27, SA 03.

Assessment 4

1. At a clear editing window, open Report 02.
2. Save the document with Save As and name it Ch 27, SA 04.
3. Make the following changes to the report:
    a. Move the insertion point to the end of the document and then press Enter.

  b. Change the title so it reads *TELECOMMUNICATIONS TECHNOLOGY* (rather than *DEVELOPMENT OF TELECOMMUNICATIONS TECHNOLOGY*).
  c. Turn on the Outline Feature Bar.
  d. Change the numbering definition to Headings.
  e. Mark the following text as headings:
    TELECOMMUNICATIONS TECHNOLOGY
    Contributions of Major Historical Events
    Development of a World Market
    The American Civil War
    Colonization
    The 1870s Depression
4. Display only the title and headings in the report.
5. Move *Contributions of Major Historical Events* below *The 1870s Depression*.
6. Display all levels in the document.
7. Save the document again with the same name (Ch 27, SA 04).
8. Print and then close Ch 27, SA 04.

Assessment 5

1. At a clear editing window, change the font to 12-point Century Schoolbook, then create the document shown in figure 27.12. Use the Outline feature to create the numbered paragraphs.
2. Save the document and name it Ch 27, SA 05.
3. Print and then close Ch 27, SA 05.

Figure 27.12

PUBLICIZING THE CLIENT SURVEY PROJECT

1. Produce Client Survey buttons.

 a. Contact the director of public relations for button design and production.
 b. Relay cost information to administrator.

2. Publicize Client Survey week in the dining room of each facility.

 a. Gather materials for the booth at the main dining room. Include brochures, slide show, and buttons.
 b. Request a poster from each team to place in the booth.
 c. Develop volunteer sign-up sheet. Make the sign-up sheet available at the booth.

3. Start bulletin board for Client Survey activities, pictures, announcements, and communications.

 a. Research bulletin board size and price.
 b. Request space from Interior Design committee.
 c. Establish and maintain bulletin board.

Assessment 6

1. At a clear editing window, open Ch 27, SA 05.
2. Save the document with Save As and name it Ch 27, SA 06.
3. Change the level and automatic numbering for the items below:
    a. Change item 1a to the previous level.
    b. Change the new item 3b to the next level.
    c. Change item 3b (what used to be 3c) to the next level.
4. Save the document again with the same name (Ch 27, SA 06).
5. Print and then close Ch 27, SA 06.

28

SORTING AND SELECTING

PERFORMANCE OBJECTIVE

Upon successful completion of chapter 28, you will be able to sort information in a properly prepared file and select specific groups of information from a larger group.

WordPerfect is a word processing program that includes some basic database functions. Database programs contain features that let you alphabetize information or arrange numbers numerically. In addition, with a database program you can select specific files or records from a larger file.

Sorting

Text established in a line, paragraph, data file, parallel columns, or a table can be sorted alphanumerically (letters and digits) or numerically (numbers). To sort text, click Tools, then Sort. This causes the Sort dialog box shown in figure 28.1 to display.

Figure 28.1

Sort Dialog Box

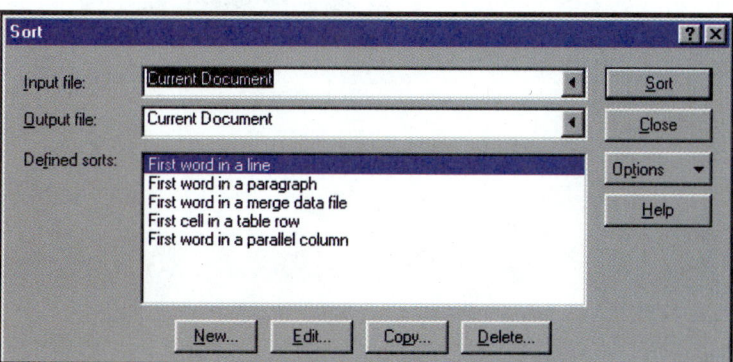

Sorting and Selecting 683

Determining Input and Output Files

The default settings for the Input file and Output file options at the Sort dialog box are Current Document. At these settings, text in the current document is sorted and then redisplayed in the editing window. To sort a document other than the one currently displayed, select the text in the Input file text box, then key the name of the file to be sorted. To send sorted text to a separate document, select the text in the Output file text box, then key a name for the document.

Using Predefined Sorts

WordPerfect displays predefined sorts in the Defined sorts list box. The type of sort selected will vary depending on the open document. For example, if you open a document containing a table, the *First cell in a table row* option is selected. If this is the type of sort you want to complete, click the Sort button. WordPerfect sorts the contents of the first cell in each table row and rearranges them alphabetically in ascending order (A to Z).

EXERCISE

Sorting a List

1. At a clear editing window, key the text shown in figure 28.2 at the left margin.
2. Save the document and name it Ch 28, Ex 01.
3. With Ch 28, Ex 01 displayed in the editing window, sort the list alphabetically by last name by completing the following steps:
   a. Click Tools, then Sort.
   b. At the Sort dialog box, make sure *First word in a paragraph* is selected, then click the Sort button.
4. After the document is sorted, save it again with the same name (Ch 28, Ex 01).
5. Print and then close Ch 28, Ex 01.

Figure 28.2

Hess, Joanna. *Desktop Publishing Projects.* Seneca, NY: Thousand Pines Publishing, 1997.
Ulrich, Thomas. *Personal Desktop Publishing.* St. Paul, MN: Patterson Publishers, 1998.
Capelino, George. *Desktop Publishing Guidebook.* Arlington, VA: Myers Press, 1996.
Bove, Emil. *Proofreading and Editing Documents.* Miami, FL: Palm West Publishers, 1997.

EXERCISE 2

Sorting Cell Contents

1. At a clear editing window, open Table 02.
2. Save the document with Save As and name it Ch 28, Ex 02.
3. Sort the contents of the cells in each table row (except the first row) by completing the following steps:
   a. Select all rows in the table except the first row.
   b. Click Tools, then Sort.
   c. At the Sort dialog box, make sure *First cell in a table row* is selected, then click the Sort button.
4. Save the document again with the same name (Ch 28, Ex 02).
5. Print and then close Ch 28, Ex 02.

Creating a New Sort Definition

With the predefined sorts, WordPerfect sorts the first line, paragraph, column, record, or row in a document. If you want to sort on different text such as the second word in a line or paragraph or the text in cells in the third column of a table, you must either create a new sort definition or edit an existing definition. To create a new sort definition, click the New button at the Sort dialog box. This causes the New Sort dialog box shown in figure 28.3 to display.

New Sort Dialog Box

Figure 28.3

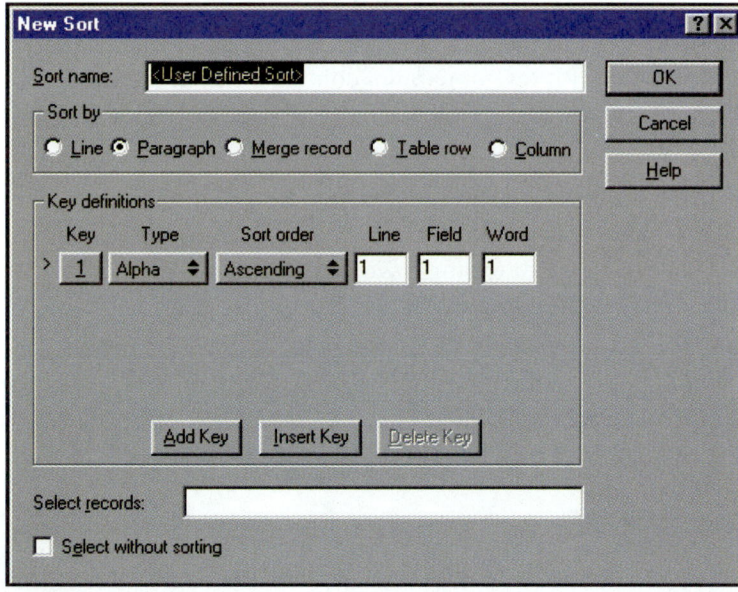

Sorting and Selecting 685

Naming a Sort Definition

At the New Sort dialog box, key a name for the new sort in the Sort name text box. The name can contain spaces and should be unique from other sort definition names. By default, WordPerfect inserts *<User Defined Sort>* in the Sort name text box. You can use this name if you do not want to give the sort definition a specific or unique name. If you change options at the New Sort dialog box with the name *<User Defined Sort>*, the changes remain in effect for only that sort. When you display the New Sort dialog box again, the options return to the default settings.

Determining the Type of Sort

You can choose to sort text established in lines, paragraphs, merge records, rows in a table, or text in parallel columns. Figure 28.4 displays the definitions of the sort types.

Figure 28.4 — Sort Types

Sort Type	Sort Definition
Line	Text that ends in a hard return.
Paragraph	Text that ends with two or more hard returns.
Merge record	Record that ends with an **ENDRECORD** code.
Table row	A row of cells in a table.
Parallel column	Each record in a row of columns.

WordPerfect automatically determines the sort type based on the sort document. For example, if you sort a document containing text established at tab settings, WordPerfect selects the Line option. If you sort a document containing records in a data file, WordPerfect automatically selects the Merge record option. WordPerfect selects Table row if the document to be sorted contains a table. If you sort a document with text in parallel columns, the Column option is selected.

Defining Keys

With options in the Key definitions section of the New Sort dialog box you can define the type of sort. WordPerfect gives key 1 first priority, key 2 second priority, and so on. A sort can be performed on more than one key. For example, you can sort states alphabetically, then sort the last names of individuals alphabetically within each state.

By default, there is one key defined. The settings for key 1 will vary depending on the text in the editing window or in the file identified for sorting. For example, if you open the New Sort dialog box in a document containing paragraphs, the default setting for Key 1 is an alphanumeric paragraph sort in ascending order on Line 1, Field 1, and Word 1.

Defining the Sort Type

The key type can be alpha or numeric. Alpha is the default setting and will sort numbers and letters together and display numbers first. This is referred to as an alphanumeric sort. Numbers in an alphanumeric sort are treated as regular characters and are read from left to right. For example, in an alphanumeric sort, the number 110 would be sorted before 23. The numbers are read from left to right and the 1 in 110 causes the number to be sorted on that value. In a numeric sort, 23 would be sorted before 110 because 23 has a lesser value.

If you are sorting text that contains both numbers and letters, complete an alphanumeric sort. You can also complete an alphanumeric sort on numbers of the same length such as ZIP Codes, telephone numbers, and Social Security numbers. Conduct a numeric sort on text that contains only numbers with values, or numbers with varying lengths.

Defining the Sort Order

By default, a sort is completed in ascending order. Letters are sorted from A to Z, and numbers are sorted from negative to positive. This sort order can be changed to Descending, which sorts letters from Z to A, and numbers from positive to negative.

Defining Divisions

Records are divided into divisions. The divisions vary depending on the record type. The divisions for each record type are shown in figure 28.5.

Figure 28.5

Record Type Divisions

Record Type	Divisions
Line	Field, Word
Paragraph	Line, Field, Word
Merge record	Field, Line, Word
Table Row	Column, Line, Word
Column	Column, Line, Word

In the Line and Paragraph sort, a field is text divided by a tab or indent. With the Merge record sort, a field is text that ends in an ENDFIELD code. In all sorts, a word is text that is divided by a space, punctuation, a forward slash (/), or a hard hyphen. In a Paragraph sort, a line is text that is divided by a soft or hard return. In a Column sort, columns are divided by hard page breaks and are numbered from left to right.

Adding a Key

When the Sort dialog box is first displayed, there is only one key specified in the Key definitions section. This is the active key. The active key is designated by the marker (>) displayed before the key. If you want to sort or select on more than one key, add a key by clicking the Add Key button. The Add Key button is located at the bottom of the Key definitions section. When you click the Add Key button, a key is added to the end of the Key list.

You can also insert a key with the Insert Key button. When you click the Insert Key button, a key is inserted above the active key. A maximum of nine keys can be defined in the Key definitions section.

Deleting a Key

A key or keys can be deleted from the Key definitions section of the New Sort dialog box. To delete a key, make the key active with the mark symbol (>) by clicking the key number. To delete the key, click the Delete Key button located at the bottom right side of the Key definitions section of the New Sort dialog box. Exercises 3 through 8 will allow you to practice all the different types of sorts.

EXERCISE 3

Sorting by Social Security Number

1. At a clear editing window, complete the following steps:
   a. Make sure the Ruler Bar is displayed.
   b. Clear all previous tabs, then set a left tab at the 1.75-inch mark, the 3.5-inch mark, and the 5.5-inch mark.
   c. Key the text in figure 28.6 in columns. (Be sure to press the Tab key before each column, even the first column.)
2. Save the document and name it Ch 28, Ex 03.
3. With Ch 28, Ex 03 displayed in the editing window, sort by Social Security number in the third column by completing the following steps:
   a. Click Tools, then Sort.
   b. At the Sort dialog box, click the New button.
   c. At the New Sort dialog box, make sure Line is selected in the Sort by section.
   d. Change the number in the Field text box to 4. To do this with the mouse, select the *1* in the Field text box, then key **4**.
   e. Make sure the number in the Word text box is *1*.
   f. Click OK.
   g. At the Sort dialog box, click the Sort button.
4. Print Ch 28, Ex 03.
5. With Ch 28, Ex 03 still open in the editing window, sort by last name in the first column by completing the following steps:
   a. Click Tools, then Sort.
   b. At the Sort dialog box, make sure *<User Defined Sort>* is selected in the Defined sorts list box, then click the New button.
   c. At the New Sort dialog box, change the number in the Field text box to *2*. (The first column is the second field.)
   d. Change the number in the Word text box to *2*. (The last name is the second word in the field.)
   e. Click OK.
   f. At the Sort dialog box, click the Sort button.
6. Print and then close Ch 28, Ex 03.

Figure 28.6

Bernice Light	Surgical Unit	423-44-9934
Ola Busching	Labor and Delivery	532-33-4923
Tina Vitali	Pediatrics	132-03-2965
Thomas Heusers	Coronary Care Unit	217-43-8613

EXERCISE 4

Sorting by Last Name

1. At a clear editing window, key the text shown in figure 28.7 at the left margin.
2. Save the document and name it Ch 28, Ex 04.
3. With Ch 28, Ex 04 displayed in the editing window, sort the list alphabetically by last name by completing the following steps:
    a. Click Tools, then Sort.
    b. At the Sort dialog box, click the New button.
    c. At the New Sort dialog box, key **Line sort on word 2** in the Sort name text box. Make sure Line is selected in the Sort by section and that *Alpha* displays in the Type text box.
    d. Change the number in the Word text box to *2*.
    e. Make sure the number in the Field text box is *1*.
    f. Click OK.
    g. At the Sort dialog box, click the Sort button.
4. Save the document again with the same name (Ch 28, Ex 04).
5. Print and then close Ch 28, Ex 04.

Figure 28.7

Krista Slater, "Advancements in CD-ROM"
Adam Perrault, "Artificial Intelligence"
Bryant Hunter, "Fuzzy Logic"
Corey Gentry, "Fifth Generation Computers"
Erik Cushman, "Innovative Input Devices"

EXERCISE 5

Sorting Paragraphs by First Word

1. At a clear editing window, open Loan doc.
2. Save the document with Save As and name it Ch 28, Ex 05.
3. With Ch 28, Ex 05 open in the editing window, sort the paragraphs alphabetically by the first word by completing the following steps:
    a. Click Tools, then Sort.
    b. At the Sort dialog box, click *<User Defined Sort>* in the Defined sorts list box, then click the New button.
    c. At the New Sort dialog box, change the number in the Field text box to *2*.
    d. Make sure the number in the Line and Word text boxes is *1* and the sort type is Alpha.
    e. Click OK.
    f. At the Sort dialog box, click the Sort button.
4. Edit the document so that the paragraph numbers are in sequential order. Check the spacing of paragraphs in the document and, if necessary, make adjustments.
5. Save the document with the same name (Ch 28, Ex 05).
6. Print and then close Ch 28, Ex 05.

EXERCISE

Sorting by Last Name

1. At a clear editing window, open Customer df.
2. Save the data file with Save As and name it Ch 28, Ex 06.
3. With Ch 28, Ex 06 open in the editing window, sort the records alphabetically by last name by completing the following steps:
   a. Display the Sort dialog box.
   b. At the Sort dialog box, click <*User Defined Sort*> in the De*f*ined sorts list box, then click the *N*ew button.
   c. At the New Sort dialog box, change the number in the Field text box to *3*.
   d. Make sure the number in the Line and Word text boxes is *1*.
   e. Click OK.
   f. At the Sort dialog box, click the *S*ort button.
4. Print Ch 28, Ex 06.
5. With Ch 28, Ex 06 open on the screen, sort the records alphanumerically by Social Security number. (The Social Security number is in the sixth field.)
6. After the records are sorted, print Ch 28, Ex 06 again.
7. Save the document with the same name (Ch 28, Ex 06).
8. Close Ch 28, Ex 06.

EXERCISE

Sorting a Table by Last Name

1. At a clear editing window, open Table 03.
2. Save the table and name it Ch 28, Ex 07.
3. With Ch 28, Ex 07 open in the editing window, sort the table by the last name by completing the following steps (the first row is established as a header row, so you do not have to select the cells first):
   a. Display the Sort dialog box.
   b. At the Sort dialog box, click <*User Defined Sort*> in the De*f*ined sorts list box, then click the *N*ew button.
   c. At the New Sort dialog box, change the number in the Word text box to *2*.
   d. Make sure the number in the Column and Line text boxes is *1*.
   e. Click OK.
   f. At the Sort dialog box, click the *S*ort button.
4. Save the document again with the same name (Ch 28, Ex 07).
5. Print and then close Ch 28, Ex 07.

EXERCISE 8

Sorting Columns by Area Code

1. At a clear editing window, open Para col.
2. Save the document with Save As and name it Ch 28, Ex 08.
3. With Ch 28, Ex 08 open in the editing window, sort the columns alphanumerically by area code by completing the following steps:
   a. Display the Sort dialog box.
   b. At the Sort dialog box, click *<User Defined Sort>* in the De<u>f</u>ined sorts list box, then click the <u>N</u>ew button.
   c. At the New Sort dialog box, change the number in the Column text box to *2*, the number in the Line text box to *4*, and the number in the Word text box to *1*.
   d. Click OK.
   e. At the Sort dialog box, click the <u>S</u>ort button.
4. Save the document again with the same name (Ch 28, Ex 08).
5. Print and then close Ch 28, Ex 08.

Editing a Sort Definition

A sort definition sorts on specific text in a document. If you decide to sort on different text, you can edit or copy an existing sort definition or create a new definition. To edit a sort definition, display the Sort dialog box, select the sort definition to be edited in the De<u>f</u>ined sorts list box, then click the <u>E</u>dit button. This causes the Edit Sort dialog box to display. The Edit Sort dialog box contains the same options as the New Sort dialog box shown in figure 28.3. Make any necessary changes to this dialog box, then click OK. Copy a sort definition in the same manner except click the Co<u>p</u>y button at the Sort dialog box.

EXERCISE 9

Editing a Sort

1. At a clear editing window, open Ch 28, Ex 01.
2. Save the document and name it Ch 28, Ex 09.
3. Edit the *Line sort on word 2* sort definition, then sort the text by the first word in the publication name by completing the following steps:
   a. Click <u>T</u>ools, then So<u>r</u>t.
   b. At the Sort dialog box, click *Line sort on word 2*, then click the <u>E</u>dit button.
   c. At the Edit Sort dialog box, key **Line sort on word 3** in the <u>S</u>ort name text box.
   d. Change the number in the Word text box to *3*.
   e. Click OK.
   f. At the Sort dialog box click the <u>S</u>ort button.
4. Save the sorted document with the same name (Ch 28, Ex 09).
5. Print and then close Ch 28, Ex 09.

Deleting a Sort Definition

A sort definition can be deleted at the Sort dialog box. To do this, display the Sort dialog box, select the sort definition to be deleted in the De_f_ined sorts list box, then click the _D_elete button. At the question, *Are you sure you want to delete this item?*, click _Y_es.

EXERCISE 10

Deleting Sort Definitions

1. At a clear editing window, delete the sort definition, *Line sort on word 3*, by completing the following steps:
   a. Display the Sort dialog box.
   b. At the Sort dialog box, click *Line sort on word 3* in the De_f_ined sorts list box.
   c. Click the _D_elete button.
   d. At the question *Are you sure you want to delete this item?*, click _Y_es.
2. Click _C_lose to close the Sort dialog box.

Sorting Considerations

Sorting can be performed on words within lines and fields. When sorting words, WordPerfect reads words within a field or line from left to right. In some situations, consideration must be given to how the sort is conducted. For example, if data file records contain a field with the city, state, and ZIP Code, and you want to sort on the state, you must identify the field number, then the second word (the city is first and the state is second). The records containing one-word cities would sort correctly, but records containing two-word cities would not. The two-word cities sort on the second word. A record containing Dover, Delaware, would sort on Delaware, but a record containing San Diego, California, would sort on Diego.

There are two methods that can be used to ensure that sorting occurs correctly. One method is to enter two-word cities (or any other words that should be kept together) with a hard space. For example, when keying San Diego, press Ctrl + space bar between San and Diego. The other method is to identify the word in a line or field reading the line or field from right to left. If the field contains the city, state, and ZIP Code, you can tell WordPerfect to sort on the second word from the right. This sorts the state correctly. To use this method, key a negative number in the Word text box. For example, to sort on the state when the line contains the city, state, and ZIP Code, key the number **-2** in the Word text box. The hyphen before the 2 tells WordPerfect to read the words from right to left.

When you key a hyphen between hyphenated last names, or use a hyphen in numbers such as Social Security numbers or telephone numbers, the name and numbers are treated as one unit. If you want to sort on parts of a number, such as the month or year in a date, separate the numbers by a slash rather than a hyphen. For example, key dates in this manner: 05/09/98. This way, the year is considered the third word (the month, 05, is the first word; the day, 09, is the second word; and the year, 98, is the third word).

Before sorting, save the document. That way, if sorting does not operate the way you intended, you can remove the sorted document from the screen and open the previously saved document.

If you want to sort only a portion of the text in a document, you must select the text first. For example, if you want to sort columns of text that appear within a letter or memo, select the columns of text (including the tab set code) before displaying the Sort dialog box.

EXERCISE 11

Sorting by ZIP Code

1. At a clear editing window, open Customer df.
2. Save the data file with Save As and name it Ch 28, Ex 11.
3. With Ch 28, Ex 11 open in the editing window, sort the records alphanumerically by ZIP Code by completing the following steps:
   a. Display the Sort dialog box.
   b. At the Sort dialog box, click *<User Defined Sort>,* then click the New button.
   c. At the New Sort dialog box, change the number in the Field text box to *4*, the number in the Line text box to *2*, and the number in the Word text box to *-1*. (Enter the hyphen before *1* to tell WordPerfect to read the words from right to left).
   d. Click OK.
   e. At the Sort dialog box, click the Sort button.
4. Save the records again with the same name (Ch 28, Ex 11).
5. Print and then close Ch 28, Ex 11.

EXERCISE 12

Sorting by Percentage

1. At a clear editing window, open Tab 04.
2. Save the document with Save As and name it Ch 28, Ex 12.
3. With Ch 28, Ex 12 open in the editing window, sort the third column numerically by percentage by completing the following steps:
   a. Select only the columns (excluding the title and the blank line spaces below the title).
   b. Display the Sort dialog box.
   c. At the Sort dialog box, click *<User Defined Sort>*, then click the New button.
   d. At the New Sort dialog box, change the sort type to Numeric and the number in the Field text box to *4*.
   e. Click OK.
   f. At the Sort dialog box, click the Sort button.
4. Remove the percent symbol after 8.25, then insert a percent symbol after 3.21.
5. Save the records again with the same name (Ch 28, Ex 12).
6. Print and then close Ch 28, Ex 12.

Selecting Records

With the Select records option at the New Sort or Edit Sort dialog boxes, you can write a *select equation* to select specific text from a document. This might be useful, for example, in a situation where you want to select records from a data file of those individuals with a specific ZIP Code.

Before selecting records from a document, save the document first. After selecting records, either save the document with the same name (overwriting the original records), or save the document with a new name.

Writing Select Equations

The symbols shown in figure 28.8 can be used to write select equations:

Figure 28.8 — Select Operators

=	Equal	>	Greater than
<>	Not equal to	<	Less than
&	And	>=	Greater than or equal to
|	Or	<=	Less than or equal to

The ampersand symbol (&) specifies two conditions and describes "and" situations. With this symbol, the record must contain both conditions—for example, all customers living in a specific state *and* having a specific area code. The vertical line (|) specifies records that match either one of two conditions and describes "or" situations. For example, with the vertical line you can retrieve all customers who live in Houston *or* Dallas. The other symbols are mathematical symbols with the conditions shown in figure 28.8. Figure 28.9 shows examples of how select equations can be written to select specific records. When keying a select equation, leave a space before and after the ampersand (&) symbol or the vertical line (|), and leave a space before the key number, but not before or after the select mathematical symbol.

Figure 28.9 — Select Equation Examples

1. Suppose key 1 is the committee assignment, and you want to select records of individuals serving on the Publicity committee. The select equation you would key at the New Sort or Edit Sort dialog boxes is **key 1=Publicity**.

2. Suppose key 1 is the software program, and you want to retrieve all records except those customers using PlanPlus software. The select equation you would key at the New Sort or Edit Sort dialog boxes is **key 1<>PlanPlus**.

3. Suppose key 1 is the company name, key 2 is the state, and you want to select records of individuals working for CompuPlus in the state of Oregon. The select equation you would key at the New Sort or Edit Sort dialog boxes is **key 1=CompuPlus & key 2=Oregon**.

4. Suppose key 1 is the Social Security number, and you want to select records of those individuals with numbers higher than 125-55-7890. The select equation you would key at the New Sort or Edit Sort dialog boxes is **key 1>125-55-7890**.

EXERCISE 13

Selecting Specific Percentages

1. At a clear editing window, open Tab 04.
2. Save the document with Save As and name it Ch 28, Ex 13.
3. With Ch 28, Ex 13 open in the editing window, select those percentages greater than 10% by completing the following steps:
   a. Select only the columns (excluding the title and the blank line spaces below the title).
   b. Display the Sort dialog box.
   c. At the Sort dialog box, click *<User Defined Sort>*, then click the New button.
   d. At the New Sort dialog box, change the sort type to Numeric and the number in the Field text box to *4*.
   e. Click in the Select records text box.
   f. Key **key 1>10**.
   g. Click OK.
   h. At the Sort dialog box, click the Sort button.
   i. Key a percent symbol (%) immediately following *16.40*.
4. Save the document again with the same name (Ch 28, Ex 13).
5. Print and then close Ch 28, Ex 13.

EXERCISE 14

Selecting Specific Cities

1. At a clear editing window, open Customer df.
2. Save the data file with Save As and name it Ch 28, Ex 14.
3. With Ch 28, Ex 14 open in the editing window, select the records of those individuals living in Bismarck with a Social Security number higher than 330-00-0000 and save the selected records into a separate document named Zip df by completing the following steps:
   a. Display the Sort dialog box.
   b. At the Sort dialog box, select the text *Current Document* that displays in the Output file text box, then key **Zip df**.
   c. Click *<User Defined Sort>*, then click the New button.
   d. At the New Sort dialog box, change the number in the Field text box to *4*, the number in the Line text box, to *2*, and the number in the Word text box to *1*. (Make sure the sort type is Alpha.)
   e. Click the Add Key button. (This adds another key.)
   f. For key 2, change the number in the Field text box to *6*.
   g. Click in the Select records text box.
   h. Key **key 1=Bismarck & key 2>330-00-0000**.
   i. Click OK.
   j. At the Sort dialog box, click the Sort button.
4. Close Ch 28, Ex 14.
5. Display the Open File dialog box, then print Zip df.

CHAPTER SUMMARY

▼ WordPerfect includes some basic database features such as Sort and Select.

▼ The Sort feature sorts text established in a line, a paragraph, a data file, parallel columns, or a table.

▼ By default, text in the current document is sorted and then redisplayed in the editing window. Begin the sort and create or edit a sort definition at the Sort dialog box.

▼ With options in the Key definitions section of the New Sort or Edit Sort dialog boxes, you can define the type of sort and/or select you want performed.

▼ Up to nine keys can be specified with key 1 given first priority and sorted first. The key is the particular division within the record that is to be sorted.

▼ With the Select records option at the New Sort or Edit Sort dialog boxes, you can write a *select equation* to select specific text from a document.

COMMANDS REVIEW

	Mouse/Keyboard
Sort dialog box	Tools, Sort

CHECK YOUR UNDERSTANDING

Completion: In the space provided at the right, indicate the correct term, command, or number.

1. In an alphanumeric sort, which number is sorted first, *235* or *31*? _____

2. In a numeric sort, which number is sorted first, *452* or *58*? _____

3. When sorting text in columns, the first tab setting is considered this field number. _____

4. If you sort a document containing records in a data file, WordPerfect automatically selects this record option. _____

5. This is the maximum numbers of keys that can be defined for sorting. _____

6. In a select equation, key this symbol for "not equal to." _____

7. In a select equation, key this symbol for "or." _____

8. Key 1 is the city. This is the select equation to choose records of people living in Seattle. _____

9. Key 1 is the city and key 2 is the last name. This is the select equation to choose people with the last name of Lee who live in Seattle. _____

696   Chapter 28

10. Key 1 is the city and key 2 is the ZIP Code. This is the select equation to choose all people living in Seattle except those with the ZIP Code of 98101. _____

SKILL ASSESSMENTS

Assessment 1

1. At a clear editing window, open Column 01.
2. Save the document with Save As and name it Ch 28, SA 01.
3. Sort the lines alphabetically by last name. The last names are the second field (because they are indented to the first tab setting) and second word. At the New Sort dialog box, change the Sort by to Line.
4. Print Ch 28, SA 01.
5. With Ch 28, SA 01 open in the editing window, sort the lines alphabetically by department. (Be sure to change the Sort by to Line.)
6. Print and then close Ch 28, SA 01.

Assessment 2

1. At a clear editing window, open Bibliography.
2. Save the document with Save As and name it Ch 28, SA 02.
3. Sort the paragraphs alphanumerically by the year as the first key and sort by last name as the second key. (*Hint:* The year is the fourth word in the first line of the first field.)
4. Save the sorted document with the same name (Ch 28, SA 02).
5. Print and then close Ch 28, SA 02.

Assessment 3

1. At a clear editing window, open Customer df.
2. Save the data file with Save As and name it Ch 28, SA 03.
3. Sort the records alphanumerically by ZIP Code. (Be sure to enter a negative number in the Word text box to ensure that WordPerfect reads the words from right to left.)
4. Save the data file again with the same name (Ch 28, SA 03).
5. Print and then close Ch 28, SA 03.

Assessment 4

1. At a clear editing window, open Table 03.
2. Save the table with Save As and name it Ch 28, SA 04.
3. Sort the third column numerically.
4. Save the sorted table with the same name (Ch 28, SA 04).
5. Print and then close Ch 28, SA 04.

Assessment 5

1. At a clear editing window, open Para col.
2. Save the document with Save As and name it Ch 28, SA 05.
3. Sort the columns alphanumerically by ZIP Code. (Be sure to enter a negative number in the Word text box to ensure that WordPerfect reads the words from right to left.)

4. Save the document again with the same name (Ch 28, SA 05).
5. Print and then close Ch 28, SA 05.

Assessment 6

1. At a clear editing window, open Table 03.
2. Save the table with Save As and name it Ch 28, SA 06.
3. Select the records of those individuals with a quota less than 100,000. (Be sure to change the type of sort to <u>N</u>umeric.)
4. Save the selected records with the same name (Ch 28, SA 06).
5. Print and then close Ch 28, SA 06.

Assessment 7

1. At a clear editing window, open Customer df.
2. Save the data file with Save As and name it Ch 28, SA 07.
3. Select the records of those individuals with a Social Security number higher than 400-00-0000 and save the selected records into a separate document named SSN df.
4. When selecting is completed, close Ch 28, SA 07.
5. Display the Open File dialog box, then print SSN df.

29 USING STYLES

PERFORMANCE OBJECTIVE

Upon successful completion of chapter 29, you will be able to maintain consistency within similar business documents using the Style feature.

Documents that are published on a regular basis, such as company newsletters, reports, or brochures, should maintain a consistency in formatting each time they are created. For example, a newsletter should maintain a consistent look from issue to issue, and a company report should contain consistent formatting each time one is created. Consistent formatting can be achieved by using a *style*. In WordPerfect, a style can include formatting codes, text, or a combination of both.

In this chapter, you will learn to create styles for formatting a document, save styles into a separate document, retrieve styles from a styles document, and edit and delete styles. Outline styles, graphics styles, template styles, and system styles can also be created. For more information on these types of styles, please refer to the WordPerfect help system.

The Style and Macro features are similar in that both are used to automate functions. A macro inserts the actual formatting codes in a document, while a style inserts the Style code that contains the formatting codes. Because formatting codes are contained within a style, a style can be edited, automatically updating any occurrence of that style within a document.

For example, suppose you create a style for subheadings that changes the font to 14-point Arrus BT bold. After using the style several times in a document, you decide the subheadings would look better if they are set in 12-point Arial bold. To change all the subheadings in the document at one time, you can display the Style List dialog box and edit the style containing the font. When the style is edited, all occurrences of that style in the document are automatically changed to the new font.

The Style feature includes several options. You can create a style, apply a style, edit a style, copy a style, delete a style, and save and retrieve a style document.

Creating a Style

A style can be created at a clear editing window or in a document that contains text. A style is created at the Style List dialog box, shown in figure 29.1. To display the Style List dialog box, click Format, then Styles.

Using Styles   699

Figure 29.1

Style List Dialog Box

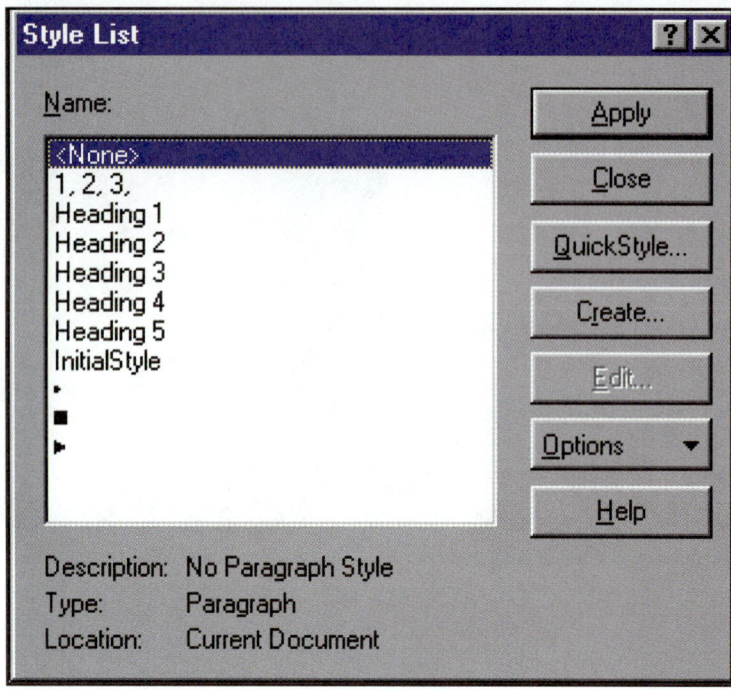

The Style List dialog box displays with default styles provided by WordPerfect. To create a new style, click the Create button. This causes the Styles Editor dialog box, shown in figure 29.2, to display.

Figure 29.2

Styles Editor Dialog Box

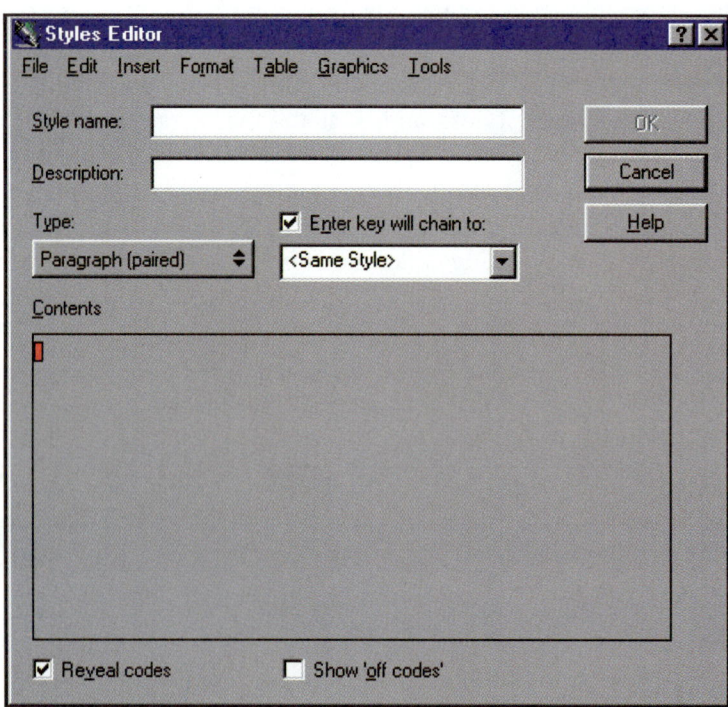

700 Chapter 29

At the Styles Editor dialog box, key a name for the style. A style name can be up to 20 characters in length and can include spaces. Click in the Description text box, then key a short description for the style. With the options from the Type drop-down menu, you determine the type of style you are creating. WordPerfect provides four types of styles—*Character (paired)*, *Paragraph (paired)*, *Paragraph (paired-auto)*, and *Document (open)*.

Character and paragraph styles are considered *paired* styles. A paired style turns on formatting to characters or paragraphs, then formatting reverts back to the settings that were in place before the style was applied. A paired-auto paragraph style automatically updates when you change the format of a paragraph to which you have applied the paired-auto style. All other paragraphs to which the style is applied are also automatically updated. For example, if you create a paired-auto style that turns on bold and italics, apply the style to a number of paragraphs, then remove the italics from one of them, the style is automatically edited to remove the italics code, and all other paragraphs to which the style is applied will have the italics removed.

A document style is considered an *open* style. An open style contains formatting that is turned on and stays on.

A character style affects text you are about to key or selected text. This type of style is useful for single words or phrases. A paragraph style will affect a paragraph where the insertion point is positioned or selected text. This type of style is useful for formatting headings in a document. WordPerfect considers a paragraph as any text followed by a hard return. This means that even a short line with no punctuation that ends in a hard return is considered a paragraph. A document style affects text from the location of the insertion point to the end of the document or until other formatting codes are encountered. This type of style is useful for formatting you want applied to the entire document.

With the Enter key will chain to option at the Styles Editor dialog box, you determine what the Enter key will do to a style. This option only affects paragraph and character styles. If a style type has been set to Document, the Enter key will chain to option is dimmed.

A style can be chained to another style using the Enter key will chain to option. For example, if you have a style named *News Banner*, and a style named *Body Text*, you can have WordPerfect automatically turn on the Body Text style when you press the Enter key at the end of the News Banner. To do this, select the Body Text style name in the Enter key will chain to text box at the Styles Editor for the News Banner style. Figure 29.3 shows an example of the Enter key will chain to drop-down list for a document. The style names that appear are styles that have been created in the current document only. The <None> option can be used to turn off the style when the Enter key is pressed. The default setting of <Same Style> means that the style remains on when the Enter key is pressed.

Figure 29.3

Enter key will chain to Text Box Drop-Down List

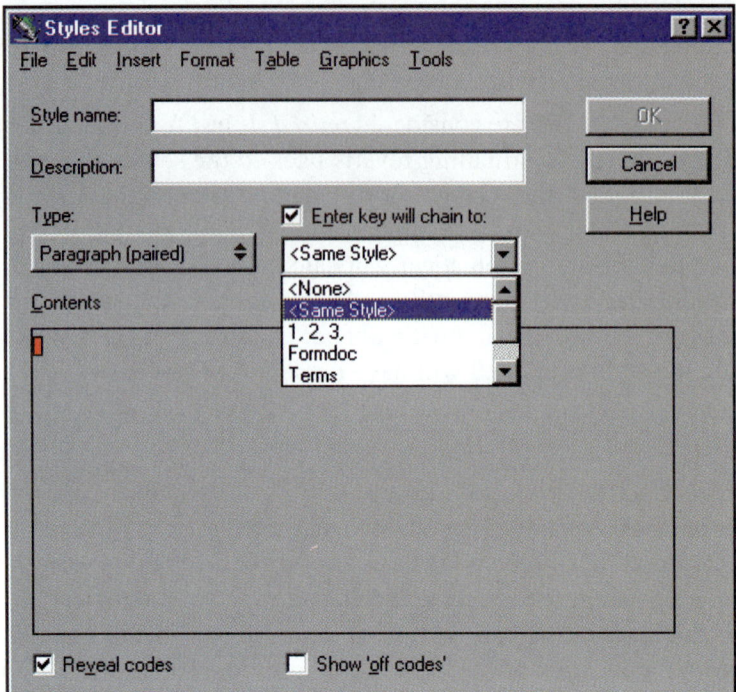

After naming the style, keying a description, and specifying what the Enter key will do in a style (if necessary), click in the Contents box. Enter codes or text in the Contents box in the same manner as in a regular document.

If you want codes to be turned on when the character or paragraph style is turned off, click Show 'off codes' at the bottom of the Styles Editor dialog box. This inserts a code with the message *Codes to the left are ON - Codes to the right are OFF* in the Contents box. Insert codes before the code that you want in effect when the style is turned on. Insert codes after the code that you want in effect when the style is turned off.

When all codes and/or text are entered in the Contents box, click OK to close the Styles Editor dialog box. At the Style List dialog box, click Close.

EXERCISE

Creating a Paragraph Style

1. At a clear editing window, open Report 06.
2. Save the report with Save As and name it Ch 29, Ex 01.
3. Search for all bold codes and delete them from the document.
4. Create a paragraph style named *Title* that turns on bold and changes the relative size of the font to Very Large by completing the following steps:
   a. Click Format, then Styles.
   b. At the Style List dialog box, click Create.
   c. At the Styles Editor dialog box, key **Title**.
   d. Press the Tab key (this moves the insertion point to the Description text box), then key **Turn on bold and change font size for title**.

e. Click in the Contents box.
f. Complete the steps to turn on bold and change the relative size to Very Large.
g. Click OK to close the Styles Editor dialog box.
h. At the Style List dialog box, click Close.

5. Create a character style named *Terms* that changes the font to 12-point Bookman Old Style italic by completing the following steps:
   a. Click Format, then Styles.
   b. At the Style List dialog box, click Create.
   c. At the Styles Editor dialog box, key **Terms**.
   d. Press the Tab key (this moves the insertion point to the Description text box), then key **Change font for terms**.
   e. Click the Type button (contains the words *Paragraph (paired)*), then click Character (paired) at the drop-down list. (When you click Character (paired), the insertion point is positioned in the Contents box.)
   f. Complete the steps to change the font to 12-point Bookman Old Style italic.
   g. Click OK to close the Styles Editor dialog box.
   h. At the Style List dialog box, click Close.

6. Create a document style named *Formdoc* that changes the font to 12-point Century Schoolbook, the left and right margins to 1.25 inches, and changes the justification to Full by completing the following steps:
   a. Click Format, then Styles.
   b. At the Style List dialog box, click Create.
   c. At the Styles Editor dialog box, key **Formdoc**.
   d. Press the Tab key, then key **Change font, margins, and justification**.
   e. Click Type, then Document (open). (This positions the insertion point inside the Contents box.)
   f. Complete the steps to change the font to 12-point Century Schoolbook, the left and right margins to 1.25 inches, and the justification to Full.
   g. Click OK to close the Styles Editor dialog box.
   h. At the Style List dialog box, click Close.

7. Save the report with the same name (Ch 29, Ex 01).
8. Close Ch 29, Ex 01 (without printing).

Creating a Style from Existing Text

A paragraph style or character style can be created with formatting codes that appear in existing text. This saves you from having to complete the steps to insert the codes in the Contents box at the Styles Editor dialog box. To create character or paragraph styles in existing text, click the QuickStyle button at the Style List dialog box, or click the Styles button on the Power Bar, then click QuickStyle at the drop-down list. This causes the QuickStyle dialog box to display as shown in figure 29.4. At the QuickStyle dialog box, key a name and description for the style, make sure the correct codes are inserted in the Contents box, then close the dialog box.

Styles

Figure 29.4

QuickStyle Dialog Box

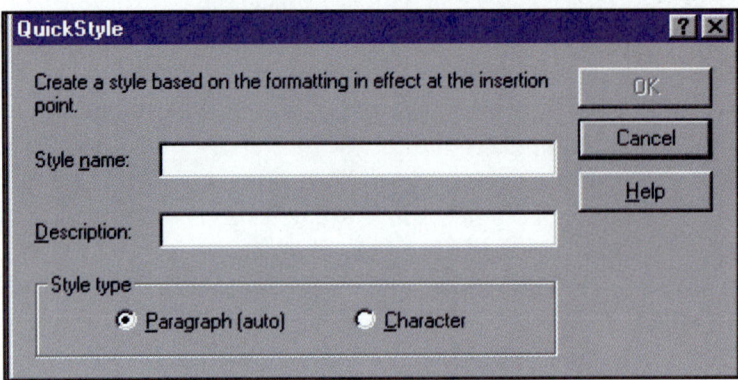

EXERCISE 2

Creating a Paragraph Style in Existing Text

1. At a clear editing window, open Notice 02.
2. Save the document with Save As and name it Ch 29, Ex 02.
3. Create a paragraph style with the existing format in the first line of the document (*NYLAND HIGH SCHOOL*) by completing the following steps:
    a. Position the insertion point anywhere in the first line of the document.
    b. Click Format, then Styles.
    c. At the Style List dialog box, click the QuickStyle button.
    d. At the QuickStyle dialog box, key **Subtitle** in the Style name text box.
    e. Press the Tab key, then key **Change font and relative size for subtitle**.
    f. Click OK.
    g. At the Style List dialog box, click Close.
4. Save the document again with the same name (Ch 29, Ex 02).
5. Close Ch 29, Ex 02 (without printing).

Applying a Style

After a style has been created, it can be turned on and/or off in a document (referred to as *applying* a style). A style can be applied before you key text or it can be applied in a document with existing text.

Applying a Paragraph Style

If a paragraph style is applied in a paragraph of existing text, the style affects only the paragraph where the insertion point is positioned. To apply a paragraph style in an existing paragraph of text, position the insertion point anywhere within the paragraph, then click Format, then Styles. At the Style List dialog box, select the desired style, then click the Apply button.

If you apply a paragraph style and then key text, the paragraph style is turned on each time you press Enter. To turn off the paragraph style, follow the same steps except click <None> at the Style List dialog box.

Applying a Character Style

A character style can be applied before text is keyed, or you can select existing text, then apply the character style. Follow the same steps used for applying a paragraph style. After keying the text, turn off the character style by clicking the Off button. When a character style is turned on, the Off button displays instead of the Apply button. You can also turn a character style off by pressing the right arrow key. This moves the insertion point to the right of the Style Off code.

Applying a Document Style

A document style contains formatting that affects the document from the location of the insertion point to the end of the document or until other codes are encountered. Document styles are turned on but not off. To turn on a document style, follow the same steps used for applying character or paragraph styles. A document style cannot be turned off but you can delete the style code in the document. Delete a document style code in Reveal Codes in the normal manner. You can also delete a document style from the Style List dialog box.

Applying Styles with the Styles Button on the Power Bar

To apply styles using the Styles button on the Power Bar, position the insertion point in the document where you want to turn on a style; click the Styles button on Power Bar (fourth button from the left), then click the style name from the drop-down list that appears. Styles can be turned off using the Styles button on the Power Bar by clicking <None> at the drop-down list.

EXERCISE 3

Applying the Formdoc Document Style

1. At a clear editing window, open Ch 29, Ex 01.
2. Save the document with Save As and name it Ch 29, Ex 03.
3. Apply the *Formdoc* document style by completing the following steps:
    a. Position the insertion point at the beginning of the document.
    b. Click Format, then Styles.
    c. At the Style List dialog box, click *Formdoc* in the Name list box, then click the Apply button.
4. Position the insertion point on any character in the title TRENDS IN TELECOMMUNICATIONS, then apply the *Title* paragraph style by completing the following steps:
    a. Click the Styles button on the Power Bar.
    b. At the drop-down list that appears, click *Title*.
5. Select the words *national telecommunications network* in the first paragraph in the *Continued Growth of Photonics (Fiber Optics)* section, then apply the *Terms* character style.
6. Select the words *light wave systems* in the first paragraph in the *Continued Growth of Photonics (Fiber Optics)* section, then apply the *Terms* character style.
7. Select the word *photonics* (it displays in italics in the document) in the first paragraph in the *Continued Growth of Photonics (Fiber Options)* section, then apply the *Terms* character style.

8. Move the insertion point to the beginning of the document, display the Tab Set dialog box, clear all previous tabs, then set a left tab 0.3 inches from the left margin.
9. Save the document again with the same name (Ch 29, Ex 03).
10. Print and then close Ch 29, Ex 03.

Saving Styles

When a style is created in a document, the style is saved with the document. If you display the Style List dialog box in a document in which styles were previously created, the styles are listed in the dialog box.

Styles can also be saved into a separate document. This lets you use a style in additional documents. To save styles in a separate document, click Options, then Save As at the Style List dialog box. At the Save Styles To... dialog box, shown in figure 29.5, key a name for the styles document, then click OK.

Figure 29.5

Save Styles To... Dialog Box

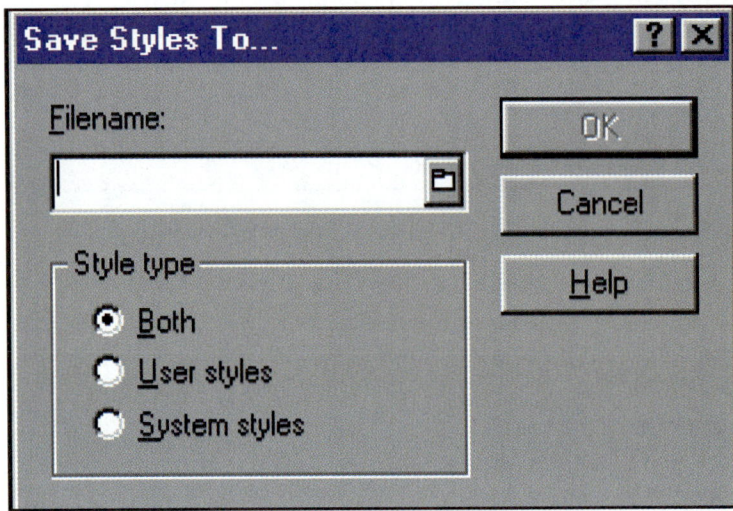

To help you remember that the document contains styles, you may want to add *styles* to the document name. The styles are saved both in the document in which they were created and in the new styles document.

Saving Styles as a Separate Document

1. At a clear editing window, open Ch 29, Ex 01.
2. Move the insertion point to the end of the document, then insert Ch 29, Ex 02 into the current document. (*Hint:* Use the File option from the Insert drop-down menu.)

3. With both Ch 29, Ex 01 and Ch 29, Ex 02 open in the current document, save the styles *Terms*, *Title*, and *Subtitle* into a separate document named *Format styles* by completing the following steps:
    a. Display the Style List dialog box.
    b. At the Style List dialog box, click Options, then Save As.
    c. At the Save Styles To... dialog box, key **a:\Format styles**.
    d. Click OK.
    e. At the Style List dialog box, click Close.
4. Close the current document without saving it.

Retrieving Styles

Styles that have been saved in a separate document can be retrieved at any time. If you want to retrieve a styles document into the document currently open in the editing window, display the Style List dialog box, click Options, then Retrieve. At the Retrieve Styles From... dialog box, shown in figure 29.6, key the name of the styles document, then click OK. At the question *Overwrite current styles?*, click Yes, and then close the box.

Figure 29.6

Retrieve Styles From... Dialog Box

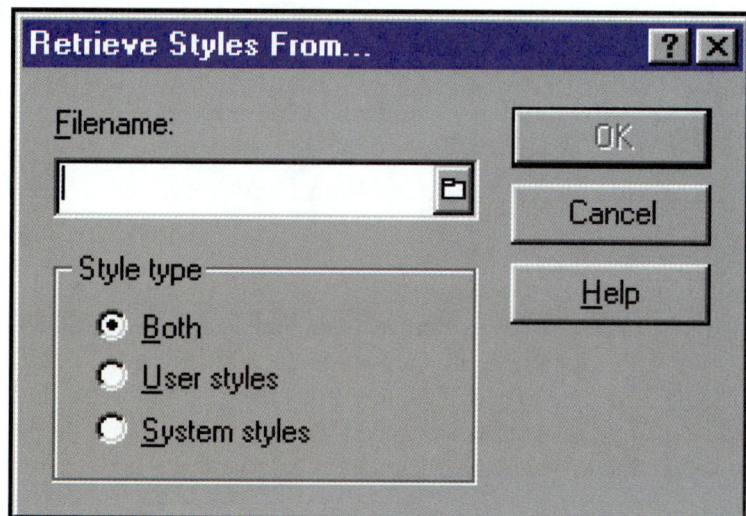

Styles do not have to be saved to a separate document to be used in another document. At the Retrieve Styles From... dialog box, you can retrieve a document containing styles, and WordPerfect retrieves just the styles from the document into the Style List dialog box of the current document.

For example, suppose you saved a document named *Newsletter* that contained a monthly company newsletter along with three styles to format the newsletter. At the Retrieve Styles From... dialog box, you would enter the entire path, including the drive letter, the folder name, and the file name.

EXERCISE 5

Retrieving a Style Document into the Current Document

1. At a clear editing window, open Report 08.
2. Save the document with Save As and name it Ch 29, Ex 05.
3. Search for and delete all bold codes.
4. Retrieve the style document named *Format styles* into the current document by completing the following steps:
   a. Display the Style List dialog box.
   b. At the Style List dialog box, click Options, then Retrieve.
   c. At the Retrieve Styles From... dialog box, key **a:\Format styles**.
   d. Click OK.
   e. At the *Overwrite current styles?* question, click Yes.
   f. At the Style List dialog box, click Close.
5. With the insertion point positioned at the beginning of the document, apply the *Formdoc* document style.
6. Move the insertion point to the beginning of the title, *IDENTIFICATION OF CI*, and apply the *Title* paragraph style.
7. Move the insertion point to each of the subheadings (*Introduction, Purpose and Scope, Application,* and *Requirements*) in the document, then apply the *Subtitle* paragraph style.
8. Position the insertion point at the beginning of the document, display the Tab Set dialog box, clear all previous tabs, then set a left tab 0.3 inches from the left margin.
9. Check page breaks in the document and, if necessary, make adjustments to the page breaks.
10. Save the report again with the same name (Ch 29, Ex 05).
11. Print and then close Ch 29, Ex 05.

Editing a Style

One of the advantages to using styles within a document is that a style can be edited and all occurrences of that style in the document are then automatically updated. To edit a style, display the Style List dialog box, click the style to be edited, then click the Edit button. At the Styles Editor insert and/or delete codes in the Contents section as needed, then click OK. Close the Style List dialog box and any occurrence of the edited style in the document is automatically updated to reflect the changes.

EXERCISE 6

Editing a Title Style

1. At a clear editing window, open Ch 29, Ex 05.
2. Save the document with Save As and name it Ch 29, Ex 06.
3. After looking at the printout of Ch 29, Ex 05, you decide that the title, *IDENTIFICATION OF CI*, would look better if the relative size of the font was Large instead of Very Large. To edit the *Title* paragraph style, complete the following steps:
   a. Display the Style List dialog box.
   b. At the Style List dialog box, click *Title*, then click the Edit button.

      c. At the Styles Editor dialog box, delete the Very Large code from the Contents box, then change the relative size to Large.
      d. Click OK.
      e. At the Style List dialog box, click Close.
4. You decide that the subheadings would look better if underlining was added. Edit the *Subtitle* paragraph style to include underlining by completing steps similar to those in step 3.
5. Save the document again with the same name (Ch 29, Ex 06).
6. Print and then close Ch 29, Ex 06.

Copying a Style

If you want to create a style that is similar to a style you have already created, you can copy the existing style, then make minor changes to the new style. You can also copy an existing style into a document.

    To copy a style and create a new style, display the Style List dialog box, select the style to be copied, click Options, then Copy. At the Styles Copy dialog box, shown in figure 29.7, make sure Current document is selected, then click OK. At the Styles Duplicate dialog box, shown in figure 29.8, key a name for the new style, then click OK. (Both the original style name and the new style name will display in the Style List dialog box.) At the Style List dialog box, position the insertion point on the new style name, then click the Edit button. Make any necessary changes to the new style, then click OK. Close the Style List dialog box.

Figure 29.7

Styles Copy Dialog Box

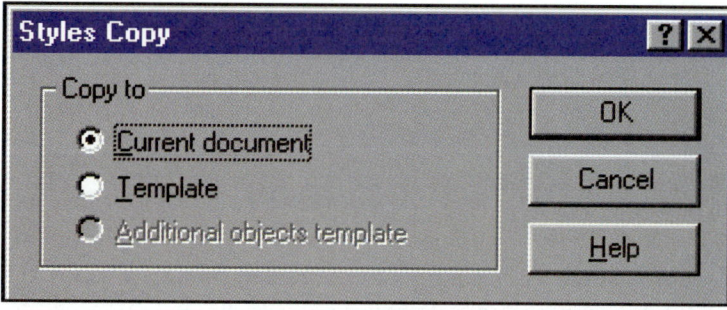

Figure 29.8

Styles Duplicate Dialog Box

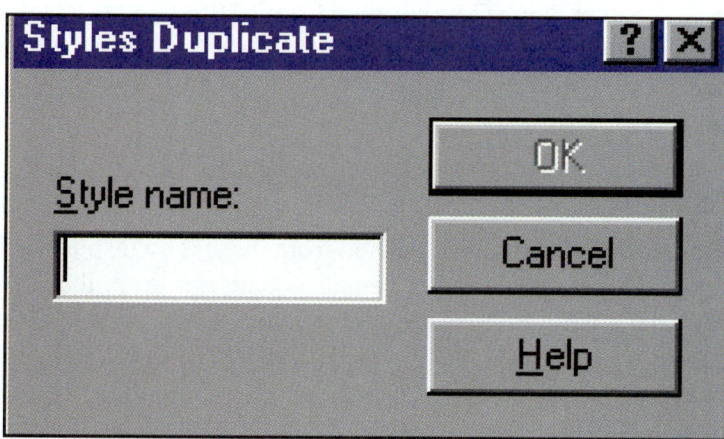

EXERCISE 7

Copying the Subtitle Style

1. At a clear editing window, open Ch 29, Ex 05.
2. Save the document with Save As and name it Ch 29, Ex 07.
3. Create a style named *Sub 2* by copying the *Subtitle* style by completing the following steps:
    a. Display the Style List dialog box.
    b. At the Style List dialog box, click *Subtitle* in the Name list box.
    c. Click Options, then Copy.
    d. At the Styles Copy dialog box, make sure Current document is selected, then click OK.
    e. At the Styles Duplicate dialog box, key **Sub 2**, then click OK.
    f. At the Style List dialog box, make sure *Sub 2* is selected in the Name list box, then click the Edit button.
    g. At the Styles Editor dialog box, make the following changes in the Contents box:
        (1) Change the Type to Character (paired).
        (2) Delete the Times New Roman Regular code.
        (3) Delete the Large code.
        (4) Add an italics code.
    h. Click OK.
    i. At the Style List dialog box, click Close.
4. Select the subheading *Requirements During Development* located toward the end of the document, then apply the *Sub 2* style.
5. Select the subheading *Requirements for Operations/Maintenance:* located toward the end of the document, then apply the *Sub 2* style.
6. Save the document again with the same name (Ch 29, Ex 07).
7. Print and then close Ch 29, Ex 07.

When you open the Style List dialog box, default styles provided by WordPerfect are displayed. These styles are located in a template document named *Wp7us.wpt*. A style or styles can be copied to the *Wp7us.wpt* template. When a style or styles are copied to this template, the style or styles will display when you display the Style List dialog box.

To copy a style to the Wp7us.wpt template, display the Style List dialog box, click the style you want to copy to Wp7us.wpt, click Options, then Copy. At the Styles Copy dialog box, shown in figure 29.7, click Template, then click OK. Close the Style List dialog box. If you display the Style List dialog box at a clear editing window, the style you copied to the template will display with the default WordPerfect styles.

Deleting a Style

A style applied to text in a document can be deleted from the text by displaying Reveal Codes and deleting the style on or style off codes. Styles can also be deleted from the Style List dialog box. To delete a style, click the style in the Name list box, click Options, then Delete. At the Delete Styles dialog box shown in figure 29.9, make sure Include codes is selected, then click OK. Close the Style List dialog box.

There are two options at the Delete Styles dialog box. The first option, Include codes, deletes the style and the contents of the style from the Style List dialog box and from the document. Use this option if you want to remove all effects of a style in a document.

The second option, Leave codes, deletes the style from the Style List dialog box and from the document but leaves the codes contained in the style. This is useful if you want to save the document in another format for another program. (The WordPerfect style codes will not convert when a document is saved in a different file format, but the codes contained in the document will.)

Delete Styles Dialog Box

Figure 29.9

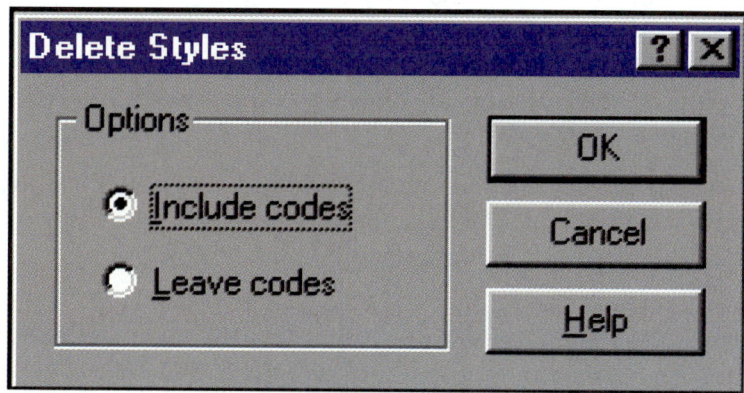

EXERCISE 8

Deleting a Character Style

1. At a clear editing window, open Ch 29, Ex 03.
2. Save the document with Save As and name it Ch 29, Ex 08.
3. Delete the character style named *Terms* by completing the following steps:
   a. Display the Style List dialog box.
   b. At the Style List dialog box, click *Terms*.
   c. Click Options, then Delete.
   d. At the Delete Styles dialog box, make sure Include codes is selected, then click OK.
   e. At the Style List dialog box, click Close.
4. Save the document again with the same name (Ch 29, Ex 08).
5. Print and then close Ch 29, Ex 08.

Using Styles 711

CHAPTER SUMMARY

▼ The Style feature automates functions, much like the Macro feature. A macro inserts the actual formatting codes in a document, while a style inserts the Style code that contains the formatting codes.

▼ A style can be edited, thus automatically updating any occurrence of that style within a document.

▼ The four types of styles are *Character (paired)*, *Paragraph (paired)*, *Paragraph (paired-auto)*, and *Document (open)*. Character and paragraph styles are considered *paired styles*, which turn on formatting to specific characters or paragraphs. The paired-auto paragraph styles are automatically updated if you change the format of a paragraph that has the style applied to it. All other paragraphs with the style applied to it are also automatically updated. A document style is an *open* style, which affects text from the location of the style to the end of the document.

▼ You can create a style that includes formatting codes, text, or a combination of both. With the Styles feature, you can create a style, apply a style, edit a style, copy a style, delete a style, and save and retrieve a styles document.

▼ A style can be created at a clear editing window or in a document containing text. A style is created at the Style List dialog box and edited at the Styles Editor dialog box.

▼ After a style has been created, it can be applied in a document by clicking the Apply button at the Style List dialog box or by clicking the Styles button on the Power Bar, then clicking the desired style at the drop-down list.

▼ A style is saved with the document in which it was created. Styles can also be saved into a separate document; this lets you use a style in different documents.

▼ Retrieve a style document into the document currently open in the editing window at the Retrieve Style From... dialog box.

▼ Styles can be copied and deleted at the Style List dialog box.

COMMANDS REVIEW

	Mouse/Keyboard
Style List dialog box	Format, Styles
Styles Editor dialog box	At the Style List dialog box, select an existing style, choose Edit
Save Styles To... dialog box	Choose Options, Save As at the Style List dialog box
Retrieve Styles From... dialog box	Choose Options, Retrieve at the Style List dialog box

CHECK YOUR UNDERSTANDING

Completion: In the space provided at the right, indicate the correct term, command, or number.

1. Maximum number of characters that can be used in a style name. _____

2. Option that can be used to chain two styles together, so that one style automatically begins when the other ends. _____

3. Four style types that can be created. _____
   _____
   _____
   _____

4. Styles are created at this dialog box. _____

5. At this dialog box you can edit styles. _____

6. A character or paragraph style is considered to be this kind of style. _____

7. A document style is considered to be this kind of style. _____

8. This type of style is useful for formatting you want applied to the entire document. _____

9. This type of style will affect a paragraph where the insertion point is positioned or selected text. _____

10. This type of style affects text you are about to key or selected text and is useful for single words or phrases. _____

SKILL ASSESSMENTS

Assessment 1

1. At a clear editing window, create a document style (be sure to change the Type to Document (open)) named *Form news* that includes the following formats:
   a. Font of 12-point Century Schoolbook.
   b. Justification of Full.
2. Create a paragraph style named *News head* that changes the font to 16-point Arial bold.
3. Create a paragraph style named *News sub* that changes the font to 14-point Arial bold.
4. Save the styles in a document named Newsltr styles.
5. Close the document without saving it.

Using Styles 713

Assessment 2

1. At a clear editing window, complete the following steps:
    a. Press Enter once.
    b. Key **DISTRICT HAPPENINGS** at the left margin.
    c. Press Enter once.
    d. Create a horizontal line at the Create Graphics Line dialog box. Change the Line thickness to the fourth option from the top in the first column.
    e. Press Enter once.
    f. Access the Flush Right command, then key **April Newsletter**.
    g. Press Enter once.
    h. Access the Flush Right command, then key **Joni Kapshaw, Editor**.
    i. Press Enter twice.
2. Insert the document named News 01 into the current document.
3. Save the document with Save As and name it Ch 29, SA 02.
4. With Ch 29, SA 02 still open in the editing window, retrieve the *Newsltr styles* style document.
5. With the insertion point positioned at the beginning of the document (on the blank line), apply the *Form news* style.
6. Move the insertion point to the beginning of the title, *DISTRICT HAPPENINGS*, then apply the *News head* paragraph style.
7. Apply the *News sub* paragraph style to the following subheadings:
    April Newsletter
    Joni Kapshaw, Editor
    Recreation Program
    Sixth Grade Camp
    Library News
8. Move the insertion point to the left margin of the line containing the subheading, *Recreation Program*, then define two balanced newspaper columns.
9. With the insertion point still positioned on the line containing *Recreation Program*, display the Tab Set dialog box, clear all previous tabs, then set a left tab 0.25 inches from the left margin.
10. Save the newsletter again with the same name (Ch 29, SA 02).
11. Print and then close Ch 29, SA 02.

Assessment 3

1. At a clear editing window, open Ch 29, SA 02.
2. Save the document with Save As and name it Ch 29, SA 03.
3. Edit the *News head* style by deleting the font code and size code for 16-point Arial bold, inserting a bold code, and inserting a code that changes the relative size of the font to Very Large.
4. Edit the *News sub* style by deleting the font code and size code for 14-point Arial bold, inserting a bold code, and inserting a code that changes the relative size of the font to Large.
5. Save the newsletter again with the same name (Ch 29, SA 03).
6. Print and then close Ch 29, SA 03.

30

CREATING TABLES, INDEXES, AND LISTS

PERFORMANCE OBJECTIVE

Upon successful completion of chapter 30, you will be able to specify information in a document to be included in a table of contents, index, list, or table of authorities.

A book, textbook, report, or manuscript often includes sections such as a table of contents, index, and lists of tables or figures in the document. Creating these sections can be tedious when done manually. With WordPerfect, these functions can be automated to make the generating of sections quick and easy.

In this chapter, you will learn the steps to mark text for a table of contents, index, list, and table of authorities, and then define and generate the table, index, or list. You will find that the steps involved in marking, defining, and generating tables, indexes, and lists are similar and include the following:

1. Locate the reference and select it.
2. Identify whether it is to be included in a table of contents, list, index, or table of authorities.
3. Define the table, list, or index.
4. Generate the table, list, or index.

WordPerfect provides a Generate Toolbar with options for working with a table of contents, list, index, and table of authorities. To display the Generate Toolbar, position the arrow pointer on the current Toolbar, then click the right mouse button. At the drop-down menu that displays, click Generate.

Creating a Table of Contents

A table of contents appears at the beginning of a book, manuscript, or report and contains headings and subheadings with page numbers. Figure 30.1 shows an example of a table of contents.

Creating Tables, Indexes, and Lists 715

Figure 30.1

Table of Contents

TABLE OF CONTENTS

Chapter 1: 1
    Leading 3
    Spacing Paragraphs 5
    Kerning 9
    Hyphenation 12
Chapter 2: 15
    Page Design 16
    Graphics 19

Marking Text

Generally, when you create a table of contents, you are working in an existing document—one that already has the headings and subheadings included. To mark text for the table of contents, you would complete the following steps:

Table of Contents

1. Click Tools, point to Generate, then click Table of Contents; or click the Table of Contents button on the Generate Toolbar.
2. With the Table of Contents Feature Bar displayed (as shown in figure 30.2), select the heading or subheading in the document.
3. Click Mark # (where # represents the level number).
4. Mark any other headings or subheadings for the table of contents.
5. Click Close to close the Table of Contents Feature Bar.

Figure 30.2

Table of Contents Feature Bar

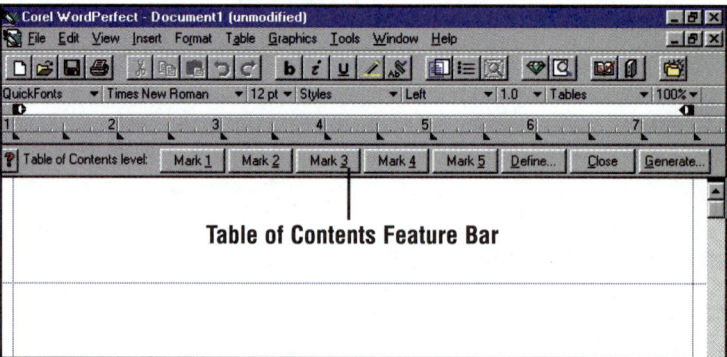

Table of Contents Feature Bar

Text to be included in a table of contents is identified by level numbering. The first level is generally reserved for headings, the second level for subheadings, and the other levels for subheadings under subheadings. A maximum of five levels can be identified.

When text is marked for a table of contents, codes are inserted before and after the text. These codes can be seen in Reveal Codes. For example, if you identified the heading *COMPUTER REVOLUTION* for a table of contents as level 1, the heading and codes appear as follows in Reveal Codes. The codes identify the beginning and end of the marked text and the level numbering.

716 Chapter 30

If you make a mistake when marking a heading for a table of contents, display Reveal Codes, delete the beginning or ending mark text code, then remark the text.

If the text that is being marked for a table of contents contains character formatting such as bold, italics, and underline, you generally do not include these codes when you select the text. If you do select the codes, the formatting will be included in the table of contents. You may want to select text with Reveal Codes on to ensure that the codes are not selected.

After all headings and subheadings have been marked in a document, the table of contents can be defined and generated.

Defining the Table of Contents

Before defining the table of contents, move the insertion point to the location in the document where the table is to appear (generally at the beginning of the document), then insert a hard page break with Ctrl + Enter. To define the table of contents, position the insertion point above the hard page break, then key a heading (such as **TABLE OF CONTENTS**). Press Enter two or three times to separate the heading from the contents of the table, then turn on the Table of Contents Feature Bar if it is not already displayed. Click Define at the Table of Contents Feature Bar. At the Define Table of Contents dialog box, shown in figure 30.3, make any necessary changes, then click OK. WordPerfect inserts the message << *Table of Contents will generate here* >> in the document at the location of the insertion point.

Figure 30.3

Define Table of Contents Dialog Box

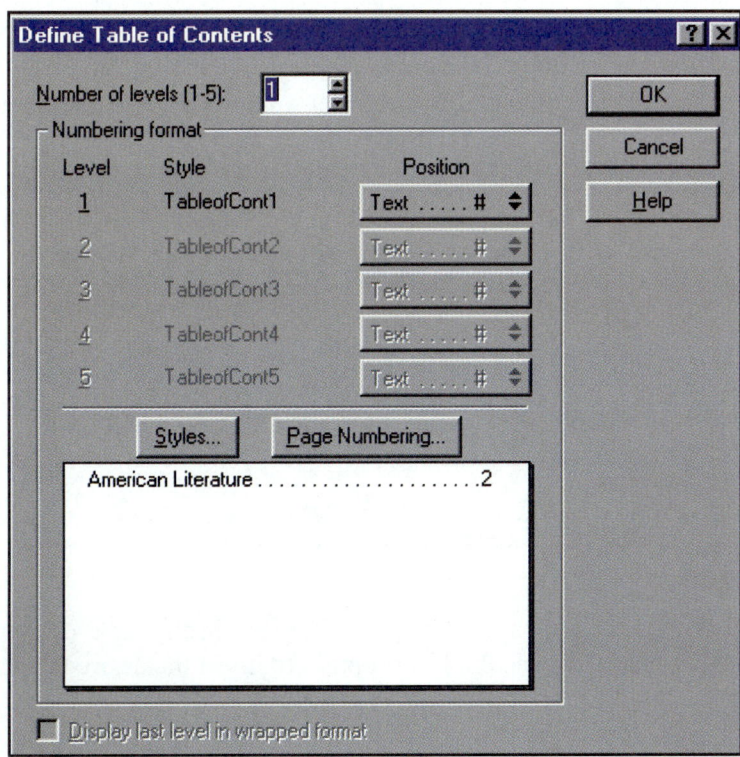

Creating Tables, Indexes, and Lists   717

The Define Table of Contents dialog box contains a number of options. At the first option, Number of levels (1-5), key the number of levels included in the table of contents (up to a maximum of 5). For example, if the table of contents includes a heading and a subheading, key **2** in the Number of levels (1-5) text box. You can also click the up- or down-pointing triangle after the text box to increase or decrease the number.

The Numbering format section of the Define Table of Contents dialog box displays the number of levels and level styles. It also shows the position of the page number for each level. For example, the Position text box for Level 1 displays with *Text .....#*. This indicates that the first level text will display in the table of contents followed by dot leaders, then the page number. By default, other levels will display in the same manner.

With options from the Position text box for each level, you can choose a different position for the page number. If you position the arrow pointer on the Position text box for Level 1, then click the left mouse button, a drop-down menu displays with numbering positions.

With the first option, No Numbering, you can eliminate page numbering. If you choose the second option, Text #, numbers will be positioned one space to the right of the heading or subheading. Choosing the third option, Text (#), will cause numbers to be positioned one space to the right of the heading or subheading surrounded by parentheses. The fourth option, Text   #, will position numbers at the right margin without preceding leaders. The last option is the default and causes numbers to display at the right margin preceded by dot leaders.

WordPerfect uses default level styles for a table of contents. With the Styles button from the Define Table of Contents dialog box, you can edit WordPerfect's table of contents styles or create your own.

By default, the page numbers in a table of contents display like the page numbers in the document. If you have inserted special page numbering in your document, such as volume, chapter, or section page numbering, you can specify how page numbering will appear in the table of contents with the Page Numbering button. When you click the Page Numbering button at the Define Table of Contents dialog box, the Page Number Format dialog box, shown in figure 30.4, displays. At this dialog box, click Document page number format if you want to customize the page number display.

Figure 30.4

Page Number Format Dialog Box

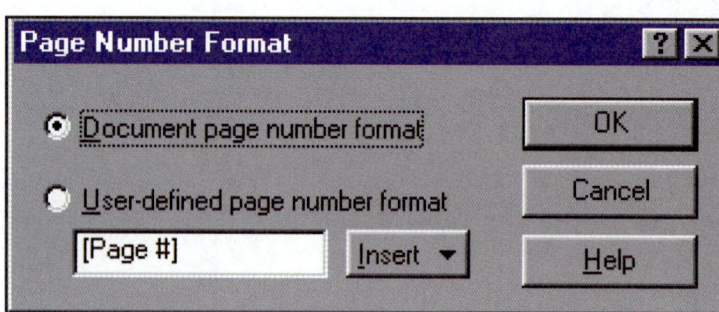

If you want to change the appearance of page numbers in the table of contents, click User-defined page number format, then use the Insert option to insert the desired page numbering code.

By default, the Display last level in wrapped format option is inactive, which means that text longer than one line is wrapped to the next line and is usually indented. This selection can be made active by clicking Display last level in wrapped format. With this option active, the last level wraps to the left margin of the next line rather than being indented. In addition, only the first three numbering selections are available for the last level. The flush right and flush right with preceding dot leaders are not available. Also, all last level headings appear on the same line rather than each appearing on its own line.

Generating the Table of Contents

After a table of contents has been defined, it can be generated. Generating a table of contents causes the table to appear on the screen with the appropriate levels and page numbers. To generate a table of contents, click Generate on the Table of Contents Feature Bar; or click the Generate button on the Generate Toolbar. At the Generate dialog box, shown in figure 30.5, click OK. WordPerfect makes several passes through the document generating any tables, indexes, or lists. When the table is generated, it is positioned at the location where the table of contents was defined. A title is not included for the table. To include a title, move the insertion point to the beginning of the page where the table of contents appears, then key the title.

Generate

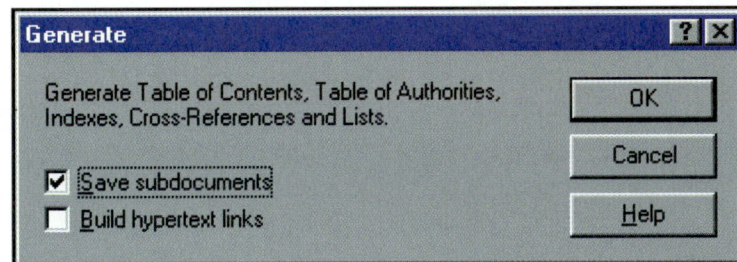

Figure 30.5

Generate Dialog Box

The pages of a table of contents itself are generally numbered with lowercase Roman numerals. To number the pages of a table of contents, turn page numbering on, then change the Page numbering format to Lowercase Roman (i, ii, iii, etc.). If you want the body of the book, report, or manuscript to begin with Arabic numbers, change the Page numbering format back to Numbers (1, 2, 3, etc.).

EXERCISE 1

Creating a Table of Contents

1. At a clear editing window, open Report 03.
2. Save the report with Save As and name it Ch 30, Ex 01.
3. Make the following changes to the report:
   a. Turn on page numbering and number pages at the bottom center of each page.
   b. Insert a hard page break at the beginning of the line containing the title *CHAPTER 2: DEVELOPMENT OF TECHNOLOGY, 1850 - 1900*.
4. Mark the title *CHAPTER 1: DEVELOPMENT OF TECHNOLOGY, 1800 - 1850* as a level 1 heading for a table of contents by completing the following steps:
   a. Click Tools, point to Generate, then click Table of Contents. (This displays the Table of Contents Feature Bar.)
   b. Select the title. (Turn on Reveal Codes before selecting and make sure that you do not include the Bold code.)

c. Click Mark <u>1</u>.
5. Mark the title *CHAPTER 2: DEVELOPMENT OF TECHNOLOGY, 1850 - 1900*, at the beginning of page 3, as a level 1 heading for a table of contents by completing steps 4b and 4c.
6. Mark the following headings in the document as level 2 headings for a table of contents. Complete steps similar to those in 4b and 4c. At step 4c, click Mark <u>2</u>.
    Industrialization
    Development of a World Market
    The American Civil War
    Colonization
    The 1870s Depression
7. After marking the headings for the table of contents, move the insertion point to the beginning of the document, then complete the following steps:
    a. Turn on Reveal Codes, then position the insertion point immediately to the right of the [Open Style: InitialStyle] code.
    b. Press Ctrl + Enter to insert a hard page break.
    c. Move the insertion point above the hard page break.
    d. Turn page numbering on at the bottom center of each page and change the page numbering method to lowercase Roman numerals.
    e. Center and bold the title *TABLE OF CONTENTS*, then press Enter three times.
    f. Define the table of contents by completing the following steps:
        (1) Click <u>D</u>efine on the Table of Contents Feature Bar.
        (2) At the Define Table of Contents dialog box, key **2** in the <u>N</u>umber of levels (1-5) text box.
        (3) Click OK.
8. Move the insertion point to the beginning of the second page. Turn on Reveal Codes, then position the insertion point immediately to the left of the first code on page 2 (the [Ln Spacing: 2.0] code), then change the page numbering method to numbers and change the beginning number to 1.
9. Generate the table of contents by completing the following steps:
    a. Click <u>G</u>enerate on the Table of Contents Feature Bar.
    b. At the Generate dialog box, click OK.
10. Save the document again with the same name (Ch 30, Ex 01).
11. Print and then close Ch 30, Ex 01. (Check with your instructor to see if you should print the entire document or just the Table of Contents page.)

Creating a List

A list is created in a manner similar to that for the table of contents. A list of illustrations or tables contains the captions of the illustrations and tables used in the document. A list can consist of illustrations, tables, figures, or other data, and is inserted at the beginning of the document. Before marking text to be included in a list, you must name a list. A list name can be text or a number. To create a list, you would complete the following steps:

List

1. Click <u>T</u>ools, point to Ge<u>n</u>erate, then click <u>L</u>ist; or click the List button on the Generate Toolbar.
2. With the List Feature Bar displayed (as shown in figure 30.6), click <u>L</u>ist.
3. Key a name for the list (or a number), then press Enter.
4. Select the text to be included in the list.

5. Click Mark.
6. Continue marking text to be included in the list.

When these steps are completed, beginning and ending codes are inserted before and after the selected text. If you make a mistake while marking text for a list, display Reveal Codes, delete the beginning or ending code, and then remark the text. You can have different lists displayed in a document. For example, you can have a separate list of tables, figures, and equations in the same document.

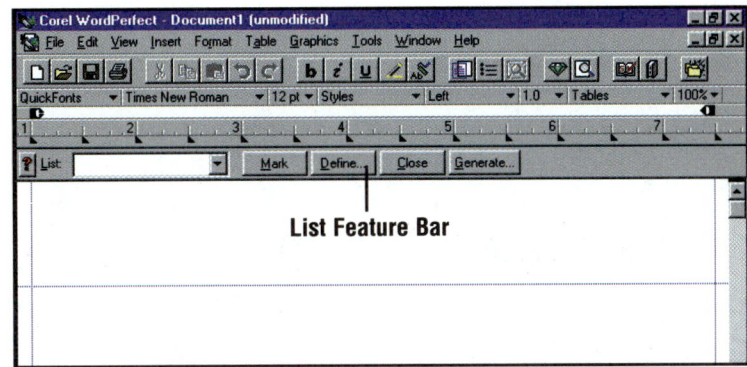

Figure 30.6

List Feature Bar

Defining the List

Generally, a list appears at the beginning of the document. Before defining the list, move the insertion point to the beginning of the document, then insert a hard page break with Ctrl + Enter. Move the insertion point above the page break, then create an appropriate title for the list. Press Enter two or three times, then define the list. To do this, you would complete the following steps:

1. Position the insertion point above the hard page break, then key a heading (such as **LIST OF ILLUSTRATIONS**).
2. Press Enter two or three times to separate the heading from the list.
3. Click Define on the List Feature Bar.
4. At the Define List dialog box, shown in figure 30.7, position the insertion point on the list you want to define, then click Edit. This causes the Edit List dialog box, shown in figure 30.8, to display.
5. Make any necessary changes to options at the Edit List dialog box, then click OK.
6. At the Define List dialog box, make sure the insertion point is positioned on the list you are defining, then click Insert. WordPerfect inserts the message << *List will generate here* >> in the document at the location of the insertion point.

The options at the Edit List dialog box are similar to the options contained in the Define Table of Contents dialog box. At the Edit List dialog box, you can name the list with the List option. You can specify the position of the page number after the text in the list as well as the type of page numbering. By default, WordPerfect uses a list style. With the Change... option, you can change this to an index, different list, table of contents, or table of authorities.

Creating Tables, Indexes, and Lists   721

Figure 30.7

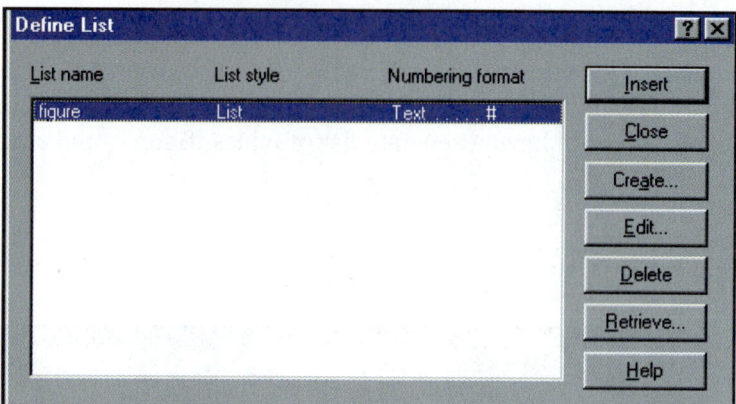

Define List Dialog Box

Figure 30.8

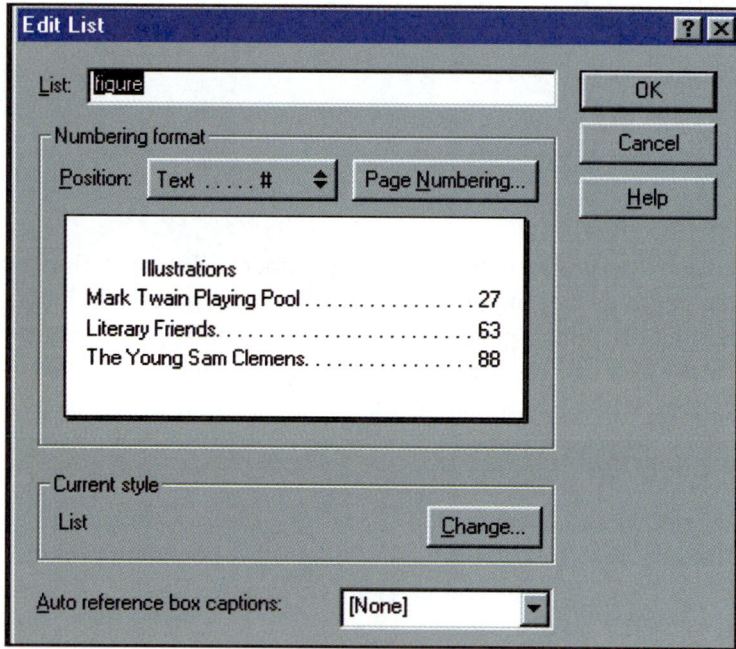

Edit List Dialog Box

Generating the List

After the list has been defined, it can be generated. Generating a list causes the list to appear in the editing window with the appropriate page numbers. To generate a list, click Generate on the List Feature Bar; or click the Generate button on the Generate Toolbar. At the Generate dialog box, click OK.

EXERCISE 2

Generating a Figure List

1. At a clear editing window, open Report 09.
2. Save the document with Save As and name it Ch 30, Ex 02.
3. Mark the first figure in the report for a list by completing the following steps:
   a. Click Tools, point to Generate, then click List. (This displays the List Feature Bar.)
   b. Position the arrow pointer inside the List text box on the List Feature Bar, then click the left mouse button.
   c. Key the name **figure** then press Enter.
   d. Select the figure caption, *Figure 1.1 Main System Components*, after the first figure on the second page. (Do not include the bold codes.)
   e. Click Mark.
4. Complete similar steps as those in 3d and 3e to mark the other two figure captions (*Figure 1.2 Input Devices* and *Figure 1.3 Output Devices*).
5. After the figure captions are marked, move the insertion point to the beginning of the document, then complete the following steps:
   a. Turn on Reveal Codes, then position the insertion point immediately to the right of the [Open Style: InitialStyle] code.
   b. Press Ctrl + Enter to insert a hard page break.
   c. Move the insertion point above the hard page break.
   d. Turn page numbering on at the bottom center of each page and change the page numbering method to lowercase Roman numerals.
   e. Center and bold the title *LIST OF FIGURES*, then press Enter three times.
   f. Define the list by completing the following steps:
      (1) Click Define on the List Feature Bar.
      (2) At the Define List dialog box, make sure *figure* is selected, then click Insert.
6. Move the insertion point to the beginning of the second page, turn on Reveal Codes, then position the insertion point immediately to the left of the [Ln Spacing: 2.0] code.
7. Change the numbering method to numbers and change the beginning number to 1.
8. Generate the list of figures by completing the following steps:
   a. Click Generate on the List Feature Bar.
   b. At the Generate dialog box, click OK.
9. Save the document again with the same name (Ch 30, Ex 02).
10. Print and then close Ch 30, Ex 02. (Check with your instructor to see if you should print the entire document or just the List of Figures page.)

Creating an Index

An index is a list of topics contained in the publication and the pages where those topics are discussed. WordPerfect lets you automate the process of creating an index in a manner similar to that used for creating a table of contents or a list.

Creating Tables, Indexes, and Lists 723

When creating an index, you mark a word or words that you want included in the index. Creating an index takes some thought and consideration. The author of the book, manuscript, or report must determine the headings desired and what subheadings will be listed under headings. Figure 30.9 shows an example of an index.

Figure 30.9

Index

```
                          INDEX

    Accents . . . . . . . . . . . . . . . . . . . . . . . . . . . . . . . . . . . . . . . . . 12
    Acute . . . . . . . . . . . . . . . . . . . . . . . . . . . . . . . . . . . . . . . . . . 41
    Advance to line . . . . . . . . . . . . . . . . . . . . . . . . . . . . . . . 71-73
        to line code . . . . . . . . . . . . . . . . . . . . . . . . . . . . . . . . 100
        to set position code . . . . . . . . . . . . . . . . . . . . . . . . . . 102
    Balance . . . . . . . . . . . . . . . . . . . . . . . . . . . . . . . . . . . . 82-85
```

Marking Text

After the decision has been made about the appearance of headings and subheadings in an index, the text to be included can be identified. To mark text for an index, you would complete the following steps:

Index

1. Click Tools, point to Generate, then click Index; or click the Index button on the Generate Toolbar.
2. With the Index Feature Bar displayed (as shown in figure 30.10), select the word or words to be marked for the index.
3. If the selected word or phrase is a heading, click the arrow pointer inside the Heading text box on the Index Feature Bar or press Alt + Shift + E. (This inserts the selected text inside the text box. If the selected word or phrase is many characters in length, you may not see all the letters in the text box.)
4. Click Mark on the Index Feature Bar.

Figure 30.10

Index Feature Bar

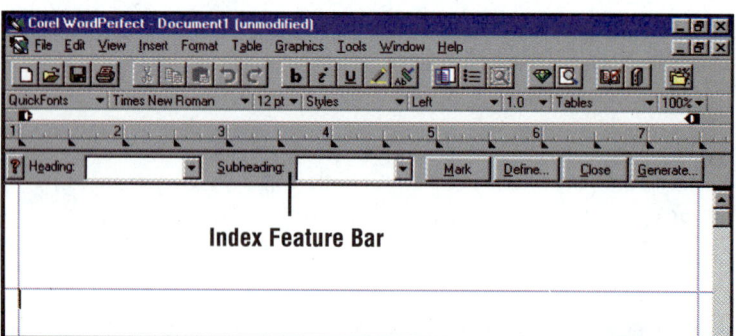

When text is marked for an index, an index code is inserted before the text. The code can be seen in Reveal Codes. If you make a mistake when marking text for an index, display Reveal Codes, delete the index code, and then remark the text.

When you position the arrow pointer inside the H̲eading text box, then click the left mouse button, the selected word or phrase appears in the H̲eading text box. If the selected word or phrase is to be identified as a subheading, select the text in the H̲eading text box, key the heading text, position the arrow pointer inside the S̲ubheading text box, then click the left mouse button. This inserts the original heading text in the S̲ubheading text box.

Creating a Concordance File

Words or phrases that appear frequently in a document can be saved in a concordance file. This saves you from having to mark each reference in the document. A concordance file is a regular WordPerfect document that contains words or phrases to be included in an index. Each word or phrase is created on a separate line.

To create a concordance file, start at a clear editing window and key the common words or phrases for the index. Put each word or phrase on a separate line followed by a hard return. When WordPerfect generates the index, it checks the document for any occurrence of the words or phrases in the concordance file and includes them in the index.

Each word or phrase in the concordance file is treated as a heading. If you want some of the words or phrases to be treated as subheadings, you must mark them as you would regular text in a document, identify to WordPerfect what heading you want, then identify the text as the subheading. When creating an index, text can come from a concordance file or it may be marked in a document or both. When all entries have been made to the concordance file, save it as you would any other document.

Defining an Index

An index should appear at the end of a document. The pages of an index are generally numbered with Arabic numbers. Before defining the index, move the insertion point to the end of the document, then insert a hard page break with Ctrl + Enter. Move the insertion point below the page break, create an appropriate heading or title for the index, press the Enter key two or three times, then define the index. To define the index, click D̲efine on the Index Feature Bar. At the Define Index dialog box, shown in figure 30.11, make any necessary changes, then click OK. WordPerfect inserts the message << *Index will generate here* >> in the document at the location of the insertion point.

Figure 30.11

Define Index Dialog Box

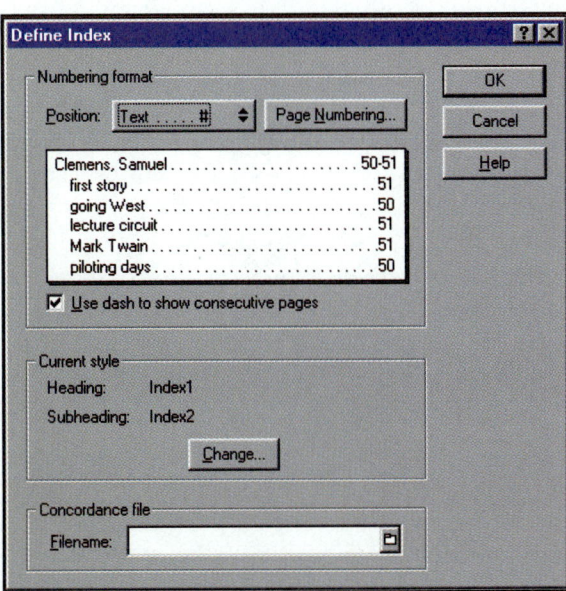

The options at the Define Index dialog box are similar to the options contained in the Define Table of Contents dialog box and the Edit List dialog box. If you want WordPerfect to include words in a concordance file for the index, click Filename at the bottom of the Define Index dialog box, then key the name of the concordance document.

By default, WordPerfect combines sequential numbers in the index. For example, if a topic in the index spans pages 24 through 27, the page numbers will display as 24-27 after the topic. If you do not want sequential numbers combined, remove the check mark from the Use dash to show the consecutive pages option at the Define Index dialog box. This will cause the numbers to display as 24,25,26,27 after the topic.

Generating the Index

After an index has been defined, it can be generated. To generate an index, click Generate on the Index Feature Bar; or click the Generate button on the Generate Toolbar. At the Generate dialog box, click OK.

EXERCISE

Creating an Index

1. At a clear editing window, open Report 09.
2. Save the document with Save As and name it Ch 30, Ex 03.
3. Turn on page numbering and number pages at the bottom center of each page.
4. Mark the first occurrence of the word *text* in the first paragraph of the report for an index by completing the following steps:
    a. Click Tools, point to Generate, then click Index.
    b. Select the word *text* in the first paragraph of the report.
    c. Position the arrow pointer inside the Heading text box on the Index Feature Bar, then click the left mouse button.
    d. Click Mark.
5. Mark the first occurrence of the words *typeset-quality* in the first paragraph of the report as a subheading for an index by completing the following steps:
    a. Select *typeset-quality* in the first paragraph of the report.
    b. Position the arrow pointer inside the Subheading text box on the Index Feature Bar, then click the left mouse button. (Make sure *text* still displays in the Heading text box.)
    c. Click Mark.
6. Mark the following words in the report for an index as a heading or subheading as identified. (To mark a word or phrase as a subheading and the current word in the Heading text box is correct, select the word or phrase, then click inside the Subheading text box. If the word in the Heading text box is not correct, select the word or phrase in the document, select the word in the Heading text box, key the correct heading word, then click inside the Subheading text box.)

    interactive in the first paragraph (subheading; *text*, heading)
    mode in the first paragraph (heading)
    batch processing in the second paragraph (subheading; *mode*, heading) (Do not include the bold codes when selecting the text.)
    Typographical characters in the third paragraph (heading)
    typefaces in the third paragraph (subheading; *typographical characters*, heading)
    sizes in the third paragraph (subheading; *typographical characters*, heading)

styles in the third paragraph (subheading; *typographical characters*, heading)
positions in the third paragraph (subheading; *typographical characters*, heading)
graphics in the third paragraph (subheading; *mode*, heading)
text in the third paragraph (heading) (Select it so the period is not included.)
typeset-quality in the third paragraph (subheading; *text*, heading)
system in the fourth paragraph (heading)
main in the fourth paragraph (subheading; *system*, heading)
input in the fourth paragraph (subheading; *system*, heading)
output in the fourth paragraph (subheading; *system*, heading)

7. After marking words for the index, save the report again with the same name (Ch 30, Ex 03).
8. With Ch 30, Ex 03 still open on the screen, display a new editing window by clicking the New Blank Document button on the Toolbar.
9. At the clear editing window, create a concordance file by completing the following steps:
    a. Key each of the following items on a separate line:
        Desktop publishing
        WYSIWYG
        Hardware
        Software
        CPU
        Memory
        Disk drive
        Expansion boards
        Ports
        Keyboard
        Mouse
        Display monitor
        Laser printer
        Dot-matrix printer
    b. Save the document and name it Ch 30 Concordance File.
    c. Close Ch 30 Concordance File.
10. With Ch 30, Ex 03 displayed in the editing window, define the index by completing the following steps:
    a. Move the insertion point to the end of the document.
    b. Press Ctrl + Enter to insert a hard page break.
    c. Change the line spacing to 1.
    d. Center and bold the title *INDEX*. (Be sure to turn off bold.)
    e. Press Enter three times.
    f. Define the index by completing the following steps:
        (1) Click Define on the Index Feature Bar.
        (2) At the Define Index dialog box, click in the Filename text box, then key **Ch 30 Concordance File.wpd**.
        (3) Click OK.
11. Generate the index by completing the following steps:
    a. Click Generate on the Index Feature Bar.
    b. At the Generate dialog box, click OK.
12. Save the document again with the same name (Ch 30, Ex 03).
13. Print and then close Ch 30, Ex 03. (Check with your instructor to see if you should print the entire document or just the Index page.)

Regenerating a Table, List, or Index

A table of contents, list, or index can be edited after being generated. If you notice that you made a mistake when marking text or you make changes to the text, mark the text again, then regenerate the table, list, or index by completing the same steps used for generation. You do not need to define the table of contents, list, or index again because the document still contains the definition code(s) inserted before the table, list, or index was generated the first time. If, after you generate a table of contents, list, or index, you decide you do not like the appearance, you can redefine it. Before redefining, delete the old definition code.

Creating a Table of Authorities

A table of authorities is a list of citations for a legal brief that lists the pages of sources where the citings occur. The table is divided into sections and can include cases, statutes, regulations, and miscellaneous categories. Figure 30.12 shows an example of a table of authorities. A table of authorities can be defined and generated in a document in a similar manner to a table of contents, list, or index.

Some thought goes into planning a table of authorities. Before marking any text in a legal brief, you need to determine what section headings you want and what should be contained in the sections. For example, sections may include headings for Supreme Court cases, state court cases, other cases, and statutes.

Figure 30.12

Table of Authorities

TABLE OF AUTHORITIES

Federal Cases

Langevin v. Kentucky, 302 U.S. 411, 426 L.Ed.2d 642, 93 S.Ct. 3412 (1973) 3, 6

Longwell v. Missouri, 218 U.S. 143, 348 L.Ed.2d 744, 96 S.Ct. 3332 (1979) 4

United States v. Collins, 433 U.S. 211, 154 n.9, 60 L.Ed.2d 733, 96 S.Ct. 3122 (1983) 2, 8

Washington Cases

Julienne v. Dalrymple, 82 Wn.2d 311, 632 P.2d 723 (1981) 5

State v. Allenmore, 72 Wn.2d 640, 423 P.2d 553 (1973) 2, 6

State v. Nasson, 101 Wn.2d 732, 534 P.2d 512 (1985) 8

Marking the Text

When marking text for a table of authorities, you need to find the first occurrence of the authority and mark it as a *full form* with the complete name and case or statute. Then any other occurrence of that case or statute can be identified as a *short form*. Using a short form once the long form has been established saves time. To mark text for a table of authorities, you would complete the following steps:

1. Click Tools, point to Generate, then click Table of Authorities; or click the Table of Authorities button on the Generate Toolbar. This causes the Table of Authorities Feature Bar to display as shown in figure 30.13.
2. Move the insertion point to the first item to be included, then select the entire citation.
3. With the citation selected, click Create Full Form.
4. At the Create Full Form dialog box, shown in figure 30.14, key the section name where the selected text is to appear in the Section name text box. For example, if the selected citation is to be marked for the Federal section of the Table of Authorities, key **Federal** in the Section name text box. An abbreviated portion of the selected text is displayed in the Short form text box. You can key a different name for the short form in the Short form text box.
5. Click OK. This causes the full form to display in the full form editing window. In this window, edit the citation, if necessary, so it appears exactly as you want it to appear in the table of authorities. When you are finished, click Close.

Table of Authorities

Figure 30.13

Table of Authorities Feature Bar

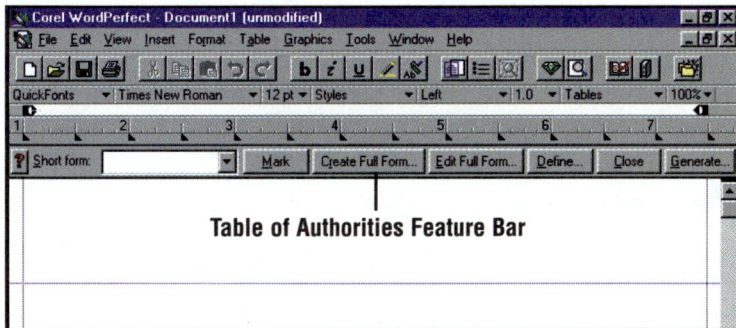

Figure 30.14

Create Full Form Dialog Box

When you click Close at the full form editing window, the insertion point is returned to the document and a code is inserted identifying the section of the table where the marked text will be inserted along with the short form name.

Creating Tables, Indexes, and Lists

An abbreviated portion of selected text displays after the Short form option at the Create Full Form dialog box. You can change this to something shorter that is easier to remember. For example, if the marked citation is Kellor v. Thurston Co., 3 Wn.2d 309,103 P.2d 355 (1951), it could be shortened to *Kellor*. The text you key in the Short form text box must be unique to that citation.

After the full form is marked, move through the document (legal brief) and locate all occurrences of the same authority and mark each one as a short form. To do this, you would complete the following steps:

1. On the Table of Authorities Feature Bar, make sure the short form displayed in the Short form text box is the correct one. If not, you would key the correct short form or choose a short form from the drop-down list. To display the drop-down list, click the down-pointing arrow to the right of the Short form text box, then click the correct short form. (There will not be any short forms displayed in the drop-down list until you have marked a full form and identified the short form.)
2. Position the insertion point anywhere in the next occurrence of the citation.
3. Click Mark on the Table of Authorities Feature Bar.
4. Continue in this manner until all necessary citations have been marked as short forms. After marking all short forms of the first citation, return to the beginning of the document and mark the remaining citations.

Defining the Table of Authorities

A table of authorities should be placed at the beginning of the document. Before defining the table of authorities, move the insertion point to the beginning of the document, then insert a hard page break with Ctrl + Enter. Move the insertion point above the hard page break, then key the table of authorities heading.

When defining a table of authorities, you need to define each section in the table. After keying the heading, press Enter two or three times, access the Center command, key the first section heading, press Enter, then define the section.

The options at the Edit Table of Authorities dialog box are similar to those contained in the Define Table of Contents dialog box and the Define Index dialog box. With the options, you can determine the position of page numbers after the reference text and specify the type of page numbering. You can also specify whether you want WordPerfect to combine sequential numbers in the table or list page numbers separately.

If the citation you marked includes any underlining, the underlining is deleted when the citation is listed in the table of authorities. If you want underlining to remain, click Underlining allowed at the Edit Table of Authorities dialog box.

After the first section of the table of authorities is defined, press Enter a few times to space between the first section and the next section, then define the next section by completing steps similar to those just described.

Generating the Table of Authorities

Before generating the table of authorities, you will need to include a new page numbering code in the document. The table of authorities should be numbered with lowercase Roman numerals. The beginning of the document should include a new page numbering code to start numbering at 1 and to change the numbering style back to Arabic numbers. If you do not insert a new page numbering code at the beginning of the document (after the table of authorities), the page numbers generated in the table of authorities will be incorrect.

Once all sections of the table of authorities have been defined and the new page numbering code and page number style codes have been inserted, generate the table of authorities. To do this, click Generate on the Table of Authorities Feature Bar; or click the Generate button on the Toolbar. At the Generate dialog box, click OK. WordPerfect makes several passes through the document generating any tables, indexes, or lists.

Editing a Table of Authorities

After a table of authorities has been generated, a full form can be edited. This might include editing the text of the full form or changing the short form identifier or the section. To edit full form text in a table of authorities, you would complete the following steps:

1. Click Edit Full Form on the Table of Authorities Feature Bar.
2. At the Edit Full Form dialog box, click the full form you want to edit, then click OK.
3. At the full form editing window, make any necessary changes to the full form text; or click Short form, then change the short form identifier; or click Section and change the section name.
4. When all changes have been made at the full form editing window, click Close. After editing a full form, generate the table of authorities again to update the full form.

EXERCISE 4

Creating a Table of Authorities

1. At a clear editing window, open Legal brief.
2. Save the legal brief with Save As and name it Ch 30, Ex 04.
3. Mark the first statute for the table of authorities by completing the following steps:
    a. Click Tools, point to Generate, then click Table of Authorities. (This displays the Table of Authorities Feature Bar.)
    b. Move the insertion point to the statute *RCW 7.89.321* (toward the end of the second page), then select the entire statute.
    c. With the statute selected, click Create Full Form.
    d. At the Create Full Form dialog box, key **Other** in the Section name text box.
    e. Click OK.
    f. Make sure the statute displays correctly in the full form editing window, then click Close.
4. Mark the following statutes for the table of authorities by completing steps similar to those in 3b through 3f.
    RCW 7.53.443
    RCW 7.72A.432(2)
    RCW 7.42A.429(1)
5. Mark the citation *State v. Connors, 73 W.2d 743, 430 P.2d 199 (1974)* for the table of authorities with the short form *Connors* by completing the following steps:
    a. Move the insertion point to the first occurrence of the citation, *State v. Connors, 73 W.2d 743, 430 P.2d 199 (1974)*, then select the entire citation (including the underline codes). You may want to turn on Reveal Codes to position the insertion point just left of the underline on code before selecting the citation.
    b. Click Create Full Form on the Table of Authorities Feature Bar.
    c. At the Create Full Form dialog box, key **Washington** in the Section name text box.

Creating Tables, Indexes, and Lists   731

d. Select all text in the Short form text box, then key **Connors**.
e. Click OK.
f. Make sure the citation displays correctly in the full form editing window, then click Close.

6. Move the insertion point to the next occurrence of the citation *State v. Connors, 73 W.2d 743, 430 P.2d 199 (1974)* and mark it as a short form by completing the following steps:
   a. Position the insertion point anywhere on the second occurrence of the citation, *State v. Connors, 73 W.2d 743, 430 P.2d 199 (1974)*.
   b. Click Mark on the Table of Authorities Feature Bar.

7. Mark the following citations for the *Washington* section of the table of authorities. (Be sure to include the underlining codes.)
    State v. Bertelli, 63 W.2d 77, 542 P.2d 751 (1971)
    State v. Landers, 103 W.2d 432, 893 P.2d 2 (1984) *(make a short form named* Landers*)*

   Move the insertion point to the next occurrence of State v. Landers, 103 W.2d 432, 893 P.2d 2 (1984), and mark it as a short form.

8. After marking all the citations for the table of authorities, move the insertion point to the beginning of the document and complete the following steps:
   a. Turn on Reveal Codes, then position the insertion point immediately to the right of the [Open Style: InitialStyle] code.
   b. Press Ctrl + Enter to insert a hard page break.
   c. Move the insertion point above the hard page break.
   d. Turn page numbering on at the bottom center of each page, and change the page numbering method to lowercase Roman numerals.
   e. Center and bold the title *TABLE OF AUTHORITIES*, then press Enter three times.
   f. Key the subheading **Washington Cases**, centered and underlined.
   g. Press Enter twice.
   h. Define the first section of the table of authorities by completing the following steps:
      (1) Click Define on the Table of Authorities Feature Bar.
      (2) At the Define Table of Authorities dialog box, click *Washington* in the Section name list box, then click Edit.
      (3) At the Edit Table of Authorities dialog box, click Underlining allowed. This inserts a check mark in the Underlining allowed check box.
      (4) Click OK.
      (5) At the Define Table of Authorities dialog box, make sure *Washington* is selected, then click Insert.
   i. Press Enter once, then key the subheading **Other Cases**, centered and underlined.
   j. Press Enter twice.
   k. Define the second section of the table of authorities by completing the following steps:
      (1) Click Define on the Table of Authorities Feature Bar.
      (2) At the Define Table of Authorities dialog box, click *Other* in the Section name list box, then click Edit.
      (3) At the Edit Table of Authorities dialog box, click Underlining allowed.

(4) Click OK.

(5) At the Define Table of Authorities dialog box, make sure *Other* is selected, then click Insert.

l. Move the insertion point to the beginning of the second page. Turn on Reveal Codes, position the insertion point immediately to the left of the [Ln Spacing: 2.0] code, then change the numbering method to numbers and change the beginning number to 1.

9. Generate the table of authorities by completing the following steps:
   a. Click Generate on the Table of Authorities Feature Bar.
   b. At the Generate dialog box, click OK.
10. Save the document again with the same name (Ch 30, Ex 04).
11. Print and then close Ch 30, Ex 04. (Check with your instructor to see if you should print the entire document or just the Table of Authorities page.)

CHAPTER SUMMARY

▼ WordPerfect includes a feature to help automate the creation of a table of contents, a list, an index, and a table of authorities in a document.

▼ When creating a table of contents, list, index, or table of authorities, four steps are necessary: (1) locate the reference and select it; (2) identify whether it is to be included in a table of contents, list, index, or table of authorities; (3) define the table, list, or index; and (4) generate the table, list, or index.

▼ To mark text for a table of contents, display the Table of Contents Feature Bar by clicking Tools, pointing to Generate, then clicking Table of Contents; or by clicking the Table of Contents button on the Generate Toolbar. The heading or subheading can then be selected.

▼ Defining the table of contents generally involves determining where the Table of Contents will be located in the document and the number of levels to be included. This is done at the Define Table of Contents dialog box.

▼ To make the table of contents appear on the screen, it must be generated. This is done at the Generate dialog box.

▼ The same basic procedures are followed when creating a list and an index as the steps followed for creating a table of contents.

▼ A concordance file can be created that includes words or phrases to be included in an index. This saves you from having to mark each reference in the document.

▼ A table of contents, index, or list can be regenerated if it has been edited or if changes have been made to the document.

▼ A table of authorities is a list of citations for a legal brief that lists the pages of sources where the citings occur. It can be defined and generated in a document in a similar manner to a table of contents, list, or index.

COMMANDS REVIEW

	Mouse/Keyboard
Table of Contents Feature Bar	Tools, Generate, Table of Contents; or click the Table of Contents button on the Generate Toolbar
List Feature Bar	Tools, Generate, List; or click the List button on the Generate Toolbar
Index Feature Bar	Tools, Generate, Index; or click the Index button on the Generate Toolbar
Table of Authorities Feature Bar	Tools, Generate, Table of Authorities; or click the Table of Authorities button on the Generate Toolbar
Generate dialog box	Tools, Generate, Generate; or click the Generate button on the Generate Toolbar

CHECK YOUR UNDERSTANDING

Completion: In the space provided at the right, indicate the correct term, command, or number.

1. A table of contents generally appears at this location in the document. _____

2. An index generally appears at this location in the document. _____

3. A table of authorities generally appears at this location in the document. _____

4. This is the maximum number of levels that can be included in a table of contents. _____

5. This toolbar contains buttons for creating a table of contents, list, index, or table of authorities. _____

6. This is the page numbering style for a table of contents. _____

7. This is the page numbering style for an index. _____

8. This is the name of the file that can be created that contains headings for an index. _____

List the four basic steps to be followed when creating a table of contents, an index, or a list.

1. _____
2. _____
3. _____
4. _____

Chapter 30

SKILL ASSESSMENTS

Assessment 1

1. At a clear editing window, open Report 10.
2. Save the document with Save As and name it Ch 30, SA 01.
3. Make the following changes to the document:
    a. Turn on page numbering and number pages at the bottom center of each page.
    b. Create, define, and generate a table of contents. (Be sure to change the page number and page numbering method for the table of contents page.)
4. Save the report with the same name (Ch 30, SA 01).
5. Print and then close Ch 30, SA 01. (Check with your instructor to see if you should print the entire document or just the Table of Contents page.)

Assessment 2

1. At a clear editing window, open Ch 30, SA 01.
2. Save the document with Save As and name it Ch 30, SA 02.
3. Make the following changes to the document:
    a. Create and define a list of figures. (The list of figures should appear on a separate page after the Table of Contents but before the beginning of the report.)
    b. Mark the title of the list of figures for inclusion in the Table of Contents.
    c. Generate the list of figures (and regenerate the Table of Contents).
4. Save the report with the same name (Ch 30, SA 02).
5. Print and then close Ch 30, SA 02. (Check with your instructor to see if you should print the entire document or just the pages with the list of figures and Table of Contents.)

Assessment 3

1. At a clear editing window, key the text shown in figure 30.15, then save the document and name it Ch 30 Cf (this is a concordance file).
2. Close Ch 30 Cf.
3. At a clear editing window, open Ch 30, SA 02.
4. Save the document with Save As and name it Ch 30, SA 03.
5. Mark the following word(s) as headings or subheadings (as described) for the index:
    eligibility in the first paragraph (subheading; heading, *Requirements*)
    active in the second paragraph (subheading; heading, *employee*)
    Earnings in figure 1.2 (heading)
    Final Average Earnings in figure 1.2 (heading)
    Year of Credited Service in figure 1.2 (heading)
    date in the first paragraph below figure 1.2 (subheading; heading, *Retirement*)
    Normal in figure 1.3 (subheading; heading, *Retirement*)
    Early in figure 1.3 (subheading; heading, *Retirement*)
    Late in figure 1.3 (subheading; heading, *Retirement*)
    death in the last paragraph (subheading; heading, *Benefits*)
6. Create and define the Index. (Include the concordance file *Ch 30 Cf* when defining the index.)
7. Mark the title of the Index for inclusion in the Table of Contents.
8. Generate the Index (and regenerate the Table of Contents and list of figures).

Creating Tables, Indexes, and Lists

9. Save the report with the same name (Ch 30, SA 03).
10. Print and then close Ch 30, SA 03. (Check with your instructor to see if you should print the entire document or just the pages with the Index, list of figures, and Table of Contents.)

Figure 30.15

participant
Requirements
employee
hour of service
Benefits
Retirement
termination

31

BROWSING THE WEB

PERFORMANCE OBJECTIVE

Upon successful completion of chapter 31, you will be able to browse the World Wide Web from within WordPerfect 7, search for specific information on the Web, create a home page and convert it to HTML using the Internet Publisher, and create hypertext links.

Increasingly, businesses are accessing the Internet to conduct research, publish product or catalog information, communicate, and market products globally. WordPerfect provides the ability to jump to the Internet and browse the World Wide Web from a WordPerfect window, and create documents that are easily converted to Web documents with HyperText Markup Language (HTML) codes. HTML "tags" attached to information in a Web document enable the links and jumps between documents and data resources to operate. Information provided by the tags also instructs the browser software how to display text, images, animations, or sounds.

Understanding the Internet

The Internet is a network of computers connected around the world. In 1969, the U.S. Defense Department created a network to allow researchers at different sites to exchange information. The first network consisted of only four computers. Since then, the number of networks that have connected has grown exponentially, and it is no longer just a vehicle of information for researchers, but can be used by anyone with a modem attached to their computer.

Users access the Internet for several purposes: to communicate using e-mail; to subscribe to news groups; to transfer files; to socialize with other users around the globe in "chat" rooms; and largely to access virtually any kind of information imaginable.

The *World Wide Web* is the most commonly used application on the Internet. The *World Wide Web* is a set of standards and protocols used to access information available on the Internet. The *Internet* is the physical network utilized to carry the data. The software program you use to access the World Wide Web is called a *Web browser*. A Web browser allows you to move around the Internet by pointing and clicking with the mouse.

Browsing the World Wide Web

In this chapter, you will be completing several exercises and assessments that require you to search for locations and information on the World Wide Web. To do this, you will need the following:

1. A modem or network connection to a server with Internet access.
2. Browser software installed and configured. (This chapter will explore the World Wide Web using *Netscape Navigator*.)
3. An Internet Service Provider account.

A modem is a hardware device that allows data to be carried over telephone lines. The word "modem" is derived from MODulator/DEModulator. The modem attached to your computer converts digital data into an analog signal that can be transferred over telephone lines. At the other end of the connection is another modem that converts the analog signal back to digital data for the receiving computer. There are internal and external modems available in a variety of speeds. Modem speed is measured in terms of the number of bits per second data is transferred. If you are using a computer connected to a network, the network server will route the data through its modem, or to another server with a modem.

Two of the more popular Web browser software packages are *Netscape Navigator*, and *Microsoft Explorer*. Both of these browsers adopt the "point and click" interface.

An Internet Service Provider (ISP) sells access to the Internet. In order to provide this access, the ISP must have in place the hardware and software necessary to support access to the Internet, phone lines to accept the modem connections, and support staff to assist their customers. The ISP is responsible for configuring their computers, routers, and software to enable connectivity to every other individual and computer that make up the Internet. Examples of Internet Service Providers include America Online, CompuServe, Prodigy, and AT&T Worldnet Service.

Locating URLs on the Internet

We all know that we can dial a telephone number for a friend or relative in any country around the world and establish a connection within seconds. The global telephone system is an amazing network that functions because of a common set of protocols and standards that are agreed upon by each country. The Internet operates on the same principle. Computer protocols known as TCP/IP (Transmission Control Protocol/Internet Protocol) form the base of the Internet. Protocols are simply agreements on how various hardware and software should communicate with each other. The Internet Service Provider becomes the Domain Name Service (DNS), *the route to the Internet*. The DNS and IP determine how to route your computer to another location/computer on the Internet. Every computer directly linked to the Net has a unique IP address.

This explanation has been overly simplified. The technical details on how computer A can "talk" to computer B do not directly involve a computer user any more than does picking up a phone in Vancouver, British Columbia and dialing a number in San Diego, California.

Uniform Resource Locators, referred to as URLs, are the method used to identify locations on the Internet. The format of a URL is *http://server-name.path*. The first part of the URL, *http://*, identifies the protocol. The letters *http* stand for Hypertext Transfer Protocol, which is the protocol or language used to transfer data within the World Wide Web. The colon and slashes separate the protocol from the server name. The server name is the second component of the URL. For example, in the URL *http://home.netscape.com*, the server name is identified as *home.netscape*. The last part of the URL specifies the domain to which the server belongs. For example, *.com* refers to "commercial" and establishes that the URL is a commercial company. Other examples of domains include *.edu* for "educational," *.gov* for "government," and *.mil* for "military." Some examples of URLs are displayed in figure 31.1.

738   Chapter 31

Figure 31.1

Sample URLs

URL	Connects to...
http://home.netscape.com	Netscape's home page
http://www.corel.com	Corel's home page
http://lcweb.loc.gov	Library of Congress
http://www.xerox.com	Xerox home page
http://www.kodak.com	Eastman Kodak home page

You can easily connect to Netscape and then browse the Web by clicking the Browse the Web button located toward the right side of the Toolbar. This causes the Netscape dialog box to display as shown in figure 31.2. You can also display this dialog box by clicking File, then Internet Publisher. At the Internet Publisher dialog box, click the Browse the Web button. At the Netscape dialog box, you can key a specific URL in the Location text box located toward the top of the dialog box. When keying a URL, you must key the address exactly as written, including any colons (:) or slashes (/).

Browse the Web

Figure 31.2

Corel Home Page

In exercise 1, you will be using Netscape to access the World Wide Web and then locate two different sites. Before completing this exercise, check with your instructor to make sure that the Internet and Netscape are available to you. You must be connected to the Internet before completing the exercises and assessments in this chapter.

EXERCISE 1

Exploring the Web Using URLs

1. Explore several locations on the World Wide Web from within WordPerfect by completing the following steps:
   a. Click the Browse the Web button on the Toolbar (last button at the right side of the Toolbar that displays with the icon of a spider web). In a few moments the Netscape dialog box will display and you will be connected to the Corel home page. (The home page will display similar to the one shown in figure 31.2.) *(If the Netscape dialog box does not open, check with your instructor to ensure you have Internet access on the computer you are using and that the Web Browser software has been properly configured.)*
   b. Select the current URL by clicking the left mouse button in the Location text box. (The Location text box is positioned just below the Netscape toolbar as shown in figure 31.2.)
   c. Key **http://www.eb.com** and then press the Enter key. In a few seconds you will see the home page for Britannica Online as shown in figure 31.3. *(Web sites are changing constantly—the home page may vary from what you see in figure 31.3.)*
   d. Scroll through the home page by clicking the down-pointing triangle on the vertical scroll bar.
   e. When you have finished viewing the page, select the current URL by clicking the left mouse button in the Location text box.
   f. Jump to the home page for NASA by keying **http://www.nasa.gov** and then pressing the Enter key.
   g. Spend a few minutes reading the information on the NASA home page. Click the down-pointing triangle on the vertical scroll bar to view the entire page.
2. After viewing the NASA home page, return to WordPerfect by clicking File on the Netscape dialog box Title Bar, then clicking Exit at the drop-down menu.

Figure 31.3

Britannica Online Home Page

740 Chapter 31

Using Hypertext Links

As you were viewing the home pages for Britannica Online and NASA, did you notice text that displayed in a different color (usually blue) and was also underlined? Text displayed in a different color and underlined indicates text that has been identified as a *hypertext link*. A hypertext link allows you to link or connect to another item. To use a hypertext link, position the mouse pointer on the desired hypertext link until the pointer turns into a hand, then click the left mouse button. For example, when you displayed the Britannica Online home page, you could have clicked the hypertext link *How to Subscribe*. Information on how to subscribe to Britannica Online would then display on the screen. Most pages contain a variety of hypertext links. Using these links, you can zero in on the exact information you are searching for.

The Netscape dialog box contains a Back and a Forward button. These buttons are located toward the top of the dialog box below the Title Bar. If you click a hypertext link, clicking the Back button will display the previous page or location. If you click the Back button and then would like to go back to the hypertext link, click the Forward button. By clicking the Back button, you can back your way out of any hypertext links and return to the Netscape dialog box.

In exercise 2, you will be using Netscape to access the World Wide Web, locating specific home pages, and then using hypertext links to display specific information.

EXERCISE

Exploring the Web and Using Hypertext Links

1. Explore several locations on the World Wide Web from within WordPerfect and use hypertext links by completing the following steps:
   a. Click the Browse the Web button on the Toolbar.
   b. At the Netscape dialog box, click in the Location text box to select the current URL.
   c. Jump to the home page for the White House by keying **http://www.whitehouse.gov** and then pressing the Enter key.
   d. Jump to another page linked to this home page using a hypertext link by completing the following steps:
      (1) Scroll down the White House page until you see the underlined text What's New:.
      (2) Position the arrow pointer on What's New: until the pointer turns into a hand, then click the left mouse button.
      (3) In a few moments, a page will display providing information on current government activities. (This page is updated regularly.)
      (4) Scroll through this page until you find a hypertext link that interests you and then click the hypertext link.
   e. After viewing information on the current page, click the Back button. This returns you to the What's New page. (Notice when you return to the previous page that the hypertext link text has changed color. This identifies the pages you have viewed.)
   f. Click the Back button again. This returns you to the White House home page.
   g. Click the Back button again. This returns you to the Netscape dialog box. (Notice that the *What's New* hypertext link text has changed color.)

Browsing the Web

    h. Click the current URL in the Location text box, then key **http://www.ups.com**.
    i. When the UPS home page displays, click the QuickCost Calculator button.
    j. At the QuickCost Calculator page, key the following text in the specified text box (you will need to scroll down the page to display some of the text boxes):
       (1) Key **99032** in the Zip® Code text box in the Origin: United States section.
       (2) Key **Spokane** in the City text box in the Destination section.
       (3) Key **98031** in the Zip®/Postal Code text box in the Destination section.
       (4) Key **1** in the Weight text box in the Package Information section.
    k. Scroll down to the bottom of the page, then click Calculate Cost.
    l. At the Security Information dialog box, click Continue.
    m. View the results of the QuickCost Calculator.
    n. Click the Print button located toward the top of the Netscape dialog box to send the cost results to the printer.
    o. Click the Back button until the Corel home page is displayed.
    p. Search for TWA flight departure times from Houston, TX to San Diego, CA by completing the following steps:
       (1) Click in the Location text box to select the current URL, then key **http://www.twa.com**.
       (2) Click the Proceed (without signing in) button (located toward the end of the page).
       (3) Click Continue at the Security Information dialog box.
       (4) At the TWA home page, scroll down the page and then click the hypertext link <u>FLIGHT SCHEDULES</u>.
       (5) At the page for flight schedules, the current date displays. (Leave this date as displayed.)
       (6) Click in the Evening (after 6 PM) check box. (You may need to scroll down the page to display this check box.)
       (7) Select Houston, TX in the City of Departure text box. To do this, scroll down the list of cities in the list box below City of Departure until Houston, TX displays, then click Houston, TX to select it.
       (8) Select San Diego, CA in the City of Arrival text box. To do this, scroll down the list of cities in the list box below City of Arrival until San Diego, CA displays, then click San Diego, CA to select it.
       (9) Click the view schedule button.
       (10) Click Continue at the Security Information dialog box.
       (11) View the flights available and then click <u>Details</u> beside the first flight displayed.
       (12) Print the page that appears by clicking the Print button on the Netscape Toolbar.
2. Click F<u>i</u>le, then E<u>x</u>it to close Netscape.

Finding Information Using Search Engines

In the previous exercises, you jumped around the Web by keying URLs, which are a fast way to move from site to site. Often, however, you will access the Web to search for information and you will not know the URL that you want to visit.

Search engines are valuable tools to assist a user in locating information on a topic by simply keying a few words or a short phrase. There are many search engines available on the Internet such as Yahoo, InfoSeek, WebCrawler, AltaVista, etc. Each offers the opportunity to search for specific information. As you use different search engines, you may find you prefer one over the others. To search for information using a search engine you would follow these basic steps:

1. Load Netscape.
2. Click the Net Search button on the toolbar located below the Location text box.
3. At the Net Search page, click the desired search engine.
4. Key a word or phrase in the Search text box and then click the button that begins the search.
5. The search engine will return with (display) a list of Web sites that have the key word or phrase in the index. Scroll through the list and read the short descriptions. You can jump to any of the sites by clicking the hypertext link. Use the Back button to return to the list and select another site.

As you gain experience searching the Web, you will develop methods to refine your search techniques and tools to limit the time spent browsing. Before you begin a research project, jot down your key words or phrases and think about ways to limit the sites that will be selected by being as specific as possible without constricting the search. As you will see in the next exercise, you can become overwhelmed with the number of sites that will be selected.

EXERCISE

Using Search Engines to Locate Information on the Web

Note: Web pages and search indexes are changing constantly. If the instructions in this exercise do not match what you are viewing, you may need to substitute different articles than the ones instructed here.

1. Jump to the World Wide Web from within WordPerfect and search for information on the world's tallest building using the Infoseek search engine by completing these steps:
    a. Click the Browse the Web button on the Toolbar.
    b. At the Netscape dialog box, click the Net Search button.
    c. At the Netscape Destinations page shown in figure 31.4, click Infoseek.
    d. Click inside the text box beside the smartseek red arrow.
    e. Key **world's tallest building** and then click the seek button to the right of the smartseek text box.
    f. In a few moments the Infoseek search engine will return with a list of sites that meet your search criteria. Scroll down the page to see the number of sites that have been selected. (The number of sites selected will vary. The Internet changes on a daily basis with new information being added constantly.)
    g. Scroll through the list until a hypertext link displays that mentions *Malaysia* in the title. (The hypertext link will vary depending on the information available at the time you conduct the search.) Click the hypertext link. (This should display information on the tallest building in the world that is located in Malaysia. If this is not the information displayed, try another hypertext link that mentions Malaysia.)

Browsing the Web 743

h. After reading the information, click the Back button.
   i. Click the Back button again to return to the Netscape Destinations page.
2. Search for information on the top 100 companies doing business on the World Wide Web using the Yahoo search engine by completing the following steps:
   a. At the Netscape Destinations page, click Yahoo.
   b. Scroll down the screen to view the list of categories that begins with Arts.
   c. Click the hypertext link Business.
   d. Scroll down the Business and Economy page until Indices displays and then click Indices. (This displays an index of topics.)
   e. Scroll down the list of topics until Web 100, The displays and then click Web 100, The. (In a few moments you will be connected with the site *http://www.w100.com*.)
   f. Scroll down this screen until the text *"The 100 largest American corporations on the Web"* displays (this text may vary slightly), then click the word *List* that displays in red and is located at the right of the text *"The 100 largest American corporations on the Web."*
   g. Scroll down the list of company names. Click a company name for which you want to find out more information. This will jump you to the company's home page.
   h. With the company's home page displayed, click the Print button on the Netscape Toolbar.
3. Click the Close button located at the right side of the Netscape Title Bar to exit Netscape.

Figure 31.4

Net Search Destinations Page

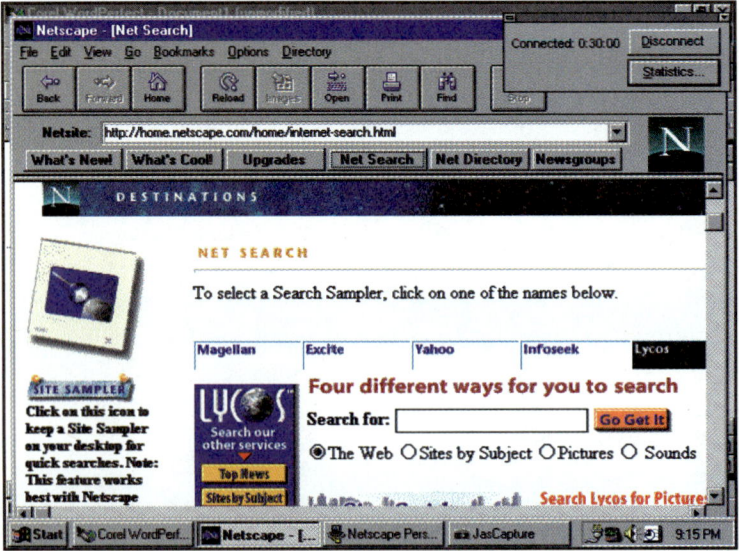

Creating a Home Page

Now that you have been "surfing the net," you have visited several home pages and have an idea how a home page displays. These home pages were designed using a language called HyperText Markup Language (HTML). This is a language that Web browsers use to read hypertext documents. In the past, a person needed knowledge of HTML to design a home page. Now a home page can be created in WordPerfect and then converted to HTML using the Internet Publisher feature.

Before creating a home page, consider the information you want contained in the home page. Carefully plan the layout of the information and where to position hypertext links. Good page design is a key element to a successful home page. Often a company will hire a professional Web page designer to do their home page. Before designing a home page, you may want to visit a variety of home pages and consider some of the following questions: What elements are included on the home page? How are the elements distributed on the page? Is the information organized logically and easy to read? Is the home page visually appealing? Evaluating home pages on the Web will help you when designing your own.

Using the Internet Publisher

WordPerfect has a built-in feature called the Internet Publisher that provides templates for creating Web documents; a conversion program to format the current document as a Web document; the ability to save a copy of the current document in HTML format for publication on the Web; and a button to browse the Web from the Internet Publisher dialog box. To view the Internet Publisher dialog box shown in figure 31.5, click File, then Internet Publisher.

Figure 31.5

Internet Publisher Dialog Box

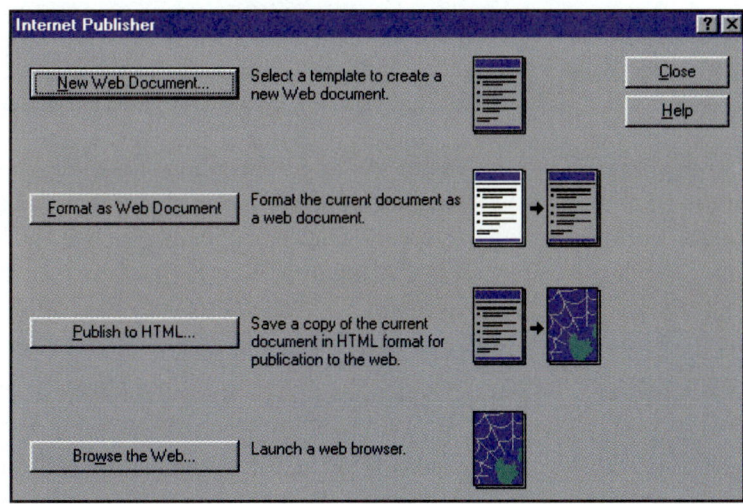

You can create a Web document in the Internet Publisher by clicking the New Web Document button, or you can convert an existing WordPerfect document to a Web document by clicking the Format as Web Document button in the Internet Publisher dialog box.

Formatting a Home Page

When a document is converted from WordPerfect to a Web document, some of the WordPerfect formatting codes are deleted. This is because the HTML does not read all WordPerfect codes. In the Internet Publisher, you can format a document as a Web document and then make formatting changes to the Web document. Then, the document can be published as an HTML format for publication on the Web.

When you open a WordPerfect document and then click the Format as Web Document button at the Internet Publisher dialog box, the editing window changes and displays similar to the one shown in figure 31.6. (The document displayed in this figure is the document you will be formatting in exercise 4.)

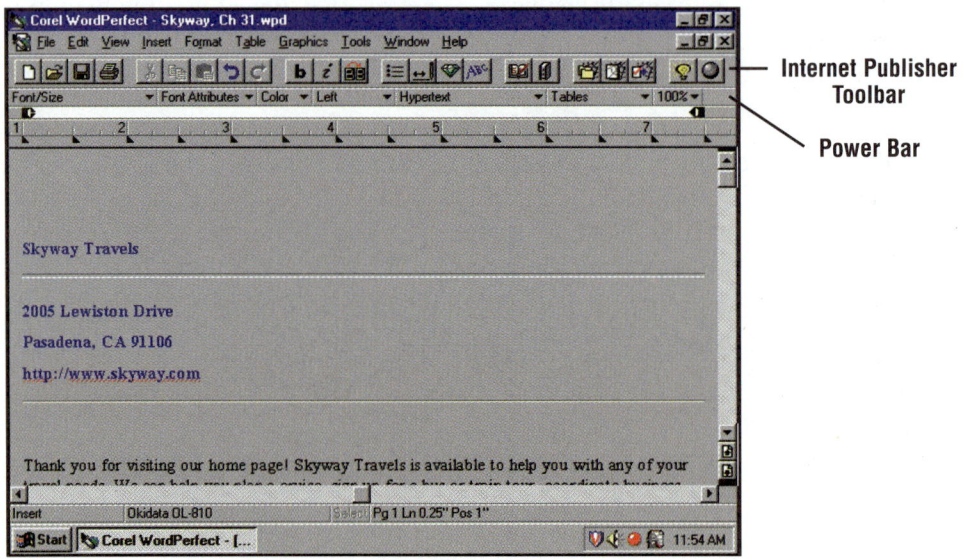

Figure 31.6 — Document Formatted as a Web Document

The toolbar that displays below the Menu Bar is the Internet Publisher Toolbar. This toolbar contains buttons at the right side for working with the Web. For example, you can access the Web by clicking the Browse the Web button or you can click the View in Web Browser button that will create a copy of the current document in HTML and display it in a browser. Position the arrow pointer on each button to display a description of what the button will accomplish.

Below the Internet Publisher Toolbar is a Power Bar. This bar contains buttons for formatting a Web document. Using these buttons, you can change the font size, attributes, and color; change the alignment of text; create a hypertext link; create a table; and change the view.

In exercise 4, you will be formatting a WordPerfect document to a Web document and then applying some basic formatting to the document. You will then save a copy of the document in HTML format for publication to the Web. When you save a document in the HTML format, the extension *.htm* is automatically added to the document name.

To view the document you converted to a Web document, you will access Netscape and then open the document. This document will be located on your student disk. For a home page to be available on the Web, you must have access to a Web server. Large businesses usually have their own server and you would have to contact the Information Systems department of the company to arrange for space on the server to store your HTML documents (home pages). The other option is to rent space from an Internet Service Provider (ISP). The ISP you use to access the Web will also arrange to store your Web page. Check out all of the fees involved, as there are many different fee structures in existence.

EXERCISE 4

Converting an Existing WordPerfect Document to an HTML Document

1. Create a Web page by converting an existing WordPerfect document to an HTML document by completing the following steps:
    a. Open Skyway home page. (This document is located on your student data disk.)
    b. Save the document with Save As and name it Skyway, Ch 31.
    c. Click File, then Internet Publisher.
    d. At the Internet Publisher dialog box, click the Format as Web Document button.
    e. At the message box stating *"This document will be formatted as a web document. Only web-compatible formatting and features are available."*, click OK. (When the document is converted, notice how the formatting has changed.)
    f. Make the following formatting changes to the document:
        (1) Select the company name *Skyway Travels*.
        (2) Click the Font/Size button on the Power Bar, then click *Heading 1* at the drop-down list.
        (3) With *Skyway Travels* still selected, click the Align text button on the Power Bar (contains the word *Left*).
        (4) At the drop-down list that displays, click *Center*.
        (5) Select the company address and e-mail address.
        (6) Click the Font/Size button on the Power Bar, then click *Heading 3* at the drop-down list.
        (7) With the text still selected, click the Align text button on the Power Bar and then click *Center* at the drop-down list.
        (8) Deselect the text.
    g. Click the Save button on the Internet Publisher Toolbar.
    h. Save a copy of the document in HTML format for publication to the Web by completing the following steps:
        (1) Click the Publish to HTML button on the Internet Publisher Toolbar.
        (2) At the Publish to HTML dialog box, make sure the path and document name display correctly in the Publish to list box (if you are saving on the data disk in drive a:, the path and name will display as *a:\Skyway, Ch 31.htm*) and then click OK.
    i. Close Skyway, Ch 31.
2. Click the Browse the Web button on the WordPerfect Toolbar.
3. At the Netscape dialog box, open the Skyway, Ch 31.htm document by completing the following steps:
    a. Click File, then Open File.
    b. At the Open dialog box, make sure drive a: is the default drive, then double-click the *Skyway, Ch 31.htm* document name in the File name list box. (This document name will vary depending on your operating system. The document name may display as *skyway~1.htm*.)
    c. Scroll through the Skyway Travels home page to see how the document appears in HTML format.
4. Exit Netscape by clicking File, then Exit.

Creating Hypertext Links

The business Web sites you have visited, such as Britannica Online and UPS, have included hypertext links to connect you to other pages or Web sites. You can create your own hypertext link in your home page. To do this, select the text you want specified as the hypertext link, click Tools, then click Hypertext/Web Links. This displays the Hypertext Feature Bar below the Ruler Bar. Click the Create button on the Hypertext Feature Bar and the Create Hypertext Link dialog box displays as shown in figure 31.7. At this dialog box, click in the circle immediately preceding the Document option, then key the Web site URL where you want to link. Click OK to close the Create Hypertext Link dialog box and then click Close on the Hypertext Feature Bar. Text identified as a hypertext link will display underlined and in blue in the document.

Figure 31.7

Create Hypertext Link Dialog Box

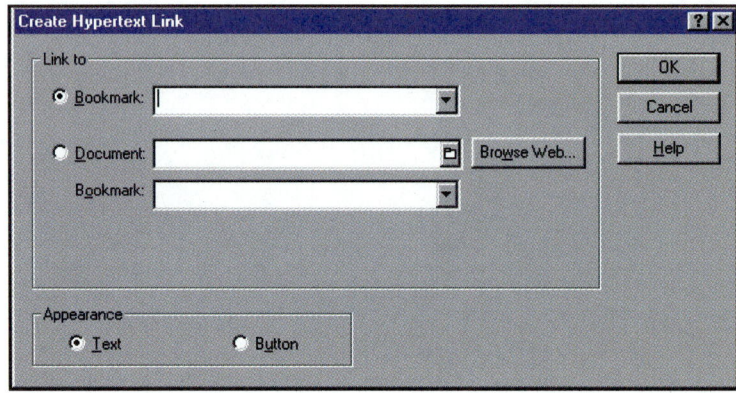

In exercise 5, you will be establishing hypertext links from the Skyway Travels home page to the airlines listed in the home page.

EXERCISE 5

Creating Hypertext Links

1. At a clear editing window, open Skyway, Ch 31. (Open the WordPerfect document and not the HTML document. The WordPerfect document displays preceded by the image of a tip of a fountain pen, while the HTML document displays preceded by the image of an envelope.) At the message telling you that the document will be formatted as a web page, click OK.
2. Create a hypertext link so that clicking *Alaska Airlines* will display the Alaska Airlines home page by completing the following steps:
   a. Select the text *Alaska Airlines* that displays toward the end of the document.
   b. Click Tools, then Hypertext/Web Links.
   c. Click the Create button that displays on the Hypertext Feature Bar.
   d. At the Create Hypertext Link dialog box, click in the circle immediately preceding the Document: option. (This moves the insertion point into the Document text box.)
   e. Key **http://www.alaska-air.com**.

  f. Click OK to close the Create Hypertext Link dialog box.
3. Complete steps similar to those in step 2 to create a hypertext link from *Northwest Airlines* to the URL *http://www.nwa.com*.
4. Complete steps similar to those in step 2 to create a hypertext link from *Transworld Airlines* to the URL *http://www.twa.com*.
5. Complete steps similar to those in step 2 to create a hypertext link from *United Airlines* to the URL *http://www.ual.com*.
6. Click the Save button on the Internet Publisher Toolbar.
7. Publish the document to HTML by completing the following steps:
  a. Click the Publish to HTML button on the Internet Publisher Toolbar.
  b. At the Publish to HTML dialog box, make sure the correct path and document name display in the Publish to list box, then click OK.
  c. At the message telling you that the file already exists and asking if you want to overwrite it, click Yes.
8. Close Skyway, Ch 31.
9. Click the Browse the Web button on the Toolbar.
10. At the Netscape dialog box, open the *Skyway, Ch 31.htm* document by completing the following steps:
  a. Click File, then Open File.
  b. At the Open dialog box, make sure drive a: is the default drive, then double-click the *Skyway, Ch 31.htm* document name in the File name list box. (This document name will vary depending on your operating system. The document name may display as *skyway~1.htm*.)
  c. Scroll to the end of the Skyway Travels home page to display the hypertext links.
  d. Click the hypertext link *Alaska Airlines*. (This will display the Alaska Airlines home page.)
  e. Scroll through the Alaska Airlines home page, clicking on any hypertext links that interest you.
  f. When you are done viewing the Alaska Airlines home page, click the Back button until the Skyway Travels home page displays.
  g. Click each of the other hypertext links (*Northwest Airlines*, *Transworld Airlines (TWA)*, and *United Airlines*) to display the home page for each of these airlines.
11. After viewing the home pages for each airline, exit Netscape.

CHAPTER SUMMARY

- The Internet is a network of computers connected around the world allowing the exchange of information.
- WordPerfect 7 provides the ability to jump to the Internet from the WordPerfect editing window.
- The World Wide Web is the most commonly used application on the Internet and is a set of standards and protocols used to access information available on the Internet.
- A software program used to access the Web is referred to as a Web browser.
- To locate information on the World Wide Web you need a modem, browser software, and an Internet Service Provider account. An Internet Service Provider sells access to the Internet.
- A modem is a hardware device that carries data over telephone lines.
- Uniform Resource Locators (URLs) are the method used to identify locations on the Web.
- A home page on the Web can contain a hypertext link. Click this link to connect to another site, location, or page.
- Use a search engine such as Yahoo, InfoSeek, or WebCrawler, to locate information on the Internet on a specific topic by keying a few words or a short phrase.
- Home pages are Web documents that describe a company, school, government, or individual and are created using a language called HyperText Markup Language (HTML).
- A home page can be created in WordPerfect and then converted to an HTML document using the Internet Publisher feature.

COMMANDS REVIEW

	Mouse	**Keyboard**
Browse the Web	Browse the Web button	File, Internet Publisher, Browse the Web
Internet Publisher	File, Internet Publisher	File, Internet Publisher
Hypertext Feature Bar	Tools, Hypertext/Web Links	Tools, Hypertext Web/Links

CHECK YOUR UNDERSTANDING

Completion: In the space provided at the right, indicate the correct term or command.

1. List three reasons why users access the Internet. _____

   _____

   _____

2. The word "modem" is derived from this. _____

3. List two of the more popular Web browser software packages. _____

   _____

4. The letters ISP stand for this. _____

5. This is the method used to identify locations on the Internet. _____

6. Click this button on the Toolbar to access the Web. _____

7. Click this in a home page to link to another page or location. _____

8. Click this button on the Netscape dialog box to display the previous page or location. _____

9. List at least three search engines that can be used to search for specific information on the Internet.
   _____
   _____
   _____

10. A home page on the Web is created using this language. _____

11. A home page can be created in WordPerfect and then converted to HTML with this feature. _____

12. Click this option at the Tools drop-down menu to display the Hypertext Feature Bar. _____

SKILL ASSESSMENTS

Assessment 1

1. Jump to the Web from within WordPerfect.
2. Access the *Library of Congress* web site using the URL *http://lcweb.loc.gov*.
   a. Click the hypertext link Copyright, then scroll down and click Copyright Basics. (If you do not find Copyright Basics, look for other text such as US Copyright Office and click this text.)
   b. List five categories of works that are protected by copyright.
      1. _____
      2. _____
      3. _____
      4. _____
      5. _____
3. Jump to the web site for *AT&T* using the URL *http://www.att.com*.
4. Click ABOUT AT&T, then click AT&T Learning Network at the next page.
5. Click Enter the AT&T Learning Network and then read what AT&T is doing to support education on the Information Superhighway.
6. Print the AT&T Learning Network home page.
7. Exit Netscape.

Assessment 2

1. Jump to the Web from within WordPerfect and then perform search for information on *endangered species* using the Yahoo search engine.

2. Scroll the list of responses and jump to the site Alberta's At-Risk Wildlife. Read the information on the home page and then jump to one of the hypertext links for one of the Alberta species that are in danger of becoming extinct.
3. Print the page that you visited.
4. Explore other sites related to this topic.
5. Exit Netscape.

Assessment 3

1. Jump to the Web from within WordPerfect and then access the UPS home page at *http://www.ups.com*.
2. Use the QuickCost Calculator to calculate the cost of shipping a 3-pound package from Atlanta, GA to Phoenix, AZ. Look up Zip Codes for these cities in a Zip Code directory.
3. Print the QuickCost Calculator results page.
4. Exit Netscape.

Assessment 4

1. Create a WordPerfect document like the one shown in figure 31.8. Substitute your first name and last name in the title, and enter descriptive text about yourself below each of the subheadings (Figure 31.8 is a sample only). Include the bold and italics as shown.
2. Save the completed document and name it Ch 31, SA 04.
3. Format the current document as an HTML document using the Internet Publisher.
4. In the HTML editing window, select the title and change it to the Heading 1 style from the Font/Size button.
5. Select the subheadings and change their color to red.
6. Publish the document as an HTML document using the same name.
7. Print and then close Ch 31, SA 04.

Figure 31.8

I. M. Graduate

Career Objective: An office administrative assistant position in a company with a vision of employing the latest technology to grow in the next century to a globally competitive leader.

Education: Office Administration Executive Diploma from **Higher Colleges of Technology** in Big City, USA.

Work Experience:
- part-time administrative assistant for school career placement office
- cashier in retail department store
- volunteer at local hospital

Hobbies and Interests: Participate in competitive volleyball, basketball, and golf. Enjoy volunteering at the college athletic center.

Relocation: Able to relocate anywhere within North America. I have a particular interest in exploring areas of Southern Ontario, Canada, and would relocate to this area at my own expense.

Unit Six

PERFORMANCE ASSESSMENTS

PROBLEM SOLVING AND DECISION MAKING

Assessment 1

1. At a clear editing window, create the document shown in figure U6.1 using the Outline feature. (Make sure the numbering definition is Paragraph.)
2. Save the document and name it Unit 6, PA 01.
3. Print and then close Unit 6, PA 01.

SCOPE OF EMPLOYEE ASSESSMENT PROJECT

1. Preventative

    a. Governing board review of bylaws
    b. Medical staff review of bylaws
    c. Annual review of policies and procedures

2. Ongoing monitoring

    a. Medical staff
        i. Medical staff department review and evaluations relating to quality and appropriateness of care
        ii. Medical record review
        iii. Morbidity/mortality review
    b. Administration
        i. Departmental review and evaluation related to quality
        ii. Utilization review reports
        iii. Risk management and litigations reports
        iv. Financial data reports

Figure U6.1

Assessment 2

1. At a clear editing window, change the font to 12-point Century Schoolbook, then create the outline shown in figure U6.2 using the Outline feature. (Be sure to change the numbering definition to Outline.)
2. Save the outline and name it Unit 6, PA 02.
3. Print and then close Unit 6, PA 02.

Optional: Create an outline for a book you are reading or for a research project you are doing.

CUSTOMER SURVEY

Presentation Agenda

I. Overview of past year with customer survey process

    A. Survey documents
    B. Survey process

II. Team presentations

    A. Evaluation of customer survey process
    B. Evaluation of customer survey team development
    C. Future employee involvement in customer survey
    D. Employee evaluation of customer survey process

III. Status report on implementation

    A. Time lines for implementation
    B. Follow-up activities

IV. Questions and discussion

V. Presentation of award letters and certificates

Figure U6.2

Assessment 3

1. At a clear editing window, create the following styles:
    a. Create a document style named *Doc Format* that changes the font to 12-point Bookman Old Style, turns on page numbers at the bottom right corner of each page, and changes the justification to Full.
    b. Create a paragraph style named *Title* that changes the font to 16-point Arial bold.
    c. Create a paragraph style named *Subtitle* that changes the font to 14-point Arial and turns on underlining.
2. Save the styles in a style document named *Report styles*.
3. Close the document without saving it.

Assessment 4

1. At a clear editing window, open Report 04.
2. Save the report with Save As and name it Unit 6, PA 04.
3. Complete the following steps:
   a. Position the insertion point at the beginning of the document (immediately to the right of the [Open Style: InitialStyle] code), then press the Enter key once.
   b. Move the insertion point to the blank line at the beginning of the document, display the Style List dialog box, then retrieve the *Report styles* style document.
   c. Apply the *Doc Format* document style.
   d. Apply the *Title* style to the Chapter 3 title of the report.
   e. Apply the *Title* style to the Chapter 4 title of the report.
   f. Apply the *Subtitle* style to each of the headings within the report.
   g. Create, define, and generate a table of contents.
4. Save the report again with the same name (Unit 6, PA 04).
5. Print and then close Unit 6, PA 04.

Assessment 5

1. Jump to the World Wide Web from within WordPerfect and search for information on a country of your choice.
2. Try to find the following information about the country you choose:
   a. the population.
   b. the language(s) spoken.
   c. the currency.
   d. the capital city.
3. At a clear editing window in WordPerfect, create a document in a report format that describes the information you learned about the country you investigated.
4. Save the document and name it Unit 6, PA 05.
5. Print and then close Unit 6, PA 05.

WRITING

The following activities give you the opportunity to practice your writing skills along with demonstrating an understanding of some of the important WordPerfect features you have mastered in this unit. In planning the documents, remember to shape the information according to the writing purpose and the audience. Use correct grammar, appropriate word choices, and clear sentence constructions.

Activity 1

Situation: Open Report 03, move the insertion point to the end of the document and then insert the document named Report 04. (Be sure to use the File option from the Insert drop-down menu.) Save the document with Save As and name it Unit 06, Act 01. Using Unit 06, Act 01, create an outline of the document at a clear editing window. Use the Outline feature to create the outline.

When the outline is completed, save the document and name it Unit 06, Outline. Print and then close Unit 06, Outline. Close Unit 06, Act 01.

Activity 2

Situation: Open Unit 06, Act 01 and then save the document with Save As and name it Unit 06, Act 02. Create styles to format the report. You determine the type of style and the formatting for the styles. Apply the styles to the report. Save the report again with the same name (Unit 06, Act 02). Print Unit 06, Act 02. With the document still open, edit at least one of the styles you created. Save the document again with the same name (Unit 06, Act 02). Print and then close Unit 06, Act 02.

Activity 3

Situation: You are the administrative assistant to Pat Windslow, the superintendent for the Omaha City School District. You have been asked by the superintendent to provide a list of books written by Samuel Clemens needed for the next English Department meeting. The superintendent tells you that there is a book company named Amazon Books located on the World Wide Web that should contain the needed information. Jump to the World Wide Web, go to the Amazon Book home page located at *http://www.amazon.com*, display a list of books written by Samuel Clemens, and then print this list.

The superintendent would also like you to compose a note to the English teachers explaining how to locate Amazon Books on the Internet. In your note, include the Web site address, directions on how to locate the Web site, a description of how to locate books by specific authors, and a description of how to display books on a specific subject.

APPENDIX A • PROOFREADERS' MARKS

Proofreaders' Mark	Example	Revised
# Insert space	lettertothe	letter to the
ℐ Delete	the commands is	the command is
lc / Lowercase	he is Branch Manager	he is branch manager
cap or UC Uppercase	Margaret simpson	Margaret Simpson
¶ New paragraph	The new product	The new product
no ¶ No paragraph	the meeting. Bring the	the meeting. Bring the
∧ Insert	pens, clips	pens, and clips
⊙ Insert period	a global search	a global search.
⊐ Move right	With the papers	With the papers
⊏ Move left	access the code	access the code
⊐⊏ Center	Chapter Six	Chapter Six
∽ Transpose	It is raesonable	It is reasonable
sp Spell out	475 Mill Ave	475 Mill Avenue
… Stet (do not delete)	I am very pleased	I am very pleased
⌒ Close up	regret fully	regretfully
ss Single-space	The margin top ss is 1 inch.	The margin top is 1 inch.
ds Double-space	Paper length is set for 11 inches.	Paper length is set for 11 inches.
ts Triple-space	The F8 function key contains commands	The F8 function key contains commands
bf Boldface	Boldface type provides emphasis.	**Boldface** type provides emphasis.
ital Italics	Use italics for terms to be defined.	Use *italics* for terms to be defined.

APPENDIX B • FORMATTING BUSINESS DOCUMENTS

There are many memo and business letter styles. This appendix includes one memo and two business letter styles.

At the end of a memo or business letter, the initials of the person keying the document appear. In exercises in this textbook, insert your initials where you see the XX at the end of a document. The name of the document is included after the initials.

Both business letters in this appendix were created with standard punctuation. Standard punctuation includes a colon after the salutation and a comma after the complimentary close.

A business letter can be printed on letterhead stationery, or the company name and address can be keyed at the top of the letter. For the examples in this text, assume that all business letters you create will be printed on letterhead stationery.

↓ *1-inch top margin*

DATE: September 28, 1998
ds
TO: Adam Mukai, Vice President
ds
FROM: Carol Jenovich, Director
ds
SUBJECT: NEW EMPLOYEES
ts

Two new employees have been hired to work in the Human Resources Department. Lola Henderson will begin work on October 1 and Daniel Schriver will begin October 14.
ds
Ms. Henderson has worked for three years as an administrative assistant for another company. Due to her previous experience, she was hired as a program assistant.
ds
Mr. Schriver has just completed a one-year training program at Gulf Community College. He was hired as an Administrative Assistant I.
ds
I would like to introduce you to the new employees. Please schedule a time for a short visit.
ds
XX:MEMO

---

758   Appendix B

Block-style Letter

→ 2-inch top margin

December 8, 1998

→ 5 Enters (Returns)

Mr. Paul Reinke
Iverson Medical Center
1290 South 43rd Street
Houston, TX 77348
ds
Dear Mr. Reinke:
ds
During the entire month of January, our laser printer, Model No. 34-454, will be on sale. We are cutting the original price by 33 percent!
ds
When you purchased your computer system from our store last month, you indicated an interest in a laser printer. Now is your chance, Mr. Reinke, to purchase a high-quality laser printer at a rock-bottom price. Once you have seen the quality of print produced by a laser printer, you will not be satisfied with any other type of printer.
ds
Visit our store at your convenience and see a demonstration of this incredible printer. We are so confident you will purchase the printer that we are enclosing a coupon for a free printer cartridge worth over $100.
ds
Very truly yours,

→ 4 Enters (Returns)

Gina Cerazzo, Manager
ds
XX: Block Letter
ds
Enclosure

Modified Block-style Letter

→ 2-inch top margin

December 8, 1998

→ 5 Enters (Returns)

Mr. Paul Reinke
Iverson Medical Center
1290 South 43rd Street
Houston, TX 77348
ds
Dear Mr. Reinke:
ds
During the entire month of January, our laser printer, Model No. 34-454, will be on sale. We are cutting the original price by 33 percent!
ds
When you purchased your computer system from our store last month, you indicated an interest in a laser printer. Now is your chance, Mr. Reinke, to purchase a high-quality laser printer at a rock-bottom price. Once you have seen the quality of print produced by a laser printer, you will not be satisfied with any other type of printer.
ds
Visit our store at your convenience and see a demonstration of this incredible printer. We are so confident you will purchase the printer that we are enclosing a coupon for a free printer cartridge worth over $100.

Very truly yours,
ds
HOUSTON COMPUTING

→ 4 Enters (Returns)

Gina Cerazzo, Manager
ds
XX: Modified Block Letter
ds
Enclosure

APPENDIX C • GRAPHICS IMAGES

 approved.wpg
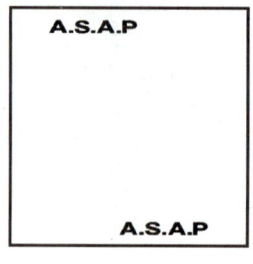 asap.wpg
 buck.wpg
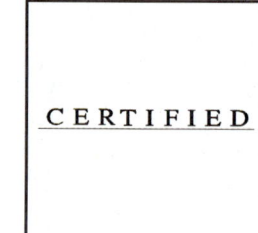 certify.wpg

 cheetah.wpg
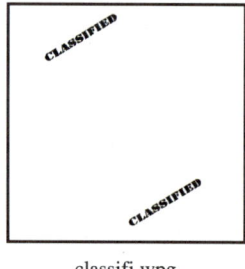 classifi.wpg
 confiden.wpg
 confirm.wpg

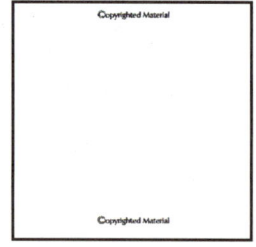 copyrite.wpg
 crane_j.wpg
 crest.wpg
 dontcopy.wpg

 draft.wpg
 dragn.wpg
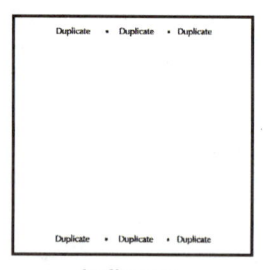 duplicat.wpg
 ender01.wpg

 ender02.wpg
 ender03.wpg
 ender04.wpg
 ender05.wpg

Appendix C

PHOTO CREDITS

The following photos are courtesy of:

Page	
3	Hewlett-Packard Company
19	Apple Computer, Inc.
39	Apple Computer, Inc.
55	Peter Fox/Apple Computer, Inc.
75	Hewlett-Packard Company
109	Hewlett-Packard Company
131	Hewlett-Packard Company
157	Hewlett-Packard Company
179	Intel Corporation
199	Peter Fox/Apple Computer, Inc.
289	Micron Electronics, Inc.
311	Frank Pryor/Apple Computer, Inc.
329	John Greenleigh/Apple Computer, Inc.
445	Jeff Haeger/Apple Computer, Inc.
477	Micron Electronics, Inc.

INDEX

Abbreviations feature, 376-378
Absolute tabs, 206, 207, 210
Active document, 272
Active key, 687
Addresses, envelopes, 529-530
Advanced Find dialog box, 122
Advancing the insertion point, 385-386
Advertising checking style, 318
Alaska Airlines home page address, 748
Alignment. *See also* Justification
    in cells, 588-589, 592, 593
    flush right, 235-236
    vertically on page, 184-185
All caps, 39
Antonyms, 166, 169
Appearance, character style, 137-145
Appending
    blocks of text, 265
    envelopes to documents, 529, 531
Application control button, 276
Archive documents, 116
Area charts, 631
Arrow pointer, xii, 7
Attaching boxes, 425-426
Auto Look Up, Thesaurus, 168

Background color, boxes, 431
Balanced newspaper columns, 540, 542
Bar charts, 624-625, 631, 643
Basic Counts dialog box, 322
Block protect, 182, 546
Blocks of text, 261
    appending, 265
    copying, 264-265
    deleting, 262
    moving, 263-264
Block-style letter example, 759
Bolding text, 40-41, 138
Bold italic type style, 132-133
Bold type style, 132-133
Booklet, print as, 305
Bookmarks, 383-384
Borders
    boxes, 428-430
    columns, 549-550, 552-553
    drop caps, 466
    page, 453-456
    paragraph, 451-452, 454-455
    table, 602-603, 607-608

Boxes
    attaching, 425-426
    border and fill styles, 428-430
    button, 418-419
    captions, 421-423, 428
    chart, 630-631
    color, 431, 436-437
    contents, 423-427
    corners, 455, 456
    deleting, 483
    in Draw, 477, 482-483
    editing, 421
    editing images, 434-437
    equation, 445-449
    figure, 414-416, 423, 427-428, 438, 456
    finding, 437
    moving, 437-438
    position, 425-426
    sizing, 426-427, 428, 438
    styles, 411, 434
    table, 416-417
    text, 413-414
    TextArt image, 506-507
    text flow around, 431-433
    user, 417, 428
Brightness, images, 436
Britannica Online home page address, 740
Browse the Web button, 739
Bulleted paragraphs, 88-89, 90, 92-93
Bullets definition, 668
Button boxes, 418-419. *See also* Boxes
BW threshold, 435

Calculating, in tables, 611-613
Calendar Expert, 402-403
Canceling a merge, 342
Caps Lock key, 39
Captions, boxes, 421-423, 428
Cascading windows, 273-274
Case of letters
    converting, 386
    matching, 293, 295
CD-ROM drive, ix, x
Cell contents, deleting, 573, 576
Cells, 559
    entering text, 562
    formatting, 588-591
    inserting tabs, 562
    joining, 574

lines and fill, 602-607
names, 561
selecting, 570-571
selecting text, 571
splitting, 575-576
Centering text, 55-56, 57, 58
Centering vertically on a page, 184-185
Change the font button, Power Bar, 135
Character (paired) styles, 701, 703, 705, 711
Character sets, 148-149
Character styles. *See* Font, appearance
Chart boxes, 630-631. *See also* Boxes
Chart Editor, 624
Charts
    area, 631
    bar, 624-625, 631, 643
    deleting, 629
    high/low, 632, 635, 642
    labels, 642-646
    layouts, 631-632, 639-642
    legends, 627-629
    line, 632, 634, 636
    pie, 632, 633, 640-641, 645-646
    positioning, 630
    radar, 632
    scatter, 632
    series, 636-638
    sizing, 630-631
    surface, 632
    from table data, 623-625
    3D, 639, 641
    tick marks, 645
    titles, 625-627
    types, 631-633
    x-axis and y-axis options, 644-645
Check boxes, xvi-xvii
Checking styles, Grammatik
    customizing, 319-320
    rule classes, 315-318, 319-320
    selecting, 313-314, 318-319
Clipboard, 265
Close button, 11
Closed Object Tools, 479
Closing
    documents, 11, 16
    windows, 272
Codes. *See* Reveal Codes
Collating and grouping while printing, 303
Color
    boxes, 431, 436-437
    in Draw, 498, 499
    font, 144-145
    images, 436-437
    lines, 460
    printing, 303

    reversed text, 469
    tables, 605-608
    TextArt, 504, 505, 506-507
Color palettes, 144
Column and row indicators, 561
Column breaks, 541, 546
Column headings
    centering, 215-216
    and chart labels, 642
Columns. *See* Columns of text; Newspaper columns; Parallel columns; Tables
Columns dialog box, creating newspaper columns, 539-541
Columns of text
    aligning visually, 213-215
    copying, 267-268
    deleting, 268-269
    headings, 215-216
    moving, 266-267
    selecting, 265-266
    tabs, 200, 204, 210. *See also* Tabs
Command buttons, xviii
Commands
    canceling, 10-11
    choosing, xii-xix
Computer hardware, ix-xi
Concordance file, 725, 727
Conditional end of page, 183
Continued footnotes, 254
Contouring text, 495-497. *See also* Shaping text
Contrast, images, 436, 437
Control Panel, xxiii-xxiv
Copying
    blocks of text, 264-265
    documents, 112-113
    formatting, 146-147
    formulas, 611, 612
    objects in Draw, 492
    styles, 709-710
    text columns, 267-268
Corel home page, 739
Corners, borders, 455, 456
Counting document elements, 321-322, 324
CPU, ix
Cursor, 6
Custom Box dialog box, 414
Custom Page Numbering dialog box, 190
Cutting and pasting, 261. *See also* Moving

DAD (Desktop Application Director), 5
Data Chart Gallery, 633
Data entry
    data files, 331-335
    keyboard merge, 344-345
Data File Feature Bar, 333
Data files, 329-335. *See also* Tables, data files
    fields, 330-331
    filename extension, 331
    moving between fields, 333
    sorting, 690, 693, 695
Data labels, chart, 642-646
Date
    format, 381-382
    inserting, 381-383
    setting, xx
Default box captions, 421
Default folder, 10
Default macros, 400-401
Default settings, tables, 609
Default styles, 710
Deleting
    blocks of text, 262
    boxes, 483
    cell contents, 573, 576
    charts, 629
    columns of text, 268-269
    documents, 114-115
    document style codes, 705
    folders and contents, 118
    hyphens, 372-373
    macros, 400
    objects in Draw, 494
    to the Recycle Bin, 116
    rows and columns from a table, 573, 576
    sort definitions, 692
    styles, 705, 710-711
    a table, table contents, or table structure, 577-578
    text, 24, 34
Desktop, Windows 95, xx, 4
Desktop Application Director (DAD), 5
Details button, displaying document names, 119-120
Diagonal lines, tables, 590
Dialog boxes, xiv-xviii
Disk drives, ix, x
Disk maintenance, xi
Displaying document information, 109-110, 171
Display options, document names, 119-121
DNS (Domain Name Service), 738
Documentation or Speech checking style, 318
Document control button, 276
Document information, displaying, 109-110, 171. *See also* Document statistics
Document Initial Font dialog box, 239
Document lists, printing, 117-118

Document names, 10
    display options, 119-121
    extensions, 164, 331, 393
Document statistics, 323-324
Document styles, 701, 703, 705
Document summary, 125-126, 304
Document window, 5
Domain Name Service (DNS), 738
Dot leaders
    changing character, 212
    Flush Right, 235
    tabs, 200-201, 203, 209
Double indenting, 83-84
Double underlining, 138
Draft mode, 66
Dragging. *See* Moving
Draw program
    attributes, 498-499
    clearing objects, 490, 494
    contouring text, 495-497. *See also* Shaping text
    copying objects, 492
    deleting a box, 483
    editing a box, 482-483
    editing objects, 491-492
    freehand drawing, 483-484
    inserting and editing images, 484-485
    inserting text, 485
    moving objects, 491, 493
    selecting objects, 489-491
    shapes, 477-481, 482
    sizing the drawing area, 487-488
    sizing objects, 494
Draw button, Graphics Toolbar, 477
Drawing shapes, 477-481, 482
Draw Power Bar, 478
Draw Toolbar, 478, 498
Draw Tool palette, 478
Draw window, 478, 482
Drive, changing, 109
Drop caps, 464-467
Drop-down menus, choosing commands, xiv
Drop shadow, borders, 455

Edit Box dialog box, 415
Editing window, 6-7, 8
E-mail, merging to, 339
Endfoot macro, 256
Endnotes and footnotes
    converting to footnotes, 256-257
    creating, 245-247, 248-249
    deleting, 251
    editing, 250
    formatting, 249, 257
    including in a search, 296
    options, 252-256

printing, 248
renumbering, 251-252
Enter key will chain to option, 701
Envelopes
   addresses, 529-530
   appending to an existing document, 529, 531
   creating as a document, 528-529
   merging, 343-344
   options, 530-531
   paper definitions, 527-528, 530
   printing, 527-528
Environment Preferences dialog box, 369
Equation boxes, 445-449. *See also* Boxes
Equation Editor, 446, 447-448
Equation Editor Toolbar, 448
Equation palette, 446, 447
Equations
   editing, 449
   font, 448
   inline, 450
   to select records, 693-695
   viewing, 448
   writing, 446-447
Esc key, 11
Exiting WordPerfect and Windows 95, 13, 16
Experts, WordPerfect, 402-405
Extensions, filename, 164, 331, 393

Fax Expert, 402
Feature Bars
   Data File, 333
   Header/Footer, 232-233
   Index, 724
   Macros, 395
   Outline, 663-664, 668
   Table of Authorities, 729
   Table of Contents, 716
Fiction checking style, 318
Fields
   data files, 330-331
   form files, 336
Figure boxes. *See also* Boxes
   captions, 421, 423, 428
   corners, 456
   editing, 427
   inserting images, 414-416
   moving, 438
Figure lists, 720-723
File lists, printing, 117-118
File menu, xiii
Filename extensions, 164, 331, 393
Filenames. *See* Document names
Files from disk, printing, 301-302
Fill
   boxes, 428-430
   cells, 602, 605-607, 609
   in Draw, 498, 499
   drop caps, 466
   gradient, 455
   images, 436
Fill styles, boxes, 428-430
Find and Replace. *See also* Searching
   codes, 292, 294-295, 297-298
   font, 293-294, 295
   options, 295-297
   text, 289-293
Flush right alignment, 235-236
Folders
   changing default, 10, 109
   deleting, 118
   new, 110-111
Font, 133
   appearance, 137-142
   chart titles, 625-626
   color, 144-145
   in Draw, 486, 487, 495
   drop caps, 466
   envelopes, 530
   equations, 448
   face, 131-132, 134-135
   Find and Replace, 293-294, 295
   in headers and footers, 238-239
   size, 132, 136-137, 143-144
   TextArt, 502
   type style, 132-133, 137
Font Toolbar, 137
Footend macro, 256
Footers. *See also* Headers
   creating, 231-233, 236
   discontinuing, 241
   distance from text, 235
   editing, 236-237
   formatting, 237-239
   in Grammatik check, 318
   including in a search, 296
   page numbering, 239-240
   printing, 234-235, 241
   on specific pages, 233
   suppressing, 241-242
   viewing, 233
Footnotes and endnotes
   continued, 254
   converting to endnotes, 256-257
   creating, 245-247, 248-249
   deleting, 251
   editing, 250
   formatting, 249, 257
   in Grammatik check, 318
   including in a search, 296
   options, 252-256
   printing, 248
   renumbering, 251-252

separator line, 254-256
spacing between notes, 254, 256
Footnote window, 246
Foreground color, boxes, 431
Foreign languages, 162, 169, 317
Formal Memo or Letter checking style, 313, 318, 319
Format Justification menu, 61
Formatting, copying, 146-147. *See also* Styles, copying
Format Toolbar, 63-64, 179
Formdoc document style, 705
Form file, 329. *See also* Merging
creating, 336-337
envelope, 343
fields, 336
formatting, 342
labels, 535-536
Formula Bar, 609-610, 611
Formulas, in tables
calculating, 611-612
copying, 611, 612
examples, 610
inserting, 609, 612, 613
operators, 610
QuickSum, 614
Freehand drawing, 483-484
Function keys, x

Generating
indexes, 726, 727
lists, 722-723
regenerating, 728
tables of authorities, 730-731, 733
tables of contents, 719, 720
Go To, 23, 543-544
Grammatik, 311-312
checking styles, 313-315, 317, 318-320
document statistics, 323-324
foreign languages, 317
parse tree, 321
parts of speech, 320
QuickCorrect, 324
readability, 322
replacements, 312-313
rule classes, 315-317, 318-319
user word lists, 317, 324
Graphical user interface (GUI), xix
Graphic elements, including in search, 296
Graphics, printing, 303
Graphics boxes. *See* Boxes
Graphics images. *See* Images
Graphics styles, 699
Graphics Toolbar, 412, 477

Grid
Draw window, 481-482
table, 560
GUI (graphical user interface), xix
Gutter, columns, 541, 548

Half-size paper definition, 526
Hanging indents, 84-86
Hard hyphens, 372
Hard page breaks, 183-184, 533
Hard spaces, 379-380
Hardware, 3
Header/Footer Feature Bar, 232-233
Header rows, tables, 597
Headers. *See also* Footers
creating, 231-233, 236
discontinuing, 241
distance from text, 235-236
editing, 236-237
font, 238-239
formatting, 237-239
in Grammatik check, 318
including in a search, 296
page numbering, 239-240
printing, 234, 241
on specific pages, 233-234
suppressing, 241
Header window, 232
Heading numbering definition, 668, 670
Headings, columns, 215-216, 642
Headings numbering definition, 668, 670
Help
Windows 95, xxi-xxii
WordPerfect, 47-50
Hidden text, 141-142
Hide documents, 116
High/low charts, 632, 635, 642
History, Thesaurus, 168, 170
Home pages, creating with Internet Publisher, 745-747
Horizontal charts, 639
Horizontal lines, 456-457, 459-464
HTML (HyperText Markup Language), 737, 745-747
http (Hypertext Transfer Protocol), 738
Hypertext links, 741-742, 748-749
HyperText Markup Language (HTML), 737, 745-747
Hypertext Transfer Protocol, 738
Hyphenation
deleting, 372-373
guidelines, 370
inserting, 372
prompt, 369, 371
suspending, 370
turning on, 368, 371
and word wrap, 367-368
zone, 367-368, 371
Hyphens, 372-373

Index 769

I

I-beam pointer, xii
Illustration lists, 720-723
Image boxes, TextArt, 506-507
Image offset for binding, printing, 304-305
Images
    in Draw, 484-485
        editing in boxes, 434-437
        in figure boxes, 414-416
        predesigned, 411-412, 760-762
        watermark, 420-421
Image Tools dialog box, 434-437
Indenting text
    first line of paragraph, 79-81
    hanging indents, 84-86
    from left and right margins, 83-84
    from left margin, 81-82
Indexes, 723-728
Index Feature Bar, 724
Informal Memo or Letter checking style, 318
Infoseek search engine, 743
Inline equations, 450
Input files, sorting, 684
Inserting
    a document into a box, 416-417
    a document into another document, 270-271
    hyphens, 372
    images, 411-412, 414-416, 484-485
    text, 23-24
    watermarks, 420-421
Insertion point, 6
    advancing, 385-386
    moving between data file fields, 333
    moving to a specific page, 23
    moving within and between columns, 543-544
    moving within a table, 563
    moving with the keyboard, 21-23, 33
    moving with the mouse, 19-21, 23, 33
    in Reveal Codes, 42
Internet, 737. *See also* Web
Internet Protocol (IP), 738
Internet Publisher, 745-747
Internet Service Provider (ISP), 738
IP (Internet Protocol), 738
ISP (Internet Service Provider), 738
Italicizing text, 44-45, 138
Italic type style, 132-133

J

Joining cells, 574
Justification, 60-66. *See also* Alignment

K

Keeping text together on a page, 181-183, 254
Keyboard, ix-x
    moving insertion point, 21-23, 33
    selecting text, 26-27, 34
Keyboard merge, 344-345
Keys, sorting, 686, 687

L

Labels
    chart, 642-646
    creating, 532-534
    form file, 535-536
Language, selecting a foreign language module
    Grammatik, 317
    Thesaurus, 169
Large Icons button, displaying document names, 119-120
Layouts, charts, 631-632, 639-642
Leader tabs, 200-201, 203, 209, 212
Leading, 374
Legends, charts, 627-629
Letter Expert, 402, 403-404
Letter styles, business, 759
Line attributes in Draw, 498, 499
Line button, Draw Toolbar, 498
Line charts, 632, 634, 636
Line color in Draw, 498, 499
Line height, 373-374
Line numbering, 374-376
Line Object Tools, 479
Lines
    cell, 602-605
    between columns, 549-552
    customizing, 459-464
    diagonal, 590
    footnote separator, 254-256
    horizontal, 456-457
    vertical, 458
Line spacing, 59-60
List boxes, xv-xvi
List button, displaying document names, 119-120
Lists, 720-723
Locking cells, 590
Logical pages, 305, 533

M

Macros
    default, 400-401
    deleting, 400
    editing, 396-397
    Equation Editor, 448
    location, 391-392
    naming, 393
    pausing, 398-400

playing, 395
recording, 392-395
Reverse, 468
watermark, 401
Macros Feature Bar, 395
Macro Tools Toolbar, 392
Mailing addresses, envelopes, 529-530
Mailing labels. *See* Labels
Main word list, 157
Make It Fit, 469-471
Margins, changing
with Margins dialog box, 77-78
with margin guidelines, 75-77
with Ruler Bar, 78-79
top and bottom, 179-181
Marking text
for indexes, 724, 726
for lists, 720-721, 723
for tables of authorities, 729-730, 731
for tables of contents, 716-717, 719-720
Maximize button, 275-276
Memo Expert, 402, 405
Memory capacity, disks, x
Memo style, 758
Menu bar, xiii, 5, 6
Merge dialog box, 332
Merge records, sorting, 686
Merging, 338-339
canceling, 342
conditions, 348-350
envelopes, 343-344
at the keyboard, 344-345
options, 339-340
output, 339
selecting records, 346-348
Microsoft Explorer, 738
Minimize button, 275
Mirror images, 435
Modem, 738
Modified block-style letter, 759
Monitor, ix
Monospaced typeface, 131
Mouse, ix, xi
Mouse pointer, xii, 7
Moving
blocks of text, 263-264
boxes, 437-438
columns, 266-267
documents, 113
objects in Draw, 491, 493
text between documents, 277-278

N

Naming
documents, 10, 114
macros, 393
sort definitions, 686
styles, 701
NASA home page address, 740
Netscape dialog box, 739
Netscape Navigator, 738
Net Search Destinations page, 744
New Document button, 401
New Page Size dialog box, 525-526
Newsletter Expert, 402
Newspaper columns
balanced, 540, 542
borders, 549-550, 551-553
column breaks, 541
column widths, 541, 548-549
creating with the Columns dialog box, 539-541
lines between, 549-552
moving insertion point, 543-544
Northwest Airlines home page address, 749
Numbering
footnotes and endnotes, 253-254, 255
lines, 374-376
outlines, 664-665, 668-669
paragraphs, 86-88, 90-91, 92
Numbering definitions, outlines, 668-670
Number of document elements, 171
Numeric format, tables, 599-601

O

Object Properties button, Draw Toolbar, 498
Objects in Draw
attributes, 498-499
copying, 492
deleting, 494
editing, 491-492
moving, 491, 493
selecting, 489-491
sizing, 494
Open dialog box, 109-110, 119-121
Opening
documents, 12, 16
multiple windows, 271-272
Open styles, 701
Option buttons, xvii-xviii
Orientation, 525
Orphan, 181
Outline Feature Bar, 663-664, 668, 672
Outlines
beginning number, 676
creating, 663-666
defining, 676
displaying or hiding body text, 673
displaying or hiding outline families, 671-673

editing outline families, 674-676
entering text, 665
numbering definitions, 668-670
numbering level, 670-671
numbering styles, 664-665, 667-668
turning off, 665
Outline styles, 699
Outlining characters, 138
Outlining mode, 664
Output files, sorting, 684

Page borders, 453-456
Page breaks
inserting, 183-184
labels, 533
between merged documents, 339
preventing, 182-183
Page icons, scrolling with, 21
Page Margins button, Format Toolbar, 179
Page mode, 66
Page numbering
adding text, 191
beginning number, 188-190
codes, 186, 189, 190
forcing odd or even, 194
in headers and footers, 239-240
inserting, 185, 186, 194
numbering method, 190-191
page x of y, 193
with Roman numerals, 190-191
secondary numbers, 192-193
specific pages, 187
suppressing, 187-188
tables of contents, 718, 719
Pages, centering vertically, 184-185
Page Size dialog box, 523
Paired styles, 701
Paper definitions
creating, 524-526
deleting, 527
editing, 526-527
envelope, 527-528, 530
half-size, 526
inserting, 523-524
Paper Size dialog box, 523
Paragraph numbering style, outlines, 664-665, 667, 668
Paragraphs
borders, 451-452, 454-455
bulleted, 88-89, 90, 92-93, 668
indenting, 79-86
numbering, 86-88, 90-91, 92
number of, in document, 321-322
sorting, 684, 686, 689
splitting and joining, 24
Paragraph styles, 701, 702-703, 704

Parallel columns, 541. *See also* Columns of text; Newspaper columns; Tables
block protect, 546
borders, 550, 552-553
column breaks, 546
column widths, 541, 548
creating, 545-547
lines between, 549-552
moving insertion point, 543-544
sorting, 686
Parse tree, Grammatik, 321
Parts of speech, Grammatik, 320-321
Pasting, 261. *See also* Moving
Pausing macros, 398-400
PerfectExpert, 49-50
Personal information for templates, 403, 405
Physical pages, 305, 533
Pie charts, 632, 633, 640-641, 645-646
Playing macros, 395
Point sizes, 132
Power Bar, 5, 6. *See also individual button names*
Previewing documents, 118-119
Preview window, 119
Printer, ix, x-xi
merging to, 339, 342
selecting, 299
Print File List dialog box, 117
Printing
booklets, 305
collating and grouping, 303
color, 303
document list, 117-118
document on disk, 301-302
documents, 13, 16, 117
document summary, 304
envelopes, 527-528
footnotes and endnotes, 248
graphics, 303
headers and footers, 234-235, 241
image offset for binding, 304-305
labels, 534
multiple copies, 302-303
resolution, 303-304
in reverse order, 303
selected text, 305-306
selecting printer, 299
specific pages, 299-301
two-sided, 304-305
Proofreaders' marks, 757
Properties, documents, 116
Properties dialog box
Information tab, 171
Summary tab, 125
Properties for Table Format dialog box
Cell tab, 588
Column tab, 568, 592

    Row tab, 595
    Table tab, 597-598
Properties for Table Lines/Fill dialog box
    Cell tab, 603
    Table tab, 607
Proportional typeface, 131
Punctuation and spacing, 8, 336, 758

Quick Check, 313, 318-319, 324
QuickCorrect, 7, 86, 88-89, 159, 164, 172-174, 324
Quick Data Entry dialog box, 333
QuickFinder, 121-124
QuickFonts button, Power Bar, 133, 147
QuickFonts menu, 147
QuickFormat, 146-147
QuickMark, 383, 384
QuickMenus, 56-57
QuickSpot, 64-66, 133
QuickStyle, 703-704
QuickSum, 614
QuickTips, 6
Quotation definition, 668

Radar charts, 632
Readability, 322, 324
Read-only documents, 116
Recording macros, 392-395
Records, 331. *See also* Data files
    divisions, 687
    selecting for a merge, 346-350
    selecting for a sort, 693-695
Recycle Bin, 116
Redline, characters, 139-141
Redo, 28-30
Regenerating indexes, lists, and tables, 728. *See also* Generating
Regular hyphens, 372
Regular type style, 132-133
Relative size, font, 143-144
Relative tabs, 206, 210
Removing. *See* Deleting
Renaming documents, 114
Replacements, Grammatik, 312-313
Replacing. *See* Find and Replace
Resolution, printing, 303-304
Restore button, 275, 276
Restoring files from the Recycle Bin, 116
Restoring text, 29, 30-31
Retrieving styles, 707-708
Reveal Codes, 43, 70
    bold, 43
    bookmarks, 383
    center, 55, 58
    conditional end of page, 183

    finding and replacing, 292, 294-295, 297-298
    font, 134
    hyphens, 368, 370, 372-373
    indent, 81, 83, 85, 93
    index, 724
    italic, 44
    line spacing, 59
    margins, 76, 93, 180
    marking, 716-717, 724
    page numbering, 186, 189, 190
    paper definition, 524
    showing or hiding merge codes, 340
    styles, 675
    symbols, 148
    tabs, 79, 208
    underlining, 46
    Widow/Orphan, 182
Reveal Codes window, 42-43
Reversed text, 468-469
Roman numerals, page numbering, 190-191
Rotating
    box contents, 424
    cell contents, in tables, 588
    images in boxes, 435, 437
    TextArt, 506
Row and column indicators, 561
Row height, tables, 595
Rows. *See* Tables
Rule class errors count, 323
Rule classes, Grammatik, 315-318, 319-320
Ruler, Draw window, 481-482
Ruler Bar
    changing column widths, 548-549, 565-567
    changing margins, 75-77
    changing tabs, 199-204
    table markers, 565-566
    visually aligning columns, 213-215

Sans serif typeface, 131-132
Save As dialog box, 9
Saving
    documents, 9-10, 16, 31
    selected text as a separate document, 269-270
    standard text, 269
    styles, 706-707
Scatter charts, 632
Screen saver, adding, xxiii
Scroll bars, 5, 7, 19-21
Scrolling with mouse, 19-21, 33
Search engines, 742-744
Searching. *See also* Find and Replace
    documents, 123-124
    graphics boxes, 437
    specific folders, 122-123
    for text, 121-124

Index 773

Secondary page numbers, 192-193
Search string, 290, 293
Selected text
    printing, 305-306
    saving as a separate document, 269-270
Select equations, 693-695
Selecting
    cells, 570-571
    columns of text, 265-266
    documents, 111, 265
    objects in Draw, 489-491
    records, 346-350, 693-695
    text, 25-28, 34
    text in cells, 571
Select operators, 694
Sentences, number of, in document, 321-322
Separator line, footnotes, 254-256
Series, chart, 636-638
Serif typeface, 131-132
Server domains, 738
Server names, 738
Shadow, characters, 138-139
Shadow pointer, 7
Shapes in Draw
    attributes, 498-499
    clearing, 480
    drawing, 477-481, 482
    inserting text into, 487, 488-489
Shaping text, 500-501, 504, 505. *See also* Contouring text
Shortcut commands. *See* Shortcut keys
Shortcut keys, xviii, 51, 69, 94
Shortcut menus, xviii-xix
Size, type. *See* Font, size
Sizing
    boxes, 426-427, 428, 438
    charts, 630-631
    drawing area, 487-488
    drop caps, 466
    lines, 462, 464
    objects in Draw, 494
    TextArt, 506
    windows, 275-277
Sizing handles, 437
Small caps, 139
Small Icons button, displaying document names, 119-120
Soft hyphens, 372, 373
Soft returns, 370
Software, 3
Sort definitions
    creating, 684-689
    editing, 691-692
    predefined, 684
    types, 686-687

Sorting. *See also* Sort definitions
    columns, 688, 691, 693
    considerations, 692
    data files, 690, 693, 695
    input and output files, 684
    keys, 686
    paragraphs, 684, 686, 689
    selecting records, 693-695
    in tables, 684, 685, 690
Spacing and punctuation, 8, 336
Spacing between notes, 254, 256
SpeedFormat, 615-616
Spell-As-You-Go, 8, 157
Spell Checker, 157-159
    customizing, 161-163
    editing while spell checking, 160-161
    user word lists, 157, 161, 162, 163-166, 317, 324
Spelling Assist, Thesaurus, 169
Spin boxes, xviii
Splitting and joining paragraphs, 24
Splitting cells, 575-576
Standard text, 269
Start menu, xxi, 4
Status bar, 5, 7
Strikeout, characters, 140-141
Styles
    applying, 704-705
    copying, 709-710
    creating new, 699-703
    creating from existing text, 703-704
    default, 710
    deleting, 705, 710-711
    editing, 708-709
    Enter key will chain to option, 701
    Formdoc, 705
    graphics, 699
    naming, 701
    outline, 699
    outline numbering, 664-665, 667-668
    retrieving, 707-708
    saving, 706-707
    system, 699
    template, 699
    turning on/off, 705
    types, 701
Styles button, Power Bar, 703, 705
Styles Editor dialog box, 237-238, 700
Subscript, 142
Subtitles, charts, 627
Sum option. *See* QuickSum
Superscript, 142
Suppressing
    headers and footers, 241-242
    page numbering, 187-188
Surface charts, 632
Suspend hyphenation, 370

Syllables, number of, in document, 321-322
Symbols
    displaying, 379, 380
    inserting, 148-149
Synonyms, 166, 167-168, 169
System documents, 116
System styles, 699

Tab Bar, 204-205
Tab codes, 208
Tab key, 39
Table boxes, 416-417. *See also* Boxes
Table contents, deleting, 577-578
Table data, charts from, 623-628
Table grid, 560
Table list, 720
Table markers, Ruler Bar, 565-566
Table menu, 587
Table of Authorities Feature Bar, 729
Table of Contents Feature Bar, 716
Tables
    borders, 602-603, 607-608
    calculating numbers, 611-613
    cell lines, 602-605
    codes, 562
    column widths, 565-569, 592-593
    creating, 559-562, 563-564
    creating charts from, 623-625
    data files, 340-341
    default settings, 609
    deleting cell contents, 573, 576
    deleting rows or columns, 573, 576
    deleting the table, contents, or structure, 577-578
    diagonal lines, 590
    entering text in cells, 562
    fill, 605-606, 609
    formatting cells, 588-591
    formatting columns, 592-593
    formatting rows, 594-596
    formatting the entire table, 597-598
    formulas, 609-611, 612, 613
    grid, 560
    header rows, 597
    inserting rows or columns, 571-572
    joining cells, 574
    locking cells, 590
    moving rows or columns, 576-577
    moving the insertion point, 563
    numeric format, 599-601
    selecting cells, 570
    selecting text in cells, 571
    sorting, 684, 690
    sorting cell contents, 685
    SpeedFormat, 615-616
    splitting cells, 575-576
Tables of authorities, 728-733

Tables of contents, 209, 715-720
Tables Toolbar, displaying, 561
Table structure, deleting, 577-578
Tab menu, 200
Tabs
    absolute and relative, 206-207, 210
    clearing, 201, 204, 206, 207
    default, 210
    evenly spaced, 210
    inserting in cells, 562
    setting with the Ruler Bar, 199-204
    setting with the Tab Bar, 204-205
    setting with the Tab Set dialog box, 206-210
    types, 200
Taskbar, xx, 5, 7
T button, Outline Feature Bar, 668
TCP (Transmission Control Protocol), 738
Technical or Scientific checking style, 313-315, 318
Templates, 401-405
Template styles, 699
Text
    boxes, 413-414
    contouring, 495-497
    deleting, 24, 34
    inserting in Draw, 485-487, 488-489
    shaping, 500-501, 504, 505
TextArt 7, 500-507
Text boxes
    dialog boxes, xv
    graphics boxes, 413-414
Text color, 144-145
Text columns. *See* Columns of text
Text flow. *See* Word wrap; Wrapping text
Thesaurus program, 166-170
Tick marks, charts, 645
Tiling windows, 274-275
Time, setting, xx
Title bar, 5-6, 275-276
Titles, charts, 625-627
Toolbar menu, 63
Toolbars, 5, 6
    choosing commands, xiii
    displaying, 63
    Draw, 478, 498
    Equation Editor, 448
    Font, 137
    Format, 63-64, 179
    Graphics, 412, 477
    Macro Tools, 392
    Tables, 561
Transmission Control Protocol (TCP), 738
Transworld Airlines home page address, 749
TWA home page address, 742
Two-Page mode, 66-67
Typeface. *See* Font, face
Type size. *See* Font, size
Type style. *See* Font, type style

Index   **775**

Undelete, 28-29
Underlining spaces, 144
Underlining text, 45-46, 138
Undo, 28-30
Uniform Resource Locators (URLs), 738-740
United Airlines home page address, 749
UPS home page address, 742
URLs (Uniform Resource Locators), 738-740
User boxes, 417, 428. *See also* Boxes
User word lists, 157, 163, 317, 324
    activating, 162
    adding or removing, 164
    adding words, 161, 164-165
USPS Bar Code, 530-531

Vertical centering on page, 184-185
Viewing mode, 66-68

Watermark macro, 401
Watermarks, 420-421
Web. *See also* Internet Publisher
    hypertext links, 741-742, 748-749
    locating URLs, 738-740
    search engines, 742-744
Web browsers, 737, 738
Web documents, 745-747
White House home page address, 741
Widow/Orphan, 181-182
Windows, 261
    Application control button, 276
    cascading, 273-274
    closing, 272
    Control Panel, xxiv
    cutting and pasting text between, 277-278
    document, 5
    Document control button, 276
    Draw, 478, 482
    footnote and endnote, 246
    header, 232
    Maximize button, 275-276
    Minimize button, 275
    opening multiple, 271-272
    Preview, 119
    Restore button, 275, 276
    sizing, 275-277
    tiling, 274-275
Windows 95
    Control Panel, xxiii-xxiv
    desktop, xx, 4
    exiting, 13, 16

    Help, xxi-xxii
    operating system, xix-xxi
Window's clipboard, 265
Word forms, finding and replacing, 291-292
Word lists. *See* Main word list; User word lists
WordPerfect
    converting to HTML, 745-747
    exiting, 13, 16
    Experts, 402-405
    Help, 47-50
    loading, 4-5, 16
    special characters, 148-149, 502-503
    template, xix
Words, number of, in document, 321-322
Word wrap, 7. *See also* Wrapping text
    and hard spaces, 379-380
    and hyphenation, 367-368
World Wide Web, 737, 738. *See also* Web
Wrapping text
    in cells, 562
    around drop caps, 467
    around graphics boxes, 431-433
    tables of contents, 718
Writing Tools dialog box
    Customize menu, 160
    Grammatik tab, 312
    Spell Checker tab, 158
    Thesaurus tab, 166

X-axis options, charts, 644-645

Yahoo search engine, 744
Y-axis options, charts, 644-645

Zoom
    in drawing area, 488
    on images, 435
    ratio, 67-68